Global Aspects and Cultural Perspectives on Knowledge Management:
Emerging Dimensions

Murray E. Jennex
San Diego State University, USA

Senior Editorial Director:	Kristin Klinger
Director of Book Publications:	Julia Mosemann
Editorial Director:	Lindsay Johnston
Acquisitions Editor:	Erika Carter
Development Editor:	Myla Harty
Production Editor:	Sean Woznicki
Typesetters:	Mike Brehm, Natalie Pronio, Deanna Zombro
Print Coordinator:	Jamie Snavely
Cover Design:	Nick Newcomer

Published in the United States of America by
Information Science Reference (an imprint of IGI Global)
701 E. Chocolate Avenue
Hershey PA 17033
Tel: 717-533-8845
Fax: 717-533-8661
E-mail: cust@igi-global.com
Web site: http://www.igi-global.com/reference

Library of Congress Cataloging-in-Publication Data
Global aspects and cultural perspectives on knowledge management: emerging dimensions / Murray E. Jennex, editor.
    p. cm.
  Includes bibliographical references and index.
  Summary: "This book presents new technologies, approaches, issues, solutions, and cases that can help an organization implement a knowledge management (KM) initiative, presenting issues that drive the technologies, processes, methodologies, techniques, and practices used to implement KM in a variety of ways and in the multi-faceted modern environment that we find ourselves in today"--Provided by publisher.
  ISBN 978-1-60960-555-1 (hbk.) -- ISBN 978-1-60960-556-8 (ebook) 1.
Knowledge management. I. Jennex, Murray E., 1956-
  HD30.2.G572 2011
  658.4'038--dc22
                              2011016062

British Cataloguing in Publication Data
A Cataloguing in Publication record for this book is available from the British Library.

All work contributed to this book is new, previously-unpublished material. The views expressed in this book are those of the authors, but not necessarily of the publisher.

Table of Contents

Preface xvi

Section 1

Chapter 1
Measuring Knowledge Management Outcomes at the Individual Level: Towards a Tool for
Research on Organizational Culture 1
    Shahnawaz Muhammed, The American University of Middle East, Kuwait
    William J. Doll, The University of Toledo, USA
    Xiaodong Deng, Oakland University, USA

Chapter 2
Using Agent Based Simulation and Game Theory Analysis to Study Knowledge Flow in
Organizations: The KMscape 19
    Richard Jolly, Portland State University, USA
    Wayne Wakeland, Portland State University, USA

Chapter 3
A Comprehensive Model for Assessing the Organizational Readiness of Knowledge Management 30
    Babak Sohrabi, University of Tehran, Iran
    Iman Raeesi, University of Tehran, Iran
    Amir Khanlari, University of Tehran, Iran
    Sakineh Forouzandeh, Shahid Beheshti University, Iran

Chapter 4
Knowledge Management Toolkit for SMEs 49
    Kerstin Fink, University of Innsbruck, Austria
    Christian Ploder, University of Innsbruck, Austria

Chapter 5
A Framework for Managing the Life Cycle of Knowledge in Global Organizations 64
    Mark Salisbury, University of New Mexico, USA

Chapter 6

Social Network Structures for Explicit, Tacit and Potential Knowledge..81
    Anssi Smedlund, Helsinki University of Technology, Finland & Tokyo Insititute of
        Technology, Japan

Section 2

Chapter 7

A Simulation System for Evaluating Knowledge Management System (KMS) Implementation
Strategies in Small to Mid-Size Enterprises (SME) 92
    Robert Judge, San Diego State University, USA

Chapter 8

Knowledge Sharing Behavior of Graduate Students 113
    Shaheen Majid, Nanyang Technological University, Singapore
    Sim Mong Wey, Nanyang Technological University, Singapore

Chapter 9

Cocreating Corporate Knowledge with a Wiki..126
    Joseph A. Meloche, University of Wollongong, Australia
    Helen Hasan, University of Wollongong, Australia
    David Willis, BlueScope Steel Research, Australia
    Charmaine C. Pfaff, University of Wollongong, Australia
    Yan Qi, University of Wollongong, Australia

Chapter 10

Reaching for the Moon: Expanding Transactive Memory's Reach with Wikis and Tagging.............144
    Mark B. Allan, NASA Ames Research Center, USA
    Anthony A. Korolis, IBM Corporation, USA
    Terri L. Griffith, Santa Clara University, USA

Chapter 11

Assessing the Impact of Knowledge Transfer Mechanisms on Supply Chain Performance 157
    Stephen McLaughlin, National University of Ireland Maynooth, Ireland

Chapter 12

Capturing Tacit Knowledge from Transient Workers: Improving the Organizational
Competitiveness..172
    Salah Eldin Adam Hamza, SOFCON Consulting Engineering Co., Saudi Arabia

Section 3

Chapter 13
Organization of Lessons Learned Knowledge: A Taxonomy and Implementation 190
    Subramanian Rama Iyer, Oklahoma State University, USA
    Ramesh Sharda, Oklahoma State University, USA
    David Biros, Oklahoma State University, USA
    Joyce Lucca, Oklahoma State University, USA
    Upton Shimp, Oklahoma State University, USA

Chapter 14
Investigating the Impact of Knowledge Management Factors on New Product Development
Performance 210
    Belbaly Nassim, GSCM–Montpellier Business School, France

Chapter 15
Knowledge Strategy and its Role in the Organization: An Exploratory Study 227
    Joseph E. Kasten, Dowling College, USA

Chapter 16
Zooming in on the Effect of National Culture on Knowledge Sharing Behavior 243
    Wei Li, Freddie Mac, USA

Chapter 17
Utilizing the Rasch Model to Develop and Evaluate Items for the Tacit Knowledge Inventory
for Superintendents (TKIS) 264
    Christian E. Mueller, University of Memphis, USA
    Kelly D. Bradley, University of Kentucky, USA

Section 4

Chapter 18
Exploring Qualitative Differences in Knowledge Sources: A Study of Hierarchical Effects of
Judgmental Confidence and Accuracy Performance 286
    Carina Antonia Hallin, University of Stavanger, Norway
    Torvald Øgaard, University of Stavanger, Norway
    Einar Marnburg, University of Stavanger, Norway

Chapter 19
An Experiment of Information Elaboration in Mediated Knowledge Transfer 311
    Kelly J. Fadel, Utah State University, USA
    Alexandra Durcikova, The University of Arizona, USA
    Hoon S. Cha, Salisbury University, USA

Chapter 20
Facilitating Knowledge Transfer and the Achievement of Competitive Advantage with
Corporate Universities: An Exploratory Model Based on Media Richness and Type of
Knowledge to be Transferred 329
    M. Suzanne Clinton, University of Central Oklahoma, USA
    Kimberly L. Merritt, Oklahoma Christian University, USA
    Samantha R. Murray, Lubbock Christian University, USA

Chapter 21
Knowledge Management Utilization: A Case Study of Two Jordanian Universities 346
    Dalal M. Zoubi, Al- Balqa' Applied University, Jordan

Compilation of References 376

About the Contributors 420

Index 430

Detailed Table of Contents

Preface xvi

Section 1

Chapter 1

Measuring Knowledge Management Outcomes at the Individual Level: Towards a Tool for
Research on Organizational Culture 1

Shahnawaz Muhammed, The American University of Middle East, Kuwait
William J. Doll, The University of Toledo, USA
Xiaodong Deng, Oakland University, USA

Extant literature has mostly focused on defining knowledge management success at an organizational
or project level. The literature lacks a framework for measuring knowledge management success at
the individual level. Individual knowledge innovation and performance make organizations more productive. This research proposes a model of the interrelationships among individual level knowledge
management success measures (outcomes) including conceptual, contextual and operational knowledge, innovation, and performance. The model is tested using a sample of 252 individuals engaged in
managerial and professional knowledge work. The results suggest that conceptual knowledge enhances
operational and contextual knowledge. Contextual knowledge also improves operational knowledge.
Contextual knowledge is the key predictor of innovations that, along with operational knowledge, enhance work performance. The results provide a model for defining and measuring knowledge management success at the individual level.

Chapter 2

Using Agent Based Simulation and Game Theory Analysis to Study Knowledge Flow in
Organizations: The KMscape 19

Richard Jolly, Portland State University, USA
Wayne Wakeland, Portland State University, USA

Knowledge sharing in organizations, especially the impact of sharing freely versus not sharing, was
studied using game theoretic analysis and a Netlogo agent-based simulation model. In both analyses,
some agents hoarded knowledge while others shared knowledge freely. As expected, sharing was found

to greatly increase the overall amount of knowledge within the organization. Unexpectedly, on average, agents who share acquire more knowledge than hoarders. This is in contradiction to the conclusion from the prisoner's dilemma analysis. This is due to the synergy that develops between groups of agents who are sharing with each other. The density of the agents is important; as the density increases, the probability increases that an agent with a large amount of knowledge to share happens to be organizationally nearby. The implications are that organizations should actively encourage knowledge sharing, and that agent-based simulation is a useful tool for studying this type of organizational phenomena.

Chapter 3

A Comprehensive Model for Assessing the Organizational Readiness of Knowledge Management 30
Babak Sohrabi, University of Tehran, Iran
Iman Raeesi, University of Tehran, Iran
Amir Khanlari, University of Tehran, Iran
Sakineh Forouzandeh, Shahid Beheshti University, Iran

Implementing knowledge management or knowledge-sharing projects in an organization require significant organizational prerequisites. Lacking proper infrastructures and prerequisite, not only make the knowledge management process unprofitable, but might incur harmful effects as well. To decrease such risks, it is proposed to introduce the readiness assessment, in order to gauge a company's appetite for the work involved in implementing the knowledge management. In this research, critical success factors have been extracted from literature reviews and surveyed through a questionnaire, distributed among 130 knowledge management experts. Then, to validate the measurement of the multi-item constructs, exploratory factor analysis (EFA) was used. Identifying effective variables and their grouping onto related factors, the second questionnaire was employed for readiness assessment of an IT firm working in Iran and its results were presented with Radar diagrams. Finally, promoting propositions were provided based on the firm's current state.

Chapter 4

Knowledge Management Toolkit for SMEs 49
Kerstin Fink, University of Innsbruck, Austria
Christian Ploder, University of Innsbruck, Austria

The discipline of knowledge management is no longer emerging in large organizations, but also small and medium-sized enterprises (SMEs) are focusing on finding the right process that will allow them to make advantages of their intellectual capital. Using survey data from 219 small and medium-sized enterprises in Austria and Switzerland, this article illustrates the four key knowledge processes (1) knowledge identification, (2) knowledge acquisition, (3) knowledge distribution, and (4) knowledge preservation for SMEs and also reports the findings of the empirical study designed to allocate cost-efficient software products to each of the four knowledge processes. As a result a knowledge toolkit for SMEs that integrates knowledge processes, methods and software tool for decision support making is given. Finally, the social view of knowledge management to SMEs is discussed, showing that the use of information technology is currently far more important than the integration of a social-cognitive perspective.

Chapter 5

A Framework for Managing the Life Cycle of Knowledge in Global Organizations...........................64
Mark Salisbury, University of New Mexico, USA

This article describes a framework for managing the life cycle of knowledge in organizations. The framework emerges from years of work with the laboratories and facilities that are under the direction of the United States Department of Energy (DOE). The article begins by describing the background of the work from which the framework emerged; this is followed by describing the problem of identifying the "right" knowledge for the "right" people at the "right" time and how the use of performance objectives addresses this problem. Next, the phases in the life cycle of knowledge in an organization, the theoretical foundation for the framework, and the other aspects of the framework (Work Processes, Learning Processes, and Methodologies) are described. Finally, a discussion section summarizes the framework and discusses future directions for enhancing and extending the framework.

Chapter 6

Social Network Structures for Explicit, Tacit and Potential Knowledge...81
*Anssi Smedlund, Helsinki University of Technology, Finland & Tokyo Insititute of
    Technology, Japan*

The purpose of this conceptual article is to develop argumentation of the knowledge assets of a firm as consisting of three constructs, to extend the conventional explicit, tacit dichotomy by including potential knowledge. The article highlights the role of knowledge, which has so far not been utilized in value creation. The underlying assumption in the article is that knowledge assets can be thought of as embedded in the relationships between individuals in the firm, rather than possessed by single actors. The concept of potential knowledge is explained with selected social network and knowledge management literature. The findings suggest that the ideal social network structure for explicit knowledge is centralized, for tacit knowledge it is distributed, and for potential knowledge decentralized. Practically, the article provides a framework for understanding the connection between knowledge assets and social network structures, thus helping managers of firms in designing suitable social network structures for different types of knowledge.

Section 2

Chapter 7

A Simulation System for Evaluating Knowledge Management System (KMS) Implementation
Strategies in Small to Mid-Size Enterprises (SME) 92
Robert Judge, San Diego State University, USA

Companies create and use information and knowledge every day. The problem all companies have is figuring out how to efficiently discover that knowledge, capture it, share it, and use it to gain competitive advantage in the marketplace. This article describes a simulation model designed to provide small to midsized enterprises (SME) with a means to understand the impact of barriers and value accelerators on the flow of organizational information. The simulation model reports the throughput of information (number of information packets received per day) and its timeliness (average duration until packet arrival) and provides for sensitivity analysis of the parameters describing a strategy. Comparisons among model instantiations allow an organization to determine the appropriate strategy for current and future KMS efforts.

Chapter 8

Knowledge Sharing Behavior of Graduate Students 113

Shaheen Majid, Nanyang Technological University, Singapore
Sim Mong Wey, Nanyang Technological University, Singapore

The concept of knowledge sharing is gaining popularity due to increased awareness and new initiatives in knowledge management. However, its implications in the educational arena have been relatively unexplored. The purpose of this study was to investigate perceptions, nature and extent of knowledge sharing among graduate students in Singapore. A questionnaire was used for data collection and 183 students from two public universities in Singapore participated in this study. The study revealed that the participants were primarily motivated to share knowledge in an attempt to build relationships with their peers and email was the preferred communication channel. However, intense competition among the students to outperform their classmates and the lack of depth in relationship were the two most cited factors hindering knowledge sharing. The study suggests that academic institutions should review their instruction approaches to make the learning process less competitive which would help improve knowledge sharing among students.

Chapter 9

Cocreating Corporate Knowledge with a Wiki 126

Joseph A. Meloche, University of Wollongong, Australia
Helen Hasan, University of Wollongong, Australia
David Willis, BlueScope Steel Research, Australia
Charmaine C. Pfaff, University of Wollongong, Australia
Yan Qi, University of Wollongong, Australia

Wikis have a growing reputation on the open Internet for producing evolving stores of shared knowledge. However, such democratic systems are often treated with suspicion within corporations for management, legal, social, and other reasons. This article describes a field study of a corporate Wiki that has been developed to capture, and make available, organisational knowledge in a large manufacturing company as an initiative of their Knowledge Management (KM) program. As this approach to KM is a controversial and rapidly changing phenomenon, a Q Methodology research approach was selected to uncover employees' subjective attitudes to the Wiki. Activity Theory was used to provide a deeper interpretation of the findings of the Q-study. The results are enabling the firm to more fully exploit the potential of the Wiki as a ubiquitous tool for successful tacit and explicit knowledge management as more employees are encouraged to participate in a process of cocreating the store of corporate knowledge. The article also demonstrates how meaningful and rigorous research on this new democratic direction of corporate KM should continue.

Chapter 10

Reaching for the Moon: Expanding Transactive Memory's Reach with Wikis and Tagging............. 144

Mark B. Allan, NASA Ames Research Center, USA
Anthony A. Korolis, IBM Corporation, USA
Terri L. Griffith, Santa Clara University, USA

Transactive memory systems (TMS) support knowledge sharing and coordination in groups. TMS are enabled by the encoding, storage, retrieval, and communication of knowledge by domain experts—knowing who knows what. The NASA Ames Intelligent Robotics Group provides an example of how TMS theoretical boundaries are stretched in actual use. This group is characterized as being highly innovative as they routinely engage in field studies that are inherently difficult due to time and technology resource constraints. We provide an expanded view of TMS that includes the technology support system available to this group, and possible further extensions to NASA's or other such dynamic groups' practice.

Chapter 11

Assessing the Impact of Knowledge Transfer Mechanisms on Supply Chain Performance 157

Stephen McLaughlin, National University of Ireland Maynooth, Ireland

With the complexity of organizations increasing, it is becoming vitally important that organizations understand how knowledge is created and shared around their core business processes. However, many organizations deploy technology without due consideration for how their employees access, create, and share information and knowledge. This article explores the subject empirically through the study of how employees work with information and knowledge around a core business function—in this case a supply chain process. In order to do this, the organization needs to be viewed from a network perspective as it relates to specific business processes. Viewing the organization in this way enabled the author to see how employees' preferred knowledge and information transfer mechanisms varied across the core process. In some cases, the identified transfer mechanisms where at odds with the prescribed organization wide mechanisms. However, when the organization considered the employees' preferred transfer mechanisms as part of an overall process improvement, the E2E supply chain performance was seen to improve significantly.

Chapter 12

Capturing Tacit Knowledge from Transient Workers: Improving the Organizational
Competitiveness.. 172

Salah Eldin Adam Hamza, SOFCON Consulting Engineering Co., Saudi Arabia

This article studies the way tacit knowledge is dealt with in a high turnover business environment through a qualitative research approach in an engineering organization with respect to organizational culture and values and the effect in competitive stance. The study found peer review process and managerial/supervisory style to be effective in enabling new employees in a short time with knowledge critical for them to do a successful job, core values, and open-door policy to be necessary factors in forming a fertile environment for a quick tacit knowledge harvesting. The study also showed that a good competitive stance and customer satisfaction can be achieved and maintained through implementation of a rigorous peer review process. The study revealed noneffective utilization of knowledge management (KM) technical resources. The study directs future research towards evaluating possible objectives for utilization of KM technological resources, timeline for effective codification of tacit knowledge, and responsibilities for handling resources.

Section 3

Chapter 13

Organization of Lessons Learned Knowledge: A Taxonomy and Implementation 190

Subramanian Rama Iyer, Oklahoma State University, USA

Ramesh Sharda, Oklahoma State University, USA

David Biros, Oklahoma State University, USA

Joyce Lucca, Oklahoma State University, USA

Upton Shimp, Oklahoma State University, USA

With knowledge management systems (KMS) containing large repositories, a major issue is content organization. The ease of finding relevant information depends on the effectiveness of knowledge organization. Ontology, thesauri, and taxonomy are some of the key words that relate to knowledge organization. In this article we propose a schema for organizing knowledge that represents lessons learned from prior experience. Such knowledge from lessons learned has distinct characteristics so that it can be organized in specific ways for ease of discovery, retrieval, and also possible incorporation in formal learning. The proposed taxonomy includes concepts from domain related hierarchy, sources of lessons learned, formal learning, and collaborative inputs (Web 2.0). We describe the proposed taxonomy for organizing the lessons learned knowledge (also termed as knowledge nuggets) and provide details of a specific implementation of this taxonomy in a military organization. Such approaches to knowledge organization have the potential to be useful in many other knowledge management (KM) projects.

Chapter 14

Investigating the Impact of Knowledge Management Factors on New Product Development
Performance 210

Belbaly Nassim, GSCM–Montpellier Business School, France

Knowledge is recognized as an important weapon for new product development (NPD) performance, and many firms are beginning to manage the knowledge detained by their new product development processes. Researchers have investigated knowledge management factors such as enablers, creation processes, and performance. However, very few studies have explored the relationship between these factors in the context of new product development (NPD). To fill this gap, this article develops a research model which applies the knowledge management factors to the NPD context. The model includes five enablers: collaboration, trust, learning, team leadership characteristics, and t-shaped skills with an emphasis on the knowledge creation processes such as socialization, externalization, combination, and internalization. The results confirm the strong support of the research model and the impact of the independent variables (knowledge management enablers) on the dependent variables (knowledge creation and NPD performance). In light of these findings, the implications for both theory and practice are discussed.

Chapter 15
Knowledge Strategy and its Role in the Organization: An Exploratory Study.................................. 227
    Joseph E. Kasten, Dowling College, USA

Knowledge strategy is defined as the set of guidelines and philosophies that guide an organization's knowledge-based activities, such as knowledge gathering, development, storage, and utilization. Much of the early literature describing knowledge strategy suggests that its role in the organization is to drive, and be driven by, organizational structure and the human resources and technology strategies. The present research utilizes semi-structured interview data to determine that knowledge strategy is less of a formal structure and more of a lens through which knowledge-based decisions are viewed and focused, resulting in organizational actions that align with the knowledge strategy of the organization.

Chapter 16
Zooming in on the Effect of National Culture on Knowledge Sharing Behavior............................... 243
    Wei Li, Freddie Mac, USA

This study investigates what are the national cultural factors that influence employees' cross-cultural knowledge sharing in online environments and in what way. The article draws on findings from 41 in-depth interviewees conducted with 20 Chinese and 21 American employees who worked for a large multinational corporation. The rich interview data identified three national cultural differences that impacted Chinese and American participants' knowledge sharing through an online system, namely, language, differences grounded in collectivism/individualism, and different levels of uncertainty avoidance. English created a barrier for Chinese users to post their ideas, but it did not seem to stop them from consuming knowledge. Differences grounded in collectivist/individualist values were mainly reflected in these two cultural groups' different logic regarding the relationship between different working contexts and the necessity to share. Chinese also showed a higher level of uncertainty avoidance than Americans. Together these cultural differences could explain why Chinese shared knowledge less frequently than their American peers. Despite these reported cultural differences, findings from this research suggest that the actual cultural differences were smaller than what literature would predict. Possible explanations for fewer cultural differences are explored. Practical implications for knowledge management practitioners are also provided.

Chapter 17
Utilizing the Rasch Model to Develop and Evaluate Items for the Tacit Knowledge Inventory
for Superintendents (TKIS)... 264
    Christian E. Mueller, University of Memphis, USA
    Kelly D. Bradley, University of Kentucky, USA

Tacit knowledge was originally introduced into the professional literature by Michael Polanyi and later made popular by researchers in a variety of domains. Measuring this implicit form of procedural knowledge requires multiple approaches to adequately "capture" what is often known, but not easily articulated. The present study combines use of Sternberg et al.'s framework for capturing domain-specific tacit knowledge with that of Rasch modeling to develop and validate items for use on a newly developed tacit knowledge inventory. Development of the Tacit Knowledge Inventory for Superintendents (TKIS) occurred in three phases, including two phases of piloting and Rasch analysis. For illustrative purposes, presentation of results is limited to the Rasch analyses conducted on interpersonal tacit knowledge items. However, the methodology extends its usefulness to researchers and practitioners to guide the development process of similar assessments.

Section 4

Chapter 18

Exploring Qualitative Differences in Knowledge Sources: A Study of Hierarchical Effects of
Judgmental Confidence and Accuracy Performance...286
    Carina Antonia Hallin, University of Stavanger, Norway
    Torvald Øgaard, University of Stavanger, Norway
    Einar Marnburg, University of Stavanger, Norway

Focusing on knowledge management (KM) and strategic decision making in service businesses through the constructs of strategic capital and knowledge sharing, the study investigates qualitative differences in domain-specific knowledge of frontline employees and executives. The study draws on cognitive theory and investigates the extent to which the knowledge of these subject groups is correct with respect to incorporating intuitive judgments by various employee groups into forecasting and following strategic decision making. The authors carried out this investigation through an exploratory study of the subject groups' confidence and accuracy (CA) performance in a constructed knowledge-based forecasting setting. The groups' intuitive judgmental performances were examined when predicting uncertain business and industry-related outcomes. The authors surveyed 39 executives and 38 frontline employees in 12 hotels. The analysis is based on a between-participants design. The results from this setting do not fully confirm findings in earlier CA studies. Their results indicate that there are no significant differences in the accuracy of executives (as experts) and frontline employees (as novices). Although executives demonstrate overconfidence in their judgments and frontline employees demonstrate under confidence, in line with earlier CA theory of experts and novices, the differences we find are not significant. Similarly, the CA calibration performance difference between the two groups is not significant. They suggest, among other reasons, that our findings differ from earlier CA studies because of organizational politics and culture by power distance, social capital, misuse of knowledge and the size of the business.

Chapter 19

An Experiment of Information Elaboration in Mediated Knowledge Transfer 311
    Kelly J. Fadel, Utah State University, USA
    Alexandra Durcikova, The University of Arizona, USA
    Hoon S. Cha, Salisbury University, USA

Understanding knowledge transfer in computer mediated contexts is becoming essential given that organizations are spread more and more globally. In this article, the authors adopt elaboration likelihood theory to investigate knowledge transfer processes in a Knowledge Management System (KMS). They report the results of an exploratory experiment conducted to examine the impact of argument quality, source credibility and validation on knowledge usefulness of a document in a KMS. Their findings indicate that while validation of knowledge in KMS positively affects perceptions of knowledge usefulness, higher argument quality was associated with lower usefulness ratings. Surprisingly, source credibility has no effect on perceptions of knowledge usefulness. The implications of these results for both researchers and practitioners are discussed.

Chapter 20

Facilitating Knowledge Transfer and the Achievement of Competitive Advantage with Corporate Universities: An Exploratory Model Based on Media Richness and Type of Knowledge to be Transferred 329

M. Suzanne Clinton, University of Central Oklahoma, USA
Kimberly L. Merritt, Oklahoma Christian University, USA
Samantha R. Murray, Lubbock Christian University, USA

The knowledge literature suggests that transferring knowledge leads to synergistic cost advantages, better implementation of organizational strategies, and competitive advantage. Organizations are implementing corporate universities to aid in knowledge transfer. There is no standardized definition for corporate universities, but rather models that allow organizations to customize them to meet their training needs. Building on recent work of managing the knowledge transfer process (Murray & Peyrefitte, 2007) and on seminal work on media richness theory (Daft & Lengel, 1986), the authors propose that the type of knowledge to be transferred, and the appropriate media to transfer that knowledge, determine the most beneficial generation of corporate university to achieve competitive advantage. The article presents a model and propositions concerning relationships between the type of knowledge to be transferred, appropriate media selection, and generation of corporate university to implement.

Chapter 21

Knowledge Management Utilization: A Case Study of Two Jordanian Universities 346

Dalal M. Zoubi, Al-Balqa' Applied University, Jordan

The interest in KM in Jordan is retalively new, since about 2003. Many Jordanian institutions, including universities are working to understand issues related to this field in order to use KM and achieve excellence and competitiveness. This study tries to highlight some of the factors affecting KM utilization at universities, such as KM awareness and the exercising of its operations, because failure to utilize KM is often due to a lack of awareness, and incrrect exercise of its operations. This study aims at identifying the impact of the workers KM awareness at YU and ANU, and exercising its operations on KM utilization. Data was collected from workers at senior and middle management levels, using a questionnaire consisting of three sub-measures. Several conclusions have been reached, and it is expected that they will contribute to helping universities utilize the KM system successfully.

Compilation of References 376

About the Contributors 420

Index 430

Preface

A REVISED KNOWLEDGE PYRAMID

Much has been written on the knowledge pyramid, usually characterized as the data, information, knowledge, wisdom, DIKW, hierarchy and its use in knowledge management, KM. This chapter continues this discussion but takes a different position. It is posited that the knowledge pyramid is an artifact of KM processes and not an artifact of reality. This is a different position in that several authors (Ackoff, Sharma, Bates, Fricke) consider the pyramid as a natural expression of the relationships between DIKW and the logical progression for the generation of IKW (Ackoff, 1989; Bates, 2005; Miller, 1996; Sharma, 2004). This chapter proposes that the natural relationship between DIKW is actually an inverted pyramid and that the knowledge pyramid is an artificially constructed artifact representing the relationship between DIKW in an organizational KM context.

Additionally, while the current knowledge pyramid expresses only the hierarchical relationships between DIKW, this chapter shows that the revised knowledge pyramid can also represent process flow relationships. This is a conceptual chapter that hopes to promote discussion and insight by researchers into the nature of KM and its relationship to the overall processes of learning. It also is the introductory chapter to a book of KM research. This book and chapter provide new insights into KM processes, concepts, and implementation. This chapter particularly starts the discussion on concepts such as filtering and selection processes. Another goal of this chapter is to create a model that integrates KM and Business Intelligence, BI, and/or the other "intelligences" such as Customer Intelligence, CI. It is also expected that this discussion will generate a better understanding of KM processes so that better KM systems, KMS, can be designed to better fit the needs of KM users. Finally, this chapter will state definitions of terms important to KM, including definitions of data, information, knowledge, and intelligence. It is hoped that these can be accepted as working, consensus definitions but it is recognized that these terms are philosophical in nature and can be debated as long as we want. This debate is embraced but not encouraged as I agree with Keen and Tan (2007) who believe that while it is important to understand KM terms, it is unproductive for researchers to get focused on trying to precisely define these terms at the expense of furthering KM research. The KM discipline needs to allow the debate but also needs to unite into a consensus set of working definitions. It is hoped this chapter and book will spur this consensus.

Methodology

This is an introductory chapter to a KM research book that focuses on concepts, however, the arguments made and conclusions presented are based on action research. The inspiration for this chapter comes from a project the author participated in with a United States based defense contractor. Specifics of the project and the company cannot be presented due to nondisclosure agreements. What can be said is that the company attempted to take technologies and experience developed/gained working with United States Department of Defense and other national intelligence agencies and generate a commercial knowledge management offering. The role of the author in this project was as a KM academic expert responsible for providing KM focus and direction. It is action research as the author had a vested interest in the success of the project and in generating a commercial KM offering and was able to reflect on the project while participating. Specific data for this chapter comes from the company's initial presentation of what was considered to be a knowledge pyramid. This pyramid cannot be presented due to nondisclosure agreement. However, the presented pyramid can be described as a fusion of the traditional knowledge pyramid with KM processes and intelligence concepts. It was analysis of this pyramid and discussions with the project team that is the basis for this chapter. The pyramid presented is the result of this reflection and is not at all similar to the project proposed pyramid.

The Traditional Knowledge Pyramid

References to a knowledge hierarchy can be found in the popular literature but generally Ackoff is given credit for the first academic publication. Figure 1 illustrates the traditional knowledge pyramid as originally proposed by Ackoff (1989). The inference from the figure is that data begets information begets knowledge begets wisdom. An additional inference is that there is more data than information, more information than knowledge, and more knowledge than wisdom. This model has been used in countless KM presentations and papers and it is stated as a given truth that it is a generally accepted model showing the DIKW hierarchy (Fricke, 2007; Hey, 2008; Sharma, 2004). The model does not philosophically define data, information, knowledge, or wisdom and it is not the purpose of this paper to do this, there are many sources already available that make arguments supporting various definitions. However, it is the purpose of this paper to propose consensus, KM focused working definitions. The traditional knowledge pyramid uses the following summarized basic definitions:

Figure 1. The knowledge pyramid (Ackoff, 1989)

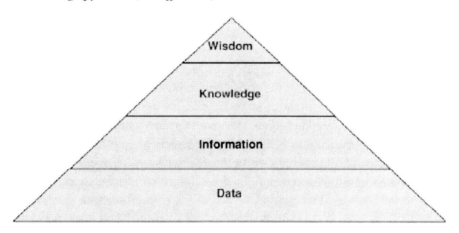

- Data: basic, discrete, objective facts such as who, what, when, where, about something.
- Information: data that is related to each other through a context such that it provides a useful story, as an example, the linking of who, what, when, where data to describe a specific person at a specific time.
- Knowledge: information that has been culturally understood such that it explains the how and the why about something or provides insight and understanding into something
- Wisdom: placing knowledge into a framework or nomological net that allows the knowledge to be applied to different and not necessarily intuitive situations

These definitions imply that there is a relationship between data, information, knowledge, and wisdom and it is the knowledge pyramid that provides a graphical representation of these relationships as a roll up hierarchy of data leading to information leading to knowledge and finally leading to wisdom (henceforth this will be referred to as the DIKW creation flow). Houston and Harmon describe this in the use of summations: $I = \sum(D)$, $K = \sum(I) = \sum\sum(D)$, and $W = \sum(K) = \sum\sum(I) = \sum\sum\sum(D)$ (Houston and Harmon, 2002).

The use of the pyramid is typically in instruction of database and KM concepts to reflect that "data," "information," "knowledge," and "wisdom" are different concepts and are in increasingly higher levels of abstraction. This chapter argues that the DIKW pyramid is a misleading representation of the relationships among these concepts for information systems research purposes. Maintaining the fuzziness of these concepts in the information systems discipline leads to confusion. We need to better define these constructs to begin to eliminate some of the ambiguities in our research.

A counter point to the traditional knowledge pyramid is provided by Tuomi (2000). Tuomi (2000) states that data is not the building block for information, knowledge, and wisdom as data is not observed, collected, or recorded in a vacuum. Rather, our understanding of the world through our wisdom and knowledge drives us to collect specific information and data to support our use of our knowledge and wisdom. In this view, the hierarchy flows down the pyramid rather than up the pyramid and data does not exist as a collection of unrelated facts as all collected facts are related to our basic knowledge and wisdom. While this is an improvement to the knowledge pyramid it still allows for confusion as it provides little insight and explanation for the relationships between DIKW. The proposed revision of the knowledge pyramid will show that flow is in both directions and introduces discussion on the relationships between DIKW.

The Revised Knowledge Pyramid

The revised knowledge pyramid attempts to place the knowledge hierarchy within the context of the natural or real world. Figure 2 illustrates the revised pyramid. What it shows is that data, information, knowledge, and wisdom exists in a global context, i.e. humans are constantly gathering and processing data into information, knowledge, and wisdom. However, the data gathered and processed is not all that is available and is limited by the abilities of the sensors to detect, interpret, and capture data. Sensors can be our human senses, other's human senses, or mechanical where mechanical sensors are anything that is not a human sense such as a light detector, radio wave detector, pressure meter, a typed in transaction record, etc.. They reflect that as sensors improve our ability to capture more data improves. A human example of improving sensors is using lasiks to improve eyesight allowing a person to "see" much

Figure 2. Revised knowledge pyramid

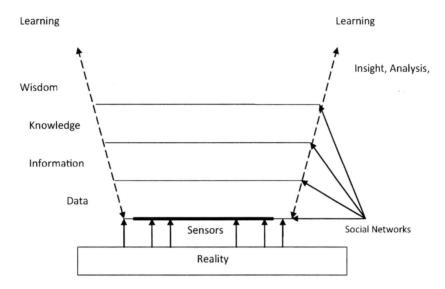

more, enriching the vision that is captured. A mechanical example is changing accuracy, range, and/or sensitivity of sensors so they can "sense" more phenomena,

The dotted arrows reflect the processing into information, knowledge, and wisdom using the processes of insight, analysis, and sense making. These lines are bi-directional indicating that the generation of information, knowledge, and/or wisdom may progress up the hierarchy or feedback down the hierarchy as the user understands more of what they are learning (this recognizes Turomi's (2000) counter view). The lines between layers reflect the social networks used to transfer to different users. Social networks are being used loosely in this context and refer to any formal or informal, direct or indirect methods used to transfer data, information, knowledge and wisdom between users. Examples include classroom settings, word of mouth, published articles, conference presentations, email, etc. Ultimately, this is a representation of the knowledge hierarchy and the general learning process for people and societies that results in multiple large bodies of knowledge being generated and used. The endpoints lead to learning. Why learning? Learning has a multitude of definitions but for this model learning is defined as the acquisition of DIWK that leads to a change in behavior or expectation within the individual or group that is doing the learning.

Why is the knowledge pyramid inverted, i.e. why is there more information than data, more knowledge than information, and more wisdom than knowledge? One reason is simply mathematical, if information is the structuring of data into meaningful combinations, then the number of possible combinations for a quantity x of data is minimally x! implying there is possibly a greater amount of information than the original amount of data. Considering that data users may have differing frames of reference for processing data in different disciplines of thought (for example accountants versus marketers or engineers versus biologists) it is very conceivable that the amount of information generated is greater than the original amount of data. This same argument can be used for the generation of knowledge and wisdom, especially when it is also considered that users may have different ethical, religious, or cultural belief systems that could cause them to interpret information and then knowledge differently (for example Christians may generate different wisdom from the same knowledge than a Buddhist would or free societies different than totalitarian societies). This is consistent with

Nonaka (1994) and Jennex (2008), and others that argue that all knowledge is context specific. An example of this is technology transfer that takes DIKW from one discipline (or context) and attempts to apply it to another discipline (or context). An example is taking the knowledge of using learning algorithms to identify meaningful sound patterns used to create sound canceling headphones and applying it to analyzing light diffraction patterns for identifying radioactive or other (such as explosive) substances.

Figure 3 represents a newly proposed KM knowledge pyramid. This pyramid is more like a traditional pyramid. The solid vertical arrows represent application of KM to the DIKW hierarchy pyramid. Jennex (2005, p. iv) defined KM as "the practice of selectively applying knowledge from previous experiences of decision making to current and future decision making activities with the express purpose of improving the organization's effectiveness." This implies that KM is not trying to capture all knowledge or wisdom. Rather, KM targets specific knowledge and wisdom needed by an organization to perform specific tasks. Specific, actionable knowledge and wisdom is defined as intelligence and it is the goal of KM to provide intelligence to the organization for use in decision making. The lines between layers reflect the filters used to focus on specific DIKW. KM needs specific data, information, knowledge, and intelligence. Additionally, KM seeks to share this with the right people at the right time (Jennex, et al., 2009). This implies that KM filters data, information, and knowledge to generate specific, actionable intelligence that is shared with specific, limited users. Filters are placed on the social networks to limit access and to separate and capture that which is needed from that which is not. This is a fairly new term for KM as the KM literature tends to use the term KM strategy. It is the position of this chapter that KM filters are the implementation of KM strategy. That filters are important is evidenced by Jennex and Olfman (2005) who found KM strategy to be a key critical success factor. The use of intelligence leads to organizational learning. Organizational learning is defined as a quantifiable improvement in activities, increased available knowledge for decision-making, or sustainable competitive advantage (Cavaleri,

Figure 3. The KM knowledge pyramid

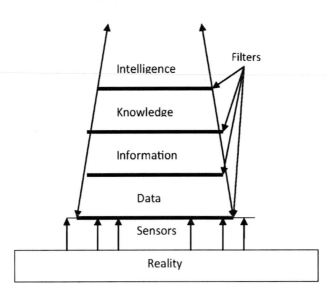

Figure 4. The revised knowledge-KM pyramid

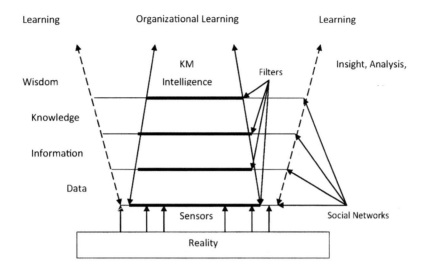

1994; Dodgson, 1993; Easterby-Smith, 1997; Miller, 1996). Huber, Davenport, and King (1998) believe an organization learns if, through its processing of DIKW, its potential behaviors are changed.

Figure 4 combines the two pyramids. The implication is that the KM knowledge pyramid is a subset of the revised knowledge pyramid as shown in Figure 2. There are other differences. KM tends not to use wisdom but is beginning to apply intelligence concepts and differentiate between knowledge needed to make a decision and specific actionable knowledge needed to make a specific decision in a specific context. For example marketing knowledge is needed to create marketing campaigns but specific customer knowledge is needed to make decisions as to how to market specific customers. For some users this is confusing as it seems to imply there are differing types of knowledge needed for KM. However, this tends to be consistent in intent to Tuomi's (2000) concept of wisdom.

This confusion between wisdom and intelligence may be a driver for those who practice Business Intelligence, BI, or Customer Intelligence, CI, etc. as they see a need for differentiating between general information and knowledge and specific decision information and knowledge (BI is defined as the collection, analysis, and presentation of business information for decision making (Wikipedia, 2008) while CI is the same only for customer information (Wikipedia, 2008)). As previously discussed, Figure 3 captures this by using the term intelligence rather than wisdom where intelligence refers to very specific actionable knowledge. The term intelligence is taken from the intelligence realm, that area that seeks to generate actionable knowledge to be used in the formulation of strategies and tactics to accomplish a specific goal, such as beating an opponent during wartime or to determine what actions should be planned. This term is not chosen lightly as it does fit into the DIKW hierarchy meaning that it is the interpretation of data, information, and knowledge to create courses of action or make specific decisions. Also, the KM arrows are shown to be double headed as the hierarchy may travel in either direction. In fact, it is expected that while the learning process will tend to generally be a bottom up process, meaning that it starts with the interpretation of data, organizational learning and KM will generally be a top down process where it is first determined what actions or decisions need to take place or be made and from that identify what intelligence, then knowledge, then information, then data is needed to support taking the specific actions or making the specific decisions.

The other major difference is in the application of filters. While the general learning process seeks to push data, information, knowledge, and wisdom out to all who wish to use it, KM does not. As stated earlier, KM seeks to support specific decision making and thus needs specific data, information, knowledge, and intelligence. Additionally, KM seeks to share this with the right people at the right time. This implies that KM filters data, information, and knowledge to generate specific, actionable intelligence that is shared with specific, limited users. Filters are placed on the social networks to limit access and to separate and capture that which is needed from that which is not. This is a fairly new term for KM as the KM literature tends to use the term KM strategy. It is the position of this paper that KM filters are the implementation of KM strategy. That filters are important is evidenced by Jennex and Olfman (2005) who found KM strategy to be a key critical success factor.

A final difference between the traditional knowledge pyramid and the revised knowledge pyramid is the removal of apex's. This was done to remove confusion as an apex tends to imply that there is an ultimate point, such as the ultimate key wisdom for the traditional knowledge pyramid or a single key datum for the revised knowledge pyramid. While it is somewhat satisfying to refer to ultimate points, this chapter does not support the idea of a "big bang" theory for data or an ultimate, supreme wisdom. Rather, the chapter does support that there is some initial level of data and some ultimate amount of wisdom or intelligence. To support this position again consider the contextual nature of knowledge and wisdom/intelligence and the multiple frames of reference and contexts that users bring to the generation of knowledge and wisdom. Also consider that most organizations do not ultimately need one key piece of intelligence as there is rarely a single decision that needs to be made. Hence the revised knowledge pyramid is pyramidal in form as that provides a visual impact as to the relative amounts of data, information, knowledge, and wisdom/intelligence but are flat topped, much like the Aztec and Mayan pyramids and not like the Egyptian pyramids (note that this is being used to illustrate the point and not to imply that there is more merit to one style pyramid over another).

Discussion

The revised knowledge pyramid recognizes Ackoff (1989) and Tuomi (2000) and finds both wanting. Ackoff (1989) assumes data generates information which generates knowledge which generates wisdom. Tuomi (2000) believes all data and information is collected based on influence from existing knowledge and wisdom. Ackoff's (1989) pyramid flows up, Tuomi's (2000) pyramid flows down and reality as observed and implemented in the revised knowledge pyramid recognizes that flow is in both directions. Tuomi (2000) is wrong in thinking that flow is only down the pyramid. Basic research often times involves collecting data about something that we do not have knowledge or wisdom. An example is physics research in the late 1800s. Scientists did not understand nor did they have knowledge about atomic structure, subatomic particles, and radiation. Data was collected an observed by scientists noting that photographic film was fogged when near certain materials. This data was gathered and then put into context as information that said specific materials caused fogging. Consideration of this information led to the formation of theories to explain why this happened, generating potential knowledge. Analysis of this knowledge led to experiments designed to prove the correctness of this potential knowledge, ultimately resulting in theories on radiation. This example shows that both Ackoff (1989) and Tuomi (2000) are right and both are wrong. Flow of creation is in both directions of the pyramid.

Another example bolstering this argument is the use of data mining to create information by discovering patterns in data. Commonly called knowledge discovery, it is the analysis of these new found patterns, or information, and the application of context, culture, and other knowledge that creates knowledge; and the positioning of this knowledge into existing problem or competitive advantage contexts that creates actionable knowledge or intelligence. In this example the predominant direction of creation flow is up the pyramid but it can also be argued that previous knowledge of business needs, processes, and behavior influenced the interpretation of discovered patterns into knowledge and intelligence so that creation flow is actually in both directions. Additionally consider analytics. Analytics seeks to gather specific data to answer specific questions. Systems are created to gather, analyze, and display specific data, information, and knowledge so that managers can monitor organizational performance and take action if warranted. Analytics is primarily a top down design that starts with the intelligence needed and then determines what data, information, and knowledge to gather.

A final example is from engineering. It is common for engineers to instrument everything they can when conducting testing, even if they are not sure of a purpose for the data. A high pressure vessel destructive test from my past illustrates this. The test called for burst testing a 2500 psi vessel pressure using water. Standard instrumentation for measuring pressure and temperature were used plus video monitoring was added. There was no real need for collecting video data other that it was thought it would be interesting to watch. Since water, a noncompressible liquid, was being used as the pressuring medium it wasn't expected to be a violent failure (violence in this case is represented by a very large, very fast release of energy) as it was expected that the vessel would crack and the water spill out or perhaps spray out. The test team was very surprised when the test resulted in a spectacular release of energy. The video data was what provided the story and it was interesting to see the test setup disintegrate during the first test and then to see that the subsequent test setups were surrounded by sand bags and other retaining walls. The point of this example is that there are many situations in which we collect data for no real reason other than we can and it is later analysis of this data that results in the generation of unexpected information, knowledge, and intelligence.

CONCLUSION

The revised knowledge-KM pyramid is visually more complex and thus less satisfying as a visual model then the traditional knowledge pyramid but is more satisfying conceptually as it fits our perception of reality to a better degree than the traditional knowledge pyramid. Is this the final model? Probably not but it is a step in the right direction and a starting point for more detailed discussion on the knowledge pyramid. Should we quit using the traditional knowledge pyramid? While I think yes, and replace it with the revised knowledge pyramid only, I also suspect that the traditional knowledge pyramid will remain as it has its use as a tool for introducing the concepts of data, information, knowledge, and wisdom to beginning students. However, it is recommended that the traditional knowledge pyramid be quickly followed by the revised knowledge-KM pyramid as this is a better model for explaining what KM is and does and for how DIKW are created.

The revised knowledge-KM pyramid also shows that BI, CI, etc. are really not new applications but are manifestations of confusion caused by the traditional knowledge pyramid. While it is expected that BI, CI, etc. practitioners may not embrace that they are within KM, the model does support the fusion of these initiatives into the KM discipline and KM researchers are encouraged to include these approaches in researching and applying KM.

Finally, this chapter proposed to provide a set of what are hoped to be consensus working definitions of KM terms from the revised knowledge-KM pyramid. These terms are summarized below:

- Data: basic, discrete, objective facts such as who, what, when, where, about something.
- Information: data that is related to each other through a context such that it provides a useful story, as an example, the linking of who, what, when, where data to describe a specific person at a specific time.
- Knowledge: information that has been culturally understood such that it explains the how and the why about something or provides insight and understanding into something
- Wisdom: placing knowledge into a framework or nomological net that allows the knowledge to be applied to different and not necessarily intuitive situations
- Intelligence: specific actionable knowledge needed to make a specific decision in a specific context.
- Learning: the acquisition of DIWK that leads to a change in behavior or expectation within the individual or group that is doing the learning.
- Organizational Learning: a quantifiable improvement in activities, increased available knowledge for decision-making, or sustainable competitive advantage. An organization learns if, through its processing of DIKW, its potential behaviors are changed (Cavaleri, 1994; Dodgson, 1993; Easterby-Smith, 1997; Huber, Davenport, and King, 1998; Miller, 1996).
- Social networks: any formal or informal, direct or indirect methods used to transfer data, information, knowledge and wisdom between users.
- Filters: KM processes that limit access and separate and capture that DIKW/I which is needed from that which is not.

The implications of this chapter are many. KMS designers have a better understanding of how KM fits in the general DIKW world. KMS can focus on strategy and strategy implementation through the design and implementation of KM filters. This leads to the possibility of creating audit mechanisms that can validate that KM strategy has been properly implemented that is similar in nature to auditing security policy implementations in firewalls. Another implication is a clearer understanding of the role of social networks in the creation and transfer of DIKW/I. KMS designers will also be focused on providing technological support for these social networks and it clarifies that KMS is more than just knowledge storage and retrieval technologies, they also incorporate communication and collaboration technologies. Another implication is a new focus on identifying specific actionable knowledge for focused decision making, or, as stated in the chapter, generating intelligence. A final implication is that KM should now be recognized as an integrated part of regular DIKW/I processing. KMS designers should be focusing on integrating KM processes into regular work processes.

The rest of this book provides current research into KM. Topics of chapters range from the use of social networking technologies to analysis of KM strategy to analysis of knowledge transfer and flow. A wide range of contexts are discussed, from schools to multinational organizations to small and medium enterprises, SMEs. Many different research methodologies are used, such as case studies, action research, and quantitative methods. A good indicator for the maturing of the KM discipline is that significantly more research is quantitative based. This indicates the discipline is moving from theory building to theory proving, a sure sign of a maturing discipline.

Murray E. Jennex
San Diego State University, USA

REFERENCES

Ackoff, R. L. (1989). From Data to Wisdom. *Journal of Applied Systems Analysis, 16*, 3–9.

Bates, M.J. Information and knowledge: an evolutionary framework for information science. Information Research 10(4), paper 239, 2005.

Cavaleri, S. (1994). Soft Systems Thinking: A Pre-Condition for Organizational Learning. *Human Systems Management, 13*(4), 259–267.

Davenport, T. H., & Prusak, L. (1998). *Working Knowledge*. Boston, MA: Harvard Business School Press.

Dodgson, M. (1993). Organizational Learning: A Review of Some Literatures. *Organization Studies, 14*(3), 375–394. doi:10.1177/017084069301400303

Easterby-Smith, M. (1997). Disciplines of Organizational Learning: Contributions and Critiques. *Human Relations, 50*(9), 1085–1113. doi:10.1177/001872679705000903

Fricke, M. The Knowledge Pyramid: A Critique of the DIKW Hierarchy. Journal of Information Science, 2007.

Hey, J. The Data, Information, Knowledge, Wisdom Chain: The Metaphorical link. Retrieved June 16, 2008 from: http://www.oceanteacher.org, 2004.

Houston, R. D., & Harmon, E. G. "Re-envisioning the information concept: systematic definitions." In H. Bruce, R. Fidel, P. Ingwersen, & P. Vakkari (Eds.), Emerging frameworks and methods: proceedings of the fourth International Conference on Conceptions of Library and Information Science (CoLIS4), pp. 305-308. Greenwood Village, CO: Libraries Unlimited, 2002.

Huber, G. P., Davenport, T. H., & King, D. "Some Perspectives on Organizational Memory." Unpublished Working Paper for the Task Force on Organizational Memory, F. Burstein, G. Huber, M. Mandviwalla, J. Morrison, and L. Olfman, (eds.) Presented at the 31st Annual Hawaii International Conference on System Sciences. Hawaii, 1998.

Jennex, M. E. (2005). What is Knowledge Management? *International Journal of Knowledge Management, 1*(4), iiv.

Jennex, M. E. (2008). The Impact of Culture and Context on Knowledge Management. In Jennex, M. E. (Ed.), *Current Issues in Knowledge Management* (pp. 6–11). IGI. doi:10.4018/9781599049168.ch002

Jennex, M. E., & Olfman, L. (2005). Assessing Knowledge Management Success. *International Journal of Knowledge Management, 1*(2), 33–49. doi:10.4018/jkm.2005040104

Jennex, M. E., Smolnik, S., & Croasdell, D. T. (2009). "Towards a Consensus Knowledge Management Success Definition." VINE. *The Journal of Information and Knowledge Management Systems, 39*(2), 174–188.

Keen, P. G. W., & Tan, M. (2007). Knowledge Fusion: A framework for extending the rigor and relevance of knowledge management. *International Journal of Knowledge Management, 3*(4), 1–17. doi:10.4018/jkm.2007100101

Markus, B. Learning Pyramids. WSVA 1 – Virtual Academy and the Surveying/ Geoinformatics Community –Virtual Academy I. 2005.

Miller, D. (1996). A Preliminary Typology of Organizational Learning: Synthesizing the Literature. *Journal of Management, 22*(3), 485–505. doi:10.1177/014920639602200305

Nonaka, I. (1994). A Dynamic Theory Of Organizational Knowledge Creation. *Organization Science, 5*(1), 14–37. doi:10.1287/orsc.5.1.14

Rowley, J. (2007). The wisdom hierarchy: representations of the DIKW hierarchy. *Journal of Information Science, 33*(2), 163–180. doi:10.1177/0165551506070706

Sharma, N. (2004) The Origin of the "Data Information Knowledge Wisdom" Hierarchy. Accessed June 17, 2008: http://wwwpersonal.si.umich.edu/~nsharma/dikw_origin.htm, 2008

Tuomi, I. (2000). Data is More Than Knowledge: Implications of the Reversed Knowledge Hierarchy for Knowledge Management and Organizational Memory. *Journal of Management Information Systems, 16*(3), 103–117.

Wikipedia, "Business Intelligence" accessed from http://en.wikipedia.org/wiki/Business_intelligence on 8/29/2008.

Wikipedia, "Customer Intelligence" accessed from http://en.wikipedia.org/wiki/Customer_intelligence on 8/29/2008.

Section 1

Chapter 1
Measuring Knowledge Management Outcomes at the Individual Level:
Towards a Tool for Research on Organizational Culture

Shahnawaz Muhammed
The American University of Middle East, Kuwait

William J. Doll
The University of Toledo, USA

Xiaodong Deng
Oakland University, USA

ABSTRACT

Extant literature has mostly focused on defining knowledge management success at an organizational or project level. The literature lacks a framework for measuring knowledge management success at the individual level. From a cultural perspective of knowledge management, individual knowledge, innovation and performance make organizations more productive. This research proposes a model of the interrelationships among individual level knowledge management success measures (outcomes) including conceptual, contextual and operational knowledge, innovation, and performance. The model is tested using a sample of 252 individuals engaged in managerial and professional knowledge work. The results suggest that conceptual knowledge enhances operational and contextual knowledge. Contextual knowledge also improves operational knowledge. Contextual knowledge is the key predictor of innovations that, along with operational knowledge, enhance work performance. The results provide a model (tool) for defining and measuring knowledge management success at the individual level. The implications of this success measurement tool for future empirical studies of organizational culture are discussed.

DOI: 10.4018/978-1-60960-555-1.ch001

INTRODUCTION

Knowledge management (KM) can be viewed from many different perspectives. From an organizational implementation point of view, these perspectives fall into one of the three categories identified by Alavi and Leidner (1999). This includes an information-based perspective, a technology-based perspective, or a culture-based perspective. From an information-based perspective, the focus of knowledge management is on the various characteristics of the information within the organization such as making information easily accessible and relevant. From an information-based perspective, competitive advantage is attained by managing information. From a technology-based perspective, the emphasis is on gaining competitiveness by providing technology infrastructure and support to connect various elements within the organization. In their survey, Alavi and Leidner (1999) found that managers who held a culture-based perspective associated KM with factors that shaped or were shaped by the organizational culture such as learning, communication and the development of intellectual property. Nayir and Uzuncarsili (2008) show the profound impact organizational culture can have on knowledge management through a case study in an emerging market, highlighting its importance in globally diverse environments.

In this chapter we adopt the cultural perspective that is widely used in the KM literature (Alavi & Leidner, 2001; Jennex, Smolnik, & Croasdell, 2007). We propose and develop some direct outcomes of knowledge management at an individual level. We also examine the interrelations between those outcome measures. We hope these direct outcomes will serve as an important measure in evaluating the success of KM, first at the individual level and subsequently at an organizational level.

From a cultural perspective, individual level learning and outcomes form an important force that shapes the organizational culture. This organizational culture determines the firm's success in the marketplace. Success of organizational level KM initiatives depends on the knowledge of individuals in these organizations and how these individuals use and share their knowledge (Grant, 1996; Grover & Davenport, 2001). Individuals' knowledge related to specific tasks is a critical component of their effectiveness and eventually leads to a favorable outcome for the organization. This task knowledge reflects the individuals' learning that takes place within the organizational context (Kim, 1993; Nonaka & Takeuchi, 1995).

Understanding how individuals' task related knowledge is impacted and how it can be quantified is generally lacking in the literature and can potentially hamper the overall research efforts in the KM field (Guo & Sheffield, 2006). Alavi and Leidner (1999) acknowledge that "…development of meaningful metrics for measuring the value, quality and quantity of knowledge is a key factor for long-term success and growth of KMS" (p.22). This research contends that enhanced task knowledge is the primary outcome of individual knowledge management. Further, we explore its relationship with other relevant individual outcomes such as individual innovation and performance.

With a cultural perspective of KM in mind, this research focuses on developing measures of individual level task knowledge including conceptual knowledge, contextual knowledge, and operational knowledge. We then explore the relationships among the three types of knowledge, and relate them to innovation and performance outcomes. The intent is to provide reliable and valid knowledge management success measures at the level of individual knowledge workers. These success measures can help validate whether cultural dimensions, organizational factors, or specific knowledge management practices enhance the success of individual knowledge workers.

KNOWLEDGE MANAGEMENT OUTCOMES AT THE INDIVIDUAL LEVEL WITHIN A CULTURAL FRAMEWORK

The goal of KM is to make knowledge available individually and collectively so that effective action can be taken (Bennet & Bennet, 2003). Organizational culture is one of the major factors that determine the effectiveness of knowledge management (Janz & Prasanphanich, 2003; Alavi, Kayworth, & Leidner, 2005). Alavi et al. (2005) and Nayir and Uzuncarsil (2008) have reported case studies that illustrate how organizational culture can have deep impacts on knowledge management. Individual level learning and outcomes can also shape the organizational culture in ways that will give the firm lasting competitiveness (Alavi et al., 2005).

The focus of this research is to develop KM outcome measures that may serve as indicators of individual level success in knowledge work contextualized within their organization. As individuals work within the context of an organization, the organizational culture and other contextual factors (see Figure 1) influence the knowledge management practices (behaviors) of individuals. These KM practices, in turn, impact the level of task knowledge and associated KM outcomes. In

assessing the impact of organizational culture on knowledge management, Alavi et al. (2005) note that "... certain types of organizational values will lead to different types of KM behavior and that these behaviors will lead to varying outcomes" (p. 197).

Knowledge management success outcomes and the factors that contribute to these outcomes are often not sufficiently differentiated in the literature (Jennex et al., 2007). Jennex and Olfman (2005) have shown a need to separate the critical success factors from the outcomes of KM/ knowledge management systems (KMS) success at an organizational level. From their perspective success factors are aspects of the organization or the environment that are needed for KM/KMS to succeed and should be viewed as distinct from the outcomes. They identify twelve such success factors that include knowledge strategy, technical infrastructure, and organizational culture/structure crucial to the success of any KM implementation. In the same vein, others have shown that the contextual factors such as organizational culture influence the KM behaviors of the individuals (Nayir & Uzuncarsili, 2008; Alavi et al., 2005). (Figure 1)

Aspects of organizational culture and other critical success factors affect individual behaviors by creating conducive or adverse work environ-

Figure 1. Knowledge management outcomes and antecedents

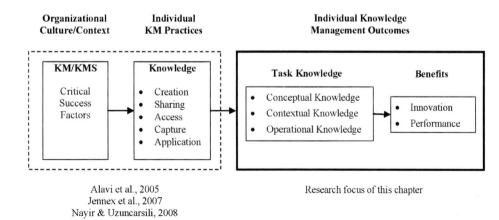

ments (Alavi et al., 2005; Jennex & Olfman, 2005). From a KM perspective, these factors enable or deter behaviors related to how individuals manage their knowledge. In a work setting, knowledge management behaviors of an individual can include processes involved in knowledge creation, knowledge sharing, knowledge access, knowledge capture, and knowledge application. By engaging in these sustained behaviors, which we call knowledge management practices, individuals should be able to improve their task knowledge and gain associated benefits.

To capture individuals' task-related knowledge in an organizational context, we conceptualized task knowledge as having conceptual, contextual, and operational factors based on Yoshioka, Herman, Yates, and Orlikowski's (2001) knowledge framework for communicative actions. Conceptual knowledge is the individual's understanding of why he/she needs to take specific actions to complete the task (know-why) (Kim, 1993; Schultze & Leidner, 2002). Contextual knowledge is an individual's understanding of the contextual factors surrounding the task at hand, such as the knowledge related to the people (know-who), locations (know-where), and timing (know-when) necessary to complete the task (Earl, 2001; Pomerol, Brezillon, & Pasquier, 2002). Operational knowledge is the individual's understanding of task requirements (know-what) and the processes of how to accomplish the task (know-how) (Dhaliwal & Benbasat, 1996; Pfeffer & Sutton, 1999). If individuals have the right knowledge at the right time, creative actions can be enacted and value added.

Possessing knowledge is desirable. However, individuals should be able to use the knowledge to make their work more creative and productive- the outcome that organizations traditionally value. Thus, in addition to the task knowledge, we also focus on innovation and performance. Innovation is the extent to which individuals' work is novel and useful. Performance is how well individuals'

work is done in terms of efficiency, effectiveness, and quality of their work.

Individual Level KM Outcomes: Task Knowledge and Benefits

Traditionally, task knowledge is measured based on skill tests or tests that are specific to each kind of job. This approach might be appropriate in certain situations but is limited as a broad measure applicable across a wide range of tasks. This is similar to the tests that students take at the end of a particular course to assess their learning during a given period of time. Such assessment is limited in usefulness for researches that are designed to test substantive relationships among broad measures for building or testing theory. Further, the assessment itself is limited to the knowledge contained in such tests and the knowledge base largely needs to be defined a priori. Such a priori and narrow definition of one's knowledge base may not be realistically achieved in a constantly changing environment on an ongoing basis, and may also be context specific (Cohen, 1998).

For this research an individual's task knowledge is defined as what an individual knows in relation to a particular task at a specific point in time; equating it to what one's mind hold as his/her mental models (Kim, 1993). Based on the 5W1H paradigm of questioning a situation reflecting the communicative questions why, who, when, where, what, and how (Yoshioka et al., 2001), and using a pragmatic approach, we conceptualize knowledge pertaining to a task to be traceable to these questions. These questions probe the conceptual, contextual, and operational knowledge involved in a task (see Table 1).

Conceptual knowledge pertaining to a task is the deeper understanding of why the person is engaged in a particular task and why it has to be done the way it is planned to be performed by that individual. This type of knowledge is often referred to as know-why (Agarwal, Krudys, & Tanniru, 1997; Garud, 1997; Schultze & Leidner,

Table 1. Knowledge management outcomes, definition and relevant literature

Construct	Definition	Literature
Task Knowledge		
Conceptual Knowledge	Conceptual knowledge is an individual's understanding of why he/she needs to take specific actions to complete the task (know-why).	Agarwal et al., 1997; Garud, 1997; Johnson et al., 2002; Kim, 1993; Schultze and Leidner, 2002; Wiig and Jooste, 2004; Yoshioka et al., 2001
Contextual Knowledge	Contextual knowledge is an individual's understanding of the people (know-who), location (know-where), and timing (know-when) aspects necessary to complete the task.	Earl, 2001; Johnson et al., 2002; Pearlson and Saunders, 2004; Pomerol et al., 2002; Rulke and Galaskiewicz, 2000; von Hippel, 1998; Yoshioka et al., 2001
Operational Knowledge	Operational knowledge is the individual's understanding of task requirements (know-what) and the processes (know-how) to complete the task.	Dhaliwal and Benbasat, 1996; Johnson et al., 2002; Kogut and Zander, 1992; Nonaka and Takeuchi, 1995; Pfeffer and Sutton, 1999; Schultze and Leidner, 2002; Yoshioka et al., 2001
Benefits		
Innovation	Innovation is the extent to which individuals generate and apply new and useful ideas in their work.	Amabile, 1996; Madjar et al., 2002; Oldham and Cummings, 1996; Scott and Bruce, 1994; Van De Ven, 1986
Performance	Performance is how well the individual's work is done. This includes efficiency, effectiveness, and quality of work.	Brockman and Morgan, 2003; Edmondson, 1999; Hackman and Oldham, 1980; Janz and Prasarnphanich, 2003; March, 1991

2002). Wiig and Jooste (2004) point to the importance of such conceptual knowledge when they refer to the metaknowledge in their classification of task knowledge. According to Kim (1993), know-why implies the ability to articulate a conceptual understanding of an experience. It is also sometimes referred to as the understanding of the principles and laws of nature, in human mind and in society (Johnson, Lorenz, & Lundvall, 2002).

Contextual knowledge in relation to a task is the knowledge that may not be central to the satisfactory execution of that task, but may be peripherally related to it. It may be considered as the backstage knowledge with respect to a particular task (Pomerol et al., 2002). Often this knowledge is centered on the (1) knowledge regarding the people that may be involved or affected by that task (know-who: for example, knowledge regarding the customers and stakeholders) or such information as who knows what and who knows what to do (Johnson et al., 2002; Rulke & Galaskiewicz, 2000), (2) knowledge regarding the location of the task or the location of the information about the

task (know-where: for example, where can I get appropriate resources to accomplish the task), and (3) the knowledge regarding the temporal aspects of the task (know-when: for example, when should each aspect of the job be done). Such knowledge helps embellish and enrich the operationalization of an act in addition to providing a broader knowledge base for innovative ideas (Earl, 2001).

Operational knowledge is the core knowledge that is needed to accomplish a task satisfactorily. This is also sometimes referred to as problem-solving knowledge or domain knowledge (Dhaliwal & Benbasat, 1996). This core minimum knowledge regarding the task involves know-what and know-how, which is sometimes referred to as declarative and procedural knowledge (Garud, 1997; Schultze & Leidner, 2002). Know-what is the knowledge as to what is it that needs to be done in performing a task successfully (Johnson et al., 2002). And know-how is the knowledge regarding how that task needs to be performed (Johnson et al., 2002). Without at least a cursory idea of this operational knowledge of the task it is unlikely that the individual will be able to complete his/her tasks satisfactorily (Kogut & Zander, 1992; Nonaka & Takeuchi, 1995; Pfeffer & Sutton, 1999).

Often the value of knowledge gained is difficult to measure (Cohen, 1998), and hence other more measurable indicators are used. For example, Janz and Prasarnphanich (2003) use worker satisfaction, personal evaluation of performance, and stakeholder perception of team performance as the indicators of knowledge outcome. Having broader task knowledge should provide more innovative work outcomes (Wiig & Jooste, 2004). Further, having better task knowledge should be helpful in effectively and efficiently performing such tasks. Thus, in this research, we focus on innovation and performance benefits (see Table 1).

Innovation is one of the important individual activities through which organizations create value (Scott & Bruce, 1994; Van De Ven, 1986). Scott and Bruce (1994) find that creativity and innovation are often used interchangeable. They argue that innovation is not only the creation of new ideas but also the use of such ideas to create new work productions.

Creativity is the central aspect of all innovation. Creativity is often defined as the production of ideas, products and procedures that are novel and useful to the organization (Amabile, 1996; Madjar, Oldham, & Pratt, 2002), as opposed to creative behavioral traits of the individual. Accordingly, the focus here is on the novelty of the external artifact rather than the internal behavioral trait. It may involve recombination of existing ideas, materials, and processes or introducing new ideas, materials, and processes (Madjar et al., 2002).

Having the right knowledge is expected to enhance quality and reduce the variability of task performance (March, 1991). For example, in a new product development context, existing knowledge of the firm, conceptualized as organizational memory, is found to affect information acquisition efficiency resulting in new product performance (Brockman & Morgan, 2003). In a study of IS professionals in knowledge manage-

ment context, Janz and Prasarnphanich (2003) used team performance along three dimensions of efficiency, effectiveness and timeliness. This was based on the outcome measures primarily conducted in job characteristic studies and learning, and can be applicable to both individual and team levels (Edmondson, 1999; Hackman & Oldham, 1980). For this research we adapt Janz and Prasarnphanich's measure of team performance and operationalize individual knowledge worker performance as efficiency, effectiveness and quality of work.

RESEARCH MODEL AND HYPOTHESES

A research model (see Figure 2) is developed that focuses on the relationships among types of task knowledge, innovation, and the performance of individuals. The types of task knowledge include conceptual, contextual, and operational knowledge. Subsequent discussions explore these relationships and propose the associated hypotheses.

Conceptual knowledge, which is a deeper and broader understanding of the situation at hand, may not always be necessary to perform many aspects of a knowledge worker's job satisfactorily. However, having such knowledge provides a sense of purpose and motivation in performing the task in the best possible manner by enhancing know-what and know-how (Agarwal et al., 1997). This broader understanding also helps the individual contextualize his or her actions in the larger scheme of things, and helps draw on appropriate and useful information in novel and useful ways. Conceptual knowledge helps the individual look at his/her actions from higher levels of abstraction. Being able to conceptualize the task from a higher level of abstraction means being able to make richer connections with other knowledge that may or may not be immediately necessary for the execution of the task at hand, and hence, enabling the creation of a richer con-

Figure 2. A model of the relationships among individual knowledge management outcomes

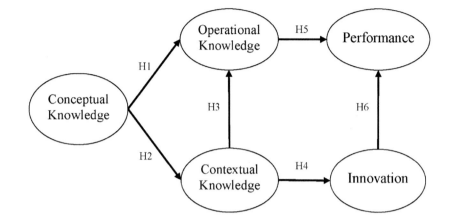

text for the execution of that task (Gasson, 2005; Johnson et al., 2002). Thus we contend:

H1: The higher the conceptual knowledge of an individual, the higher the operational knowledge of the individual.

H2: The higher the conceptual knowledge of an individual, the higher the contextual knowledge of the individual.

Know-who, know-where, and know-when knowledge creates a rich background for individual actions to take place. Even in situations where the task is primarily centered on this type of knowledge, there still exists a potential to draw upon more of such background information. Such knowledge helps in contextualizing and enriching the primary information that individuals need to use in any of their organizational actions (Johnson et al., 2002). The greater contextual knowledge individuals can bring to bear, the better the individuals can embellish their direct task-related knowledge. Especially in today's knowledge intensive environment there is an increasing need to combine and negotiate such knowledge from multiple domains (Gasson, 2005). Thus, we hypothesize:

H3: The higher the contextual knowledge of an individual, the higher the operational knowledge of the individual.

A key aspect of being innovative in the work place is the ability to generate and apply creative and useful ideas in one's work. Creative artifacts originate from ideas in an individual's mind. Novelty is the hallmark of a creative production and requires that individuals connect disparate knowledge in novel ways in their minds. In such situations, rich contextual knowledge provides the potential for the individuals to draw upon seemingly unimportant data to connect them in novel ways to the task at hand. Knowing who the stakeholders are and understanding their needs and expectations can positively contribute to making the outcomes of a knowledge worker's actions useful, novel, and interesting. Being able to easily access knowledge about where to get appropriate resources and information regarding a particular task, and knowing when to use such information and take appropriate actions can help the individuals ease the task of performing those actions. This frees their mental prowess for more creative work. Further, it is often essential to make use of disparate, multi-domain contextual information to produce hybrid and novel solutions

(Engestrom, Engestrom, & Karkkainen, 1995). Thus, we contend:

H4: The higher the contextual knowledge of an individual, the higher the innovativeness of the individual's work.

Operational knowledge is the primary knowledge that an individual needs to have in performing the task. This knowledge includes knowing what needs to be done to accomplish a task and how to do it. When an individual has such information readily accessible to his or her mind, performing the task becomes substantially effortless. Wiig and Jooste (2004) contend that having such knowledge and understanding provides workers with the basic ability to be efficient. When more such information is available, the implementation of such actions becomes more effective and efficient. In this case, the individual can focus on performing the task rather than making sense of the situation and performing the task at the same time.

H5: The higher the operational knowledge of an individual, the higher the performance of the individual's work.

Organizational productivity gains are achieved by making people work more efficiently through many work improvements including better innovations (Wiig & Jooste, 2004). Especially, in non routine work such as in knowledge work, individual innovations help them create procedures and artifacts that help them accomplish the task faster and more effectively (Scott & Bruce, 1994; Van De Ven, 1986). Over time, even small innovations in work can accumulate to produce significant performance improvement for the individual and the firm. Thus, we hypothesize:

H6: The higher the innovativeness of an individual's work, the better the performance of the individual.

RESEARCH METHODS

Following a pretest of the items, measures were further refined by conducting a pilot test. The pilot test involved a small scale data collection and assessment of validity, dimensionality and reliability of the scales. Subsequently, a large scale data collection targeting managerial and professional knowledge workers was implemented using a web-based questionnaire. The following sections briefly describe the pilot, the large scale sample, and the measurement development. Structural equation modeling software package LISREL is employed for measurement assessment and for testing the structural model and hypotheses.

Pilot Testing

A pilot test was performed based on 53 responses obtained out of 68 survey requests from knowledge workers in the United States. Twenty four responses were received from the individuals working in the various functions within organizations involved in design, manufacturing or consulting and the rest of the 29 responses were received from MBA students working for manufacturing firms. The respondents were identified by their managers or themselves as knowledge workers who used information technology heavily for their daily work. The pilot stage data analysis involved item purification using corrected item-total correlation (CITC) scores, evaluation of unidimensionality using principal component factor analysis, evaluation of convergent and discriminant validity using structural equation modeling and reliability assessment using Cronbach's alpha. Items pertaining to each construct were modified or eliminated based on the feedback from the pilot results.

Large Scale Sample

To implement the large scale data collection, a web based survey was implemented. An email list from Manufacturer's News Inc targeting managerial and professional knowledge workers were used to reach the target respondents. The website implemented tracking of click-through based on the email invitations requesting the individual to complete the survey online. After administering two waves of emailing, 252 usable and complete responses were obtained yielding a 31.6% response rate based on click-through. Thus, the response rate is based on those who read the email and clicked on the link. Respondents include individuals from a wide range and size of industries. The majority of the respondents are professionals or in middle management or above positions. Non-response bias is evaluated using a Chi-square test of goodness-of-fit of various demographic variables between the first and second wave of data collection (Smith, 1983). Results indicated no significant difference (p-value > 0.10) between the various demographic variables. Measures were then evaluated in steps similar to the pilot stage involving item purification, evaluation of factor structure, unidimensionality, and convergent and discriminant validity.

Measures

Respondents were asked to answer the survey items based on a particular project or an assignment, or based on their work during the last six months if they did not typically work on a specific project. Providing a more specific framework as mentioned above was expected to help respondents recall the work situation and answer the question with a consistent frame of reference. It is important to provide such a consistent framework to elicit the level of respondents' knowledge within the specified duration because, conceptual and contextual task-knowledge at any given time may be the result of knowledge that may have been accumulated over a long period of time, whereas the operational knowledge is often acquired closer to when the task needs to be performed. The specific measures for the three dimensions of task knowledge is newly developed in this research

and uses a five point Likert type scale where 1= None or to a very little extent and 5= To a very great extent (see Table 2).

Innovation is measured using three items as indicated in Table 2 based on Oldham and Cummings' (1996) creative performance and Scott and Bruce's (1994) innovative behavior with the focus on the work outcome. Performance is measured based on Janz and Prasarnphanich's (2003) measure used in a team performance context.

For innovation, a seven point Likert type scale ranging from 1= Not at all to 7= To an exceptionally high degree, is used, and a scale ranging from 1= Strongly disagree to 7= Strongly agree is used for performance. The final items for each construct after purification and measurement analysis are listed in Table 2.

RESULTS

First, the data is examined using exploratory factor analysis to validate that the five factors have a simple structure. Next, data is analyzed using LISREL in a two step process (Anderson & Gerbing, 1988) where (a) the measurement model is evaluated and then (b) the structural model is evaluated. In step (a) descriptive statistics are presented along with the analysis of reliability, convergent validity and discriminant validity of the measures. In step (b), the structural model is evaluated to test the substantive hypotheses H1 through H6.

Factor Analysis

All the items were factor analyzed with five factor specified, oblimin rotation, and maximum likelihood extraction. The five factor solution yielded a simple structure with all the items loading on their respective factors. Table 3 reports the results of factor analysis with the factors sorted in the descending order with the strongest factor listed first. No cross loadings were above 0.30. The two

Table 2. Measurement items for task knowledge and performance outcomes

Construct	Items	
	Towards the end of the assignment/project/work to what extent did you have FULL knowledge of…	
Conceptual Knowledge	CONC1	the reasons behind your actions
	CONC2	the philosophy behind your actions
	CONC3	the purpose of your actions
	CONC4	the rationale behind your actions
Contextual Knowledge	CONT1	whom to go to for the necessary resources
	CONT2	who were the most knowledgeable people at work
	CONT3	where you could get the required resources
	CONT4	when different things had to be done
	CONT5	when to share information
Operational Knowledge	OPER1	how to implement your work routines
	OPER2	the relevant know-how
	OPER3	your job requirements
Innovation	During the assignment/project/work compared to other people in similar position…	
	INNV1	I was the first to use certain ideas in my kind of work
	INNV2	my work was original and practical
	INNV3	my work was creative
Performance	Towards the end of the assignment/project/work compared to other people in similar position…	
	PERF1	I was very efficient at my work
	PERF2	I was very effective in my work
	PERF3	my work was of very high quality

lowest factor loadings were for items OPER3 (-0.517) and CONT5 (0.576). All the other items loaded on their respective constructs with loadings above 0.60.

Measurement Model Results

The descriptive statistics, Cronbach's alpha, average variance extracted (AVE) and correlations between the variables are reported in Table 4. The means range from 3.99 for contextual knowledge (on a 5 point scale) to 5.85 for performance (on a 7 point scale). The standard deviations range from 0.66 for contextual knowledge to 1.24 for Innovation. The skewness values are between -2 and +2 and the kurtosis values are all lower than 5.0, suggesting that the scales do not violate the assumption of normality.

The Cronbach's alpha indicates adequate reliability and ranges from 0.81, for operational knowledge, to 0.94 for conceptual knowledge. Correlations range from 0.14 to 0.59, and are all significant at p-value < 0.01 except for correlation between operational knowledge and innovation (0.14) which is significant at p-value < 0.05.

AVE scores range from 0.53 for contextual knowledge to 0.80 for conceptual knowledge. Scores above 0.50 are an indication of convergent validity. Convergent validity is also assessed by how well the items load on their respective latent variable. Figure 3 shows standardized item-factor loadings for all the five constructs. All standardized item-factor loadings are 0.70 or higher, except for one item for contextual knowledge (which has a loading of 0.69), indicating good convergent validity for the items measuring each of these

Table 3. Exploratory factor analysis: Pattern matrix with maximum likelihood extraction and oblimin rotation

Item Labels	Factors				
	Conceptual Knowledge	Innovation	Performance	Contextual Knowledge	Operational Knowledge
CONC3	.947				
CONC4	.908				
CONC1	.843				
CONC2	.796				
INNV2		.925			
INNV3		.899			
INNV1		.724			
PERF2			.921		
PERF3			.812		
PERF1			.706		
CONT2				.873	
CONT1				.695	
CONT3				.679	
CONT4				.601	
CONT5				.576	
OPER1					-.834
OPER2					-.631
OPER3					-.517

constructs. Further, all loadings are significant at p-value < 0.01.

An analysis of AVE scores and the squared correlations in Table 4 indicates that the AVE scores are greater than the square of the correlation between the focal factor and other factors, suggesting adequate discriminant validity. A more rigorous chi-square (χ^2) test of discriminant validity indicates whether a unidimensional rather than a two-dimensional model can account for the inter-correlations among the observed items in each pair. For ten comparisons, the chi-square value for the test of discriminant validity between pairs of latent factors must be equal to or greater than 10.83 for significance at p-value 0.01. Chi-

square difference between the correlated model and the measurement model with correlations fixed to 1 indicate that all values are significant at p < 0.01 (Table 5), suggesting discriminant validity between all pairs.

The five factor correlated measurement model (Figure 3) is judged to have good model-data fit with $\chi^2 = 186.47$ for 125 degrees of freedom (chi-square per degree of freedom = 1.49), Root Mean Square Error of Approximation (RMSEA) = 0.044, Non-Normed Fit Index (NNFI) = 0.99, and Comparative Fit Index (CFI) = 0.99. Values of RMSEA less than 0.05, and NNFI and CFI values above 0.95 indicate good model-data fit (Hu & Bentler, 1999). All items have item-

Table 4. Reliability, average variance extracted, correlations, and convergent validity of task knowledge and performance measures

	Conceptual Knowledge	Contextual Knowledge	Operational Knowledge	Innovation[!]	Performance[!]
Conceptual Knowledge	AVE=0.80 α=0.94				
Contextual Knowledge	r=0.56**	AVE=0.53 α=0.85			
Operational Knowledge	r=0.53**	r=0.59**	AVE=0.59 α=0.81		
Innovation	r=0.25**	r=0.22**	r=0.14*	AVE=0.73 α=0.89	
Performance	r=0.25**	r=0.29**	r=0.45**	r=0.39**	AVE=0.71 α=0.88
Mean=	4.19	3.99	4.08	5.12	5.85
SD=	0.81	0.66	0.68	1.24	0.88
Skewness=	-1.14	-0.81	-0.69	-0.60	-1.14
Kurtosis=	1.28	1.04	0.17	0.24	1.64

* Correlation is significant at the 0.05 level (2-tailed).

** Correlation is significant at the 0.01 level (2-tailed).

! a seven point Likert scale is used for this variable.

factor loadings equal to or greater than 0.69 (p-value < 0.01). The major modification index (12.05) is an error correlation between two items in conceptual knowledge. The expected value of the change for this modification is only 0.05. There are two cross-loadings from conceptual knowledge to items OPER3 and INNO3 with modification indices of 9.07 and 8.92, respectively. The expected value of change for OPER3 is 0.19, indicating a relatively weak cross loading as compared to a much stronger standardized loading (0.73) on the respective construct.

Structural Model Results

In order to test the substantive hypotheses a combined measurement and structural LISREL model is developed (see Figure 4). The result of this analysis is used to accept or reject the hypotheses based on the significance of the standardized structural coefficients of the relationships. In order to evaluate the significance of the structural coefficients, a reasonable model-data fit is necessary and is evidenced based on the various fit statistics. All item loadings and structural relationships are significant at p-value < 0.01.

Modification indices indicate three correlations among error terms. These correlated error terms are relatively weak with the largest modification index being 11.47 between CONC3 and CONC4. The model indicates good model-data fit upon examination of the various absolute and incremental fit indices (RMSEA=0.046, NNFI=0.99, CFI=0.99). The structural coefficient from conceptual knowledge to contextual knowledge has the strongest relationship with a standardized coefficient of 0.63. Weakest direct link is from conceptual knowledge to operational knowledge (0.24). However, all structural coefficients are significant (p-values < 0.01) and support all six proposed hypotheses.

Figure 3. The measurement model: standardized solution

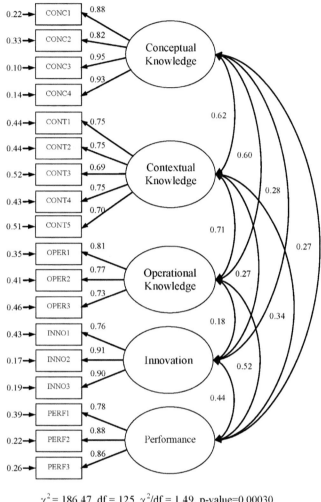

$\chi^2 = 186.47$, df $= 125$, $\chi^2/\text{df} = 1.49$, p-value$=0.00030$, RMSEA$=0.044$, NNFI$=0.99$, CFI$=0.99$

DISCUSSION

Critical success factors (CSFs) represent an organizational context that is necessary for the success of knowledge management initiatives at the organizational level. They are factors that contribute to an organization's success at building knowledge-based competencies or taking advantage of the knowledge created by individuals. Knowledge is primarily created by individuals and then shared among a community of knowing in an organization.

The success of knowledge management depends upon: the knowledge management practices used by individuals; the extent that these knowledge management practices enhance the conceptual, operational, or contextual knowledge of individuals; and whether this enhanced task knowledge improves individual innovation and performance. Increased task knowledge is the enhancement of an individual's mental model of frameworks and routines (declarative and procedural knowledge) related to the work.

Table 5. Chi-Square test of discriminant validity

Construct Pair	Δ Chi-Square	Δ Degree of Freedom	Discriminant Validity *
Conceptual Knowledge - Contextual Knowledge	387.52	1	Yes
Conceptual Knowledge - Operational Knowledge	155.60	1	Yes
Conceptual Knowledge - Innovation	977.91	1	Yes
Conceptual Knowledge - Performance	366.02	1	Yes
Contextual Knowledge - Operational Knowledge	106.90	1	Yes
Contextual Knowledge - Innovation	650.38	1	Yes
Contextual Knowledge - Performance	364.07	1	Yes
Operational Knowledge - Innovation	248.77	1	Yes
Operational Knowledge - Performance	202.62	1	Yes
Innovation - Performance	345.70	1	Yes
* Indicates significance at p < 0.01, based on the Δ Chi-square greater than 10.83 for the ten comparisons conducted.			

Figure 4. Hypotheses testing using structural model: standardized solution

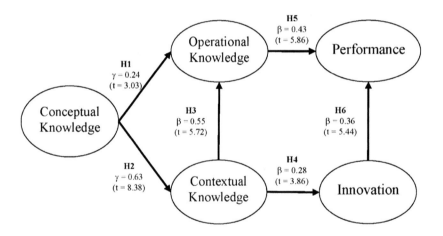

$\chi^2 = 197.58$, df=129, χ^2/df= 1.53; P-value = 0.00010, RMSEA = 0.046, NNFI=0.99, CFI=0.99

The results indicate that conceptual knowledge has an indirect rather than a direct effect on innovation and performance. Conceptual knowledge works through contextual and operational knowledge to impact innovation and performance, respectively. Thus, it is a necessary, but not a sufficient condition for achieving benefits such as innovation and performance.

Contextual knowledge helps enhance operational knowledge. Know-what and know-how can be enhanced by having greater knowledge of know-who, know-where, and know-when. This suggests that operational knowledge may not be fully usable for improving performance without a specified context for action. Contextual knowledge has not been conceptualized and researched explicitly as a separate variable. The relationship between process and context has not been adequately studied. For example, people may know the product development process but their success in this process will be enhanced if they have identified a specific target market, have better knowledge of their customers' needs, and know when the product needs to be introduced to provide a first-to-market advantage.

The results indicate that contextual knowledge also plays an important role in predicting innovation. For example, the knowledge of customer requirements will help knowledge workers identify innovations that meet or exceed customer expectations. Enhanced contextual knowledge provides a richer background to generate novel ideas.

Most research on knowledge management has focused on the organizational level, providing case studies or conceptual papers that suggest organizational factors that improve knowledge management in general or knowledge sharing in particular (Earl, 2001; Jennex & Olfman, 2005). Recent conceptual papers have focused on the role of culture in influencing organizational knowledge management practices (Albescu, Pugna, & Paraschiv, 2009) or global cross-cultural project teams (Ajmal, Kekäle, & Takala, 2009). While these conceptual or case studies provide anecdotal support for how organizational culture influences KM success, they are suggestive rather than conclusive (Jennex, 2008). A notable exception is the work of Furner, Mason, Mehta, Munyon, and Zinko (2009) who conducted a large sample empirical study of how cultural dimensions (individualism, power distance, uncertainty avoidance, masculinity) effected the learning preferences (structure and group) of individuals.

Measures of individual level knowledge management success (see Figure 1) can stimulate empirical research and enrich our understanding of the linkages among organizational culture/ practices, individual knowledge management practices (e.g., knowledge creation, knowledge sharing, and knowledge application), and success outcomes. We suggest a more empirical research agenda that explores how organizational differences might make knowledge management more difficult, influence the level of individual

knowledge management practices, and thereby influence the accumulation of the task knowledge so essential for the innovation and performance of individuals and organizations. To provide tools for this type of research, this chapter provides measures of knowledge management success at the individual level. Future research efforts will focus on the linking individuals' knowledge management practices with the measures of knowledge management success reported in this chapter. We suggest that this upstream research agenda can provide new empirical insights into how organizational practices and culture can influence knowledge management success.

LIMITATIONS AND CONCLUSION

The results should be interpreted with caution as they are based upon one sample. Further research is necessary to cross validate these success measures as well the structural relationship among them. If cross validated, these instruments can be used in future research as a set of criteria for evaluating the effectiveness of antecedent factors such as KM practices or KMS CSFs.

Another limitation of this study is that only knowledge that the respondents consciously reflect as task related knowledge is measured in this research. It is possible that the work related outcomes are also affected by knowledge that may not be directly related to an individual's work. For example, when taking up a new job, individuals bring with them a set of skill that they have developed over time through their previous work and life experiences. This may include processes and thought patterns that have evolved with their earlier experiences which may or may not bear directly with the requirements of the new work. However, such knowledge may have impact on their work in subtle ways, both positive and negative. Future research needs to focus on assessing the extent of impact of such knowledge that may not be captured in such reflective measures.

The conceptual, contextual and operational knowledge dimensions seem to be valid for the overall general task related knowledge when considered for a period of time such as when accomplishing a particular project. However, whether such a conceptualization holds true for a more specific domain of knowledge is unsure. Similarly, whether the current conceptualization of knowledge used in this research is valid when considering a more broader and general human knowledge needs to be investigated, especially when used in predictive models. Future research is needed to examine the range of knowledge abstractions for which the conceptualization used in this research is applicable.

Another possible avenue for further research is to examine the applicability of the current model of knowledge management success measures used in this research in organizational or team level. Though a greater effort may be needed for the data collection for such investigation, a wealth of statistical tools such as hierarchical linear modeling should facilitate such multilevel analysis.

In this chapter we have developed and tested a model of KM success measures at the individual level and explored their interrelationships. The model is developed based on conceptualization of individuals' work place knowledge as task knowledge and relating it to the work place outcomes of innovation and performance. Task knowledge is successfully modeled as comprising of three dimensions of conceptual, contextual and operational knowledge. Conceptual knowledge is found to have a significant impact on contextual and operational knowledge. Operational knowledge is also impacted by contextual knowledge. Contextual knowledge has the greatest impact on innovation. However, individual performance is affected by their operational knowledge and their innovativeness. The valid and reliable measurement instruments for evaluating KM success at the individual level would be a critical tool for advancing empirical research in this area. Further,

they are short and should be easy to incorporate into other studies of KM success.

REFERENCES

Agarwal, R., Krudys, G., & Tanniru, M. (1997). Infusing Learning into an Information Systems Organization. *European Journal of Information Systems*, 6(1), 25–40. doi:10.1057/palgrave.ejis.3000257

Ajmal, M. M., Kekäle, T., & Takala, J. (2009). Cultural Impacts on Knowledge Management and Learning in Project-based Firms. *Vine*, 39(4), 339–352. doi:10.1108/03055720911013634

Alavi, M., Kayworth, T. R., & Leidner, D. E. (2005). An Empirical Examination of the Influence of Organizational Culture on Knowledge Management Practices. *Journal of Management Information Systems*, 22(3), 191–224. doi:10.2753/MIS0742-1222220307

Alavi, M., & Leidner, D. E. (1999). Knowledge management systems: issues, challenges, and benefits. *Communications of the Association for Information Systems*, 1(7), 1–28.

Alavi, M., & Leidner, D. E. (2001). Knowledge Management and Knowledge Management Systems: Conceptual Foundations and Research Issues. *Management Information Systems Quarterly*, 25(1), 107–133. doi:10.2307/3250961

Albescu, F., Pugna, I., & Paraschiv, D. (2009). Cross-cultural Knowledge Management. *Informatica Economica*, 13(4), 39–50.

Amabile, T. (1996). *Creativity in Context*. Boulder, Colorado: Westview Press.

Anderson, J. C., & Gerbing, D. W. (1988). Structural Equation Modeling in Practice: A Review and Recommended Two-step Approach. *Psychological Bulletin*, 103(3), 411–423. doi:10.1037/0033-2909.103.3.411

Bennet, A., & Bennet, D. (2003). *The partnership between organizational learning and knowledge management.* In C.W. Holsapple (Ed.), Handbook of Knowledge Management, Volume 1: Knowledge Matters. 439-460. Heildelberg: Springer-Verlag

Brockman, B. K., & Morgan, R. M. (2003). The Role of Existing Knowledge in New Product Innovativeness and Performance. *Decision Sciences, 34*(2), 385–420. doi:10.1111/1540-5915.02326

Cohen, D. (1998). Toward a Knowledge Context: Report on the First Annual U.C. Berkeley Forum on Knowledge and the Firm. *California Management Review, 40*(3), 22–40.

Dhaliwal, J., & Benbasat, I. (1996). The Use and Effects of Knowledge-based System Explanations: Theoretical *Foundations and a Framework for Empirical Evaluation. Information Systems Research, 7*(3), 342–362. doi:10.1287/isre.7.3.342

Earl, M. (2001). Knowledge Management Strategies: Toward a Taxonomy. *Journal of Management Information Systems, 18*(1), 215–234.

Edmondson, A. (1999). Psychological Safety and Learning Behavior in Work Teams. *Administrative Science Quarterly, 44*(2), 350–384. doi:10.2307/2666999

Engestrom, Y., Engestrom, R., & Karkkainen, M. (1995). Polycontextuality and boundary crossing in expert cognition: Learning and problem solving in complex work activities. *Learning and Instruction, 5*(4), 319–336. doi:10.1016/0959-4752(95)00021-6

Furner, C. P., Mason, R. M., Mehta, N., Munyon, T. P., & Zinko, R. (2009). Cultural Determinants of Leaning Effectiveness from Knowledge Management Systems: A Multinational Investigation. *Journal of Global Information Technology Management, 12*(1), 30–51.

Garud, R. (1997). On the Distinction between Know-how, Know-what and Know-why. In Huff, A., & Walsh, J. (Eds.), *Advances in Strategic Management* (pp. 81–101).

Gasson, S. (2005). The Dynamics of Sensemaking, Knowledge, and Expertise in Collaborative, Boundary-Spanning Design. *Journal of Computer-Mediated Communication, 10*(4).

Grant, R. M. (1996). Toward a Knowledge-based Theory of the Firm. *Strategic Management Journal, 17*(Special Issue), 109–122.

Grover, V., & Davenport, T. H. (2001). General Perspectives on Knowledge Management: Fostering a Research Agenda. *Journal of Management Information Systems, 18*(1), 5–17.

Guo, Z., & Sheffield, J. (2006). *A Paradigmatic and Methodological Examination of KM Research: 2000 to 2004.* Proceedings of the 39th Annual Hawaii International Conference on System Sciences (HICSS 2006), Hawaii, USA.

Hackman, J. R., & Oldham, G. R. (1980). *Work redesign.* Reading, Massachusetts: Addison-Wesley.

Hu, L., & Bentler, P. M. (1999). Cutoff Criteria for Fit Indexes in Covariance Structure Analysis: Conventional Criteria versus New Alternatives. *Structural Equation Modeling, 6*(1), 1–55. doi:10.1080/10705519909540118

Janz, B. D., & Prasarnphanich, P. (2003). Understanding the Antecedents of Effective Knowledge Management: the Importance of a Knowledge-centered Culture. *Decision Sciences, 34*(2), 351–384. doi:10.1111/1540-5915.02328

Jennex, M. E. (2008). *Current Issues in Knowledge Management.* New York, NY: IGI Global.

Jennex, M. E., & Olfman, L. (2005). Assessing Knowledge Management Success. *International Journal of Knowledge Management, 1*(2), 33–49. doi:10.4018/jkm.2005040104

Jennex, M. E., Smolnik, S., & Croasdell, D. T. (2007). *Towards Defining Knowledge Management Success*. Proceedings of the 40th Annual Hawaii International Conference on System Sciences (HICSS 2007), Hawaii, USA.

Johnson, B., Lorenz, E., & Lundvall, B. A. (2002). Why all this fuss about codified and tacit knowledge? *Industrial and Corporate Change, 11*(2), 245–262. doi:10.1093/icc/11.2.245

Kim, D. H. (1993). The Link between Individual and Organizational Learning. *Sloan Management Review, 35*(1), 37–51.

Kogut, B., & Zander, U. (1992). Knowledge of the Firm, Combinative Capabilities, and the Replication of Technology. *Organization Science, 3*(3), 383–398. doi:10.1287/orsc.3.3.383

Madjar, N., Oldham, G. R., & Pratt, M. G. (2002). There's No Place Like Home? The Contributions of Work and Nonwork Creativity Support to Employees' Creative Performance. *Academy of Management Journal, 45*(4), 757–768. doi:10.2307/3069309

March, J. G. (1991). Exploration and Exploitation in Organizational Learning. *Organization Science, 2*(1), 71–87. doi:10.1287/orsc.2.1.71

Nayir, D. Z., & Uzuncarsili, U. (2008). A Cultural Perspective of Knowledge Management: The Success Story of Sarkuysan Company. *Journal of Knowledge Management, 12*(2), 141–155. doi:10.1108/13673270810859578

Nonaka, I., & Takeuchi, H. (1995). *The knowledge-creating company: How Japanese companies create the dynamics of innovation*. New York, NY: Oxford University Press.

Oldham, G. R., & Cummings, A. (1996). Employee Creativity: Personal and Contextual Factors at Work. *Academy of Management Journal, 39*(3), 607–635. doi:10.2307/256657

Pfeffer, J., & Sutton, R. I. (1999). Knowing 'what' to do is not enough: Turning knowledge into action. *California Management Review, 42*(1), 83–109.

Pomerol, J., Brezillon, P., & Pasquier, L. (2002). Operational Knowledge Representation for Practical Decision-Making. *Journal of Management Information Systems, 18*(4), 101–115.

Rulke, D. L., & Galaskiewicz, J. (2000). Distribution of Knowledge, Group Network Structure, and Group Performance. *Management Science, 46*(5), 612–625. doi:10.1287/mnsc.46.5.612.12052

Schultze, U., & Leidner, D. (2002). Studying Knowledge Management in Information Systems Research: Discourses and Theoretical Assumptions. *Management Information Systems Quarterly, 26*(3), 213–242. doi:10.2307/4132331

Scott, S. G., & Bruce, R. A. (1994). Determinants of Innovative Behavioral Path Model of Individual Innovation in the Workplace. *Academy of Management Journal, 37*(3), 580–607. doi:10.2307/256701

Smith, T. W. (1983). The Hidden 25 Percent: an Analysis of Nonresponse on the 1980 General Social Survey. *Public Opinion Quarterly, 47*(3), 386–404. doi:10.1086/268797

Van De Ven, A. (1986). Central Problems in the Management of Innovation. *Management Science, 32*(5), 570–607. doi:10.1287/mnsc.32.5.590

Wiig, K., & Jooste, A. (2004). *Chapter 45: Exploiting Knowledge for Productivity Gains*. In C. W. Holsapple (Eds.), Handbook on Knowledge Management Vol.2: Knowledge Directions, 289-308. B.V.: Springer Science and Business Media.

Yoshioka, T., Herman, G., Yates, J., & Orlikowski, W. J. (2001). Genre Taxonomy: A Knowledge Repository of Communicative Actions. *ACM Transactions on Information Systems, 19*(4), 431–456. doi:10.1145/502795.502798

Chapter 2
Using Agent Based Simulation and Game Theory Analysis to Study Knowledge Flow in Organizations:
The KMscape

Richard Jolly
Portland State University, USA

Wayne Wakeland
Portland State University, USA

ABSTRACT

Knowledge sharing in organizations, especially the impact of sharing freely versus not sharing, was studied using game theoretic analysis and a Netlogo agent-based simulation model. In both analyses, some agents hoarded knowledge while others shared knowledge freely. As expected, sharing was found to greatly increase the overall amount of knowledge within the organization. Unexpectedly, on average, agents who share acquire more knowledge than hoarders. This is in contradiction to the conclusion from the prisoner's dilemma analysis. This is due to the synergy that develops between groups of agents who are sharing with each other. The density of the agents is important; as the density increases, the probability increases that an agent with a large amount of knowledge to share happens to be organizationally nearby. The implications are that organizations should actively encourage knowledge sharing, and that agent-based simulation is a useful tool for studying this type of organizational phenomena.

DOI: 10.4018/978-1-60960-555-1.ch002

INTRODUCTION

In 1988, Peter Drucker (1988) predicted a fundamental shift in corporations towards knowledge as the basis for competitive advantage. The management of knowledge became a prime concern, and has been the topic of many academic studies and organizational projects (c.f., Davenport & Prusak, 1998; Tiwana, 2002). But knowledge management (KM) endeavors often encounter a variety of problems and challenges (c.f., Gupta, Iyer, & Aronson, 2000; Sharp, 2003; Lin & Kwok, 2006). Invariably, these studies indicate that the problems are due to unforeseen side effects manifested by the *system* being manipulated—namely the organization. Sterman (2000) argues, however, that there is no such thing as a side effect; only effects. The study of structural complexity (e.g., feedback, nonlinearity and delay) and interaction effects (e.g., emergence) is the domain of the science of systems and the science of complexity (c.f., Senge, 1990; Bar-Yam, 1997; Resnick, 1997). The present article applies tools from these fields to the study of knowledge sharing in order to gain new insights into organizational KM.

Problem Statement

A KM system requires that members of the organization share their knowledge. This may simply mean making explicit knowledge accessible to others or transforming tacit knowledge into explicit knowledge for sharing. Brown and Duguid (2000) argue for the importance of this process and its critical dependence on the environment especially the social work situation. Studies have shown that individuals may be motivated to share knowledge in some cases and not share in other cases (Ardichvili, Page, & Wentling, 2003). What are the dynamics of a situation where there is a mix of individuals with different motivations within an organization? What might management do in order to enhance knowledge sharing?

The Present Study

The present study begins by applying a game-theoretic approach to examine the result of interactions between individuals in the organization with different preferences regarding knowledge sharing. Given this basic framework, agent-based simulation is then used to model these interactions in an artificial organization made up of individuals' (agents) that either share knowledge or do not share (hoard) knowledge. The knowledge properties of the organization as a whole *emerge* from the interactions of the individuals.

THEORETICAL BACKGROUND

Motivations to Share Knowledge or Not to Share

There are a number of reasons an individual may be willing to share their knowledge including (Wasko & Farja, 2000; Ardichvili, Page, & Wentling, 2003):

- The desire to be viewed as an expert
- The desire for recognition and credit
- Viewing their knowledge as a public good (which does not belong to them individually)
- Feeling a moral obligation to share
- "Generalized reciprocity"—that is, sharing with one in the community while expecting to be reciprocated by another in the future

However, in other cases, individuals may not be willing to share their knowledge (Ciborra & Patriotta, 1998). There are a number of potential reasons for this (Gilmour, 2003; Schutte & Snyman, 2006):

- Individuals may feel their *proprietary* knowledge is a competitive advantage versus their fellow employees

- They may fear loss of power or control
- They may fear ridicule or criticism

In some cases the relative *fairness* of the transaction may determine the specific response, as described by experimental economics research (Sigmund, Fehr, & Nowak, 2002). In any case, organizational culture is clearly an important factor regarding the tendency to share knowledge (Long & Fahey, 2000).

The Request to Share: A Game Theory Analysis

Consider two employees who have the outlook that controlling their own knowledge and not sharing is in their own best interest. The possibility of sharing knowledge represents a prisoner's dilemma. To see this, examine the payoff table of the two-player version of the game shown in Table 1.

Consider the position of the row player, whose payoffs (shown in utils—the basic unit of utility value—and shown in bold italics in Table 1) are as follows:

- Row player does not share but column player shares: The payoff is 4 utils. This affords the highest payoff. The row player has the column player's knowledge and also keeps their own knowledge private.
- Neither player shares: The payoff is 2 utils. The row player is worse off than in the last situation described because he does not have the column player's knowledge.

- The row player shares, but the column player does not share: The payoff is 1 utile. Here the row player gets his lowest payoff. He does not control his own knowledge anymore, but the column player does.
- Both players share their knowledge: The payoff is 3. The reason the corporation is trying to promote the sharing of knowledge is the organizational benefit from both employees having more knowledge. The sharing of knowledge helps the entire corporation in its business goals. This in turn, helps the row player and increases the payoff from the Don't share/Don't share cell.

This payoff matrix represents the classic prisoner's dilemma (c.f., Axelrod, 1984). Both players have dominant strategies—'Don't Share.' So, it is individually rational for each player to choose this strategy. However, as is the classic attribute of the prisoner's dilemma, the individually rational choices leads to collective irrationality—that is each player (and the organization) is worse off.

Now consider the interaction between two employees whose tendency is to share (consider for example that their motivation is to be viewed as an expert). The payoff table is shown in Table 2. The case where the row player shares and the column player do not share affords the highest number of utils to the row player because he is seen as the expert and the column player is not. The rest of the payoff matrix is completed using a similar analysis. This is game 9 in Rappaport's (Rapoport & Guyer, 1978) taxonomy and has a

Table 1. Payoffs when players prefer to hoard knowledge. Row players payoffs shown in bold italics.

	Share	*Don't Share*
Share	3,3	1,4
Don't Share	4,1	2,2

Table 2. Payoffs when players prefer to share knowledge

	Share	*Don't Share*
Share	3,3	4,1
Don't Share	1,4	2,2

Table 3. Payoffs when one player prefers to share and one prefers not to share

		Non-Sharer	
		Share	Don't Share
Sharer	*Share*	3,3	4,4
	Don't Share	1,1	2,2

dominant strategy for both players and a stable equilibrium—both will share.

Finally, what if a non-sharer meets a sharer? The game's payoff will be as shown in Table 3.

This is a no-conflict game with both players having dominant strategies. The sharer will share his knowledge, the knowledge hoarder will keep his knowledge and both will be happy about it.

SIMULATION METHOD

Agent-Based Simulation

Agent-based simulation (ABS) employs autonomous agents operating within a spatial grid that represents the agents' environment. Each cell (patch) in the grid, and each agent, run a particular set of rules, algorithms and procedures that describe how it interacts with other cells or agents. The macro behavior of the system may look very different from what one might assume by inspecting the local rules. See (Gilbert & Troitzsch, 2005) for a more complete description.

ABS is a good choice for the present research because the knowledge sharing process being studied takes place between individual people (agents), and it is easy to see the spatial grid as representing the agent's location within the organization. Rules can be used to describe how employees decide whether or not to share knowledge, and the outcomes of interactions between agents.

Epstein and Axtell suggest that ABS provides a different way to explain social phenomenon (Epstein & Axtell, 1996). They argue that being able

to explain a phenomenon is equivalent to asking if one can "grow" it in an artificial environment. They label this process as "a generative kind of social science."

The Landscape for Sharing: The KMscape

The authors took an approach similar to that chosen by Epstein and Axtell in the development of Sugarscape (Epstein & Axtell, 1996). Accordingly, we have named the landscape for our simulation the KMscape. Organizational members exist in a two dimensional space. The proximity of two agents represents organizational distance. Being close together on the KMscape represents a combination of close physical proximity, close reporting relationships, common work groups, virtual sharing opportunities, and so on. For example, Allen (1993) has shown that physical proximity has a direct relationship on the probability of organization members communicating. Agents who are close together are more likely to interact. The grid is wrapped into a torus to eliminate boundary effects.

On each clock tick, new information is grown on each patch. This process represents the constant availability of new information—whether it be organizational (e.g., manufacturing process information) or environmental (e.g., customer or competitor information) data. The amount is randomly distributed between 0 and a maximum value set at the start of the simulation.

Organization Members: The Agents

Organizational members are modeled as agents. The agents are assigned to be one of two breeds at the beginning of the simulation—either sharers or hoarders—and are randomly distributed across the KMscape in a ratio set at the outset of the simulation.

This point represents the first major simplifying assumption—that an agent is solely one of two breeds and acts that way consistently through the lifetime of the simulation. There are probably some organization members who do fall in this category; however, it is likely that one exhibits both tendencies depending on the context of the individual request for knowledge sharing (e.g., who is asking, what is being asked for, the current organizational environment, etc. [Gilmour, 2003]).

Agents have an ability to detect knowledge in their surrounding environment and within other agents, which we call their *knowledge vision*. As in the Sugarscape example, we limited the agent's vision to their von Neumann-extended neighborhood (that is, north, south, east and west, but not diagonally). Each agent's vision range is randomly distributed between 0 and a maximum value set at the start of the simulation.

In this model, agents are able to assess another agent's breed. Having the neighbor agent's breed being initially unknown would be another valid approach that could be investigated in future simulations. However, the author's used the first approach staying consistent with the idea that agents have good information about their neighbor's knowledge levels and tendencies.

Model Dynamics: Collecting and Sharing Knowledge

First, on each clock tick, agents are able to harvest the new information from the environment. Each agent can harvest the information from a single patch—the patch with the largest information value within their vision range. The agent then assimilates this information into knowledge.

Next, agents request to share knowledge with the nearby organizational member with the most knowledge within their vision range that is willing to share. Only agents with the sharer breed share knowledge. Sharing is implemented as the requesting agent's knowledge being increased by a percentage of the sharing agent's knowledge (this percent is also a variable value).

On each clock tick, some of the agent's knowledge *evaporates*. This represents two effects: actual loss of knowledge from human memory or perhaps files being deleted due to their age; and, knowledge is perishable—its value tends to decay with time. The rate of evaporation is set at the start of the simulation.

The simulation has the option for a random amount of movement—representing organizational movement. The movement probability is set with a variable. The percentage indicates the probability that a given agent will move on that clock tick.

Simulation Implementation and Verification

Netlogo 3.1.3 was used for the simulation. Figure 1 is a screen shot of the simulation interface. All sliders and buttons are shown on the left. Two plots are displayed: a histogram of the knowledge held by the agents, and a plot of the total organizational knowledge. An output window is used for the testing phases. Monitors below the grid show the key parameters. The simulation is available at http://www.sysc.pdx.edu/faculty/Wakeland/papers/InfoScape.nlogo.

To summarize, on each clock tick:

- New information is grown
- Agents harvest new information and assimilate it into knowledge
- Agents attempt to retrieve more knowledge from a sharing agent
- Some of the agent's knowledge evaporates
- The agent may move to a new location on the grid

Ticks can be repeated as many times as desired to yield a time history. Each tick represents a unit of time in the organization (e.g., a few days). As the simulation progresses, a pattern of knowledge emerges on the KMscape.

Figure 1. Screen shot showing simulation interface

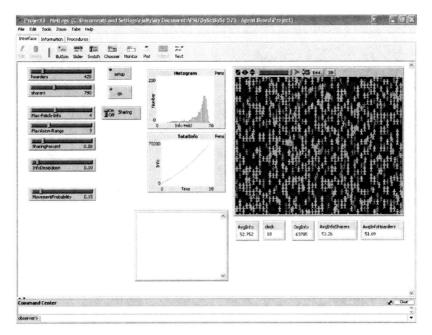

To verify that the model's logic correctly reflected the designer's intentions, a number of activities and tests were carried out. To assure that the logic for harvesting and sharing knowledge was correct, the attribute data for individual patches and agents was inspected, clock tick by clock tick, as the simulation proceeded. Many test displays and plots were placed on the user interface screen so that multiple aspects of the model could be viewed simultaneously. Input parameters were skewed to their extreme values to stress the logic, to ferret out unanticipated effects, and to explore the full range of possible model behaviors. Special test cases were run for which the correct behavior was

Figure 2. Simulation with sharing on and off; note the different scales on the plots. The top plots show total knowledge over time and the bottom plots show the distribution of the amount of knowledge held by individual agents.

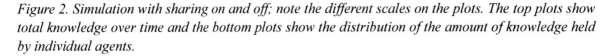

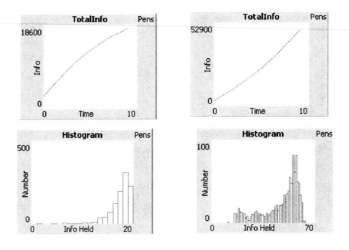

known in advance. Once the model passed these tests, it was considered to be sufficiently verified to proceed with experimentation.

RESULTS AND DISCUSSION

Results

Figure 2 shows a typical simulation result. In the left column all agents are hoarders. In the right column all agents are sharers.

As expected, with sharing, there is substantially more organizational knowledge. One can also see that sharing impacts the trajectory for total organizational knowledge over time—sharing causes the curve to bend upwards in an exponential fashion. This indicates an effect that might be considered amplification. Figure 2 also shows that sharing causes greater variance in the amount of knowledge held by the agents. This indicates that locality is playing a role—proximity to knowledge *wealthy* sharers is an important effect. These results agree with our intuition about the system.

Next the relative rate of knowledge growth is compared across the two breeds of agents:

hoarders and sharers. We examined this across various simulation parameters to reveal that under most conditions sharers do better than hoarders. However, from the prisoner's dilemma analysis, one would expect that a hoarder next to a sharer would create a knowledge-rich hoarder and a knowledge-poor sharer.

To understand the dynamics of this situation, consider Table 4. This represents three pairs of agents located next to each other on the KMscape. In the left two columns, a sharer is located next to a hoarder (S and H, respectively). In the middle two columns, two sharers are located next to each other. In the right two columns, two hoarders are adjacent. The figure shows the total accumulated knowledge level of each agent over four clock ticks. Table 4 assumes two units of information are available in the collect phase (note: this value changes at random in the simulation, but a constant value is used in Table 4 to illustrate the logic more easily) and sharing is set at 20%.

First, consider the left two columns—a sharer next to a hoarder. In the first phase of the clock tick, both agents harvest the information from the environment. They assimilate the information into knowledge and their knowledge-held account goes up to two units. In the second phase of clock

Table 4. Analysis of the synergy from sharing

		S	H	S	S	H	H
Clock 1	Collect	2	2	2	2	2	2
	Share	2	2.4	2.4	2.4	2	2
Clock 2	Collect	4	4.4	4.4	4.4	4	4
	Share	4	5.2	5.3	5.3	4	4
Clock 3	Collect	6	7.2	7.3	7.3	6	6
	Share	6	8.4	8.8	8.8	6	6
Clock 4	Collect	8	10.4	10.8	10.8	8	8
	Share	8	12.0	13.0	13.0	8	8

1, they ask each other to share. The sharer gives the hoarder 20% of his knowledge (.4 units), but the hoarder gives none. So, they end clock 1 with unequal amounts of knowledge. This continues through the 4 clock ticks shown until this difference has been magnified due to the unequal sharing to the point where the hoarder has 50% more knowledge than the sharer. This is consistent with the prisoner's dilemma's prediction.

Now, consider the middle two columns of Table 4 which illustrates two sharers next to each other. Through the same analysis, the sharers collect the knowledge from the environment and then proceed to share with each other. Since each is sharing, both agents' knowledge caches are increasing. Thus, the sharers have more knowledge to share. As a result, these two adjacent sharers conclude the four clock ticks with 13 units of knowledge. That is over 8% more knowledge that the hoarder in column 1.

Finally, consider the two hoarders shown in the rightmost two columns of Table 4. They conclude the four clock ticks with only eight units of knowledge each. Now, if we consider the six agents in Table 4 residing in the same KMscape, then the three sharers do better *on average* than the three hoarders (the sharers have 11.3 units on average while the hoarders have 9.3 units on average). The *synergy* effect between the two middle sharers is the key.

This makes sense on average, but should not a single hoarder be able to collect more knowledge if all the others are sharing? This is the classic 'free rider' scenario. To study this question, a single hoarder was simulated in a sea of sharers on the KMscape. The knowledge of the lone hoarder was compared to the average knowledge of all the sharers. The experiments were repeated 100 times to determine if any observed differences were statistical significant. Surprisingly, it was found that over most simulation conditions the sharers, on average, did better than the single hoarder.

Figure 3 summarizes the results of another set of simulations on the KMscape. The numbers in the matrix represent the mean value for knowledge held by agents, including both sharers and hoarders (over 100 replications). In these simulations, the density of agents on the KMscape grid was varied, as was the relative percentage of sharers and hoarders. Agent density represents the number of agents per unit of organizational distance as described earlier. A denser environment may result from combinations of closer physical proximity, organizational closeness (e.g., a flatter reporting hierarchy), better virtual sharing mechanisms and so on.

Figure 3 has some unexpected characteristics. Given the earlier results, it would be natural to expect to see the largest value in the top right corner, where the density is highest, and everyone is a sharer. However, the highest value for average knowledge occurs in the *middle* of the top row. Further, notice that with 0% sharers (100% hoarders) the average knowledge *decreases* as the density is increased. This can be explained as a carrying capacity of the environment. Since hoard-

Figure 3. Average knowledge per agent as the percentage of sharers and the density of agents is varied

	100%	48.5	55.5	57.7	57.2	56.0	56-65
%	75%	43.7	51.9	56.1	55.6	54.6	46-55
Sharers	50%	34.1	46.6	51.0	51.3	52.2	36-45
	25%	27.6	34.3	40.1	41.1	43.8	26-35
	0%	18.4	17.7	16.9	16.0	14.5	<26
		0.24	0.48	0.72	0.96	1.20	
				Density			

ers do not share, there is no advantage to density. But, as density increases, there is a greater chance an information rich patch has already been harvested by another agent! So, in effect, we see three effects going on simultaneously in this chart:

- An increase in the average knowledge per agent as the percentage of sharers increases; this is due to the higher probability an agent will be located near an agent who will share
- An increase in the average knowledge per agent as the density increases (given there are some sharers). This is due to the higher probability that an agent will have a sharing agent within its vision range
- A *decrease* in the average knowledge per agent as the density increases; this is due to the carrying capacity of the environment

Next, the effect of random movement was studied. One might expect this to have a large effect. Networking theory (c.f., Watts, 2003) argues that occasional random links in a network substantially reduces the overall path length. However, simulations showed that the degree of random movement had a very small effect. This may be explained by again considering the synergy effect shown in Table 4. While moving a knowledge-rich sharer into a relatively knowledge-poor area will have a locally positive effect, the movement also disrupts the synergy effect between sharers that had built the knowledge-rich agent in the first place.

Finally, the effects of various knowledge dissipation and sharing percentage values were also studied. While increased knowledge dissipation impacted the knowledge held by the agents, it did not have a major impact on the effects discussed above. The sharing percent (per transaction) has a substantial positive effect on average agent knowledge—as would be intuitively expected. The greater the sharing percentage, the faster the sharing synergy builds.

CONCLUSION

Even with the assumptions and simplifications of the model, interesting conclusions and implication can be drawn. For organizations, the results suggest that techniques to foster a culture of sharing would prove to be very beneficial.

Further, organizations should consider measures which would cluster employees to enhance the opportunity for knowledge sharing. This pertains to organizational as well as physical nearness. For example, a flatter (higher span) reporting structure may foster sharing. In the physical realm, possibilities might be the use of cubicles versus offices. Or, organizations could foster occasions for employees to come together and network (for example, communal cafeterias, group meetings, brown bag events, etc.).

For employees located in an environment of sharers and hoarders, who are concerned with the no-win conclusion of the prisoner's dilemma, the research by Axelrod (1984) outlines a potential course of action. Due to the repeated nature of the interactions, a strategy such as tit-for-tat can be employed to maximize the employee's own results as well as enhance overall cooperation. With a tit-for-tat strategy, the employee would first share with a partner. Then, if this partner reciprocates, then sharing would continue. However, if the partner does not reciprocate, then the best strategy for the agent is not to share at the next exchange.

The research also demonstrates that game theory and agent-based simulation methods can be a powerful aid in the study of organizational phenomena. While these methods are not well-suited for prediction, they provide a very versatile laboratory for studying the possible effects of parameter changes and potential interventions. And, the ability to generate phenomenon can be a powerful tool in its explanation. It is vital, of course, that the processes used to develop the model, to verify and validate the model, and to carry out the experimental analysis must be well thought out and complete.

Limitations

One potential argument against the validity of the modeling of the sharing synergy is that the *same* knowledge may be shared back and forth between neighbors over subsequent clock cycles, implying potential knowledge double counting. This is a valid concern. While it may lead to an overstatement of the total amount of unique knowledge in the organization, re-sharing the same knowledge could in fact be beneficial, since an agent may have lost or forgotten a particular bit of knowledge.

Future Work

The results of this study suggest that further work is warranted. Potential next steps could include:

- Examining the possibility of a tipping point effect—that is, some critical density of sharers to trigger enhanced organizational benefits
- Adding the ability to save the shistory of sharing transactions, and examining the characteristics of the sharing networks— for example, are they random or scale-free (Barabasi & Bonabeau, 2003)
- Examining alternative implementations to the knowledge sharing and vision algorithms, such as having the agent look for the neighboring agent with the most knowledge (not knowing if he is a hoarder or a sharer) and asking that agent to share; in the case of asking a hoarder, the result would be no sharing; an agent might or might not lose his *turn* for a given clock tick after an unsuccessful attempt to share
- Creating a model where the agent cannot determine which of its neighbors has the most knowledge; the current model assumes the agent has perfect information about their neighbors; this could be embellished by having the agent keep track of their neighbors (that is, once you have attempted to share with an agent, you have an idea of how much knowledge they have and their breed), this would also allow the testing of different sharing strategies (such as the tit-for-tat strategy mentioned earlier)

- Examining different vision algorithms— for example, implementing a radius vision which would allow the agents to see diagonally
- Making the sharing process reciprocal— something akin to the trade algorithm in Sugarscape (Epstein & Axtell, 1996)— here agents in a group would attempt to determine who they should share with; sharing would be a dyad between the two agents who will receive the greatest mutual benefit from the transaction
- Making the sharing or hoarding tendency a variable—it could begin with some base tendency and modify over the course of the simulation—perhaps based on the history of outcomes from the agent's previous sharing transactions, or their "model" about their trading partner's current state
- Addressing the concerns raised earlier about knowledge uniqueness, by making the bits of knowledge being shared unique

ACKNOWLEDGMENT

This is an extended version of the authors' paper presented at the 41st Hawaiian International Conference on System Sciences, on January 7-10, 2008.

REFERENCES

Allen, T. (1993). *Managing the flow of technology: Technology transfer and the dissemination of technological information within the R&D organization*. Cambridge, MA: The MIT Press.

Ardichvili, A., Page, V., & Wentling, T. (2003). Motivation and barriers to participation in virtual knowledge-sharing communities of practice. *Journal of Knowledge Management, 7*(1), 64–77. doi:10.1108/13673270310463626

Axelrod, R. (1984). *The evolution of cooperation.* New York: Basic Books.

Bar-Yam, Y. (1997). *Dynamics of complex systems.* Boulder, CO: Westview Press.

Barabasi, A.-L., & Bonabeau, E. (2003). Scale-free networks. *Scientific American, 5,* 60–69. doi:10.1038/scientificamerican0503-60

Brown, J., & Duguid, P. (2000). *The social life of information.* Boston, MA: Harvard Business School Press.

Ciborra, C., & Patriotta, G. (1998). Groupware and teamwork in R&D: Limits to learning and innovation. *R & D Management, 28*(1), 43–52. doi:10.1111/1467-9310.00080

Davenport, T., & Prusak, L. (1998). *Working knowledge.* Boston: Harvard Business School Press.

Drucker, P. (1988). The coming of the new organization. *Harvard Business Review, 66*(1), 45–53.

Epstein, J., & Axtell, R. (1996). *Growing artificial societies: Social science from the bottom up.* Boston: Brookings Institute Press, The MIT Press.

Gilbert, N., & Troitzsch, K. (2005). *Simulation for the social scientist.* Berkshire, England: Open University Press.

Gilmour, D. (2003). How to fix knowledge management. *Harvard Business Review,* 17–18.

Gupta, B., Iyer, L., & Aronson, J. (2000). Knowledge management: Practices and challenges. *Industrial Management & Data Systems, 100*(1), 17–21. doi:10.1108/02635570010273018

Lin, L., & Kwok, L. (2006). Challenges to KM at Hewlett Packard China. *KM Review, 9*(1), 20–23.

Long, D., & Fahey, L. (2000). Diagnosing cultural barriers to knowledge management. *The Academy of Management Executive, 14*(4), 113–127.

Rapoport, A., & Guyer, M. (1978). A taxonomy of 2x2 Games. *General Systems, XXIII,* 125–136.

Resnick, M. (1997). *Turtles, termites, and traffic jams: Explorations in massively parallel microworlds.* Cambridge, MA: The MIT Press.

Schutte, M., & Snyman, M. (2006). Knowledge flow elements within a context—a model. *South African Journal of Information Management, 8*(2).

Senge, P. (1990). *The fifth discipline: The art & practice of the learning organization.* New York: Doubleday.

Sharp, D. (2003). Knowledge management today: Challenges and opportunities. *Information Systems Management,* (Spring): 32–37. doi:10.1201/1078/43204.20.2.20030301/41468.6

Sigmund, K., Fehr, E., & Nowak, M. (2002). The economics of fair play. *Scientific American, 286*(1). doi:10.1038/scientificamerican0102-82

Sterman, J. (2000). *Business dynamics: Systems thinking and modeling for a complex world.* Boston: Irwin.

Tiwana, A. (2002). *The knowledge management toolkit.* Upper Saddle River, NJ: Pearson Education.

Wasko, M., & Farja, S. (2000). It is what one does: Why people participate and help others in electronic communities of practice. *The Journal of Strategic Information Systems, 9,* 155–173. doi:10.1016/S0963-8687(00)00045-7

Watts, D. (2003). *Six degrees: The science of a connected age.* New York: Norton & Company.

Chapter 3
A Comprehensive Model for Assessing the Organizational Readiness of Knowledge Management

Babak Sohrabi
University of Tehran, Iran

Iman Raeesi
University of Tehran, Iran

Amir Khanlari
University of Tehran, Iran

Sakineh Forouzandeh
Shahid Beheshti University, Iran

ABSTRACT

Nowadays, the key to an organization's success is the ability to assess its readiness to create and improve the processes underlying its strategy. Realizing the fact that knowledge plays important roles in attaining competitive edge and strategic goals, managers give much emphasis on Knowledge Management (KM). However, implementing knowledge management or knowledge-sharing projects in an organization require significant organizational prerequisites. Lacking proper infrastructures and prerequisites, not only make the knowledge management process unprofitable, but also it might incur harmful effects as well. To decrease such risks, it is proposed to introduce the readiness assessment, in order to gauge a company's appetite for the work involved in implementing the knowledge management. In this research, critical success factors have been extracted from comprehensive literature reviews and they have been surveyed through a questionnaire, distributed among 130 knowledge management experts. Then, to validate the measurement of the multi-item constructs, Exploratory Factor Analysis (EFA) was used. Identifying effective variables and their grouping into related factors, the second questionnaire was employed for readiness assessment of an IT firm working in Iran. The final results were presented with Radar diagrams. Finally, promoting propositions were provided based on the firm's current status.

DOI: 10.4018/978-1-60960-555-1.ch003

1. INTRODUCTION

According to Alavi and Leidner (2001), knowledge is the information processing that takes place in human minds, as well as personalized information related to facts, procedures, concepts, interpretations, ideas, observations, and judgments. Hoffman et al. (2005) believe that sustained competitive advantage occurs when a firm develops a distinctive core competency such as Knowledge Management. Knowledge Management (KM) comprises a range of practices used by organizations to identify, create, represent, and distribute knowledge. In recent decades, there has been a proliferation of KM projects in many organizations. Correspondingly, corporate spending on KM projects has increased substantially over the years (Ithia, 2003). The theoretical benefits of knowledge management are clear; hence, in order to maximize internal efficiency, internal coordination, service to clients, and overall profitability, one needs to make tacit knowledge explicit, updated and accessible. Simple one might think but one must go through the reasons as why organizations fail to make KM work possible (Guptara, 2000).

Knowledge power can be distinguished in the following items:

1. knowledge is distinct from information in enabling competitive advantage;
2. knowledge is distributed unevenly, hence, must flow for organizational performance;
3. tacit knowledge supports greater appropriateness for competitive advantage than explicit knowledge does;
4. knowledge flows must balance exploration through learning with exploitation through doing; and
5. enhancing knowledge flows requires simultaneous attention to personnel, work processes, organizations, and technologies (Nissen, 2006).

According to Karkoulian et al. (2008), organization can maximize returns through knowledge utilization. Weber and Weber (2007) introduce knowledge as a source of sustainable competitive advantage. Wills-Johnson (2008) supposes ability to manage and coordinate knowledge amongst resources provide comparative advantage to a firm. It is evident that in the new economy, knowledge assets are grounded in the experience and expertise of those individuals working in a company and the firm has to therefore provide the right structures to shape knowledge into competencies.

There are several definitions and constructs of the term 'knowledge' and its importance for the firms. Kogut and Zander (1992) for instance, describe knowledge as an embedded resource of the firm. Birkinshaw et al (2002) see it as 'contingency variable'. Like many other managerial innovations, knowledge management also appears to be adopted first by manufacturing firms, and is beginning now to permeate the service sector, predominantly in professional services such as consulting firms (Hansen et al., 1999). Knowledge, and consequently its management, is currently being touted as the basis of future economic competitiveness. Many large companies have resources dedicated to Knowledge Management, often as a part of 'Information Technology' or 'Human Resource Management' departments. Nevertheless, implementing KM projects or knowledge-sharing philosophies in organizations often require significant organizational changes. In essence, assessment of an organization's readiness could serve a guideline to leaders as they plan and implement KM initiatives (Holt et al., 2004).

Based on the dismal success rates of change implementation, managers are being encouraged to be proactive by utilizing change measurement instruments to gauge their organization's demeanor before implementing changes (Jansen, 2000; Simon, 1996) because of changes effect, which imposes risk and uncertainty onto organization. Assessment readiness provides thorough answers to two fundamental questions: What is a firm's current Knowledge Management capability? And what changes must be in place before embarking on a Knowledge Management initiative? An instrument to assess readiness should be developed based on the premise that Knowledge Management is enhanced through the critical success factors (CSFs). Before investing scarce resources in such risky projects, corporate leadership is calling for a means to decrease uncertainty surrounding Knowledge Management.

A failure to assess organizational and individual Knowledge Management readiness might result in significant loss of time and energy of managers dealing with resistance to Knowledge Management. Knowledge may be accessed at three stages: before, during, or after knowledge-related activities. However, creating Knowledge Management readiness before any attempt at organizational renewal necessitates later action to cope with resistance. An investment in developing Knowledge Management readiness – at both individual as well as whole-of-organization level – can achieve double benefits.

2. KNOWLEDGE MANAGEMENT

As the economy shifts to the postindustrial era, intangible assets (such as knowledge) gain importance over more traditional resources (e.g., land and capital) in organizations (Alavi, 2000). Knowledge is defined in different perspectives. From one perspective it has been verified from its content and constituent (Talebi et el., 2008). Content of knowledge includes "Know what", "Know why", and "Know how" and "Know who" which all are relevant to knowledge application. Knowledge constituent includes explicit and tacit knowledge (Talebi et al., 2008). "Explicit knowledge is codified and embedded in objects such as books and blue prints, but tacit knowledge is experiential and intuitive" (Ratten and Suseno, 2006). Research suggests that more than half of the knowledge that exists in firms is largely of

a tacit nature (Ratten and Suseno, 2006). Tacit knowledge leads to a sustainable competitive advantage (Weber and Weber, 2007) since it is not easily transferable or reproducible (Magnier-Watanabe and Senoo, 2008).

Individual knowledge is knowledge that resides in an individual mind while Organizational knowledge is knowledge that is formed through interactions between technologies, techniques and people. The pattern and form of interactions depend on an organization's history and culture (Monnavarian and Amini, 2009; Monavvarian and Kasaei, 2007). It has been shown that having strong human resources policies in an organization will affect how the organization manages its knowledge (Monavvarian and Kasaei, 2007). KM leverages the intellectual assets of company to meet defined business objectives. It also adds value to the organization when human capital is transformed to structured intellectual assets (Karkoulian et al., 2008).

Organizational knowledge is an evolving mix of framed experience, values, contextual information and expert insight that provides a framework for evaluating and incorporating new experiences and information into corporate decision making processes (Davenport and Prusak, 1998). Organizational knowledge often becomes embedded in documents or repositories and in organizational routines, processes, practices, and norms. In addition, organizational knowledge provides meaning in the sense that it is context-specific (Croasdell et.al., 2003; Nonaka, 1994).

The shared information and materials allow researchers to build on each others' work and achieve results faster. Thus, scientific progress and its societal benefits hinge on the sharing of information (Thursby et al., 2009). This holds true for science in both the academic and the industrial context (Haeussler, 2011). Comprehensive research in the area of knowledge sharing in universities has been rather limited (Sohail and Daud, 2009).

Knowledge Management (KM) today emerges as one of the most popular, important areas of inquiry in academic researches and management practices (Argote, McEvily, and Reagans, 2003; Ruggles, 1998). KM first appeared in industries and functional areas that basically sell knowledge – professional services, pharmaceuticals, research, and development functions – in the late 1980s and 1990s. It is now quickly moving into other industries, including manufacturing, financial services, government and military organizations, and even non-government organizations (NGOs) (Grover and Davenport, 2001). Many organizations are increasingly viewed as knowledge-based enterprises in which, formal knowledge management is essential. Being typically tied to organizational objectives, KM is rapidly becoming an integral business activity for organizations as they realize that competitiveness pivots around the effective management of knowledge (Grover and Davenport, 2001).

Knowledge Management can also be more effective in integrating and administering a firm's information technology base as well as assisting to develop a systemized information model. Knowledge management systems (KMS) are becoming increasingly important to organizations, both for their strategic potential and as a crucial resource (Ahn and Chang, 2004; Apostolou and Mentzas, 1999a, 1999b; Liebowitz and Wright, 1999; Wasko and Faraj, 2005). These systems are important for organizations, primarily to help manage a key organizational resource – intellectual capital with the potential to produce a competitive advantage (Rao and Osei-Bryson, 2007).

Although, today, there is a great deal of interest in knowledge management, there exists no universally accepted definition of it (Earl, 1999). KM can be comprehensively defined as "an emerging set of organizational design and operational principles, processes, organizational structures, applications and technologies that help knowledge workers dramatically leverage their creativity and ability to deliver business values" (Gurteen, 1998).

Basically, we follow the definition of Alavi and Leidner (2001)," KM is managing the corporation's knowledge through a systematically and organizationally specified process for acquiring, organizing, sustaining, applying, sharing and renewing both the tacit and explicit knowledge of employees to enhance organizational performance and create value ".(Allee, 1997; Davenport, 1998; Alavi and Leidner, 2001).

One of the key concerns emerging in KM is how to accomplish it. Many companies attempting to initiate KM are unsure of the best approach to adopt (Moffett et al., 2002). Literally, there seems to be general agreement that a combined social and technological approach is ideal one. Davenport and Prusak (1998) believe that knowledge management projects have one of the three aims: a) to make knowledge visible and show its role in an organization, mainly through maps, yellow pages and so on, b) to develop a knowledge-intensive culture by encouraging and aggregating behaviors such as knowledge sharing and proactively seeking and offering knowledge, c) to build a knowledge infrastructure- used not only as a technical system, but also a connecting web of people by giving space, time, tools, and encouragement to interact and collaborate.

Nevertheless, knowledge is not easily measured or audited; therefore, organizations must manage knowledge effectively in order to take full advantage of skills and experiences inherent in their systems and structures as well as the tacit knowledge belonging to the firm's employees. Road to success is eminent. It will certainly go forward, if organizations are aware of the key factors that make its adoption successful.

3. KNOWLEDGE MANAGEMENT READINESS

This section first deal with literature about critical success factors; then it goes ahead with readiness for knowledge management; and finally it provides measures extracted from the discussions.

3.1. Literature Review

KM is a conscious strategy of getting the right knowledge to the right people at the right time and helping people share and put information into action in ways that strive to improve organizational performance (Monavvarian and Kasaei, 2007). For organizations striving for innovation and competitive advantage, new knowledge as well as knowledge transfer are critical since they open new productive opportunities and enhance the firm's ability to exploit them (Weber and Weber, 2007). The majority of models used in the KM field, such as the tacit and explicit knowledge, are typically non-technology oriented (Wang and Wang, 2008). The general definitions supplied in the existing literature use the word "readiness" as a necessary precondition for a person or an organization to succeed in facing organizational change (Holt, 2000). Knowledge Management-readiness is the ability of an organization, department or workgroup to successfully adopt, use and benefit from KM. It is important for companies seeking to adopt KM to analysis their businesses to ensure a productive and beneficial implementation of Knowledge Management. It is worth mentioning that the readiness assessment analyzes the organization's environment and readiness to adopt and support an enterprise-wide project management methodology.

Knowledge Management strategies are getting matured including their ability to assess an organization's readiness for such systems (Ruppel and Harrington, 2001; Siemieniuch and Sinclair, 2004; Tsai, 2002). Since many KM initiatives do not evolve as successfully as their directors had planned, researchers explored potential barriers and facilitators of KS in organizations (Damodaran and Olphert, 2000; Desouza, 2003; Pumareja and Sikkel, 2005). DeLone and McLean (2003) use the terms 'success' and 'effectiveness' interchange-

ably and propose some factors to be considered to enhance effectiveness of KM projects. Critical enablers of KM have been validated and organized in an integrative framework along with organizational processes and performance (Lee and Choi, 2003). Jennex and Olfman (2000) studied three KM projects to identify design recommendations for building a successful KMS. Jennex (2005) summarized various definitions of KM to propose a success KM model. Again, Jennex and Olfman (2005) summarized and synthesized the literature on KM/KMS critical success factors into an ordered set of 12 KM CSFs. CSFs were ordered based on the number of studies identifying the CSF. There were 17 studies looking at over 200 KM projects. Based on the DeLone and McLean's IS Success Model, Jennex and Olfman (2006) extended their works with a KM Success Model and combined and utilized KM and KMS success (Jennex et al., 2007).

Siemieniuch and Sinclair (2004) propose a framework for organizational readiness, by introducing knowledge lifecycle management (KLM) processes. Hung and Chou (2005) give a three-dimensional Knowledge Management Pyramid Model (KMPM) for assessing the maturity of its organizational capabilities. KMPM is comprised of three components i.e. maturity levels, knowledge management processes, and knowledge management capabilities or enabling infrastructures. Holt et al. (2004) also did a study to develop an instrument for assessing KM readiness. This study draws on the literature dealing with KM and organizational change to propose a synergistic instrument to measure readiness for KM and apply it in an organizational setting. This instrument considers individual, context, content, process measures and KM attitudes.

Further, Hung et al. (2006) examined relationship between KM readiness and intellectual capital while, Keith et al. (2006) accomplished a case-based field study from a large Fortune 500 financial firm transitioning its structure to SOE and considering agile software development methodologies. Survey data was collected along with a series of interviews with key managers and developers. Findings indicate significant statistical differences in KM readiness between groups and the need for alignment. As explained, many instruments purportedly assessed readiness for an organization to embrace changes but it was not surprising that these instruments were designed to assess readiness from some limited perspectives only i.e. technologic and typical information system, lacking enough considerations on special system and project.

3.2. KM Readiness Measures

Based on literature reviews on readiness and success factors in the proposed area, we listed measures influencing on Knowledge Management readiness. These critical success factors have been extracted from various papers dealing with KM in general, KM success factors and KM readiness, in particular. Hence, this study provides a comprehensive view on knowledge management for firms embarking to KM project. It is shown that firms need to be ready for Knowledge Management which has specifically essentials with the research objective of identifying factors significantly influencing the Knowledge Management process. Table1 shows the extracted measures which are all implicitly or explicitly explained in the related sources:

4. METHODOLOGY

This section includes two parts: First, discusses sample and descriptive statistics of respondents' data; and second part is about questionnaires, type of scaling and data analysis.

4.1. Sample

There are two basic respondent strategies: sampling and census. However, we decided not to apply any sampling approach or collect data from the whole population, due to required levels of respondent expertise and limited amount of KM expert in Iran as a developing country. The population includes knowledge management experts from academic environment in Iran as well as those working in software companies and has already participated in several KM projects. The questionnaires were distributed among 130 experts and as such, a total of 93 surveys were completed at the response rate of 71%. The average age and experiences of the respondents was 39 years (SD=11 years) and 5.3 years (SD=1.9 years), respectively.

4.2. Instrument and Data Analysis

As mentioned earlier, critical success factors affecting KM readiness were extracted from literature reviews and questionnaire based surveys. The responses about the agreement or disagreement were analyzed using a five-point Likert scale. Further, their reliability or internal consistency was assessed by Cronbach's alpha. It was observed that consistency was above 0.8 (0.86), higher than the 0.7 threshold normally considered as minimum (Nunnally, 1978).

To validate the measurement of the multi-item constructs, we used exploratory factor analysis (EFA), a procedure that allowed us to drop some invalid items from the scale and include valid items to the relevant groups. One variable (knowledge strategy) was deleted in this approach, while 18 variables including 5 factors remained there. After identifying effective variables and their grouping onto related factors, the second questionnaire was employed for readiness assessment of an IT firm working in Iran (see Appendix). The questionnaire was designed based on above-mentioned factors and consisting a series of statements (92 statements) relevant to a particular area to which, respondents (or end users) from several functional units may either agree or disagree with varying degrees (using a five-point Likert scale). These

Table 1. KM readiness measures

Measures	Sources
Trust	Lee and Choi (2003); Davenport et al. (1998); Andersson and Westterlind (1999); Chua and Lam (2005); Allee (1997); Monnavarian and Amini, (2009); Monavvarian and Kasaei, (2007).
Training	Hasanali (2002); Choi (2000); Chung et al. (2005); Singh et. al., (2009); Wang and Noe (2010).
A culture of altruism	Andersson and Westterlind (1999); Davenport and Prusak (1998)
Open leadership climate	Chung et al. (2005); Davenport et al. (1998); Taylor and Wright (2004); Andersson and Westterlind (1999); Forcadell and Cuadamillas)2002); Brand (1998); Allee (1997); Monnavarian and Amini, (2009)
Learning from failure	Taylor and Wright (2004); Soliman and Spooner (2000); Brand (1998).
Knowledge strategy	Sunassee and Sewary (2003); Taylor and Wright (2004); Snyman and Krugere (2004); Chung et al. (2005); Wang and Noe, (2010); Monavvarian and Kasaei, (2007).
Management support	Davenport et al. (1998); Holt (2000); Chung et al. (2005); Chua and Lam (2005); Ross et al. (2005); Choi (2000); Streels (2000); Hasanali (2002); Singh et. al., (2009); Monavvarian and Kasaei, (2007).
Participation	Chua and Lam (2005); Choi (2000).
Centralization	Andersson and Westterlind (1999); Lee and Choi (2003); Forcadell and Cuadamillas (2002); Ruikar et al. (2006(; Walczak (2005); Monavvarian and Kasaei, (2007).
Formalization	Taylor and Wright (2004), Lang (2001); Lee and Choi (2003); Monavvarian and Kasaei, (2007).
Quality of information	Holt (2000); Hasanali (2002); Streels (2000); Davenport and Prusak. (1998); Gupta (2000); Wang and Noe, (2010); Monavvarian and Kasaei, (2007).
Team work	Chung et al. (2005); Ross et al. (2005); Choi (2000); Soliman and Spooner (2000); Forcadell and Cuadamillas (2002); Monnavarian and Amini, (2009)
Benefit	Holt (2000); Hasanali (2002); Ross et al. (2005); Wang and Noe, (2010)
Appropriateness	Holt (2000); Siemieniuch and Sinclair (2004); Monavvarian and Kasaei, (2007).
Discrepancy	Taylor and Wright (2004); Holt (2000); Monavvarian and Kasaei, (2007).
Reward system	Guptara (2000); Chung et al. (2005); Snyman and Krugere (2004); Wiig et al. (1997)Andersson and Westterlind (1999); Monnavarian and Amini, (2009).
Information systems infrastructure accessibility	Mathi (2004); Taylor and Wright (2004); Ruikar et al. (2006); Macdonald (1998); Hasanali (2002); Monavvarian and Kasaei, (2007).
Verbal skill	Polkinghorne (1989); Lang (2001);
T-shape skill	Chua and Lam (2005); Lee and Choi (2003).

questions were extracted from some reliable and valid instruments mentioned in references such as Clark (2003). Nevertheless, managers of the firms were also asked to comment on the questions and their relevance to factors wanted to measure. Assessment relies on the judgment of a respondent (or end-user) as to whether or not he/she agrees with the statement/s in the context of their department or work group.

The respondent(s) need to ensure that their responses are consistent with their assumptions e.g. if responses re about the department (and not the organization), then that assumption must be reflected throughout. The extent to which the respondent agrees or disagrees with the statement is graded on a scale of 1 to 5, where 1: Strongly Disagree, 2: Disagree, 3: Neutral, 4: Agree and 5: Strongly Agree. The statements are orchestrated in a way that a response of 'strongly agree' generates the highest score of 5 points. An average score is also calculated for each category. Higher the average score the more likely it is that the firm is ready for Knowledge Management. Based on Ruikar et al. (2006), an average score greater than or equal to zero and less than 2.5 is weak, indicating that several aspects (within a category) need urgent

Table 2. Results of exploratory factor analysis (EFA)

Items	Factors				
	Support for change	Vision for change	Culture of knowledge	Structure	Infrastructure
Training	0.79				
Management support	0.8				
Participation	0.79				
Reward system	0.78				
Benefit		0.84			
Appropriateness		0.87			
Discrepancy		0.88			
A culture of altruism			0.67		
Open leadership climate			0.87		
Learning from failure			0.82		
Trust			0.86		
Centralization				0.78	
Formalization				0.82	
Team work				0.814	
Quality of information					0.76
Information systems infrastructure accessibility					0.76
Verbal skill					0.73
T-shape					78.8
% of variance explained	14.93	12.81	15.85	12.36	13.75
Cumulative % of variance explained	14.93	27.74	43.59	55.95	69.70

attention to achieve readiness; whereas, an average score greater than or equal to 2.5 and less than 3.5 is medium, indicating that certain aspects (within a category) need attention to achieve readiness in Knowledge Management; and, an average score greater than or equal to 3.5 is high, indicating that the firm has adequate capability and maturity in these aspects and therefore has Knowledge Management-readiness (in those respects). On successful completion of the questionnaire, results are presented with Radar diagrams that summarize overall Knowledge Management readiness in each factor and its related variables. This allows companies to focus on, and improve on, those specific aspects within each category, even if they

have achieved Knowledge Management-readiness in that category.

5. RESULTS

This section also includes two parts where the first part discusses exploratory factor analysis and the second focuses on empirical results of the assessment in the firm.

5.1. Factor Analysis Results

The critical assumptions underlying factor analysis were tested using the Bartlett test of Sphericity and the Kaiser-Meyer-Olkin measure of sampling ad-

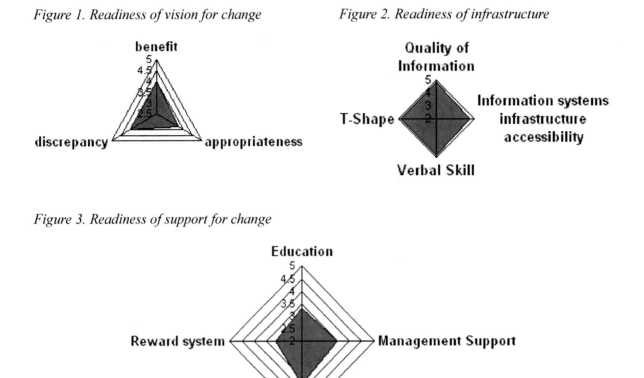

Figure 1. Readiness of vision for change

Figure 2. Readiness of infrastructure

Figure 3. Readiness of support for change

equacy (KMO=0.65). The independent variables were subjected to exploratory factor analysis using Principal Components Analysis as the extraction method and Varimax rotation with Kaiser Normalization. All factors which have the value greater than 0.5 were extracted. This iterative process is recommended as an effective way of deriving a stable factor structure (Rao et al., 1996; Sethi and King, 1991). After five iteration processes, all 18 variables were loaded satisfactorily onto the five latent factors. The factor analysis was also examined to ensure acceptable levels of variable communality and multicollinearity. The factors are associated with culture, information infrastructure of the organization, vision of change, management support and structure which explain almost 70% of the variance of KM readiness. Table2 shows exploratory factor analysis results.

5.2. Empirical Results

This section shows the findings on the KM-readiness of a firm based on responses which includes the average scores of the firm in the categories including management support for change, culture of knowledge, structure, infrastructure and vision for change. The evaluations were conducted by managerial staffs (e.g. senior project manager, project director, senior systems manager, etc.) and bottom-line staffs in the relevant departments. Average scores obtained in each category are plotted on a radar diagram as illustrated in Figures 1 to 5. These figures highlight specific points within each category that need attention to achieve Knowledge Management-readiness.

As seen in Table 3, the firm's state of infrastructure factor is excellent. All measures of this factor are greater than 3.5 (even greater than 4.7)

Table 3. Readiness scores of the firm

Factors	Measures	Score	Readiness
Vision for Change	Benefit	3.9	High
	Appropriateness	3.3	Medium
	Discrepancy	3.9	High
Infrastructure	Quality of Information	4.8	High
	Information systems infrastructure accessibility	4.7	High
	Verbal Skill	4.8	High
	T-Shape	4.8	High
Structure	Centralization	3.9	High
	Formalization	3.3	Medium
	Teamwork	3.9	High
Support for change	Education	3.3	Medium
	Management Support	3.4	Medium
	Participation	3.7	High
	Reward system	3.1	Medium
Culture of knowledge	Trust	3.7	High
	Open leadership climate	3.9	High
	Learning from Failure	3.9	High
	A culture of altruism	4.1	High

Figure 4. Readiness of structure

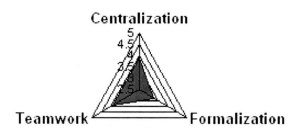

Figure 5. Readiness of culture

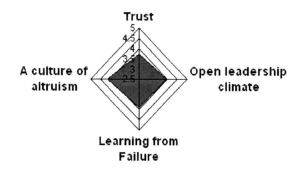

indicating that the firm has adequate capability and maturity. Also, the average scores of each item in change factor are high i.e. the firm can empower or devote the organizational resources on to the other factors. All items in the management support factor are the least KM-readiness with the lowest scores compared to the other four categories. Three measures are in medium state and only participation is high ready. In culture, all the items have high level of KM-readiness with scores greater than 3.5. At the same time,

verbal skill and T-shape have higher score in readiness assessment.

This firm tried to implement Knowledge Management in 2004 but its first attempt failed because of its emphasis merely on technological aspect. Project failure caused to managers defines this research project to assess organizational dimensions, needed before embarking on the KM project. After identifying factors influencing readiness as well as weak areas in the firm, all the people involving in the first attempt seems to agree on weakness discovered by this assessment tool. Hence, managers defined projects to improve current state of the firm to the extent to which all organizational functions and dimensions will be fully ready for this risky project.

6. CONCLUSION

This study is one of the first systematic studies to determine the KM readiness implementation in firms, especially in the SME[1] sector. This assessment survey profile offers a valuable source of information to firms, which are still lagging far behind when comes to KM practices.

Present research has identified five organizational antecedents to effective knowledge management within the context. We have tried to illuminate the unique challenges managers encounter while implementing knowledge management processes to the aforementioned dimensions. By investigating, managers acknowledge that they have considerable scope to improve current attitudes and practices within these constraints. They can use the developed instrument as a framework in assessing their current readiness in factors influencing on the success of KM project. The instrument in a way provides pointers to what needs to be addressed. The acquired results would help managers to facilitate its adoption and to prioritize its practices. At the same time, academics can use the outcomes to build models that would further expand the KM domain. Although technological infrastructure and KM systems are vital for successful implementation, firms should give more emphasis on soft components of organization such as people and culture because most failure is encountered from narrow view to such a project and a mere emphasis on technology. It causes to ensure the successful implementation of KM as well as to attain full advantages from KM in organization.

7. LIMITATIONS AND SUGGESTIONS FOR FUTURE RESEARCH

There are some limitations/constraints to this study, including its focus on one enterprise. In addition, self-selection bias not only limits to conclude the results of the study rather it might lead our choice of industry or firm narrow. Although, the instrument can be applied to IT firms, it must be handle prudently while applying in other industries. As a matter of fact, additional research must be carried out to validate conclusions and to add to our understanding about knowledge management readiness in other commercial or governmental enterprises. It is believed that the number of KM experts and their responses was small since it is a new and emerging discipline, and not many SMEs have formally implemented it, especially in a developing country like Iran. Furthermore, we think that there are other influencing factors on readiness that were probably left out, especially environmental ones that was excluded because of difficulty in developing universally applicable questionnaire, suitable to organizations. Finally, assessment instrument applied in the firm was attitude-based that in reality may be biased.

However, this instrument needs further improvement and evaluation. The instrument should be less attitude-based and more rely on current documents and statements of firms. Also, researchers are advised to implement those instruments in different areas of industries, in order to determine and enhance their applicability. Also, they should also work on developing comprehensive and integrated maturity model to help practitioners implement Knowledge Management. To that end, there is a growing commitment by scholars towards empirical and conceptual research especially in knowledge management.

ACKNOWLEDGMENT

The authors sincerely thank referees and the Area Editor for their valuable and constructive comments on an earlier version of this chapter. We are also thankful to all who participated and contributed during the course of this research.

REFERENCES

Ahn, J. H., & Chang, S. G. (2004). Assessing the Contribution of Knowledge to Business Performance: The KP3 Methodology. *Decision Support Systems*, 36, 403–416. doi:10.1016/S0167-9236(03)00029-0

Alavi, M. (2000). Managing organizational knowledge. In Zumd, R. (Ed.), *Framing the domains of it management: projecting the future through the past*. New York: Pinnaflex.

Alavi, M., & Leidner, D. E. (2001). Review: knowledge management and knowledge management systems: conceptual foundations and research issues. *Management Information Systems Quarterly*, 25(1), 107–136. doi:10.2307/3250961

Allee, V. (1997). *The knowledge evolution: Expanding organizational intelligence*. Oxford, UK: Butterworth- Heinemann.

Andersson, T., & Westterlind, T. (1999). *Sharing Knowledge over Company Borders Managing Knowledge in Key Customer Relations at ABB Sweden*. Master Thesis, Linköpings university, Sweden.

Apostolou, D., & Mentzas, G. (1999a). Managing Corporate Knowledge: A Comparative Analysis of Experiences in Consulting Firms: Part 1. *Knowledge and Process Management*, 6(3), 129–138. doi:10.1002/(SICI)1099-1441(199909)6:3<129::AID-KPM64>3.0.CO;2-3

Apostolou, D., & Mentzas, G. (1999b). Managing Corporate Knowledge: A Comparative Analysis of Experiences in Consulting Firms: Part 2. *Knowledge and Process Management*, 6(3). doi:10.1002/(SICI)1099-1441(199909)6:3<129::AID-KPM64>3.0.CO;2-3

Argote, L., McEvily, B., & Reagans, R. (2003). Introduction to the special issue on managing knowledge in organizations: creating, retaining and transferring knowledge. *Management Science*, 49(4), 5–8. doi:10.1287/mnsc.49.4.0.14421

Birkinshaw, J., Nobel, R., & Ridderstrale, J. (2002). Knowledge as a Contingency Variable: Do the Characteristics of Knowledge Predict Organization Structure. *Organization Science*, 13(3), 274–289. doi:10.1287/orsc.13.3.274.2778

Brand, A. (1998). Knowledge Management and Innovation at 3M. *Journal of Knowledge Management*, 2(1). doi:10.1108/EUM0000000004605

Choi, Y. S. (2000). *An Empirical Study of Factors Affecting Successful Implementation of Knowledge Management*. Doctoral Dissertation, University of Nebraska, Lincoln, NE

Chua, A., & Lam, W. (2005). Why KM projects fail: a multi-case analysis. *Journal of Knowledge Management*, 9(3), 6–17. doi:10.1108/13673270510602737

Chung, H. Y., Ming, H. S., Pin, L. Q., & Tsai, M. L. (2005). Critical Factors In Adopting a Knowledge Management System For The Pharmaceutical Industry. *Industrial Management & Data Systems*, 105(2), 164–183. doi:10.1108/02635570510583307

Clark, S. W. (2003). *The development of an integrated measure of readiness for change instrument and its application on ASC/PK*. Master Thesis, Department of the air force, Air University, Ohio, USA.

Croasdell, D. T., Jennex, M., Yu, Z., & Christianson, T. (2003), *A Meta-Analysis of Methodologies for Research in Knowledge Management, Organizational Learning and Organizational Memory: Five Years at HICSS*. Proceedings of the 36th Hawaii International Conference on System Sciences

Damodaran, L., & Olphert, W. (2000). Barriers and facilitators to the use of knowledge management systems. *Behaviour & Information Technology, 19*(6), 405–413. doi:10.1080/014492900750052660

Davenport, T., De Long, D., & Beers, M. (1998). Successful knowledge management projects. *Sloan Management Review, 39*(2), 43–57.

Davenport, T., & Prusak, L. (1998). *Working Knowledge-How Organizations Manage What They Know*. Boston, MA: Harvard Business School Press.

DeLone, W. H., & McLean, E. R. (2003). The DeLone and McLean Model of Information Systems Success: A Ten-Year Update. *Journal of Management Information Systems, 19*(4), 9–30.

Desouza, K. C. (2003). Barriers to Effective Use of Knowledge Management Systems in Software Engineering. *Communications of the ACM, 46*(1), 99–101. doi:10.1145/602421.602458

Earl, M. J. (1999). Opinion: what is a chief knowledge officer? *Sloan Management Review, 40*(2), 29–38.

Forcadell, F. J., & Cuadamillas, F. (2002). A Case Study on the Implementation of A Knowledge Management Strategy Oriented to Innovation. *Knowledge and Process Management, 9*(3), 162–171. doi:10.1002/kpm.143

Grover, V., & Davenport, T. H. (2001). General perspectives on knowledge management: fostering a research agenda. *Journal of Management Information Systems, 18*(1), 5–21.

Guptara, P. (2000). *Why Knowledge Management Fails: How to avoid the common pitfalls*. Washington, DC: Melcrum Publishing Ltd.

Gurteen, D. (1998). Knowledge, creativity and innovation. *Journal of Knowledge Management, 2*(1), 5–13. doi:10.1108/13673279810800744

Haeussler, C. (2011). Information-sharing in academia and the industry: A comparative study. *Research Policy, 40*, 105–122. doi:10.1016/j.respol.2010.08.007

Hansen, M., Nohria, N., & Tierney, T. (1999). What's your strategy for managing knowledge. *Harvard Business Review*, (March-April): 106–116.

Hasanali, F. (2002). *Critical Success Factors of Knowledge Management*. APQC.

Hoffman, J., Hoelscher, M. L., & Sherif, K. (2005). Social capital, knowledge management, and sustained superior performance. *Journal of Knowledge Management, 9*(3). doi:10.1108/13673270510602791

Holt, D. T. (2000). *The measurement of readiness for change: A review of instruments and suggestions for future research* Annual meeting of the Academy of Management, Toronto, Canada.

Holt, D. T., Bartczak, S. E., Clark, S. W., & Trent, M. R. (2004). *The Development of an Instrument to Measure Readiness for Knowledge Management*. Proceedings of the 37th Hawaii International Conference on System Sciences

Hung, Y. H., Chen, Y. L., & Chou, S. C. T. (2006). *On the Relationship between Knowledge Management Readiness and Intellectual Capital*. APRU DLI.

Hung, Y. H., & Chou, S. C. (2005). *On Constructing a Knowledge Management Pyramid Model*. The IEEE International Conference on Information Reuse and Integration.

Ithia, A. (2003). UK lawyers spend more on KM. *KM Review, 5*(6), 11.

Jansen, K. J. (2000). The emerging dynamics of change: Resistance, readiness, and momentum. *Human Resource Planning, 23*(2), 53–55.

Jennex, M. E. (2005). What is Knowledge Management? *International Journal of Knowledge Management, 1*(4), 1–15.

Jennex, M. E., & Olfman, L. (2000). *Development recommendations for knowledge management/ organizational memory systems*.Proceedings of the Information Systems Development Conference.

Jennex, M. E., & Olfman, L. (2005). Assessing Knowledge Management Success. *International Journal of Knowledge Management, 1*(2), 33–49. doi:10.4018/jkm.2005040104

Jennex, M. E., & Olfman, L. (2006). A Model of Knowledge Management Success. *International Journal of Knowledge Management, 2*(3), 51–68. doi:10.4018/jkm.2006070104

Jennex, M. E., Smolnik, S., & Croasdell, D. (2007). Defining Knowledge Management Success. *Proceedings of the 6th Annual ISOnEworld Conference*, Las Vegas, NV.

Karkoulian, S., Halawi, L. A., & McCarthy, R. V. (2008). Knowledge management formal and informal mentoring: an empirical investigation in Lebanese banks. *The Learning Organization, 15*(5), 409–420. doi:10.1108/09696470810898384

Keith, M., Goul, M., Demirkan, H., Nichols, J., & Mitchell, M. C. (2006). Contextualizing Knowledge Management Readiness to Support Change Management Strategies. *Proceedings of the 39th Hawaii International Conference on System Sciences*

Kogut, B., & Zander, U. (1992). Knowledge of the Firm, Combinative Capabilities, and the Replication of Technology. *Organization Science, 3*(3), 383–397. doi:10.1287/orsc.3.3.383

Lang, J. C. (2001). Managerial concerns in knowledge management. *Journal of Knowledge Management, 5*(1), 43–57. doi:10.1108/13673270110384392

Lee, H., & Choi, B. (2003). Knowledge Management Enablers, Processes, an Integrative View and Empirical Examination. *Journal of Management Information Systems, 20*(1), 179–228.

Lee, H., & Choi, B. (2003). Knowledge Management Enablers, Processes, and Organizational Performance: An Integrative View and Empirical Examination. *Journal of Management Information Systems, 20*(1), 179–228.

Liebowitz, J., & Wright, K. (1999). Does measuring knowledge make "cents"? *Expert Systems with Applications, 17*(5), 99–103. doi:10.1016/S0957-4174(99)00027-5

MacDonald, S. (1998). *Information for Innovation: Managing Change from an Information Perspective*. Oxford, UK: Oxford University Press.

Magnier-Watanabe, R., & Senoo, D. (2008). Organizational characteristics as prescriptive factors of knowledge management initiatives'. *Journal of Knowledge Management, 12*(1), 21–36. doi:10.1108/13673270810852368

Mathi, K. (2004). *Key success factors for knowledge management*. Retrieved from http://www.dmreview.com/whitepaper.

Moffett, S., McAdam, R., & Parkinson, S. (2002). Developing a model for technology and cultural factors in knowledge management: a factor analysis. *Knowledge and Process Management, 9*(4), 237–255. doi:10.1002/kpm.152

Monavvarian, A. & Kasaei, M. (2007).KM model for public administration: the case of Labour Ministry.*VINE: The journal of information and knowledge management systems, 37* (3), pp. 348-67.

Monnavarian, A., & Amini, A. (2009). Do interactions within networks lead to knowledge management? *Business Strategy Series*, *10*(3), 139–155. doi:10.1108/17515630910956561

Nissen, M. E. (2006). *Harnessing knowledge dynamics: Principled Organizational Knowing and Learning.* IRM Press.

Nonaka, I. (1994). A Dynamic Theory of Organizational Knowledge Creation. *Organization Science*, *5*(1). doi:10.1287/orsc.5.1.14

Norton, R. C. (2003). Projects that succeed: seven habits of IT executives who understand how to prevent project failure. *The E-business Executive Daily*, available at: http://www.strategit.com/Pdfs/Boardroom_ProjectsThatSucceed.pdf (accessed 10 August 2004).

Nunnally, J. (1978). *Psychometric Theory.* New York, NY: McGraw-Hill.

Polkinghorne, D. (1988). *Narrative Knowing and the Human Sciences.* Albany, NY: State University of New York Press.

Pumareja, D. T., & Sikkel, K. (2005). *The Role of Dissonance in Knowledge Exchange: A Case Study of a Knowledge Management System Implementation.* Proceedings of the 38th Hawaii International Conference on System Sciences, 42b.

Rao, L., & Osei-Bryson, K. M. (2007). Towards defining dimensions of knowledge systems quality. *Expert Systems with Applications*, *33*, 368–378. doi:10.1016/j.eswa.2006.05.003

Ratten, V., & Suseno, Y. (2006). Knowledge development, social capital and alliance learning. *International Journal of Educational Management*, *20*(1), 60–72. doi:10.1108/09513540610639594

Ross, M. V., & Schulte, W. D. (2005). Knowledge Management in a Military Enterprise: a Pilot Case Study of the Space and Warfare Systems Command. In Stankosky, M. (Ed.), *Creating the Discipline of Knowledge Management: The Latest in University Research, 157-70.* London, UK: Elsevier/Butterworth-Heinemann. doi:10.1016/B978-0-7506-7878-0.50014-4

Ruikar, K., Anumba, C. J., & Carrillo, P. M. (2006). VERDICT-An e-readiness assessment application for construction companies. *Automation in Construction*, *15*(1). doi:10.1016/j.autcon.2005.02.009

Ruppel, C. P., & Harrington, S. J. (2001). Sharing Knowledge through Intranets: A Study of Organizational Culture and Intranet Implementation. *IEEE Transactions on Professional Communication*, *44*(1), 37–52. doi:10.1109/47.911131

Siemieniuch, C. E., & Sinclair, M. A. (2004). A framework for organizational readiness for knowledge management. *International Journal of Operations & Production Management*, *24*(1), 79–98. doi:10.1108/01443570410511004

Simon, N. J. (1996). Meeting the challenge of change: The issue of readiness. *Competitive Intelligence Review, 7*(2), 86-88.

Snyman, R., & Krugere, J. (2004). The Interdependency between Strategic Management and Strategic Knowledge Management. *Journal of Knowledge Management*, *8*(1), 5–19. doi:10.1108/13673270410523871

Sohail, M.S., Daud. S., (2009). Knowledge sharing in higher education institutions: Perspectives from Malaysia. *VINE: The journal of information and knowledge management systems*, 39 (2), 125-142.

Soliman, F., & Spooner, K. (2000). Strategies for implementing knowledge management: role of human resources management. *The Journal of Knowledge Management*, I4), 337-345.

Streels, N. (2000). Success factors for virtual libraries. *Wilton, 23*(5), 68–71.

Sunassee, N. N., & Sewry, D. A. (2003). *A Theoretical Framework for Knowledge Management Implementation* Proceedings of the 2002 annual research conference of the South African institute of computer scientists and information technologists on Enablement through technology, Port Elizabeth, South Africa.

Talebi, K., Mohammadi, H. R., & Rahimi, M. (2008).*Framework for implementing knowledge management in small and medium sized enterprises'*.Paper presented at 1st Iranian Knowledge Management Conference, Tehran, Iran, February 2/3.

Taylor, W. A., & Wright, G. H. (2004). *Organizational Readiness for Successful Knowledge Sharing: Challenges for Public Sector Managers*. Hershey, PA: Idea Group Inc.

Thursby, M., Thursby, J., & Haeussler, C. Jiang., L. (2009). Do academic scientists freely share information? Not necessarily. *Vox News* Nov 29, 2009. Retrieved from http://www.voxeu.org/index.php?q=node/4264 (accessed 30.11.09).

Tsai, W. (2002). Social Structure of 'Coopetition' Within a Multiunit Organization: Coordination, Competition, and Intraorganizational Knowledge Sharing. *Organization Science, 13*(2), 179–190. doi:10.1287/orsc.13.2.179.536

Walczak, S. (2005). Organizational knowledge management structure. *The Learning Organization, 12*(4), 330–339. doi:10.1108/09696470510599118

Wang, H., & Wang, S. (2008). A knowledge management approach to data mining process for business intelligence. *Industrial Management & Data Systems, 108*(5), 622–634. doi:10.1108/02635570810876750

Wasko, M., & Faraj, S. (2005). Why Should I Share? Examining Social Capital and Knowledge Contribution in Electronic Networks of Practice. *Management Information Systems Quarterly, 29*(1), 35–37.

Weber, B., & Weber, C. (2007). Corporate venture capital as a means of radical innovation: relational fit, social capital, and knowledge transfer. *Journal of Engineering and Technology Management, 24*(1/2), 11–35. doi:10.1016/j.jengtecman.2007.01.002

Wiig, K. (1997). *Leveraging knowledge for business performance*. Pretoria, USA: Wits Business School.

Wills-Johnson, N. (2008). The networked firm: a framework for RBV. *Journal of Management Development, 27*(2), 214–224. doi:10.1108/02621710810849344

ENDNOTE

[1]   Small-Medium size Enterprise (SME)

APPENDIX

Respondents were asked to rate their agreements with the following statements, on a scale of 1-5.

		1	2	3	4	5
Benefit	I believe in the value of such knowledge sharing changes.	1	2	3	4	5
	My future in this job will be limited because of such changes.	1	2	3	4	5
	I like the available situation.	1	2	3	4	5
	The time we would spend on such changes should be spent on something else.	1	2	3	4	5
	Such changes give me ability to make decisions as how my work is done.	1	2	3	4	5
	Changes that improve knowledge sharing will make my job easier.	1	2	3	4	5
	Implementation of knowledge sharing changes will disrupt many of the personal relationships I have developed.	1	2	3	4	5
	My past experiences make me confident that I will be able to perform successfully after such changes.	1	2	3	4	5
	I am worried I will lose some of my status in the organization when such changes are implemented.	1	2	3	4	5
Participation	The information I received about such knowledge sharing changes was timely.	1	2	3	4	5
	I am able to participate in the implementation of such changes.	1	2	3	4	5
	I have some control over the knowledge sharing changes that will be proposed.	1	2	3	4	5
	The information I received about such changes, has adequately answered my questions.	1	2	3	4	5
	The information I received about this changes, helped me understand changes	1	2	3	4	5
	When we implement such knowledge sharing changes, I feel I can handle it with ease.	1	2	3	4	5
	Trade planning has been done regularly and each person in organization participates and includes in this process to some extent.	1	2	3	4	5
Discrepancy	There is a clear need to change knowledge sharing activities.	1	2	3	4	5
	Attempts to make things better are necessary around here.	1	2	3	4	5
	Our organization has problems about knowledge saving.	1	2	3	4	5
T-shape	I have the knowledge of my job.	1	2	3	4	5
	Familiar to other tasks in organization it is useful for doing my job.	1	2	3	4	5
	I have general understanding organizational processes.	1	2	3	4	5
Appropriateness	There are a number of rational reasons for such changes to be made	1	2	3	4	5
	There are legitimate reasons for us to make changes that will improve knowledge management activities.	1	2	3	4	5
	Changes that will improve knowledge sharing, match the priorities of our organization.	1	2	3	4	5
	Managing knowledge is as organizational values.	1	2	3	4	5
	Applying new information technology is appropriate with organizational purpose.	1	2	3	4	5
	Change in information distribution is a major goal of the organization.	1	2	3	4	5
Management support	This organization's most senior leader is committed to such change	1	2	3	4	5
	Management has sent a clear signal that this organization is going to make changes that will improve knowledge management.	1	2	3	4	5
	The top manager is committed to making such knowledge sharing change efforts a success.	1	2	3	4	5
	Major managers encourage everybody to the changes which improve knowledge management.	1	2	3	4	5
	Managers and leaders put their word into action.	1	2	3	4	5

Reward System	Rewards are paid according to the needs of a person.	1	2	3	4	5
	People, who have more roles in the organization, are rewarded more.	1	2	3	4	5
	Rewards are paid according to the needs of a person.	1	2	3	4	5
	Based on experiences, the organization reward system do fairly.	1	2	3	4	5
	Organization has the pool of rewords.	1	2	3	4	5
Verbal Skill	In communication, I use words that others understand easily.	1	2	3	4	5
	My colleagues can understand the words I use.	1	2	3	4	5
Centralization	How much directly does the major manager of the organization control the decisions made by others?	1	2	3	4	5
	How much freely and independently does your unit headman act in employing or firing the personnel?	1	2	3	4	5
	How mach does the major manager of the organization act directly in collecting information for making his decision?	1	2	3	4	5
	Each one can be a decision maker in the organization without being controlled by others.	1	2	3	4	5
	How much freely and independently does your unit head man act in personnel's rewards?	1	2	3	4	5
	How much freely and independently does your unit head man act in evaluating his unit function?	1	2	3	4	5
	How much freely and independently does your unit head man act in evaluating his unit function?	1	2	3	4	5
Open leader-ship climate	Usually, some meetings are held in manager's presence to hear employee's ideas.	1	2	3	4	5
	Management encourages active participation in expressing ideas.	1	2	3	4	5
	Does the manager pay attention to employee's ideas with regard to work affairs?	1	2	3	4	5
	Do they behave honestly?	1	2	3	4	5
	Do employees express ideas freely?	1	2	3	4	5
	Do employees feel relaxed in expressing their ideas?	1	2	3	4	5
Team work	The organization uses different team in order to solve its problems and requirements.	1	2	3	4	5
	The organization focuses on the team work.	1	2	3	4	5
	To do a work, team work is used instead of organizational hierarchy.	1	2	3	4	5
	Every one does his work in the team.	1	2	3	4	5
	Do teams have much power in relation to decision making and performance?	1	2	3	4	5
Formalization	Most will make their regulations on their own.	1	2	3	4	5
	Every one in the organization is permitted to work quite in the way they are satisfied.	1	2	3	4	5
	In order to the deal whit any condition, there are special procedures.	1	2	3	4	5
	The situation is available for the personnel to express ideas.	1	2	3	4	5
Trust	My success is important for my colleagues.	1	2	3	4	5
	I am sure my colleagues put their words into action.	1	2	3	4	5
	I am sure my colleagues handle me accurate information.	1	2	3	4	5
	I am sure my colleagues are honest with me.	1	2	3	4	5
Learning of failure	The employees can detect other methods to do the affairs, without fear of being reprimanded for previous failure.	1	2	3	4	5
	In case of procedure failure, the organization encourages the employees to analyze it.	1	2	3	4	5
	The organization pays no attention to the cause of failed procedure of other organizations.	1	2	3	4	5
	The organization patience to making mistakes is high.	1	2	3	4	5
	I am annoyed when others talk about my mistakes over and over again.	1	2	3	4	5
	The organization encourages creative endeavors even when it is not successful.	1	2	3	4	5
	I consider my failures as an educating source.	1	2	3	4	5

Education	In case of encountering questions, they are answered while the new systems are used.	1	2	3	4	5
	The organization holds training and introduction with the new technology courses for the employees.	1	2	3	4	5
	A lot of investment is done to educate the employees.	1	2	3	4	5
Information systems infrastructure accessibility	What extent are software systems of the organization capable of coordinating with the new systems?	1	2	3	4	5
	What extent are the internal nets in the organization capable of supporting the new systems?	1	2	3	4	5
	How is the quality of supporting the systems and the network?	1	2	3	4	5
Quality of information	How much standard is used for planning data in the organization?	1	2	3	4	5
	How is the security strategy to data in the organization?	1	2	3	4	5
	How much do you gain the required information in the appropriate time?	1	2	3	4	5
	How much do you have access to your needed information?	1	2	3	4	5
	We have a well defined good policy for using management information systems.	1	2	3	4	5
A culture of altruism	I help my colleagues without any rewards.	1	2	3	4	5
	I try to help others without any compensation.	1	2	3	4	5
	Helping my colleagues is enjoyable for me.	1	2	3	4	5
	Solving the problem of my colleagues is my job.	1	2	3	4	5

Chapter 4
Knowledge Management Toolkit for SMEs

Kerstin Fink
University of Innsbruck, Austria

Christian Ploder
University of Innsbruck, Austria

ABSTRACT

The discipline of knowledge management is no longer emerging in large organizations, but also small and medium-sized enterprises (SMEs) are focusing on finding the right process that will allow them to make advantages of their intellectual capital. Using survey data from 219 small and medium-sized enterprises in Austria and Switzerland, this article illustrates the four key knowledge processes (1) knowledge identification, (2) knowledge acquisition, (3) knowledge distribution, and (4) knowledge preservation for SMEs and also reports the findings of the empirical study designed to allocate cost-efficient software products to each of the four knowledge processes. As a result a knowledge toolkit for SMEs that integrates knowledge processes, methods and software tool for decision support making is given. Finally, the social view of knowledge management to SMEs is discussed, showing that the use of information technology is currently far more important than the integration of a social-cognitive perspective.

INTRODUCTION

The academic literature on knowledge management has become a major research field in different disciplines in the last ten years (Nonaka & Takeuchi, 1995; Ruggels, 1997; Sveiby, 1997; Davenport & Prusak, 1998; Back, Enkel, &

Krogh, 2007). Through knowledge management, organizations are enabled to create, identify and renew the company's knowledge base and to deliver innovative products and services to the customer. Knowledge management is a process of systematically managed and leveraged knowledge in an organization. In a global and interconnected society, it is more difficult for companies to know where the best and most valuable knowledge is.

DOI: 10.4018/978-1-60960-555-1.ch004

The term knowledge has a wide range of definitions in the knowledge management literature. The authors follow the definition by Davenport and Prusak (1998, p. 5) "knowledge is a fluid mix of framed experiences, values, contextual information, and expert insight that provides a framework for evaluating and incorporating new experiences and information. It originates and is applied in the mind of knowers." For a better understanding of knowledge management Jennex (2007, p. 4) points out that the concepts of organizational learning and memory should be integrated. Therefore, knowledge management can be defined as "the practice of selecting applying knowledge from pervious experiences of decision making to current and future decision-making activities with the express purpose of improving the organization´s effectiveness" (Jennex, 2007, p. 6).

Knowledge management is more than the technological solutions provided to give people access to better and more relevant information (Wang & Plaskoff, 2002, p. 113). It is important that the design of the knowledge management systems reflect the mindset of the knowledge workers and their way of offering highly qualitative knowledge solutions with quick solution processes. An effective knowledge management system must integrate people, processes, technology and the organizational structure.

Historically, knowledge management focused on the domain of larger organizations and issues of culture, networking, organizational structure and technological infrastructure are applied upon the implementation of knowledge management initiatives in large multi-national organizations and seem to give little relevance (Delahaye, 2003) to small and medium-sized enterprises (SMEs). SMEs are playing a key role in European economic performance because they account for a high proportion of the gross domestic product (GDP) and employ some two- thirds of the European workforce. According to the OECD (Organisation for Economic Co-operation and Development) *Small and Medium-sized Enterprise Outlook 2002 and 2005* (OECD, 2005), the role of SMEs in OECD economic is very important for strengthening economic performances. SMEs represent over 95% of enterprises in most OECD countries, and generate over half of private sector development. A similar impact of SMEs to economic value can be found in the report of the Asia-Pacific Economic Cooperation (APEC, 2006), where about 90% of enterprises are SMEs. During their 2006 meeting in Beijing, the members agreed to strengthen the SME's competitiveness for trade and investment. For example, SMEs account for more than 95% of companies in Australia. Of the 624.010 SMEs in Australia, more than two-thirds employ between one and four people. A further 180,880 SMEs employ between five and 19 people meaning that 93.5% of people employed by SMEs in Australia are employed by what can be described as 'micro-SMEs,' namely companies with less than 20 employees. However, the success and growth of SMEs depends on how well they manage the knowledge of their knowledge workers. In 2000, the European Council set the clear strategic goal for the European Union (EU) of becoming "the most competitive and dynamic economy in the world, capable of sustaining economic growth with more and better jobs and greater social cohesion" by the year 2010 (EC, 2000). Dezouza and Awazu (2006) point out that SMEs have to compete on the know-how in order to gain competitive advantages. Even more, SMEs do not have much money to spend on knowledge management initiatives, so knowledge must be leveraged that goals can be achieved in an effective and efficient manner (Fink & Ploder, 2007c). Ordanini (2006) discusses the issue that the adoption of information technology by SMEs began to be discussed during the 1980s. Furthermore, it has to be stated that the adoption of information technology for SMEs was slower than that of larger organizations, which can be referred to as the so-called digital divide phenomenon.

Looking to the European countries of Austria and Switzerland including Liechtenstein, a similar landscape of SMEs can be identified. According to the *Austrian Statistical Year Book* (SA, 2006) and the Austrian Institute for SMEs Research (ASME, 2006) for the year 2006, 99.7% which are 297,800 companies are SMEs in Austria. In Switzerland, also 99.7% of the companies are SMEs, looking at the data from CHSME (2006). There are several research articles dealing with knowledge management in SMEs (Sveiby, 1997; Beijerse, 2000; McAdam & Reid, 2001; Salojärvi, Furu, & Sveiby, 2005), but only a few empirical studies are conducted to see the impact of knowledge processes in SMEs. McAdam and Reid (2001) found out that the time is right for knowledge management within the SME-sector. The results of their comparative study of large organizations and SMEs showed that both sectors have much to gain by the development of knowledge management systems. Salojärvi, Furu and Sveiby (2005) have observed that SMEs should be able to enhance their performance and competitive advantages by a more conscious and systematic approach to knowledge management.

In this article, the focus lies on the impact of knowledge process modeling for SMEs to help them getting a framework to be more innovative (Donnellan, Conboy, & Hill, 2006). In research methodology, the theoretical framework for the identification of knowledge processes in SMEs will be discussed. The section that follows that covers the use of cost-efficient software products for the implementation of knowledge processes in SME and introduces a SME knowledge toolkit. Discussion and future research gives an outlook of future research and a discussion of social factors influencing knowledge management in SMEs.

RESEARCH METHODOLOGY

Definition of SMEs

There are several quantitative and qualitative definitions of the term small and medium-sized en-terprise (SME) depending on regional and national differences. In the United States, the definition of small business is set by a government department called the Small Business Administration (SBA) Size Standards Office. The SBA uses the term "size standards" which is a numerical definition to be considered as a small or medium-sized business. It must also be independently owned and operated. Unlike the European Union, which has simple definitions applied to all industries, the United States has chosen to set size standards for each individual industry. This distinction is intended to better reflect industry differences. SMEs are also of high importance for in the U.S. Economy. Similar to Europe, more than 97% of the firms in the U.S. can be defined as SMEs.

The definition of SMEs of the European Commission 2005 (EC, 2000) is used for this research design. The European Commission analyzes SMEs by using the following three characteristics: (1) number of employees, (2) annual revenue and (3) total assets. Characterized through these three factors, the European Commission differs: (1) middle enterprises (less than 250 employees and less than 50 million euro annual revenue or less than 43 million total assets); (2) small enterprises (less than 50 employees and less than 10 million euro annual revenue or less than 10 million euro total assets); and (3) micro enterprises (less than 10 employees and less than 2 million euro annual revenue or less than 2 million euro total assets).

Since the authors focus on the definition of the European Commission of SMEs, they follow the research view of a quantitative perspective of SMEs. This means that all enterprises with less than 250 employees and less than 50 million euro annual revenue or less than 43 million euro total assets in Austria and Switzerland including Liechtenstein are the target population.

Research Framework

The basic research model is the "building block" approach by Probst, Raub and Romhardt (2002)

Figure 1. Knowledge building block approach by Probst, Raub and Romhardt (2002)

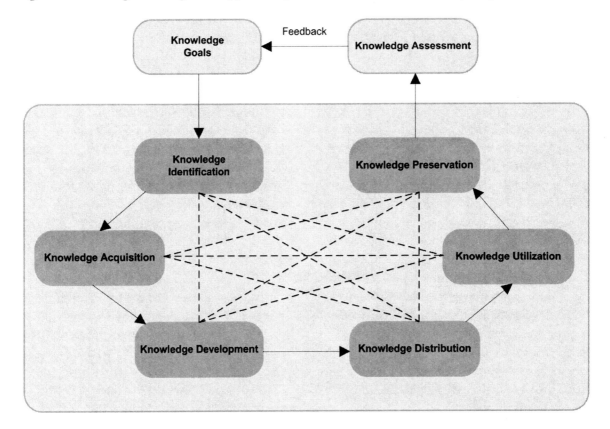

with the description of the knowledge processes (Figure 1). Involved are eight components that form two cycles: an inner cycle and an outer cycle. The inner cycle is composed of six key knowledge processes:

- *Knowledge identification* is the process of identifying external knowledge for analyzing and describing the company's knowledge environment.
- *Knowledge acquisition* refers to what forms of expertise the company should acquire from outside through relationships with customers, suppliers, competitors and partners in co-operative ventures.
- *Knowledge development* is a building block which complements knowledge acquisition. It focuses on generating new skills, new products, better ideas and more

efficient processes. Knowledge development includes all management actions consciously aimed at producing capabilities.

- *Knowledge distribution* is the process of sharing and spreading knowledge which is already present within the organization.
- *Knowledge utilization* consists of carrying out activities to ensure that the knowledge present in the organization is applied productively for its benefit.
- *Knowledge preservation* is the process where the selective retention of information, documents and experience required by management takes place.

In addition, there are two other processes in the outer cycle, knowledge assessment and knowledge goals, which provide the direction to the whole knowledge management cycle:

- *Knowledge assessment* completes the cycle, providing the essential data for strategic control of knowledge management.
- *Knowledge goals* determine which capabilities should be built on which level.

Among other knowledge process models (Nonaka & Takeuchi, 1995; Laudon & Laudon, 2006; Jennex, 2007), the building block approach of Probst, Raub and Romhardt (2002) has the advantage that it is well known in European companies as well as in SMEs and furthermore it is a very unique and complete design of knowledge processes. Business process modeling (Hammer & Champy, 1993) has become a major research field in the information systems discipline in the last ten years. Davenport sees the term business process as 'a structured, measured set of activities designed to produce a specified output from a particular customer or market' (Davenport, 1995). The linkage of business process modeling and knowledge management is called knowledge process modeling. Richter-von Hagen et al. describes knowledge-intensive processes as sequences of activities based on knowledge intensive acquisitions and handling (Richter-von Hagen, Ratz, & Povalej, 2005). Edwards and Kidd (Edwards & Kidd, 2003, p. 124) named the following five characteristics to enforce the argument that knowledge management and business process management should be integrated:

- Knowledge management is important for business if the initiative implied an advantage for the customers. The idea to implement the customer's requests—may be internal or external—is the base for including the customer (Fink, Roithmayr, & Ploder, 2006).
- Knowledge does not follow the business borders. Business processes also model activities by global trading companies and build the base for modeling knowledge intensive processes.

- Knowledge management can only be efficient if it follows a structured model. Business processes are modeled by structured actions and they are necessary to deduce knowledge-intensive processes.
- The success of knowledge management depends on the measurement of knowledge. There exists a similarity to the measurement of business processes. The measurement of the knowledge potential provides a central position and biases the success (Fink, 2004).
- Knowledge management is affected by a holistic approach. Every part of the business process modeling is important for success but every aspect should be considered.

Data Collection for Knowledge Processes

At the beginning of our research was the identification of knowledge processes for SMEs. Therefore in the first step, the authors conducted a study with the objective to find the key knowledge processes—based on the framework of (Probst et al., 2002)—for SMEs. In a second step, the authors conducted empirical studies in order to identify which software products support the identified knowledge processes and can be used in practice. The interviews were conducted at the Department of Information Systems (University of Innsbruck) in 2005. The key objective of the expert interview was to analyze which of the eight knowledge processes from Probst et al. (2002) are relevant for SMEs. The data sample was 20 expert interviews which were conducted by the authors in summer 2005. Ten experts from science and ten experts from practice were asked about the most important knowledge processes in SMEs. The result of these expert interviews showed that SMEs are only determined by three key knowledge processes: (1) knowledge identification, (2) knowledge acquisition, and (3) knowledge distribution. In addition, for SME the concept of

Figure 2. Theoretical concept of knowledge process model and method repositories for SMEs

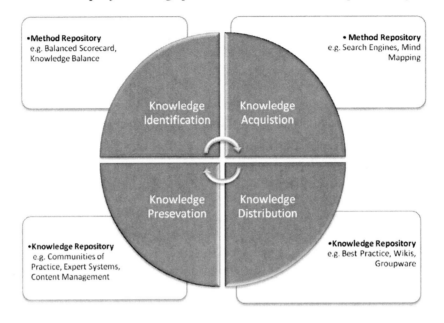

(4) knowledge disposal played a key role during the expert interviews and was extended as the fourth process called "knowledge preservation" indicating the disposal as well as actualization of knowledge. This knowledge process model for SMEs was the first step in the research work and the general research framework. The second step was to find out which process can be supported by which knowledge method. The research method was a literature review for the identification of knowledge methods (Coakes & Clarke, 2006; Smolnik, Kremer, & Kolbe, 2007) in order to build a method repository for each knowledge process.

Figure 2 describes the four key knowledge processes with the corresponding method repositories for SMEs (Fink & Ploder, 2006; 2007a) illustrating the validated research framework through interviews by the experts.

Quality Model (ISO/IEC 9126) for the Evaluation of Software Products

In a third step, the objective was to match a cost-efficient software product to each knowledge method which are usable in practice. In the research

design the focus lies on Freeware and Shareware software products in order to fulfil the pre-setting of cost-efficient software support. The research method was an online research with the result of a list of evaluated cost-efficient software products. The evaluation of each software product was conducted by applying the ISO/IEC 9126 norm. The quality model of the norm (ISO/IEC 9126-1) is divided into two parts which are important for the evaluation of the software products to support knowledge methods:

- the internal and the external quality of the software
- the quality for use

The ISO norm lists five characteristics to evaluate software products: (1) functionality, (2) reliability, (3) usability, (4) efficiency and (5) assign ability. For each characteristic, a different number of items were assessed by a Likert scale from -2 to +2. The data sample of the quality model was more than 200 different software products. A key research finding was that some of the software products cannot be used in practice because their quality was not sufficient. Finally there were 45 software products which are efficient for use in SME.

Data Collection for Cost-Efficient Software Products

The 2006 survey was developed and executed by the authors and is an update and extension of the empirical study conducted in 2004-2005. Balmisse et al. (2007) present a knowledge management tool review including the vendor perspective. The article focuses on eight tool clusters. In comparison to our research, the authors focus primarily on the tool with the corresponding vendor side, while our research framework concentrates on the methods used in SMEs with a cost-efficient software support. So the objective of the empirical study was to find out which cost-efficient software products can support the efficient methods of the four knowledge processes. For this approach the authors differ between two categories of software. At the one hand side there are the standard software products which are already in use in SMEs (for example: MS Office, Internet Explorer, Operating System, etc.) and on the other hand there are software products like Shareware, Freeware and Open Source products characterized by the issue of cost-efficient software installation in SME. This described issue is the key objective of the empirical study. The research method for this study was the online questionnaire technique. The questionnaire was built with HTML, PHP and based on a MySQL database.

The data sample of 537 SMEs were the average allocated over the regional federal states of Austria, Switzerland and Liechtenstein to get a representative result for the whole sector and were opted stochastically. The total number of SMEs was 540,000. The online questionnaire was carried out in summer 2006 after a successful pre-test with 20 respondents. The online questionnaire was partitioned into three parts:

- Generally questions referring to the IT support and application of knowledge management within the enterprise itself
- Rating relevance of the methods concerning the four knowledge processes for SME and get an idea of the favor supporting software tool
- Information about future capital investment plans referring to knowledge management

The return quote of the survey was 40%. This means that 220 SME filled out the questionnaire. The failure rate was calculated as 6.63%. So, all statements out of the survey are correct at a percentage of 93.61%. In the following section the research findings of the methods and the supporting software tools are presented and discussed. The knowledge toolkit for SMEs integrates processes, methods and software tools in a decision support framework.

RESULTS

The distribution of industries can be described as follows. Thirty percent of the SMEs were from the industry sector and 22% from the consulting and information technology sector. The retail sector was represented by 13% and the trade and handcraft sector by 19%. The rest of 21% were divided to banks and insurances with 9%, transportation 2% and Tourism 10%. Fifty-seven percent of the SMEs already use knowledge management and 85% of the SMEs use a connected infrastructure. A Web space is (hosted intern or extern) available in 78% which is necessary to deal with software products which need such an IT-infrastructure.

Mapping of Cost-Efficient Software Products with Knowledge Processes

Table 1 gives an overview of all methods supporting the four knowledge processes for SMEs and the corresponding cost-efficient software products (Fink & Ploder, 2007c). The ranking of each method is the calculated value based on the Likert scale ("absolutely adequate": +2 pt. – "not adequate": -2 pt.). The "ISO ranking" illustrates the assessment of the software based on the quality model of the ISO/IEC 9126 norm ("absolutely appropriate": +2 – "not appropriate´: -2). For example, the Software Tools Gama for supporting business games is ranked with 15 points in the ISO/IEC 9126 and 75 of the data sample find Gamma is a good tool to support business games. The absolute frequency of naming of the software through the respondents can be seen in the last column (ranking survey). The naming of "no cost-efficient software support" indicates that only high-priced software products are available on the market.

Knowledge balance (92) was ranked highest among the methods for the first process of the *identification of knowledge*. Fifty-six percent of SMEs think that this is the best method. Further methods are the balanced scorecard (89) and the Skandia navigator (74). The methods market-asset value-method (-5) and Tobin`s q (-15) were rated by less than 30% to be of good use in SMEs.

Brainstorming (225) and knowledge network (203) are popular methods for the *knowledge acquisition*. Mind mapping (195), e-mail systems (134), scenario technique (126) and system simulation (98) are also suitable methods for this knowledge process, while business games (91) are also a possibility. The method of "Synektik" was rated very low because of its complexity. The favorite for the knowledge acquisition is the search engine (232) with over 70% for efficient use in SMEs. In this case, the Google desktop search engine was the prior selection software. Sixty percent of the respondents chose e-mail systems which can be supported, for example, by the software Thunderbird1.5. For brainstorming a practical tool is Concept X7, while for mind mapping the tools Free Mind (42%) and Think Graph (41%) were rated highly. As support software to a

business game, 64% rated Gamma as a possible software tool.

As illustrated in Table 1 the methods e-mail system (185), handbook FAQs (159), communities of practice (152), groupware (139), questionnaire (110) and best practice (108) are the favorites for the k*nowledge distribution*. It has to be pointed out, that the methods micro article (2) and chat room (29) are rated not as well in the survey. The software products for the methods of transferring knowledge are InfoRapid supporting knowledge maps, EasySurvey supporting questionnaire, Skype and MSN supporting chat room, eGroupware 1.2 and AlphaAgent 1.6.0 supporting groupware, CUCards 2000 supporting checklists and Pegasus Mail, Thunderbird 1.5 and Amicron Mailoffice 2.0 for the support of e-mail systems.

Databases (242) are a recognized method of *the knowledge preservation process*. Eighty percent of the SMEs think that they will organize their knowledge with databases. Mind mapping (200), document management system (195) and checklists (164) are further efficient methods. Content management systems (126), project review (122), expert systems (74) and conceptualization (40) are methods which can be chosen but are not the prior choice. Neural network (-10) is not an adequate method for preserving knowledge. There were many different software products to support this process. MySQL is the favorite database software followed by the MSDE from Microsoft. Document management can be realized by Office Manager, UDEX dotNETContact or QVTutto.

Investment Allocation

Seventy-five percent of the respondents assumed that they are still using knowledge management in their SME. As shown in Figure 3, the attendance to invest into knowledge management in the next year exists with 60% and up to 40% cannot imagine to invest into knowledge management in the next year. Twenty percent of SMEs are planning an investment in the future and want to spend less

Table 1. Ranking of methods and cost-efficient software products (Fink & Ploder, 2007a)

	Ranking	Supporting cost-efficient software products	ISO Ranking	Ranking Survey
Knowledge Identification				
Knowledge Balance	92	no cost-efficient software product, Office similar products		
Balanced Scorecard	89	no cost-efficient software product, Office similar products		
Skandia Navigator	74	no cost-efficient software product, commercial Software		
Market - Asset Value - Method	-5	no cost-efficient software product, Office similar products		
Tobin's q	-15	no cost-efficient software product, Office similar products		
Knowledge Acquisition				
Search Engine	232	Google Desktop Search; MSN Toolbar; Yahoo Desktop Search	not possible	25; 12; 10
Brainstorming	225	Brainstorming Toolbox; Concept X7	6;17	44; 88
Knowledge Network	203	no cost-efficient software product		
Mind Mapping	195	Free Mind; Think Graph, Tee Tree Office	16; 12; 8	69; 53; 28
E-mail System	134	Pegasus Mail; Thunderbird Mail; Amicron Mailoffice 2.0	21; 21; 12	63; 165; 26
Scenario Technique	126	no cost-efficient software product, Office similar products		
System Simulation	98	no cost-efficient software product, commercial Software		
Business Game	91	Gamma	15	75
Synektik	-17	no cost-efficient software product, commercial Software		
Knowledge Distribution				
E-mail System	185	Pegasus Mail; Thunderbird Mail; Amicron Mailoffice 2.0	16; 12; 8	63; 165; 26
Handbook FAQs	159	no cost-efficient software product, Office similar products		
Communities of Practice	152	no cost-efficient software product, Office similar products		
Groupware	139	eGRoupware1.2; AlphaAgent 1.6.0; TikiCMS-Groupware	15; 14; 16	40; 26; 24
Questionnaire	110	Easy Survey	10	61
Best Practice	108	no cost-efficient software product, Office similar products		
Checklist	103	CUEcards 2000	8	128
Lessons Learned	103	no cost-efficient software product, Office similar products		
Knowledge Maps	82	InfoRapid KnowledgeMap	13	69
Story Telling	42	no cost-efficient software product, Office similar products		
Chat room	29	Skype; MSN, ICQ	not possible	71; 33; 25
Micro article	2	no cost-efficient software product, Office similar products		
Knowledge Preservation				
Database	242	MySQL; MSDE		86; 44
Mind Mapping	200	Free Mind; Think Graph, Tee Tree Office	16; 12; 8	69; 53; 28
Document Management System	195	Office Manager; UDEX dotNETContact; QVTutto	15; 15; 14	74; 35; 22
Checklist	164	CUEcards 2000	8	128
Content Management	126	CONTEX; ContentKit; VIO MATRIX	16; 13; 13	0; 47; 13
Project Review	122	no cost-efficient software product, Office similar products		
Experts System	74	KnowIT; KnowME	10; 7	38; 52
Conceptualization	40	no cost-efficient software product		
Neural Network	-10	no cost-efficient software product, commercial Software		

Figure 3. Investment allocation in SMEs for knowledge initiatives

Imaginable Investment

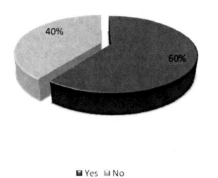

■ Yes ■ No

Level of Investment

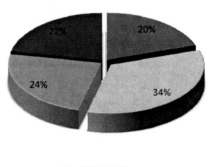

■ < 500 EURO / year
■ < 1.500 EURO / year
■ < 3.000 EURO / year

than 500 euro, 58% will spend between 500 euro and 3,000 euro and only 22% will invest more than 3,000 euro.

SME Knowledge Toolkit

The SME knowledge toolkit (Figure 4) is one of the results of our empirical research. Tiwana (2002) discusses in her book *The Knowledge Management Toolkit* a 10-step roadmap for implementing knowledge management in a company. The key objective of the toolkit is to guide a company through the complex process of analyzing the infrastructure, designing the knowledge system and linking the business strategy to knowledge management and make a performance evaluation. Jashapara (2004, p. 92) uses the term knowledge management suite that should offer a multitude of knowledge management systems in order to build an individualized toolset. The toolkit developed by the authors is an implementation for portraying knowledge processes, methods and software tools for SMEs. Therefore, the use of the toolkit can reveal the gap between the defined knowledge processes and implemented knowledge methods that could trigger further evidence to use different knowledge methods or to rearrange the knowledge

processes. The explicit identification of knowledge processes allows the user of the toolkit to match knowledge methods with cost-efficient software products that fit into the culture of SMEs. At the same time, the knowledge toolkit calculates the estimated costs for changes. The SME knowledge toolkit (Figure 4) supports all aspects of knowledge management relevant for SMEs and is divided into four key steps:

- **Step 1:** Definition of the characteristics by applying the national limitations and definitions
- **Step 2:** Identification of the knowledge processes and modeling of these processes in the SME context
- **Step 3:** Designing a knowledge method repository which enables SMEs to match the methods with the supporting knowledge processes
- **Step 4:** Designing of a software repository which helps to evaluate cost-efficient software products for knowledge management in SMEs

These four key steps are supported by the knowledge culture in an SME and by a knowledge

Figure 4. SME knowledge toolkit

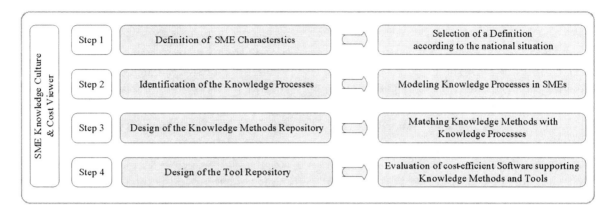

cost viewer which has the function of a controlling instrument. The SME knowledge toolkit is tailored toward the special needs of SMEs during knowledge management initiatives.

DISCUSSION AND FUTURE RESEARCH

Knowledge process modeling for SMEs uses the building block approach from Probst, Raub and Romhardt (2002) and models corresponding knowledge methods for the SME-domain. A significant emphasis in this empirical study has been the development of a flexible and usable knowledge management toolkit to implement knowledge initiatives in SMEs. This article addresses one of the currently perceived issues surrounding knowledge management, namely the lack of defining key knowledge processes for SMEs to handle knowledge methods in specific settings. The study has drawn on an extensive review of the literature as well as reported on empirical studies concerning the Austrian and Swiss SME sector.

Social Impact to SMEs

Even if the information technology infrastructure is a key dimension of knowledge management, the social and cognitive aspect may also be considered. Cognitive activity takes place in a complex, information-rich, and ever-changing environment. Tomasello (1999) notes that all human beings share their cognitive skills and knowledge with other individuals. The try to understand other persons, changes the way of interaction and social learning. A successful implementation of knowledge management only can be achieved in a culture (Holden, 2002) that supports knowledge sharing and transfer. Nakra (2000) addresses the issue that a knowledge culture is the most important value for the implementation of knowledge management because one important aspect of knowledge management is having a culture that fosters collaboration and sharing. Organizations often fail to acknowledge that it is the people, not technologies, that are the source of knowledge" (Nakra, 2000, p. 54). Organizational knowledge resides in the culture, structure, and individuals who make up the organization.

Especially in SMEs the success depends on the social system in which a knowledge worker operate. SMEs need a culture that facilitates a knowledge transfer through a more human factor because knowledge workers want to share their knowledge through communication and interaction. The social ecology of the company drives people's expectations, defines their motivation to share knowledge and pursues actions to interact with others inside or outside the organization.

Ein-Dor (2005, p. 848ff) defines taxonomies of knowledge and sees the social-individual dimension as a key success factor to knowledge diffusion. A similar view is presented by Alavi und Leidner (2001). SMEs need a culture that facilitates a knowledge transfer through a more human factor because knowledge workers want to share their knowledge through communication and interaction (Trompenaars & Hampden-Turner, 2006). The use of information technology, especially Web sites, is recognized as a critical success factor for knowledge management initiatives in the SME sector (Wong & Aspinwall, 2005). Wong (2005) sees information technologies as a key enabler for the implementation of knowledge management, and considers in the development of a knowledge management system factors such as the simplicity of technology, ease of use, suitability of users' needs, relevancy of knowledge content, and standardization of a knowledge structure as key factors for knowledge diffusion. The SME culture greatly influences the communication processes inside and outside the organization. The impact of the culture to networking processes is highly significant. Skyrme (1999, p. 15) lists two fundamental descriptions of networking:

- Networking organizations are less about organizational structures per se, and more about the informal human networking processes
- The technology of computer networking undergirds and enhances human networking.

Knowledge networking is a dynamic process in which knowledge, experiences, and expertise are shared, developed, and evolved. A knowledge-sharing culture can be developed through human interaction supported by information technology to foster new and innovative knowledge. Knowledge networking is connectivity to achieve new levels of interactivity, usability, and understanding across organizations and communities. The first results of an empirical study conducted by the authors (Fink & Ploder, 2007b) indicate that the social view is almost not taken into consideration for European SMEs. The focus lies primarily on the technical solution of knowledge management, meaning that an IT support is essential for knowledge initiatives.

Therefore, future research will direct into the development of a framework for SMEs that integrates the information technology view with the social-cognitive view. One future problem for the implementation of different software products are the interfaces of the different applications. With service-oriented architecture (SOA), it would be possible to solve this problem of interoperability and the problem of security (Kang, Kim, Lo, Montrose, & Khashnobisch, 2006). Future research will deal with SOA and should also consider open source software (OSS) (Ploder & Fink, 2007) and extending the knowledge toolkit for SMEs.

ACKNOWLEDGMENT

This article is an extended version of the paper presented at the International Resource Management Conference (IRMA) May 2007 in Vancouver. Sincere thanks to Dr. Murray Jennex for the opportunity of consideration it in the *International Journal of Knowledge Management*.

REFERENCES

Alavi, M., & Leidner, D. (2001). Review: Knowledge management and knowledge management systems. *Management Information Systems Quarterly, 25*(1), 107–136. doi:10.2307/3250961

APEC. (2006). Asia-Pacific Economic Corporation. http://www.apec.com.

ASME. (2006). Austrian Institute for SME Research. http://www.kmuforschung.ac.at.

Back, A., Enkel, E., & Krogh, G. (Eds.). (2007). *Knowledge networks for business growth*. Heidelberg: Springer Verlag.

Balmisse, G., Meingan, D., & Passerini, K. (2007). Technology trends in knowledge management tools. *International Journal of Knowledge Management, 3*(2), 118–131. doi:10.4018/jkm.2007040106

Beijerse, R. (2000). Knowledge management in small and medium-sized companies: Knowledge management for entrepreneurs. *Journal of Knowledge Management, 4*(2), 162–179. doi:10.1108/13673270010372297

CHSME. (2006). SME-Portal of Switzerland. http://www.kmu.admin.ch/index.

Coakes, E., & Clarke, S. (2006). Communities of practice. In Schwartz, D. (Ed.), *Encyclopedia of knowledge management* (pp. 30–33). Hershey, PA: Idea Group Publishing. doi:10.4018/9781591405733.ch005

Davenport, T. (1995). *Process Innovation. Reengineering work through information technology*. Boston: Harvard Business School Press.

Davenport, T., & Prusak, L. (1998). *Working knowledge. How organizations manage what they know*. Boston, MA: Harvard Business School Press.

Delahaye, D. (2003). Knowledge management at SMEs. *International Journal of Organizational Behavior, 9*(3), 604–614.

Dezouza, K., & Awazu, Y. (2006). Knowledge management at SMEs: Five peculiarities. *Journal of Knowledge Management, 10*(1), 32–43. doi:10.1108/13673270610650085

Donnellan, B., Conboy, K., & Hill, S. (2006). IS to support innovation: Weapons of mass discussion. In Khosrow-Pour, M. (Ed.), *Emerging trends and challenges in information technology management* (pp. 623–626). Hershey, PA: Idea Group Publishing.

EC. (2000). Report of the Meeting of the European Commission 23.03.2000. http://ec.europa.eu/growthandjobs.

Edwards, J., & Kidd, J. (2003). Bridging the gap from the general to the specific by linking knowledge management to business process management. In Hlupic, V. (Ed.), *Knowledge and business process management* (pp. 124–132). Hershey, PA: Idea Group Publishing.

Ein-Dor, P. (2005). Taxonomies of knowledge. In Schwartz, D. (Ed.), *Encyclopedia of knowledge management* (pp. 848–854). Hershey, PA: Idea Group Publishing.

Fink, K. (2004). *Knowledge potential measurement and uncertainty*. Wiesbaden: Dt. Univ.-Verl.

Fink, K., & Ploder, C. (2006). The impact of knowledge process modeling on small and medium-sized enterprises. In: K. Tochtermann & H. Maurer (Eds.), *Proceedings of I-KNOW '06: 6ᵗʰ International Conference on Knowledge Management*, (pp. 47-51). Graz: J.UCS.

Fink, K., & Ploder, C. (2007a). A comparative study of knowledge processes and methods in Austrian and Swiss SMEs. In: H. Österle, J. Schelp, & R. Winter (Eds.), *Proceedings of the 15ᵗʰ European Conference on Information Systems (ECIS2007)*, (pp. 704-715). St. Gallen.

Fink, K., & Ploder, C. (2007b). Knowledge diffusion through SME Web sites. In Stary, C., Brarachini, F., & Hawamdeh, S. (Eds.), *Knowledge management: Innovation, technology and cultures* (pp. 91–100). New Jersey: World Scientific. doi:10.1142/9789812770592_0008

Fink, K., & Ploder, C. (2007c). Knowledge process modeling in SME and cost-efficient software support: Theoretical framework and empirical studies. In Khosrow-Pour, M. (Ed.), *Managing worldwide operations and communications with information technology* (pp. 479–484). Hershey, PA: IGI Publishing.

Fink, K., Roithmayr, F., & Ploder, C. (2006). Multi-functional stakeholder information system for strategic knowledge management: Theoretical concept and case studies. In Khosrow-Pour, M. (Ed.), *Emerging trends and challenges in information technology management* (pp. 152–155). Hershey, PA: Idea Group Publishing.

Hammer, M., & Champy, J. (1993). *Reengineering the corporation: A manifesto for business revolution*. New York: Harper Business.

Holden, N. (2002). *Cross-cultural management: A knowledge perspective*. Harlow: Prentice Hall.

Jashapara, A. (2004). *Knowledge management: An integrated Approach*. Upper Saddle River, NJ: Prentice Hall.

Jennex, M. (2007). *Knowledge management in modern organizations*. Hershey, PA: Idea Group Pub.

Kang, M., Kim, A., Lo, J., Montrose, B., & Khashnobisch, A. (2006). Ontology-based security specification tools for SOA. In Khosrow-Pour, M. (Ed.), *Emerging trends and challenges in information technology management* (pp. 619–622). Hershey, PA: Idea Group Publishing.

Laudon, K., & Laudon, J. (2006). *Management information systems: Managing the digital firm* (9., 2. print. ed.). Upper Saddle River, NJ: Pearson Education.

McAdam, R., & Reid, R. (2001). SME and large organization perception of knowledge management: Comparison and contrast. *Journal of Knowledge Management, 5*(3), 231–241. doi:10.1108/13673270110400870

Nakra, P. (2000). Knowledge management: The magic is in the culture. *Competitive Intelligence Review, 11*(2), 53–60. doi:10.1002/(SICI)1520-6386(200032)11:2<53::AID-CIR8>3.0.CO;2-W

Nonaka, I., & Takeuchi, H. (1995). *The knowledge creating company. How Japanese create the dynamics of innovation*. New York, Oxford: Oxford University Press.

OECD. (2005). OECD SME and Entrepreneurship Outlook 2002/2005. Retrieved November 4, 2006, from http://www.oecd.org/document/.

Ordanini, A. (2006). *Information technology and small businesses: Antecedents and consequences of technology adoption*. MA: Edward Elgar Publishing.

Ploder, C., & Fink, K. (2007). An orchestration model for knowledge management tools in SMEs. In: K. Tochtermann & H. Maurer (Eds.), *Proceedings of I-KNOW '07: 7th International Conference on Knowledge Management*, (pp. 176-183). Graz: J.UCS.

Probst, G., Raub, S., & Romhardt, K. (2002). *Managing knowledge: Building blocks for success*. Chichester, UK: Wiley.

Richter-von Hagen, C., Ratz, D., & Povalej, R. (2005). Towards self-organizing knowledge-intensive processes. *Journal of Universal Knowledge Management, 0*(2), 148–169.

Ruggels, R. (1997). *Knowledge management tools*. Boston: Butterworth-Heinemann.

SA. (2006). Statistical Yearbook of Austria. http://www.statistik.at.

Salojärvi, S., Furu, P., & Sveiby, K. (2005). Knowledge management and growth in Finnish SMEs. *Journal of Knowledge Management, 9*(2), 103–122. doi:10.1108/13673270510590254

Skyrme, D. (1999). *Knowledge networking. Creating the collaborative enterprise*. Oxford: Butterworth-Heinemann.

Smolnik, S., Kremer, S., & Kolbe, L. (2007). The role of context and its explication for fostering knowledge transparency in modern organizations. In Jennex, M. (Ed.), *Knowledge management in modern organizations* (pp. 256–277). Hershey, PA: Idea Group Publishing. doi:10.4018/9781599042619.ch014

Sveiby, K. (1997). *The new organizational wealth: Managing and measuring knowledge-based assets*. San Francisco: Berrett-Koehler.

Tiwana, A. (2002). *The knowledge management toolkit: Orchestrating IT, strategy, and knowledge platforms* (2nd ed.). Upper Saddle River, N.J.: Prentice Hall.

Tomasello, W. (1999). *The cultural origins of human cognition*. Boston, London: Harvard University Press.

Trompenaars, F., & Hampden-Turner, C. (2006). *Riding the waves of culture: Understanding cultural diversity in business* (2. reprint. with corr. ed.). London: Brealey.

Wang, F., & Plaskoff, J. (2002). An integrated development model for KM. In Bellaver, R., & Lusa, J. (Eds.), *Knowledge management strategy and technology* (pp. 113–134). Boston: Artech House.

Wong, K. (2005). Critical success factors for implementing knowledge management in small and medium enterprises. *Industrial Management & Data Systems*, *105*(3), 261–279. doi:10.1108/02635570510590101

Wong, K., & Aspinwall, E. (2005). An empirical study of the important factors for knowledge—management adoption in the SME sector. *Journal of Knowledge Management*, *9*(3), 64–82. doi:10.1108/13673270510602773

This work was previously published in International Journal of Knowledge Management, Volume 5, Issue 1, edited by Murray E. Jennex, pp. 46-60, copyright 2009 by IGI Publishing (an imprint of IGI Global).

Chapter 5
A Framework for Managing the Life Cycle of Knowledge in Global Organizations

Mark Salisbury
University of New Mexico, USA

ABSTRACT

This chapter describes a framework for managing the life cycle of knowledge in global organizations. The approaches described in this chapter were initially used to successfully build a knowledge dissemination system for the laboratories and facilities that are under the direction of the United States Department of Energy (DOE) (Salisbury & Plass, 2001). The follow-on work to this effort was the development of a collaboration application that fed the dissemination system for the DOE laboratories and facilities. The resulting system managed the life cycle (creation, preservation, dissemination and application) of knowledge for the DOE laboratories and facilities (Salisbury, 2003). While seen as a highly successful system, a significant problem was the difficulty in identifying the right knowledge that needed to get to the right people at the right time. This is also a significant problem for global organizations that need to share their knowledge across international boundaries. What is needed to solve this problem for global organizations is a systemic way that can be applied as an organizational strategy to identify this knowledge, the people that needed it, and the time it should be accessible. This chapter focuses on the use of performance objectives for managing the "right" knowledge in a global organization. In the next section, the background of the projects that inspired the framework is introduced. Next, the framework itself is discussed: the theoretical foundation for the framework, Work Processes, Learning Processes, and Methodologies for managing the life cycle of knowledge in a global organization. (For a full discussion of this approach in book form, see Salisbury, 2009).

BACKGROUND

The project that started this work was the design and development of the Process Realization Pro-

cess Online Website that is used by the United States Department of Energy (DOE) and its affiliates. Over the last several years, DOE has streamlined its operations to make production more efficient in a variety of coordinated engineering, manufacturing, assembly, and management

DOI: 10.4018/978-1-60960-555-1.ch005

activities. In so doing, eight separate laboratories and plants around the United States (a subset of all DOE labs and facilities) have agreed to utilize the Product Realization Process (PRP) with a common set of Technical Business Practices (TBPs) that both prescribe and guide operations. The goal was to get a potential user community of one to two thousand individuals at these eight sites to be aware of, understand, and apply the TBPs, related documents, and terminology to their projects. In addition, the user community is an aging population, not unlike the rest of the DOE. While these experienced users are highly knowledgeable about how business has been or should be conducted, others are being asked for the first time to subscribe to the common set of business practices. Experienced employees with the TBPs, approaching their retirement, have a large amount of tacit knowledge about the TBPs that would be lost to their organization if this expertise were not captured. In addition, newcomers to these eight DOE facilities need to have an orientation while, at the same time, get a more complete picture of processes, procedures, and practices. The PRP Online Website was developed to be a dissemination system for process documents, instruction, examples, and nuggets of expert advice on applying the TBPs to the daily work of the eight laboratories and plants under the direction of DOE.

The follow-on work to this effort was the development of a collaboration application — the Team Collaboration System (TCS) — that fed the dissemination system for the DOE laboratories and facilities (Salisbury and Dickinson, 2006). TCS was developed for process improvements on the TBPs with team comprised of representatives from the laboratories and facilities of DOE. This multi-organizational and geographically dispersed team needed a system that would support complex collaboration and yet be easy to use. They also needed project management capabilities for team members to recommend improvements, other members to review the improvements, and of-

ficials with oversight responsibilities to approve the improvements before they become policy. With TCS, there was a complete and integrated system in place that supported the creation of new knowledge (process improvements), the preservation of the knowledge (stored in TCS), and the dissemination of that knowledge (documented process improvements are automatically transferred after approval to the PRP Online Website). However, complications did arise. The process improvements that were approved in the TBPs would have to be traced through the associated instruction, examples, and nuggets of expert advice that were also disseminated through the PRP Online Website. It became quite a difficult task to ensure that the associated instruction, examples, and nuggets of expert advice were updated for each process improvement.

In examining the process improvements, it was apparent that they were almost all were the result of changing a "requirement" in one of the TBP documents. These requirements were wide ranging in nature from spelling out specific handling details to outlining general rules of manufacturing. However, it was clear they were the focal point of the knowledge work that was to be completed under the guidance of the TBPs for the Product Realization Process. So, these requirements described in the TBPs became the way that the "right knowledge" was indentified and served up to the "right people" at the "right time" for following the Product Realization Process. Users could logon to the PRP Online Website, drill down to a process, find the TBP that listed the requirements for that process, and have access to the instruction, examples, and expert advice that were associated with those requirements.

The resulting system based on these requirements seemed to work remarkably well for identifying and managing the "right" knowledge for the combined system made up of TCS and the PRP Online Website. The thought of "generalizing" this way of identifying and managing knowledge came as a natural response. However, it was immediately apparent that the use of requirements in this way was particular to DOE and its labs and facilities. (Requirements in this sense were really guidelines that must be followed. Some were very general and cut across development phases while others were quite detailed and only related to a certain material used in a specific manufacturing step.) How to generalize such a promising approach became an issue. The way to solve this issue, described in this chapter, came from the field of Instructional Systems Design (ISD) in the form of performance objectives. Instead of focusing on the varying requirements that were to be addressed during a process, the focus changed to the performance objectives for the people doing the work.

Borrowing from the field of ISD, one way to go about identifying performance objectives is to conduct a content analysis. A content analysis always starts off with the same question, "What knowledge does a person need to know to create this knowledge product?" (Davis, Alexander, and Yelon, 1974). Knowledge products are the focus of knowledge work and are such artifacts as design documents, quality plans, and testing reports. Content analysis, in this setting, focuses on identifying the cognitive skills needed to create the knowledge product. Cognitive skills underlie learning how to learn, that is, getting at the heart of the problem (Gagne, Briggs, and Wager, 1992). Once the knowledge is identified, it is listed by topic and each topic is rewritten as a performance objective. For example, the topic "Completeness and Correctness Criteria" may be identified as an important topic for teaching someone how to write a Quality Plan. Once identified as a topic for instruction, it is rewritten as the performance objective, for example, "In the Quality Plan, the developer will list all approved criteria for judging the plan as complete and correct." (For a complete description of the steps for conducting a content analysis and an overview of the ISD process, see Rothwell & Kazanas, 2004). The process of writing performance objectives begins by identifying

the kind of objective that must be written. The most commonly used classification system for performance objectives was first described in 1956 by Bloom and his colleagues (Bloom, 1956). In all cases, performance objectives make a precise statement of what learner should "do" in order to accomplish the stated performance (Mager, 1997). They contain a performance component, a criterion component, and a condition component. The performance component describes how proficiency will be demonstrated. The criterion component describes how well the proficiency must be preformed. And, the condition component describes what conditions must exist when the proficiency is demonstrated.

The use of performance objectives extends the framework for managing the life cycle of knowledge in organizations reported previously (Salisbury, 2003). This extension addresses the problem of getting the right knowledge to the right people at the right time in the life cycle of knowledge in a global organization.

THE LIFE CYCLE OF KNOWLEDGE IN A GLOBAL ORGANIZATION

Figure 1 illustrates the ongoing life cycle of knowledge in global organizations. The first phase is the creation of new knowledge. This takes place when members in the organization solve a new unique problem, or when they solve smaller parts of a larger problem such as the ones generated by an ongoing project. The next phase is the preservation of this newly created knowledge. This includes recording the description of the problem as well as its new solution. This phase feeds the next one, the dissemination and application of this new knowledge. The dissemination and application phase involves sharing this new knowledge with the other members of the organization. It also includes sharing the solutions with the stakeholders affected by the problems that were solved. Disseminated knowledge then becomes an input

Figure 1. The life cycle of knowledge in a global organization

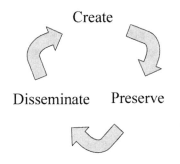

Create

Disseminate   Preserve

for solving new problems in the next knowledge creation phase. An organization's ability to solve problems increases with the utilization of this disseminated knowledge. In this way, each knowledge life cycle phase provides input for the next phrase — creating an ongoing cycle. Since this cycle continues to build upon itself, it becomes a *knowledge spiral* in the organization as described by Nonaka and Takeuchi (1995).

While the growth and sharing of knowledge is recognized as one of the most important elements in becoming a learning organization (Easterby-Smith, 1997; Marsick & Watkins, 1994; Senge, 1990), what has been missing, according to many researchers and practitioners in the field, is the development of a theoretical foundation for describing how people learn and perform in an organization (Raybould, 1995; Salisbury, 2000). This theoretical foundation is needed by today's organizations to avoid the development of technological solutions that do not support their entire life cycle of knowledge (Plass & Salisbury, 2002). To address this situation, the *Collaborative Cognition Model,* a theoretical foundation, was developed. It describes how learning can take place with one individual, be preserved, and transferred to other individuals in an organizational setting (Salisbury & Plass, 2001; Salisbury, 2003).

THEORETICAL FOUNDATION

To represent the complexity of organizational knowledge, a revision of Bloom's Taxonomy (Bloom, 1956) developed by Anderson, Krathwohl, Airasian, Cruikshank, Mayer, Pintrich, Raths and Wittrock (1998) was used to provide the basis for extending the description of knowledge utilized within the Collaborative Cognition Model. One of the major differences in the revised taxonomy by Anderson et. al. (1998) is the identification of knowledge as a separate dimension that describes it as *factual, conceptual, procedural,* and *metacognitive.* Another major difference is that Anderson and colleagues recast Bloom's other categories into a "process dimension" which describes the learner's cognitive processes when processing knowledge of that category. These process dimension categories were also renamed from Bloom's original "knowledge, comprehension, application, analysis, synthesis, and evaluation" to "remember, understand, apply, analyze, evaluate, and create." Note that Anderson and colleagues place "create" as the highest level of cognition; it describes individuals putting elements together to form a novel coherent whole or make an original product.

Anderson et al. (1998) describe factual knowledge as terminology, specific details, and elements. Conceptual knowledge relates to theories, models, principles, and generalizations. Procedural knowledge includes skills, algorithms, techniques, and other methods that are specific to a product or process. Metacognitive knowledge was added by Anderson and colleagues to Bloom's Taxonomy. It is "knowledge about knowledge" and involves general strategies for learning, thinking, and problem solving. Metacognitive knowledge also includes knowledge concerning the appropriate contexts and conditions for the use of the strategies themselves. Additionally, it includes the "heuristics" or "rules of thumb" that experts use to solve problems.

At the individual level, the Collaborative Cognition Model has elements of Situated Cognition as described by Brown, Collins and Duguid (1989). The Collaborative Cognition Model supports learning in the context of the work at the moment – creating an "authentic context" for learning. Knowledge workers can access knowledge – and other people -- to learn how to construct solutions to pressing organizational problems in a just-in-time manner. Furthermore, the Collaborative Cognition Model supports Situation Cognition for learners with differing cognitive needs by providing different types of knowledge as defined by Anderson and his colleagues (1998) in their revision to Bloom's Taxonomy (factual, conceptual, procedural, and metacognitive). As a result, the Collaborative Cognition Model supports work and learning to "live in the same space, "occur at the same time," and become interdependent. As a result, learning is situated in the authentic task of organizational work and takes place during that work.

At the team level, the Cognitive Collaboration Model is an extension of the theory of distributed cognition (see Salomon, 1996, for an overview of distributed cognition). One of the best documented examples of distribution cognition in a work environment is by Edwin Hutchins in his book "Cognition in the Wild" (Hutchins, 1996). Hutchins studied how a crew collaborated to operate a large ship at sea. According to his description of the theory of distributed cognition, cognition is distributed across individuals. That is, no one individual has complete knowledge as to how to accomplish a complex task such as operating a large ship. Hutchins also describes that cognition is distributed across the artifacts of an organization's work. On the ship that means the instruments provide critical decision-making information to the crew members. And, according to the theory of distributed cognition, cognition is in the history of those artifacts. On the ship, the previous version of an instrument gives a context for the present version of that instrument. In an office environment, artifacts are the knowledge products

of the organization. These are the "intermediate products" of a larger process and are such things as design documents and quality plans. Another set of artifacts are the knowledge assets that document the organization's processes, instruction, work examples, and expert advice that are used as resources by the members of the organization to make the knowledge products. In the Collaborative Cognition Model, the theory of distributed cognition is extended to involve different types of knowledge as defined by Anderson and his colleagues (1998) in their revision to Bloom's Taxonomy (factual, conceptual, procedural, and metacognitive); these different types of knowledge are present in the distribution of cognition across individuals, their artifacts, and the history of their artifacts.

At the organizational level, the Collaborative Cognition Model is an extension of Nonaka and Takeuchi's (1995) description of creating a knowledge spiral in an organization. Nonaka and Takeuchi theorize that knowledge is created in evolutionary stages through personal discovery, shared understanding, combining/reusing, and researching. In personal discovery there is a tacit-to-tacit exchange while a person develops understanding through experience – such as writing a Quality Plan. Shared understanding is a tacit-to-explicit exchange such as presenting a Quality Plan to another engineer. Combining/reusing is an explicit-to-explicit exchange – swapping Quality Plans for example. And researching is seeking or absorbing information in the public sector – such as examining Quality Plans provided by a professional engineering society. This means that transferring knowledge from one organizational member to another begins by the first member converting tacit knowledge (intuitions, unarticulated mental models and embodied technical skills) into explicit knowledge (a meaningful set of information articulated in clear language including numbers or diagrams). This explicit knowledge can then be passed on to another member of the organization -- who must convert it into tacit knowledge (internalization) before he or she may use it. Again, the Collaborative Cognition Model extends Nonaka and Takeuchi's (1995) description of knowledge creation by identifying the different categories of knowledge as defined by Anderson and his colleagues (1998) -- factual, conceptual, procedural, and metacognitive -- that are involved in the knowledge spiral of an organization.

DISSEMINATING AND APPLYING ORGANIZATIONAL KNOWLEDGE

Figure 2 shows the phase of disseminating and applying knowledge in the life cycle of knowledge in an organization. In this example, disseminating and applying knowledge begins with an engineer that needs to make a quality plan for a new product. The engineer goes to the system, clicks on the area of Design, then clicks on the area of "Detailed (Design)," and drills down to the area of "Quality Plan." There the engineer finds all the materials that he or she will need to develop a Quality Plan. There will be documents describing what needs to be addressed in the Quality Plan. There will be instruction available on the general principles and techniques behind a Quality Plan. The instruction addresses the "why" part — that is, why do we need a quality plan? There are also examples available of successful quality plans. They illustrate how someone applied the general principles of developing Quality Plan to a specific project. Finally, there is expert advice available that provides some direction as to when to use one approach over another when developing a Quality Plan.

But that's not all the engineer would find at that Quality Plan area in the system. The engineer would also find links to the people that are responsible for the content of the area. There is contact information for the creators of the documents, instruction, examples, and expert advice. In contacting these content providers directly, the engineer has the opportunity to understand the subtleties of the content and its application to specific projects.

Note that with these resources – materials and an opportunity for an exchange with the people who created them – the engineer can learn what is needed to get the job done. In this case, it's the creation of a Quality Plan. With adequate materials and the help of others, the engineer learns – only what is needed, in a "just in time" manner to create the Quality Plan. This is learning situated in the context of an authentic task – the pressing work of the moment. It describes the essence of Situated Cognition as described by Brown, Collins, and Duguid (1989).

It needs to be noted that when the engineer creates the Quality Plan – it is just the first step in completing a finished Quality Plan in a collaborative work environment. The next step is a review step – followed by an approval step. Note that all the assets that were available to the engineer to create the Quality Plan – materials and an opportunity for an exchange with the people who created them – are available to the other people involved in the review and approval steps. They, along with the engineer that created the Quality Plan, have integrated learning as they work together in a collaborative work environment.

FRAMEWORK FOR MANAGING THE LIFE CYCLE OF KNOWLEDGE

This example described above is the result of managing the life cycle of knowledge in an organization. However, what we have seen is simply the technology that serves up the information. Technology-based solutions leave us here – wondering how the information gets into the system – and more importantly, how is it updated and maintained. It's quickly apparent that the technology is simply the "tip of the iceberg" – a byproduct of managing the life cycle of knowledge -- that has provided this information. As Figure 3 shows, this chapter discusses the foundations,

Figure 2. Disseminating and applying organizational knowledge

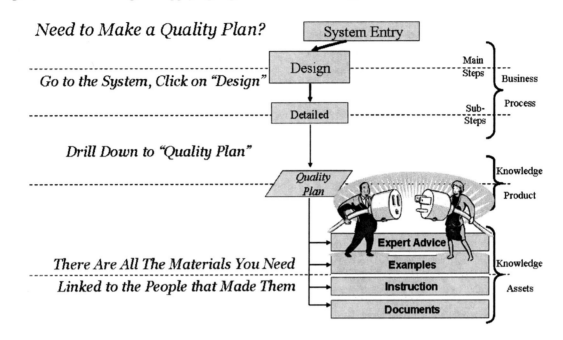

Figure 3. Framework for managing the life cycle of knowledge

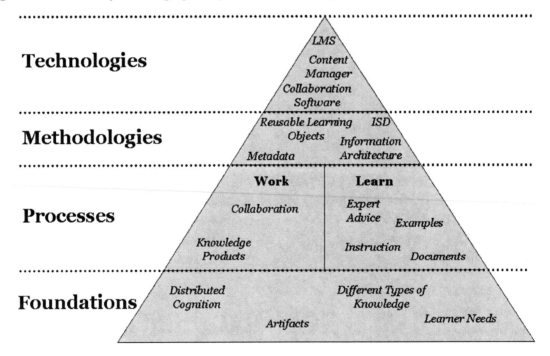

Figure 4. Cognition is distributed across individuals, artifacts, and the history of those artifacts

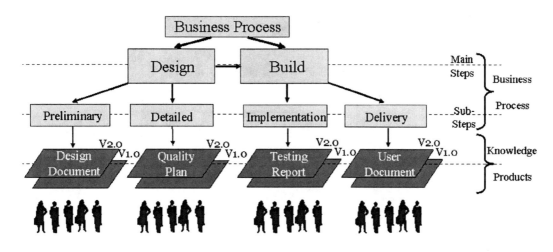

processes, and methodologies needed to support the technologies for managing the life cycle of knowledge in an organization.

WORK PROCESSES

Figure 4 shows the business process for an example manufacturing company with the two main steps of "Design" and "Build" for the manufacturing process. The Design step contains two sub-steps – "Preliminary" and "Detailed." The Build step also contains two sub-steps – "Implementation" and "Delivery." According to the theory of distributed cognition (Solomon, 1996, Hutchins, 1996), all the subtleness of a complex process does not reside in the head of one individual. While each member of the organization knows how to do his or her part of the process, the larger process is known only collectively – the ability to make informed decisions within the process is distributed across all people who work the process.

Figure 4 also illustrates the second aspect of the theory of distributed cognition (Solomon, 1996, Hutchins, 1996). That is, cognition is distributed in the artifacts of the workflow process. Artifacts are used to capture decisions and information about the work that has been done in the

workflow process The Design Document, the Quality Plan, the Testing Report, and the User Document are the artifacts for the example workflow process shown in Figure 4. Since they each have embedded knowledge about decisions that concern a unique aspect of the process, they each also represent a subset of the cognition needed to complete the entire workflow process. (See Nemeth, Cook, O'Connor, & Klock, 2004 for an overview on the importance of cognitive artifacts to the theory of distributed cognition.).

Additionally, Figure 4 shows the third aspect of the theory of distributed cognition -- the history of an artifact reveals the context for decisions and information about the process over time (Solomon, 1996, Hutchins, 1996). For example, the Quality Plan in Figure 4 is currently in version 2.0. This means that there were some major changes in the Quality Plan since version 1.0. The history of changes in an artifact tells the reasons "why" those changes were made. Frequently, it turns out that artifacts are historically related to one another. For example, when the Design Document goes from version 1.0 to 2.0, the Quality Plan will also go from version 1.0 to version 2.0 since the Quality Plan is dependent on the Design Document. In this way, the histories of artifacts provide important reasoning about their present form.

Figure 5. Identifying performance objectives for knowledge products

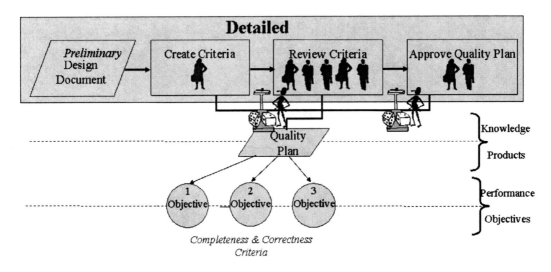

Up until this point in the chapter, the product of work was referred to as an "artifact." Recognizing the embedded nature of knowledge in these artifacts, they are referred to as "knowledge products" throughout the rest of this chapter. Figure 5 shows that every knowledge product has a set of criteria, or performance objectives that need to be met by its developers for its successful completion. These performance objectives are sometimes implicit – or in the "eye of the beholder." Recognizing the existence of these performance objectives but not able to easily articulate them is found in such phrases as "I know a good Quality Plan when I see one" or "shouldn't a Quality Plan have a..." Using content analysis from ISD, discussed earlier, is a means to "uncover" these underlying performance objectives and is essential for improving the quality of the ongoing work in an organization. These performance objectives tell an organization what needs to be done and how well it should be done.

Figure 5 also shows that the performance objectives of a knowledge product provide the basis for creating metrics to measure the knowledge work of organizations. Measuring how well the performance objectives have been met provides data relating to the "quality" of the knowledge product. Measuring how much time is spent in creating a knowledge product provides data relating to scheduling and cost for the knowledge product.

LEARNING PROCESSES

Figure 6 shows the four different types of knowledge taken from the revision of Bloom's Taxonomy (Bloom, 1956) developed by Anderson and his colleagues (1998). Figure 6 also shows that documents provide access to factual knowledge. While other media forms can be used to capture factual knowledge, documents are probably the most well known and used medium for capturing and disseminating factual knowledge (i.e., terminology, specific details, and elements) The color coding in Figure 6 shows that for most organizations, it would be desirable to have most of the factual knowledge reside in an explicit form. That is, most organizations would not want most of their factual knowledge floating around in the heads of its members.

Figure 6 also shows that instruction provides access to conceptual knowledge. As with the factual knowledge, other resources can provide access to conceptual knowledge, but instruction

Figure 6. Differentiating types of knowledge

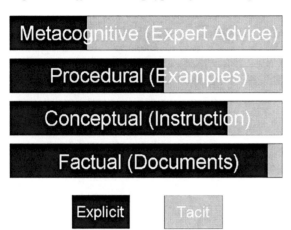

provides the best medium for capturing and disseminating this kind of knowledge (i.e., general principles and concepts). As for desired visibility of knowledge, the same idea is true for conceptual knowledge as for factual knowledge. While access to conceptual knowledge may be provided in an informal way, as with individual "on the job" instruction, most organizations would want to make most of their conceptual knowledge explicit. This is what is done when new courses are developed. The conceptual knowledge residing in the heads of the members of the organization is made explicit in the form of course materials. However, as Figure 6 shows, not all conceptual knowledge can be made explicit; this means that some informal instruction will always exist in organizations.

Also shown in Figure 6, examples provide access to procedural knowledge. Examples describe the step-by-step process for applying conceptual and factual knowledge to create a unique solution for a specific problem. While other means can provide access to procedural knowledge, examples are the best medium for providing access to this kind of knowledge. Figure 6 also shows the desired visibility for procedural knowledge in an organization. Most organizations will want to make many of their examples of good work explicit so they can provide access to procedural knowledge for

the members of their organization. Some of these "best examples" may become "best practices" for the organization. Note that it will not be possible to 'write up" each example and make the knowledge that went into that example explicit. Consequently, a large amount of procedural knowledge will remain tacit in an organization.

And Figure 6 shows that expert advice provides access to metacognitive knowledge -- "knowledge about knowledge." Again, while other means can be used to provide access to metacognitive knowledge, expert advice is the oldest, most direct, and accepted means for providing access to this kind of knowledge. Figure 6 also shows that organizations will want to make some of the "gems" of expert advice explicit for all the members of the organization. However, since it is not possible to make all metacognitive knowledge in an organization explicit, most of it will remain tacit in the organization.

Even though Figure 6 shows that large amounts of knowledge will remain in the tacit domain in an organization, organizations can still manage that knowledge. And it can be managed through the direct connection between two or more people. For example, a member of an organization can provide specific details, on the job instruction, step by step description of previous work, or some expert advice to other members of the organization. In all these cases, the knowledge begins as tacit knowledge in the first person. Next, it becomes explicit through the first person's elaboration. This explicit form is internalized by a second person and resides as tacit knowledge in that person. Using Nonaka and Takeuchi's model (1995), shared understanding through a tacit-to-explicit exchange was initiated by the first person and was followed with personal discovery by the second person where the second person put to work what he or she learned. The managing piece comes in by facilitating a work environment where those who need to know something can be connected to those who know it (French & Bazalgette, 1996). It

Figure 7. Differentiating learners and the knowledge they seek

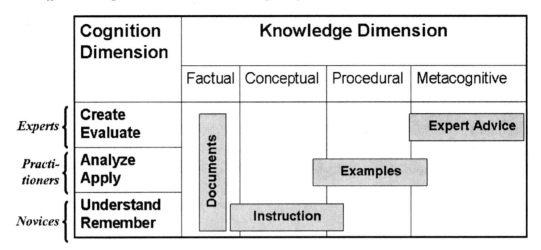

also creates another link between individual and organizational learning (Kim, 1993).

Figure 7 shows that when Anderson and colleagues revised Bloom's taxonomy, they made knowledge a separate dimension with four categories: factual, conceptual, procedural, and metacognitive (Anderson, et.al., 1998). They recast Blooms' other categories into a "process dimension" which describes the learner's cognitive processes when solving a problem in that category. Figure 7 also shows that novices are usually working at the level of trying to understand and remember. This is why it takes novices so long to get anything done. They are really "stuck" at the level of just trying to "get what's going on" and put it to memory. Also, Figure 7 shows that practitioners are usually working at the level of analyzing the situation and applying knowledge to form a solution. They already understand what to do and remember how to do it. Give them a problem similar to one that they have solved before and they will quickly analyze the problem and take a previous solution, adapt it, and apply it to their new problem. Finally, Figure 7 shows that experts should be working at the level of evaluating solutions and creating new and unique ones. The word "should" is put in this explanation because if an organization is using its experts like

practitioners – doing the everyday work – then the organization is not getting the most from its experts. If the organization's experts are spending all their time on the work of the day, then the opportunity is lost for better ways to do tomorrow's work.

Figure 7 illustrates how to provide learners with appropriate knowledge assets. Of course, an appropriate knowledge asset depends on the type of knowledge that they seek. Novices use the system to become practitioners, practitioners use the system to become experts, and experts utilize the system to create new knowledge. In the process of becoming practitioners, novices seek to understand and remember conceptual knowledge. Instructional materials are appropriate knowledge assets for them as they provide access to conceptual knowledge. Note that novices will still require factual knowledge to fully understand and remember the conceptual knowledge -- similar to a student requiring access to the manual to understand the instruction presented in the classroom. In the process of becoming experts, practitioners utilize examples to analyze and apply procedural knowledge. Note that practitioners will still require factual and conceptual knowledge to apply and analyze procedural knowledge. Experts create and evaluate expert advice. By doing so, they

Figure 8. Reusing knowledge assets

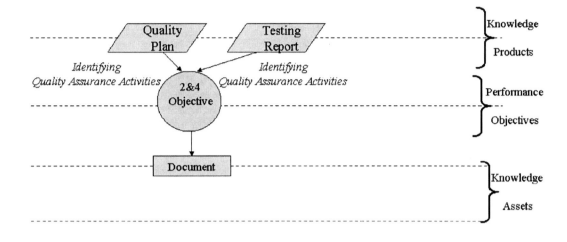

provide access to metacognitve knowledge for others in the organization.

METHODOLOGIES

Considerable attention has gone into developing methodologies for reusing knowledge work in recent years. Much of it has focused on the methodologies for developing "learning objects" or "content objects" (Barritt and Alderman, 2004; Hamel and Ryan-Jones, 2002; Rehak, 2003; Robson, 2002). However, while quite a bit has been published on sharing knowledge, especially, in the area of communities of practice (Brown and Duguid, 2001; Lave and Wenger, 1991), little has focused on the mechanics of how to identify and track knowledge for reuse (Osterlund and Carlile, 2005; Wiley, 2004). The result has been that for most organizations, reuse is addressed only at the institutional level, if at all (Davenport, 2004).

Figure 8 describes how performance objectives can be utilized for reusing knowledge work. It shows two performance objectives that were originally developed for different tasks (writing Quality Plans and Testing Reports) and described differently -- but were later found to be fundamentally the same. This created the opportunity for *reusing* a knowledge asset. Since both performance objec-

tives could now have the same identical text, this text can be a single document that is referenced by both performance objectives. Now, when users click on Performance Objective 2 & 4, they are taken to the same text – regardless of if they are addressing the performance objective for a Quality Plan or a Testing Report. (The "&" operator means that the two performance objectives have been combined into one objective.) This way, whenever the document for this combined performance objective is changed, it will be changed for users no matter which knowledge product they are working on (Quality Plan or Testing Report).

Figure 9 shows four performance objectives that are almost the same. Performance Objective 3 and Performance Objective 7 are both labeled "creating completeness and correctness criteria" for a Quality Plan. While they are written very similarly, there are some subtle differences. Performance Objective 3 is specifically written for the workers at Site A. Performance Objective 7 is written specifically for workers at Site B. In a similar situation, Performance Objective 6, "applying completeness and correctness criteria" for a Testing Report is written for workers at Site C. It has some subtle differences from Performance Objective 8 "applying completeness and correctness criteria" for a Testing Report which is written for workers at Site D.

Figure 9. Repurposing knowledge assets

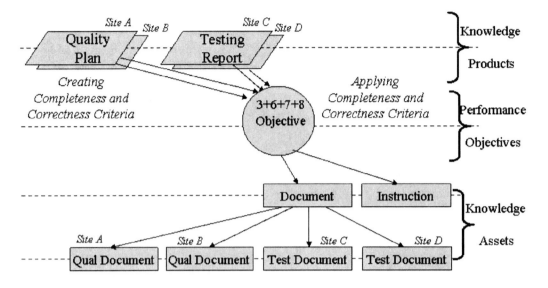

As in Figure 8, Figure 9 shows that since Performance Objectives 3, 6, 7, and 8 are very similar; knowledge workers will apply the same general principles and techniques to satisfy them. That means that the instruction module for all four performance objectives can be the same. This situation forms the basis for *repurposing* a knowledge asset. The instruction is a shared knowledge asset. However, not all knowledge assets are shared between the four performance objectives. Each performance objective has its own unique set of knowledge assets that describes the *context* (place in the process, physical site) in which the performance objective is addressed.

As in the Figure 8, Figure 9 shows that one of the documents has text that describes the common elements of the performance objective. This text is the same regardless if the Performance Objective 3+6+7+8 is accessed by a worker writing a Quality Plan from Site A or Site B – or a worker writing a Testing Report from Site C or Site D. (The "+" operator means that the four performance objectives share common knowledge assets, but each has additional knowledge assets that are not shared with the other others.) Note that all workers that access this performance objective

will also access the same instructional module as well. However, depending on what part of the process they are coming from (Quality Plan or Testing Report) or what site they are coming from (Site A, Site B, Site C, Site D), workers will see a different contextual document. For example, a worker from Site A trying to write a Quality Plan would see "Qual Document - Site A," while a worker from Site B trying to write a Quality Plan would see "Qual Document - Site B." On the other hand, a worker from Site C trying to write a Testing Report would see "Test Document - Site C." And to be complete, a worker from Site D trying to write a Testing Report would see "Test Document - Site D."

DISCUSSION

This chapter describes a framework for managing the life cycle of knowledge in global organizations. The theoretical foundation for the framework, the Collaborative Cognition Model, details how learning can be supported at the individual, team, and organizational levels. At the individual level, the Collaborative Cognition Model supports learning in the context of the work at the moment – creating an "authentic context" for learning. At the team level, the Collaborative Cognition Model supports learning in the context of a "distributed environment" where cognition is distributed across individuals, their artifacts, and the history of their artifacts. And, at the organizational level, the Collaborative Cognition Model supports creating a knowledge spiral in an organization where transferring knowledge from one organizational member to another begins by the first member converting tacit knowledge into explicit knowledge before passing it on to another member of the organization -- who must convert it into tacit knowledge before he or she may use it. The Collaborative Cognition Model also supports "different types" of learning at the individual, team, and organizational levels. It supports novices, practitioners, and experts in their need of different types of knowledge: factual, conceptual, procedural, and metacognitive.

Another aspect of the framework and the focus of this chapter is the use of performance objectives to identify the right knowledge that needs to get to the right people at the right time. In addressing this problem, performance objectives provide the key for improving the workflow process and overall knowledge worker productivity. They determine what to measure for providing feedback and how to go about making improvements in the knowledge work. They also determine what knowledge to reuse and repurpose and why it should be reused and repurposed. Furthermore, the use of performance objectives to manage this "right knowledge" provides a means for improving learning in a continuous and integrated way in global organizations.

In the last twenty years, there has been a lot of thought and work in the area of managing work processes. Organizations have recognized the value for examining how they do their work and how best to optimize their processes to get the work done better and faster. At the same time organizations have recognized the value that learning as a

group – or organization – improves the organization's ability to get the work done under changing circumstances. While a lot has been written about the learning that goes on in organizations, little attention has been placed on modeling that learning – at least, not in the same vigor that has been done with modeling and optimizing work processes. This chapter has put forth a means to model the "learning processes" of an organization through the use of performance objectives. The premise is that for organizations to reach their potential, they must integrate learning into their work. Or said another way, effective organizations must be able to work and learn together -- concurrently. That means that the "learning processes" must be modeled and combined with the work processes. That's why the "pyramid" model for this chapter (Figure 3) has the work processes and learning processes on the same layer – it shows they "live in the same space, "occur at the same time," and are interdependent.

The view of learning presented in this chapter is an entirely different view of learning than the one based upon the "learning occurs after training" approach. In the learning occurs after training approach, training is done for tomorrow's production. When training is complete, workers will be able to apply that training when the opportunity presents itself. As a result of this view, training is typically looked upon as a "non-critical" input to production. It can be delayed, or eliminated, because there is enough time to develop a work-a-around for the missed training before it can affect tomorrow's production.

In a contrary view presented in this chapter, learning is part of the work process in the "learning during work" approach, and it has to occur during today's work process to get today's work done. It is essential to today's production, and without it, the work does not get done right and on time. In this view, eliminating learning, or delaying it, only reduces an organization's ability to get today's work done. Consequently, learning is looked upon as a critical part of the work process.

Methodologies are built upon the work and learning processes. That is, methodologies are used to model the products of knowledge work, the performance objectives of knowledge work, and the knowledge assets that are applied to complete the work. These methodologies define the granularity of knowledge assets, how they will be created, stored, displayed, and updated. Finally, readers are shown that managing knowledge assets by the performance objectives they address is the key to the reuse and repurposing of those assets.

FUTURE DIRECTIONS

Further work is needed to develop the interventions necessary to realize the whole of the pyramid for managing the life cycle of knowledge in a global organization. One area should focus on empowering a leader to create a vision for managing the life cycle of knowledge in his or her organization. This vision includes why the "whole brainpower" of a global organization is greater than the sum of its parts. It shows that value lies in the knowledge provided to customers and the only way to increase that value is by bringing more brainpower to it. And most importantly, it helps organizational members to paint a picture of what managing the life cycle of knowledge will look like in their global organization.

Further work is also needed to utilize performance objectives for evaluating the performance of knowledge workers. From this perspective, performance should be evaluated in terms of the knowledge that individuals bring to bear on the problems of the global organization. The contribution of individuals to the organization's "stockpile" of factual, conceptual, procedural, and metacognitive knowledge can be used as an information source for individual performance assessments. Obviously, a "count" could be conducted to quantify contributions to procedure manuals, online instructional modules, documented work examples, and recorded expert

advice. However, as discussed in the section on learning processes, these contributions can take place informally -- sharing a fact, providing on the job instruction, sharing an example, or giving a nugget of expert advice. Further research is needed into the development of new methods for using performance objectives to "measure" and track these contributions.

REFERENCES

Anderson, L. W., Krathwohl, D. R., Airasian, P. W., Cruikshank, K. A., Mayer, R. E., & Pintrich, P. R. (1998). *Taxonomy for learning, teaching and assessing: A revision of Bloom's taxonomy of educational objectives*. New York: Longman.

Barritt, C., & Alderman, F. (2004). *Creating a Reusable Learning Objects Strategy: Leveraging Information and Learning in a Knowledge Economy*. San Francisco, CA: Pfeiffer.

Bloom, B. (1956). *Taxonomy of Behavioral Objectives: Handbook I: Cognitive Domain*. New York: David McKay.

Brown, J., Collins, A., & Duguid, P. (1989). Situated Cognition and the Culture of Learning. *Educational Researcher*, *18*, 32–42.

Brown, J., & Duguid, P. (2000). Knowledge and Organization: A Social-Practice Perspective. *Organization Science*, *12*, 198–213. doi:10.1287/orsc.12.2.198.10116

Davenport, T. (2004). *Thinking for a Living*. Boston: Harvard Business School Press.

Davis, R., Alexander, L., & Yelon, S. (1974). *Learning Systems Design*. New York: McGraw-Hill.

Easterby-Smith, M. (1997). Disciplines of Organizational Learning: Contributions and Critiques. *Human Relations*, *50*(9), 1085–1113. doi:10.1177/001872679705000903

French, R., & Bazalgette, J. (1996). From 'learning organization' to 'teaching-learning organization'? *Management Learning, 27*(1), 113–128. doi:10.1177/1350507696271007

Gagne, R., Briggs, L., & Wager, W. (1992). *Principles of Instructional Design* (4th ed.). Fort Worth: Harcourt Brace Jovanovich.

Hamel, C., & Ryan-Jones, D. (2002). Designing Instruction with Learning Objects. *International Journal of Educational Technology, 3*(1), 111–124.

Hutchins, E. (1996). *Cognition in the Wild*. Cambridge, MA: MIT press.

Kim, D. H. (1993). The link between individual and organizational learning. *Sloan Management Review, 35*(111).

Lave, J., & Wenger, E. (1991). *Situated Learning: Legitimate Peripheral Participation*. Cambridge, UK: Cambridge University Press.

Mager, R. (1997). *Preparing Instructional Objectives: A Critical Tool in the Development of Effective Instruction* (3rd ed.). Atlanta: The Center for Effective Performance.

Marsick, V., & Watkins, K. (1994). The Learning Organization: An Integrative Vision for HRD. *Human Resource Development Quarterly, 5*(4), 353–360. doi:10.1002/hrdq.3920050406

Nemeth, Cook, O'Connor, & Klock. (2004). Using Cognitive Artifacts to Understand Distributed Cognition. *IEEE Transactions on Systems, Man, and Cybernetics, 34*(6), 726–735. doi:10.1109/TSMCA.2004.836798

Nonaka, I., & Takeuchi, H. (1995). *The Knowledge-Creating Company*. New York: Oxford University Press.

Nonaka, I., & Toyama, R. (2000). SECI, Ba and Leadership: a Unified Model of Dynamic Knowledge Creation. *Long Range Planning, 33*, 5–34. doi:10.1016/S0024-6301(99)00115-6

Osterlund, C., & Carlile, P. (2005). Relations in Practice: Sorting Through Practice Theories on Knowledge Sharing in Complex Organizations. *The Information Society, 21*, 91–107. doi:10.1080/01972240590925294

Plass, J., & Salisbury, M. (2002). A Living System Approach to the Development of Knowledge Management Systems. *Educational Technology Research and Development, 50*(1), 35–57. doi:10.1007/BF02504960

Raybould, B. (1995). Performance Support Engineering: An Emerging Development Methodology for Enabling Organizational Learning. *Performance Improvement Quarterly, 8*(1), 7–22. doi:10.1111/j.1937-8327.1995.tb00658.x

Rehak, D. (2003). *SCORM Best Practice Guide for Content Developers*. Pittsburg: Learning Systems Architecture Lab at Carnegie-Mellon.

Robson, R. (2002). SCORM Steps Up. *E-learning, 3*(8), 48–50.

Rothwell, W., & Kazanas, H. (2004). *Mastering the Instructional Design Process*. San Francisco, CA: Pfeiffer.

Salisbury, M. (2000). Creating a Process for Capturing and Leveraging Intellectual Capital. *Performance Improvement Quarterly, 13*(3), 202–219. doi:10.1111/j.1937-8327.2000.tb00182.x

Salisbury, M. (2003). Putting Theory into Practice to Build Knowledge Management Systems. *Journal of Knowledge Management, 7*(2), 128–141. doi:10.1108/13673270310477333

Salisbury, M. Dickinson, M (2006). *The Team Collaboration System: An E-Mail Based Collaborative Work System*. US Department of Energy's 2006 Annual Information Management Conference (AIMC), Austin TX.

Salisbury, M. (2009). *iLearning: How to Create an Innovative Learning Organization*. San Francisco, CA: Pfeiffer (Imprint of Wiley).

Salisbury, M., & Plass, J. (2001). A Conceptual Framework for a Knowledge Management System. *Human Resource Development International, 4*(4), 451–464. doi:10.1080/13678860010016913

Salomon, G. (1996). *Distributed Cognitions.* Cambridge, UK: Cambridge University Press.

Senge, P. M. (1990). *The Fifth Discipline: The Art and Practice of the Learning Organization.* New York: Doubleday/Currency.

Wiley, D. (2004). Overcoming the Limitations of Learning Objects. *Journal of Educational Multimedia and Hypermedia, 13*(4), 507–521.

Chapter 6
Social Network Structures for Explicit, Tacit and Potential Knowledge

Anssi Smedlund
Helsinki University of Technology, Finland & Tokyo Institute of Technology, Japan

ABSTRACT

The purpose of this conceptual article is to develop argumentation of the knowledge assets of a firm as consisting of three constructs, to extend the conventional explicit, tacit dichotomy by including potential knowledge. The article highlights the role of knowledge, which has so far not been utilized in value creation. The underlying assumption in the article is that knowledge assets can be thought of as embedded in the relationships between individuals in the firm, rather than possessed by single actors. The concept of potential knowledge is explained with selected social network and knowledge management literature. The findings suggest that the ideal social network structure for explicit knowledge is centralized, for tacit knowledge it is distributed, and for potential knowledge decentralized. Practically, the article provides a framework for understanding the connection between knowledge assets and social network structures, thus helping managers of firms in designing suitable social network structures for different types of knowledge.

INTRODUCTION

This article starts from the notion that knowledge is an asset for the firm in value creation (e.g., Spender, 1996). According to research in social networks and in the theory of the firm, value creation with knowledge can be considered as something that is embedded in the relationships between individuals, thus making the research on firms' social network structures important (Nelson & Winter, 1982; Granovetter, 1985; Winter, 1987; Kogut & Zander, 1992; Uzzi, 1996). A common saying in the social networks literature is "it's not what you know, it's who you know" (e.g., Cohen & Prusak, 2001).

The main message of this article is that there are fundamentally different types of knowledge assets that produce value with fundamentally dif-

DOI: 10.4018/978-1-60960-555-1.ch006

ferent types of social network structures. Based on a short overview of knowledge management literature, an idea is proposed that there are three types of knowledge assets in a firm: explicit, tacit and potential, as well as corresponding three ideal types of social network structures: centralized, distributed and decentralized. The general purpose of this article is to develop convincing arguments to show that knowledge should be described with three constructs, to extend the conventional dichotomous view of knowledge. This line of thought makes it possible to start thinking of unrealized, not yet implemented, knowledge as a strategic asset, in addition to the knowledge assets already utilized by the firm.

The dichotomous view of knowledge as either explicit or tacit has been dominant in the theory of knowledge management after Nonaka and Takeuchi (1995) introduced their model of knowledge creation, the so-called SECI model. It has been claimed, however, that although the SECI model is excellent in describing a process after the initial idea has been developed for a new innovation, it does not necessarily explain the time before clarifying the idea (Engeström, 1999). One possible explanation for this is that the constructs of explicit and tacit knowledge alone are not sufficient to explain the varying nature of knowledge, and how knowledge should be utilized in the very early phases of innovation processes.

This article elaborates arguments about a third knowledge construct, potential knowledge. Potential knowledge is first explained through theory, and illustrated with social network structures. Potential knowledge is defined as a *knowledge asset either in codified or experience-based form that has not yet been utilized in value creation.*

A so-called Coleman-Burt debate on ideal social network structure appears in the social networks literature. This debate is about whether the most optimal network should be structurally sparse and decentralized (Burt, 1992; 2004) or dense and distributed (Coleman, 1988; Uzzi,

1996). There are empirical suggestions towards solving this debate, arguing that the optimal network structure is a combination of sparseness and density, including network ties among the actors that enable both closure and reach simultaneously (Uzzi & Spiro, 2005; Baum, van Liere, & Rowley, 2007; Schilling & Phelps, 2007).

As a result of this theoretical article, it is suggested that the type of knowledge asset—explicit, tacit or potential—is a contingency for the social network structure. It is suggested that there is no one ideal social network structure. Instead, the social network structure of a firm includes a centralized structure for explicit knowledge, a distributed structure for tacit knowledge, and a decentralized structure for potential knowledge. All the types of knowledge and the corresponding social network structures are needed, and individuals can belong to many types of networks simultaneously.

Besides categories of knowledge, another approach to the concept is to consider knowledge as a continuum. There, knowledge is never purely either tacit or explicit, but a combination of both (e.g., Jasimuddin, Klein, & Connell, 2005). Following this line of thought, knowledge that is utilized in the creation of value can be thought to include all three types, with the weighting of the different types changing from one situation to another. The role of potential knowledge is essential in the early phases of the innovation process, whereas tacit knowledge is important in the development phases, and explicit knowledge in the commercialization phases (c.f., Nonaka & Takeuchi, 1995). Based on the knowledge continuum insight, it is proposed in the discussion section that the weights of the different knowledge types, and also the social network structures are different in the idea, development and commercialization phases of the innovation process. Implications for managers are presented and further research issues suggested in the concluding section.

EXPLICIT, TACIT AND POTENTIAL KNOWLEDGE OF A FIRM

An epistemological definition suitable of describing the nature of potential knowledge is "knowing about the thought origins for doing things" (Scharmer, 2001, p. 6). Potential knowledge is knowledge whose value for the organization has not been discovered yet. To borrow from physics, potential energy is stored and available to call on when needed, while kinetic energy is in use, in motion. In the context of an expert's work at the individual level, potential knowledge has been defined as the total amount of knowledge the person has, in contrast to the "actual" knowledge that the individual uses in his or her work (Hollnagel, Hoc, & Cacciabue, 1995).

In the categorical approach to knowledge, knowledge is usually seen as either explicit or tacit. Explicit knowledge is knowledge that is codified, in the form of books, documents and written procedures, "knowledge about things." Tacit knowledge, on the other hand, can be defined as "knowledge about how to do things" (Scharmer, 2001, p. 6), and it is located in the routines of individuals and the organization, as well as in the ways of working between the individuals in the firm (Nelson & Winter, 1982).

Tacit knowledge, according to Polanyi's (1966) original definition, cannot be made explicit, but in the knowledge management theory, a fundamental insight of Nonaka's SECI model (1995) includes the transformation of tacit knowledge into explicit and back during the innovation process in a firm, as highlighted in the cases presented in Nonaka and Takeuchi's (1995) book.

Definitions for tacit knowledge vary in the literature. Hansen (1999) sees tacit knowledge in the firm as corresponding to knowledge that has a low level of codification, that is complex and hard, but not impossible to articulate, or can be acquired only through experience. According to Teece (1986), knowledge in the tacit form is transferable, but it has to be transferred by those who posses the knowledge, due to difficulties in the articulation of tacit knowledge.

The discussion on the definitions and types of knowledge has been guiding the knowledge management literature since the birth of the field. Snowden (2002) states that knowledge management as a discipline has gone through three phases since the early 1990s. The first phase considered the efficient use and storing of codified knowledge, the second phase was started by Nonaka and Takeuchi's (1995) book, and the attention was directed towards learning and conversion between tacit and explicit knowledge. The third phase deals with innovation, complexity and self-emergence of knowledge.

A shortcoming that Nonaka and Takeuchi's SECI model has, despite of its undisputed explanation power on the knowledge creation process, is that it does not take into account the emergence of knowledge in the very early phases of the innovation process (Engeström, 1999; Scharmer, 2001). Scharmer illustrates this with the well- known home bakery example of Nonaka and Takeuchi (1995, p. 100) by arguing that certain kinds of information about bread, such as weight, price and ingredients are explicit knowledge. The activities of baking and producing the bread are examples of tacit knowledge. Finally, the knowledge that enables a baker to create the baking process in the first place is self-transcending, emergent type of knowledge. This is the type of knowledge that could be labeled as potential, and that is what the SECI model lacks. Potential knowledge is the starting point for the knowledge spiral in the SECI model of Nonaka and Takeuchi (1995).

To position the concept of potential knowledge in conjunction with the value creation of the firm, it can be reflected through the explicit-tacit dichotomy (Table 1). Firm-level explicit knowledge, knowledge about things, is knowledge in a codified form that can be stored, managed and used electronically with data mining and document mining techniques in the organization. Firm-level tacit knowledge, respectively, is knowledge that

Table 1. Potential knowledge defined through explicit and tacit types of knowledge

Tacit	Experience-based knowledge	Experience-based or codified knowledge that has not yet been utilized in value creation.
Explicit	Codified knowledge	
	Realized knowledge assets	**Potential knowledge assets**

exists in the skills and perceptions of the employees or groups of employees in a given area, is stored in organizational routines (Nelson & Winter, 1982), and cannot be handled electronically. Potential knowledge is a knowledge asset either in a codified or experience-based form that has not yet been utilized in value creation.

Table 1 describes potential knowledge as an unrealized form of tacit or explicit knowledge. The three knowledge assets pose a challenge in the management of social network structures— what kinds of social network structures are needed, and what managerial action should be taken to create these structures?

SOCIAL NETWORK STRUCTURES FOR EXPLICIT, TACIT AND POTENTIAL KNOWLEDGE IN A FIRM

In this section, the ideal social network structures for explicit, tacit and potential knowledge are presented. By leveraging social network structures, a firm can produce most value with its knowledge assets. It has been argued that decentralized, distributed and centralized social network structures (see Barabási, 2002) are ideal for potential, tacit and explicit knowledge. These networks make it possible not only to search for new, non-redundant sources of potential knowledge, but also to transfer experience-based, tacit knowledge, and to implement explicit knowledge in the firm.

The management of potential knowledge requires scanning the firm's environment through social network ties and seizing the value creation potential in that network. Therefore, the management challenges related to building a social

network structure for potential knowledge are twofold: 1) how to increase the span of the network in order to increase the knowledge potential, and 2) how to transform potential, unrealized knowledge into realized knowledge.

In the case of tacit knowledge, which is hard to transfer due to its experience-based, un-codified and complex nature, the management challenge is how to arrange the social network structure to allow close, personal and reciprocal social network relationships for the transfer of tacit knowledge across the organization.

Explicit knowledge, which is exact, codified knowledge about things, poses the challenge of how to implement that knowledge in practice. The main topic of interest in the implementation of explicit knowledge is creating a structure of accuracy and discipline to ensure flawless flow of explicit knowledge. Table 2 summarizes the three classifications of knowledge and the management challenges related to the social network structure in each type of knowledge.

From the point of view of the contingency theory (e.g., Burns & Stalker, 1961), it has been stated that environmental conditions affect the structures of networks. For example, Podolny and Baron (1994; 1997) argue that under uncertainty, and when facing authoritative power, social network ties are formed more likely with similar others, which leads to the formation of strong ties. Also, cultural traditions and institutions have been found to influence the social network structures in a way that in the environment with highly profound institutions, such as the lifetime employment and seniority-based promotion in Japan, taller hierarchies and greater formal centralization can be found (Lincoln, Hanada, & McBride, 1986).

Table 2. Three classifications of knowledge and social network structure-related management challenges

Type of knowledge	Definition	Social network management challenge
Potential knowledge	Codified or experience-based knowledge that has not yet been utilized in value creation	How to build an extensive social network and how to scan and seize knowledge from this structure?
Tacit knowledge	Experience-based knowledge	How to transfer experience-based knowledge in the social network structure?
Explicit knowledge	Codified knowledge	How to implement codified knowledge in value creation with the social network structure?

The type of knowledge is a contingency for the social network structure. The explicit knowledge of a firm is used to reach efficiency in producing already designed products or services, because it includes well-codified rules, documents and procedures. This knowledge is, for example, knowledge related to stock levels or blueprints of products. Therefore, an ideal social network structure for explicit knowledge is the centralized structure (see Barabási, 2002), in the sense of the mechanic management system presented by Burns and Stalker (1961).

Tacit knowledge is a knowledge asset that has accumulated through past experiences in the firm. It is mainly used for gradual improvement of existing products, services or production methods and processes. Tacit knowledge can be, for example, the know-how of the employees, or past customer experiences. It is experiences that are difficult to transfer and require reciprocal and close relationships with the individuals. The distributed social network structure (see Barabási, 2002) is the most suitable one for tacit knowledge. In the traditional contingency theory, Burns and Stalker's (1961) organic management system resembles the distributed social network structure.

Potential knowledge is either codified or experience-based, an unrealized knowledge asset that has future value creation potential. It is used to initiate the innovation of something totally new in the very early phases of the innovation process. Potential knowledge is characterized with connections to many non-redundant sources of knowledge, which makes the ideal network

structure for potential knowledge decentralized (see Barabási, 2002). There are no equivalent structures of decentralized networks in the contingency theory. Table 3 summarizes this chapter by presenting the social network structures for explicit, tacit and potential knowledge.

Decentralized, distributed and centralized social network structures have notable differences in their functioning mechanisms. The decentralized social network is built on individuals as hubs of knowledge who gather and broker knowledge from different sources. The distributed social network structure does not have brokers, because there the relationships are distributed evenly, and individuals are connected with a few links to a couple of others. In the centralized social network, the functioning mechanism is based on a focal individual who manages the flows of knowledge with disconnected others. In the next section, the types of knowledge and social network structures are connected to different tasks in the firm.

DISCUSSION

Based on a common presupposition in the theory of the firm, and in the social network literature, knowledge can be thought of as embedded in the interactions between individuals in the firm (i.e., Nelson & Winter, 1982; Kogut & Zander, 1992; Uzzi, 1996). Therefore, each of the three knowledge constructs poses different challenges for the management of social network relationships in

Table 3. Social network structures for explicit, tacit and potential knowledge in a firm

	Potential knowledge	**Tacit knowledge**	**Explicit knowledge**
Illustration			
Network structure	Decentralized	Distributed	Centralized
Functioning mechanism	There are hubs in the knowledge network that control the flows of knowledge and intermediate between different groups. Some of the actors are more connected than the others.	There is no specific actor who manages the knowledge flows. The knowledge flows horizontally from one actor to another. Every actor has knowledge links to a couple of other actors.	The focal node in the network manages the knowledge flows. The knowledge flows hierarchically from the top down and from the bottom to the top. There are no knowledge exchange links between the subordinates.

a firm. In order to produce value with potential knowledge, the firm must be able to grow the reach of its network to include non-redundant, new sources of knowledge. In explicit knowledge, the social network should allow quick and flawless implementation, and in tacit knowledge comprehensive and reciprocal transfer.

There has been a debate among knowledge management scholars about whether the concept of knowledge should be treated as a categorical construct (e.g., Nonaka & Takeuchi, 1995), or as a continuum (e.g., Jasimuddin, Klein, & Connell, 2005). The starting point of this article has been the categorical perspective to knowledge, although the continuum perspective that sees knowledge as existing along a continuum of tacitness and explicitness is usable also in the context of the theory of the firm. The suggestion towards knowledge consisting of both tacit and explicit components at the same time is plausible for example in the context of absorptive capacity (Cohen & Levinthal, 1990). There, a firm must posses a certain knowledge base before it is able to learn anything new.

Figure 1 integrates the categorical and continuum perspectives of knowledge in the value

creation of a firm. Here, a firm creates value basically in three ways: 1) invention, 2) development, and 3) commercialization. These three ways of value creation are present in the innovation process of product innovation. In the invention phase, the role of potential knowledge is emphasized, and the management of the firm should concentrate on building a decentralized social network structure to support free and fast flow of ideas from distant and non-redundant sources. However, based on the insight of absorptive capacity and the knowledge continuum view, the invention phase needs also tacit knowledge and explicit knowledge, but to a lesser extent. This is because without certain explicit procedures and methods, or without some kind of individual's past experiences in ideation work, new invention is not possible.

Similarly with the invention phase, also the development and commercialization phases include all three types of knowledge, but with different weights (see Figure 1). In the development phase, an idea is gradually developed, based on the expertise of the individuals, with the reciprocal and distributed social network structure. Finally, in the commercialization phase, the developed product is produced as efficiently as

Figure 1. Potential, tacit and explicit knowledge in different phases of the innovation process

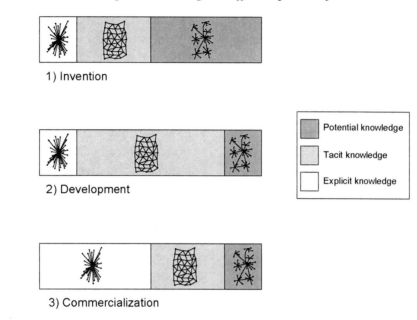

1) Invention

2) Development

3) Commercialization

possible along the unambiguous rules and procedures in the centralized social network structure.

Jasimuddin et al. (2005) present the paradoxes and difficulties related to the concept of knowledge convincingly in their literature review. There is confusion in the field of knowledge management about the concept, not only because different scholars have their own theoretical backgrounds, but also because it is not always clear whether knowledge is discussed from the point of view of the individual or the organization, from the epistemological or managerial standpoint.

Connecting potential, tacit and explicit knowledge constructs to the different phases in the innovation process makes it possible to see knowledge as both a categorical and a continual concept. Categorizations are needed to distinguish different aspects of knowledge assets that create value for the firm, and the knowledge continuum is needed when the categories are applied into practice in the value creation process.

CONCLUSION AND FURTHER RESEARCH

The cycles of the economy are becoming shorter, and firms are expected to bring new products and services to the market at an increasing pace. Rapid, centralized implementation of explicit knowledge is essential, because firms must be able to transform their product definitions, processes and production methods rapidly across a possibly globally distributed hierarchical demand-supply chain. Besides efficient production, firms must be capable of improving their products or services gradually to meet the needs of the customers. Gradual development can be achieved by allowing reciprocal and thorough transfer of tacit knowledge in a distributed social network. Last but not least, firms face a challenge of innovativeness, scanning and seizing their environment for new possible trends and ideas. There, the decentralized social network structure for potential knowledge comes into place.

It is clear that there is no one optimal social network structure for a firm but many, and each social network type requires unique management initiatives. Potential knowledge can be harnessed with managerial actions that aim to create a decentralized social network structure, for example, by investing in search capabilities or by increasing the pool of different types of talent in the firm, and emphasizing creativity and sharing of ideas in the leadership style. In order to create decentralized structures, individuals with knowledge broker capabilities (c.f., Burt, 2004) should be encouraged to improve the sharing, gathering and flow of ideas across the firm.

Tacit knowledge can be leveraged with managerial actions that aim for distributed social network structures. This can be achieved by emphasizing learning and trust building in the leadership style of managers. Investments in team building, team cohesion, and building of cross-functional teams with members from different parts of the organization should be made to ensure a timely transfer of tacit knowledge.

Finally, the management of explicit knowledge should focus on efficiency and a time-to-market mindset. There, a centralized social network structure can be achieved by investing in efficient, hierarchical management systems and systems engineering with industrial organization logic.

The divisions according to the type of knowledge presented in this article offer one theoretical framework for managing the complex whole of the social network ties in a firm. Decentralized, distributed and centralized social network structures all exist in the firm, and the same individuals can be a part of a social network for potential, tacit and explicit knowledge at the same time. The plethora of types of relationships between individuals in an organization is vast. The fundamental question for future research is which kinds of layers of relationships should be investigated more thoroughly, and how the social networks that the different types of relationships uncover should be operationalized. More work should be done in terms of defining the potential knowledge construct to find answers to why some firms are essentially better in sensing new opportunities in the market than others.

By influencing the social network structures in the firm with managerial action, the use of knowledge assets in value creation can be encouraged. The aim of further research based on this article is to connect different types of knowledge assets to different value-creating tasks in the firm, and to study empirically the inter-firm and intra-firm management initiatives suitable for each of the social network types. From the intra-firm social network perspective, possible interesting research questions would be related to the ideal structures in, for example, transferring ideas across the firm, business development, or in efficient production. Also individual-level research questions on, for example, the social network characteristics of highly innovative individuals should be studied from the knowledge management perspective.

In many cases, innovation occurs in the relationships between different firms (Powell, Kogut, & Smith-Doerr, 1996), and also development and production functions are increasingly operated across firm and industry borders. The three types of knowledge and the corresponding three social network types should be investigated from the point of view on how the three knowledge types can be separated from each other in inter-firm relationships. Creating awareness of different types of knowledge assets in the collaboration relationships between many firms, and different types of social networks to support them, would allow more efficient management of globally distributed innovation, development and production activities.

REFERENCES

Barabási, A.-L. (2002). *Linked: The new science of networks*. Cambridge, MA: Perseus Publishing.

Baum, J., van Liere, D., & Rowley, T. (2007). Between closure and holes: Hybrid network positions and firm performance. Working paper, Rotman School of Management, University of Toronto.

Burns, T., & Stalker, G. (1961). *The management of innovation*. London: Tavistock Publications Ltd.

Burt, R. (1992). *Structural holes: The social structure of competition*. Cambridge, MA: Harvard University Press.

Burt, R. (2004). Structural holes and good ideas. *American Journal of Sociology, 110*(2), 349–399. doi:10.1086/421787

Cohen, D., & Prusak, L. (2001). *In good company: How social capital makes organizations work*. Boston: Harvard Business School Press.

Cohen, W., & Levinthal, D. (1990). Absorptive capacity: A new perspective on learning and innovation. *Administrative Science Quarterly, 15*(1), 128–152. doi:10.2307/2393553

Coleman, J. (1988). Social capital in the creation of human capital. *American Journal of Sociology, 94*(1), 95–120. doi:10.1086/228943

Engeström, Y. (1999). 23 Innovative learning in work teams: Analyzing cycles of knowledge creation in practice. In Engeström, Y., Miettinen, R., & Punamäki-Gitai, R.-L. (Eds.), *Perspectives on activity theory*. Cambridge: Cambridge University Press.

Granovetter, M. (1985). Economic action and social structure: The problem of embeddedness. *American Journal of Sociology, 91*(3), 481–510. doi:10.1086/228311

Hansen, M. (1999). The search-transfer problem: The role of weak ties in sharing knowledge across organization subunits. *Administrative Science Quarterly, 44*(1), 82–111. doi:10.2307/2667032

Hollnagel, E., Hoc, J., & Cacciabue, P. (1995). Expertise and technology: I have a feeling we are not in Kansas anymore. In Hoc, J., Cacciabue, P., & Hollnagel, E. (Eds.), *Expertise and technology* (pp. 279–286). New Jersey: Lawrence Erlbaum Associates Publishers.

Jasimuddin, S., Klein, J., & Connell, C. (2005). The paradox of using tacit and explicit knowledge. Strategies to face dilemmas. *Management Decision, 43*(1), 102–112. doi:10.1108/00251740510572515

Kogut, B., & Zander, U. (1992). Knowledge of the firm, combinative capabilities, and the replication of technology. *Organization Science, 3*(3), 383. doi:10.1287/orsc.3.3.383

Lincoln, J., Hanada, M., & McBride, K. (1986). Organizational structures in Japanese and U.S. manufacturing. *Administrative Science Quarterly, 31*(3), 338–364. doi:10.2307/2392827

Nelson, R., & Winter, S. (1982). *An evolutionary theory of economic change*. Cambridge, MA: Belknap.

Nonaka, I., & Takeuchi, H. (1995). *The knowledge-creating company: How Japanese companies create the dynamics of innovation*. New York: Oxford University Press.

Podolny, J. (1994). Market uncertainty and the social character of economic exchange. *Administrative Science Quarterly, 39*(3), 458. doi:10.2307/2393299

Podolny, J., & Baron, J. (1997). Resources and relationships: Social networks and mobility in the workplace. *American Sociological Review, 62*(5), 673–693. doi:10.2307/2657354

Polanyi, M. (1966). *The tacit dimension*. London: Routledge & Kegan.

Powell, W., Kogut, K., & Smith-Doerr, L. (1996). Interorganizational collaboration and the locus of innovation: Networks of learning in biotechnology. *Administrative Science Quarterly, 41*(1), 116–145. doi:10.2307/2393988

Scharmer, C. (2001). Self-transcending knowledge: Organizing around emerging realities. In Nonaka, I., & Teece, D. (Eds.), *Managing industrial knowledge: Creation, transfer and utilization.* London: Sage Publications.

Schilling, M., & Phelps, C. (2007). Interfirm collaboration networks: The impact of large-scale network structure on firm innovation. *Management Science, 52*(11), 1113–1126. doi:10.1287/mnsc.1060.0624

Snowden, D. (2002). Complex acts of knowing: Paradox and descriptive self-awareness. *Journal of Knowledge Management, 6*(2), 100–111. doi:10.1108/13673270210424639

Spender, J.-C. (1996). Making knowledge the basis of a dynamic theory of the firm. *Strategic Management Journal, 17*(Winter Special Issue), 45-62.

Teece, D. (1986). Profiting from technological innovation: Implications for integration, collaboration, licensing and public policy. *Research Policy, 15*(6), 285–305. doi:10.1016/0048-7333(86)90027-2

Uzzi, B. (1996). The sources and consequences of embeddedness for the economic performance of organizations: The network effect. *American Sociological Review, 61*(4), 674–698. doi:10.2307/2096399

Uzzi, B., & Spiro, J. (2005). Collaboration and creativity: The small world problem. *American Journal of Sociology, 111*(2), 447–504. doi:10.1086/432782

Winter, S. (1987). Knowledge and competence as strategic assets. In Teece, D. (Ed.), *The competitive challenge: Strategies for industrial innovation and renewal.* Centre for Research Management.

This work was previously published in International Journal of Knowledge Management, Volume 5, Issue 1, edited by Murray E. Jennex, pp. 78-87, copyright 2009 by IGI Publishing (an imprint of IGI Global).

Section 2

Chapter 7

A Simulation System for Evaluating Knowledge Management System (KMS) Implementation Strategies in Small to Mid-Size Enterprises (SME)

Robert Judge
San Diego State University, USA

ABSTRACT

Companies create and use information and knowledge every day. The problem all companies have is figuring out how to efficiently discover that knowledge, capture it, share it, and use it to gain competitive advantage in the marketplace. This chapter describes a simulation model designed to provide small to mid-sized enterprises (SME) with a means to understand the impact of barriers and value accelerators on the flow of organizational information. The simulation model reports the throughput of information (number of information packets received per day) and its timeliness (average duration until packet arrival) and provides for sensitivity analysis of the parameters describing a strategy. Comparisons among model instantiations allow an organization to determine the appropriate strategy for current and future KMS efforts.

INTRODUCTION

Corporations are faced with tradeoffs every day in the process of deciding where best to invest their capital. Information System (IS) departments serve a critical role in advising the company on the best

means to use IS and Information Technology (IT) to achieve its strategies while limiting capital, time and risks. A Knowledge Management System (KMS) is one IS solution that may be considered important to a company's strategy. Implementing a KMS is generally a large, complex, and costly undertaking, although it may be approached stepwise. This raises the question of just what is the

DOI: 10.4018/978-1-60960-555-1.ch007

correct sequence of KM Infrastructure, methods, and processes to implement. There is little research that has looked into strategies related to the sequence of systems and processes for knowledge processing (Becerra-Fernandez, 2001; Chalmeta & Grangel, 2008; Choi, Poon, & Davis, 2008). However, it is clear a KM strategy is needed to minimize risks and uncertainties with budget and to encourage acceptance (M. Jennex & Olfman, 2003).

Key factors that influence the acceptance of a KMS in a SME have been identified in the literature: management leadership and support, culture, information technology, strategy and purpose, measurement, and organizational infrastructure (Wong & Aspinwall, 2005). Although no study appears to have looked at the differential ranking of critical success factors based on the number of company employees, it may be safe to assume that some factors are. In particular, any factors associated with the creation, input, and linking of knowledge in the KMS are likely to be influenced by the number of personnel available to create, input and link that new knowledge. (Becerra-Fernandez, González, & Sabherwal, 2004) indicate that organizational size has a direct influence on various KM processes. This company size factor provides a strong reason for researching Small to Midsize Enterprises (SME) organizations since they exist at the point where the knowledge flows and processes are likely to be in transition.

SMEs are a critical part of the U.S. economy, accounting for 96 percent of all companies in the U.S. (Moss, Ashford, & Shani, 2003) and approximately 75 percent of new employment (SBA, 2001). A SME, with less capitalization than large companies, may face considerable risk in taking on a large IS project such as the implementation of a KMS. This research will strive to provide information that may be valuable to those SMEs facing a decision on whether to move forward with implementing a KMS. Knowledge of key success factors, especially quantifiable ones, may greatly improve their ability to make informed decisions

on whether to move forward with a KMS project. However, quantifiable factors alone do not provide enough information for sound decision making. Accounting for the interactions of those factors and how they operate in a specific entity can provide a much stronger foundation for effective decisions.

A SME's organizational knowledge is limited relative to that of larger organizations. When an employee leaves, they potentially leave with a relatively larger share of the organizational knowledge. How large that share is, would be influenced by the number of employees, the degree of previous knowledge socialization and the cognitive capabilities of fellow employees. Given this potential large loss of knowledge, it should be an imminent concern of SMEs to find a means to capture and store that knowledge. Implementing appropriate KMS strategies will provide for such capability. There are other advantages that a SME can realize from an effective KMS: reduction of repetitive solutions to the same problem, reduction of redundancy in knowledge based activities, knowledge made available quickly and easily, and an increase employee satisfaction by enabling greater personal development and empowerment. The ultimate advantage, however, is to obtain a strategic advantage over competitors (Knapp, 1998). Knowledge-based resources may be essential to providing a sustainable competitive advantage because of the difficulty competitors have in duplicating it (McEvily & Chakravarthy, 2002).

There are two categories of knowledge that IT systems must support in some fashion. Explicit knowledge, is generally in a recorded form, and can be read, viewed, distributed, stored and manipulated in many ways for advantage (e.g., knowledge base, data warehouses, DSS, portals, etc). The second form of knowledge, tacit knowledge, encompasses perspectives, know-how, expertise and context-specific skills and is not easily put in writing (Nonaka & Takeuchi, 1995; Polanyi, 1962). Therefore, it requires entirely different systems to assist in its creation, storage and dissemination. IT tools helpful with the creation and transfer of tacit knowledge are those that encourage dialog: communities of practice, portals, E-mail, groupware, intranets, the Internet, links, and videoconferencing (Scott, 2000). All the above IT tools, methods, and management are components of a KMS. These components cost money and time to implement. Their use should be driven by strategy that is in turn directed by useful data and information.

The contribution of this research is in providing a mechanism for the SME business community to gather useful data and information for use in evaluating potential strategies when considering or moving forward with the implementation of a KMS. A company that can better understand what affects the flow of its knowledge can then understand the timing of investments in resources to support an evolving KMS. This research may also prove valuable to those involved in the design of future KMS simulation tools: to create a more effective interface to allow users to capture their corporate knowledge structure and the parameters for factors affecting the flow through that structure. This research and model could also be employed to understand large companies as well. However, SME's provide an advantage in the simulation because they experience the point where the flow of knowledge through personal contact becomes impacted by growth.

MODELING CONCEPT

The simulation model is based on the concept that knowledge is created or acquired and then must flow to others who can apply it in the same or new ways, or combine it with other knowledge to create new knowledge. Nonaka and Takeuchi (page 5, 1995) identified four modes of knowledge creation: socialization, externalization, combination, and internalization. In the context of this chapter, these modes can be conceptualized as knowledge processing flows. The knowledge

flows as either tacit or explicit information packets from its source in the organizational memory to where it will be used or converted to another form (e.g. tacit to explicit). Socialization is the pathway for tacit information to flow between people. Sometimes this tacit information can be converted to explicit information and flow through the pathway of externalization. Combination occurs when someone is able to take explicit information and add more explicit information to it. Lastly, information that is received as explicit and converted into tacit occurs through internalization. Thus, there are several ways that information packets can flow from someone motivated to exchange that knowledge to someone motivated to receive it. Something must induce the flow of knowledge. This chapter assumes a push-pull concept. Push represents the capture and storage of created knowledge and the willingness to share it. If there is someone who has the desire for that knowledge, they will pull it towards themselves by actively searching for it or being receptive to new knowledge. The problem is that this flow of knowledge rarely occurs efficiently, rapidly and without loss of content. Something gets in the way of the knowledge process flows; a barrier. The role of barriers has been observed and described by many authors. Table 1 provides a listing and description of barriers.

Barriers to knowledge flow occur in two primary categories: those of the individual and those of the organization (Von Krogh, Nonaka, & Ichijo, 2000). Barriers may also occur under two situations: 1) something prevents the initiation or efficiency of transfer, and 2) the receiver of the knowledge loses motivation to complete the full transfer of knowledge (Szulanski, 1996, 2003).

Barriers related to an individual may arise due to a variance in education, attitudes, norms, life experiences, and cognitive capabilities. In some cases these factors may cause them to be open or closed to new topics and knowledge flow. Potential new knowledge can confront a person's beliefs and self-image and thus incur resistance to change.

Table 1. Types of barriers and their description

Barriers	Author(s)	Description
System not user friendly – difficult to use	(Damodaran, 2000)	Relates to the user interface of information management systems. If an interface is poor, the users may encounter difficulty, become discouraged and use the system less.
Infrastructure	(Fichman, 1992)	Lack of infrastructure may impact the acquisition, evaluation and proper use of knowledge by an entity.
Complexity	(Simonin, 1999)	The amount of complexity in the knowledge to be transferred may impact the acquisition, evaluation and proper use of knowledge by an entity. This may well be a subfactor of causal ambiguity.
Ambiguity	(Simonin, 1999; Szulanski, 1996)	The difficulty to communicate knowledge and information in a readily understood and assimilated form associated with a given context.
Motivation	(Ardichvili, Page, & Wentling, 2003; Hendriks, 1999)	There are two categories of motivations: to contribute knowledge and to use it. A lack of either motivation will disrupt the smooth flow of knowledge within an organization.
Absorptive capacity	(Cohen & Levinthal, 1990; Fichman, 1992; Szulanski, 1996)	The ability of an entity to recognize the value of information and to assimilate, transform, and use it. If an entity is overloaded with information, it may impact the acquisition, evaluation and proper use of knowledge by an entity.
Physical space	(Cross & Cummings, 2004; Von Krogh et al., 2000)	The physical space that separates employees and makes it less likely that frequent interaction will occur.
Organizational structure	(McDermott & O'Dell, 2001)	How entities within an organization share knowledge: the tools, interactions, and existing transfer networks. The structure of the organization may legitimize and make possible more frequent interactions and opportunities for sharing of knowledge.
Critical mass (network externalities)	(Katz & Shapiro, 1986)	The value of an information exchange system will increase when more users are involved in adding to or changing information.
Relationships	(Szulanski, 1996; Wunram, Weber, Pawar, & Gupta, 2002)	Successful transfer of knowledge may require several exchanges between provider and recipient. A difficult or untrusting relationship may impact the acquisition, evaluation and proper use of knowledge by an entity.
Language	(Gupta & Govindarajan, 2000; Hu & Jaffe, 2003)	The lack of shared verbal, written and body language used to communicate knowledge may impact the acquisition, evaluation and proper use of knowledge by an entity.
Culture	(De Long & Fahey, 2000; Ford & Chan, 2003; McDermott & O'Dell, 2001)	The lack of shared values and beliefs of an entity and the assumptions used to make sense of other's behavior and communications may impact the acquisition, evaluation and proper use of knowledge by an entity.
Cognitive Capabilities	(Alavi & Leidner, 2001)	The lack of ability in an individual to understand provided knowledge may impact the acquisition, evaluation and proper use of knowledge by an entity.
Perceived Value	(Damodaran, 2000)	Individuals may decide not to use the KMS because they perceive there are other means to locate and acquire the knowledge they need. The other source may be less efficiently located and the knowledge may be of lower actual quality.
Density of Employees	(Leenders, van Engelen, & Kratzer, 2003)	As a company grows, it becomes less likely that each employee will have equal opportunity to interact with every other employee – this in turn will slow the flow of tacit knowledge in the company. More individuals interacting with one another may become a distraction.
Security	(Hall, Sapsed, & Williams, 2000; Riege, 2005)	Confidence that any knowledge supplied will only be used within the organization and in proper context. If belief exists that this is not the case, entities may be hesitant to share or codify their knowledge. Fear of losing one's job could also impact willingness to share knowledge.
Trust/Credibility	(Alavi & Leidner, 2001; Cross, Parker, Prusak, & Borgatti, 2001)	If employees are not confident that their knowledge will be properly used or attributed to them, they may hesitate in sharing that knowledge. Also, if employees do not trust the source of knowledge provided, they will be less likely to use it.

Figure 1. Conceptual model

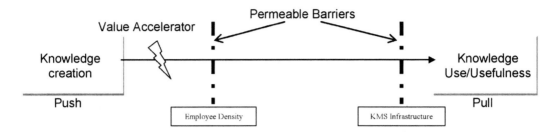

Organizations also have barriers that must be overcome in order for knowledge to flow freely. Examples of barriers that may exist in any given organization are: cultural, language, trust, physical separation, existing procedures/processes, IT/IS infrastructure and knowledge systems, incentive systems, and lack of opportunity and time for face-to-face communication to occur.

There may are also exist "value accelerators" (facilitators) that will improve the ability of an information packet to move through the barrier more readily. A summary of technology that can be used to facilitate knowledge flows through the above mentioned four modes of knowledge creation was written by (Marwick, 2010). Examples of value accelerators are:

1. Linking of packets to other packets: improving context or broadening to other contexts.
2. Knowledge Repositories: storage of explicit information packets in a readily searchable form.
3. Email: will increase the flow of knowledge among those employees who may not have the chance of meeting face-to face.
4. Brown Bag Lunches – open discussions and storytelling to socialize tacit information.
5. Linking of competence to packets: providing links to experts who can provide additional details and context related to particular information packets.
6. Expert systems and A.I.: Sophisticated systems that aid the search for key information.

7. Data warehousing and Data Mining: providing the tools necessary to consolidate key information and look for unexpected relationships in the information.
8. Communities of practice (Ardichvili et al., 2003): Online discussion with others interested and dealing with similar issues – provides for give and take of explicit information.

The permeability of the barriers and the value of the knowledge will determine how effectively the knowledge flows from creator to user. These barriers and value accelerators will vary from organization to organization. The model must allow for the selective inclusion of the relevant barriers and value accelerators and adjustment of their respective parameters. (Figure 1)

The process proposed for using such a simulation system entails working with a SME to understand the knowledge flows, barriers, value accelerators, and portals that exist in the company. These constructs will determine the parameters necessary to configure the system's algorithms (percent of tacit vs. explicit packets, number of employees, number of packets generated by employee, etc.) and distributions (probability of a useful packet of information being found, impact of the number of employees on socialization, etc.) to properly model the SME's KMS structural characteristics. A discrete-stochastic simulation, using the model and parameters will simulate the flow of information packets throughout the organizational structure as modeled. A representative baseline will be developed by adjusting the construct parameters until the flows and usage rates approximate those measured by the organization. This baseline will be stored for comparison to models representing changes to the organizational structure (KM infrastructure, technology and mechanisms, and processes). The comparison of simulations will allow for an understanding of sensitivity of the knowledge flows to changes in the organizational structure and the associated costs/benefits. The organization may then develop a better informed knowledge management strategy.

SIMULATION CONSTRUCTION

The simulation constructed to represent the above model concepts was accomplished using iGrafx simulation software and is composed of the following components:

1. Knowledge Packet generator
    a. Poisson random number generator
    b. Percent of tacit versus explicit packets
    c. Prioritization of packets (determination of packet value)
2. Barriers
    a. Employee Density (Socialization pathway)
    b. KMS usefulness (Externalization pathway)
3. Value Accelerators
    a. Scheduled brown bag meeting (Socialization pathway)
    b. Email (Externalization pathway)
    c. Knowledge repository (Externalization pathway)
4. Receiver of Knowledge Packets

KNOWLEDGE PACKET GENERATOR

The knowledge packet generator controls the time between the arrivals of information packets each day. The interarrival time is based on the exponential distribution and adjusted to account for the number of employees. The Exponential distribution has repeatedly been found to be a good approximation of the time between arrivals (information packets being generated) (Render, 2003). The key assumption associated with the use of an Exponential distribution is that the arrivals are independent of one another. Although there may be circumstances where two people generate information packets at the same time because of collaborated content, this is probably rare and not a serious constraint in the use of the Exponential distribution.

The average interarrival time is based on the observation that a small company has frequent interactions among its members and with that stimulation of new ideas and knowledge. Also, a small company is generally composed of founders who have considerable expertise and inventiveness. Thus a company of five may generate information packets twice per day on average. As the company grows, other employees are brought in for support functions and may not contribute new information as frequently. The time between new packets will decrease because there are more employees, however, the rate of new information generated per person will be less. This reduction in the rate of generating new information per person may also be driven by the new employees being less informed in the technology or having less cognitive capacity to generate knowledge than the initial founding team. Prior to simulating a given organization, its average interarrival time would need to be determined by expert opinion or empirical observations.

Each information packet is randomly determined to be tacit or explicit and will, respectively, be directed to either the socialization pathway or the externalization pathway of the model. Since there are only two options, the Bernoulli distribution was selected for random assignment. The Bernoulli distribution will assign a given percent of the information packets as either tacit or explicit based on a provided probability of one of these occurring. This probability will change over time as the number of previously generated explicit packets increases. As more explicit packets enter and reside in the KMS, the usefulness of the system will increase because the users will have a greater likelihood of locating valuable packets of information. The percent of tacit and explicit packets will be adjusted in the simulation to increase the probability of explicit packets being created as the volume of existing explicit packets grows.

The last function of the knowledge packet generator is to assign a priority to represent the value of a particular packet just created. Not all packets are created equal. Some have more valuable content that will be desired by one or more people in the company. The normal distribution is used to represent the assignment of priority which has a range of 1 to 127. It is not unreasonable to assume that in any company, there are some low value and some high value packets, but in general most will be somewhere in between in value. The normal distribution should reflect this condition reasonably well.

Barriers

There are several barriers in this model, two of which will be implemented in the evaluation instantiations described below. One barrier will be placed on the socialization pathway and represents a barrier to information flow caused by employee density. It will be found in all four instantiations. The other barrier, KMS usefulness, will be placed on the externalization pathway in the last two instantiations.

The employee density barrier addresses the observation that the communication of ideas flows unimpeded in a small company where employees are all proximally close, but less so

as the company grows and personnel are spread out into different rooms and buildings (Monge, Rothman, Eisenberg, Miller, & Kirste, 1985). Research has shown that communication among personnel drops rapidly after the first 75-100 feet of separation (Zahn, 1991). The employee density barrier is concerned with the decrease in flow of tacit packets due to more people and greater separation among them. The priority of a packet also plays a role in this barrier. A high priority packet will stimulate a person to tell it to more employees and thus increase the likelihood of the packet getting to the right person. The impact of the barrier in the model represents a delay in the transfer of a packet, which depending on its priority may range from a portion of a day to its never reaching another company employee. This barrier is simulated by the following function:

Delay due to Employee Density = f (Packet Priority, Number of Employees, Normally distributed random number)

The KMS Usefulness Barrier will be implemented in the externalization pathway. This barrier represents the difficulty of motivating employees to capture, codify and retrieve information: to use the KMS. When there are relatively few packets in the system, the users will perceive the KMS to be of little use to them and use it infrequently. This is because the probability of a desired packet being found will be very low when there are few packets. Therefore, any explicit packets initially entered into the system may be unused for a long period of time until the users see an adequate base of packets to search through to find useful information. Employees will understand this and feel less motivation to capture and codify since few will see and use their information. They will perceive low value to their efforts. However, with more employees, gradually more packets will input in the KMS system and thus there will be a greater probability of reaching a critical mass of packets and perceived usefulness. This greater number of packets will then make the KMS more useful to the employees. The packet priority affects the barrier delay by motivating employees to capture and codify the information for rapid location in the KMS system.

The function used to simulate this barrier has parameters representing the packet priority, number of employees, number of explicit packets in the system, and a random generator. The result of this function is a delay attributed to a given explicit packet.

KMS Barrier delay = f (Packet Priority, Number of Employees, Number of Explicit Packets in System, Normally distributed random number)

Value Accelerators

Just as both the socialization and externalization pathways may have barriers, they may also have various value accelerators. The value accelerators perform the function of increasing an information packet's priority. The higher the priority, the more rapidly the packet will pass through any barriers it encounters. There are three value accelerators used in the evaluation section of this chapter: Brown Bag Meetings, Email, and Knowledge Repositories. The Brown Bag Meetings serve as a value accelerator in the socialization pathway by providing a time and place for employees to exchange ideas and build on each other's knowledge. This is accomplished in the simulation by a function that increases an existing tacit packet's priority. The Brown Bag Meeting value accelerator is represented by a function which takes into account the existing priority of the packet as well as a randomization component.

The Email (including IM, SMS, etc.) Value Accelerator increases the value of explicit packets in the externalization pathway by increasing their priority. This has the subsequent effect on movement through barriers as seen above in the Brown Bag Value Accelerator. The increase in priority is based on a randomness component plus the number of information packets being sent and

viewed. The accelerator assumes that as the email system is used more frequently, the probability of receiving a valuable packet will increase. The Email Value Accelerator is represented in the simulation by the following function:

Email Value Accelerator = f (Existing Priority, Normally distributed random number, Probability of finding a Good Packet)

The last value accelerator is the Knowledge Repository. This value accelerator also operates by increasing the priority of explicit packets. A knowledge repository allows for packets of information to be stored and easily searched. This in turn allows packets to pass from the point and time of creation to an end user more rapidly than by email alone. This effect of the knowledge repository is simulated by the following function:

Knowledge Repository Value Accelerator = f (Existing Priority, Normally distributed random number, Probability of finding a Good Packet)

Receiver of Good Packets

This last function in the simulation gathers statistics on how many packets, either Tacit or Explicit, were selected and the average length of time they were in the system prior to selection. This function only counts those packets that have a priority higher than 60. This gate can be adjusted for any given simulation. The packets as initially generated, receive priorities normally distributed between 1 and 127, so a value of 60 establishes that about 50% of the packets will make it through at some point in time. The percent that ultimately make it through will vary depending on the length of the simulation and more importantly on the number of value accelerators each packet encounters. This follows from the logic that as you add value to your KMS (value accelerators),

Figure 2. Instantiation #1

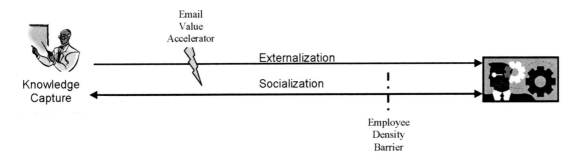

it will be used more often and thus more packets will be located and used for multiple purposes.

EVALUATION METHODOLOGY: SME MODEL INSTANTIATION COMPARISONS

The concepts and simulation model developed above was applied to a theoretical SME environment for the purpose of evaluation. A basic model (see Figure 2) was developed that could then be modified to represent alternative configurations of a KMS infrastructure for the SME. The model was adapted by addition of barriers, value accelerators, and parameter changes to reflect four alternative KM infrastructures for the SME. The artifact was evaluated by comparing simulations of these separate SME organizational structures of barriers and value accelerators. The four instantiations evaluated in this study were:

1. *Instantiation #1 - Baseline SME organizational structure:* This instantiation will consist of the socialization pathway (tacit packets) with a barrier (Employee density) and an externalization pathway (explicit packets) with one value accelerator (Email). This organizational instantiation represents one of an organization with few initial personnel, and a poor KM infrastructure and technologies. It is reflective of a small startup

company with few employees and little infrastructure.

2. *Instantiation #2 - Enhanced socialization pathway:* This instantiation builds directly on the preceding one by adding one value accelerator to the socialization pathway. In this situation, the additional value accelerator (Brown Bag Lunches), will represent a means to increase the flow of tacit knowledge by regular open exchanges of knowledge that might not happen by simple meetings in the hallway. This communication helps to promote the flow of knowledge through the employee density barrier found in this instantiation and instantiation #1. (Figure 3)

3. *Instantiation #3 - Initial externalization pathway:* This instantiation builds directly on the second instantiation by adding a barrier to the externalization pathway. The barrier is titled "Usefulness" and represents that a KM system provides little "usefulness" when the number of explicit information packets available for searching is low. As the number of packets in the system increases, so does the probability of finding a useful packet. The barrier's permeability increases as the number of packets increase. (Figure 4)

4. *Instantiation #4 - Enhanced externalization pathway:* This instantiation will build on the third instantiation by adding a value accelerator (Knowledge Repository) to the exter-

Figure 3. Instantiation #2

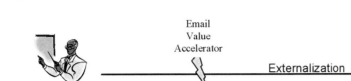

Figure 4. Instantiation #3

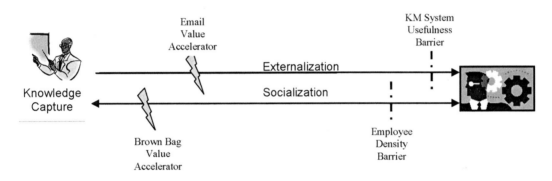

nalization pathway. The value accelerator will improve throughput of knowledge packets by allowing for storage and future use. It also adds value by allowing for better categorization to aid in the search for specific information. (Figure 5)

Each of the four above instantiations were simulated 20 times: four categories of company size (5, 10, 20 or 50 employees) times five categories of the number of days (50, 100, 250, 500, and 1000). The simulation will report the average number of packets received per person per day for both tacit and explicit packets. These key indicators of the efficiency and usefulness of the system will be plotted to evaluate the effectiveness of the model. The four instantiations represent a sequential improvement that one might expect to see in a SME over time. The first instantiation represents the baseline and perhaps could be

considered a very early stage startup. The second instantiation represents an improvement to the socialization pathway. This difference can be addressed by the following hypotheses:

H1a: The use of an appropriate value accelerator in the socialization pathway will significantly reduce the average time tacit packets spend in the system.

H1b: The use of an appropriate value accelerator in the socialization pathway will significantly increase the number of tacit packets received per person per day in the system.

Instantiation # 3 represents the inclusion of a barrier on the externalization pathway to account for low usefulness of a KMS until a critical mass of packets are available for searching and finding valuable information. The fourth instantiation installs a knowledge repository to improve the

Figure 5. Instantiation #4

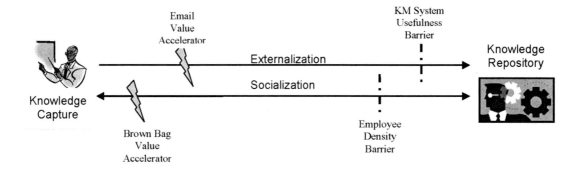

usefulness of the KMS. This leads to the following hypotheses:

H2a: The use of an appropriate value accelerator in the externalization pathway will significantly reduce the average time explicit packets spend in the system.

H2b: The use of an appropriate value accelerator in the externalization pathway will significantly increase the number of explicit packets received per person per day in the system.

RESULTS

The statistics collected for each simulation were: 1) the average time until a "tacit" packet reached a user of that packet, 2) the average time until an "explicit" packet reached a user of that packet, 3) the average number of "tacit" packets received by a user each day, and 4) the average number of "explicit" packets received by a user each day. The following figures report this data and are used to validate the model is operating as instantiated.

The first set of figures (Figures #6 – #10) look at the baseline instantiation. This first instantiation, as detailed in the above evaluation section, incorporates an Employee Density Barrier and an Email Accelerator. The expectation for such an instantiation is that we would see evidence that the larger the employee population is, the longer

the average time a tacit packet takes getting to the user of that packet. This might occur for two primary reasons: 1) as a company brings on more employees, some will be in support roles and not likely to be large contributors of new knowledge, and 2) the original small team, which had a relatively rapid exchange of that sharing, now are spending time managing and working with the new employees and less time exchanging new information. Figure 6 shows us that our expectations are met. The line for 50 employees shows an average increase of 20 days per packet in the system – about a 400% increase from when there were only 5 employees. The expectation of a longer time through the system was met, but is the difference seen too excessive or maybe not excessive enough? These results may be excessive because as a company grows larger, subgroups would form around job responsibilities and the need for similar information. These subgroups would facilitate the knowledge exchange among themselves. So perhaps a less drastic difference might be more realistic.

Figure 7 looks at the impact of this baseline instantiation on the flow of explicit packets. Since this instantiation does not have any barriers to explicit packets flowing through the externalization pathway, we would expect the time spent in the system to be invariant to the number of employees and the number of days simulated. Other

Figure 6. Instantiation #1: Tacit packet average time (days) in system

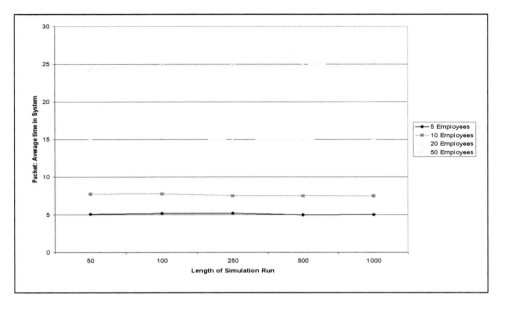

Figure 7. Instantiation # 1: Explicit packet average time (days) in system

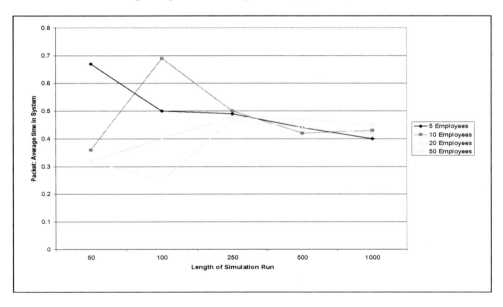

than initial random noise, which disappears after about 250 days, this expectation seems to be met.

The next two figures look at the number of packets per person per day received. Figure 8 shows this for the tacit packets and Figure 9 for the explicit packets. The expectations are that the number of tacit packets per person per day should

be highest with a small employee population and lowest with the larger population. This is because in a smaller group there is more interaction and opportunity for exchange of information. As the group grows the odds of a person with a valuable packet of information serendipitously running into the person who should receive that packet,

Figure 8. Instantiation # 1: Tacit packets/person/day

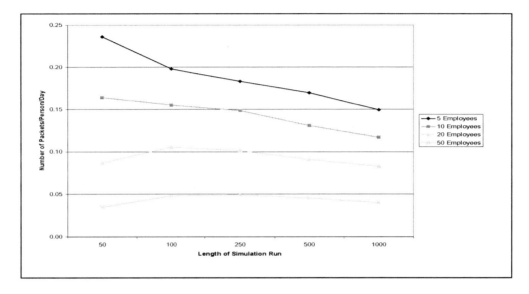

Figure 9. Instantiation #1: Explicit packets/person/day

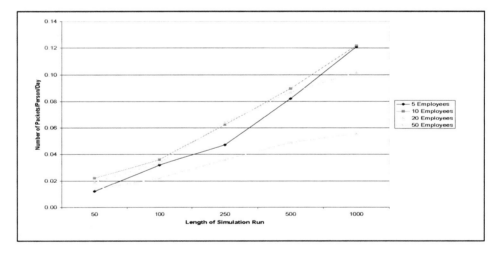

decreases. This is what the figure validates. What is also apparent in this figure is a downward slope for all lines. The downward slope is due to the transition over time from primarily tacit information flow to one of an increasing proportion of explicit packets. Initially, there are few explicit packets generated, but as the number of days of simulation increase, more explicit packets enter the system. The more explicit packets in the system, the more interest the users have in looking for those packets, which further encourages the production of explicit packets as all members see this value.

The externalization pathway carries the explicit packets and in instantiation #1 there are no barriers in this pathway. We would expect to see an increase in explicit packets over time. As more explicit packets are accumulated - the "usefulness" of the KMS increases and proportionately more explicit than tacit packets are generated by users.

Figure 10. Instantiation #2: Tacit packet average time (days) in system

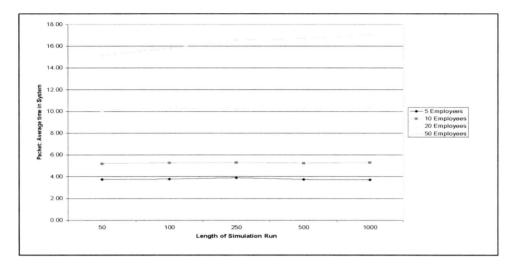

This is validated in Figure 9. This Figure also highlights the effects of adding new personnel as the company grows: 1) as a company brings on more employees, some will be in support roles and not likely to be large contributors of new knowledge, and 2) the original small team, which had a given level of sharing and relatively rapid exchange of that sharing, now are spending time managing and working with the new employees and less time exchanging new information. The figure illustrates this effect as a distinctly lower increase in packets per person per day for a company with 50 employees relative to that of the smaller companies.

The next figure looks at the second instantiation, which adds in a value accelerator: brown bag lunches. This accelerator offers a means for a company to improve the flow of tacit packets, which will become more crucial as the company grows. When Figure 6 is compared with Figure 10, it can be seen that the number of days a tacit packet spends in the organization decreases. This comparison validates (supports H1a) the expectations of the impact of a value generator both in terms of its effect on the time spent in the system and also on the greater value to a larger company.

Figure 11 can be compared with Figure 8 to understand the effect of the brown bag value accelerator on the number of packets received per person per day. This comparison validates (supports H1b), that the average number packets per person per day increases due to the beneficial impact of the brown bag lunches on facilitating tacit information exchange.

The third instantiation adds the barrier: KMS Usefulness. The purpose of this barrier is to reflect the impact perceived usefulness has on actual use of the system. If the users do not perceive the system as useful, because the information desired is not available, then they will not use it. The premise of this barrier is that as more explicit packets enter the externalization pathway and build up, the perceived and actual usefulness will increase. Users will have a greater likelihood of locating the information they require in a bigger pool of packets. By adding this barrier, the expectation is that the average time an explicit packet spends in the organization will increase to a point (critical mass), and then begin decreasing as more use of the system occurs. This is validated (supports H2a) in Figure 12.

The effect of adding a value generator (knowledge repository) to the externalization pathway

Figure 11. Instantiation # 2: Tacit packets/person/day

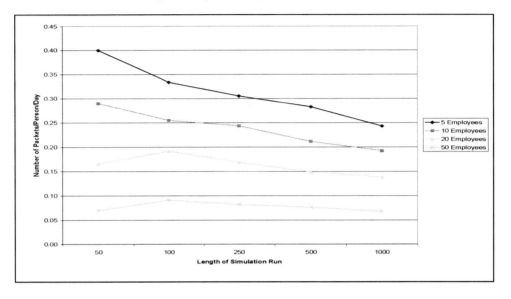

Figure 12. Instantiation #3: Explicit packet average time (days) in system

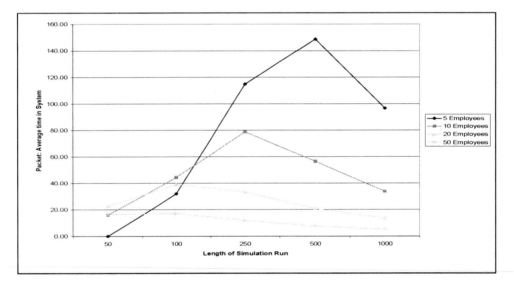

occurs in the simulation of the fourth instantiation and is seen Figure 13. The figure looks similar to Figure 12, but the scale is shifted downward representing a faster throughput of packets in the organization. This validates (supports H2b) the externalization pathway for barriers and accelerators.

The last figure in the series (Figure 14) shows the average number of explicit packets created per person per day. It is a snapshot at day 250 and provides insight into how the various instantiations perform as the number of employees increase. Simulations for this figure were run up to 500 employees. The results appear reasonable at lower populations. Instantiation 2 starts out

Figure 13. Instantiation # 4: Explicit packet average time (days) in system

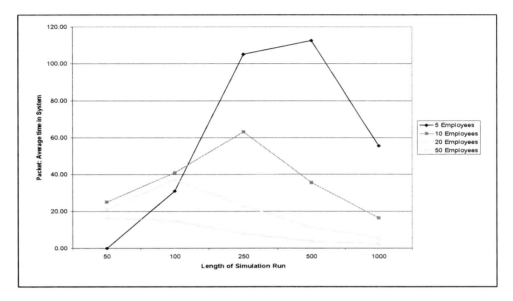

higher than 3 because 3 has a barrier to knowledge flow. Instantiation 4 starts out highest of all because the value accelerator (knowledge repository) is associated with externalization: the explicit pathway. However, as the number of employees increases the difference among the instantiations shrinks until by the time the company reaches 500 employees the results are the same. The assumption in the model which influences this is

that the level of individual knowledge contribution decreases over time due to the law of diminishing returns. The focus of all employees in a small company is on creation of core competence. However, as the company grows, more employees are involved with support functions and contribute on the average less to the core competency.

Figure 14. Explicit packets per person per day (snapshot at day 250)

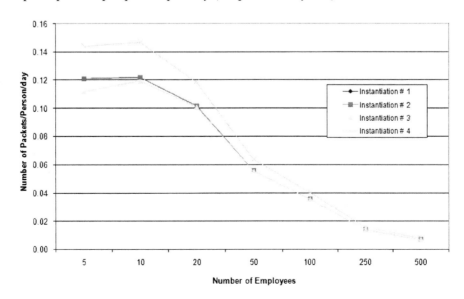

CONTRIBUTION TO RESEARCH

Knowledge management research faces many difficulties. Knowledge is hard to define and hard to measure. Experiments are not easy to perform and data for analysis is frequently indirect. The systems to manage the flow of knowledge are equally difficult to define and measure (M. E. Jennex, Smolnik, & Croasdell, 2007). This research took the approach of tying together generally accepted concepts of knowledge and knowledge management to develop a model that might be used to simulate a subset of the flows of knowledge in a small organization. With further development of this model (Judge, 2008), the flows, barriers, and value accelerators might be configured to simulate specific companies. This would allow management teams to assess the options to reduce existing barriers to knowledge flows, the cost to do so, and the potential benefits. Having the ability to predict these benefits and costs as the organization grows will allow the development of successful KM strategies.

The process of developing and validating this artifact identified numerous areas where future research is required:

- How do multiple barriers interact with one another? Are they multiplicative or additive?
- What value accelerators are most effective given various barriers? Can specific value accelerators only assist knowledge flow through certain barriers?
- What are the real barriers to flow of information and knowledge and what factors define them?
- How are all these questions affected by size and age of company, environmental turbulence, and industry of the company (Judge, 2008)?
- How does one measure the number and flow of tacit and explicit information? How does this flow change over time and growth of the company?
- What drives the ratio of tacit to explicit information? Does this ratio change with the size of an organization?

The design itself is an iterative process and as new theory or data on parameters becomes available the design will be improved. Using the knowledge gained from this study will provide insight into what researchers might look for and what they might see when studying knowledge flows in situ.

This research also provides some support that the number of employees, the type of information packet, and time can be modeled to understand how these variables interact. Future research may provide additional insight into how organizational structure, KM infrastructure, motivators, physical workspace, quality of information, organizational climate, and actual behaviors work together to produce "usefulness" in a KMS for a SME.

CONCLUSION

In "Working Knowledge: How Organizations Manage What They Know" (Davenport & Prusak, 1998) the authors state, "In general, the greatest value of modeling knowledge processes lie not in exact understanding of knowledge input, output, and flow rates but in identifying the variability in the model that can be affected by management action." This model with its four instantiations is an initial attempt to demonstrate that a simplified model of knowledge flows in a company is possible. It points out a means for management to represent the flow of knowledge through the barriers found within their organization. They can then configure potential value accelerators to determine which might be most effective. It will also allow them to understand the effects of both of these as the company grows.

Future development of the model might consider:

- External validation of distributions used to simulate packet creation, barrier induced wait time, and probability of finding good packets.
- How cost information can be combined with the model to better analyze strategies for implementation of value accelerators (relevance to the business community).
- Looking at how value accelerators not only alter priority for faster movement through barriers, but may also generate new packets themselves (i.e., Brown Bag Lunches provide opportunities to exchange knowledge – but they may also stimulate new knowledge).
- Genetic Algorithms: information as genes, barriers as fitness function, changing environment changes fitness function, recombination of ideas to form better ones.
- Use of agent modeling to represent the complex adaptive behaviors that arise and modify the knowledge flow (Nissen & Levitt, 2004) as the organization grows.
- How knowledge flows can be represented more fully by building a simulation model that integrates the acquisition, creation, capture, storage and retrieval, and use of knowledge in an organization.

Building a simulation model is an iterative process and is limited in the degree of detail it implements. There is always the temptation to reduce each construct into further sub-constructs. The question that must always be asked is: does the additional level of detail add to the validity and usefulness of the model? This simulation model is limited to a flow of tacit and explicit information packets. How they were created, captured, acquired or stored is not addressed. There was no discussion or modeling of Organizational Memory (OM). More detail could have been built into this model. For example, it could have addressed the OM. It could have defined human, electronic and other media as forms of storage. It could also have further deconstructed human storage into individuals. It could then further model that some individuals have different levels of cognitive capabilities, absorptive capacities, and specialize in certain domains of knowledge. This additional detail comes with a price: it must be quantitatively described. Even at the level the model for this research was constructed, many of the variables were estimated based on limited theory and experience. At lower levels of model description, the values for parameters would be even more likely to be unrealistic at this point. This is a serious limitation and opportunity. It provides for slowly constructing models of what we know we know and hypothesizing what we know we don't know. In some cases the models also allow for serendipitously discovering those things we don't know we know and don't know we don't know.

REFERENCES

Alavi, M., & Leidner, D. E. (2001). Review: Knowledge management and knowledge management systems: Conceptual foundations and research issues. *Management Information Systems Quarterly, 25*(1), 107. doi:10.2307/3250961

Ardichvili, A., Page, V., & Wentling, T. (2003). Motivation and barriers to participation in virtual knowledge-sharing communities of practice. *Journal of Knowledge Management, 7*(1), 64–77. doi:10.1108/13673270310463626

Becerra-Fernandez, I. (2001). Organizational Knowledge Management: A Contingency Perspective. *Journal of Management Information Systems, 18*(1), 23–55.

Becerra-Fernandez, I., González, A. J., & Sabherwal, R. (2004). Knowledge management: challenges, solutions, and technologies.

Chalmeta, R., & Grangel, R. (2008). Methodology for the implementation of knowledge management systems. *Journal of the American Society for Information Science and Technology, 59*(5), 742–755. doi:10.1002/asi.20785

Choi, B., Poon, S., & Davis, J. (2008). Effects of knowledge management strategy on organizational performance: a complementarity theory-based approach. *Omega, 36*(2), 235–251. doi:10.1016/j.omega.2006.06.007

Cohen, W. M., & Levinthal, D. A. (1990). Absorptive Capacity: A New Perspective on Learning and Innovation. *Administrative Science Quarterly, 35*(1). doi:10.2307/2393553

Cross, R., & Cummings, J. N. (2004). Tie and network correlates of individual performance in knowledge-intensive work. *Academy of Management Journal, 47*(6), 928–937. doi:10.2307/20159632

Cross, R., Parker, A., Prusak, L., & Borgatti, S. P. (2001). Knowing what we know: Supporting knowledge creation and sharing in social networks. *Organizational Dynamics, 30*(2), 100–120. doi:10.1016/S0090-2616(01)00046-8

Damodaran, L. (2000). Barriers and facilitators to the use of knowledge management systems. *Behaviour & Information Technology, 19*(6), 405–413. doi:10.1080/014492900750052660

Davenport, T. H., & Prusak, L. (1998). *Working knowledge*. Boston, MA: Harvard Business School Press.

De Long, D. W., & Fahey, L. (2000). Diagnosing cultural barriers to knowledge management. *The Academy of Management Executive, 14*(4), 113–127.

Fichman, R. G. (1992). Information Technology Diffusion: A Review of Empirical Research. *Proceedings of the Thirteenth International Conference on Information Systems*, 195–206.

Ford, D. P., & Chan, Y. E. (2003). Knowledge sharing in a multi-cultural setting: a case study. *Knowledge Management Research & Practice, 1*(1), 11–27. doi:10.1057/palgrave.kmrp.8499999

Gupta, A. K., & Govindarajan, V. (2000). Knowledge Management's Social Dimension: Lessons from Nucor Steel. *Sloan Management Review, 42*(1), 71–80.

Hall, J., Sapsed, J., & Williams, K. (2000). Barriers and Facilitators to Knowledge Capture and Transfer in Project-Based Firms.

Hendriks, P. (1999). Why share knowledge? The influence of ICT on the motivation for knowledge sharing. *Knowledge and Process Management, 6*(2), 91–100. doi:10.1002/(SICI)1099-1441(199906)6:2<91::AID-KPM54>3.0.CO;2-M

Hu, A. G. Z., & Jaffe, A. B. (2003). Patent citations and international knowledge flow: the cases of Korea and Taiwan. *International Journal of Industrial Organization, 21*(6), 849–880.

Jennex, M., & Olfman, L. (2003). Organizational Memory. *Handbook on Knowledge Management, 1*, 207–234.

Jennex, M. E., Smolnik, S., & Croasdell, D. (2007). Towards Defining Knowledge Management Success. *Proceedings of the 40th Annual Hawaii International Conference on System Sciences*.

Judge, R. (2008). *Simulating knowledge flows to formulate strategies for implementing Knowledge Management in small organizations*. University Microfilms International, P. O. Box 1764, Ann Arbor, MI, 48106, USA.

Katz, M. L., & Shapiro, C. (1986). Technology Adoption in the Presence of Network Externalities. *The Journal of Political Economy, 94*(4), 822–841. doi:10.1086/261409

Knapp, E. M. (1998). Knowledge Management. *Business and Economic Review, 44*(4), 3–6.

Leenders, R., van Engelen, J. M. L., & Kratzer, J. (2003). Virtuality, communication, and new product team creativity: a social network perspective. *Journal of Engineering and Technology Management, 20*(1-2), 69–92. doi:10.1016/S0923-4748(03)00005-5

Marwick, A. (2010). Knowledge management technology. *IBM Systems Journal, 40*(4), 814–830. doi:10.1147/sj.404.0814

McDermott, R., & O'Dell, C. (2001). Overcoming cultural barriers to sharing knowledge. *Journal of Knowledge Management, 5*(1), 76–85. doi:10.1108/13673270110384428

McEvily, S. K., & Chakravarthy, B. (2002). The persistence of knowledge-based advantage: an empirical test for product performance and technological knowledge. *Strategic Management Journal, 23*(4), 285–305. doi:10.1002/smj.223

Monge, P. R., Rothman, L. W., Eisenberg, E. M., Miller, K. I., & Kirste, K. K. (1985). The Dynamics of Organizational Proximity. *Management Science, 31*(9), 1129–1141. doi:10.1287/mnsc.31.9.1129

Moss, D., Ashford, R., & Shani, N. (2003). The forgotten sector: Uncovering the role of public relations in SMEs. *Journal of Communication Management, 8*(2), 197–210. doi:10.1108/13632540410807655

Nissen, M. E., & Levitt, R. E. (2004). Agent-based modeling of knowledge flows: illustration from the domain of information systems design. *System Sciences, 2004. Proceedings of the 37th Annual Hawaii International Conference on*, 8.

Nonaka, I., & Takeuchi, H. (1995). *The knowledge-creating company*. New York City, NY: Oxford University Press.

Polanyi, M. (1962). Tacit Knowing: Its Bearing on Some Problems of Philosophy. *Reviews of Modern Physics, 34*(4), 601–616. doi:10.1103/RevModPhys.34.601

Render, B. (2003). *Stair, R. and Balakrishnan, N. (2003) Managerial Decision Modeling with Spreadsheets*. Prentice Hall.

Riege, A. (2005). Three-dozen knowledge-sharing barriers managers must consider The Authors. *Journal of Knowledge Management, 9*(3), 18–35. doi:10.1108/13673270510602746

Scott, J. E. (2000). Facilitating interorganizational learning with information technology. *Journal of Management Information Systems, 17*(2), 81.

Simonin, B. L. (1999). Ambiguity and the process of knowledge transfer in strategic alliances. *Strategic Management Journal, 20*(7), 595–623. doi:10.1002/(SICI)1097-0266(199907)20:7<595::AID-SMJ47>3.0.CO;2-5

Szulanski, G. (1996). Exploring internal stickiness: Impediments to the transfer of best practice within the firm. *Strategic management journal, 17*(winter), 27-43.

Szulanski, G. (2003). *Sticky Knowledge: barriers to knowing in the firm*. Sage Publications Inc.

Von Krogh, G., Nonaka, I., & Ichijo, K. (2000). *Enabling Knowledge Creation: New Tools for Unlocking the Mysteries of Tacit Understanding*. New York City, NY:xOxford University Press.

Wong, K. Y., & Aspinwall, E. (2005). An empirical study of the important factors for knowledge-management adoption in the SME sector. *Journal of Knowledge Management, 9*(3), 64. doi:10.1108/13673270510602773

Wunram, M., Weber, F., Pawar, K. S., & Gupta, A. (2002). Proposition of a Human-centred Solution Framework for KM in the Concurrent Enterprise. *Proceedings of the 8th International Conference on Concurrent Enterprising–Ubiquitous Engineering in the Collaborative Economy, Rome, Italy, 17*, 151–158.

Zahn, G. L. (1991). Face-to-Face Communication in an Office Setting: The Effects of Position, Proximity, and Exposure. *Communication Research, 18*(6), 737. doi:10.1177/009365091018006002

Chapter 8
Knowledge Sharing Behavior of Graduate Students

Shaheen Majid
Nanyang Technological University, Singapore

Sim Mong Wey
Nanyang Technological University,Singapore

ABSTRACT

Active knowledge sharing is considered an important activity in the learning process. However until now, the focus of many studies has been on understanding the impact of information and knowledge sharing on the performance of corporate and public organizations. On the other hand, its implications in the educational arena have been relatively unexplored. The purpose of this study was to investigate perceptions, nature and extent of knowledge sharing among graduate students in Singapore. It also investigated the factors and class activities that would either promote or inhibit knowledge sharing among students. A questionnaire was used for data collection and 183 students from two public universities in Singapore participated in this study. The study revealed that the participants were primarily motivated to share information and knowledge in an attempt to build relationships with their peers and email was the preferred communication channel for this purpose. However, intense competition among the students to outperform their classmates and the lack of depth in relationship were the two most important factors hindering the knowledge sharing activity. The study suggests that academic institutions should review their instruction approaches to make the learning process less competitive which would help improve knowledge sharing among students.

INTRODUCTION

The emergence of *knowledge-based economy* and complexity of work environment have reinforced the need for effective exploitation of knowledge and making knowledge management an essen-tial area of activity in organizations. Therefore, knowledge is now regarded as a precious resource for augmenting traditional factors of production (Choi, Lee & Yoo, 2010). In fact, knowledge is increasingly viewed as a crucial determinant of an organization's competitive advantage (Chia et al., 2005; Almahamid, Awwad & McAdams, 2010) which can help organizations survive in

DOI: 10.4018/978-1-60960-555-1.ch008

a highly competitive, dynamic, and volatile environment. Among the knowledge management activities, the notion of *knowledge sharing* has generated much interest among academics and practitioners in recent years. Many studies have focused on investigating factors that influence various aspects of knowledge sharing, although most of such studies were conducted in the context of business and public organizations. This is not surprising, given the fact that many of the knowledge management initiatives were initially implemented in these organizations. Although education institutions, to some extent, are different from business and public organizations, active information and knowledge sharing is considered vital for the learning process. In general, problems attributed to the lack of knowledge sharing among students can also be studied on the same lines as in corporate and public organizations.

Factors Affecting Knowledge Sharing

Knowledge sharing is considered as a social behavior and many physical, technological, psychological, cultural, and personality factors either promote or inhibit this activity (Chiri & Klobas, 2010; Cyr & Choo, 2010; Wu & Munir, 2010). Often people feel pleased by helping others through sharing their knowledge because for them it is a satisfying, fulfilling and meaningful activity (Beitler & Mitlacher, 2007). However, literature suggests that strong personal ties and mutual respect can motivate individuals to share knowledge with their peers. Cyr & Choo (2010) also highlighted that reciprocity together with trust promotes knowledge sharing. Alstyne (2005) also agreed that **trust** is an important factor in developing positive interpersonal relationships which encourages knowledge sharing. Mutual trust is often developed over time through frequent interactions and that is why it is important that adequate time and opportunities should be provided for developing cordial relations.

Despite the immense benefits of knowledge sharing, as often advocated by researchers and practitioners, it is a fact that in many situations, people avoid sharing their knowledge. Davenport (1997) argued that the act of knowledge sharing is unnatural and there are plenty of reasons why people avoid sharing their knowledge. The lack of in-depth relationship between the source and recipient of knowledge, lack of motivation or rewards to share (Smith & McKeen, 2003), lack of time, and non-existence of *knowledge sharing culture* (Siakas, Georgiadou & Balstrup, 2010) are some of the factors that are likely to impede knowledge sharing among peers. In addition, lack of understanding of what to share and with whom to share, limited appreciation for knowledge sharing, and the fear of providing wrong information can also hamper the knowledge sharing activity (Majid & Wey, 2008; Ardichvili, Page & Wentling, 2003; Skyrme, 2002).

Knowledge Sharing in Academic Institutions

Many studies have highlighted the fact that information and knowledge sharing plays an important role in the learning and development of individuals (Chiu, 2010). In addition to lecturer-centric approaches, several new instruction strategies such as problem-oriented teaching, contextualized teaching, target-oriented teaching, and interactive and collaborative teaching are gaining popularity. These innovative teaching methods have already turned instruction into sharing (Zhou, Knoke, Sakamoto, 2005).

Majid and Tina (2009) noted that many academic institutions are now emphasizing their teaching staff to incorporate group discussions, team projects, and other cooperative activities in their *instruction approaches*. These *cooperative learning activities* can bring many benefits such as better student achievements, improved communication skills, and a positive attitude towards knowledge sharing (Emmer & Gerwels, 2002).

Similarly, teamwork can also help students emotionally in coping with the pressure of academic work, fulfilling personal needs and goals, and enhancing interpersonal relations (Educational Broadcasting Corporation, 2004). It can also assist students in seeking answers to their queries, learn new things, better understanding regarding a particular subject, or merely helping one another. It is, therefore, quite evident that interaction and knowledge sharing among students is a vital component of their learning process (Ma & Yuen, 2011).

Access to a wide array of online collaborative tools is providing ample opportunities to students for interacting and sharing knowledge with their peers (Giacoppo, 2008). Eveleth, Eveleth and Sarker (2005) believe that social fragmentation of students can be addressed through creating online 'third space' which would allow students to construct knowledge collaboratively. They feel that *incentives* such as participation points would motivate students to participate in such online forums. Similarly, the online third space communities help students acquire knowledge actively through co-construction, not just passively receive knowledge encoded in a lecture delivered in a traditional classroom. Neto and Correia (2009) noted that *social collaboration tools* such as online discussion forums, virtual communities, instant web messengers, Weblogs, and Wikis provide a broad range of knowledge sharing options and capabilities.

Many studies suggest that the use of online discussion boards enhance student learning (Ma & Yuen, 2011; Krentler & Flurry, 2005). Their studies show that, regardless of subject of study and the Internet experience, all students participating in discussion boards show an improvement in their learning. Majid and Mokhtar (2007) found that students actively participating in discussion forums also obtained higher scores for their assignments and group projects. Their study also revealed that full-time students contributed more in the online forums than part-time students. Graff

(2006) studied the relationship between students' performance on coursework assignments and their perceptions of online community as well as relationship between students' online community scores and their engagement with an online assessment. A positive correlation was found between student coursework performance and involvement in online assessments. Similarly, students' online community scores were related to their coursework performance. These studies suggest that online collaboration tools help students in learning and knowledge sharing as well as in improving their academic performance.

Although the importance of knowledge sharing in the learning process is widely discussed and recognized, only recently studies on different aspects of knowledge sharing by students have started appearing. Chua (2003) reported that students' knowledge sharing tendency is driven by a set of contextualized concerns, and the decision to share or withhold knowledge depends on the expected payoff. He found that student's perceived payoff of sharing knowledge was contingent on the knowledge sharing behavior of other students. In another study, Majid and Yuen (2006) found that although students exhibited a positive attitude towards information and knowledge sharing, it was restricted to only certain individuals and situations. They noted that students avoided sharing knowledge with their peers if the individual or group projects were to be graded. Other *barriers* to information and knowledge sharing revealed by their study were the lack of depth in relationship, limited socializing opportunities, and too much pressure to academically outperform classmates. They recommended that the learning environment should be less competitive and threatening, and to some extent, it could be achieved by assigning team projects and activities. Chiu (2010) reported that students may not be willing to share their knowledge as it is critical to their *academic performance*. Wolfe and Loraas (2008) studied knowledge sharing by MBA students and concluded that proprietary knowledge sharing occur when students' competitiveness is team-oriented. A cross-culture study of American and Chinese undergraduate students revealed that students were more willing to share their personal knowledge with in-group members than out-group members (Zhang et al. 2006). He (2010) identified factors influencing knowledge sharing among Health Services Administration students and found that mutual influence and team cohesion are two major factors directly influencing knowledge sharing within virtual teams.

As active and voluntary sharing of knowledge is considered an essential element of the learning process, it is highly desirable that educators and other academic stakeholders should properly understand the *knowledge sharing behaviour* of students and the barriers that restrict it. Unfortunately, most of the information and knowledge sharing studies have been done in organisational settings and very little is known about the knowledge sharing patterns of tertiary students. The main objectives of this study were to investigate the knowledge sharing patterns of graduate students in Singapore, the type of knowledge shared, and the preferred *communication channels* for this purpose. In addition, those factors that were likely to inhibit or promote knowledge sharing among students were also investigated. It was an exploratory study with no hypothesis testing involved.

METHOD

The study used a modified version of the questionnaire used previously by Majid and Yuen (2006) to investigate knowledge sharing patterns of undergraduate students in Singapore. One purpose of using this questionnaire was to find out commonalities and differences in knowledge sharing by undergraduate and graduate students. Some questions were adjusted keeping in view the findings of previous study as well as to make them more relevant to graduate students. The modi-

fied questionnaire was pre-tested on six graduate students at Nanyang Technological University to assess the clarity and validity of the instrument.

The sample for the study was drawn from graduate students enrolled with two public universities in Singapore - Nanyang Technological University and the National University of Singapore. Websites of both the universities were searched for identifying coursework based graduate programmes and six core courses, having more students, were short listed for conducting the survey. An email was sent to the respective course instructors for seeking permission for administering the questionnaire in their classes. All of them agreed and the questionnaire was given out to the students at the entrances of classrooms. Students were informed that they could return the completed questionnaire to a collection box, placed at the back of the classroom. Most of the students chose either to complete the questionnaire before the start of the class or during the lecture break time. A total of 264 questionnaires were distributed and 183 filled-in questionnaires were received back, resulting in a response rate of 69.3%. This data collection approach was considered more appropriate as many previous studies in Singapore, using pure random sampling techniques, failed to achieve higher response rates (Majid & Kowtha, 2008; Sum, Kow & Chen, 2004).

FINDINGS

Profile of Respondents

The respondents from both the participating universities were almost evenly distributed – 49.1% from National University of Singapore (NUS) and 50.9% from Nanyang Technological University (NTU). One-half of the respondents were from various engineering departments of NTU and NUS, while the remaining one-half of the participants were from the graduate programmes in

Table 1. Knowledge sharing for study-related purposes

Situation	N	Mean Score (1 ~ 7)	Std Deviation
To share ideas with **own group members** while working on group projects or assignments	181	5.34	1.131
To discuss or clarify the requirements of projects or term papers or tutorial assignments	182	4.84	1.290
To discuss or clarify examination-related matters	179	4.56	1.476
To discuss or clarify concepts learnt in the class	183	4.34	1.295
To tackle or solve study-related questions	182	4.31	1.260
To share ideas with classmates while working on **individual projects or assignments**	182	3.85	1.398
To share ideas with students from **other groups** while working on group projects or assignments	182	3.57	1.484

Information Studies and Knowledge Management at the School of Communication and Information in NTU. Seventy-seven (42.1%) of the respondents were female while remaining 106 (57.9%) were male. Around one-third of the respondents have up to 5 years' of work experience while one-quarter of the respondents did not have any such experience. The mean score for years of working experience for all the participants was 5.05 years.

Purposes of Information and Knowledge Sharing

Through an indirect question, the respondents were asked to give their opinion, on a scale of 1-7, on how often their peers share knowledge with their classmates for various study-related activities (Table 1). The respondents felt that most often the sharing of knowledge occurs with one's own team mates whilst undertaking team projects or group assignments (mean score: 5.34). Interestingly, in stark comparison to the above, knowledge sharing with students from other groups whilst working on group projects or assignments was perceived to be the least prevalent (mean score: 3.57). In addition, the sharing of knowledge with other students whilst working on individual assignments was also considered less common (mean score: 3.85). These findings confirm Zhang, et al. (2006) finding that students prefer sharing knowledge with their group members than students from other groups.

A similar trend was also reported by some other studies (Majid & Yuen, 2006; Mäkelä & Brewster, 2009) where intra-group knowledge sharing was more prevalent than inter-group sharing.

The respondents were also asked, on a scale of 1 to 7, to indicate the type of materials often shared by their peers with other classmates (Table 2). Two most commonly shared materials were the URLs of useful websites (mean score: 4.22) and the class notes or handouts (mean score: 4.20). However, it was observed that variation in the mean scores for all the materials listed in the survey fell in a narrow range of 3.72 to 4.22. This implies that the respondents did not think there was much difference in the type of materials shared by the students. Majid and Yuen (2006) also found that undergraduate students prefer sharing URLs of useful websites with their peers than books and copies of articles. Probably, they thought it was wastage of their time and money to provide hard-copies of materials as well as they wanted their class fellows to search and locate their own information.

Factors Encouraging Knowledge Sharing

The respondents, on a scale of 1-7, were asked what factors are likely to motivate their peers to share information and knowledge with other classmates (Table 3). A majority of the respondents

Table 2. Type of materials shared

Information Type	N	Mean Score (1 ~ 7)	Std Deviation
URLs of useful websites	183	4.22	1.432
Class notes/handouts	183	4.20	1.653
Powerpoint slides of class presentations	183	3.90	1.705
Previous assignments/term papers	183	3.89	1.647
Printouts/photocopies of articles	183	3.84	1.564
Books/photocopies of book chapters	183	3.72	1.488

Table 3. Factors motivating knowledge sharing among students

Factor	N	Mean Score (1 ~ 7)	Std Deviation
To build or develop relationships with other students	180	4.81	1.264
To further one's own understanding of concepts learnt in the class through sharing ideas with other students	181	4.75	1.269
To feel belonged to and fit into a group	182	4.55	1.281
Out of altruism to help others	178	4.27	1.376
For rewards e.g. class or online forum participation marks	176	4.00	1.568
To gain respect by portraying the image of an expert	181	3.99	1.436
Heightening of one's self-esteem	181	3.72	1.415

believed that the desire to build or develop close relationships with fellow students was the most important motivator for knowledge sharing (mean score: 4.81), closely followed by another factor that it would improve one's own understanding of the concepts learnt in the class (mean score: 4.75). The factors that were considered the least likely to encourage knowledge sharing were the desire to develop image of an expert among peers (mean score: 3.99) and to satisfy personal ego (mean score: 3.72). It appeared that a majority of the respondents perceived knowledge sharing as a positive and desirable activity rather than a source for achieving personal gains. A similar trend was observed in studies by Majid and Yuen (2006) and Alstyne (2005) where developing relationships and trust building were considered motivating factors for sharing knowledge. However, in contract to Chua (2003) study which concluded that

knowledge sharing by students depends on the perceived payoffs, the respondents of this study felt that rewards in the form of academic grades were not so important.

The respondents were also asked to identify those class activities that were likely to encourage information and knowledge sharing among students. The two activities that emerged at the top of the list, with mean scores of 5.35 and 5.27, were group projects and small group discussions respectively (Table 4). On the other hand, activities that were considered the least likely to encourage information and knowledge sharing were the school level seminars (mean score: 4.02) and the invited speakers (mean score: 4.13). This finding supports Grantham's (2005) argument that team projects and group discussion enhance learning experience of students.

Table 4. Class activities encouraging knowledge sharing

Study-Related Activities	N	Mean Score (1 ~ 7)	Std Deviation
Group projects	181	5.35	1.272
Small group discussions	182	5.27	1.208
Class discussions	182	4.70	1.402
Student presentations	182	4.43	1.331
Invited speakers	181	4.13	1.445
School/division seminars	181	4.02	1.437

Table 5. Knowledge sharing for graded and non-graded assignments

Scenario	N	Mean Score (1 ~ 7)	Std Deviation
Scenario 1 Individual assignments **to be graded**	182	4.46	1.393
Scenario 2 Individual assignments **not to be graded**	182	4.77	1.377

Information and Knowledge Sharing for Assignments

The respondents were give two scenarios to understand their knowledge sharing behaviour in different situations. They were asked to indicate the likelihood of information and knowledge sharing activity while working on individual assignments in situations where the grades may or may not matter (Table 5). It was interesting to note that the respondents felt it was less likely for their peers to share knowledge with their classmates if individual assignments were to be graded (mean score: 4:46), as compared to a situation where these assignments were not to be graded (mean score: 4.77). The paired sample T-test also revealed a significant difference (P = 0.0006 <0.05) between the mean scores of these two scenarios. This finding confirms the result of an earlier study by Majid and Yuen (2006) which concluded that students avoid sharing knowledge for those learning activities that are to be graded.

Types of Information and Knowledge Sharing Channels

The participating students were asked to indicate, on a scale of 1 to 7, that how often various channels of communication were used by them for sharing information and knowledge with their peers. The mean scores for email and face-to-face communication were the highest, at 5.51 and 5.16 respectively. As it can be seen from Table 6, there was a considerable gap between the mean scores of these two channels and the rest of the communication modes, testifying the popularity of the former channels. On the other hand, online forum discussion boards and online chat rooms were the least utilized channels for sharing knowledge with fellow students. This finding is not in line with Wagner and Bolloju's (2005) claim that communication tools such online discussion forums, virtual communities, instant web messengers, Weblogs, and Wikis promote knowledge sharing. It also does not support Krentler and Flurry (2005) conclusion that online discussion boards

Table 6. Channels used for information and knowledge sharing

Channels	N	Mean Score (1 ~ 7)	Std Deviation
Email	183	5.51	1.157
Face-to-face	182	5.16	1.314
Short Messaging Service (SMS)	181	3.92	1.639
Telephone	183	3.86	1.596
Instant messaging services (e.g. MSN)	183	3.42	1.825
Online forum discussion boards	182	3.41	1.708
Online chat rooms	183	3.02	1.664

Table 7. Reasons for using various communication channels (multi responses)

Channels	Reasons for Using (No. of respondents)			
	Convenient accessibility	Minimal message distortion	Minimal response time lag	Personal & warmness
Email	130	67	41	12
Face-to-face	95	103	96	102
Short Messaging Service (SMS)	115	32	46	11
Telephone	114	61	93	32
Instant messaging services (e.g. MSN)	84	35	51	8
Online forum discussion boards	90	40	31	8
Online chat rooms	72	32	47	11

improve student learning process. As Singapore is a hi-tech and IT-savvy society, it will be interesting to further explore this topic, particularly the impact of culture on the use of online discussion forums and chat rooms for knowledge sharing by students.

Reasons for Using Various Communication Channels

The respondents were further asked about the factors they often consider while making use of different communication channels for sharing information and knowledge with their peers (Table 7). Two main reasons given for using email were its convenient accessibility and minimal message distortion during the transmission. The face-to-face communication was preferred because of minimal distortion of message, and the personal touch and warmness that can be received by using this communication channel. The factors respondents considered while making use of certain other channels such as telephone, Short Messaging Service (SMS), online chat rooms and Instant Messaging were firstly convenience or accessibility, and subsequently due to minimal time lag for responses. It appeared those communication channels were preferred for information and knowledge sharing that were easily accessible, able to transmit messages instantly, and cause minimum distortion during the transmission.

Table 8. Factors inhibiting information and knowledge sharing

Inhibiting Factors	N	Mean Score (1 ~ 7)	Std Deviation
Too busy; lack of time	182	5.13	1.577
Lack of depth in relationship	182	5.03	1.338
Students only share with those who share with them	181	4.73	1.471
Limited opportunities for face-to-face interaction with other students	180	4.60	1.440
Lack of avenues to voluntarily share information	180	4.51	1.404
Lack of knowledge sharing culture on the campus	181	4.45	1.451
Fear of providing wrong information	180	4.05	1.481
Fear that others may outperform me in the studies	180	3.75	1.494
Fear of being perceived as a "show-off" person	180	3.60	1.444
Fear that a clash of opinion may spoil relationship	177	3.24	1.455

Factors Inhibiting Knowledge Sharing

The respondents were asked, on a scale of 1 to 7, to identify factors that were likely to hinder information and knowledge sharing among students (Table 8). Two most likely factors identified by them were the lack of time (mean score: 5.13) and lack of depth in relationships (mean score: 5.03). These factors were followed by the perception that students only share knowledge with those who share with them (mean score: 4.73). In addition, the respondents felt that lack of opportunities for face-to-face interaction with other students on campus was another factor inhibiting information and knowledge sharing. On the other hand, factors such as the fear of being perceived as a "show-off" by peers or that a clash of opinion might strain relationships were deemed the least likely to discourage sharing. One respondent pointed out that language could pose a barrier to sharing, especially for international students.

Several earlier studies have also identified somewhat similar factors that impede knowledge sharing such as lack of time; lack of trust and depth in relationship (Wu & Munir, 2010); and lack of knowledge sharing culture (Siakas, Georgiadou & Balstrup, 2010).

Suggestions for Improving Information and Knowledge Sharing

Through an open-ended question, the respondents were asked to suggest measures for encouraging information and knowledge sharing among students. Nine broad categories of measures emerged after the respondents' suggestions were analyzed and related suggestions were grouped together. Some 41 respondents believed that group assignments or projects would be very useful in encouraging students to actively share knowledge with peers (Table 9). Following that, the respondents also thought that a less stressful environment with reduced emphasis on academic competition would be more conducive for information and knowledge sharing to take place. In addition, they felt that concrete measures of encouragement and sharing facilities ought to be put in place by the universities and the lecturers to inculcate a culture of sharing among the students.

CONCLUSION

New approaches to learning put a lot of emphasis on *peer learning* and, therefore, active and voluntary sharing of knowledge is crucial for its success.

Table 9. Suggestions for improving knowledge sharing among students

	Suggestion	No. of Responses
1	Assign group assignments or projects to students	41
2	Place less emphasis on grades or academic outcomes	18
3	Put in place measures to encourage sharing or cultivate a culture of sharing	17
4	Require student to make presentations	15
5	Encourage interaction, communication or discussion among students	15
6	Give recognition or make sharing an academic requirement e.g. award grade	10
7	Help build relationships among students	8
8	Encourage sharing via online facilities	7
9	Provide informal settings to encourage sharing	5

Although on the whole, students in this study exhibited a positive attitude towards information and knowledge sharing, it appeared that certain academic requirements were hindering this vital activity. It was found that students avoid sharing information and knowledge for those assignments, student projects, and academic activities that were to be graded. Probably the intense competition among students to academically outperform others was compelling them to hoard knowledge from their peers. This attitude, if left unchecked, is likely to persist at the workplace which may be aggravated due to intense work pressures and competition among colleagues for better career advancement. It is, therefore, desirable for the academic institutions to reconsider their student assessment policies and procedures to make them less competitive and threatening. However, it is also a fact that instructors need to use some assessment scheme to differentiate students based on their performance. Similarly, if students know that certain academic activity is not to be graded, they are less likely to work hard as well as make the desired level of effort. Therefore, a balanced approach could be to assign more group projects and other team activities. Although competition will not be fully eliminated, as it will still exist among the project groups, the knowledge sharing activity will at least occur within each project

team. In addition, students in this study also clearly indicated that group based assignments and projects would help them share information and knowledge with their peers.

Another barrier to knowledge sharing, as revealed by this study, was the lack of mutual trust and in-depth relationships between students. As a large number of graduate students in Singapore pursue their studies on a part-time basis, they often spend limited time on campus thus there are inadequate opportunities to interact with fellow students. Academic institutions need to provide ample opportunities to these students to socialize and develop cordial relationships which would help promote mutual trust and respect. Once they start regarding their classmates as their learning partners instead of competitors, they are likely to share their ideas and knowledge more frequently.

Though this study has offered some interesting and meaningful insights into knowledge sharing mechanisms of graduate students, some of the findings might be influenced by local culture and the existing education system in Singapore. It would be interesting to conduct a similar study in other countries or regions to identify commonalities and differences. Such studies may also draw pure random samples and use a combination of data collection techniques. I will also be interesting to explore knowledge sharing behavior of full-time, part-time and distance learning students. A longitudinal study can also be conducted to investigate if students continue demonstrating the same knowledge sharing habits and behaviour at their workplace. Similarly, it is also important to highlight here that students' knowledge sharing behavior not necessarily reflects knowledge sharing clusters of the surveyed universities. In addition to students, there are other distinct communities in universities such as professors, researchers, and administrative and management staff and their work situations are often completely different from students. Therefore, the findings of this study cannot be generalized to the whole university community.

REFERENCES

Almahamid, S., Awwad, A., & McAdams, A. C. (2010). Effects of Organizational Agility and Knowledge Sharing on Competitive Advantage: An Empirical Study in Jordan. *International Journal of Management, 27*(3), 387–404.

Alstyne, M. W. V. (2005). Create Colleagues, not Competitors. *Harvard Business Review, 83*(9), 24–25.

Ardichvili, A., Page, V., & Wentling, T. (2003). Motivation and Barriers to Participation in Virtual Knowledge-sharing Communities of Practice. *Journal of Knowledge Management, 7*(1), 64–78. doi:10.1108/13673270310463626

Beitler, M. A., & Mitlacher, L. W. (2007). Information Sharing, Self-directed Learning and its Implications for Workplace Learning: A Comparison of Business Student Attitudes in Germany and the USA. *Journal of Workplace Learning, 19*(8), 526–536. doi:10.1108/13665620710831191

Chia, H. B., Kamdar, D., Nosworthy, G. J., & Chay, Y. W. (2005). *Motivating Knowledge Sharing.* NUS Business School Research Paper Series, RPS#2005-016.

Chiri, K., & Klobas, J. (2010). *Knowledge Sharing and Organisational Enabling Conditions.* Proceedings of the 11th European Conference on Knowledge Management, p246-256. Universidade Lusíada de Vila Nova de Famalicão Portugal.

Chiu, S. H. (2010). Students' Knowledge Resources and Knowledge Sharing in the Design Studio – An Exploratory Study. *International Journal of Technology and Design Education, 20*(1), 27–42. doi:10.1007/s10798-008-9061-9

Choi, S. Y., Lee, H., & Yoo, Y. (2010). The Impact of Information Technology and Transactive Memory Systems on Knowledge Sharing, Application, and Team Performance: A Field Study. *Management Information Systems Quarterly, 34*(4), 855–870.

Chua, A. (2003). Knowledge Sharing: A Game People Play. *Aslib Proceedings, 55*(3), 117–129. doi:10.1108/00012530310472615

Cyr, S., & Choo, C. W. (2010). The Individual and Social Dynamics of Knowledge Sharing: An Exploratory Study. *The Journal of Documentation, 66*(6), 824–846. doi:10.1108/00220411011087832

Davenport, T. H. (1997). *Some Principles of Knowledge Management* (1997). Retrieved on January 21, 2011 from http://www.itmweb.com/essay538.htm.

Educational Broadcasting Corporation. (2004). *What are the Benefits of Cooperative and Collaborative Learning?* Retrieved on January 21, 2011 from http://www.thirteen.org/edonline/concept2class/coopcollab/index_sub3.html

Emmer, E. T., & Gerwels, M. C. (2002). Cooperative Learning in Elementary Classrooms: Teaching Practices and Lesson Characteristics. *The Elementary School Journal, 103*(1), 75–92. doi:10.1086/499716

Eveleth, L. B., Eveleth, D. M., & Sarker, S. (2005). An Emerging On-line "Third Place" for Information Systems (IS) Students: Some Preliminary Observations. *Journal of Information Systems Education, 16*(4), 465–475.

Giacoppo, A. S. (2008). Integrating Social Software into a Student Teacher Education Program: Enabling Discourse, Knowledge Sharing, and Development in a Community of Learning. *Dissertation Abstracts International Section A: Humanities and Social Sciences, 68*(9-A), 3811.

Graff, M. (2006). The Importance of Online Community in Student Academic Performance. *Electronic Journal of e-Learning, 4*(2), 127-131.

Grantham, D. (2005). *Understanding Student Learning Styles and Theories of Learning.* Retrieved on January 21, 2011 from: www.ukcle. ac.uk/resources/postgraduate/grantham2.html.

He, J. (2010). Examining Factors that Affect Knowledge Sharing and Students' Attitude toward their Learning Experience within Virtual Teams. *Dissertation Abstracts International Section A: Humanities and Social Sciences, 71*(3A), 925.

Krentler, K. A., & Flurry, L. A. W. (2005). Does Technology Enhance Actual Student Learning? The Case of Online Discussion Boards. *Journal of Education for Business, 80*(6), 316–321. doi:10.3200/JOEB.80.6.316-321

Ma, W. W. K., & Yuen, A. H. K. (2011). Understanding Online Knowledge Sharing: An Interpersonal Relationship Perspective. *Computers & Education, 56*(1), 210–219. doi:10.1016/j.compedu.2010.08.004

Majid, S., & Kowtha, R. (2008). *Utilizing Environmental Knowledge for Competitive Advantage.* International Conference on Information Resources Management (Conf-IMR), 18-20 May, 2008: Niagara Falls, Canada.

Majid, S., & Mokhtar, I. A. (2007). *From Virtual to Real Discourse: Relating Online Student Participation and their Academic Performance.* 3rd International Conference on Open and Online Learning (ICOOL), 11-14 June, 2007: Penang, Malaysia.

Majid, S., & Tina, R. R. (2009). *Perceptions of LIS Graduate Students of Peer Learning.* Asia-Pacific Conference on Library & Information Education and Practice (A-LIEP): Preparing Information professional for International Collaboration, 6-8 March 2009, Japan.

Majid, S., & Wey, S. M. (2009). Perceptions and Knowledge Sharing Practices of Graduate Students in Singapore. *International Journal of Knowledge Management, 5*(2), 21–32. doi:10.4018/jkm.2009040102

Majid, S., & Yuen, T. J. (2006). Information and Knowledge Sharing by Undergraduate Students in Singapore. In M.K. Pour (ed.), *IRMA International Conference: Proceedings of the 17th IRMA International Conference.* Hershey, PA: Idea Group Publishing.

Mäkelä, K., & Brewster, C. (2009). Interunit Interaction Contexts, Interpersonal Social Capital, and the Differing Levels of Knowledge Sharing. *Human Resource Management, 48*(4), 591–613. doi:10.1002/hrm.20300

Neto, M., & Correia, A. M. (2009). *BIWiki – Using a Business Intelligence Wiki to Form a Virtual Community of Practice for Portuguese Master's students.* Proceedings of the 10th European Conference on Knowledge Management, 570-577. Università Degli Studi Di Padova, Vicenza, Italy.

Siakas, K. V., Georgiadou, E., & Balstrup, B. (2010). Cultural Impacts on Knowledge Sharing: Empirical Data from EU Project Collaboration. *The Journal of Information & Knowledge Management Systems, 40*(3/4), 376–389.

Skyrme, D. J. (2002). *The 3Cs of Knowledge Sharing: Culture, Competition and Commitment.* Retrieved on January 21, 2011 from: http://www.skyrme.com/updates/u64_f1.htm.

Smith, H. A., & McKeen, J. D. (2003). *Instilling a Knowledge-sharing Culture.* Retrieved on January 21, 2011 from: http://business.queensu.ca/centres/monieson/docs/working/working_03-11.pdf.

Sum, C., Kow, L. S., & Chen, C. (2004). A Taxonomy of Operations Strategies of High Performing Small and Medium Enterprises in Singapore. *International Journal of Operations & Production Management, 24*(3/4), 321–345. doi:10.1108/01443570410519051

Wagner, C., & Bolloju, N. (2005). Supporting Knowledge Management in Organizations with Conversational Technologies: Discussion Forums, Weblogs, and Wikis. *Journal of Database Management, 16*(2), 1–8.

Wolfe, C., & Loraas, T. (2008). Knowledge Sharing: The Effects of Incentives, Environment, and Person. *Journal of Information Systems, 22*(2), 53–76. doi:10.2308/jis.2008.22.2.53

Wu, W., & Munir, S. B. (2010). Why Should I Share? Examining Consumers' Motives and Trust on Knowledge Sharing. *Journal of Computer Information Systems, 50*(4), 11–19.

Zhang, Q., Chintakovid, T., Sun, X., Ge, Y., & Zhang, K. (2006). Saving Face or Sharing Personal Information? A Cross-cultural Study on Knowledge Sharing. *Journal of Information & Knowledge Management, 5*(1), 73–79. doi:10.1142/S0219649206001335

Zhou, Y. R., Knoke, D., & Sakamoto, I. (2010). Rethinking Silence in the Classroom: Chinese Students' Experiences of Sharing Indigenous Knowledge. *International Journal of Inclusive Education, 9*(3), 287–311. doi:10.1080/13603110500075180

Chapter 9
Cocreating Corporate Knowledge with a Wiki

Joseph A. Meloche
University of Wollongong, Australia

Helen Hasan
University of Wollongong, Australia

David Willis
BlueScope Steel Research, Australia

Charmaine C. Pfaff
University of Wollongong, Australia

Yan Qi
University of Wollongong, Australia

ABSTRACT

Wikis have a growing reputation on the open Internet for producing evolving stores of shared knowledge. However, such democratic systems are often treated with suspicion within corporations for management, legal, social, and other reasons. This article describes a field study of a corporate Wiki that has been developed to capture, and make available, organisational knowledge in a large manufacturing company as an initiative of their Knowledge Management (KM) program. As this approach to KM is a controversial and rapidly changing phenomenon, a Q Methodology research approach was selected to uncover employees' subjective attitudes to the Wiki. Activity Theory was used to provide a deeper interpretation of the findings of the Q-study. The results are enabling the firm to more fully exploit the potential of the Wiki as a ubiquitous tool for successful tacit and explicit knowledge management as more employees are encouraged to participate in a process of cocreating the store of corporate knowledge. The article also demonstrates how meaningful and rigorous research on this new democratic direction of corporate KM should continue.

DOI: 10.4018/978-1-60960-555-1.ch009

INTRODUCTION

The Internet, through the use of social technologies such as Wikis, is enabling data, information, and knowledge to have a ubiquitous quality where people take for granted their ability and right to access, and contribute to, the global knowledge repository that is the World Wide Web. This is transforming the knowledge culture from one where control rests with established authority and power to one where knowledge repositories continually evolve being created and maintained by society as a whole. Within corporations, knowledge management (KM) initiatives strive to collect organisational knowledge to be available as a strategic resource, but corporate cultures are often not well disposed to the sharing of knowledge in the open, participatory manner afforded by a Wiki (Warne, Hasan, & Ali, 2005). Organisational KM initiatives usually incorporate the development of formal knowledge management systems (KMS) that support employees in regard to knowledge processes (Jennex, 2005). Some enlightened, learning organisations (Senge, 1990) are now seeking the capability to cocreate such open knowledge repositories where all workers are motivated and empowered to take responsibility for their own KM processes. Emerging from the social arena into the corporation, the Wiki is, however, bound to challenge management authority by attempting to engage the knowledge worker in a more participatory KM capability and environment. Even with traditional KMS, it has often been difficult to determine what factors contribute to their success and to know that they have succeeded (Jennex & Olfman, 2005). As a new, emerging phenomenon, corporate Wikis pose an even greater challenge in this regard.

This article critically examines the prospects for Wiki technology to be a tool to successfully support a contemporary, yet challenging, view of corporate KM that is participatory, holistic, collective, and contextual. The research described here involved a field study of a pioneering case where a corporate Wiki was developed to capture, and make available, organisational knowledge in a large manufacturing company as an initiative of their KM program. The study aimed to tease out the range of attitudes of employees to the Wiki and determined perceptions of Wiki attributes that influenced their willingness to contribute to it. Due to the ground-breaking nature of the topic and this case, innovative research techniques were adopted that would allow issues to emerge from the participant employees, rather than predetermined by the researchers. The results of the data analysis are re-interpreted in terms of critical success factors (CSF) or KMS success.

The article begins with an overview of changing user perceptions of KM through the use of a Wiki, and creating receptive environments for a Wiki in organisations. The Wiki is defined and lessons from unsuccessful corporate Wiki projects are presented. The context of the field study of the Wiki implementation is introduced together with an outline and justification of the Q methodology approach adopted for the data collection of the study. Activity Theory is also introduced as a richer framework for understanding the topic. Findings from the Q-study on employee attitudes to the Wiki are presented and Activity Theory is then used to interpret them. The results of this analysis and their implication for an expanded use of the Wiki are discussed.

BACKGROUND

Knowledge and Wikis

A Wiki is an open author system for a conjoined construction and maintenance of Web sites (Fuchs-Kittowsk & Köhler, 2002). Technically, a Wiki is a collection of interlinked HTML Web pages and has cross links between internal pages where each page can be edited, keeping a complete record of such changes. Thus a Wiki can be accessed from any Web browser and no other special tools are needed to create and edit existing pages. Any change can be easily reverted to any of its previous states. A working definition of a Wiki is an evolving knowledge repository where users are encouraged to make additions to this repository by adding new documents or working on existing ones (Pfaff & Hasan, 2006a). It opens up ownership, and responsibility for, the store of record knowledge to all those who have access to it. The implications of this can be felt in legal, social, and cultural areas.

In many cases, organisations try to "manage knowledge" by organising and categorising large volumes of information so that it can be easily retrieved (Hildreth & Kimble, 2002). However, research indicates that this may be detrimental because knowledge by its very nature cannot be "managed," in the traditional sense (Hart & Warne, 2005). Organisations often implement KM programs by adopting a well-structured and ordered approach that must be aligned with current organisational goals (Maholtra, 2004). There are assumptions that all relevant knowledge, including that which is tacit, can be stored in carefully designed computerised databases, software programs, and institutionalised rules and practices (Maholtra, 2004). The process of building these structured knowledge repositories has been criticised as being time-consuming, laborious, and costly (Lam & Chua, 2005). Viewed as a superficial implement of management, official corporate knowledge repositories are often not kept up-to-date and are rarely accessed when real knowledge is sought (Lam & Chua, 2005).

In contrast, a Wiki transforms users into active participants receiving and creating ubiquitous knowledge. Wiki technology can take advantage of the collaborative efforts of all members of the organisation to create an effective library of organisational knowledge. Organisational knowledge is equated with the collective wisdom of the organisation when this knowledge is collected and shared (Rich & Duchessi, 2000). The Wiki challenges holders of opposing viewpoints to build consensus so that collective knowledge is created and innovative work can be done. Users can create knowledge collaboratively in groups or through individual efforts and disseminate knowledge anywhere and anytime. Weiser (1993) argues that users live through their practices and tacit knowledge so that the most powerful things are those that are effectively invisible in use. By invisibility, Weiser means that the tool does not intrude on human consciousness but the focus is on the task and not the tool. The challenge is making the invisibility visible through the study of human factors and the user interface (Linger & Warne, 2001). It is the invisible work of finding, interpreting, and connecting relevant pieces of information, negotiating meanings and eliciting knowledge in conversations with others, creating new ideas and using them to come up with a final product, which occurs in the head or as part of communication or doing work (Efimova, 2004), that constitutes as knowledge work. The creators and users of such knowledge are known as knowledge workers.

Traditionally the main elements of computer-based systems in organisations are data and information (Alavi & Leidner, 2001). On the contrary, knowledge, now recognised as a critical organisational resource (Kelloway & Barling, 2000), is the province of people. It makes sense to bring the capability of social technologies to play in organisational KM initiatives because social technologies such as Wikis support the concept of knowledge as the *social practice of knowing*, where knowledge is considered to be embedded in a community rather than just in one individual (Boyd, 2006). A Wiki can become a *peer production information commons* (Benkler, 2006) functioning as common spaces where people can share experiences and have unanticipated, unchosen exposures to the ideas of other people. Moreover, due to the association of knowledge with people, it seems sensible to view KMS as an advanced information systems (IS) that are essentially sociotechnical in nature (Hasan & Crawford, 2007). A considerable

Table 1. Twelve CSF for KMS success (Jennex et al., 2008)

A knowledge strategy that identifies users, sources, processes, storage strategy, knowledge, and links to knowledge
Motivation and commitment of users including incentives and training
Integrated technical infrastructure, including networks, repositories, computers, software, and KMS experts
An organisational culture and structure that supports learning and the sharing and use of knowledge
A common enterprise-side knowledge structures that is clearly articulated and easily understood.
Senior management support including allocation of resources leadership and training
Learning organisation
The KMS has a clear goal and purpose
Measures are established to assess the impacts of the KMS and use of knowledge, as well as verification that the right knowledge is being captured
The search, retrieval, and visualisation functions of the KMS support facilitated use of knowledge
Work processes are designed that incorporate knowledge capture and use
Knowledge is secure/protected

body of knowledge has been created over the past few decades on IS development and success in organisations (e.g., Klein & Hirschheim, in press) that can be applied to KMS.

The situation with KMS is generally more complex than it is with IS. IS development is typically top-down, expensive, and controlled by formal methodologies and procedures, where managers set specific performance targets and are looking for a measurable return on their substantial investment within a few years (Cleetus, Cascaval, & Matsuzaki, 1996). While some traditional KMS may be created this way, this is certainly not the case with the Wiki project we have studied. According to the Australian Standard (AS5037, 2005), KM success is determined indirectly by improvement in organisational performance, which can be difficult to attribute directly to the KMS as other factors could be involved. While recognising this, considerable progress has been made in adapting IS success models to one for KMS success (Jennex & Olfman, 2006). This has led toward a definition (Jennex, Smolnik, & Croasdell, 2007) and measures of KM and KMS success (Jennex, Smolnik, & Croasdell, 2008). Table 1 contains a list of 12 CSF that have been identified to assist with the analysis of KM/KMS

success dimensions (Jennex et al., 2008). These appear to be relevant to the corporate Wiki as a KMS and this list provides a dimension against which results of this study of employee attitudes to their Wiki can be reviewed.

Previous Wiki Research

In previous research (author's references removed for reviewing), we have reported corporate Wiki projects that were unsuccessful. This research identified management, social, and legal issues that mitigate against the easy uptake of Wikis in corporations. The informal network approach that is currently favoured in a Wiki implies a loss of central management control of corporate knowledge and changes to organisational structure and culture (Pfaff & Hasan, 2006b). The Wiki is described as a "social software" (Swisher, 2004), implying that there are social factors that must undergo some changes before the Wiki will be accepted to improve the organisation's knowledge management. Legal issues concerning rights to intellectual property and possible libellous material see a Wiki as a risky endeavour. Yahoo!, Disney, SAP, and Motorola have been cited in literature as having successfully used corporate Wikis to reap the benefits of economic savings, increased efficiency in understanding the elements of knowledge work, and easy dissemination of knowledge to disconnected teams (Gonzalez-Reinhart, 2005; Pfaff & Hasan, 2006b).

There are some informal and networked enterprises where flexible participatory modes of information and knowledge management are ubiquitous (e.g., O'Brien & Ali, 2006). The adaptability and leaderless development capability of the Wiki makes it eminently suitable as a knowledge repository in such enterprises, as has been shown emergency situations (Murphy & Jennex, 2006a, 2006b; Raman, Ryan, & Olfman, 2006). Such projects show how, in contrast to many organisational IS and KMS, Wikis can be acquired with low cost software and bottom up design where its structure and content are set up through the ongoing efforts of users (Pfaff & Hasan, 2006a).

Current Research

In this article, we report the findings of an exploratory field study of a corporate Wiki called a Technology Encyclopaedia (TE) that has been developed and implemented to capture organisational knowledge for a large manufacturing company and make it widely available as an initiative of their Knowledge Management (KM) program. We sought to employ techniques for data collection and analysis that would not preclude issues to emerge in the study that were not anticipated by the researchers. Consequently, Q Methodology and Activity Theory are employed as research tools because of their suitability for this purpose. They are described in the following sections of the article in sufficient detail so that their use in the data collection, analysis, and interpretation of the study can be understood.

Q Methodology consists of procedures for data collection and analysis with the ability to reveal communicative subjectivity, giving a voice to the understandings of what are the key issues and letting the people involved share their views and opinions. Q Methodology also allows the researchers to further explore and understand the experiences of participants in the study and expand on knowledge of their behaviours and attitudes (Brown, 1986). A Q Methodology research approach was therefore selected to uncover employees' subjective attitudes to the TE so that the firm could more fully exploit its potential as a ubiquitous tool for tacit KM.

Activity Theory provides a solid theoretical basis for understanding human experience through the discovery and observation of how humans develop through the use and creation of tools within their culture. According to Kaptelinin and Nardi (1997), it is really a "set of conceptual principles that constitute a general conceptual system, rather than a highly predictive theory." Activity Theory can, however, be quite a practical holistic way of analysing a complex situation as seems to be the case in this study. Activity, that is, what people do, is the basic unit of analysis, and is mediated through the use of tools. The TE is the tool, although significant; is not neutral, but an integral part of the activity. In our research, the process of identifying and revealing the aspects of the activities mediated by the TE add to the findings from the data analysis of the Q-study.

Q Methodology

Q Methodology was selected as a technique for data collection and analysis to better understand how Wiki technology can contribute to the area of KM by drawing out and examining the views of TE users. As the corporate Wiki is an emergent technology having complex ramifications that are not yet well understood, this approach can help to expose issues, which may otherwise be invisible. Q Methodology has been frequently associated with quantitative forms of analysis due to its involvement with factor analysis of Q-sort technique. However it is important to note that the Q Methodology uncovers the *range of views,* such

Figure 1. A Q sort triangle for ranking of the statement if there were a sample of 11

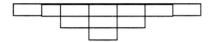

as the users' subjective views, attitudes, opinions, understandings, and experiences on a specific topic of investigation, as opposed to most methods that offer one composite view. The following will describe the concourse, the sorting procedure, and the analysis of the results from the sort process that form the Q Methodology.

A Q study normally starts with the concourse, which involves having the participants provide their thoughts and views. This activity of statement generation may not occur in a single session but may transpire over time or amongst various groups, but always on the same topics. A Q sample of 30 to 50 individuals has the ability to produce meaningful results, that is, provide an accurate picture of the range of views on a topic (McKeown & Thomas, 1988).

The Q sort involves eliciting the individual views of participants by choosing amongst the statements called a Q sample, and demonstrating the extent of their agreement or disagreement with them. For example they may be instructed as follows:

You are being asked to sort statements in accordance with your degree of concurrence/agreement with the statements where +4 is high agreement and –4 is high disagreement and the scales between –4 and +4 reflect shades/levels of agreement. You will find the statements on a pack of cards that will be given to you. You are asked to sort the cards in accordance with the rating given to each card. The largest number of statements will be placed in the centre and the least amount of statements at each extreme point. Figure 1 is similar to the sample form that you will need to record your ranking of the statements. (Meloche & Crawford, 1998)

The analysis stage occurs when all participants have completed the individual sorting process. The Q Sorts are statistically analysed by any of the standard Q factor analysis computer programs to find correlations and identify factors that are common to the sorts of several individuals (Stephenson, 1953). The results contain clusters of those individuals who appear to hold similar views in their ranking of the statements. Each of these clusters may reveal a distinct activity for which the TE is being used.

Activity Theory

Once clusters of like-minded participants are determined in the Q-study, we have found that a deeper understanding of these clusters can be made if each is interpreted as an activity using the language and framework of Activity Theory.

The Cultural-Historical Activity Theory is a social-psychological theory that has its roots in the work of the Russian psychologist Vygotsky during the first half of the 20th century. Vygotsky (1997) saw human activity as quite distinct from that of nonhuman entities in that it is mediated by tools, the most significant of which is language. Vygotsky defined human activity as a dialectic relationship between subject and object, simply a person or group of people, working at something. He also proposed that all human activity is purposeful, is carried out through the use of tools and is essentially social. Vygotsky believed that tools play a mediating role in all human activities and mental processes.

To be able to analyse complex interactions and relationships, Engeström (1987) proposed a research framework with an activity system as the unit of analysis. This is represented in the triangle shown in Figure 2, which has been widely used in social science research over the last 2 decades (Hasan, 2001). Here the core of an activity is a dialectic relationship between subject (human) and object (purpose) where the subject can be individual or collective, as in a group or

Figure 2. Engeström's (1987) activity theory

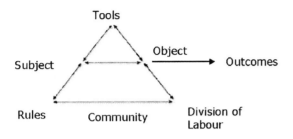

team working on a common project. The subject-object relationship, which defines the activity, is mediated by tools and community. Tools which mediate activities can be physical, that is, technica, or psychological such as language, ideas, and business models. This is a two-way concept of mediation where the capability and availability of tools mediates what is able to be done and tools, in turn, evolve to hold the historical knowledge of how the communities behaves and is organised.

This is particularly powerful when the tools are computer-based. Engeström (1987) proposed that the formal, or informal, rules and division of labour of the community, in which the activity occurs, also dynamically mediate the subject-object relationship. Engeström (1987) suggests that it is the internal tensions and contradictions of such an activity system, which includes both historical continuity and locally situated contingency that are the motive for change and development.

In research, there are normally two sets of activities of interest namely those of the researchers and those of the situation being studied. While traditional scientific research is built on objectivity where there is assumed to be no influence of the researchers on the object of the study, there is an equally valid approach to research which focuses on subjectivity. Here the researchers recognised that the activities of the researcher and the situation being studied impact on each other to mutual advantage. In this approach Q Methodology and Activity Theory come together to provide ap-

propriate techniques for conducting the research and interpreting the results.

Activity Theory imposes the following concepts on the design, conduct, and interpretation of the research activity for which Q Methodology is a tool:

- The *holistic* nature of the object of study, that is, in the activities involving the TE, the subjects (employees), the tool (TE), and the culture of the work community are all inter-related and any attempt to study them individually may be misleading.
- All human activity is driven by some *purpose* but people always have a variety of *motives* for doing what they do, some personal and some for the common good.
- Human activity is *dynamic* and is always changing. What works one day may not work the next. Opinions and motives change.
- Human activity is always influenced by the *context* in which it takes place. The Concourse is quite public yet the sorts can be a private activity.

It is always useful to explicitly identify the activities of the study. In this case there are at least four:

- The activity of contributing to the TE which is the focus of the Q-study
- The activity of accessing and using the content of the TE, its main purpose
- The researchers' activity in conducting the study
- (for some employees) Participating in the study

The key activity of accessing and using the content of the TE can be generalised to the activity of knowledge work as depicted in the Activity Theory Triangle of Figure 3.

Figure 3. The activity triangle of Figure 2 labelled for the activity of knowledge work

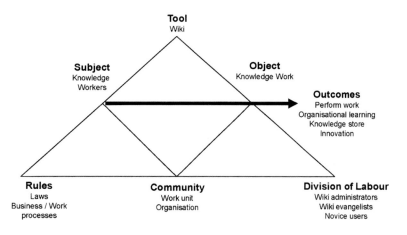

Table 2. Categories of statements as determined by the researchers responding to the question: "What would (from your point of view) help you to contribute to the TE?"

Category Type	Number	Example Statement
Usefulness	11	If I could see tangible benefits to customers
Ongoing	2	Knowing that this type of system is going to be around " for the long haul" and not be a "flavour of the month"
Acknowledgement	10	If contributions were recognised and rewarded
Time	2	If I had the time to contribute
Ease of Use	12	If I could easily get attachments in right format before entering
Security	5	If confidentiality issues are resolved
Mainstream	5	If it was universally regarded as a necessary job function
Support	6	(39) If it had a specialist entry person/editor
Exposure to Risk	4	(16) If I knew it would not make me redundant

The Wiki Case Study

This research project was initiated by the manager of the unit where the TE is implemented and who is its main sponsor. He approached the other authors, researchers of KM at the local university, to conduct a study of employee attitudes in contributing to the TE in order to suggest interventions that might improve their involvement.

The Concourse

A Concourse was held with a selected group of employees at their worksite. It consisted of a general discussion with the members of the research team and the client representative on what they would like or expect of a TE. Using ZING Technology, which is a group decision support tool. Participants were asked to supply their ideas for the topic as brief statements. A total of 57 statements were collected and researchers organised these statements into categories that included usefulness, ongoing, acknowledgement, time, ease of use, security, mainstream, support, and exposure to risk (Table 2). These categories helped in the subsequent analysis but were not shown to the individuals who participated in the sort.

*Table 3. 18 sorts in 3 factors * (Reflected Negative Factor)*

	Interpreted as:	Sorts per Factor
1	Corporate Knowledge Worker (CKW)	7
2	CKW with Customer Focus *	4
3	Main Stream View *	7

The Sort

The statements generated by the Concourse concerned "What would (from your point of view) help you to contribute to the TE?" and individuals sorted the statements in accordance with the instructions "the extent to which you agree or disagree with the statements." A "forced sort" methodology was applied where each statement need to be placed in one of the provided squares on the Q Grid. The process involves correlation and by-person factor analysis where the analysis is performed not by variables, such as traits, or statements, but rather by persons, where people correlate to others with similar views based upon their sorts. The three factors (opinion types with reference to contributing to the TE) were titled as shown in Table 3.

The following section includes the high agree (positive) and the high disagree (negative) statements from each of the Factors and the respective Factor scores, which indicate the relative level of the statements. The aim is two fold: first, to see the continuality among the high and positive statements: and second, to compare the prior with the high negative statements and the contrast between them. This comparison is done with each of the Factors in turn so as to allow for a more rigorous examination of the Factors, both individually and in comparison with each other.

Factor 1: Corporate Knowledge Worker (CKW)

For Factor 1, the 10 statements given the highest weighting are shown in Table 4.

For Factor 1, the ten statements given the lowest weighting are shown in Table 5.

Factor 1 contains the statements most aligned with a good corporate knowledge worker—concerned with the value and usability of the TE.

The main concern of the individuals is the ongoing use/status/reliability of the TE. The other positive statements reflect a desire for ease of use and for client feedback. The negative statements indicate that CKWs are not concerned about acknowledgement, awards, and job security.

Factor 2: Reflected (Negative Factor) CKW with Customer Focus

The following statements are the strongest agreement statements for Factor 2; the ones following these are the strongest disagreement statements. For Factor 2, the nine statements given the highest weighting are shown in Table 6.

For Factor 2, the nine statements given the lowest weighting are shown in Table 7. Factor 2 also reflects the views of the CKW and its focus on customers. There is concern and a desire for assurance, that confidentiality issues will be resolved and that the objectives be made clear, that is, tangible benefits of the TE. The negative statements showed a disregard for additional rewards or acknowledgement. They were not concerned with acknowledgement, publicity, or any possible negative impact on their job security.

Factor 3: Negative Factor—Main Stream View

For Factor 3, the five statements given the highest weighting are shown in Table 8.

For Factor 3, the three statements of Table 9 were given the lowest weighting:

Table 4. Factor 1: strongly agree statements

High Positive Statement	Z-Value	Category
If I thought the system was not going to be redundant in couple of years	2.064	Ongoing
If its usefulness was apparent	1.595	Usefulness
If I could see tangible benefits to customers	1.539	Usefulness
If it was of more value	1.520	Usefulness
If I had the time to contribute	1.520	Time
Knowing that this type of system is going to be around "for the long haul" and not be a "flavour of the month"	1.388	Ongoing
If the system allowed direct entry of existing data without the need to re-format	1.351	Ease of use
If I thought someone was going to read what I wrote	1.295	Usefulness
If it accepted dot points/not essay	1.051	Ease of use
If I could easily get attachments in right format before entering	1.051	Ease of use

Table 5. Factor 1: strongly disagree statements

High Negative Statement	Z-Value	Category
If I knew it would not make me redundant	-1.013	Exposure to Risk
If contributions were recognised and rewarded	-1.032	Acknowledgement
If it had an improved authentication process	-1.220	Security
If contributions were tracked to me so that my boss can see my contributions	-1.257	Acknowledgement
Knowing who was reading it	-1.370	Acknowledgement
If it provided the ability to make anonymous entries	-1.426	Exposure to Risk
If I could use it in focus groups with limited team members	-1.539	Security
If there was a Wiki award	-1.782	Acknowledgement
If guys in the control room could browse it in the middle of the night	-1.895	Usefulness
If there was a Wiki newsletter	-2.008	Acknowledgement

Table 6. Factor 2: strongly agree statements

High Positive Statements	Z-Value	Category
If it gave something back to the organisation	1.995	Usefulness
If I had the time to contribute	1.448	Time
If the system captured info requests—so you could write on a topic for a known audience.	1.408	Support
If confidentiality issues are resolved	1.215	Security
If customers could access the information	1.201	Usefulness
If it was of more value	1.188	Usefulness
If I could see tangible benefits to customers	1.161	Usefulness
If the objectives was made clear	1.128	Usefulness
If I thought the information was useful to the users	1.121	Usefulness

Table 7. Factor 2: strongly disagree statements

High Negative Statements	Z-Value	Category
If I was not limited by my ability to contribute	-1.101	Exposure to Risk
If I knew it would not make me redundant	-1.188	Exposure to Risk
Having people who could capture information for me as its produced	-1.368	Support
If it had a specialist entry person/editor	-1.448	Support
If I thought the system was not going to be redundant in a couple of years	-1.415	Ongoing
If it provided the ability to make anonymous entries	-1.502	Exposure to Risk
If it was linked to STI (an incentive scheme)	-1.515	Acknowledgement
If there was a Wiki newsletter	-1.949	Acknowledgement
If there was a Wiki award	-2.276	Acknowledgement

Table 8. Factor 3: strongly agree statements

High Positive Statements (Reflected)	Z-Value	Category
If I had the time to contribute	1.752	Time
If it was universally regarded as a necessary job function	1.700	Mainstream
If it was linked to STI	1.607	Acknowledgement
If there was a higher level of commitment to Wiki from management	1.246	Mainstream
Knowing that this type of system is going to be around "for the long haul" and not be a "flavour of the month"	1.129	Ongoing

Table 9. Factor 3: strongly disagree statements

High Negative Statement (Reflected)	Z-Values	Category
If I thought that customers wanted information added as part of their project	-1.002	Usefulness
If it provided the ability to make anonymous entries	-1.433	Exposure to Risk
If I knew it would not make me redundant	-1.677	Exposure to Risk

Factor 3 reflects the views of those who want the TE to be "mainstream" and acknowledged as an ongoing part of their work. It contains the individuals whose statements are both concerned about their status, how they will be acknowledged and whether the TE will fully supported by management. Note, however, that the statement "If it was linked to STI" could be a surrogate for mainstream rather than a concern about acknowledgement and reward since STI job goals are always assigned in key performance areas. They are not concerned with being made redundant or being able to make anonymous entries.

ANALYSIS OF THE RESULTS

The Factors as Revealed from the Q-Study

The study revealed the following three factors representing clusters of participants with similar opinions.

Factor 1: This Factor consists of individuals whose statements are most aligned with a progressive and dedicated "corporate knowledge worker." They are concerned with how useful the TE is for knowledge sharing and expect that it is easy to use. It is interesting to note that CKWs in this particular organisation are not concerned with acknowledgement, which goes against the assumed innate need by workers for recognition (Pfaff & Hasan, 2006a) This defies Wiki critics who have pointed that a disadvantage of the Wiki is that there is no recognition of authorship because pages can be freely written or edited by anybody. Although this group of workers may not all be young workers, people on this Factor exhibit characteristics typical of "Gen Y," the generation that has grown up in the digital age. For them it is natural and rewarding to share information and knowledge using new social technologies on the Internet (Li & Bernoff, 2008). They do this at home so expect to do so at work as a normal part of what they do.

Factor 2: The people who make up this Factor, like those in Factor 1, are concerned with the value and its usefulness of the TE. However the CKWs on this factor also have a strong customer focus in their selection of "usefulness" statements. The workers on Factor 2 are willing to share knowledge not because it is natural but because it has the potential to improve their service to customers. The openness of the Wiki invites opportunities for improvement so that coordination and corporate learning across product groups and departments will become easier. The usefulness of the Wiki depends on its CKWs to contribute and maintain this growing repository of knowledge in the organisation. In response to CKWs concerns about assurance and confidentiality issues, it is assumed that management hires competent employees, and thus any inaccurate entries will either be corrected voluntarily by the original contributor, or by others. Qualified peers will be responsible for information quality and for acquiring information with a strong customer focus. The Wiki is, therefore, an information repository whose relevance and accuracy undergoes continuous peer review.

Factor 3: People in Factor 3 are concerned with how mainstream the TE is. They currently see it as experimental and something extra to do. As everyone at work is time poor, these workers would do their bit to maintain the Wiki content if management directed that this should be a component of the central organisational business process and a recognised part of their job. They are also not comfortable with the free-form nature of the Wiki and so they would also like someone to be responsible for specifying the type of content that it is intended to contain. For instance, reports, reference articles, and other useful information pertaining to their research and projects could be made available on the Wiki so that the Wiki will "write itself." They would like the Wiki to be an information commons where project managers could include regular updated information of their projects on the Wiki and encourage workers to make it part of their ongoing work routine to put up new reports and edit old entries to update the data. Another concern of these workers is whether the TE will be always be fully supported by management.

Interpretation as Activities

As understood in Activity Theory, human activity is a dialectic relationship between subject (a person or people) and the object of work (which includes its purpose) or, in other words, activity provides a holistic unit of analysis for people doing things together. Ostensibly the use of the TE to store information could be considered one activity, namely the employees (the subjects) creating a store of corporate knowledge (the object), and this almost certainly reflects the view of organisational management. However, the factors identified by the Q-study could be considered to reveal three separate activities, each with a different object or purpose and undertaken by a different cluster of employees as follows.

Figure 4. The activity triangle for knowledge work with a customer focus (Factor 2)

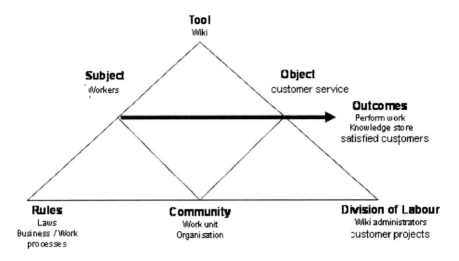

The Activity of Factor 1: CKWs are subjects engaged in the activity of knowledge sharing for its own sake (i.e., knowledge sharing is the object of the activity). They are motivated by the capability and open form of the Wiki. These CKWs use the TE in an informal and interactive way. They may even spend, or even waste, too much time on this activity and enter content without consideration of its relevance or importance. They may not be careful about the spelling and grammar of their entries and be more interested in sharing their knowledge than setting up a well structured knowledge repository for practical access and application. An outcome of their activity will however be increased content in the TE, much of which could be valuable to the organisation. This is consistent with the representation of the activity of knowledge work depicted in Figure 3.

The Activity of Factor 2: These CKWs are subjects engaged in the activity of creating a knowledge store (a concrete object) that will improve customer service the main motive of the activity as shown in Figure 4. These subjects are motivated to create a useful resource for the organisation so will probably give time and effort to the structure of TE, making it easy to retrieve useful knowledge, and they will be more careful about the standard of English. They will only put up what they think would be useful and may ignore other content that they believe does not do this but may have other value.

The Activity of Factor 3: These traditional workers are subjects engaged in the activity for which they were employed, as mandated by management, to conduct research and development for the company. This is their normal work activity and determines their motive for using the TE as shown in Figure 5. They do not give much credence to the usefulness of the TE content but would make entries if this were made a part of their job description. They would probably spend time making sure they did not put up anything that was controversial or did not look right as they would be conscious of doing the right thing as determined by management. The Wiki would not be a work tool that came easily to them.

As a knowledge repository, the TE will become much more valuable to the company as more people contribute more useful content. So one of the expected outcomes of our research activities was that it would encourage more people to see its value and purpose, and hence they would make more entries. This outcome would be more likely if management understood that the activities

Figure 5. The activity triangle for the mainstream workers of Factor 3

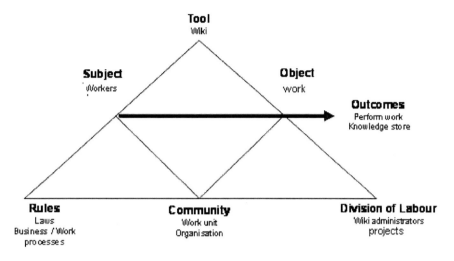

of the subjects on the different Factors have different motives and perceived purpose. At the same time they should acknowledge that this is not a value judgment that any of these activities are any better or worse that any other. They do, however, need to be considered separately by a manager wanting to increase employee contribution. As the different type and form of content from different activities may not sit well with others, there may need to be separate spaces in the TE for each of the activities. The interactive discussion from activity 1 needs to be separated from structured content of activity 2 and from activity 3 to decide where more formal content (project reports, minutes of meetings etc) goes—in the TE or just as lists or links.

A Review of the KMS Critical Success Factors

The study of the TE has focussed on the activities through which knowledge workers make contributions to a corporate Wiki. The findings of the study not only add to our understanding of KMS in general but also demonstrate some aspects of Wikis that distinguish them from more traditional organisational systems. There is less tangible investment of resources in a Wiki, with little expenditure on the software and the initial design leaving users to develop the content and structure. There may, however, be a greater commitment of intangible resource in changes to organisational culture. Table 1 contains a list of CSF developed for traditional KMS. In Table 10, we indicate how these may need some expansion or revision for the case of corporate Wikis based on our research.

CONCLUSION

As the impending retirement of Baby Boomers looms closer, the retention of corporate knowledge becomes more crucial. The path to decentralisation of IS, and hence KMS, control is seen as a pragmatic, step-by-step approach, which can achieve its aim only in the long run. The Wiki is in line with such a pragmatic approach to the incremental evolution of corporate KM. It is in the management's interest to support the Wiki as a KMS because the Wiki will be maintained by CKWs and acquire and disseminate "living knowledge." For future sustainability and a demonstration of management support, corporate incentives should be given so that the new generation of employees

Table 10. The KMS CSFs of Table 1 augmented with findings from the Wiki study

KMS CSF	Comments regarding Corporate Wikis
A knowledge strategy that identifies users, sources, processes, storage strategy, knowledge, and links to knowledge	Still important but allow for emergence of these elements
Motivation and commitment of users including incentives and training	Even more critical with a Wiki because of its participatory nature
Integrated technical infrastructure, including networks, repositories, computers, software, and KMS experts	A Wiki encourages links and references to other knowledge sources
An organisational culture and structure that supports learning and the sharing and use of knowledge	Critical for success with a Wiki where management must allow democratisation of corporate knowledge work
A common enterprise-wide knowledge structure that is clearly articulated and easily understood.	A Wiki structure emerges from the users rather than imposed top-down
Senior management support including allocation of resources leadership and training	Wikis are a challenge on this one as they allow democratisation of knowledge thus changing power structures associated with knowledge in organisations
Learning organisation	Critical always but with a Wiki, learning becomes the responsibility of all CKWs
The KMS has a clear goal and purpose	The goal and purpose of a Wiki may initially be broader and more exploratory
Measures are established to assess the impacts of the KMS and use of knowledge, as well as verification that the right knowledge is being captured	Measures need to be in keeping with the open nature of a Wiki
The search, retrieval, and visualisation functions of the KMS support facilitated use of knowledge	Usability is important but this has been a criticism of some Wiki software
Work processes are designed that incorporate knowledge capture and use	Critical: knowledge work needs to be part of the job description, explicit workload agreements with appropriate rewards and incentives
Knowledge is secure/protected	Knowledge and users' are perceived to be safe

will be CKWs who are motivated and fully committed to contributing and maintaining a Wiki. Management is encouraged to take a discretionary approach in terms of rewarding participation, productivity, quality articles, and good ideas.

The Wiki has been described as a democratisation of knowledge (Hasan & Pfaff, 2006). In previous research with corporate Wikis, organisations that favour a top down management approach can be seen as undermining the process of the democratisation of knowledge. Management of this case study acknowledged this fact and is committed to finding a solution to maximise the potential of their CKWs through the use of the Wiki. The feedback obtained from employees has given management a valuable insight into CKWs' expectations of the value and usability of a Wiki and greater management support is required for

the sustainability and further development of the Wiki. In keeping with the theme of democracy and promoting a nonthreatening, ubiquitous environment for employees to elicit helpful feedback, Q Methodology was chosen. The Q study demonstrated its effectiveness to community building activities, open discussion, reflection, individual decision making, and providing outcomes that can guide the development and use of ubiquitous knowledge creation and dissemination technologies. Activity Theory has informed the interpretation of results in that it provides a language to describe the less tangible outcomes of the research. It is expected that Activity Theory will inform the directions and structure of future research. This will provide a holistic and dynamic framework for study with a focus on collective activity for the advancement of knowledge work where all employees ubiquitously participate in the cocreation of a store of corporate knowledge for effective knowledge based practice.

REFERENCES

Alavi, M., & Leidner, D. (2001, March). Review: Knowledge management and knowledge management systems: Conceptual foundations and research issues. *Management Information Systems Quarterly, 25*(1), 107–136. doi:10.2307/3250961

AS 5037 (2005). Australian Standard Knowledge Management, Standards Australia.

Benkler, Y. (2006). *The wealth of networks: How social production transforms markets and freedom.* New Haven: Yale University Press.

Boyd, S. (2006). *Are you ready for social software?* Retrieved October 15, 2008, from http://www.stoweboyd.com/message/2006/10/are_you_ready_f.html

Brown, S. R. (1986). Q technique and method: Principles and procedures. In Berry, W. D., & Lewis-Beck, M. S. (Eds.), *New tools for social scientists* (pp. 57–76). Beverly Hills, CA: Sage.

Cleetus, K. J., Cascaval, G. C., & Matsuzaki, K. (1996). PACT – a software package to manage projects and coordinate people. In *Proceedings of the 5th International WET ICE '96.*

Efimova, L. (2004). *Discovering the iceberg of knowledge work: A weblog case.* OKLC 2004.

Engeström, Y. (1987). *Learning by expanding: An activity-theoretical approach to developmental research.* Helsinki: Orienta-Konsultit.

Fuchs-Kittowski, E., & Köhler, A. (2002). Knowledge creating communities in the context of work processes. *ACM SIGCSE Bulletin, 2*(3), 8–13.

Gonzalez-Reinhart, J. (2005). Wikis and the Wiki way. *Information Systems Research,* 1–22.

Hart, D., & Warne, L. (2005). Comparing cultural and political perspectives of data, information, and knowledge sharing in organisations. *International Journal of Knowledge Management, 2*(2), 1–15. doi:10.4018/jkm.2006040101

Hasan, H. (2001). An overview of techniques for applying activity theory to information systems. In H. Hasan, E. Gould, & P. Larkin (Eds.), *Information systems and activity theory: Vol. 2. Theory and practice* (pp. 3-22). Wollongong University Press.

Hasan, H., & Crawford, K. (2007). Knowledge mobilisation in communities through socio-technical system. *Journal of KMRP, 5*(4), 237–248.

Hasan, H., & Pfaff, C. C. (2006). Emergent conversational technologies that are democratising information systems in organisations: The case of the corporate Wiki. In *Proceedings of the ISF,* Canberra.

Hildreth, P.M., & Kimble, C. (2002, October 1). The duality of knowledge. *Information Research, 8*(1).

Jennex, M. (2005). Editorial preface: Knowledge management systems. *International Journal of Knowledge Management, 1*(2), i–iv.

Jennex, M. E., & Olfman, L. (2005). Assessing knowledge management success. *International Journal of Knowledge Management, 1*(2), 33–49. doi:10.4018/jkm.2005040104

Jennex, M. E., & Olfman, L. (2006). A model of knowledge management success. *International Journal of Knowledge Management, 2*(3), 51–68. doi:10.4018/jkm.2006070104

Jennex, M. E., Smolnik, S., & Croasdell, D. (2007a, January). Towards defining knowledge management success. In *40th Hawaii International Conference on System Sciences, HICSS40, IEEE Computer Society.*

Jennex, M. E., Smolnik, S., & Croasdell, D. (2007b). Knowledge management success. *International Journal of Knowledge Management, 3*(2), i–vi.

Jennex, M. E., Smolnik, S., & Croasdell, D. (2008, January). Towards measuring knowledge management success. In *41st Hawaii International Conference on System Sciences, HICSS41, IEEE Computer Society.*

Kaptelinin, V., & Nardi, B. A. (1997). *The activity checklist: A tool for representing the space of context* (Working paper). Umeå University: Dept. of Informatics.

Kelloway, E. K., & Barling, J. (2000). Knowledge work as organizational behaviour. *International Journal of Management Reviews, 2*, 287–304. doi:10.1111/1468-2370.00042

Klein, H., & Hirschheim, R. (in press). The structure of the IS discipline reconsidered. *Information and Organization.*

Lam, W., & Chua, A. (2005). Knowledge management project abandonment: An exploratory examination of root causes. *Communications of the Association for Information Systems, 16*, 723–743.

Li, C., & Bernoff, J. (2008). *Groundswell: Winning in a world transformed by social technologies.* Boston, MA: Harvard University Press, Forrester Research Inc.

Linger, H., & Warne, L. (2001). Making the invisible visible: Modelling social learning in a knowledge management context [Special issue on knowledge management]. *Australian Journal of Information Systems*, 56-66.

Malhotra, Y. (2004). Why KMS fail? Enablers and constraints of KM in human enterprises. In M.E.D. Koenig & T. Kanti Srikantaiah (Eds.), *KM lessons learned: What works and what doesn't* (pp. 87-112). American Society for Information Science and Technology Monograph Series: Information Today Inc.

McKeown, B. F., & Thomas, D. B. (1988). *Q methodology. Quantitative applications in the social sciences.* Newbury Park, CA: Sage.

Meloche, J., & Crawford, K. (1998). A metaphorical approach to information seeking, a Q study. In *14th Annual Conference of the Internal Society for the Scientific Study of Subjectivity*, Seoul Korea.

Murphy, T., & Jennex, M. E. (2006a). Knowledge management, emergency response, and hurricane Katrina. *International Journal of Intelligent Control and Systems, 1*(4), 199–208.

Murphy, T., & Jennex, M. E. (2006b). Knowledge management and hurricane Katrina response. *International Journal of Knowledge Management, 2*(4), 52–66.

O'Brien, F., & Ali, I. (2006). Formal and informal networks during emergency situations: The impact for information strategy. In *Proceeding of 11th ICCRTS.*

Pfaff, C. C., & Hasan, H. (2006a). Overcoming organizational resistance to using Wiki technology for knowledge management. In *Proceedings of the 10th Pacific Asian Conference on Information Systems.*

Pfaff, C. C., & Hasan, H. (2006b). The Wiki: A tool to support the activities of the knowledge worker. In *Proceedings of the Transformational Tools for 21st Century (TT21C) Conference 2006* (pp. 38-48).

Raman, M., Ryan, T., & Olfman, L. (2006). Knowledge management systems for emergency preparedness: The Claremont University consortium experience. *International Journal of Knowledge Management, 2*(3), 51–68. doi:10.4018/jkm.2006070103

Rich, E., & Duchessi, P. (2000). Models for understanding the dynamics of organizational knowledge in consulting firms. In *Proceedings of the Hawaii International Conference on System Sciences.*

Senge, P. (1990). *The fifth discipline. The art and practice of the learning organization.* London: Random House.

Stephenson, W. (1953). Postulates of behaviorism. *Philosophy of Science, 20,* 110–120. doi:10.1086/287250

Swisher, K. (2004, July 29). Boomtown: Wiki may alter how employees work together. *Wall Street Journal,* p. B1.

Vygotsky, L. S. (1978). *Mind and society.* Cambridge, MA: Harvard University Press.

Warne, L., Hasan, H., & Ali, I. (2005). Transforming organizational culture to the ideal inquiring organization. In Courtney, J., Haynes, J., & Paradice, D. (Eds.), *Inquiring organizations: Moving from knowledge management to wisdom* (pp. 316–336). Hershey, PA.

Weiser, M. (1993, October). Hot topics: Ubiquitous computing. *IEEE Computer,* 71-72.

This work was previously published in International Journal of Knowledge Management, Volume 5, Issue 2, edited by Murray E. Jennex, pp. 33-50, copyright 2009 by IGI Publishing (an imprint of IGI Global).

Chapter 10

Reaching for the Moon:
Expanding Transactive Memory's Reach with Wikis and Tagging

Mark B. Allan
NASA Ames Research Center, USA

Anthony A. Korolis
IBM Corporation, USA

Terri L. Griffith
Santa Clara University, USA

ABSTRACT

Transactive memory systems (TMS) support knowledge sharing and coordination in groups. TMS are enabled by the encoding, storage, retrieval, and communication of knowledge by domain experts—knowing who knows what. The NASA Ames Intelligent Robotics Group provides an example of how TMS theoretical boundaries are stretched in actual use. This group is characterized as being highly innovative as they routinely engage in field studies that are inherently difficult due to time and technology resource constraints. We provide an expanded view of TMS that includes the technology support system available to this group, and possible further extensions to NASA's or other such dynamic groups' practice.

INTRODUCTION

The United States National Aeronautics and Space Administration (NASA) is pushing to return astronauts to the Moon by 2020, and then on to Mars (Lawler, 2007). Robots will play a crucial role in this vision by performing time consuming, repetitive tasks that have little to gain from high-level

human reasoning. The Intelligent Robotics Group (IRG) at NASA Ames Research Center develops software enabling space exploration robots of the future to carry out their tasks in unstructured environments without requiring human guidance at every step.

The dynamics of innovative, research-oriented groups such as IRG present a considerable challenge to capturing and reusing knowledge. In their discussion of knowledge management in research

DOI: 10.4018/978-1-60960-555-1.ch010

and development, Armbrecht et al. (2001) note that managing knowledge is not literally possible in R&D environments, and that facilitating knowledge flows is a more productive approach. Support for the development, maintenance, and augmentation of cognitive Transactive Memory Systems is one way to facilitate these knowledge flows.

Transactive Memory System (TMS) theory provides a framework based on group-level cognition describing how individuals in a group can cooperatively learn, store, use, and coordinate their knowledge to increase the group's effectiveness (Brandon & Hollingshead, 2004; Lewis, Belliveau, Herndon, & Keller, 2007; Moreland, Argote, & Krishnan, 1998; Wegner, 1987). TMS are the cognitive memory systems through which teams know who knows what, who needs what knowledge, and how to coordinate given the distribution of this knowledge. Much of the research on TMS has focused on small, stable groups. However, simulation models suggest that TMS may be of even more value to larger groups, groups in a dynamic task environment, and groups that deal with volatile knowledge environments (Ren, Carley, & Argote, 2006). At the same time, more dynamic and emergent environments present difficulties around the boundaries of TMS mechanisms (Majchrzak, Jarvenpaa, & Hollingshead, 2007; Nevo & Wand, 2005).

Just as returning to the Moon and sending humans to Mars push our technical capabilities, the demands of the required tight time horizons, technical integration, and fluid teams push our understanding of team dynamics and support as well. In the sections of this article, we extend the concept and application of TMS to focus on fluid teams that interact with technology. We review the TMS literature with a specific focus of highlighting areas where knowledge management systems and practices can augment the TMS. We see knowledge management as intertwined technical systems and organizational practices supporting knowledge coordination, transfer, and reuse (e.g., Sambamurthy & Subramani, 2005).

Whereas most TMS research focuses on TMS development through teams working face to face on the task, we focus on how to extend TMS development in settings where computer mediated communication is prevalent and technology augmentation is part of the general task environment. We use IRG as an exhibit for this discussion, and conclude with further design ideas to generalize from this setting to organizational settings more broadly.

TRANSACTIVE MEMORY: A FOUNDATION FOR SUCCESSFUL TEAM WORK

Organizational knowledge is useful to the extent that knowledge is high quality, transfers across users, and is used in a coordinated fashion—for example, when team process knowledge supports the link between task knowledge and performance outcomes (Griffith & Sawyer, 2007; Griffith, Sawyer, & Neale, 2003; Haas & Hansen, 2007; Reagans, Argote, & Brooks, 2005). In this context, task knowledge is knowledge about the task at hand while process knowledge is about how to apply that task knowledge toward performance. Transactive memory, a type of process knowledge, is a team's way of knowing who knows what and how to coordinate as a result (Wegner, 1987). Transactive memory is a powerful force in team performance and provides our focus here (Kanawattanachai & Yoo, 2007; Lewis, 2004).

More specifically, a TMS describes how individuals in a group learn, store, use, and coordinate their knowledge to increase the group's effectiveness (Wegner, 1987). One of the main advantages of the TMS is that it provides individuals with more extensive and higher quality knowledge than they have access to in their individual memories (Moreland & Myaskovsky, 2000). TMS theory builds upon what is known about individual memory functions. There are three stages in individual memory systems: (1) knowledge enters the system during the encoding stage, (2) it is retained in the individual's memory in the storage stage, and (3) it is accessed for use during the retrieval stage (Wegner, 1987). The TMS is a network of individual memory systems with communication links that have been established. These communication links are not created arbitrarily, but can be facilitated by design of the organization or information technology tools that exist within the environment. These links rely on the creation of metamemories (or memories about the memories of others) by individuals in the group. A "TMS is a shared division of cognitive labor" (Lewis et al., 2007, p. 160) in terms of a group managing the three memory stages noted above.

The structure of these systems includes an awareness of knowledge specialization amongst the team members, a level of credibility related to the specialized knowledge, and the ability to coordinate given this specialization (for recent summaries, please see, Kanawattanachai & Yoo, 2007; Lewis, 2003). The literature has established a variety of benefits for groups with TMS. First, the cognitive load on the individual is decreased, thus allowing people to focus on their domain expertise instead of redundantly storing knowledge (Wegner, 1987). Second, individuals have access to more knowledge than they would through their own individual memories (Wegner, 1987). Third, the best qualified person (domain expert) for a given problem will be assigned, thereby increasing group efficiency. Fourth, knowledge coordination should allow members to be proactive rather than reactive in their work (Murnighan & Conlon, 1991). Thus, TMS also refers to the group's ability to coordinate given the knowledge of where the knowledge resides and who should have access to what (Liang, Moreland, & Argote, 1995; Wegner, 1987). Finally, problems should be able to be solved more quickly and with higher quality knowledge since problems will be aligned with domain expertise (Moreland & Levine, 1992).

Wegner (1987) discussed three issues with TMS which are especially important to the features of technology-enabled systems: directory updating, information allocation, and retrieval coordination. Directory updating is the process of keeping meta-memories current to enable efficient retrieval within the system. That is, if domain experts change or new knowledge emerges, the directory must be updated in a timely manner. One of the solutions to this problem is to create directory structures that enable more efficient searching. Information allocation is the process of routing incoming knowledge to the correct location in the directory structure. This is especially important in technology-enabled solutions and the rules for knowledge routing must be established at the system onset, but remain adaptable as the knowledge evolves. When new knowledge enters the system, it should be allocated to the member who is perceived as the domain expert (Nevo & Wand, 2005). In certain cases, an individual retainer is elected based on circumstantial knowledge responsibility (Wegner, 1987). That person may not be the knowledge expert, but they fill the role because they had initial contact with the knowledge. Retrieval coordination is the process of deciding where to look for a memory item. During retrieval, there is an evaluation of perceived expertise before the knowledge is accessed (Nevo & Wand, 2005). An effective TMS also requires a common language for tasks, assignments, roles, and locations of expertise (e.g., Faraj & Sproull, 2000). These issues have implications for technology tools in the areas of user interface design and search algorithms.

Prior research has considered the role knowledge technology plays regarding TMS. Moreland and Myaskovsky (2000) provide one of the most primitive, yet effective versions. They used hard-copy handouts summarizing each team member's skills (based on an earlier performance period). The results indicated that this knowledge was used to form the TMS. Teams that were given the handouts performed significantly better than those that did not have prior knowledge of teammates' skills, and on a par with teams that had been trained as a group. Using a more technically sophisticated approach, Nevo and Wand (2005) designed "meta memory" support via information technology. We note that their work focused on being able to extend the mechanisms of TMS to communities, not teams, and that theirs is a presentation of a design, not a test. Nevertheless, they argue effectively that information technology can support TMS via directories of who knows what, and metaknowledge including the quality of the knowledge held by the person, the cost of obtaining that knowledge, and so forth.

Nontechnical sources can also support TMS development. Baumann (2001) (cited in Lewis et al., 2007) found that role structures from prior groups facilitated TMS in new groups even when group members had not worked together before—if the new task had a similar role structure. Brandon and Hollingshead (2004) suggest that the basics of TMS are created from a variety of sources (memories, overheard conversations, memos, handbooks, etc.). Over time and with interaction, the TMS is refined. Additionally, ongoing maintenance is important. Individuals have an ongoing process of encoding, storing, and retrieving knowledge that serves to update the TMS and keep it aligned with the reality of the group. TMS is "not just any static association of task, expertise, and person information" (Brandon & Hollingshead, 2004, p. 637). We believe that TMS can be supported either by ongoing direct interaction with others, or generalized exchange via communal repositories (e.g., Yuan, Fulk, & Monge, 2007).

The literature has also identified several difficulties in the design of information systems that support knowledge management and transactive memory. First, the often contextualized nature of knowledge presents difficulties, especially during the encoding stage. Second, a considerable amount of knowledge is tacit. Tacit knowledge first exists within individual memories and is difficult to codify and retain, especially in large organizations. Third, the different knowledge locations present problems in a TMS. For example, in the IRG system, individuals retain knowledge in their individual memories; machines or robots contain structured data; organizational procedures and rules exist with embedded knowledge; organizational structure and roles can be captured, but are changing. These various retainer memories may be difficult to combine in a technology tool. Fourth, the volatility of organizational knowledge presents problems. Finally, all of this assumes that the needed information has gotten into the repository—a difficult assumption if people must actively enter this information versus it being collected more passively (Goodman & Darr, 1998; Griffith & Sawyer, 2006).

Several other factors have been identified in the literature as affecting TMS function. Ren et al. (2006) note that larger groups, groups with higher task volatility (the frequency with which the group changes its tasks), and groups with higher knowledge volatility (cases where knowledge quickly becomes irrelevant—that is, decays) are likely to benefit more from TMS than other teams. The key is to maintain an up-to-date view of the expertise distribution. The role of the TMS is to provide access to knowledge when it is needed. This role is more valuable to the extent that there are more places to look (i.e., larger groups), and to the extent that the task and or knowledge is likely to change (requiring new searches).

Dynamic teams are receiving increasing attention. Brandon and Hollingshead (2004) note that it is more difficult to achieve optimal TMS in dynamic contexts (ill-structured problems, uncertain environments, or settings with shifting goals). Lewis et al. (2007) focus specifically on group membership change and note that a key issue is to trigger the reevaluation of the TMS given new members—attempting to put a round peg in a square hole just because that is the vacant hole is not effective. Majchrzak et al. (2007) examined the teams at work during the response to Hurricanes

Katrina and Rita. They considered TMS in the context of teams with: sense of great urgency, high levels of interdependence, and constantly changing environments and resources. Moreover, these teams had to manage unstable task definitions, flexible task assignments, fleeting membership, differing purposes (firefighting, security, animal care). However, they also note that these "teams" often violated the boundaries around which TMS was developed, namely, known membership, members perceiving interdependence, and shared goals—the boundaries of the definition for a true team (Hackman, 2002).

THE INTELLIGENT ROBOTICS GROUP

The Intelligent Robotics Group (IRG) at NASA Ames Research Center is comprised of 24 permanent staff members with a diverse skill set and little overlap of these skills within the group. Space robotics is a broad field, spanning the areas of mechanical engineering, controls theory, computer engineering, computer science, through to the nascent social science of human-robotic interaction. The vast scope of developing a robotic space mission requires closely coordinated efforts across many organizations and suborganizations. IRG's research approach is to develop systems-level software and concepts for supervisory control of robotic activities, then validate those concepts in field test scenarios.

The group's core development spans several technical areas, including applied computer vision, robot software architectures, interactive 3D visualization, science instrument integration, and frameworks to support human-robot interaction. Staff members frequently rotate between teams as project requirements evolve, and every project involves external collaborations. Virtual teaming is common and necessary, and the teams are comprised of people from diverse organizational cultures: other NASA centers, academia, large

corporations, and small technology start-ups. Virtual teams are assembled from several organizations to develop an innovative technology within a fixed timeframe, then disbanded at the end of the project. Personnel may come and go over the lifetime of each project, and members participate in these fluid virtual teams on a part-time basis.

IRG frequently supplements its workforce by employing interns through various educational outreach programs. Interns will work for the group for anywhere between 2 to 12 months, and at peak times the number of interns may match the number of permanent staff. The level of education of the interns covers a wide range, from high school to doctoral students. Similarly, there is a wide variation in the amount and quality of work accomplished through intern labor. All of the students are bright and motivated, and most make valuable contributions over the course of their employment. Although there are usually a few students that never quite hit stride, every year there are one or two "star" interns that surpass all expectations and make contributions at the level of permanent staff. The departure of star interns often has a disruptive effect on the group's effectiveness. High performing interns acquire trust through action (e.g., Majchrzak et al., 2007) and rapidly become first class participants in their team's TMS. Loss of the intern fractures the stable interdependence of the team as the intern's knowledge role has to be reassigned and relearned.

Paradoxically, the more capable the intern, the less the knowledge transfer to the permanent team. Whereas most interns receive sustained mentoring from a permanent staff member, high performing interns are often trusted to perform their roles with little supervision. Under current methods, this provides little opportunity for knowledge to transfer from the intern to the team.

The dynamics in this setting push the boundaries of TMS development, maintenance, and augmentation. The transient nature of the intern workforce affords them limited time to work on specific projects, and it is critical that the group effectively integrate the knowledge of the intern population before their departure. Additionally, the research focus of the IRG's work is at odds with traditional TMS in that roles and tasks are dynamic, with permanent staff often rotating between projects.

Managing TMS in Dynamic Teams: Quick Start TMS

We will present a sociotechnical approach to "Quick Start" TMS. Our approach focuses on training for team assimilation and systems assimilation via a Wiki[1] platform. Additionally, we will highlight the sociotechnical hurdles imposed for such teams when largely voluntary "Web 2.0" tools are utilized. For example, while everyone in each team should be contributing to the Wiki, the temporary members may be reluctant to do so if they equate temporary with lower status and do not feel it is their place.

We define a "Quick Start" TMS as an approach that provides everything a newcomer to the group needs to rapidly form a mental map of the group as a whole. It goes beyond simply mapping knowledge roles to individuals in the group; it is a mapping of how those knowledge roles apply to the group's projects, how those projects have evolved, how the projects interrelate, and how external organizations and individuals fit into the group's "big picture." It provides high level connective meta-information between projects and existing applied knowledge, as well as conduits to concrete work products as examples, and insertion points for contributing new work products to the knowledge base.

Two mechanisms for achieving these goals follow from the discussion of public goods theory (Fulk, Flanagin, Kalman, Monge, & Ryan, 1996) in communication systems. Yuan et al. (2007) build from this theory to distinguish between two types of TMS information access. The first, connective access, is the direct exchange of information through social interaction. Effective connective information exchange depends on individuals having well developed expertise directories of "who knows what" in order to coordinate knowledge at the team level. Information system support for the development and maintenance of these individual expertise directories has taken the form of online expertise directories, which map areas of expertise to people.

The second type of information access is through communal sources. Communal sources are broadly defined as external information repositories where knowledge can be contributed and consumed by multiple people. Yuan et al. (2007) argue that communal repositories such as corporate intranets, Wikis, blogs, and e-mail lists not only complement connective information sources, they may serve as effective substitutes. One significant advantage of communal sources is that they permit asynchronous access to information, which is a crucial aspect to consider in the context of virtual teams and fluid teams where the information holder may no longer be with the organization.

We draw our confidence in Wikis and other communal sources from experiences across a wide range of organizational settings. Majchrzak et al. (2007), for example, note that Wikis can be used to coordinate within and across emergent groups in disaster relief settings. Rech, Bogner, and Haas (2007) document effective application for software reuse. Cress and Kimmerle (2008) effectively differentiate between the information sharing capabilities of blogs and file sharing systems, and the knowledge development and learning supported by the more collaborative/ interactive Wiki process.

We believe the Quick Start TMS approach supports traditional TMS development, and may substitute for access to a particular individual's knowledge. We outline two technology mechanisms that can be foundational Quick Start TMS. The first, a Wiki, is in use in the IRG. The second, tagging information within the Wiki, is under development.

THE WIKI

The IRG has a base system through which they can implement an approach for Quick Start TMS, which will benefit both new and permanent team members. IRG began using an integrated Wiki/ Software Configuration Management (SCM)/ bug tracking system in 2006. The historical logs maintained by SCM tools and bug tracking systems allow new developers to re-experience the step-by-step evolution of a software code base. Re-experience of the development process through the combination of SCM commit logs, bug tracking logs, code comments, and archived forum discussions constitutes the fundamental mechanism for learning in collaborative open-source communities (Hemetsberger & Reinhardt, 2006) and we think it has application here.

Some of the teams in the group, primarily those that were software development intensive, rapidly adopted the system. Many of the group members have a history of contributing to open source software efforts and were familiar with the potential benefits of the system. Management sponsored use of the system and the group was encouraged to consolidate information that had been spread out among disparate repositories into the Wiki system. The deployment found several champions who promoted Wiki use, created foundation pages, and imported existing documentation into the system.

An informal practice evolved during early adoption of the system wherein if a team member asked a question regarding a project relevant task and the answer required more than two sentences, the information holder was asked, "Is it on the Wiki?" If the answer was "no," the information holder was asked to create a summary information page. However, during the summer of 2007, IRG encountered operational realities that pushed them to formalize the "is it on the Wiki" process for mission-critical operations. The group carried out a field test of simulated lunar operations involving two planetary robot rovers performing a systematic

site survey to map local topography and surface substructure. The robots carried out their survey at a lunar analog site located at the rim of an ancient meteor impact crater in the Arctic Circle (Fong et al., 2008). Operations involved teams at three locations: local operations located at a simulated lunar outpost in the Arctic, a ground-operations team located at NASA Johnson Space Center in Houston, Texas, and a remote monitoring team located at NASA Ames Research Center in Mountain View, California. All three teams shared the same tool chain, but experts for the individual tools were distributed amongst the three teams. All exercise participants had well developed knowledge of who knew what, and operational readiness tests preceding the field exercise had gone smoothly. However, communication barriers and time constraints significantly impeded knowledge coordination during the exercise. Network bandwidth constraints prohibited voice communication to the field site, e-mail turn-around was too slow, and instant messaging did not provide sufficiently rich communication.

Following the field test, IRG developed a cross-training procedure mediated by the Wiki to mitigate future coordination problems. The process begins with the subject matter expert training another group member face to face. Following the training, the trainee summarizes their experience on the Wiki. The trainer then reviews the Wiki page, corrects any miscommunications, and provides supplementary information. Later, a third member of the group is assigned to the knowledge role in question during a test exercise, using the Wiki as their only source of information. During testing, the third party makes note of any questions or operational issues directly into the Wiki. The subject matter expert amends the document, and this process iterates as the document is refined. This process has low overhead as the trainee's notes are augmented, refined, and validated by collaborative Wiki-mediated exchanges between the subject matter expert and other group members. By artificially inserting the Wiki as a communication medium following the initial face to face transactive information exchange, the information is effectively encoded into the knowledge repository for future asynchronous retrieval, and the iterative validation process assists in transforming the subject matter expert's knowledge from tacit to explicit.

The Wiki is used in a similar fashion across all areas of IRG's workflow. During meetings, notes are typed into the Wiki in real time. The Wiki is used for software development discussions and requirements gathering; links between the Wiki, bug tracking system, and SCM commit notes provides a comprehensive view of current software status as well as historical context. Test plans are created in the Wiki for operational exercises and results are noted in the Wiki in real time by participants during the test. At the test debrief sessions which are held upon completion, the test director enters a detailed recap of the day's events and begins a skeleton test plan for the next iteration.

The Wiki system is a rich communal repository that retains information about virtually every aspect of IRG's workflow and knowledge products, and as such, provides a solid foundation for a Quick Start TMS. Information is available for asynchronous access from the repository, and it also provides a level of connective support as all information entered into the system can be traced to the individual who entered it. However, as the amount of information in the system grows, access and retrieval become more challenging.

TAGS

There is an additional dynamic quality to the Quick Start TMS approach: tagging, where users freely assign keywords to objects in the information repository using their own understanding of the information. Tagging is nonhierarchical and inclusive, as the group members themselves form the directory structure with their input (Golder & Huberman, 2006). Tagging has been applied

in several practical Web 2.0 solutions, including Del.ico.us, a social bookmarking site; Flickr, a photo sharing and cataloging site; and Technorati, a blog search engine. The metadata generated by this activity is shared with the other members and forms the directory structure. The collective metadata has three components: (i) the person doing the tagging, (ii) the information object being tagged, and (iii) the tag data itself.

These processes are closely tied to Wegner's (1987) discussion of directory updating and information allocation in transactive memory systems. Directory updating is fundamentally learning who knows what in the group. It often contains the metamemory or information about the memory. Tagging supports directory updating in that the tag contains information about the contributor, the information object and the descriptive tag information itself. Furthermore, information allocation is the process of assigning memory items to group members. Tagging further supports information allocation in that tags contain information on the person doing the tagging. Generally, the first person to receive any information is assigned to keep it in personal memory and could be the subject expert. In performing a tag-based keyword search, the pointer to this domain expert is thus created.

Tags also add to the Quick Start process via their relationship to sensemaking. Sensemaking is supported as team members process labels, categorize information, and the information's meaning becomes apparent to the individual or the group. Tagging provides "triggers for sensemaking" as taggers and readers of tags are confronted with requests to make sense and/or situations where an other's sensemaking may not match their own (Louis & Sutton, 1991). In their study of tagging using the Del.ico.us social network, Golder and Huberman (2006) found the vocabulary formed quickly, a consensus was formed and it was not significantly affected by the addition of more tags. Even though a stable language emerges, minority opinions can still exist without disturbing the established vocabulary. This flexibility allows tagging systems to change over time with shifts in group membership or the sensemaking patterns of the group.

Tagging has been identified as an alternative to the structured taxonomy or ontology-based approach. Tagging relies on people to contribute to the directory structure to classify information objects (Titus, Subrahmanian, & Ramani, 2007). Taxonomies are hierarchical and exclusive, with regard to the participants' input. Tagging, as noted above, is non-hierarchical and inclusive (Golder & Huberman, 2006). In practice, users freely assign keywords to objects in the information repository using their own understanding of the information. The metadata generated by this activity is shared with the other members and forms the directory structure. In taxonomies, a subset of the user population designs the keywords used in the system. In the NASA IRG environment, an informal tagging approach was favored rather than a top-down ontology as this supports the features needed for Quick Start TMS.

Presently, the IRG Wiki does not use tags. The loosely organized Wiki information causes much of the sensemaking in the group to occur outside the domain of IT tools and through shared experiences. We submit that the Wiki environment is an ideal candidate for asynchronous sensemaking, especially for the transient interns. The interns have not had the benefit of shared experiences and can instead rely on stored knowledge to enable sensemaking.

Current Situation in the IRG and Generalizing Beyond

Dynamic groups need Quick Start TMS. NASA's IRG provides an example where one component exists, the Wiki, but there is room for improvement in the social implementation of the Wiki, and in the use of tags. However, even in this limited form, we offer that there is evidence of success. The Intelligent Robotics Group holds a yearly, off-site retreat in order to reflect on the past year's work,

stimulate ideas for future areas of research, and discuss ways to make the group more effective. Two comments were made during the 2007 retreat that had direct relevance to TMS. The first was made by the principal investigator for a recently completed project that had only a few dedicated staff, but involved many of the group members on an as-needed, part-time basis. He thanked those involved, adding:

Robotics covers so many areas, and it was really great this year, with all the people in the group - knowing what person to go to to get the necessary bits and pieces, and pulling it all together to make the magic happen.

The second comment came from a new permanent staff member who had been with the group for only a few months. During a discussion on how the Wiki could be improved, he said that it would be helpful for him to have a list of past projects, what software components were reused and developed for those projects, who had worked on the projects, and in what role. Despite being familiar with the individual group members and their core competencies, he was having a difficult time developing a cohesive view of the organization and where his expertise would be most valuable. It became apparent in the discussion that followed that the evolution of projects within IRG—previous projects, technology offshoots, funding sources, project collaborators, and so forth—provided valuable connective information about the group's diverse application areas that mapped organizational goals to technology development. This prompted the creation of a current and historical project directory to provide organizational context for development efforts.

IRG has enhanced group knowledge sharing and retention by integrating a communal information repository into their workflow and evolving social strategies to capture information adequately. But as they reach for the Moon we think there are further opportunities and that these opportunities can support dynamic groups in general. Below we summarize how groups can support their TMS with technology systems that they may already be using. While this generalization is limited in that our main focus has been a highly technical team, these ideas also build on research spanning a broad variety of teams and TMS literature.

Wiki with Tagging as a "Quick Start" TMS Enabler

When used as a main part of team work, Wikis, tagging, and search functionality can be used to support transactive memory in the organization. Directory updating is supported by the tagging components as the tag contains a pointer to the contributor, the content and an indication of the content's significance within the group. Knowledge allocation is supported by the tagging feature as incoming information can be dynamically assigned to various knowledge domains based on the tag. Retrieval coordination is achieved as most open source Wiki software contains search functionality for both the Wiki contents as well as the tags.

An additional feature of the Wiki is an indicator of validation. This feature benefits both the information contributor and the seeker as everyone can view contributions and whether they are still in an experimental phase or are a validated method. However, research and development work is iterative and ongoing and the validity of documentation may change over time. Wikis provide a flexible framework for this scenario allowing users to iteratively add to knowledge and change its level of validation as perceived by the group's contributors.

Expertise Directory for People and Projects

The Wiki environment should contain a directory of the staff which provides visibility to the contributor for all content. This system user name would be linked to other metadata, including: (i) self-reported and peer-nominated expertise domains, (ii) past and current projects, and (iii) technology expertise (e.g., hardware or software products). Linking the Wiki content with individuals invites information seekers to seek out the domain expert for face-to-face knowledge exchange if information retained in the repository is inadequate. For groups with dynamic task environments, a directory of past and current projects provides organizational context to enhance coordination. Cross linking the expertise and project directories allows shared resources to be easily identified and provides links to individuals with project-specific task knowledge.

Encourage Contributions from All, but Especially from Temporary Members

Temporary members face challenges with contribution to a knowledge repository due to their transient status and the training required to use a knowledge repository. We overcome this by recommending the use of technologies which are becoming prevalent with the emergence of Web 2.0 and that require little training. When temporary members join the team, permanent members should encourage contribution as part of their mentoring. The message should be made clear that the temporary members were brought in for specialized skills and their knowledge needs to be captured by the organization's memory before their departure.

Adjust Team Design such that Wiki Contribution is Part of Standard Workflow

Teams have enough to do. Teams also have a lot to gain from better dynamics and stronger TMS. We see benefit to teams if systems such as the Wiki and tagging approach described above are how the team does its work—rather than an extra step.

Research results, reports, project management, and the like can be managed via collaborative spaces such as a Wiki. These work products then become searchable and traceable—allowing for newcomers and temporary members to get a head start on understanding the work process of the group.

CONCLUSION

Dynamic teams need extra support to manage who knows what—known as Transactive Memory (e.g., Moreland et al., 1998; Wegner, 1987). NASA's Intelligent Robotics Group provides a setting that highlights how Transactive Memory Systems can be pushed to their boundaries given dynamic tasks and team membership. This group also provides an opportunity to evaluate how technology tools and related organizational practices can support TMS at these boundaries—and how a "Quick Start" approach to TMS may provide value in dynamic team environments. We believe the use of Wikis and tagging provides a rich communal repository that supports Quick Start TMS. There are several sociotechnical design considerations in the implementation of this system, including: (i) creating an expertise directory of people and projects in the Wiki, (ii) encouraging Wiki contributions from temporary workers and (iii) making Wiki contribution an unobtrusive task and part of the standard workflow. These technologies can be an effective tool to assist dynamic groups in knowledge sharing and coordination.

REFERENCES

Armbrecht, F. R., Chapas, R., Chappelow, C. C., Farris, G. F., Friga, P. N., & Harz, C. A. (2001). Knowledge management in research and development. *Research Technology Management, 44*, 28–48.

Baumann, M. R. (2001). The effects of manipulating salience of expertise and membership change on transactive memory. Unpublished doctoral dissertation: University of Illinois, Urbana-Champaign.

Brandon, D. P., & Hollingshead, A. B. (2004). Transactive memory systems in organizations: Matching tasks, expertise, and people. *Organization Science, 15*, 633–644. doi:10.1287/orsc.1040.0069

Cress, U., & Kimmerle, J. (2008). A systemic and cognitive view on collaborative knowledge building with Wikis. *Computer-Supported Collaborative Learning, 3*, 105–122. doi:10.1007/s11412-007-9035-z

Faraj, S., & Sproull, L. (2000). Coordinating expertise in software development teams. *Management Science, 46*, 1554–1568. doi:10.1287/mnsc.46.12.1554.12072

Fong, T. W., Allan, M., Bouyssounouse, X., Bualat, M. G., Deans, M., Edwards, L., et al. (2008). *Robotic site survey at Haughton Crater.* Paper presented at the 9th International Symposium on Artificial Intelligence, Robotics, and Automation in Space.

Fulk, J., Flanagin, A., Kalman, M., Monge, P. R., & Ryan, R. (1996). Connective and communal public goods in interactive communication systems. *Communication Theory, 6*, 60–87. doi:10.1111/j.1468-2885.1996.tb00120.x

Golder, S., & Huberman, B. A. (2006). Usage patterns of collaborative tagging systems. *Journal of Information Science, 32*, 198–208. doi:10.1177/0165551506062337

Goodman, P. S., & Darr, E. D. (1998). Computer-aided systems and communities: Mechanisms for organizational learning in distributed environments. *Management Information Systems Quarterly, 22*, 417–440. doi:10.2307/249550

Griffith, T. L., & Sawyer, J. E. (2006). Supporting technologies and organizational practices for the transfer of knowledge in virtual environments. *Group Decision and Negotiation, 15*, 407–423. doi:10.1007/s10726-006-9048-4

Griffith, T. L., & Sawyer, J. E. (2007). *Multilevel knowledge and team performance in a Fortune 100 technology company*. Unpublished manuscript.

Griffith, T. L., Sawyer, J. E., & Neale, M. A. (2003). Virtualness and knowledge in teams: Managing the love triangle of organizations, individuals, and information technology. *Management Information Systems Quarterly, 27*, 265–287.

Haas, M. R., & Hansen, M. T. (2007). Different knowledge, different benefits: Toward a productivity perspective on knowledge sharing in organizations. *Strategic Management Journal, 28*, 1133–1153. doi:10.1002/smj.631

Hackman, J. R. (2002). *Leading teams: Setting the stage for great performances*. Cambridge, MA: Harvard Business School Press.

Hemetsberger, A., & Reinhardt, C. (2006). Learning and knowledge-building in open-source communities - a social-experiential approach. *Management Learning, 37*, 187–214. doi:10.1177/1350507606063442

Kanawattanachai, P., & Yoo, Y. (2007). The impact of knowledge coordination on virtual team performance over time. *Management Information Systems Quarterly, 31*, 783–808.

Lawler, A. (2007). Lunar science: Asking for the Moon. *Science, 315*, 1482–1484. doi:10.1126/science.315.5818.1482

Lewis, K. (2003). Measuring transactive memory systems in the field: Scale development and validation. *The Journal of Applied Psychology, 88*, 587–604. doi:10.1037/0021-9010.88.4.587

Lewis, K. (2004). Knowledge and performance in knowledge-worker teams: A longitudinal study of transactive memory systems. *Management Science, 50*, 1519–1533. doi:10.1287/mnsc.1040.0257

Lewis, K., Belliveau, M., Herndon, B., & Keller, J. (2007). Group cognition, membership change, and performance: Investigating the benefits and detriments of collective knowledge. *Organizational Behavior and Human Decision Processes, 103*, 159–178. doi:10.1016/j.obhdp.2007.01.005

Liang, D. W., Moreland, R., & Argote, L. (1995). Group versus individual training and group performance: The mediating role of transactive memory. *Personality and Social Psychology Bulletin, 21*, 384–393. doi:10.1177/0146167295214009

Louis, M. R., & Sutton, R. I. (1991). Switching cognitive gears: From habits of mind to active thinking. *Human Relations, 44*, 55–76. doi:10.1177/001872679104400104

Majchrzak, A., Jarvenpaa, S. L., & Hollingshead, A. B. (2007). Coordinating expertise among emergent groups responding to disasters. *Organization Science, 18*, 147–161. doi:10.1287/orsc.1060.0228

Moreland, R. L., Argote, L., & Krishnan, R. (1998). Training people to work in groups. In Tindale, R. S., Heath, L., Edwards, J., Posvoc, E. J., Bryant, F. B., & Suarez-Balcazar, Y. (Eds.), *Applications of theory and research on groups to social issues* (*Vol. 4*, pp. 37–60). New York: Plenum.

Moreland, R. L., & Levine, J. M. (1992). Problem identification by groups. In Worchel, S., Wood, W., & Simpson, J. A. (Eds.), *Group process and productivity*. Newbury Park, CA: Sage.

Moreland, R. L., & Myaskovsky, L. (2000). Explaining the performance benefits of group training: Transactive memory or improved communication? *Organizational Behavior and Human Decision Processes, 82*, 117–133. doi:10.1006/obhd.2000.2891

Murnighan, J. K., & Conlon, D. E. (1991). The dynamics of intense work groups: A study of British string quartets. *Administrative Science Quarterly, 36*, 165–186. doi:10.2307/2393352

Nevo, D., & Wand, Y. (2005). Organizational memory information systems: A transactive memory approach. *Decision Support Systems, 39*, 549–562. doi:10.1016/j.dss.2004.03.002

Reagans, R., Argote, L., & Brooks, D. (2005). Individual experience and experience working together: Predicting learning rates from knowing who knows what and knowing how to work together. *Management Science, 51*, 869–881. doi:10.1287/mnsc.1050.0366

Rech, J., Bogner, C., & Haas, V. (2007). Using Wikis to tackle reuse in software projects. *IEEE Software, 24*, 99–104. doi:10.1109/MS.2007.183

Ren, Y., Carley, K. M., & Argote, L. (2006). The contingent effects of transactive memory: When is it more beneficial to know what others know? *Management Science, 52*, 671–682. doi:10.1287/mnsc.1050.0496

Sambamurthy, V., & Subramani, M. (2005). Special issue on information technologies and knowledge management. *Management Information Systems Quarterly, 29*, 1–7.

Titus, N., Subrahmanian, E., & Ramani, K. (2007). *Folksonomy and designing: An exploration.* Paper presented at the ASME 2007 International Design Engineering Technical Conferences & Computers and Information in Engineering Conference.

Wagner, C. (2004). Wiki: A technology for conversational knowledge management and group collaboration. *Communications of the Association for Information Systems, 13*, 265–289.

Wegner, D. (1987). Transactive memory: A contemporary analysis of the group mind. In Mullen, B., & Goethals, G. R. (Eds.), *Theories of group behavior* (pp. 185–208). New York: Springer-Verlag.

Yuan, Y. C., Fulk, J., & Monge, P. R. (2007). Access to information in connective and communal transactive memory systems. *Communication Research, 34*.

ENDNOTE

[1] A Wiki is a type of server software that hosts Web sites that allow users to add, edit or remove content collectively. Wikis allow users to edit the organization of content as well as the content itself. These features promote open contribution to the Web site and allow submissions from nontechnical users. For more information, please see Wagner (2004).

This work was previously published in International Journal of Knowledge Management, Volume 5, Issue 2, edited by Murray E. Jennex, pp. 51-63, copyright 2009 by IGI Publishing (an imprint of IGI Global).

Chapter 11
Assessing the Impact of Knowledge Transfer Mechanisms on Supply Chain Performance

Stephen McLaughlin
National University of Ireland Maynooth, Ireland

ABSTRACT

With the complexity of organizations increasing, it is becoming vitally important that organizations understand how knowledge is created and shared around their core business processes. However, many organizations deploy technology without due consideration for how their employees access, create and share information and knowledge. This chapter explores the subject empirically through the study of how employees work with information and knowledge around a core business function – in this case a supply chain process. In order to do this the organization needs to be viewed for a network perspective as it relates to specific business processes. Viewing the organization in this way enabled the author to see how employee's preferred knowledge and information transfer mechanisms varied across the core process. In some cases the identified transfer mechanisms where at odds with the prescribed organization wide mechanisms. However, when the organization considered the employee's preferred transfer mechanisms as part of an overall process improvement, the E2E supply chain performance was seen to improve significantly.

INTRODUCTION

Organizations are waking up to the fact that the supply chain is not simply a support function for its business, but is in fact the key capability against which a competitive advantage can be developed (Kulp *et al*, 2003). An organization's supply chain capability is now regarded as a key contributor to any organization striving to maximise competitive advantage (Toyer, 1995), and no longer is the

DOI: 10.4018/978-1-60960-555-1.ch011

'supply chain' simply the preserve of procurement, logistic, or manufacturing specialists (Porter & Miller, 1985; Malhotra *et al*, 2005).

As organizations start to compete within global market places the complexity of their supply chains increase significantly. In order to address and manage the increased complexity many organizations look to enterprise 'supply chain' software solutions to ensure a smooth scalable supply chain operation. This was the case with IBM's Integrated Supply Chain (ISC) operation in their Europe, Middle East and Africa (EMEA) region. Recent strategy initiatives had seen manufacturing and distribution for PC products handed over to third party providers. As part of the partnership agreement the manufacturing and logistics partners shared, or had access to IBM data feeds thus enabling a continuous data flow from the IBM handled fulfilment front end through to the third party distribution engine. The data flowed; however, end-to-end performance began to deteriorate significantly. Whilst developing a recovery plan the organization identified the fact that the performance issues were down to a failure to understand how employees, situated in different parts of the supply chain accessed, created, and shared information and knowledge (McLaughlin *et al*, 2006). What this chapter will do is show how knowledge and information needed to be accessed, created, and shared, and how the recovery plan, by focusing on the identified preferred knowledge and information needs at different points across the supply chain, was able to drive significant end-to-end core process improvements.

Before proceeding it is important that the difference between 'information' and 'knowledge' as terms of reference are clearly defined in the context of this research. Although many authors and academics use the terms information and knowledge as though they were interchangeable (Fuller, 2001; Tsoukas, 2005), there is a subtle, but significant difference between the two. This in effect has reduced the significance of knowl-

edge, often reducing it to merely information, and thus the qualities of knowledge, as a classic philosophical concept are lost. In order to try and distinguish between information and knowledge Fuller (2001) looks at the original meaning of information. 'Information' was derived, during the middle ages, from a Latin word used to describe the process by which documents were transferred, or communicated, from one entity to another. As for 'knowledge', this was the mind's representation of this process, which in turn was usually understood in relatively passive terms. Knowledge, in effect, was the result of the minds receptiveness to what lies outside it. So, in the context of this problem facing IBM, and for clarity in this chapter, the author will define information and knowledge as follows:

- *Information* – This is taken to mean codified data. Data that is captured and shared via hard-copy or electronic documentation, which in turn may be stored in databases or spreadsheets, or in report form.
- *Knowledge* – Simons (1945) found that according to his model humans act as information processing systems that extract 'meaning structures' from information inputs through sensory organs, and store these meaning structures as new knowledge. Simons (1945) viewed that information only becomes knowledge within the context of the human mind is supported by Davenport and Prusak (1998), Fuller (2001) and Von Hayek (1952) and Polanyi (1962). Accepting that knowledge creation and use is dependant on human interaction within an organization or process, Davenport *et al* (1998) provide the most commonly accepted definition of knowledge within organizational and business research.

"Knowledge is a fluid mix of framed experience, values, contextual information, and expert insight that provides a frame work for evaluating and incorporating new experiences and information."
(Davenport & Prusak, 1998)

RESEARCH CONTEXT AND METHODOLOGY

The core IBM supply chain processes are supported by integrated information systems such as SAP, i2, and IBM's own DB2 database system. Certainly information in the form of performance data was available at all points across the supply chain. However, core performance, in the case of IBM, was under target. In this case the key performance metric was the time taken to process, build and deliver a customer's order. IBM was quick to apply resource and executive focus to addressing the problem. However, as outlined in McLaughlin *et al* (2006) if sustainable process improvement was to be achieved a different approach would be needed to identify where best to implement performance-improving change. The first issue the organization faced in improving performance was to identify and separate the real problems from the apparent problematic symptoms. In order to do this an end-to-end process description would need to be developed for the supply chain. This would be a significant undertaking, and not practical considering the time pressure, and resource constraints. Therefore, it was decided that a process description would be defined for the core business process responsible for customer order delivery times; this process was the Order Flow Process (OFP).

As information and data was available across the process, the author would look at how both information and knowledge was being used along the core order flow process (OFP). In order to do this along with defining the OFP, the author would also have to identify the key employee groups that operated along the OFP, and then determine their information and knowledge habits. By then looking at how the employee groups are constrained in their information and knowledge habits (by organisation, technology, and people (Barson *et al*, 2000; McLaughlin *et al*, 2008; Skyrme *et al*, 1997)), and comparing this to how the employee groups would like to work, a list of information and knowledge related performance improvements could be identified.

The research methodology follows an action research approach in identifying best knowledge transfer practice across a complex supply chain organization. The research is exploratory in nature and a case study (Yin, 2002) methodology is used to support this line of inductive theory building. The findings presented in this chapter are based on data collated within and across IBM's Integrated Supply Chain. For the purpose of the research the author surveyed over 150 individuals working across an IBM core end-to-end business process; in this case the supply chain order flow process (OFP) was used. The author identified all the employees to be surveyed by mapping the organization's departments and workgroups to the OFP. Once the different departments and workgroups were correctly mapped to the different parts of the OFP the respective employees were identified through the internal on-line directory system. The author used a semi-structured questionnaire and one-to-one interviews to identify the organization's knowledge habits with respect to the order flow business process. The on-line questionnaire was used to elicit a response from those employees directly involved with running the OFP, whilst the one-to-one interviews were conducted with the members of the senior management team. The content and structure of both the on-line questionnaire, and the one-to-one interviews was identical. It was just felt that senior management would be more likely to respond to an interview, than take the time to answer an on-line questionnaire. The structure and contents of the questionnaire / interview is contained in appendix at the end of this chapter. The analysis of the data has been used to understand the different explicit and tacit knowledge sharing habits of the workforce, and the perceived barriers that influence these habits along a core business process. The analysis also identified where along the core process the existing knowledge management approach (codified or personalised) was at odds with employee tacit and explicit knowledge sharing habits. By understanding the different knowledge creation and sharing practices along the core process the author has been able to develop a picture of the preferred knowledge approaches, not just by business function but more importantly by the different collaborative working groups who interact along the core business process. The information gathered through the primary research allowed the organization to re-focus on how to improve knowledge and information flows in order to improve process performance (McLaughlin *et al*, 2006).

As there is little academic research on actual barriers to information and knowledge transfer along process pathways the author, as a former employee, relied on pre-understanding (Gummesson, 1991) of the process and organization as a valid starting point for conducting this research.

DEFINING THE SUPPLY CHAIN PROCESS

Organizations, in general, are now well aware of the components that make up their supply chain; indeed these components are often well established and embedded. However, many still struggle with the problem of effective component alignment (Day, 1994; Teece, 1998). Functionally aligned organizations may understand and individually manage their supply chain components, but performance can only be maximised once they achieve the transformation to process alignment. Process aligned organizations focus on core process performance as opposed to functional business unit performance. This is a fundamental and key change for most organizations and one that they must make in order to fully develop their supply chain capabilities (van Weele, 2002).

However, this shift in focus does not come easily to many organizations, as internal business unit boundaries can be difficult to remove (Argote *et al*, 2000). The problem is exacerbated within complex organizations where capabilities such as manufacturing, logistics, and procurement have been outsourced, as is the case with IBM's supply chain.

IBM's supply chain organization (ISC) is functionally aligned as opposed to process aligned. Therefore, although functional organization charts provide a good initial indication as to how the organization is structured, they do not give any real indication as to how the different departments and workgroups actually interact with the OFP. The importance of viewing the supply chain from a process, as opposed to functional alignment, is not new (van Weele, 2002), so although the IBM ISC organization is functionally aligned, the author would need to define the organization from a

Table 1. Order flow process key components

OFP Components	Description
1. Order Receipt (OR) to Order Entry (OE).	*Process for getting an order from a customer and loading into the IBM fulfilment system.*
2. Order Entry (OE) to Order Drop (OD).	*Process for clearing the order through the fulfilment system to a point where order is ready to 'drop into manufacturing for building.*
3. Order Drop (OD) to Order Ship (OS).	*Process for getting an order through manufacturing to a point where it is ready to ship.*
4. Order Ship (OS) to Order Delivery (ODel).	*Process for consolidating an order into a shipment and delivering the order to the customer.*

process perspective. The OFP can be broken down in to four basic components as shown in Table 1.

From the OFP components outlined in Table 1 certain departments and workgroups across the ISC can be quickly associated to the core process. However, other departments and workgroups will also have an impact, be it directly or indirectly, on the performance of the OFP. Therefore, in order to develop an accurate understanding of information and knowledge habits an extended view of how departments and workgroups interact with the OFP would need to be developed. In order to identify how different business groups across the organization interact along to OFP the author used the IDEF methodology to map the OFP from end-to-end and then social network analysis to link ISC departments to the core process (OFP).

Mapping Employees to the Core Process

Once the OFP process had been mapped the author reviewed over 45 departmental operating manuals to see how and where they interacted with the OFP. The departments were identified from a functional overview of the ISC's organization. Each department was assessed against the following criteria in order to insure all those impacting the OFP were flagged for inclusion in the research.

1.   Select the department if its operational role clearly identifies it as having operational ownership of any part of the process that touches orders as they pass through the process.

Figure 1. Departments associated with OFP

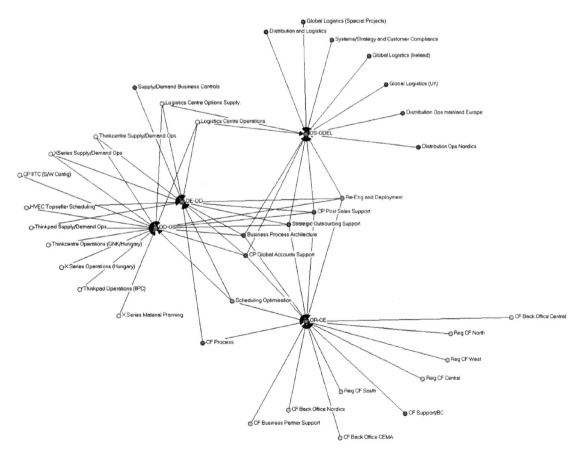

2. Select the department if its operational role clearly identifies it as having operational ownership of any part of the process that can directly or indirectly impact orders in real time as they pass through the process.

3. Select the department even if its operational role does not identify it as having operational ownership of any part of the process but where practical experience shows the department to be involved in a direct or indirect way which impacts order flow in real time.

By using the selection criteria outlined above the number of relevant departments reduced from 45 to 35 in number. Through a further review of the department's operating manuals, and using social network analysis a sociogram was generated to show how the respective departments related to the core OFP components. (Figure 1)

From the social network analysis 8 distinct workgroups could be identified. These groups were made up of departments that were not necessarily from the same business functions, but did share common aspects of process interaction. The 8 groups are identified in Table 2.

What was also important to note was the interdependent relationship the different workgroups had on each other; some departments had a direct interaction with the OFP, whereas other departments impacted the OFP through more indirect means. The interdependent relationship between the different workgroups is shown in Figure 2.

By defining the end-to-end order flow process and then identifying and mapping the different workgroups to the OFP diagram a new view of the organization emerges, based not on hierarchical structure, but on relative impact to the OFP and interdependent relationship.

IDENTIFYING KNOWLEDGE USAGE ACROSS A CORE PROCESS

Two key components to knowledge as generated and used within any organization are Explicit and Tacit (Polanyi, 1958; Nonaka *et al*, 2000; Smith 2001). Tacit is very much dependant on the individual's experiences and perspectives. This is difficult to capture from a systems perspective, with most knowledge management (KM) systems relying on explicit knowledge capture as the main

Table 2. Workgroups linked to OFP

OFP Groups	Description
OR – OE	*Primarily responsible for order receipt and loading activities, and ensuring customer orders are valid prior to loading.*
OE – OD	*Primarily responsible for supply availability against order forecast/expectation, and demand planning.*
OD – OS	*Primarily responsible for order build scheduling, and ensuring manufacturing is ready from a material and resource perspective to build customer orders.*
OS – ODel	*Primarily responsible for ensuring orders enter the distribution phase as soon as manufacturing is complete.*
E-2-E Order Management	*Made up of departments that have E2E customer responsibility of order within ISC organization, but do not directly manage orders through any stage of the process.*
E-2-E Re-Engineering	*Not responsible for actual orders in process, but are responsible for system availability and compliance with process requirements.*
E-2-E Administration	*Support groups such as business controls departments that although do not directly process orders are responsible for business guidelines that in turn can impact the E2E process.*
Senior Management	*Responsible for operational decisions impacting order scheduling, resource allocation, and prioritising organizational and process change.*

focus. In fact some researchers make the point that in order to improve KM efficiency an organization must focus on ICT, and intelligent agents (Carneiro, 2001). According to Johannessen *et al* (2001) there is a real danger that because of the focus ICT solutions have on mainly explicit knowledge this may relegate tacit knowledge to the background and hence a knowledge mismatch. Therefore, in order for KM systems to maximise their potential they need to be able to address the question of how to capture and work with tacit, as well as explicit knowledge, but not just through the use of ICT systems. From an organizational perspective this means understanding how knowledge becomes embedded in organizations, what form this knowledge takes, and how individuals react to, and draw on it.

In order to determine how information and knowledge are utilised around the OFP, Nonaka *et al's* (2000) breakdown of knowledge into tacit and explicit components needs to be considered. The reason for this is because Nonaka *et al* (2000) identified four distinct knowledge transfer mechanisms that are inherent in any learning organization. The mechanisms are tacit to tacit, tacit to explicit, explicit to explicit, and explicit to tacit.

Before considering the different types of knowledge transfer mechanisms, consideration must also be given the manner in which organizations can best manage the mechanisms. Hansen (1999) identified two distinct approaches; codified and personalised.

1. *Codified Systems*– (**Technology Driven**). The use of technology to support and manage explicit knowledge.
2. *Personalised Systems*–(**Team Driven**). The development of teams and the flow of tacit knowledge via the team dynamic.

Although Hansen (1999) suggest that an organization's approach will be either dominantly codified or personalised, a more balanced approach where neither a codified or personalised approach is dominant can be realised (Jennex & Olfman, 2006). It is this view that is fundamental to the research presented in this chapter. Indeed both codified and personalised systems can be used to manage the different knowledge transfer mechanisms, as shown in Table 3.

Knowledge Gap Analysis

The identified employees belonging to the 8 OFP workgroups were then questioned using a mixture

Figure 2. Relationships between OFP workgroups

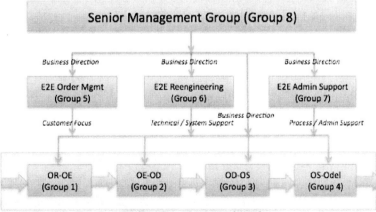

Table 3. A codified / personalised view of knowledge transfer

Knowledge Tx Mechanisms.	Approach	Description.
Tacit to Tacit	*Codified*	Change requests that enable better face to face interaction through the use of technology and available systems.
	Personalised	Change requests that allow better face to face/ information sharing through formal/informal network development.
Tacit to Explicit	*Codified*	Change requests that improve the capture of information through improved systems interfaces.
	Personalised	Change requests which improve an individual's ability to input valuable information into appropriate systems.
Explicit to Explicit	*Codified*	Change requests that improve system-to-system data transfer.
	Personalised	Change requests that look to improve how information is manually pulled from systems, reformatted, and then re-entered to different systems.
Explicit to Tacit	*Codified*	Change requests which look at improving the way systems present information in a format acceptable to the user.
	Personalised	Change requests that look to improve users contextual understand of the information on systems, and their ability to analyse the said information.

Table 4. Level of response to OFP survey

OFP Groups	% of population responding	n	N
OR-OE	15.51%	38	245
OE-OD	25.00%	8	32
OD-OS	53.33%	16	30
OS-ODel	22.45%	11	49
E2E Management	20.59%	21	102
E2E Re-Engineering	26.00%	13	50
Administration	54.17%	13	24
Snr Management	87.50%	7	8
Total	23.52%	127	540

n = Sample size. N = Population size.

of on-line and one to one questionnaires. The response rate for the 8 groups can be seen in Table 4.

The questionnaire focused on identifying how employees currently accessed information and knowledge in order to do their respective jobs. The employees were also asked to comment on how effective they believed the existing approach (codified or personalised) was in supporting them in doing their jobs. From the responses collated the view from the employees was that the dominant approach was a codified one; with the focus on integrated enterprise systems such as SAP, i2 etc., Although it was felt that these systems where important to the overall supply chain operation, the dominant focus on these systems meant that individual employees and groups did not have systems that supported more effective control and interaction within their work environment. This view supported Marwick (2001) and Johannessen *et al* (2001) who both identified the fact that an over dependency on technology would result in a failure to fully address the knowledge needs of an organization. If we then consider Porter *et al* (1985) who identify knowledge as a key compo-

Table 5. Workgroups knowledge approach gap analysis

OFP Groups	Dominant Current Approach	Desired Approach
OR – OE	Codified	Mixed (more focus on Personalised)
OE – OD	Codified	Codified
OD – OS	Codified	Mixed (more focus on Personalised)
OS – ODel	Codified	Mixed (more focus on Personalised)
E-2-E Order Management	Codified	Personalised
E-2-E Re-Engineering	Codified	Mixed (more focus on Personalised)
E-2-E Administration	Codified	Codified
Senior Management	Codified	Personalised

nent for competitive advantage, a failure by any organization to fully address its knowledge needs will result in underperformance.

From the analysis (Table 5) only two groups seemed to have the right knowledge system approach; OE-OD (*codified systems*) who mainly ensure supply is available to build before allowing an order to drop into manufacturing, and E-2-E Administration (*codified systems*) who ensure business control guidelines and reporting guidelines are followed. From the responses obtained from the remaining groups there was a belief that the existing dominant knowledge system approach did not support the knowledge and information sharing needs of the employees.

Changing the Process in Line with Knowledge Needs

How IBM, or any other complex organization, manages the re-alignment of supply chain relationships must surely impact both immediate and future performance (Lee *et al*, 1997; Troyer, 1995). Therefore, the senior management team implemented a change programme dependant on developing more effective cross-organizational working relationships in order to improve the end-to-end performance of the OFP. Performance is not simply down to the implementation of elaborate IT systems (Kotter, 1995), but requires the alignment of key personnel in an understanding of the

knowledge management aspects relating to the end-to-end processes (Wiig, 1997; Tsoukas, 1996). This requires management to think about how the business operates from a process as opposed to a functional perspective (van Weele, 2002). In order to see if the changes driving performance improvement correlated to the desired knowledge approaches a process optimisation team was setup which in turn was made up of key practitioners from all of the identified workgroups, with the exception of senior management (McLaughlin *et al*, 2006). The reason for excluding senior management from this part of the change process was because the author wanted to develop a 'bottom-up' solution for change. Senior management would then be re-engaged to review and prioritise the changes for improvement in line with organization's strategic direction. In total the optimisation team identified and implemented 90 changes across the OFP over a period of 4 months. Each change was assessed to determine the type of knowledge transfer mechanism it supported, the workgroups it impacted, and the type of knowledge systems approach used to solution the change. Figure 3 shows how the implemented changes to the OFP were seen to impact the different knowledge transfer mechanisms.

Figure 3 also shows the knowledge approaches that the implemented changes would drive. So, as expected those changes relating to tacit to tacit transfer were implemented using personalised

Figure 3. Changes and knowledge transfer mechanisms

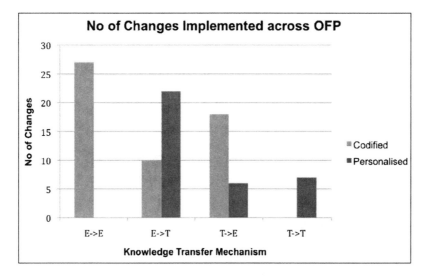

knowledge systems, and those changes relating to explicit to explicit transfer were implemented using codified knowledge systems. What is interesting here is the tacit to explicit and explicit to tacit transfer related change implementations. In the case of tacit to explicit knowledge transfer the majority of changes (75%) were implemented using codified type changes. What this tells us is

that the majority of changes have focused on improving system and user interfaces. The personalised aspect relates to training and personal knowledge sharing issues such as trust. With the explicit to tacit transfer mechanism the changes were implemented mainly (66%) through personalised type changes. Most of the focus was on raising the employee's ability to extract data from

Figure 4. Types of codified OFP changes

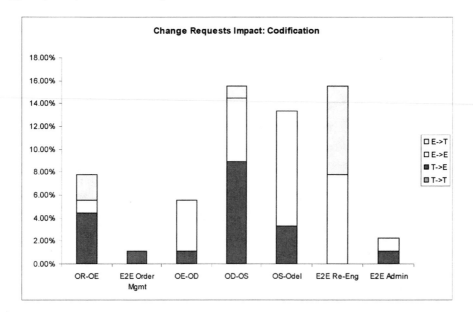

Figure 5. Types of personalised OFP change

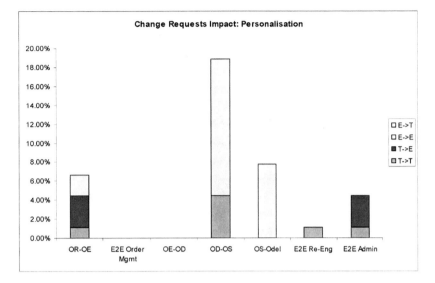

the systems, and then correctly interpreting the data. However, this information, to be of relevance to this case, needs to show how the changes impacted across the different workgroups, and the type of knowledge systems then used to implement the changes. Figure 4 and 5 show this for codified and personalised systems respectively. Note that Senior Management are not included in these findings, as there were no changes identified that directly impacted this group.

The majority of codified system changes can be seen to impact OD-OS (manufacturing), OS-Odel (distribution) and E2E Re-Eng (BPR). Across these three groups a significant amount of change related to explicit to explicit knowledge transfer. This in turn relates to how ICT systems transfer, manipulate, and store data between them. Within E2E Re-Eng significant focus is also placed on explicit to tacit knowledge transfer. These changes focused on removing ambiguity and improving the way the E2E Re-Eng ICT systems present OFP data. Across all groups (with the exception of E2E Re-Eng) tacit to explicit related changes were present. These related to the way in which employees accessed systems, and improving the flexibility they had in data entry. This was cer-

tainly important in the case of OR-OE (front end order entry) where fulfilment specialists need to add context to orders where they related to additional customer information. In the case of OD-OS (manufacturing) the tacit to explicit changes related to improving the user interfaces of the manufacturing systems. Prior to the changes the systems provided little flexibility to change order parameters once the order had been accepted into the manufacturing system.

From a personalised system perspective E2E Order Management and OE-OD (supply & demand planning) required no personalised system changes. This is due to the fact that the main focus of their work relies heavily on codified systems (data manipulation, storage, transfer and retrieval). What was interesting was the significant number of personalised system related changes impacting the OD-OS (manufacturing) group. The majority of these changes directly related to improving employee ability to interpret system-generated data (explicit to tacit). Focus within this group was also given to improving manufacturing employees' ability to socially network with other employees along the OFP, and supply chain in general (tacit to tacit). Figure 6 shows an overall

Figure 6. Focus of knowledge transfer improvements across OFP workgroups

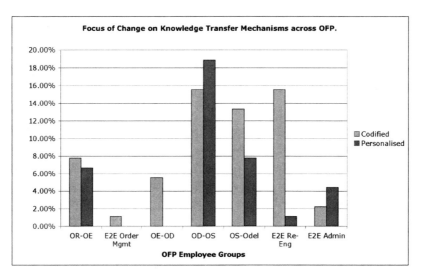

view as to how codified and personalised related knowledge transfer changes impacted the different workgroups interacting along the OFP.

The changes identified and implemented by the optimisation team were the only changes used to drive OFP end-to-end performance improvement. Over a period of 4 months the changes drove overall end-to-end performance up by 23%. From a knowledge management perspective the changes focused on certain knowledge transfer mechanisms, with the change implementation being driven from either a codified or personalised systems approach. Table 6 compares the perceived

knowledge approaches along the OFP prior to the process improvements being implemented, the desired knowledge approaches based on employee knowledge habits, and finally the actual knowledge approaches used to drive end-to-end performance.

Although the senior management group did not have any changes that directly impacted them, the formation of the optimisation team, and the integration of the optimisation team's input into the existing management system allowed for better tacit to tacit and explicit to tacit knowledge transfer, which in turn was supported through a

Table 6. Workgroups knowledge approach gap analysis

OFP Groups	Current knowledge Approach	Desired Knowledge Approach	Actual Knowledge Approaches
OR – OE	Codified	Mixed (more focus on Personalised)	Mixed (more focus on Personalised)
OE – OD	Codified	Codified	Codified
OD – OS	Codified	Mixed (more focus on Personalised)	Codified
OS – ODel	Codified	Mixed (more focus on Personalised)	Mixed (more focus on Personalised)
E-2-E Order Management	Codified	Personalised	Mixed (more focus on Personalised)
E-2-E Re-Engineering	Codified	Mixed (more focus on Personalised)	Mixed (more focus on Codified)
E-2-E Administration	Codified	Codified	Mixed (more focus on Personalised)
Senior Management	Codified	Personalised	Mixed (more focus on Personalised)

personalised system; the optimisation team and senior management review meeting (McLaughlin *et al*, 2006). Prior to the implementation of the OFP changes only two workgroups believed they had the right knowledge approach to support their roles. However, on completion of the process improvements 6 of the 8 workgroups had knowledge approaches that more closely matched their desired knowledge approach.

CONCLUSION

Every supply chain will be different, and certainly the knowledge approaches identified across IBM's order flow process will differ to those experienced in other organizations. However, what the research identifies is the need to understand how knowledge and information is created, accessed, stored, interpreted, and shared along core business processes, and not just from an organization wide, functional perspective. The research shows that where an organization looks at how knowledge and information are created and shared from a process perspective, as opposed to how they are created and shared from a functional perspective, real performance improvements can be realised. This finding supports the view of Smolnik *et al* (2005) that the real value of information and knowledge can best be understood when assesses in the context of environment (and processes) in which it is being utilised. In the case of IBM's ISC a high degree of focus had been placed on technology in order to drive supply chain performance. However, the findings from this case study support the belief of Marwick (2001) that technology alone cannot yet fully support all aspects of knowledge transfer, and Johannessen *et al* (2001) that an over dependency on technology can result in the tacit aspect of knowledge creation being overlooked. What the author also found was that the knowledge and information needs of employees will vary along the supply chain, and in order to drive end to end performance, the

best results will be when changes address these knowledge and information needs. In particular, process improvements need to focus not just on codified systems, but also on personalised systems. In effect, supply chain organizations also need to be clear about where along the process codified and personalised systems need to be implemented. It is the author's belief (supported by this research) that this cannot be done, especially in a complex organization, without directly researching the knowledge habits of their employees.

The findings put forward in this chapter are limited in the fact that only one organization was analysed. However, the author feels that the findings identify a need to review complex supply chain processes from a knowledge perspective, with particular focus on the types of knowledge transfer mechanisms at work along the core processes. What this chapter sets out to do is identify a starting point from which organizations can understand how employees utilise knowledge and information at key points along the supply chain. By taking this perspective organizations can better target knowledge and information barriers along core processes with their process improvement initiatives, and by so doing focus on changes that more effectively impact core process performance.

REFERENCES

Argote, L., & Ingram, P. (2000). Knowledge transfer: a basis for competitive advantage in firms. *Organizational Behavior and Human Decision Processes*, *82*(1), 150–169. doi:10.1006/obhd.2000.2893

Barson, R., et al. (2000). *Inter and intra organizational barriers to sharing knowledge in the extended supply chain*. e2000 Conference Proceeding.

Carneiro, A. (2001). The role of intelligent resources in knowledge management. *Journal of Knowledge Management, 5*(4), 358–367. doi:10.1108/EUM0000000006533

Davenport, T., & Prusak, L. (1998). *Working Knowledge*. Boston: Harvard Business Press.

Day, G. S. (1994). The capabilities of market driven organizations. *Journal of Marketing,* 37–52. doi:10.2307/1251915

Fuller, S. (2001). *Knowledge Management Foundations*. Boston: Butterworth-Heinemann Press.

Gummesson, E. (1991). *Qualitative Methods in Management Research*. London: Sage Publishing.

Hansen, M. T. (1999). The search transfer problem: The role of weak ties in sharing knowledge across organizational sub-units. *Administrative Science Quarterly, 44*(2), 82–122. doi:10.2307/2667032

Jennex, M. E., & Olfman, L. (2006). A model of knowledge management success. *International Journal of Knowledge Management, 2*(3), 51–68. doi:10.4018/jkm.2006070104

Johannessen, J., Olaisen, J., & Olsen, B. (2001). The mismatch of tacit knowledge: The importance of tacit knowledge, the dangers of information technology, and what to do about it. *International Journal of Information Management, 21*(1), 3–21. doi:10.1016/S0268-4012(00)00047-5

Kotter, J. P. (1995). *Leading Change: Why Transformation Efforts Fail*. Boston, MA. *Harvard Business Review*, (March-April): 59–67.

Kulp, S. C., Ofek, E., & Whitaker, J. (2003). Supply chain coordination. In Harrison, T., Lee, H. L., & Neale, J. L. (Eds.), *The Practice of Supply Chain Management: where theory and application converge*. Boston: Kluwer Academic Publishing.

Lee, H. L., Padmanabhan, V., & Whang, S. (1997). The bullwhip effect in supply chains. *Sloan Management Review, 38*(3), 93–102.

Malhotra, A., Gosain, S., & El Sawy, O. (2005). Absortive capacity configurations in supply chains: Gearing for partner-enabled market knowledge creation. *Management Information Systems Quarterly, 29*(1), 145–187.

Marwick, A. D. (2001). Knowledge Management Technology. *IBM Systems Journal, 40*(4), 814–831. doi:10.1147/sj.404.0814

McLaughlin, S., & Paton, R. A. (2008). Identifying Barriers that Impact Knowledge Creation and Transfer within complex organisations. *Journal of Knowledge Management, 12*(2), 107–123. doi:10.1108/13673270810859550

McLaughlin, S., Paton, R. A., & Macbeth, D. (2006). Managing Change within IBM's complex supply chain. *Management Decision, 44*(8), 1002–1019. doi:10.1108/00251740610690586

Nonaka, I., & Takeuchi, H. (1995). *The knowledge creating company: How Japanese companies create the dynamics of innovation*. London: Oxford Press.

Polanyi, M. (1954). *Personal knowledge: towards a post-critical philosophy*. Chicago, IL: University of Chicago Press.

Porter, M. E., & Millar, V. E. (1985). How information gives you competitive advantage. *Harvard Business Review*, (Jul-Aug): 149–161.

Prusak, L. (2001). Where did Knowledge Management come from? *IBM Systems Journal, 40*(4), 1002–1007. doi:10.1147/sj.404.01002

Simons, R. (2005). *Leavers of Organizational Design*. Boston: Harvard Business School Press.

Skyrme, D. J., & Amidon, D. M. (1997). *Creating the knowledge based business*. London: Business Intelligence.

Smolnik, S., Kremer, S., & Kolbe, L. (2005). Continuum of context explication: Knowledge discovery through process-orientated portal. *International Journal of Knowledge Management, 1*(1), 27–46. doi:10.4018/jkm.2005010102

Teece, D. J. (1998). Capturing value from knowledge assets: the new economy, markets for know how, and intangible assets. *Californian. Management Review, 40*(3), 55–78.

Tiwana, A. (2000). *The Knowledge Management toolkit.* New Jersey: Prentice Hall PTR.

Troyer, C. R. (1995). Smart movers in supply chain coordination. *Transport and Distribution, 36*(9), 55.

Tsoukas, H. (1996). The firm as a distributed knowledge system: A constructivist approach. *Strategic Management Journal, 17*, 11–25.

Van Weele, A. J. (2002). *Purchasing and Supply Chain Management* (3rd ed.). London: Thompson Publishing.

Von Hayek, F. (1952). *The counter revolution in science.* Chicago: University of Chicago Press.

Wiig, K. (1997). Knowledge Management: An Introduction and Perspective. *Journal of Knowledge Management, 1*(1), 6–14. doi:10.1108/13673279710800682

Yin, R. K. (2002). *Case Study Research* (3rd ed.). London: Sage Publications.

Chapter 12

Capturing Tacit Knowledge from Transient Workers:
Improving the Organizational Competitiveness

Salah Eldin Adam Hamza
SOFCON Consulting Engineering Co., Saudi Arabia

ABSTRACT

This article studies the way tacit knowledge is dealt with in a high turnover business environment through a qualitative research approach in an engineering organization with respect to organizational culture and values and the effect in competitive stance. The study found peer review process and managerial/ supervisory style to be effective in enabling new employees in a short time with knowledge critical for them to do a successful job, core values, and open-door policy to be necessary factors in forming a fertile environment for a quick tacit knowledge harvesting. The study also showed that a good competitive stance and customer satisfaction can be achieved and maintained through implementation of a rigorous peer review process. The study revealed noneffective utilization of knowledge management (KM) technical resources. The study directs future research towards evaluating possible objectives for utilization of KM technological resources, timeline for effective codification of tacit knowledge, and responsibilities for handling resources.

INTRODUCTION

Knowledge transfer in an organization occurs when members of the organization pass tacit and explicit knowledge to each other. Information

technology assists knowledge transfer by providing knowledge means for capturing, storing, and retrieving. Knowledge that is primarily in the tacit dimension requires that more context be captured with the knowledge in which context is the information used to explain what the knowledge means and how it is used. That is why this study focuses

DOI: 10.4018/978-1-60960-555-1.ch012

on how tacit knowledge can be transferred into explicit in order to make it retrievable and helpful for organization members to achieve a better organizational competitive advantage.

The speed of making tacit knowledge tangible is an issue in a high employee turnover environment. This is important especially when the process of engaging new engineers and project managers in designing projects is faster and the time for training new employees is limited. While it takes the organization time and effort to enable new employees with tacit knowledge necessary for them to do a successful job, knowledgeable employees emigrate to other organizations seeking better employment opportunities. This situation attracts future research focus. The implementation of learning-based systems development is a challenge for organizations as the basic training and education offered by them and the particular experiences of the individuals on their own and other factors such as fear and ignorance prevent such actions (Selamat & Choudrie, 2007). It is important for the development of people that we create a suitable organizational culture and infrastructure such that knowledge sharing is promoted. Literature reveals examples of effective learning communities and illuminates that even within one single company there is no one-size-fits-all solution (Kohlbacher & Mukai, 2007).

All are considered good justifications for this study to explore how tacit knowledge can be handled in a high employee turnover engineering organization, what are the cultural values that can help the organization to achieve the mission of tacit knowledge management (KM), and what is the effect tacit knowledge may influence on the organization competitive stance.

Literature on knowledge, KM, KM success/ failure factors, KM success models, organizational learning, learning culture, and competitive advantage are first reviewed. The background of the case study and research methodology are then presented. Afterward, the success and failure of the engineering organization are discussed in light of the findings. Finally, conclusions and future research directions are drawn.

KNOWLEDGE/KM

Organizational knowledge usually resides embedded in various types of forms including records, documents, procedures, processes, databases, routines, and practices. Davenport and Prusak (1998, p. 5) define knowledge as "a fluid mix of framed experience, values, contextual information, and expert insight that provides a framework for evaluating and incorporating new experiences and information. It originates and is applied in the minds of knower." Several other definitions of knowledge were given by Nonaka and Takeuchi (1995), Alavi and Leidner (1999), Lai and Chu (2000), Murray (1996), Sveiby (1997), Polanyi (1966), and Biggam (2001). Since 1990, organizations realized that knowledge could be about diverse organizational aspects such as products, processes, customers, employees, partners, competitors, and good and bad experiences. Many organizations started since then to pay attention to manage this knowledge until it became a hot topic nowadays as many business communities trying to properly understand and implement it (Jennex, 2007).

In order to make the best use of knowledge, many initiatives emerged and evolved in the past seventeen years forming what has been known as KM. Nevertheless, still experts are debating and bearing different opinions on KM (Corral, Griffin, & Jennex, 2005). Jennex (2005, p. iv) gave one of the most recent definitions of KM when they state:

KM is the practice of selectively applying knowledge from previous experiences of decision making to current and future decision-making activities with the express purpose of improving the organization's effectiveness.

Further, search in literature reveals that many other definitions, taxonomies, and dimensions of knowledge have been published. Jennex and Croasdell (2005) cited that the most commonly used taxonomy is Polyani's (1967). Further, Polanyi (1967) made a distinction between two types of knowledge; explicit—knowledge that has been captured and codified into manuals, procedures, and rules, and is easy to disseminate (Stenmark, 2000) and tacit—that is understood within a knower's mind (Jennex, 2007, p. 3). Explicit and tacit knowledge form two endpoints of a knowledge continuum with a varying degree of explicitness in between. Jennex (2007) supports this notion, as he views that what may be tacit to one person may be explicit to another. This fact has encouraged many researches to recognize the importance of transferring tacit knowledge into explicit and stimulate studies on how to arm a broader spectrum of organization members with tacit knowledge.

The theory of tacit and explicit knowledge may necessitate the development of a scale that can be used to identify whether individuals rely more on tacit or explicit knowledge in the completion of a task and to identify what tasks might be more conducive to either tacit or explicit knowledge. Instruments designed to elicit perceptions regarding the nature of knowledge used by workers and their degree of reliance on tacit knowledge would help managers identify pockets of tacit knowledge within the firm that could either be made explicit or prevent it from becoming explicit should its strategic value requires protection (Chilton & Bloodgood, 2007). Further, collaborative techniques that support a team of success-critical stakeholders in surfacing tacit knowledge during systems development projects help accessing tacit knowledge (Grunbacher & Briggs, 2001).

An agent-based retrieval system technology could act as a facilitator in the knowledge managing process of capturing tacit knowledge on an intra-organizational Web and make it tangible (Stenmark, 2000). This approach has two benefits:

first, the otherwise hard to solve problem of being able to produce an exhaustive definition of one's interests is replaced with the much simpler task of determining whether a given document is interesting or not. This is because the latter is based on tacit knowledge. This is also illustrated by the fact that users prefer pointing to documents rather than inventing keywords when searching the Web. Second, since a good profile results in more accurate information, a natural incentive to set up and maintain the profile exists. It may be claimed that the explication of tacit knowledge is both difficult and costly, and not always desired. Knowledge does not move without motivating forces, and people will not give away valuable possessions such as knowledge without concern for what they may gain or loose in the process. The author's contribution was the suggestion that profiles based on the tacit knowledge of our interests and identified by practice are conveyed as more trustworthy than the espoused theory-based job descriptions.

KM SUCCESS/KM FAILURE FACTORS

Various sets of factors for success of knowledge management systems (KMS) were pointed out by Mandviwalla, Eulgem, Mould, and Rao (1998), Davenport, DeLong, and Beers (1998), Ginsberg and Kambil (1999), Alvai and Leinder (1999), Jennex and Olfman (2000), Holsapple and Joshi (2000), Cross and Baird (2000), Koskinen (2001), Jennex and Olfman (2002), Barna (2003), and Yu, Kim, and Kim (2004). Some of the factors pointed out by those studies included provision for knowledge creation, storage/retrieval, transfer, and application, user motivation to share and use knowledge, leadership, top management support, the ability to identify, capture, and transfer critical tacit knowledge, efficiency to facilitate the transference of tacit knowledge to new members, creating and promoting a culture of knowledge sharing management, creating communities of practice, and creating a best practices repository, creating a learning organization, and creation of organizational memory.

KM SUCCESS MODELS

In 1992 DeLone and McLean published their seminal work that proposed a taxonomy and an interactive model for conceptualizing and operationalizing IS Success (DeLone & McLean, 1992). Jennex, Olfman, Pituma, and Yong-Tae (1998) and Jennex and Olfman (2002) adopted the generic framework of the DeLone and McLean IS Success Model and customized its dimensions to reflect the System Quality and Use constructs needed for an organizational memory information system (OMS). DeLone and McLean (2003) revisited the DeLone and McLean IS Success Model by incorporating subsequent IS Success research and by addressing criticisms of the original model. Jennex and Olfman (2006) adapted DeLone and McLean (2003) to KM Success by applying KM research.

Bots and de Bruijn (2002) developed the knowledge value chain as the best way to judge good KM through which KM is assessed for effectiveness at each step of the knowledge process. They developed the model by viewing and contrasting KM through an analytical (technical) perspective and an actor (user) perspective. These perspectives are conflicting, and KM assessment occurs by determining how well the KMS meets each perspective at each step.

Massey, Montoya-Weiss, and O'Driscoll (2002) derived a process-based KM success model from their Nortel case study that suggested that KM cannot be applied commonly and that a process approach to KM will help an organization to realize how it can apply KM to improve its performance. The model is based on the framework proposed by Holsapple and Joshi (2001), and reflects that KM success is based on understanding a process-oriented KM strategy and its effects on

the organization, its knowledge users, and how they use knowledge. It recognizes that KM is an organizational change process and KM success cannot split itself from the organizational change success with the result the KM success is defined as improving organizational or process performance. The model key components are KM Strategy, Key Managerial Influences, Key Resource Influences, and Key Environmental Influences.

Lindsey (2002) proposed a conceptual KM effectiveness model based on combining Organizational Capability Perspective theory (Gold, Malhotra, & Segars, 2001) and Contingency Perspective Theory (Becerra-Fernandez & Sabherwal, 2001). The model defines KM effectiveness in terms of two main constructs: knowledge infrastructure capability and knowledge process capability, with the knowledge process capability construct being influenced by a knowledge task.

Maier (2002) also proposed a KMS success model based on the DeLone and McLean IS Success Model (1992). This model is similar to the Jennex Olfman model. This model uses seven dimensions: system quality, information/communication/knowledge quality, knowledge-specific service, system use/user satisfaction, individual impact, impact on collectives of people, and organizational impact.

ORGANIZATIONAL LEARNING/ LEARNING CULTURE

Organizational Learning (OL) is identified as a quantifiable improvement in activities, increased available knowledge for decision-making or sustainable competitive advantage (Brown & Duguid, 1991;Lave & Wenger, 1991; Lesser & Prusak, 1999; Walker, Kogut, & Shan, 1997). Another definition refers to OL as the process of detection and correction of errors (Burt, 1997). In this view, organizations learn through individuals acting as agents for them. Individual learning activities are seen as being facilitated or inhibited by an ecological system of factors that may be called an organizational learning system. Learning in this perspective is based on Kolb's (Portes, 1998) model of experiential learning where individuals learn by doing. An organization can also learn if, through its processing of information, its potential behaviors are changed (Jacobs, 1961). This incorporates the concept of OM into OL. In this view, OM is the process by which experience is used to modify current and future actions.

Just implementing KMS and transferring tacit knowledge into explicit may not improve the organizational competitive advantage unless the organization becomes a learning society (Senge, 1990, 1994). Numerous organizations have found that becoming a learning organization requires specific widespread organizational primary competencies, including systems thinking, personal mastery, mental models, building shared vision, and team learning (Senge, 1990). The works of Child and Kieser (1981) and Schein (1993) have elevated the status of the learning organization as many believe that all organizations engage in collective learning as work progresses. Learning is enhanced when people gather for dialogue, which is defined as a sustained collective inquiry into the processes, assumptions, and certainties that compose everyday experience (Isaacs, 1993).

While creating a knowledge-enabled culture, English and Baker (2006) emphasized that every organization must search for and import best practices, learn/understand and share, create intellectual capital, and convert intellectual capital into value and profits.

Barna (2003) identified creating and promoting a culture of knowledge sharing within the organization and creating a learning organization as the main factors important to a successful KMS. That is in addition to articulating a corporate KM vision, rewarding employees for knowledge sharing, creating communities of practice, creating a best practices repository, obtaining senior management support, providing KMS training, and precisely defining KMS project objectives.

Further, Yu, Kim, and Kim (2004) explored the linkage of organizational culture to KM success and found that KM drivers such as a learning culture (Davenport & Prusak, 1998), knowledge sharing intention, KMS quality, rewards, and KM team activity significantly affected KM performance. According to Yeung, Ulrich, Nason, and Glinow (1999), organizations with routines and competencies designed to retain and nurture transferred knowledge are better able to support the process of learning by doing than less fertile organizations.

Schein (1992) define culture as the shared values, beliefs, and practices of the people in the organization, and Smith and McLaughlin (2003) included the impact of nonrational people-factors that are so often un-discussable in organizations. Nevertheless, McDermott and O'Dell (2001) indicated that many well-designed KM efforts have failed because of people's nonsupportive beliefs.

The success or failure of knowledge sharing activities depends on how individuals and/or groups feel about the process, that is, the rumor mill shares knowledge highly effectively if not necessarily accurately because people enjoy the social activity and how they feel about the network of people with whom they are socializing in sharing knowledge (Smith, 2005). A successful implementation of KM requires building the KM approach to fit by linking sharing knowledge to solving practical business problems, tying sharing knowledge to a pre-existing core value, introducing KM in a way that matches the organization's style, building on the existing networks that people use in their daily work, and encouraging peers and supervisors to exert pressure to share (McDermott & O'Dell, 2001).

COMPETITIVE ADVANTAGE

Knowledge is recognized as a key economic resource, and obviously, organizations must possess the right knowledge in the desired form and context under all circumstances in order to be successful. Several studies have shown that KM is critical and plays an important source for competitive advantage (Adams & Lamont, 2003; April, 2002; Carneiro, 2000; Grover & Davenport, 2001; Kalling, 200; 3Sharkie, 2003).

Knowledge about customers, products, processes, and past successes and failures are assets that may produce long-term sustainable competitive advantage (Huber, 2001; Stewart, 2001). This understanding was supported by Nonaka (1994), Teece (1998), and Spender (1996) as they stressed that competitive advantage through KM is realized through identifying the valuable tacit knowledge possessed by organizational members and making that knowledge explicit. Reducing costs, enhancing product or service quality, or creating value to customers are necessary business strategies for designing and implementing KM in order to create competitive advantage (Ofek & Sarvary, 2001).

Today's businesses challenges have led the organizations to look for more creativity in management practices, products, services, and production processes that leads to competitive advantage (Higgins, 1995). Organizational learning is identified as a quantifiable improvement in activities, increased available knowledge for sustainable competitive advantage or decision-making (Easterby-Smith, 1997; Miller, 1996). Few business owners would disagree that one of their most valuable assets is the reputation of their business, because a stellar reputation builds a competitive advantage (Kartalia, 2000). For knowledge-based organizations, competitive advantage and profits are generated through the successful management of intangible assets (Sveiby, 1997).

The need to understand the relationship between KM and competitiveness is not new (Dutta, 1997). In order for practitioners to manage knowledge effectively, it is imperative that they have some type of guidelines when developing their KM initiatives (Holsapple & Jones, 2007). Such guidance could come from a definitive model

that gives practitioners a structure for organizing their analyses of activities involved in KM and for understanding how they impact competitiveness.

The knowledge chain model is an initial step in this direction (Holsapple & Singh, 2000). It identifies nine activity classes that are performed by organizations in their conduct of KM. Each class is a potential source of competitive advantage that can be approached from one or more of four angles: productivity, agility, innovation, and/or reputation—the PAIR directions (Holsapple & Singh, 2001). Each of the nine basic KM activities can be performed in ways that enhance a firm's performance in one or more of the PAIR directions (Holsapple & Singh, 2005).

Holsapple and Jones (2007) furnished an understanding of contemporary practices and views regarding the relationships between performance of KM activities and impacts on competitiveness, with particular emphasis on the role of technology in performing KM activities in ways that enhance competitiveness. That understanding can help practitioners in recognizing both needs and opportunities as they evaluate and plan their own organizations' KM initiatives, can inform and help researchers stimulate future investigations of the relationship between KM and competitiveness, and can point out gaps in present KM technologies and, perhaps, spur advances in those areas for technology vendors.

BACKGROUND OF THE CASE STUDY

The study performed a detailed investigation of tacit knowledge performance in a Middle East engineering design organization specializes in engineering designs for the oil and gas sector. The organization handles project types including process plants, refineries, pipelines, control systems, wastewater, and infrastructures. Performance of these projects is vital to the global economy as well as to the local because of the importance the oil and gas sector plays worldwide. Schedule delays or design quality problems have direct impact in the rate of flow of oil and gas into the world market and therefore a diverse impact in the economy.

The organization structure divides into seven departments headed by the general manager. The general manager reports to the CEO who heads a group of companies. The departments include engineering, business development, commercial, information technology (IT), human resources (HR), quality, and finance. In addition to the managers of the departments, the organization mainly employs project managers and engineers as core staff in addition to support staff for non-engineering departments.

Over the past 6 years, the organization has expanded its range of business capacities and resources in order to get hold of more market opportunities and has enjoyed a healthy growth in terms of business and profits. In the last two years, the organization acquired a leading company in the design of transmission and power projects and accomplished a major engineering software refurbishment to cope with market needs that emerged from oil prices increase. Nevertheless, the organization realized a continuous loss of experienced engineers and project managers and therefore a loss of critical knowledge needed for completion of current projects and for competition to new projects. This was due to staff transition from one job to another and migration from one country to another chasing better employment.

The organization establishes databases warehousing completed and current project information, engineering standards, repetitive design details, customer related processes, customer satisfaction/complaints records, and organizational knowledge.

METHODOLOGY

This study aims to address three research questions: (1) How can tacit knowledge be captured, shared, and transferred in a high turnover business environment? (2) What are the cultural aspects and values necessary to prevail in a high turnover business environment to make tacit knowledge manageable? and (3) How can tacit knowledge affect organizational competitive stance?

Denkin and Lincoln (1994) qualitative approach was followed in this study to investigate the research questions. Unstructured in depth face-to-face interviews were conducted with key personnel, project managers, lead engineers, and new employees for exploring the case study. Interview questions were asked by the same interviewer and answers were hand-recorded by the interviewer and each of two assistants. Answers were confirmed by the interviewees to ensure correct understanding and that all information and details were accurately recorded and not missed out. The respondents were asked open-ended questions. "How do you evaluate the peer review process and how do you rate it with work practices in your previous organizations," "How do you find the knowledge base beneficial to provide information you need to do your daily work and what contribution you make towards maintaining the knowledge base," and "What is your opinion about the resources provided by the organization to facilitate knowledge exchange between employees" are examples of the questions to the employees. "As a manager, can you tell me what practices do you exercise to ensure that a new staff has been fully oriented and how long does it take you to achieve that" is one example of the questions for the managers. The respondents have proofread transcripts of their interviews to ensure validity. Reviews of corporate organizational and project records and procedures were also studied. Finally, observations of the researcher, been a participant, occupied a part in the setting. These different data sources were explored in order to provide data triangulation (Denzin, 1970) and to lead to greater validity (Coolican, 1992).

The participants consisted of 19 staff: the engineering manager, four project managers (including two new), five lead engineers, and nine engineers (including six new). Staff members that had spent less than a year with the organization were considered new. Being the manager for the main department in the organization, the engineering manager was selected. Project managers were selected to study the tacit knowledge transfer process between them and the engineering manager, their project team members and the reflections in customer satisfaction performance. Lead engineers were selected as their category weighs more than 80% of the organization's workforce, therefore the role lead engineers play in transferring tacit knowledge upward, and downward the organizational hierarchy is essential. New engineers were interviewed to explore the benefit from the tacit knowledge transfer process.

Records of nine projects handled by project managers other than those interviewed were studied. Six projects were competed between years 2003 and 2006, and three were ongoing. Records reviewed included contract documents, minutes of meetings, customer complaints, objectives, and revenue performance.

Finally, observations by the researcher were recorded and confirmed by interviewees.

RESEARCH FINDINGS

In this section, we discuss the findings concluded from the study as emerged in four categories: business processes, managerial/supervisory practices, technological resources, and core values. The business processes category embeds two elements concerned with tacit knowledge in the engineering design organization; the peer review as a mechanism in project execution process and secondly the process of incorporating captured knowledge into work procedures. The managerial/supervisory practice category concerns the way a manager/supervisor distributes work to his subordinates, oversees their daily performance, and guides them to resolve issues. The technological resources category included four elements: e-mail accounts, public employee network folders, knowledge database, and Internet access. The fourth category is organizational core values intended to control

Figure 1. A peer review model at project level

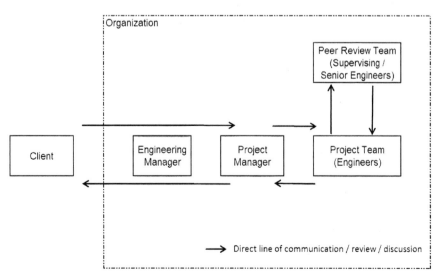

the behavior of the organization members among each other. The four categories are detailed here.

Business Process Category

The first finding in terms of business process category is the peer review process—independent review for work either by supervisor or by a senior colleague nominated by the supervisor—implemented consistently in developing project designs. Figure 1 illustrates the peer review model at project level. Two sources were consulted and led to different findings; a review of organizational work procedure and an interview with engineers. An excerpt from design work procedure is given here:

The lead engineer shall carry out or shall appoint a senior engineer to carryout a discipline peer review on a daily basis to ensure that engineer's performance is in accordance with organizational practices, clients' standards and requirements, business practices and is technically sound. Upon completion of a design package, the peer reviewer shall provide a sign off copy of the design confirming his direct involvement in the stages through which the design has been accomplished.

On the other hand, new engineers appear to have benefited much from the peer review and gained rising confidence to gear up with their new business. Interviews with four new engineers (less than a year with the organization) revealed the following feedback:

We were hesitant to pass three months probation when selected for recruitment with the organization, as it was a new industry to us. The peer review process has promoted our confidence and enriched our knowledge to take the right action. It offered us the chance to observe through actions and learn through experience and practice. The face-to-face interaction with our peers taught us what we would have not learned in years in our own.

The other element identified in the context of business process is how knowledge has been exchanged, captured, and deposited in database. There is a specific database developed and reserved for collecting and publishing knowledge. Supervisors and department managers can browse its contents through a shared drive. The supervisor of the knowledge base informed:

The organization is certified for Quality Management System 9001:2000 and the system provides for a systematic incorporation of suggested ideas into the knowledge base for improvement and learning through a proposal; logging, review, approval, circulation and updating life cycle. The only few proposals received to add to the knowledge base were from exclusively department heads. Middle and bottom line employees are not motivated to pursue submitting proposals. It might be a good idea to include this issue to our criteria for selecting the best employee for monthly award. The project close out reports been prepared by project managers have provisions for proposals, but never been utilized.

One further finding in this category concerns the time suitable for the organizations to extract knowledge from project records. A lead engineer indicated that:

Sometimes we recall experience we encountered with a project in the past. The problem is that we cannot search those projects records as they have been destroyed in compliance to clients' policy. Some clients' policies prevent keeping project sensitive documents beyond closeout. Extraction and writing of knowledge should take place while projects are live.

Managerial/Supervisory Practice Category

The findings in terms of managerial/supervisory practice were of two elements: the engineering / project manager daily interaction and filling the vacant lead positions from within the organization. These findings are tackled as follows.

The engineering manager was the most senior function responsible for project performance and dealing with clients. A number of project managers handle projects under the supervision of the engineering manager. The engineering manager does not handle projects on his own, but oversees all projects to ensure quality, schedule and cost effectiveness. He keeps an eye on performance of all projects, reviews incoming correspondence prior to action by project managers and initials outgoing correspondence prior to issue by project managers. In this regard the engineering manager response was:

Need for close and deep face-to-face involvement with project managers newly recruited to projects is critical. Although, the organization employs staff with ten years minimum experience for project management, project managers coming from other business environments showed lack for sense of contractual obligations, absence of documented commitments and financial impact. The close supervision and involvement have helped me remarkably reduce client problems with new project managers. I do nominal and procedural interaction with long-term employed staff. Face-to-face communication with my subordinates offers me the chance to share and personalize experience. It is the practice been followed in all departments. I served this organization for more than a decade and my observation is valid throughout my career.

A top management member relating to the project/engineering manager interaction results stated another case. He told a story in the name of the CEO:

The CEO received a call from a client representative desiring demobilization of a project manager newly recruited by the organization. The client was not satisfied initially as the project manager was slow to cope with client's demands on time. He was not fully aware of the way the client wanted his project to be handled. The CEO requested the client for three weeks time to get a replacement to the project manager. The CEO instructed the engineering manager to work closely with the project manager to enable him grasp the business aspects. After three weeks of close involvement and guidance, the project manager harvested enough knowledge to deal with the client. The CEO informed the client that he would get a replacement in two days. The client said he is doing well with the project manager and does not want a replacement. The project was ultimately completed successfully.

In their first day of employment, new employees go through an orientation cycle with all departments. The HR department starts the orientation program and issues every employee a wallet-size card with the company's core values that read:

We accomplish more together than we could do alone and are willing to do more than we receive. We challenge ourselves and will continually examine and raise our expectations. We respect our clients, our competitors, and the law. We respect and take pride in our firm and each other. We are loyal to our clients, our firm, each other, our profession, and our community.

The other element identified in the context of managerial/supervisory practice is the way the organization fills vacant lead positions. It is the management first choice to search within current staff for suitable candidates to fill those positions. Individuals across projects stated:

The organization viewpoint is important for two reasons; it ensures maintaining project team's morale and relations. We feel fear that we may not be in harmony with new leaders as some come with their own policies and agenda. The second, we think the organization should reward good performers, encourage, and motivate others to excel through promotion to upper positions. We believe in special cases when high skills are required.

Technological Resource Category

The study identified several technological resources in support of business requirements as well as organizational learning and knowledge. E-mail accounts, databases, public folders, and Internet access, employees' public network folders—folders assigned to employees with limited capacity to share information for a limited time and not to be backed-up—were the major identified. These findings are explained as follows.

The organization was committed to enable employees with e-mail accounts, each with a two-mega byte attachment capacity. Eighty four per cent of the respondents stated that:

We appreciated providing e-mail facilities across the organization. Sometimes, we need to send drawing files to vendors or client in sizes more than permitted. This is a frustrating situation. However, the organization provides bigger bandwidth to senior people.

On the other hand, respondents expressed concerns about granting e-mail accounts to all employees. A senior manager feedback was:

Some employees exchange e-mails to a group of people within the organization domain just for leisure. They do not think if their message may disturb recipients from doing their business. I noticed that one staff kept forwarding to others and me several e-mails he receives everyday. I was

not interested in most of them. Some employees do not appropriately select their addresses resulting in overwhelming us with irrelevant and uninteresting material.

The organization adopts lessons learned program comprises of two aspects: collection and implementation. At the end of each project, project teams conduct collection workshops for capturing useful knowledge, so their significant positive and negative experiences can be made easily available for application to improve other projects. At the start of each project, the project teams conduct implementation workshops for selection of applicable existing lessons from the knowledge base to help new or ongoing project teams improve their performance. The program has successfully improved project quality, reduced cost, and enhanced schedule. The program faces collection limitations as most of project teams are demobilized to other projects immediately when projects approach their end. By the time collection workshops are held only few members remain available to participate and share their experience, thereby limiting workshops effectiveness. Two engineers stated that:

Databases been used by business units served analysis of performance and extracting information for planning for future business. We have concerns about the speed of extracting knowledge and transferring it into the knowledge base. The best time to collect and extract lessons learned is during project lifetime. Most clients' security policies call for destroying records when projects are closed. We lost the chance to capture, extract, and register some lessons learned while the projects were live. The IT policies restrict direct access to databases only to senior staff while juniors were not permitted free search and browsing for confidentiality and control reasons. Also, we don't have access to computer assisted design and drafting (CADD) files.

Core Values Category

The study identified a business environment inspired by core values guiding staff toward mutual respect and personal relations maintenance. These findings are explained as follows.

The author has participated in developing and establishing several and cross-functional practices. As a participant, the author noted observations and discussed them with interviewees for confirmation. Those observations included:

Core values were displayed in offices, conference rooms, and hallways. Top management and senior staff continuously recall the core values especially in public speeches and the company annual festivals. There is no historical track record of harassment or discrimination to race, color, or sex.

Eighty-nine per cent of the respondents agreed with the observations on harassment and misconduct and another set of 95% of them indicated that:

The management adopts an open-door policy whereby they listen to employees regarding different organizational issues. Employees across the organization have the liberty to discuss and exchange individual experience, ideas, emotions, and values. The management does not respond to every issue raised through the open-door-policy.

CONCLUSION

This article explores how tacit knowledge can be handled in a high employee turnover engineering organization, the cultural values that can help the organization achieve the mission of tacit KM, and the effect tacit knowledge may influence on the organization competitive stance. The findings indicate that tacit knowledge can be shared, exchanged, and promoted between new and existing knowledgeable staff in a high employee-turnover business environment. New employees can adapt into the organization culture and practices effectively and timely should a shield of an internal review process is created to ensure that performance is in line with customer expectations. A structured internal peer review facilitates knowledge sharing and exchange between project teams and eliminates organizational dependence on a single employee's effort that might put the business performance at risk. Therefore, an employee leaving the organization may not severely affect the knowledge assets of the company as most of what transient workers know should have been exposed to other members through the review process.

It is not enough for sharing tacit knowledge just to have staff get involved in peer review processes. The organization needs to have human relations maintained while they exercise such interactions. People coming from different cultures and ethnics have different understandings and interpretations as well. Deployment of codes of conduct, core values, and open-door policies within multicultural organizations forms strong grounds and fertile environments for tacit knowledge sharing.

Another major conclusion regards the use of technological resource dedicated for KM capturing, dissemination, and codification for future use. It was obvious that objectives were not fully met, as specific measurable goals were not set for resources to achieve. Literature reviewed indicated that KM strategy that identifies users, sources, processes, and storage is a key factor for success of the KMS. This study concluded that the strategy should include objectives, timeline, and responsibilities of tacit KM activities and resources.

The concluding remark is that sharing tacit knowledge through a well-established organizational culture leads to a better competitive stance.

A key direction for future research would be to evaluate possible objectives for utilization of KM technological resources, timeline for effective codification of tacit knowledge, and responsibilities for handling resources.

REFERENCES

Adams, G. L., & Lamont, B. T. (2003). Knowledge management systems and developing sustainable competitive advantage. *Journal of Knowledge Management, 7*(2), 142–154.

Alavi, M., & Leidner, D. (1999). Knowledge management systems: Emerging views and practices form the field. In *Proceedings of the 32th Hawaii International Conference on System Sciences*, IEEE Computer Society.

April, K. D. (2002). Guidelines for developing a k-strategy. *Journal of Knowledge Management, 6*(5), 445–456.

Barna, Z. (2003). *Knowledge management: A critical e-business strategic factor.* Unpublished Masters Thesis, San Diego State University, USA.

Becerra-Fernandez, I., & Sabherwal, R. (2001). Organizational knowledge management: A contingency perspective. *Journal of Management Information Systems, 18*(1), 23–55.

Biggam, J. (2001). Defining knowledge: An epistemological foundation for knowledge management. In *Proceedings of the 34th Hawaii International Conference on System Sciences*, IEEE Computer Society.

Bots, P. W. G., & de Bruijn, H. (2002). Effective knowledge management in professional organizations: Going by the rules. In *Proceedings of the 35th Hawaii International Conference on System Sciences*, IEEE Computer Society.

Brown, J., & Duguid, P. (1991). Organizational learning and communities-of-practice: Toward a unified view of working, learning, and innovation. *Organization Science, 2*(1), 40–57.

Burt, R. (1997). The contingent value of social capital. *Administrative Science Quarterly, 42*(2), 339–365.

Carneiro, A. (2000). How does knowledge management influence innovation and competitiveness? *Journal of Knowledge Management, 4*(2), 87–98.

Child, J., & Kieser, A. (1981). Development of organizations over time. In Nystrom, N. C., & Starbuck, W. H. (Eds.), *Handbook of organizational design*. Oxford: Oxford University Press.

Chilton, M. A., & Bloodgood, J. M. (2007). The dimensions of tacit and explicit knowledge: A description and measure. In *Proceedings of the 40th Hawaii International Conference on System Sciences*, IEEE Computer Society.

Coolican, H. (1992). *Research methods and statistics in Psychology*. London: Hodder & Stoughton.

Corral, K., Griffin, J., & Jennex, M. E. (2005). Expert's perspective: The potential of knowledge management in data warehousing. *Business Intelligence Journal, 10*(1), 36–40.

Cross, R., & Baird, L. (2000). Technology is not enough: Improving performance by building organizational memory. *Sloan Management Review, 41*(3), 41–54.

Davenport, T. H., DeLong, D. W., & Beers, M. C. (1998). Successful knowledge management projects. *Sloan Management Review, 39*(2), 43–57.

Davenport, T. H., & Prusak, L. (1998). *Working knowledge: How organizations manage what they know*. Boston, MA: Harvard Business School Press.

Delone, W. H., & McLean, E. R. (1992). Information systems success: The quest for the dependent variable. *Information Systems Research, 3*, 60–95.

DeLone, W. H., & McLean, E. R. (2003). The DeLone and McLean model of information systems success: A ten-year update. *Journal of Management Information Systems, 19*(4), 9–30.

Denkin, N. K., & Lincoln, Y. S. (1994). *Handbook of qualitative research*. London: Sage.

Denzin, N. K. (1970). *The research act: A theoretical introduction to sociological methods*. Chicago: Aldine.

Dutta, S. (1997). Strategies for implementing knowledge-based systems. *IEEE Transactions on Engineering Management, 44*(1), 79–90.

Easterby-Smith, M. (1997). Disciplines of organizational learning: Contributions and critiques. *Human Relations, 50*(9), 1085–1113.

English, M.J., & Baker, W.H. (2006, February). Rapid knowledge transfer: The key to success. *Quality Progress, ASQ,* 41-84.

Ginsberg, M., & Kambil, A. (1999). Annotate: A Web-based knowledge management support system for document collections. In *Proceedings of the 32nd Hawaii International Conference on System Sciences*, IEEE Computer Society.

Gold, A. H., Malhotra, A., & Segars, A. H. (2001). Knowledge management: An organizational capabilities perspective. *Journal of Management Information Systems, 18*(1), 185–214.

Grover, V., & Davenport, T. (2001). General perspectives on knowledge management: Fostering a research agenda. *Journal of Management Information Systems, 18*(1), 5–21.

Grunbacher, P., & Briggs, R. O. (2001). Surfacing tacit knowledge in requirements negotiation: Experiences using easy win win. In *Proceedings of the 34th Hawaii International Conference on System Sciences*, IEEE Computer Society.

Higgins, J. M. (1995). Innovate or evaporate: Seven secrets of innovative corporations. *The Futurist, 29*(5), 42–48.

Holsapple, C. W., & Jones, K. G. (2007). Knowledge chain activity classes: Impacts on competitiveness and the importance of technology support. *International Journal of Knowledge Management, 3*(3), 2–5.

Holsapple, C. W., & Joshi, K. D. (2000). An investigation of factors that influence the management of knowledge in organizations. *The Journal of Strategic Information Systems, 9*, 235–261.

Holsapple, C. W., & Joshi, K. D. (2001). Knowledge management: A three-fold framework. *The Information Society, 18*(1), 47–64.

Holsapple, C. W., & Singh, M. (2000). The knowledge chain. In *Proceedings of the Annual Conference of the Southern Association on Information Systems*, Atlanta, Georgia.

Holsapple, C. W., & Singh, M. (2001). The knowledge chain model: Activities for competitiveness. *Expert Systems with Applications, 20*(1), 77–98.

Holsapple, C. W., & Singh, M. (2005). Performance implications of the knowledge chain. *International Journal of Knowledge Management, 1*(4), 1–22.

Huber, G. P. (2001). Transfer of knowledge in knowledge management systems: Unexplored issues and suggested studies. *European Journal of Information Systems, 10*(2), 72–79.

Isaacs, W. N. (1993). Taking flight: Dialogue, collective thinking, and organizational learning. *Organizational Dynamics, 22*(2), 24–39.

Jacobs, J. (1961). *The decline and rise of American cities*. New York: Random House.

Jennex, M. E. (2005). What is KM? *International Journal of Knowledge Management, 1*(4), i–iv.

Jennex, M. E. (2007). *Knowledge management in modern organizations*. Idea Group Publishing.

Jennex, M. E., & Croashell, D. (2005). Knowledge management: Are we a discipline? *International Journal of Knowledge Management, 1*(1), i–v.

Jennex, M. E., & Olfman, L. (2000). Development recommendations for knowledge management/ organizational memory systems. In *Proceedings of the Information Systems Development Conference.*

Jennex, M. E., & Olfman, L. (2002). Organizational memory/knowledge effects on productivity: A longitudinal study. In *Proceedings of the 35th Annual Hawaii International Conference on System Sciences,* IEEE Computer Society.

Jennex, M. E., & Olfman, L. (2006). A model of knowledge management success. *International Journal of Knowledge Management, 2*(3), 51–68.

Jennex, M. E., Olfman, L., Pituma, P., & Yong-Tae, P. (1998). An organizational memory information systems success model: An extension of DeLone and McLean's I/S success model. In *Proceedings of the 31st Annual Hawaii International Conference on System Sciences,* IEEE Computer Society.

Kalling, T. (2003). Knowledge management and the occasional links with performance. *Journal of Knowledge Management, 7*(3), 67–81.

Kartalia, J. (2000). Managing your most valuable asset: The corporate reputation. Entegra. Retrieved October 18, 2008, from www.senet.com/articles_managing_assest.htm

Kohlbacher, F., & Mukai, K. (2007). Japan's learning communities in Hewlett-Packard consulting and integration: Challenging one-size fits all solutions. *The Learning Organization, 14*(1), 8–20.

Koskinen, K. U. (2001). Tacit knowledge as a promoter of success in technology firms. In *Proceedings of the 34th Hawaii International Conference on System Sciences,* IEEE Computer Society.

Lai, H., & Chu, T. H. (2000). Knowledge management: A review of theoretical frameworks and industrial cases. In *Proceedings of the 33th Hawaii International Conference on System Sciences,* IEEE Computer Society.

Lave, J., & Wenger, E. (1991). *Situated learning: Legitimate peripheral participation.* Cambridge, UK: Cambridge University Press.

Lesser, E., & Prusak, L. (1999). Communities of practice, social capital and organizational knowledge. *Information Systems Research, 1*(1), 3–9.

Lindsey, K. (2002). Measuring knowledge management effectiveness: A task-contingent organizational capabilities perspective. In *Proceedings of the Eighth Americas Conference on Information Systems.*

Maier, R. (2002). *Knowledge management systems: Information and communication technologies for knowledge management.* Berlin, Germany: Springer- Verlag.

Mandviwalla, M., Eulgem, S., Mould, C., & Rao, S. V. (1998). *Organizational memory systems design.* Unpublished Working Paper for the Task Force on Organizational Memory. In F. Burstein, Massey, A.P., Montoya-Weiss, M.M., & O'Driscoll, T. M. (2002). Knowledge management in pursuit of performance: Insights from Nortel Networks. *Management Information Systems Quarterly, 26*(3), 269–289.

McDermott, R., & O'Dell, C. (2001). Overcoming cultural barriers to sharing knowledge. *Journal of Knowledge Management, 5*(1), 76–85.

Miller, D. (1996). A preliminary typology of organizational learning: Synthesizing the literature. *Journal of Management, 22*(3), 485–505.

Murray, P. (1996). Information, knowledge and document management technology. *Knowledge Management Briefs, 1*(2), Retrieved October 18, 2008, from http://www.ktic.com/resource/km2/Information,%20knowledge,%20and%20document%20management%20technology.htm

Nonaka, I. (1994). A dynamic theory of organizational knowledge creation. *Organization Science, 5*(1), 14–37.

Nonaka, I., & Takeuchi, H. (1995). *The knowledge-creating company - how Japanese companies create the dynamics of innovation*. New York: Oxford University Press.

Ofek, E., & Sarvary, M. (2001). Leveraging the customer base: Creating competitive advantage through knowledge management. *Management Science INFORMS, 47*(11), 1441–1456.

Polanyi, M. (1966). *The tacit dimension*. Gloucester: Routledge and Kegan Paul.

Polanyi, M. (1967). *The tacit dimension*. London: Routledge and Keoan Paul.

Portes, A. (1998). Social capital: Its origins and applications in modern sociology. *Annual Review of Sociology, 24*, 1–24.

Schein, E. H. (1992). *Organizational culture and leadership* (2nd ed.). San Francisco: Jossey-Bass.

Schein, E. H. (1993). How can organizations learn faster? The challenge of entering the green room. *Sloan Management Review, 34*(2), 84–92.

Selamat, M. H., & Choudrie, J. (2007). Using meta-abilities and tacit knowledge for developing learning based systems: A case study approach. *The Learning Organization, 14*(4), 321–344.

Senge, P. (1994). *The fifth discipline: The art and practice of the learning organization*. Currency/Doubleday.

Senge, P. M. (1990). *The fifth discipline*. New York: Doubleday.

Sharkie, R. (2003). Knowledge creation and its place in the development of sustainable competitive advantage. *Journal of Knowledge Management, 7*(1), 20–31.

Smith, P. A. C. (2005). Knowledge sharing and strategic capital: The importance and identification of opinion leaders. *The Learning Organization, 12*(6), 563–574.

Smith, P. A. C., & McLaughlin, M. (2003). Succeeding with knowledge management: Getting the people-factors right. In *Proceedings of the 6th World Congress on Intellectual Capital and Innovation*, McMaster University, Hamilton.

Spender, J.-C. (1996). Organizational knowledge, learning and memory: Three concepts in search of a theory. *Journal of Organizational Change Management, 9*, 63–78.

Stenmark, D. (2000). Turning tacit knowledge tangible. In *Proceedings of the 33rd Hawaii International Conference on System Sciences*, IEEE Computer Society.

Stewart, T. (2001). *The wealth of knowledge: Intellectual capital and the twenty-first century organization*. New York: Doubleday.

Sveiby, K. E. (1997). *The new organizational wealth: Managing and measuring knowledge-based assets*. San Francisco: Berrett-Koehler.

Teece, D. (1998). Capturing value from knowledge assets: The new economy, markets for know-how, and intangible assets. *California Management Review, 40*(3), 55–79.

Walker, G., Kogut, B., & Shan, W. (1997). Social capital, structural holes and the formation of an industry network. *Organization Science, 8*(2), 109–125.

Yeung, A. K., Ulrich, D. O., Nason, S. W., & von Glinow, M. A. (1999). *Organizational learning capability*. New York: Oxford University Press.

Yu, S.-H., Kim, Y.-G., & Kim, M.-Y. (2004). Linking organizational knowledge management drivers to knowledge management performance: An exploratory study. In *Proceedings of the 37th Hawaii International Conference on System Sciences*, IEEE Computer Society.

Section 3

Chapter 13
Organization of Lessons Learned Knowledge:
A Taxonomy and Implementation

Subramanian Rama Iyer
Oklahoma State University, USA

Ramesh Sharda
Oklahoma State University, USA

David Biros
Oklahoma State University, USA

Joyce Lucca
Oklahoma State University, USA

Upton Shimp
Oklahoma State University, USA

ABSTRACT

With knowledge management systems (KMS) containing large repositories, a major issue is content organization. The ease of finding relevant information depends on the effectiveness of knowledge organization. Ontology, thesauri, and taxonomy are some of the key words that relate to knowledge organization. In this article we propose a schema for organizing knowledge that represents lessons learned from prior experience. Such knowledge from lessons learned has distinct characteristics so that it can be organized in specific ways for ease of discovery, retrieval, and also possible incorporation in formal learning. The proposed taxonomy includes concepts from domain related hierarchy, sources of lessons learned, formal learning, and collaborative inputs (Web 2.0). We describe the proposed taxonomy for organizing the lessons learned knowledge (also termed as knowledge nuggets) and provide details of a specific implementation of this taxonomy in a military organization. Such approaches to knowledge organization have the potential to be useful in many other knowledge management (KM) projects.

DOI: 10.4018/978-1-60960-555-1.ch013

INTRODUCTION

Humans learn effectively through stories, analogies, and examples. Davenport and Prusak (1998) argue that knowledge is communicated effectively when it is conveyed with a convincing narrative. Family-run businesses transfer the secrets of business learned through experience to the next generation. Knowledge through experience does not necessarily reside in any business textbook, but the transfer of such knowledge facilitates its profitable use. Nonaka (1991) used the term *tacit knowledge* for the knowledge that exists in the head but not on paper. Tacit knowledge is difficult to capture, manage, and share. He also observed that organizations that use tacit knowledge as a strategic weapon are innovators and leaders in their respective business domains. There is no substitute for the substantial value that tacit knowledge can provide. Therefore, it is necessary to capture and codify tacit knowledge to the greatest extent possible.

Knowledge management is noted to be one of the cornerstones of business success. U.S. companies spent an estimated US$73B on knowledge management software in 2007, with the average spending on knowledge management per employee growing to US$1224 (WirelessNews, 2007). According to a report by INPUT, the U.S. government spending on knowledge management solutions is projected to increase 35% over the next 5 years to reach US$1.3 billion by fiscal year 2010 (PRNewswire, 2005).

Despite spending billions of dollars on knowledge management both by industry and government, there is no guarantee that knowledge management projects will attain their objective. Usually it is the successful projects that see the limelight. Chua and Lam (2005) have noted that the amount of published material on failures pales in number when compared to the number of success stories. Yet, Storey and Barnett (2000) quote Charles Lucier, chief knowledge officer at Booz-Allen & Hamilton, as saying that 84% of all knowledge management projects fail to have any real impact. Much research has focused on successful knowledge management initiatives as well as factors that could lead to a successful knowledge management project (Davenport, De Long, & Beers, 1998). On the other hand, many researchers have studied the issue of why knowledge management initiatives fail (e.g., Storey & Barnet, 2000). Some have also presented case studies of knowledge management failures (Chua & Lam, 2005). One of the causes for such failures is that the prospective users of such knowledge cannot easily locate relevant information. Knowledge compiled in a knowledge management system does no good to the organization if it is not easily found by the likely end users.

Every knowledge management initiative must have a schema for knowledge organization. Multiple techniques have been tried for knowledge organization with varying results. *Taxonomy, ontology, thesauri*, and *knowledge maps* are some of the terms which are usually associated with knowledge organization. Many researchers have used "taxonomy" and "ontology" interchangeably (Gilchrist, 2003). The need to categorize or organize arises from the need to provide structure to any system. A knowledge repository is an integral part of any knowledge management system (Walsh & Ungson, 1991). If a knowledge repository is revised on a periodic basis, an increasing number of knowledge assets will be added to it, thus increasing the need for an effective knowledge organization scheme.

Sherif (2006) explored the complexities in the nature of the pieces of knowledge and the interrelationships that can exist between these pieces of knowledge in an organization. She notes that the ability of the innovative organization to exploit its knowledge depends on its ability to retrieve it. Knowledge retrieval depends on an effective knowledge organization scheme. In this article we propose a schema for knowledge organization and also illustrate the implementation of the schema with a case study.

Even though we have identified and understood the critical nature of knowledge organization, there is very little research on knowledge organization schemes that specifically focus on lessons learned knowledge (LLK). Such knowledge and its successful organization can be critical for sharing real-world experiences of individuals involved in a task or activity (e.g., those in the military deployed in austere locations) with those who have yet to experience the phenomenon. Furthermore, LLK can be valuable when traditional training and other knowledge transfer options are suboptimal for meeting the knowledge receivers needs. Organization of such lessons learned knowledge is our focus in this article.

The article is organized as follows. The next section provides a brief literature review including the definitions of the terms commonly used in knowledge organization. The third section presents our proposed schema for knowledge organization. The next section presents the case study that describes our specific implementation. The final section concludes the article with our observations on the implementation.

LITERATURE REVIEW

A few terms in knowledge organization appear to be used interchangeably. We provide a brief explanation of these and attempt to mitigate the confusion, then provide a very brief overview of representative knowledge management literature from which we can glean lessons for developing a knowledge organization scheme. Lastly, we describe relevant studies on knowledge organization.

Common Terms in Knowledge Organization

Various terms are used in connection with knowledge organization. Considerable confusion and overlap exists among these terms (Gilchrist, 2003). The list of terms discussed in this section is not exhaustive; however, we have chosen those terms which are often associated with knowledge organization.

A taxonomy is a hierarchical classification system. In other words, *taxonomy* is defined as the science of classification. Taxonomy is slightly different from ontology. An *ontology* is a collection of the items in a domain and the relationships that exist between those items. Taxonomy assumes a hierarchical structure, whereas ontology is merely a collection of items and the relationships among them. Ontology does not mandate a hierarchical structure. We can argue that hierarchical structures or taxonomies are better for the purposes of organization than ontologies. Ontology deals with the logic but taxonomy provides a structured way to think about the domain. The next related concept is a thesaurus. As a classification system, *thesaurus* is an extension of the taxonomy concept. Every thesaurus incorporates a taxonomy (Garshol, 2004) and also has a controlled vocabulary.

Other related concepts are metadata and tags. Metadata (Tan, 2008) can be broadly defined as data about data. Tagging is the process of designating a piece of information according to the users' association (Fitzgerald, 2006). *Gold* is a single word, but with various implications for users. Chemistry students may tag *gold* as an element; investors see *gold* as an important hedging tool; painters view *gold* as an important color-shade. Users may view *gold* differently and attach meanings according to their associations.

Tagging may help individual users to more efficiently retrieve the knowledge they need. However, such approaches can be challenging to incorporate in knowledge management projects. Nonetheless, successful KM projects employ various organization schemes to promote user acceptance. Informal knowledge organization techniques such as tagging, linguistic linking, and navigation path are assuming more importance nowadays. The following section provides examples of knowledge management projects from which we can gather lessons for successful knowledge organization.

Representative (Sample) of KM Projects Success and Failure Issues

Knowledge management projects provide very important lessons for organizing and building knowledge repositories. We begin by briefly reviewing literature on the knowledge organization related factors that contributed to successful or failed knowledge management projects. Very little research has focused on construction of frameworks for knowledge organization in a knowledge management context. This literature review deals with not only taxonomies but also ontologies, thesauri, and the like. We believe that the basic principles of design are common to every schema for knowledge organization.

Davenport et al. (1998) studied 31 knowledge management projects in 24 companies and noted that the structure of knowledge is constantly changing. A key recommendation by Davenport et al. (1998) is that knowledge management systems should provide multiple channels for knowledge transfer. On the other hand, Garland (2007) studied the organizational factors that need to be considered while implementing knowledge management in an e-learning environment. His study at the Department of National Defense of the Canadian Forces found that an environment conducive to knowledge sharing is essential and that a Web-based knowledge approach helps foster knowledge sharing.

The lessons learned system (LLS) (Weber & Aha, 2003) is a knowledge management initiative most commonly used in governmental organizations such as the departments of defense. At the core of the LLS is a knowledge repository where all the knowledge is stored and from where it may be retrieved. Members contribute to the repository as well as use the knowledge from the repository (see Figure 1).

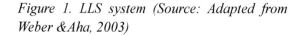

Figure 1. LLS system (Source: Adapted from Weber &Aha, 2003)

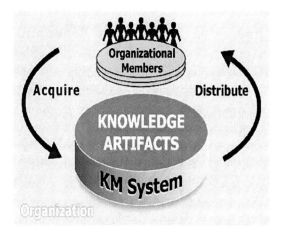

However, Weber and Aha (2003) found that, usually, there is a lesson distribution gap between the repository and the end user. Either knowledge is sought by the user and cannot be readily found or it is pushed to the user without being requested. Deficiencies in knowledge distribution cannot be solved easily. Weber and Aha (2003) proposed monitored distribution (MD) as a solution to the distribution gap. The MD approach converts all the knowledge assets into case studies and the end users can search for the assets which most closely resemble their organizational processes. The authors conclude that the knowledge delivery process needs to be tightly integrated with the task where knowledge is applicable. In a follow-up study, Weber (2007), focusing on repository-based knowledge management initiatives, finds that textual representations of knowledge may be difficult and cumbersome to follow, which may create hurdles for users in accessing and contributing to the knowledge management effort.

Chua and Lam (2005) analyzed five documented cases of knowledge management failure and found that unstructured and noncurrent knowledge systems resulted in the knowledge management application tool becoming too cumbersome. They also found that tacit aspects of knowledge were forsaken due to an over-reliance on knowledge management tools.

Knowledge Organization Research

Knowledge organization is closely related to knowledge development and sharing phases of the knowledge management process proposed by Probst, Raub, and Romhardt (2000).[1] We now turn to the review of the literature in the knowledge organization area. Researchers have approached the basic task of organizing knowledge by proposing a framework or structure for building a taxonomy or ontology. Knowledge management systems need order if users are to utilize their contents meaningfully. The volume of information and knowledge has grown exponentially; organizations need to categorize it in order to find what is relevant. This need to categorize and provide order to knowledge repositories has given rise to the interest in taxonomy building, ontology, and thesauri creation. Categorization arises from the following requirements (Feldman, 2004):

- To provide browsing and searching capabilities on the intranet or Web site
- To improve the accuracy of searches
- To group results by topic
- To remove ambiguous terms that may communicate different meanings
- To improve navigation by guiding users to the most relevant knowledge
- To provide an overview of a complex topic

Feldman (2004), commenting on the validity of categorization schemes, notes that not all schemes are applicable for every situation. Lessons learned knowledge (LLK) has its own unique characteristics, justifying further study in knowledge organization.

Any classification system is essentially a means to organize and communicate information, and it should also facilitate information retrieval (Mayr, 1969). Côté (2005) finds that taxonomies are very effective in untangling the modern information access mess. He used the model taxonomies architecture presented by Bedford (2004). The four model taxonomy architectures are flat, facet, hierarchical, and network. In a flat taxonomy architecture, the taxa are arranged with no apparent relationship between them. Facet taxonomy focuses on a center piece and all other taxa related to the center piece. A hierarchical taxonomy is the most common taxonomy with a single parent and different taxa classified under the parent; each taxon may itself be a parent for many other taxa to be classified under it. The visualization may look like a tree architecture. Each taxon can have only one parent. Moving up the architecture broadens the subject and moving down the architecture narrows the subject. Network taxonomy architecture, in contrast, is complex. Each taxon can have more than one parent, and any taxon in the architecture can be connected to any other taxon by meaningful links.[2]

Research has also focused on taxonomy design. Rich (1992) points out that the classification systems are judged by their utility and portrayal of the real world. Pack (2002) argues that a taxonomy should employ language that is familiar to the users and content should be evenly distributed across the taxonomy. The focus of research regarding the effectiveness of taxonomies has been on taxonomy design; however, the user is an important element. Taxonomy designers need to integrate the user and solicit feedback from the user regarding the taxonomy design and category views (Connelly 2007). Vogel (2003) provided a conceptual explanation of the principles of good taxonomy design. He argues that taxonomy development should precede any phase in a knowledge management project. Taxonomy development begins with identifying the nature of the knowledge asset the users are interested in accessing. The next step is to find the appropriate thesauri for the organization if a thesaurus exists. Vogel (2003) also provides a few tips on taxonomy creation. Organizations need to develop multiple taxonomies, rather than a single multipurpose taxonomy, that incorporate the right number of levels, eliminate confusing terms, and provide balance between the levels in the taxonomies. Each knowledge asset also needs to be identified using appropriate tag/s.

We next propose a knowledge organization schema that could be applied to multiple domains in organizing lessons learned knowledge. The following section explains our proposed lessons learned knowledge organization schema.

KNOWLEDGE ORGANIZATION SCHEMA

The human brain is able to process massive amounts of information only because it is an expert organizer, categorizing each piece of input and dropping it into relevant slots of existing categories (Feldman, 2004). It is likely that people searching for knowledge might expect a hierarchical form of organization. A taxonomy, as we have noted, is a hierarchical classification system. It has been recognized as the most suitable broad scheme for knowledge organization because it provides a structured way to think about knowledge. The next step, obviously, is to identify the taxa. We propose several taxa, in the form of knowledge views, that could be used to organize knowledge,

which are detailed next. Figure 2 provides an illustration of the taxa that we propose.

Subject View

A very common approach to knowledge organization is to group like items together. This view is so common that it is somewhat elementary. Nonetheless, it can be an effective view for a user unfamiliar with the knowledge domain. A good example of the view would be a book store. A customer may wish to find a book about traveling in Spain. Since book stores often group like publications together, the customer simply has to deduce that the book would likely be in the travel section and not the self-help, fiction, or nonfiction sections. This view may not be optimal as it may be difficult to classify a book or piece of knowledge into a single subject area. However, for an individual that does not know where to begin looking for knowledge, this may be the only option.

Source View or Subject Matter Expert (SME) View

Knowledge originates from different sources. In an organization, employees in different strata, who are experts in a specific area, contribute knowledge to the repository when their expert knowledge

Figure 2. Knowledge organization schema

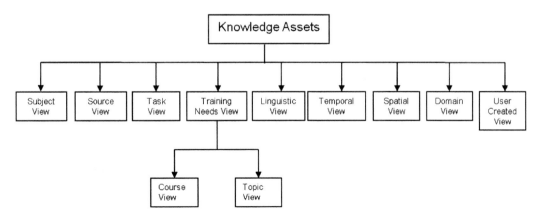

is captured and transferred. Nonaka (1991) has explained that tacit knowledge, knowledge that resides in the heads of employees, is very difficult to capture, and transfer. Knowledge transfer in any multinational organization with thousands of employees is a difficult task. If users want to locate the knowledge source for further interaction, the source view or contributor view will enable them to locate the employee who has contributed the knowledge. The source view also serves the purpose of recognizing the employee as a SME. It may also result in accentuating or decreasing the validity of the knowledge asset. For example, Jane Doe may have a considerably larger reputation and her knowledge assets may carry more weight than the knowledge assets contributed by John Doe.

Task View (Taskonomy)

One of the earliest references to *taskonomy* can be found in Dougherty and Keller (1982). *Taskonomy* is nothing but a taxonomy of tasks undertaken (Byrne, John, Wehrle, & Crow, 1999). Cichelli and Shimp (2007) describe a taskonomy for organizing knowledge objects in U.S. Army domains. Knowledge can be organized in numerous ways (Dougherty et al., 1982); however, we need to understand why knowledge is organized in a particular fashion. In their study of organizing the tools used by blacksmiths, Dougherty and Keller (1982) found that each tool has a specific task, and it is better to organize those tools based on the task that they are meant for. A whole task can be broken down into subtasks. The tools can be organized according to the subtasks that they are meant to accomplish. Drawing similarities between organizing tools and organizing knowledge, knowledge can be organized based on the tasks and sub-tasks it is meant for. Knowledge need not be tied to any one task or sub-task; it can be found in many subtasks. The taskonomy should be flexible enough to handle new knowledge to accomplish the tasks which were associated with earlier knowledge.

Training Needs View

Any business organization can be viewed as a collection of different departments based on the function that they serve. For example, the marketing department takes care of all matters related to marketing, and the finance department takes care of all matters related to finance. Knowledge relevant to these departments can be found, obviously, within the departments, and in other departments as well, or even outside the organization. This knowledge can be used for training new employees or even existing employees (Larry, 2002; Psarras, 2007). The training function could contain topics and courses. For example, the finance department could be divided into subdepartments and microdepartments. These subdepartments based on their need could have many topics of interest. Further, when it comes to training, the course view provides a collection of all the courses available pertaining to any function. These courses can have knowledge assets categorized under each course.

Linguistic or Alphabetic View

One of the common knowledge organization schemes followed by many is the linguistic scheme. Knowledge assets can be pooled in one place and can be arranged alphabetically. For example, in an encyclopedia, knowledge is arranged alphabetically without reference to the representative discipline. If the user needs to find information on a topic, and has no idea of the discipline, an alphabetical arrangement will help to locate it. However, this system can open the door for significant clutter, and may result in the user being lost in a sea of knowledge without proper guidance. Despite the drawbacks, the linguistic or alphabetic view is useful when the user does not know where to look for knowledge assets. Users can find the knowledge assets by browsing through the linguistic organization scheme.

Temporal View

Knowledge can be harvested in organizations in different years or be constantly created. The arrival of new knowledge may sound the bell for replacement of existing knowledge or may signal a complement to the existing knowledge. A knowledge repository needs to be updated constantly to keep knowledge fresh and provide users with the latest information. A temporal organization scheme can provide suitable guidance for users to search for knowledge (Marshall, 2008). Very old knowledge assets may not carry much value if there has been a significant time lapse between the time the knowledge was created and the time the knowledge was accessed. Therefore, a temporal view could guide users to look for recent knowledge and discard old knowledge assets if they are irrelevant. This view could also interact with the SME view the context of knowing when and how a particular lesson was learned can be very helpful in actually making use of that knowledge. For example, a knowledge asset from an expert whose knowledge is based upon the Vietnam War may be less relevant in a recent war environment.

Spatial View

A geographical view may also be important in learning about the context of the knowledge being saved. Knowledge relevant to Malaysia may not be relevant to Argentina because the two present a whole host of differences. Therefore, when we consider knowledge assets harvested in different regions of the world, a spatial organization scheme can be useful (Fonseca, Biscaya, Aires-De-Sousa, & Lobo, 2006). The spatial organization scheme can be created for nations and the national view can be further broken down into regional views. We are living in an ever shrinking global village. Individuals being deployed in foreign countries, away from their homeland, can learn about the vital aspects of the new place such as culture, survival

tactics, and so on. As with the temporal view, the spatial view also interacts with the SME view.

Domain View

General Electric (GE) is a multinational corporation with 327,000 employees worldwide and with a research budget of US$6 billion (GE, 2008). GE has five strong businesses with many subsidiaries under each business (i.e., technology, energy, GE capital, NBC Universal, and consumer and industrial). Each business may cater to a specific market niche. The money spent on research alone signals the amount of knowledge being generated within each business. Each market niche can be thought of as a domain. These domains can be helpful in creating a domain view for organizing knowledge. Domain views are not just limited to multinational corporations but can be employed in organizations sufficiently large to incorporate multiple domains.

User Generated View

Knowledge retrieval is a critical success factor in any knowledge management system. Users think differently and may attach different meanings to the same knowledge asset. In earlier sections we noted the importance of tagging and metadata. Users can associate different meanings and suggest key words for each knowledge asset. These key words or tags can be used to group knowledge assets. Thus, the tags provide a user defined view. Sherif (2006) emphasized the need for tagging each knowledge asset. Tagging helps organizations associate each asset with a specific functionality, department, or domain. Tagging also helps to connect knowledge assets. Tagging has now become indispensable to information retrieval. As the world moves towards establishing online communities for each interest area, tagging is a vital tool to identify relevant information. This concept is part of the Web 2.0 phenomenon (Rabinovitch, 2008). Another Web 2.0 concept is to organize knowledge assets on the basis of user ratings or recommendations. This could result in displaying assets that are most highly rated, high viewed, and so forth.

The taxa described in this section could have many knowledge assets classified under them. The taxonomy used within these taxa depends on the number of knowledge assets and the nature of the knowledge assets. The taxa can take different names and some taxons can be completely omitted based on the nature of the repository. The architecture of each knowledge repository depends on the domain and the type of knowledge assets. The next section presents a case study of the knowledge organization approaches we have proposed above in a U.S. Army organization.

A knowledge asset could be found in any of the views described above. A knowledge asset could be classified under subject view, but the same knowledge asset could be found through the linguistic view or source view. To put it formally, consider the following relational expression:

$K \in \{S_b, S_o, T_k, T_r, L, T_m, S_p, D, U)$

K = Knowledge asset

S_b = Subject View

S_o = Source View

T_k = Task View

T_r = Training Needs View

L = Linguistic View

T_m = Temporal View

S_p = Spatial View

D = Domain View

U = User Created View

This expression states that the knowledge asset could belong to any of the mentioned classifications. The knowledge asset may be listed in any one or multiple views. The taxonomy should be flexible so that the user can reach the required knowledge asset navigating through multiple views.

CASE STUDY: DAC-ETS KNOWLEDGE HARVESTING REPOSITORY

The Defense Ammunition Center (DAC) is part of the U.S Army Joint Munitions Command (JMC). DAC provides ammunition safety training to the Army (and other Department of Defense components) along with other training services such as civilian ammunition training. Some of the major activities of DAC are as follows (DAC, 2008):

- Impart ammunition training through its Ammunition School
- Manage two Department of the Army career programs for ammunition expertise—
  - ◦ QASAS—Quality assurance specialists (ammunition surveillance), and
  - ◦ Ammunition managers
- Provide explosives safety support the Department of the Defense
- Support logistics engineering

As we can see, training is an integral part of the DAC activities. Logistics support is another major area. In the process of providing logistic support many DAC employees get deployed to battle fields such as Iraq and Afghanistan. Thus, DAC must support its personnel in garrison and in more austere and deployed environments.

DAC personnel are charged with the safe handling of over 400 types of ammunition. Their duties include inspecting, packing, storing, and transporting ammunition either in the United State or while deployed in remote locations around the world. At deployed locations, they may also have to deal with captured enemy ammunition (CEA) and handle it in the same safe manner as U.S. produced munitions. Deployed condition can make their job even more hazardous as poor road condition, lack of necessary tools, and unusual climates can hamper their ability to accomplish their mission. Furthermore, the military operations tempo in Iraq and Afghanistan require that more novice DAC personnel deploy. These people need to quickly gather all the ammunition related knowledge they can before being deployed.

Because DAC employees operate in this highly demanding and dangerous environment, we have developed a knowledge harvesting process and created a repository to share the knowledge. The DAC Knowledge Harvesting Repository is a virtual storehouse of knowledge assets harvested from federal employees (QASAS) returning from temporary overseas assignments in support of military operations. The fundamental nature of the knowledge assets is primarily related to ammunition and explosives operations on the battlefield.

Knowledge Nuggets

We chose to call the harvested knowledge assets *knowledge nuggets* (KN). Of the many definitions or explanations provided by a thesaurus (www.thesaurus.com) for *nugget*, two explanations stand out: 1) a lump of precious metal, and 2) anything of great value or significance. A knowledge nugget assumes even more importance since knowledge already is of great value. A KN can be just one piece of knowledge like a video or text. However, a KN can also be a combination of video, text, documents, figures, maps, and so forth. The tools used to transfer knowledge have a central theme, which is the knowledge itself. In our DAC repository we have a combination of knowledge statements, videos, corresponding transcripts, causal maps and photographs. The following sub section provides an idea of the knowledge harvesting process.

Knowledge Harvesting Process

The knowledge harvesting process began with videotaping interviews with DAC employees regarding their deployment experience. Speech in the interviews, in some cases, was converted manually to text by DAC. In other cases the knowledge harvesting team (hereinafter referred to as

the *team*) employed voice recognition technologies to convert the speech to text. The text was checked for accuracy and then passed through the text mining division of the team. The text mining group read through the transcript and employed text mining software to extract some preliminary knowledge from the transcript. The text mining division provided a one-sentence summary for the knowledge nugget, which became the knowledge statement or commonly known among the team as the "punch line." The punch line is created from the transcripts along with the excerpts, relevant video from the interview, and causal maps make the entire knowledge nugget. The knowledge nugget is further refined by checking for quality of general appearance, errors in text, and so on. The concept of knowledge nugget is described elsewhere (Sharda, Biros, Lucca, & Upton, 2008) and is thus not repeated here. A sample knowledge nugget is represented seen in Figure 7.

Knowledge Nugget Organization

The knowledge nuggets are used by instructors, students, and others associated with DAC. The knowledge nuggets primarily deal with the experiences in the field (i.e., "war stories"). As highlighted earlier, the knowledge nuggets can relate to ammunition malfunction to foreign weather conditions to food conditions. Knowledge about food may seem trivial; however, it is a quality of life issue and virtually every knowledge nugget is vital for employees getting ready for deployment. The knowledge nuggets are no less significant for instructors and others accessing the knowledge repository.

Given the critical nature of the knowledge nuggets, it is a difficult yet challenging task to provide elegantly refined knowledge that is organized according to a taxonomy. Creating a digital library for the harvested knowledge is not complex but streamlining the knowledge nuggets to enable easy retrieval is an important objective. It will be counterproductive if instructors, students and users must wade through multiple pages to find relevant knowledge. Therefore, the goal is to prepare a properly organized knowledge repository with search capabilities.

We employed the lessons learned knowledge organization schema proposed in this article to organize and display the knowledge nuggets through many different views. Figure 3 provides the basic idea of the overall taxonomy. We will describe each taxon in detail. The taxonomy was organized in the following fashion to guide the user to the most relevant nugget. It includes multiple ways to locate a single nugget. Obviously a nugget which may be listed in one view will also be found navigating another way. Figure 7 provides an illustration of the knowledge nugget organization.

View by Subjects

In the repository, broad subject areas are used to classify the knowledge nuggets. The View by Subjects provides the user a view of the different subjects in the repository. View by Topics is synonymous with the "subject view," in our proposed schema for knowledge organization. This view was designed for the user who knows little or nothing about the DAC course and course topic structure. Each subject has many knowledge nuggets listed within it. Therefore, the Subject view follows a hierarchical taxonomy as depicted in Figure 4.

"View by subject" provides a way to locate a relevant nugget if the user is aware of the broad areas of interest and would like to find a course that covers the subject. A subject may contain multiple nuggets and each of those nuggets may

Figure 3. DAC knowledge harvesting repository: taxonomy

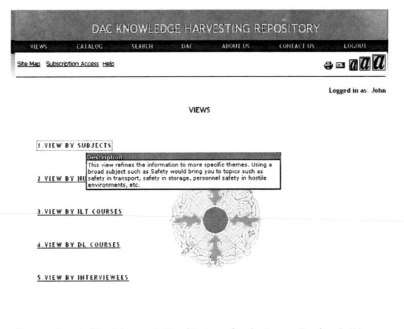

Figure 4. Subject view taxonomy: schematic form

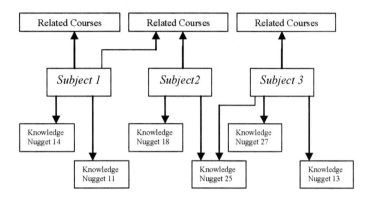

belong to other topics. To help the user find a course related to a particular subject, we have developed "related courses view" that provides a list of all those courses which a particular subject is related. The user can navigate to the courses through the subject view. For example, if users want to find a distance learning course that covered ammunition transportation, they could quickly scan the "view by subjects" list, locate a subject

area, view related KNs, and find links to associated courses. Figure 5 provides an illustration of the view by subjects taxonomy.

"TC 10-220—Chain of Command, Civilian vs. Military Interface on the Battlefield" is a topic, which is related to "Ammo-54—Risk Management and Preparation of SOPS for Ammunition and Explosive Operations". TC 10-220 has many knowledge nuggets classified under it. TC 10-220

Figure 5. View by subjects taxonomy

DAC KNOWLEDGE HARVESTING REPOSITORY

| VIEWS | CATALOG | SEARCH | DAC | ABOUT US | CONTACT US | LOGOUT |

Site Map Help Back

Logged in as: John

SUBJECTS

SUBJECT ID ▼	SUBJECT NAME ▼
TC10-220	CHAIN OF COMMAND, CIVILIAN VS MILITARY INTERFACE ON THE BATTLEFIELD
TC115	FOREIGN WEATHER CLIMATE AWARENESS
TC25	CRITICAL KNOWLEDGE & INFORMATION TRANSFER ON THE BATTLEFIELD
TC30	QUALITY OF LIFE ISSUES ON THE BATTLEFIELD
TC310	SERVICE REGULATIONS ON THE BATTLEFIELD
TC350	AMMUNITION TRAINING REQUIREMENTS ON THE BATTLEFIELD
TC385-55	TRANSPORT SAFETY ON THE BATTLEFIELD
TC385-740	STORAGE SAFETY ON THE BATTLEFIELD
TC530	PERSONAL SAFETY IN HOSTILE EVIRONMENTS
TC550	MISSION IMPACTS FROM FOREIGN TURMOIL
TC550-75	FOREIGN AMMO HANDLING IN REMOTE AREAS
TC570	TOOLS & EQUIPMENT REQUIREMENTS IN REMOTE LOCATIONS
TC614	POSITION DESCRIPTION AWARENESS PRIOR TO DEPLOYMENT
TC735	INVENTORY & ACCOUNTABILITY ON THE BATTLEFIELD
TC742	AMMUNITION SERVICEABILITY ON THE BATTLEFIELD
TC746	RETROGRADE PREPARATION ON THE BATTLEFIELD
TC75	AMMUNITION DEMIL PROCEDURES ON THE BATTLEFIELD

RETURN TO TOP

Figure 6. Nugget relation with courses and topics

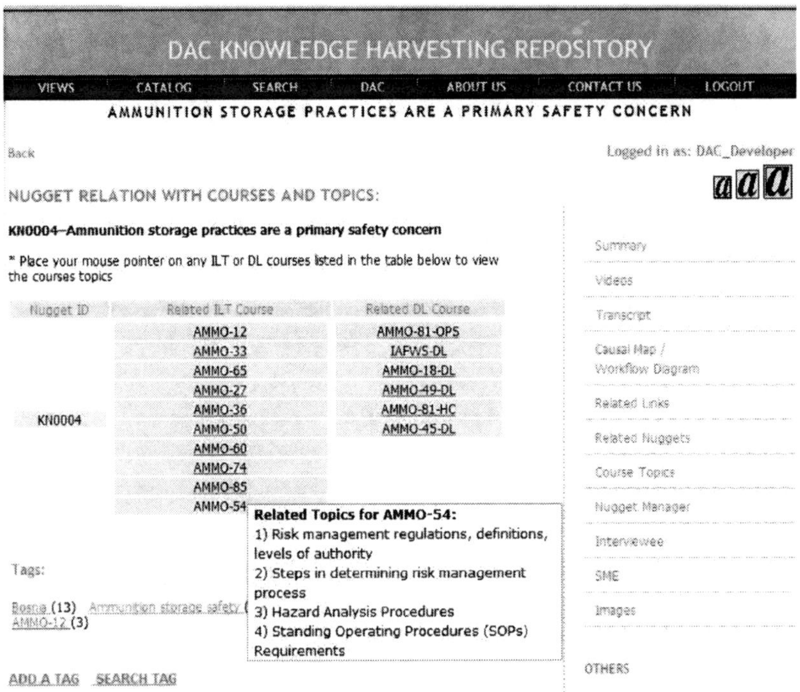

is related to Ammo-54, however, there could be other topics that belong to multiple courses. Figure 6 provides the relation between nuggets, courses and topics.

View by Interviewee

DAC personnel deployed on the field come back with rich personal experience, which is then harvested into knowledge nuggets. Some might have just one deployment while some might have been deployed more than once. Each deployment opens new vistas of knowledge. The interviewees may be experts in some subject area; the interviewee view helps the user locate a knowledge nugget. View by interviewee follows a hierarchical taxonomy architecture. View by interviewee is synonymous with "source view" in our proposed schema for knowledge organization.

- **Temporal view:** We have not included a "temporal view" explicitly in the reposi-

tory. However, a close look at Figure 7 reveals that SME and temporal view are intertwined, as mentioned earlier. The user can search for the deployment periods of the interviewees and look for nuggets.

- **Spatial view:** If a user chooses to explore the deployment periods of DAC personnel by clicking on deployment periods, the following screen provides a list of deployment locations. Thus, we have also incorporated the "spatial view."

View by ILT Courses

DAC conducts multiple traditional, instructor led training (ILT) courses and distance learning (DL) courses. There are multiple courses being offered by DAC. The developed knowledge nuggets are relevant in some of the courses. The ILT course view enables the user to scan for nuggets in any particular ILT course. The ILT course view is the same as "course view" in our proposed schema

Figure 7. "View by interviewee" screen shot

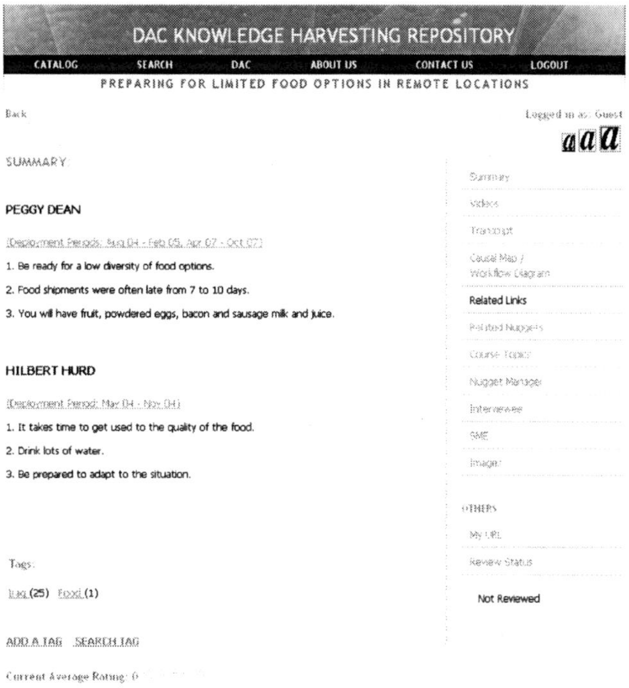

for knowledge organization. The ILT course view follows a hierarchical taxonomy.

Course is the highest order in this view of the taxonomy. Topics are classified under courses, and topics have knowledge nuggets classified under them. The topics for each course were derived by SMEs and army ammunition community leaders based on environmental need. Since this taxonomy is institutionalized in the schoolhouse, organizing nuggets in this manner is natural to DAC instructors and students alike.

Courses may have stand-alone knowledge nuggets; these knowledge nuggets are not classified under any topic. For example, knowledge nugget 10 is not classified under any topic; however, knowledge nugget 10 is classified directly under course 1. A situation may arise where a particular topic may be classified under two courses. In Figure 8, topic 3 belongs to course 1 and to course 4. A knowledge nugget may be classified under one topic or even multiple topics. Knowledge nugget 25 in Figure 8 belongs to topic 2 as well as topic

3. Figure 9 illustrates the course view taxonomy through a screen shot. "Ammo 12—Ammunition Storage" is a course and "TC-30—Quality of life issues on the battlefield" is a topic under Ammo 12. TC-30 has multiple knowledge nuggets classified under it.

There could be multiple knowledge nuggets under topics. For example, Topic TC-30 may have multiple knowledge nuggets. Figure 10 shows the knowledge nuggets classified under TC-30.

View by DL Courses

As pointed out in the previous section, DAC trains people through the distance learning mode. The relevant nuggets pertaining to each particular distance learning courses are listed in the view by DL courses. The taxonomy followed is similar to the ILT course view.

Figure 8. ILT course view taxonomy: schematic form

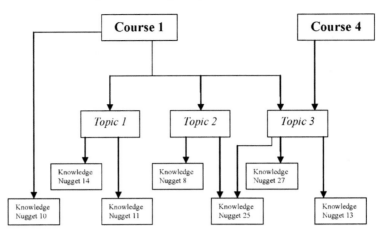

View by Nuggets

A linguistic arrangement is provided for the user who may find difficulty in locating a particular knowledge nugget within any topic. All the knowledge nuggets in the repository are listed here, and they can be sorted alphabetically. A flat taxonomy architecture is employed in view by nuggets. This view is similar to the "linguistic view" in our proposed schema for knowledge organization. Figure 11 illustrates the view by nuggets through a screen shot.

User-Generated Views

We have explained the importance and usefulness of tagging in the literature review section. While not a specific "view" like other "views," a user

Figure 9. "View by ILT course" taxonomy: screen shot

DAC KNOWLEDGE HARVESTING REPOSITORY

| CATALOG | SEARCH | DAC | ABOUT US | CONTACT US | LOGOUT |

Site Map Help Back

Logged in as: John

ILT COURSES CATALOG

AMMO-1: CONVENTIONAL AMMUNITION
AMMO-10: AMMUNITION QUALITY ASSURANCE
⊟ AMMO-12: AMMUNITION STORAGE
  ⊞ TC30 QUALITY OF LIFE ISSUES ON THE BATTLEFIELD
AMMO-13: AMMUNITION SUPPLY AND INVENTORY
AMMO-14: AMMUNITION SURVEILLANCE
AMMO-19: CHEMICAL ACCIDENT/INCIDENT RESPONSE AND ASSISTANCE
AMMO-20: CHEMICAL AGENT SAFETY
⊟ AMMO-27: CONVENTIONAL AMMUNITION RADIATION HAZARDS
  ⊞ TC30 QUALITY OF LIFE ISSUES ON THE BATTLEFIELD
AMMO-28: ELECTRICAL EXPLOSIVES SAFETY FOR ARMY FACILITIES
AMMO-29: ELECTRICAL EXPLOSIVES SAFETY FOR NAVAL FACILITIES
⊟ AMMO-33: EXPLOSIVES SAFETY AND ENVIRONMENTAL RISK MANAGEMENT
  ⊞ TC30 QUALITY OF LIFE ISSUES ON THE BATTLEFIELD
⊟ AMMO-36: EXPLOSIVES SAFETY FOR NAVAL FACILITIES PLANNING
  ⊞ TC28 CRITICAL KNOWLEDGE & INFORMATION TRANSFER ON THE BATTLEFIELD

Figure 10. Knowledge nuggets under TC-30

SUBJECT : QUALITY OF LIFE ISSUES ON THE BATTLEFIELD

ID▼	NUGGET NAME▼
KN0012	PREPARING FOR LIMITED FOOD OPTIONS IN REMOTE LOCATIONS
KN0038	EXPECT LIVING CONDITIONS TO CHANGE AT ANY TIME DURING DEPLOYMENT

These nuggets are tacit knowledge generated from interviews and are for classroom discussion only. Unless otherwise stated, they are not considered to be official doctrine of the DoD. The developer disclaims all responsibility from use of this information.

may associate a particular knowledge nugget with ammunition safety, while another user may associate the same nugget with location. Multiple tags for the same nugget help in clearly associating a nugget with a particular topic without ambiguity. Over time, a consensus emerges as to what tags

Figure 11. View by nuggets: screen shot

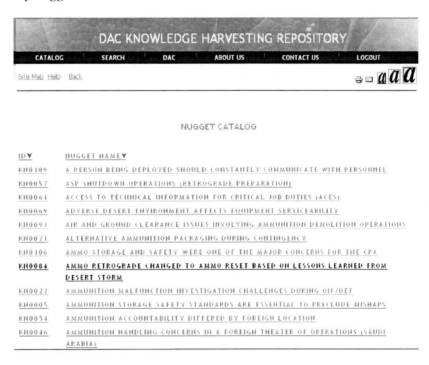

NUGGET CATALOG

ID▼	NUGGET NAME▼
KN0109	A PERSON BEING DEPLOYED SHOULD CONSTANTLY COMMUNICATE WITH PERSONNEL
KN0057	ASP SHUTDOWN OPERATIONS (RETROGRADE PREPARATION)
KN0061	ACCESS TO TECHNICAL INFORMATION FOR CRITICAL JOB DUTIES (ACES)
KN0069	ADVERSE DESERT ENVIRONMENT AFFECTS EQUIPMENT SERVICEABILITY
KN0093	AIR AND GROUND CLEARANCE ISSUES INVOLVING AMMUNITION DEMOLITION OPERATIONS
KN0071	ALTERNATIVE AMMUNITION PACKAGING DURING CONTINGENCY
KN0106	AMMO STORAGE AND SAFETY WERE ONE OF THE MAJOR CONCERNS FOR THE CPA
KN0084	**AMMO RETROGRADE CHANGED TO AMMO RESET BASED ON LESSONS LEARNED FROM DESERT STORM**
KN0022	AMMUNITION MALFUNCTION INVESTIGATION CHALLENGES DURING OIF/OEF
KN0005	AMMUNITION STORAGE SAFETY STANDARDS ARE ESSENTIAL TO PRECLUDE MISHAPS
KN0051	AMMUNITION ACCOUNTABILITY DIFFERED BY FOREIGN LOCATION
KN0046	AMMUNITION HANDLING CONCERNS IN A FOREIGN THEATER OF OPERATIONS (SAUDI ARABIA)

should be used for a particular knowledge nugget. Figure 7 provides a typical nugget view. Tags are identical to the "user defined view" in our proposed knowledge organization schema. In a nugget, we let the users define the nugget using key words or tags that feel are appropriate. For example, Figure 7 provides a view of the knowledge nugget related to limited food options. Some users have tagged the nugget under "Iraq," while other users have tagged it under "food."

In the DAC repository we have not incorporated "taskonomy" and "domain view." Taskonomy refers to an organization of knowledge nuggets based on tasks alone. The DAC repository, which is primarily used for training purposes, does not have many nuggets that relate to well-defined tasks. The experience of DAC personnel is captured within various nuggets. Therefore, the experiences do not call for a taskonomy. Also, the domain is fixed in this case, not needing a separate domain view.

Evaluation of DAC Knowledge Harvesting Repository

We tested the proposed schema with DAC Knowledge Harvesting Repository. The knowledge harvesting system described was demonstrated to many military customers at different levels. We presented the proposed schema to a group of 22 ammunition managers and QASAS professionals (16 male, 6 female) who also happened to be instructors at the DAC technical training facility. The average time in the QASAS career field was 14 years, and the average time as QASAS instructors was 4 years. The concept of capturing the lessons from the field and developing them as KNs in the expertise transfer system was met with overwhelming approval from the participants. All agreed that capturing the lessons learned would be quite beneficial in their classrooms; however, the groups did provide input for some refinements. First, the QASAS professionals helped us to understand that the lessons learned were really lessons to be learned. The term *lessons learned* suggests

that that the knowledge contributor applied a solution to a problem that he or she knew to be correct. This is not the case in deployed military environments. The individuals returning from the field often reported KNs in the form of situations where they had to think and devise solution to problems quickly. Until those solutions are either vetted by SMEs or can be found in Army doctrine, they should not be considered lessons learned and taken as valid. Thus, we note them as lessons to be learned. For example in one KN, QASAS came across captured enemy ammunition (CEA) and did not know how to handle it. She took a digital photo of it, sent it to the explosive ordinance disposal professionals, and they provide her with proper handling guidance. Our QASAS experts told us that while she performed her job correctly, there were other ways to handle the situation. From that feedback, we worked with the QASAS to develop a vetting process whereby SMEs would evaluate the KNs for accuracy and consistency with DoD doctrine. Second, the QASAS experts also assisted by helping us refine the various views. Through their feedback we made some refinements in the training course views to be more consistent with the course structure. Also, it was the QASAS experts who suggested "view by interviewee" to provide a more robust spatial orientation. Based on the feedback received from our customers we conclude that the proposed knowledge organization schema is effective for application in different domains and we are waiting to scale the repository to even higher levels.

CONCLUSION

The need to organize knowledge is critical to the success of any knowledge management system. Many researchers have identified the importance of a refined knowledge organization scheme, and some have even gone to the extent of highlighting the lack of knowledge organization scheme as a cause of failure of knowledge management projects. There is a wide body of research on creation of taxonomies of corporate libraries and the ease of obtaining knowledge. However, published literature on a knowledge organization scheme was found to be lacking. This article provides a specific example of an implemented knowledge organization.

We recognize the limitations of generalizability of our results. Ours is a case study and not a controlled experiment. Therefore, we do not have data collected on the number of users, the diversity among users, their skill level, and so on. Hence, it is impossible to make a comparison of the usability of these specific categories or to make a comparison between different repositories.

We also note that there are a few issues that exist with the creation of the taxonomy. First, it is quite difficult to identify the relevant points to be included in the knowledge nuggets. We recognize that the success of the taxonomy also depends on "catchy" phrases for the titles of knowledge nuggets. To find a solution to this issue, we use data mining techniques. Second, populating the knowledge nuggets in different taxa is critical for expedient content retrieval. Assigning knowledge nuggets to different categories and then validating those assignments is a major task in such knowledge organization efforts.

Given the importance of a knowledge organization scheme, there is a need for a schema for knowledge organization that could be applied in different domains. Our contribution, through this article, is to propose a knowledge organization schema that can be employed in different domains, and to validate the approaches using a live case study.

REFERENCES

Bedford, D. A. D. (2004). *Enterprise taxonomies—Context, structures & integration.* Paper presented at the American Society of Indexers Annual Conference, American Society of Indexers, Arlington, VA, USA.

Byrne, M. D., John, B. E., Wehrle, N. S., & Crow, D. C. (1999). The tangled Web we wove: A taskonomy of WWW use. In *Proceedings of the SIGCHI conference on Human Factors in Computing Systems: The CHI Is the Limit.* Pittsburgh, PA: ACM.

Chua, A., & Lam, W. (2005). Why KM projects fail: A multi-case analysis. *Journal of Knowledge Management. Kempston, 9*(3), 6.

Cichelli, J. J., & Shimp, R. U. (2007). *Taskonomy vs. taxonomy: Human-centered knowledge management design.* Paper presented at the Interservice/Industry Training, Simulation & Education Conference, Orlando, FL.

Connelly, J. (2007). Eight steps to successful taxonomy design. *Information Management Journal, 41*(6), 40–46.

Côté, J. A. (2005). Knowledge taxonomies. *Information Outlook, 9*(6), 45–52.

Davenport, T. H., De Long, D. W., & Beers, M. C. (1998, Winter). Successful knowledge management projects. *Sloan Management Review, 39*(2), 9843–9857.

Davenport, T. H., & Prusak, L. (1998). *Working knowledge: How organizations manage what they know.* Boston: Harvard Business School Press.

Defense ammunition center.(2008). Retrieved August 2008, from www.dac.army.mil

Dougherty, J. W. D., & Keller, C. M. (1982). Taskonomy: A practical approach to knowledge structures. *American Ethnologist, 9*(4), 763–774. doi:10.1525/ae.1982.9.4.02a00090

Feldman, S. (2004). Why CATEGORIZE? *KM World, 13*(9), 8.

Fitzgerald, M. (2006). Tagging tools offer powerful ways to organize information.

Fonseca, A. M., Biscaya, J. L., Aires-De-Sousa, J., & Lobo, A. M. (2006, January). Geographical classification of crude oils by Kohonen self-organizing maps. *Analytica Chimica Acta, 556*(2), 374–382. doi:10.1016/j.aca.2005.09.062

Garland, G. (2007). *Organizational factors and solutions to be considered when implementing knowledge management in a military e-learning environment*. Canada: Royal Roads University.

Garshol, L. M. (2004). Metadata? Thesauri? Taxonomies? Topic maps! Making sense of it all. *Journal of Information Science, 30*(4), 378–391. doi:10.1177/0165551504045856

GE. (2008). *GE fact sheet,* Retrieved August 2008 from www.ge.com

Gilchrist, A. (2003). Thesauri, taxonomies and ontologies—An etymological note. *The Journal of Documentation, 59*(1), 7–18. doi:10.1108/00220410310457984

Larry, W. C. (2002). Knowledge management and training the value of collaboration. *Performance Improvement, 41*(4), 37–43. doi:10.1002/pfi.4140410407

Marshall, L. (2008). The usefulness of chronological arrangement for subheadings in book indexes: An examination of the literature (Part 2). *Key Words, 16*(2), 56–59.

Mayr, E. (1969). *Principles of systematic zoology*. New York: McGraw-Hill.

Nonaka, I. (1991). The knowledge-creating company. *Harvard Business Review, 69*(6), 96–104.

Pack, T. (2002). *Taxonomy's role in content management. EContent* (p. 26). Information Today.

PRNewswire. (2005). INPUT predicts federal knowledge management spending will reach $1.3 billion by FY10; Katrina-highlighted weaknesses spur OMB and Congress to push agencies to develop more information sharing processes and systems. *PRNewswire*, Reston, VA.

Probst, G., Raub, S., & Romhardt, K. (2000). *Managing knowledge: Building blocks for success*. New York: Wiley.

Psarras, J. E. (2007). Education and training in the knowledge-based economy: The application of knowledge management. *International Journal of Information Technology & Management, 6*(1), 6–6.

Rabinovitch, E. (2008). WEB 2.0 is here and ready for use. *IEEE Communications Magazine, 46*(3), 24–24. doi:10.1109/MCOM.2008.4463764

Rich, P. (1992). The organizational taxonomy: Definition and design. *Academy of Management Review, 17*(4), 758–781. doi:10.2307/258807

Sharda, R., Biros, D., Lucca, J., & Upton, S. (2008). *A knowledge representation model for lessons learned knowledge*. Stillwater: Oklahoma State University.

Sherif, K. (2006). An adaptive strategy for managing knowledge in organizations. *Journal of Knowledge Management. Kempston, 10*(4), 72.

Storey, J., & Barnett, E. (2000). Knowledge management initiatives: learning from failure. *Journal of Knowledge Management, 4*(2), 145. doi:10.1108/13673270010372279

Tan, M. (2008). Metadata and its applications in the digital library: Approaches and practices. *Journal of Academic Librarianship, 34*(3), 271–271. doi:10.1016/j.acalib.2008.03.019

Vogel, C. (2003). A roadmap for proper taxonomy design part 1 of 2. *Computer Technology Review, 23*(7), 42–44.

Walsh, J. P., & Ungson, G. R. (1991). Organizational memory. *Academy of Management Review, 16*(1), 57–91. doi:10.2307/258607

Weber, O. R., & Aha, W. D. (2003). Intelligent delivery of military lessons learned. *Decision Support Systems, 34*(3), 287. doi:10.1016/S0167-9236(02)00122-7

Weber, R. (2007). Knowledge management in call centres. *Electronic Journal of Knowledge Management*, 5(3), 333–346.

WirelessNews. (2007). *AMR research: Spending on knowledge management will hit $73B in 2007.* AMR Research.

ENDNOTES

[1] Probst et al. (2000) explored the core problems in different industries and identified number of activities as core processes of knowledge management, which are fairly closely related. These activities are knowledge identification, knowledge acquisition, knowledge development, knowledge sharing and distribution, knowledge utilization, and knowledge retention.

[2] Some readers may notice a similarity to the hierarchical database model by IBM and the network database model of CODASYL.

This work was previously published in International Journal of Knowledge Management, Volume 5, Issue 3, edited by Murray E. Jennex, pp. 1-20, copyright 2009 by IGI Publishing (an imprint of IGI Global).

Chapter 14
Investigating the Impact of Knowledge Management Factors on New Product Development Performance

Belbaly Nassim
GSCM–Montpellier Business School, France

ABSTRACT

Knowledge is recognized as an important weapon for new product development (NPD) performance, and many firms are beginning to manage the knowledge detained by their new product development processes. Researchers have investigated knowledge management factors such as enablers, creation processes, and performance. However, very few studies have explored the relationship between these factors in the context of new product development (NPD). To fill this gap, this article develops a research model which applies the knowledge management factors to the NPD context. The model includes five enablers: collaboration, trust, learning, team leadership characteristics, and t-shaped skills with an emphasis on the knowledge creation processes such as socialization, externalization, combination, and internalization. The results confirm the strong support of the research model and the impact of the independent variables (knowledge management enablers) on the dependent variables (knowledge creation and NPD performance). In light of these findings, the implications for both theory and practice are discussed.

It seems that firms that could manage effectively the knowledge embedded in their NPD processes would perform better. Firms that misuse their knowledge are losing out on the benefits of efficient NPD processes. It is no surprise that each stage of the NPD process requires the combination of knowledge and skills to perform useful actions, to solve ill-structured problems which involve continuous information acquisition, sharing and utilization (Griffin & Hauser, 1992; Hutt, Reingen,

DOI: 10.4018/978-1-60960-555-1.ch014

& Ronchetto, 1988). This places a premium on the ability to effectively capture the knowledge created during the NPD process so that it can be reused in the next generation of products to reduce development time (Belbaly & Benbya, 2006). Companies attempting to manage the knowledge detained by their NPD performance have followed the knowledge management initiatives that have already been used (Davenport, Long, & Beers, 1998; Wiig, 1997). These initiatives have taken on subjects of very different natures including information technology (Davenport & Prusak, 1998; Liebowitz & Wilcox, 1997; O'Leary, 1998; Ruggles, 1998), organizational structure (Wenger, Mcdermott, & Snyder, 2002) or even new human-resources policies, to change the organizational culture. However, despite the acknowledged importance of knowledge, few studies have investigated how companies can leverage knowledge for the improved NPD performance. In fact, most studies have explored the underlying organizational variables influencing NPD performance: development time, productivity, commercial success of new products, and quality (Clark & Fujimoto, 1991; Henderson & Cockburn, 1996; Pisano, 1996; Ulrich & Eppinger, 2004). To fill this gap, studies have tried to explore which factors are essential for managing NPD knowledge effectively. One challenge is to understand the relationships among these factors. Many studies have examined the relationship between knowledge management enablers, processes, or performance. For example, while some research has focused on the relationship between knowledge management enablers and processes (Lee & Choi, 2003; Zander & Kogut, 1995); the emphasis of

other studies is on the relationship between knowledge management enablers and organizational performance (Becerra-Fernandez & Sabherwal, 2001; Bierly & Chakrabarti, 1996; Gold, Malhotra, & Segars, 2001). Researchers and practitioners have not tried to examine these relationships in a NPD context, thus a NPD perspective of the knowledge enablers, processes and performance based on relevant theories is a necessity.

The objective of this article is to propose a research model in the NPD context that interconnects two knowledge management enablers: organizational culture and people (Chase, 1997; Davenport et al., 1998; Graham & Pizzo, 1996; Long, 1997; O'Dell & Grayson, 1999) with the knowledge creation process (Nonaka & Takeuchi, 1995) and NPD performance (Rosenau, 1988). For this purpose, this article analyses the previous empirical studies and attempts to support the relationship among knowledge management enablers, the knowledge creation process and NPD performance by testing it empirically.

CONCEPTUAL FRAMEWORK

Studies have emphasized three factors for managing knowledge: enablers, processes, and NPD performance (see Figure 1) (Beckman, 1999; Belbaly & Benbya, 2006; Demarest, 1997; O'Dell & Grayson, 1999). Knowledge management enablers are organizational mechanisms for fostering knowledge consistently (Ichijo, Krogh, & Nonaka, 1998) and provide the infrastructure necessary for the organization to increase its efficiency of knowledge processes (Sarvary, 1999). Knowledge

Figure 1. Research framework for studying knowledge management factors

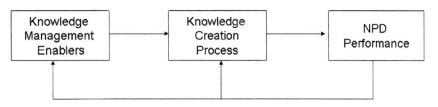

management enablers can stimulate knowledge creation, protect knowledge, and facilitate the sharing of knowledge in an organization (Stonehouse & Pemberton, 1999). Knowledge processes can be thought of as a structured coordination for managing knowledge effectively (Gold et al., 2001), including activities such as creation, sharing, storage, and usage (Alavi & Leidner, 2001; Beckman, 1999). Finally, NPD performance may be defined as the degree to which companies achieve their business objectives (Davenport, 1999). The relationship among these three factors can be found in the input-output process model by Hackerman and Morris (1978) and explained in the knowledge-chain model (Holsapple and Singh, 2001). In this article, we have used these two models assuming that the input Knowledge management factors affect the output NPD performance through certain kinds of interaction processes; this means that the knowledge management enablers affect NPD performance throughout the knowledge creation process (Lee & Choi, 2003).

The two sets of knowledge management enablers dealt with in this article are organizational culture, and people (Chase, 1997; Davenport et al., 1998; Graham & Pizzo, 1996; Long, 1997; O'Dell & Grayson, 1999). Organizational culture is a key element of managing organizational change and renewal and remains the most important and most thoroughly studied factor for successful knowledge management (Davenport et al., 1998). Organizational culture acts as an influencing factor of the knowledge creation process (Quinn, Anderson, & Finkelstein, 1996). In reality, culture defines not only what knowledge is valued, but also what knowledge must be kept inside the organization for sustaining NPD performance. A culture of collaboration, trust and learning is required to encourage the application and development of knowledge within the NPD process of an organization (Krogh, 1998; Miller 1996), and as a consequence to enhance the NPD performance.

The second knowledge management enabler is at the heart of organizational knowledge creation (Choi & Lee, 2003; Holsapple et al., 2001); this is because it's people who create and share knowledge. Therefore, managing people who are willing to create and share knowledge is important (O'Dell & Grayson, 1999). In a NPD context, the people within an organization may encourage knowledge creation (Choi & Lee, 2003; Holsapple et al., 2001). Our study includes two key structural enablers that influence the knowledge creation process for the people: team leader characteristics and T-shaped skills (Leonard-Barton, 1995; Muczyk & Reimann, 1987).

These enablers (or influencing factors) have a direct impact on the knowledge creation processes that occur during the product development (Stonehouse & Pemberton, 1999). The knowledge creation process adopts the SECI model (socialization, externalization, combination, and internalization) proposed by Nonaka and Takeuchi (1995), which has the capability to improve the efficient management of the knowledge embedded in the NPD processes. The efficient management of both the enablers and the knowledge creation process will provide real-time responses to firm problems and will consequently lead to outcomes that enhance NPD performance. The understanding of these outcomes is possible because the SECI model focuses on where knowledge is created and expanded through social interaction between tacit and explicit knowledge (Nonaka 1994; Nonaka, Byosiere, & Konno, 1994; Nonaka & Takeuchi, 1995). These authors specify four knowledge creation modes as an interplay between tacit[1] and explicit[2] knowledge that lead to the creation of new knowledge: socialization (tacit to tacit), externalization (tacit to explicit), combination (explicit to explicit), and internalization (explicit to tacit). They are explained hereafter:

Socialization yields new tacit knowledge that is built through informal interaction between individuals, usually through an exchange of tacit knowledge that occurs during joint activities rather than through written or verbal instructions (Hedlund, 1994; Nonaka 1994; Nonaka et al. 1998; Nonaka et al. 1995). *Externalization* involves the expression of tacit knowledge and its conversion into comprehensible forms that are easier to understand. It's an act of codifying or converting tacit knowledge into explicit knowledge, characterized by more formal interactions such as interviews with experts, or the sharing of lessons learned in a previous project (Nonaka 1994; Nonaka & Konno, 1998; Nonaka & Takeuchi, 1995). *Combination* involves the conversion of explicit knowledge into more complex sets of explicit knowledge (Nonaka 1994). Combination occurs through communication, diffusion, integration, and systemization of knowledge and contributes to knowledge at the group level as well as at the organizational level (Nonaka & Takeuchi, 1995). And finally, *internalization* is the conversion of explicit knowledge into the organization's tacit knowledge. This requires the individual to identify the knowledge relevant to oneself within the organization's explicit knowledge. Learning by doing, on the job training, learning by observation, and face-to-face meetings are some of the internalization processes by which individuals acquire knowledge (Nonaka, 1994); Nonaka & Takeuchi, 1995).

Given that the knowledge creation occurs in an NPD context, the challenge for NPD projects is to recognize the different contexts (knowledge management enablers) that have a significant influence on NPD performance. Once this realization has been achieved, the next challenge will be to ensure that the sources of knowledge creation are available to the NPD teams so that they are able to measure NPD performance (Lambkin 1988; Rosenau, 1988). NPD performance is measured through time to market (Griffin, 1993).

The championing recognition of the knowledge management factors (knowledge management enablers—organizational culture, people- processes-; the knowledge creation process; and NPD performance) has permitted us to construct our research model (see Figure 2). This research model enables the knowledge creation process to meet NPD performance, because each of the knowledge management enablers creates the necessary conditions for knowledge creation to enhance the NPD performance.

Figure 2. Research model

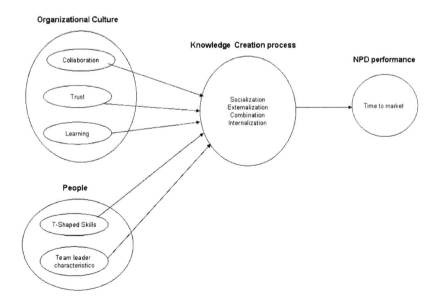

HYPOTHESES

Collaboration: Collaboration occurs when people from different organisations (or within the same organisation) produce something through shared effort, resources, and decision making and then take joint ownership of the final product or service (Linden, 2003; Hurley & Hult, 1998). Effective collaboration generally requires a greater degree of trust among project participants (DeFillippi, 2002) and also reduces individual differences (Leonard-Barton, 1995). For example, NPD interdepartmental collaboration needs several departments working closely together to share information, ideas, resources, and decision authority in order to shape a new product idea and then bring it into existence. Collaborative culture fosters this type of exchange by reducing fear and increasing openness to other members in NPD projects. Thus, collaborative culture affects knowledge creation by increasing the knowledge exchange among different NPD members (Krogh, 1998).

H1: Collaboration is positively associated with the knowledge creation process.

Learning: Learning is the acquisition of new knowledge by actors who are able and willing to apply that knowledge to making decisions or influencing others in the organisation (Damanpour, 1991; Miller, 1996). The learning capability gives the organisation the ability to learn the lessons of its experiences and to pass on those lessons across boundaries and time (Ashkenas, Ulrich, Jick, & Kerr, 1995). Many companies have formalized a process whereby lessons learned within individual business units are being collected and shared for overall use to enhance the learning capability of its people. This capability provides an important link between learning and knowledge creation because knowledge creation is a dynamic process and requires learning new sets of capabilities (Cohen & Levinthal, 1990). This outcome was supported by Quinn et al. (1996), which stated that for successful knowledge creation, organizations should develop a deeply ingrained learning culture. Kanevsky and Housel (1998) insisted that the amount of time spent on learning is positively related to the amount of knowledge created.

H2: Learning is positively associated with the knowledge creation process.

Trust: Trust can be defined as maintaining reciprocal faith in each other in terms of intention and behavior (Kreitner & Kinicki, 1992). Trust is based on the expectation that the trustee will perform certain desired behaviours or actions of importance to the trustier. When the relationships between the trustee and the trustier are high, people are more willing to participate in knowledge exchange (Nahapiet & Ghoshal, 1998). Szulanski (1996) empirically found that the lack of trust among employees is one of the key barriers to knowledge exchange. The increase in knowledge exchange brought on by mutual trust results in knowledge creation (Lee et al. 2003). Thus, trust nurtures the knowledge creation process by creating a context which facilitates the knowledge exchange for the socialisation process of the NPD team. Firms like 3M and Hewlett Packard attempt to create high levels of trust in their NPD teams to increase knowledge creation, by providing material and nonmaterial expressions of commitment to their employees (Adler, 2001). Trust also encourages a climate conducive to better knowledge creation by alleviating the fear of risk. The presence of a high level of trust can reduce this risk (Nelson & Cooprider, 1996).

H3: Trust is positively associated with the knowledge creation process.

Team Leader Characteristics

During the past decade, a shift in emphasis has occurred toward the participation of followers in leadership, to the extent that leadership is now often defined as the process of leaders and followers in a situation of mutual influence (Rosenbach & Taylor, 1993). Management styles of leaders can differ along several styles of leadership—democratic/facilitative—(Muczyk & Reimann, 1987; Stogdill, 1963). A democratic and participatory style of leadership makes the communication among team members more effective (Kidd & Christy, 1961; Wilemon & Thamhain, 1983). A facilitative style of leadership encourages the establishment of trust and collaboration within teams (Norrgren & Schaller, 1999), which in turn promotes an increase in knowledge exchange. The challenge for most team leaders is to develop capacity in others by creating a climate in which acquiring and sharing knowledge is encouraged or even demanded (Politis, 2002). Leaders encourage employees to share their ideas by creating a climate that is receptive to new ideas. Employees may be more likely to share knowledge when they are praised by managers, when they are given financial or nonfinancial rewards as part of their performance evaluation for sharing (Bryant, 2003). Team leaders encourage employees to develop new ideas and new knowledge during the creation process by converting their personal experiences and images into personal insights shared with others on the NPD team (Bryant, 2003).

H4: Team leader characteristics are positively associated with the knowledge creation process.

T-shaped skills: T-shaped skills are both deep (the vertical part of the "T") and broad (the horizontal part of the "T"); that is, their possessors can explore particular knowledge domains and their various applications in particular products (Leonard-Barton, 1995). People with T-shaped skills would have a desired ability to understand the technical facets of their discipline, while also understanding the direction of the company as a whole. People with T-shaped skills are extremely valuable for creating knowledge because they can integrate diverse knowledge assets (Leonard-Barton, 1995). They have the ability both to combine theoretical and practical knowledge and to see how their branch of knowledge interacts with other branches. Therefore, they can expand their competences across several functional NPD areas, and thus create new knowledge (Johannenssen, Olsen, & Olaisen, 1999; Madhavan & Grover, 1998).

H5: T-shaped skills are positively associated with the knowledge creation process.

NPD Performance

New product development has received much attention over the last 10 years because it is seen as an important source of competitive advantage (Brown & Eisenhardt, 1995; Wheelwright & Clark, 1992). The NPD literature is dedicated to identifying NPD performance dimensions that drive business success and it has generally been examined at the project level (Cooper and Kleinschmidt, 1987, 1993, 1994) and has only recently been extended to the product development function as a whole (Cooper & Kleinschmidt, 1995; Loch et al., 1996). NPD dimensions are changing across industries (Brown & Eisenhardt, 1995; Loch, Stein, & Tersheisch, 1996) and include the length of development cycles, the first to market, development productivity, percentage of distinctive and financially successful new products, or the proportion of sales from new products (Griffin & Page, 1993). The use of time as a metric for measuring product development performance has gained significant popularity in the academic and practitioner literature (Griffin, 1993). Time to market refers to how fast a firm completes its product development projects from concept generation to market introduction. It's often referred to in the literature as speed-to-market or time to market (Tatikonda & Rosenthal, 2000). Time to market reduction is possible when the NPD team has in-depth knowledge and experience in particular technologies and market applications that increase the knowledge exchange and facilitate the knowledge creation process. Thus, time to market reduction is sustained by the ability to use the knowledge created during the NPD process so that it can be reused in the next generation of products to reduce development time (Belbaly & Benbya, 2006).

H6: The knowledge creation process is positively associated with NPD performance.

METHODOLOGY AND DATA ANALYSIS

A questionnaire-based survey was conducted. Questionnaires were sent to a total of 225 middle managers in 16 organizations. Depending on each individual firm's size, 2 to 15 middle managers were surveyed from each firm. Middle managers were reached through their VP of product development, directors of product development or senior product managers. A typical job title of a middle manager was product manager. Middle product managers were surveyed because they play a key role in managing product knowledge. Middle product managers are positioned at the intersection of the vertical and horizontal flows of product knowledge. Thus, they can synthesize the tacit knowledge of both top managers and frontline employees, make it explicit, and incorporate it into new products and services (Nonaka & Takeuchi, 1995).

Considerable variations in the effect of individual factors upon time to market reduction often exist across various new product ventures and product groups of the same firm. It is unrealistic to expect that the same elements will be responsible for reducing time in all product cases. Consequently investigation of the time to market reduction at an aggregate level (i.e., the level of the overall firm or a level higher than an individual new product development process) will result in amalgamated finding and misleading interpretation. Therefore, the position taken in this research is that new individual product develop-

ment processes must be selected as the unit of the study, to obtain a more precise measurement of the knowledge management factors affecting the time to market reduction and as potential effects on NPD performance. This stance is in line with the majority of research in NPD (Mascarenhas, 1992).

We relied on multiple-item measures that have already been tested by previous studies (see Table 1). Research constructs were operationalized on the basis of related studies and pilot tests that have been already tested by several authors which operational definitions of instruments and their related literature concerning the different variables and items used in this study are summarized in Table 1 and Appendix 1. Each item of our questionnaire was based on a 5-point Likert scale ranging from 1 (*strongly disagree*) to 5 (*strongly agree*). A pilot study was carried out initially. The number of respondents to the survey was 52, of which 6 were eliminated because they had incomplete responses. The usable sample contained 46 completed questionnaires, indicating a response rate of 20%, which is an acceptable rate of response according to the principles of survey design. In this dataset, 21 data points were missing and have been replaced by the maximum likelihood techniques.

Most of the research constructs have already been validated and used for other studies on knowledge management, organizational design, marketing, learning, NPD or IT management (see Table 1). For example, questionnaire items for the knowledge creation process, which were used in this study, had been validated and used by Nonaka and Takeuchi (1995).

This measurement model was estimated using PLS that incorporated the model, parameters and estimation summary on the one hand, and the model assessment as a whole on the other. PLS allows to both specify the relationships among the conceptual factors of interest and the measures underlying each construct, resulting in a simultaneous analysis of (1) how well the measures relate to each construct and (2) whether the hypothesized relationships at the theoretical level

Table 1. Constructs used in the study

Variables	Operational definition	Related literature
Team leader characteristics	Degree of leaders influence on followers	Norrgren & Schaller (1999); Edmondson (1999); Muczyck & Reimann (1987)
T-shaped skills	Degree of knowledge domains exploration and their various applications	Iansiti (1992); Johannenssen et al. (1999); Leonard-Barton (1995)
Collaboration	Degree of active support and helps in organization	Huemer, Krogh, & Johan (1998), ; Kreitner & Kinicki (1992)
Trust	Degree of reciprocal faith in others' intentions. behaviors, and skills toward organizational goals	Davenport et al. (1998) ; Ichijo et al. (1998)
Learning	Degree of opportunity, variety, satisfaction, and encouragement for learning and development in organization	Hurley & Hult (1998); Junnarkar (1997); Quinn et al. (1996); Swieringa & Wierdsma (1992)
Socialization	Degree of tacit knowledge accumulation, extra-firm social information collection, intra-firm social information gathering, and transfer of tacit knowledge	Nonaka & Takeuchi (1995) ; Nonaka et al. (1994)
Externalization	Degree of creative dialogue, deductive and inductive thinking, use of metaphors, and exchanged ideas	Nonaka (1994); Nonaka & Takeuchi (1995)
Combination	Degree of acquisition and integration, synthesis and processing, and dissemination	Nonaka (1994); Nonaka & Takeuchi (1995)
Internalization	Degree of personal experiences, simulation, and experimentation	Nonaka & Takeuchi (1995) ; Nonaka et al. (1994)
NPD performance	Degree of overall success, market share, growth rate profitability, and innovativeness in comparison with major competitors	Rosenau (1988); Cohen & Levinthal (1990)

Table 2. Summary of constructs

Construct Name	Construct identifier	AVE	Initial number of items	Cronbach's alpha
Collaboration	CO	0.91	5	0.98
Trust	TU	0.73	3	0.83
Learning	LE	0.71	3	0.81
Team leader Characteristics	TL	0.74	3	0.84
T-Shaped Skills	TS	0.73	5	0.91
Knowledge Socialization	KS	0.67	5	0.88
Knowledge Externalization	KE	0.60	4	0.78
Knowledge Combination	KC	0.71	4	0.86
Knowledge Internalization	KI	0.62	4	0.79
Time to Market	TM	0.62	4	0.80

are empirically true. The objective of the research is to explain the variance and measures using PLS because it is more appropriate than the alternatives, such as LISREL and AMOS, when sample size is small and models are complex (Fornell, 1981). The properties of the measurement model are summarized in Table 2.

Results

Following the two-step analytical procedures (Hai, Anderson, Tatham, & Black, 1998), we first examined the measurement model and then the structural model. The rationale of this two-step approach was to ensure that our conclusion on structural relationships was drawn from a set of measurement instruments with desirable properties.

Instrument Reliability: One measure of reliability using the confirmatory factor analysis used here is composite reliability (Fornell, 1981). Composite reliability is also called Cronbach alpha. The Cronbach's alpha, which reflects the internal consistency of the indicators, ranges from 0.78 to 0.98 for the 10 constructs, indicating a high internal consistency. These statistics are shown in Table 2.

Instrument validity: A recommended method to examine the validity of constructs is by assessing the convergent validity, which can be established at the multimethod level of analysis by measuring the degree of agreement in responses of the informants to different survey items (Phillips & Bagozzi, 1986). Convergent validity of an indi-

cator is used to assess whether individual scale items are related. A confirmatory factor analysis was performed to test for validity (Bagozzi, 1980). The t values for all of the standard factor loadings exceeded the critical value of 3.29, at a p level of 0.01. Thus the measures support convergent validity (Anderson & Gerbing, 1988).

The structural model: While the factor analysis results provide evidence of convergent validity in the PLS methodology (see Agarwal & Karahanna, 2000), divergent validity is also assessed using the average variance extracted (i.e., the average variance shared between a construct and its measures, AVE). All the constructs of our study have an AVE higher than 0.5 (see Table 2). The results of the PLS analysis are shown in Figure 2 and Table 3. To allow for the possibility of effects other than those hypothesized, we tested a saturated model, including paths from all independent variables to each of the measures of effectiveness. To present an uncluttered picture, the nonsignificant relationships have been omitted from Figure 3 but are displayed in Table 3.

As shown in Figure 3, all the knowledge management factors (collaboration, trust, learning, T-shaped skills, team leader characteristics) have

Figure 3. Structural model

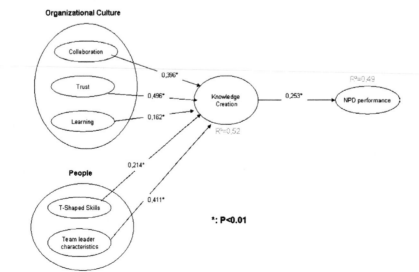

Table 3. Structural model

	Path Coefficients		Path Coefficients
Knowledge Creation ($R^2 = 0.52$)		**NPD performance** ($R^2 = 0.49$)	
		Collaboration	0.100
Collaboration	0.396	Trust	0.001
Trust	0.496	Learning	0.215
Learning	0.162	T-shaped Skills	0.371
T-shaped Skills	0.214	Team leader characteristics	0.024
Team leader characteristics	0.411	Knowledge creation	0.253

significant effects on the knowledge creation process, with a path coefficient of 0.396, 0.496, 0.162, 0.214, 0.411 respectively. Knowledge management factors explain 52% of the knowledge creation process. NPD performance is found to be statically significant with a path coefficient of 0.100, 0.215, 0.371 and 0.253 for collaboration, learning, T-shaped skills, and knowledge creation, respectively. The previous variables explain 49 percent of NPD performance.

Motivated by the need to better understand the impact of the knowledge creation process on NPD performance, this study develops an interconnected theoretical model that reflects the impact of knowledge management factors on the knowledge creation process, and NPD performance. The findings present strong support to the existing theoretical links between knowledge management factors, knowledge creation and NPD performance. These results have several implications for theory and practice.

CONCLUSION

Our Study is of interest from both theoretical and practical perspectives. Theoretically, a research model is establishing the impact of knowledge management factors on the knowledge creation process and NPD performance. Our framework is linking organizational culture and people factors which are crucial for a firm's ability to manage its knowledge creation process and NPD efficiently. We have adopted a process-oriented perspective of knowledge by using Nonaka's (1985) creation

model. In our case, our findings confirm that knowledge creation is associated with organizational culture factors such as collaboration trust and learning and also with people factors such as team leader characteristics and T-shaped skills. Thus, our research framework facilitates firm's adoption of a flexible organizational culture and people strategy that will enhance the knowledge creation process and NPD performance.

From a practical point of view, the relationships among knowledge creation and NPD performance may provide a clue as to how NPD managers can adjust knowledge management factors and knowledge creation processes to sustain their NPD performance. As NPD managers may face difficulties in building their organizational knowledge by creating the adequate environment, the importance to find which knowledge management factors are critical for knowledge creation and NPD performance. The current findings of this study indicate strong link between the knowledge management factors and the knowledge creation process with NPD performance which will allow NPD managers to manage efficiently their organization's knowledge. This framework can be applied as a tool by NPD managers to assess the performance of their knowledge management activity. This tool should also facilitate the adaptation and change that NPD managers need to do in order to enhance the knowledge creation process and reduce time to market. Another major managerial implication is based on the ability of the firms to benchmark themselves with direct competitors.

During the development of this study, we recognized that some limitations are related to the focus, sample size, and model assessment of the research. Firstly, this research focuses on the specific software development industry in the Silicon Valley. This community is following specific standards for software development that are shared by the majority of these companies. Several research questions need to be raised as they were not considered in this study: Would these results be repeated in another industry? What is the impact of company location? What happens in the case of a decentralized new product development team? Is there a difference in the impact between services and products, and between complex and simple services and products on NPD performance? What is the real impact of the storage, retrieval, and usage on NPD performance? Does the market influence the NPD performance and the way it's organized? Does the level of implementation of the NPD process have an impact on NPD performance?

The second limitation of this research is related to the sample size that has to be increased in order to improve the existing result and also to be able to use other type of data analysis like LISREL and AMOS. In our case, due to the timeframe that was very short, it was also very difficult to get more respondents to our survey.

Final limitation; this research would have given better results if we had conducted a longitudinal study.

REFERENCES

Adler, P. (2001). Market, hierarchy, and trust: The knowledge economy and the future of capitalism. *Organization Science*, *12*(2), 215–234. doi:10.1287/orsc.12.2.215.10117

Agarwal, R., & Karahanna, E. (2000). Time flies when you're having fun: Cognitive absorption and beliefs about information technology usage. *Management Information Systems Quarterly*, *24*(4), 665–694. doi:10.2307/3250951

Alavi, M., & Leidner, D. E. (2001). Review: Knowledge management and knowledge management systems: Conceptual foundations and research issues. *Management Information Systems Quarterly*, *25*(1), 107–136. doi:10.2307/3250961

Anderson, J. C., & Gerbing, D. W. (1988). Structural equation modeling in practice: A review and recommended two-step approach. *Psychological Bulletin*, *103*(3), 411–423. doi:10.1037/0033-2909.103.3.411

Ashkenas, R. U., Ulrich, D., Jick, T., & Kerr, S. (1995). *The boundary-less organisation: Breaking the chains of the organisational structure*. San Francisco: Jossey-Bass.

Bagozzi, R. P. (1980). The nature and causes of self-esteem, performance, and satisfaction in the sales force: A structural equation approach. *The Journal of Business*, *53*, 315–331. doi:10.1086/296088

Becerra-Fernandez, I., & Sabherwal, R. (2001). Organizational knowledge management: A contingency perspective. *Journal of Management Information Systems*, *18*(1), 23–25.

Beckman, T. (1999). The current state of knowledge management. In Liebowitz, J. (Ed.), *Knowledge management handbook* (pp. 1–22). Boca Raton, FL: CRC Press.

Belbaly, N., & Benbya, H. (2006). A stage model for NPD process maturity and IKMS implementation. In *Artificial Intelligence and Integrated Intelligent Information Systems: Emerging Technologies and Applications* (pp. 428–447). Hershey, PA: IGI Global. doi:10.4018/9781599042497.ch020

Bierly, P., & Chakrabarti, A. (1996). Generic knowledge strategies in the U.S. pharmaceutical industry. *Strategic Management Journal*, *17*(10), 123–135.

Brown, S. L., & Eisenhardt, K. M. (1995). Product development: Past research, present findings, and future directions. *Academy of Management Review*, *20*(2), 343–378. doi:10.2307/258850

Bryant, S. E. (2003). The role of transformational and transactional leadership in creating, sharing and exploiting organisational knowledge. *Journal of Leadership & Organizational Studies, 9*(4). doi:10.1177/107179190300900403

Chase, R. (1997). The knowledge-based organization: An international survey. *Journal of Knowledge Management, 1*(1), 38–49. doi:10.1108/EUM0000000004578

Choi, B., & Lee, H. (2003, Summer). Knowledge management enablers, processes, and organizational performance: An integrative view and empirical examination. *Journal of Management Information Systems, 20*(1), 179–228.

Clark, K. B., & Fujimoto, T. (1991). *Product development performance: Strategy, organisation and management in the world auto industry*. Boston: Harvard Business School Press.

Cohen, W. M., & Levinthal, D. A. (1990). Absorptive capacity: a new perspective on learning and innovation. *Administrative Science Quarterly, 35*, 128–152. doi:10.2307/2393553

Cooper, R. G., & Kleinschmidt, E. J. (1987). New products: What separates winners from losers? *Journal of Product Innovation Management, 4*, 169–184. doi:10.1016/0737-6782(87)90002-6

Cooper, R. G., & Kleinschmidt, E. J. (1993). Major new products: What distinguishes the winners in the chemical industry? *Journal of Product Innovation Management, 10*, 90–111. doi:10.1016/0737-6782(93)90002-8

Cooper, R. G., & Kleinschmidt, E. J. (1994). Determinants of timeliness in product development. *Journal of Product Innovation Management, 11*, 381–396. doi:10.1016/0737-6782(94)90028-0

Cooper, R. G., & Kleinschmidt, E. J. (1995). New product performance: Keys to success, Profitability and cycle time reduction. *Journal of Marketing Management, 11*, 315–337. doi:10.1080/0267257X.1995.9964347

Damanpour, F. (1991). Organizational innovation: A meta-analysis of effect of determinants and moderators. *Academy of Management Journal, 34*(3), 555–590. doi:10.2307/256406

Davenport, T., & Prusak, L. (1998). *Working knowledge. How organizations manage what they know*. Boston: Harvard Business School Press.

Davenport, T. H. (1999). Knowledge management and the broader firm: Strategy, advantage, and performance. In Liebowitz, J. (Ed.), *Knowledge management handbook* (pp. 2-1–2-11). Boca Raton, FL: CRC Press.

Davenport, T. H., Long, D., & Beers, M. C. (1998). Successful knowledge management projects. *Sloan Management Review, 39*(2), 43–57.

DeFillippi, R. J. (2002). Organizational models for collaboration in the New Economy. *HR: Human Resource planning, 25*(4), 7.

Demarest, M. (1997). Understanding knowledge management. *Long Range Planning, 30*(3), 374–384. doi:10.1016/S0024-6301(97)90250-8

Edmondson, A. (1999). Psychological safety and learning behaviour in work teams. *Administrative Science Quarterly, 44*, 350–383. doi:10.2307/2666999

Fornell, C., & Larcker, D. F. (1981). Evaluating structural equation models with unobservable variables and measurement error. *JMR, Journal of Marketing Research, 18*(1), 39–50. doi:10.2307/3151312

Gold, A. H., Malhotra, A., & Segars, A. H. (2001). Knowledge management: An organizational capabilities perspective. *Journal of Management Information Systems, 18*(1), 185–214.

Graham, A. B., & Pizzo, V. G. (1996). A question of balance: Case studies in strategic knowledge management. *European Management Journal, 14*(4), 338–346. doi:10.1016/0263-2373(96)00020-5

Griffin, A. (1993). PDMA research on new product development practices: Updating trends and benchmarking best practices. *Journal of Product Innovation Management, 14*(6), 429–458. doi:10.1016/S0737-6782(97)00061-1

Griffin, A., & Hauser, J. R. (1992). Patterns of communication among marketing engineering and manufacturing—A comparison between two new product teams. *Management Science, 38*(3), 360–373. doi:10.1287/mnsc.38.3.360

Hackerman, J., & Morris, C. (1978). Group tasks, group interaction process, and group performance effectiveness: A review and proposed integration. In Berkowltz, L. (Ed.), *Group Process* (pp. 1–15). New York: Academic Press.

Hair, J. F., Anderson, R. E., Tatham, R. L., & Black, W. C. (1998). *Multivariate data analysis* (5th ed.). Prentice Hall.

Hedlund, G. (1994). A model of knowledge management and the N-form corporation. *Strategic Management Journal, 15*(5), 73–90.

Henderson & Cockburn. (1996, Spring). Scale, scope, and spillovers: The determinants of research productivity in drug discovery. *RAND Journal of Economics, RAND, 27*(1), 32–59. doi:10.2307/2555791

Holsapple, C. W., & Joshi, K. D. (2001). Organizational knowledge resources. *Decision Support Systems, 31*(1), 39–54. doi:10.1016/S0167-9236(00)00118-4

Huemer, L., Krogh, G., & Johan, R. (1998). Knowledge and the concept of trust. In Krogh, G., Roos, J., & Kleine, D. (Eds.), *Knowing in firms* (pp. 123–145). Thousand Oaks, CA: Sage.

Hurley, R., & Hult, T. (1998). Innovation, market orientation, and organizational learning: An integration and empirical examination. *Journal of Marketing, 62*(3), 42–54. doi:10.2307/1251742

Hutt, M., & Reingen, P., & Ronchetto, Jr. (1988). Tracing emergent processes in marketing strategy formation. *Journal of Marketing, 52*(1), 4–19. doi:10.2307/1251682

Iansiti, M. (1992). *Science-based product development: An empirical study of the mainframe computer industry* (Working paper). Cambridge, MA: Harvard Business School.

Ichijo, K., Krogh, G., & Nonaka, I. (1998). Knowledge enablers. In Krogh, G., Roos, J., & Kleine, D. (Eds.), *Knowing in Firms* (pp. 173–203). Thousand Oaks, CA: Sage.

Johannenssen, J.-A., Olsen, B., & Olaisen, J. (1999). Aspects of innovation theory based on knowledge management. *International Journal of Information Management, 19*(2), 121–139. doi:10.1016/S0268-4012(99)00004-3

Junnarkar, B. (1997). Leveraging collective intellect by building organizational capabilities. *Expert Systems with Applications, 13*(1), 29–40. doi:10.1016/S0957-4174(97)00020-1

Kanevsky, V., & Housel, T. (1998). The learning-knowledge-value cycle. In Krogh, G., Roos, J., & Kleine, D. (Eds.), *Knowing in firms* (pp. 269–284). Thousand Oaks, CA: Sage.

Kidd, J. A., & Christy, R. T. (1961). Supervisory procedures and work-team productivity. *The Journal of Applied Psychology, 45*, 388–392. doi:10.1037/h0040865

Kreitner, R., & Kinicki, A. (1992). *Organizational behavior*. Homewood, IL: Richard D. Irwin.

Krogh, G. (1998). Care in the knowledge creation. *California Management Review, 40*(3), 133–153.

Lambkin, M. (1988). Order of entry and performance in new markets. *Strategic Management Journal, 9*, 127140. doi:10.1002/smj.4250090713

Lee, H., & Choi, B. (2003). Knowledge management enablers, process, and organizational performance: An integrative view and empirical examination. *Journal of Management Information Systems, 20*(1), 179–228.

Leonard-Barton, D. (1995). *Wellsprings of knowledge: Building and sustaining the sources of innovation.* Boston: Harvard Business School Press.

Liebowitz, J., & Wilcox, L. (1997). *Knowledge management and its integrative elements*. CRC Press.

Linden, R. (2003). Learning to manage horizontally: The promise and challenge of collaboration. *Public Management, 85*(7), 8.

Loch, C., Stein, L., & Terweisch, C. (1996). Measuring development performance in the electronics industry. *Journal of Product Innovation Management, 13*(1), 3–20. doi:10.1016/0737-6782(95)00089-5

Long, D. D. (1997). Building the knowledge-based organizations: How culture drives knowledge behaviours. *Working Paper of the Center for Business Innovation*, Cambridge, MA: Ernst & Young LLP.

Madhavan, R., & Grover, R. (1998). From embedded knowledge to embodied knowledge: New product development as knowledge management. *Journal of Marketing, 62*(4), 1–12. doi:10.2307/1252283

Mascarenhas, B. (1992). Order of entry and performance in international markets. *Strategic Management Journal, 13*, 499–510. doi:10.1002/smj.4250130703

Miller, D. A. (1996). A preliminary typology of organizational learning: Synthesizing the literature. *Journal of Management, 22*(3), 484–505. doi:10.1177/014920639602200305

Muczyk, J. P., & Reimann, B. C. (1987). The case for directive leadership. *Academy of Management Review, 12*, 637–647.

Nahapiet, J., & Ghoshal, S. (1998). Social capital, intellectual capital, and the organizational advantage. *Academy of Management Review, 23*(2), 246–266. doi:10.2307/259373

Nelson, K. M., & Cooprider, J. G. (1996). The contribution of shared knowledge to IS group performance. *Management Information Systems Quarterly, 20*(4), 409–429. doi:10.2307/249562

Nonaka, I. (1994). A dynamic theory of organizational knowledge creation. *Organization Science, 5*(1), 14–37. doi:10.1287/orsc.5.1.14

Nonaka, I., Byosiere, P., & Konno, N. (1994). Organizational knowledge creation theory: A first comprehensive test. *International Business Review, 3*(4), 337–351. doi:10.1016/0969-5931(94)90027-2

Nonaka, I., & Konno, N. (1998). The Concept of "Ba": Building a foundation for knowledge creation. *California Management Review, 40*(3), 40–54.

Nonaka, I., & Takeuchi, H. (1995). *The knowledge-creating company*. Oxford University Press.

Norrgren, F., & Schaller, J. (1999). Leadership style: Its impact on cross-functional product development. *Journal of Product Innovation Management, 16*, 377–384. doi:10.1016/S0737-6782(98)00065-4

O'Dell, C., & Grayson, J. (1999). Knowledge transfer: Discover your value proposition. *Strategy and Leadership, 27*(2), 10–15. doi:10.1108/eb054630

O'Leary, D. E. (1998). Enterprise knowledge management. *IEEE Computer, 31*(3), 54–61.

Phillips, L. W., & Bagozzi, R. P. (1986). On measuring organizational properties of distribution channels: methodological issues in the use of key informants. In L. Bucklin & J. M. Carman (Eds.), *Research in Marketing, 8*, 313-369.

Pisano, G. P. (1996). *The development factory: Unlocking the potential of process innovation.* Harvard Business School Press.

Politis, J. D. (2001). The relationship of various leadership styles to knowledge management. *Leadership and Organization Development Journal, 22*(8), 354–364. doi:10.1108/01437730110410071

Quinn, J. B., Anderson, P., & Finkelstein, S. (1996). Leveraging intellect. *The Academy of Management Executive, 10*(3), 7–27.

Rosenau, M. D. (1988). Speeding your product to market. *Journal of Consumer Marketing, 5,* 23–40.

Rosenbach, W. T. (1993). *Contemporary issues in leadership* (3rd ed.). Boulder, CO: Westview.

Ruggles, R. (1998). The state of the notion: Knowledge management in practice. *California Management Review, 40*(3), 80–89.

Sarvary, M. (1999). Knowledge management and competition in the consulting industry. *California Management Review, 41*(2), 95–107.

Stogdill, R. M. (1963). *Manual for leadership behavior. Description Questionnaire Form, 12.* Columbus, OH: Bureau of Business Research.

Stonehouse, G. H., & Pemberton, J. D. (1999). Learning and knowledge management in the intelligent organization. *Participation & Empowerment: An International Journal, 7*(5), 131–144. doi:10.1108/14634449910287846

Swieringa, J., & Wierdsma, A. (1992). *Becoming a learning organization: Beyond the learning curve.* Wokingham, UK: Addison-Wesley.

Szulanski, G. (1996). Exploring internal stickiness: Impediments to the transfer of best practice within the firm. *Strategic Management Journal, 17*(10), 27–43.

Tatikonda, M. V., & Rosenthal, S. R. (2000). Technology novelty, project complexity, and product development execution success. *IEEE Transactions on Engineering Management, 47,* 74–87. doi:10.1109/17.820727

Ulrich, K. T., & Eppinger, S. D. (2004). *Product design and development* (3rd ed.). McGraw-Hill.

Wenger, E., Mcdermott, R., & Snyder, W. M. (2002). *Cultivating communities of practice: A guide to managing knowledge.* Boston: Harvard Business School Press.

Wheelwright, S., & Clark, K. (1992). *Revolutionizing new product development.* New York: Free Press.

Wiig, K. (1997). Knowledge management: An introduction and perspective. *Journal of Knowledge Management, 1*(1), 6–14. doi:10.1108/13673279710800682

Wilemon, D., & Thamhain, H. (1983, June). Team building in project management. *Project Management Quarterly,* 73-80.

Zander, D., & Kogut, B. (1995). Knowledge and the speed of the transfer and imitation of organizational capabilities: An empirical test. *Organization Science, 6*(1), 76–92. doi:10.1287/orsc.6.1.76

ENDNOTES

[1] Tacit knowledge is not easily shared, and cannot be codified, but can be transmitted via training or gained through personal experience. Tacit knowledge has been described as know-how, skills, and routines.

[2] Explicit knowledge can be articulated, codified, and stored in certain media. The most common forms of explicit knowledge are manuals, documents, procedures, and stories.

APPENDIX

Questionnaire

Please rate your degree of satisfaction with the following items presented hereafter:
1 = Strongly Disagree, 2 = Disagree, 3 = No Opinion, 4 = Agree, 5 = Strongly Agree

Knowledge Management Enablers

Collaboration (CO; five items)
CO1: Our organization members are satisfied by the degree of collaboration.
CO2: Our organization members are supportive.
CO3: Our organization members are helpful.
CO4: There is a willingness to collaborate across organizational units within our organization.
CO5: There is a willingness to accept responsibility for failure.

Trust (TU; three items)
Our company members...
TU1: are generally trustworthy.
TU2: have reciprocal faith in other members' intentions and behaviors.
TU3: have reciprocal faith in others' ability.

Learning (LA; three items)
Our company...
LA1: provides various formal training programs for performance of duties.
LA2: provides opportunities for informal individual development other than formal training such as work assignments and job rotation.
LA3: encourages people to attend seminars, symposia, and so on.

T-shaped skills (TS; five items)
Our company members...
TS1: can understand not only their own tasks but also others' tasks.
TS2: can make suggestion about others' task.
TS3: can communicate well not only with their department members but also with other department members.
TS4: are specialists in their own part.
TS5: can perform their own task effectively without regard to environmental changes.

Team leader characteristics (TL; three items)
Our company members...
TL1: Team members can exert influence regarding how the team should function.
TL2: Team members can influence decisions of the team leader regarding things concerning the team.
TL3: Our team leader frequently asks the team members for their opinion when a problem comes up that involves the project.

Knowledge Creation Processes

Socialization (KS; five items)

Our company stresses...

KS1: gathering information from sales and production sites.

KS2: sharing experience with suppliers and customers.

KS3: engaging in dialogue with competitors.

KS4: finding new strategies and market opportunities by wandering inside the firm.

KS5: creating a work environment that allows peers to understand the craftsmanship and expertise.

Externalization (KE; four items)

Our company stresses...

KE1: creative and essential dialogues.

KE2: the use of deductive and inductive thinking.

KE3: the use of metaphors in dialogue for concept creation.

KE4: exchanging various ideas and dialogues.

Combination (KC; four items)

Our company stresses...

KC1: planning strategies by using published literature, computer simulation and forecasting.

KC2: creating manuals and documents on products and services.

KC3: building databases on products and service.

KC4: building up materials by gathering management figures and technical information.

Internalization (KI; four items)

Our company stresses...

KI1: enactive liaison activities with functional departments by cross-functional development teams.

KI2: forming teams as a model and conducting experiments, and sharing results with entire departments.

KI3: searching and sharing new values and thoughts.

KI4: sharing and trying to understand management visions through communications with fellows.

NPD Performance

Time to market (TM; four items)

TM1: This product was developed much faster than other comparable products developed by our organization.

TM2: This product was developed much faster than similar products developed by our nearest competitors.

TM3: This product could have been developed in a short time.

TM4: The product concept formation (i.e. opportunity identification and product design) took longer than expected.

This work was previously published in International Journal of Knowledge Management, Volume 5, Issue 3, edited by Murray E. Jennex, pp. 21-37, copyright 2009 by IGI Publishing (an imprint of IGI Global).

Chapter 15
Knowledge Strategy and its Role in the Organization:
An Exploratory Study

Joseph E. Kasten
Dowling College, USA

ABSTRACT

Knowledge strategy is defined as the set of guidelines and philosophies that guide an organization's knowledge-based activities, such as knowledge gathering, development, storage, and utilization. Much of the early literature describing knowledge strategy suggests that its role in the organization is to drive, and be driven by, organizational structure and the human resources and technology strategies. The present research utilizes semistructured interview data to determine that knowledge strategy is less of a formal structure and more of a lens through which knowledge-based decisions are viewed and focused, resulting in organizational actions that align with the knowledge strategy of the organization.

INTRODUCTION

As the age of the knowledge-enabled organization nears the middle of its second decade, and the field of knowledge management reaches some level of maturity as evidenced by the behavior of its associated literature (Ponzi & Koenig, 2002), it is appropriate that the study of the strategic implica-

DOI: 10.4018/978-1-60960-555-1.ch015

tions and management of knowledge takes a more central role. The importance of knowledge to the success of firms in many industries has become well-rooted in the literature. It is necessary now to address the manner in which the management of knowledge is linked to the business strategy. This linkage is crucial to the successful application of knowledge and the systems utilized to manage it. This linkage ensures that the knowledge obtained, developed, stored, or applied by the firm is derived from, and supports, the business strategy currently in place.

The linkage between the business strategy and the knowledge activities of the organization exists in the form of a knowledge strategy (KS). A KS is defined as the set of guidelines and rules that help to define and steer the organization's knowledge-based activities and processes (Kasten, 2006). The nature of a KS, as well as the manner in which it directs the operations of the organization, is somewhat difficult to specifically define. Knowledge strategies, like other strategic plans, can be explicit or implicit. They can be prescriptive or emergent. And, they can be comprehensive or very specific. Of course, like most other strategic plans, there is little to quantify in a KS so its identity must consist of qualitative, contextual descriptions rather than values or scores.

The purpose of this article is two-fold. First, the various approaches to KS creation and implementation by various authors are synthesized into one comprehensive model. The second purpose is to collect empirical data that will enable the revision of that literature-based model to more accurately reflect the nature and application of knowledge strategy in the field. Ultimately, this article is important because it creates a framework within which we can begin to understand the role of knowledge strategy in the organization. By understanding the role played by an organization's KS and the manner in which it shapes organizational processes, researchers and practitioners alike can then understand how the KS can be used to link the business strategy with the knowledge-based activities of the firm. Without this understanding, it is unlikely that we can fully leverage the knowledge strategy, not to mention the KS creation process, to the creation of competitive advantage. The study consists of both a comprehensive review of the knowledge strategy literature as well as semistructured interviews with nine executives from a wide range of industries who are directly involved in the creation and implementation of their organization's knowledge strategy.

LITERATURE REVIEW

The literature review is divided into three subsections. The first section defines and develops the topic of knowledge strategy. This leads into the second subsection, which condenses the literature concerning the external and organizational drivers of KS creation. The last subsection details the empirical evidence supporting the existence of many of these drivers.

Theoretical KS Literature

The earliest writings directed at the strategic use of knowledge come from the business strategy development literature. Feurer, Chaharbarghi, and Distel (1995) wrote about the part played by knowledge in the implementation of business strategy. Their research stresses the importance of matching the type of knowledge maintained in the firm with its proper level in the firm. Specifically, they assert that horizontal knowledge, or wide knowledge of the industry and market, is necessary at the top of the organization to enable executives to evaluate and implement strategic plans. Vertical knowledge, or specialized knowledge, belongs at the business unit level or lower to enable them to better carry out the tasks of the firm.

Zack (1999) explicitly defines KS as "balancing knowledge-based resources and capabilities to the knowledge required for providing products or services in ways superior to those of competitors." This definition directly links the knowledge characteristics of the organization with performance and competitive advantage. Zack (1999) continues on to identify certain traits of the knowledge-based organization such as being a creator or exploiter of knowledge and whether knowledge is sought inside or outside the firm.

Bierly (1999) takes a similar approach to KS when he defines four basic drivers involved in the creation of a KS: internally vs. externally sourced knowledge, enhanced vs. new knowledge, fast vs. slow speed of learning, and depth vs. breadth of knowledge base. With these dimensions, Bierly (1999) proposes four generic knowledge strategies: explorer, exploiter, imitator, and passive learner.

KS in an Organizational Context

To understand fully the role that KS, and its creation, plays in the organization, its relationship and interactions with other characteristics of the organization should be explored. Many of these interactions have been discussed in the literature already, but primarily from a prescriptive perspective and never in one place. This subsection represents the partial compilation of this body of literature.

A critical influence on a firm's approach to knowledge gathering and creation is the environment within which it operates (Buckley & Carter, 2004). The environmental characteristics that might influence knowledge acquisition are the type of product or service the firm produces, the level of turbulence or instability in the industry, and the degree of fusion that exists between the industry and those that complement it (Bierly & Chakrabarti, 2001). The knowledge gained by the firm assists in understanding both the marketplace and the manner in which the firm should respond to changes in it. An understanding of the industrial environment also affects the scope and scale of the organization and its operations. These characteristics of the organization also have a direct influence on its knowledge-seeking and manipulation behavior.

The external environment is, of course, one of the key ingredients in the organization's overall business strategy. While the creation of the business strategy is not the topic of this article, the business strategy should, and usually does, very directly affect the creation of KS (Ursic, Nikl, Muleg, & Smogave, 2006). Nickerson and Silverman (1998) contend that most of the mishaps in a firm's strategic posture result from the failure

to integrate and align their business strategy with their knowledge and technology strategy.

Bierly and Chakrabarti (2001) point out that a number of KS drivers are identified based upon the firm's business strategy. The scope of the knowledge sought is determined by the business strategy. A focused business strategy calls for a focused knowledge acquisition and development plan. Likewise, firms with a broader business approach must develop a wider and deeper knowledge base in order for them to be able to adapt to changes in the marketplace as well as the products they offer. The rate of development called for by a business strategy determines the temporal aspects of knowledge development, both in terms of time allocated for knowledge development and the size of the technological jump sought. Other characteristics of KS, such as the manipulation and disposition of knowledge, are also driven by the needs of the business strategy.

Due to the interdisciplinary nature of knowledge, KS cannot be created in isolation. It must be informed by other aspects of the organization's plans. Three of the most important drivers of KS, in addition to the business strategy, are the organization's human resources strategy, technology strategy, and the organizational structure. Human resources policies dictate the incentive plans, training structures, and retention plans, all of which contribute directly to a firm's ability to retain tacit knowledge (Kim, Yu, & Lee, 2003).

Knowledge, especially in its explicit form, is often shared through the use of information technology. The relationship between information technology and knowledge sharing and transmittal requires that the approach to technology taken by the organization has a significant impact on its ability to capture, store, and transmit knowledge. Therefore, it is incumbent upon the creators of KS to include the technology strategy as one of its key inputs (Nickerson & Silverman, 1998; Kim et al., 2003; Shankar, Singh, Gupta, & Narain, 2003).

Shankar et al. (2003) describe the impact of the organization upon the KS process, which was earlier introduced by Liebeskind (1996). This influence might be the result of the organizational structure, the culture of the organization, or the management systems in place within the organization. The organizational structure dictates the location and flow of knowledge stores by dictating the location of people, both geographically and organizationally, and their prescribed interactions. These knowledge assets are also affected by the management processes in place within the organization, such as those that determine access to resources and employee mobility.

In order for a KS, or any strategic plan, to remain responsive to the needs of the organization and environment, a firm must establish a mechanism for the monitoring of its effectiveness and its periodic realignment with the other aspects of a firm's strategy. Since KS is influenced by the business strategy, human resources strategy, technology strategy, and the organizational structure, the organization must allow the KS to influence these other aspects of the firm's strategic infrastructure, as well.

Given the relationship between knowledge and IT, it is clear that the requirements of the KS must have an impact on the technology strategy. Johannessen, Olaisen, and Olsen (1999) describe in detail how the technological capabilities of the organization directly affect its ability to collect, control, and disseminate knowledge. This relationship is so important to the execution of KS that some authors suggest that the formulation of a firm's technology strategy should not proceed until the KS has been determined (Felton & Finnie, 2003; Hughes, 1997).

The organization is also required to react to the KS. Changes in the manner in which knowledge is acquired and managed within a firm often call for a revision in structure or management processes. Certainly, the flow of knowledge will be made more efficient if the people creating and sharing the knowledge are managed in a way that encourages, rather than discourages, knowledge sharing. In some cases, the required adjustments

to organizational structure are minor in nature, centering perhaps upon things such as job titles or performance appraisal processes. However, some organizations have completely restructured their operations around their need for knowledge creation and application (Chase, 1997).

An important strategic link exists between the KS and the knowledge management processes undertaken by the firm. The approach taken in this research places the knowledge management processes and architectures as primary methods through which the KS is implemented. The KS drives the development of the knowledge management tools, organizational processes, system content, and development cycle (Maier & Remus, 2003; Snyman & Kruger, 2004). By forming the link between KS and knowledge management, the firm is able to ensure that the knowledge management processes are truly aligned with the strategic needs of the firm rather than merely satisfying the immediate requirement to "do something."

The literature is unambiguous in its call to allow the KS of the firm to influence the business strategy. This ensures that the business strategy is aligned with and supported by the KS, just as it should be with the other substrategies such as technology and human resource strategies (von Krogh & Roos, 1995). This enables the firm to link its knowledge base, or intellectual capital, with the strategy of the organization as a whole (Huang, 1997).

The literature reviewed in this section forms the basis for the place of KS within the organization's strategy creation and implementation process. The authors contributing to this stream of literature illustrate the network of influence within the organization, as well as the influences that originate from outside the organization, that help to shape the KS. The following section discusses the empirical studies that have been conducted to explore the concept of KS and specifically the relationships presented in this portion of the literature review.

Empirical Research on KS Drivers

The literature reviewed in this section represents research that lends empirical support to the influence of the KS drivers identified in the literature. KS is directly influenced by the organization's environment, including the external board of advisors (Southon, Todd, & Seneque, 2002). In a study of three knowledge-intensive organizations (law firm, school, and city council), the authors analyze the treatment of knowledge as it applied to the organization's functions. They find that all three organizations fit their knowledge processes (location, acquisition, sharing, etc.) around their environment. More recent research suggests that while external factors are still influencers of KS, variables such as firm size and age might not play as significant a role as first thought (Gopalakrishnan & Bierly, 2006). Even more recent is the study conducted by Lane and Probert (2007) analyzing the effects of internal and external knowledge acquisition on firm performance.

Using data collected by the Danish government, Laursen and Mahnke (2001) are able to show that the human resources practices of firms vary with respect to their KS. Firms whose knowledge strategies call for an emphasis on external learning and linkages (e.g., consultants or universities) have a greater propensity to employ human resource practices that encourage knowledge sharing such as quality circles and job rotation. In addition, they identify certain human resources policies that are complementary to each other under specific knowledge strategies.

Not surprisingly, there is significant research linking the organization's technology strategy with the KS. The link between technology and knowledge management was forged when the term knowledge management first came into the language because it was mainly driven by technology. Syed-Ikhsan and Rowland (2004) find a significant correlation between the IT infrastructure and the creation and transfer of knowledge within the organization.

The last set of drivers for which evidence exists in the empirical literature is the influence of the organization upon the KS. Girard (2005) shows that the organizational approach to knowledge sharing, including the use of such techniques as social networks, tend to be preferred over any other knowledge-sharing strategy. Jang, Hong, Bock, and Kim (2002) find that the sociocultural aspects of the firm as well as the processes that were mentioned earlier influence the knowledge management strategy. After surveying 195 Spanish firms, López, Peón, and Vázquez Ordás (2004) find a significant link between the organizational culture of a firm and its learning capabilities. These learning capabilities, in turn, are linked to the firm's performance. The learning capabilities of the firm are often the result of the KS in place, so this study also provides a linkage between the organizational structure and the KS.

INITIAL MODEL

To further the understanding of the context within which these KS drivers exist, Figure 1 is provided. The model represents the various entities, both internal and external to the organization, which the literature reviewed in the previous sections suggest drives the creation of KS. Each of the works cited in the literature review was selected because it describes, theoretically or empirically, a driver of knowledge strategy. As a group, this body of literature draws a picture of the set of KS creation drivers, which is graphically presented in Figure 1. The arcs between the entities represent the influence of those entities on KS and, in the case of some, the influence of KS on the entity.

Following is a brief description of the 10 linkages shown in the initial model.

1. Characteristics of the external environment that indirectly influence KS, including the industrial characteristics such as turbulence

Figure 1. Drivers of knowledge strategy

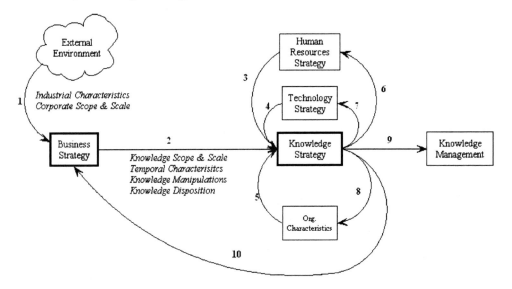

and fusion, and the scope and scale of the organization (Buckley & Carter 2004).

2. Characteristics of knowledge needed by the organization that are driven by the business strategy. These include the scope and scale of the knowledge, the temporal aspects of knowledge acquisition, the degree of manipulation undergone by the knowledge (e.g., tacit vs. explicit), and the manner in which knowledge is disseminated (e.g., internal vs. external, for sale or free) (Nickerson & Silverman, 1998).

3. The influence of the human resources strategy on KS. These drivers might include the incentive and retention plans for employees and the approach to training taken by the firm (Kim et al., 2003).

4. Technology strategy influences KS both in the approach to information technology taken by the firm as well as the level of technology of the products or services provided by the firm to the customer (Nickerson & Silverman, 1998; Kim et al., 2003).

5. The influence of the organization on KS includes the management processes, orga-

nizational structure, organizational culture, and political climate (Shankar et al., 2003).

6. The KS might require adjustments to the human resources strategy of the organization in order to accommodate the specified treatment of knowledge workers.

7. As the KS develops and new paths for knowledge sharing are identified, the technological requirements will also change. The technology strategy of the organization must reflect the knowledge flow needs of the KS (Hughes, 1997; Felton & Finnie, 2003).

8. As noted in the literature, the organizational structure often poses the largest obstacle to the implementation of knowledge-based activities such as knowledge management (Chase, 1997). Therefore, the organization will often be required to develop along with the knowledge needs specified by the KS.

9. A primary reason to have a KS is to provide guidance to the knowledge management processes implemented by the organization. The influence of the KS on the knowledge management processes ensures that the knowledge management tools and techniques are applied to properly support the

business strategy (Maier & Remus, 2003; Snyman & Kruger, 2004).

10. The development of a KS should be an input to subsequent business strategy development. This link ensures that the knowledge needs of the organization are aligned with the business strategy as well as ensuring that the business strategy is developed in keeping with the knowledge capabilities and assets of the organization (Huang, 1997; von Krogh & Roos, 1995).

METHODOLOGY AND RESEARCH FOCUS

In keeping with the stated purpose of the article, the research focus that guides the gathering of empirical data and its analysis is straightforward: How should the set of relationships between the KS drivers and the KS, which is derived from the largely prescriptive literature, be modified to reflect the practices of actual organizations engaged in the application of knowledge as a competitive asset? With an understanding of the real, vs. presumed, place of the knowledge strategy in the organization, a research model more reflective of reality can be created and act as a foundation for future research.

The research performed in this study consists of semistructured interviews with nine top executives from a number of industries: banking, healthcare (one standalone hospital and one healthcare system), financial services, insurance, software development, and government. The research subjects are all at the highest levels of the organization: CEOs, CTOs, CIOs, senior vice-presidents, and a county executive. Each of the subjects participated in interviews lasting approximately 1 hour. The participants were asked questions regarding the existence of their organization's KS, how their organization's knowledge strategy was created, its characteristics, and its manner of application. The initial interview script is included as Appendix

A. The interviews were digitally recorded, transcribed by the author, and analyzed using content analysis. Initial coding consisted of identifying KS drivers and influencers, with subsequent coding for underlying causal relationships as well as indicators of departure from those relationships noted in the literature. Throughout, linkages and differences within firms, within industries, and between industries were noted and explored with numerous follow-up questions via telephone and e-mail. As the data revealed differences between the suggestions of the literature and actual events, these differences were compiled and formed the basis of the revised research model, introduced in the next section. In most cases, the revisions to the initial model are based upon multiple observations of similar results.

A qualitative methodology was chosen for two primary reasons. First, qualitative methods are very effective at uncovering relationships between concepts that do not lend themselves to direct measurement, such as the KS. Second, qualitative methods are particularly useful when a field is relatively new and has not generated a great deal of empirical studies or theory upon which to base quantitative methodologies.

REVISION OF THE INITIAL MODEL

The data collected during this study suggest that the initial model is in need of revision. Specifically, five aspects of the model must be revised to describe more accurately the existing use and understanding of KS and its relationship with the rest of the organization and the external environment.

The first change is to remove the direct link between the external environment and KS. This is not to suggest that the external environment does not influence the knowledge needs and activities of the organization. The industry and its characteristics are a major driver of KS. However, the existence of the external environment as a separate entity on the model is misleading. Based upon the data, any influences of the industrial environment are modulated by the business strategy and therefore should not be considered separately from it. Rather, the influences of the external environment are only important as they are addressed by the business strategy.

A good example of this phenomenon is the two hospitals in the study. Both face similar external environments as far as regulations and demographics are concerned. However, when faced with a requirement to develop knowledge about process improvement, one turned inward for knowledge development and the other first looked outside and then developed an internal training program. The character of the training program also differed, one being rather formal and the other being a largely informal group of employees who met on their own time. Ultimately, these responses differ because the strategic outlook of the institution differed. The difference is only slight, because both hospitals' strategies were to be low-cost providers of healthcare to the community. The difference in their responses was due to management decisions about the best way to meet both the strategic imperative of cost control and their mandate to serve their population. One hospital is an independent institution that has to rely on its own resources, thus choosing the internal training program, while the other is part of a healthcare system. Interestingly, this hospital chose not to make use of the system's training center but instead to go right to the developer of the process, General Electric, for training of key people. Resources did not drive the difference in response; the system-associated hospital receives no financial support for this training. The difference is in the beliefs of the individual management teams as to how to deal with the environment in which they operate. Thus, the revised model reflects the importance of the business strategy in dealing with external issues.

The original model does not show a direct linkage between business strategy and the human resources strategy, technology strategy, or the organizational structure. In fact, there are direct linkages between all three substrategies and the business strategy, and much of the interplay between them does not involve knowledge, so to show the connection through the KS is unduly limiting in describing their relationship. A further modification to this aspect of the model is to make the arrows connecting the business strategy to these three elements double-ended, reflecting the two-way flow of influence between them. The abilities of the human resources department, the level of technological competence of the organization, and the organization's form and function each play a part in shaping business strategy.

While on the topic of the various substrategies supporting the business strategy, the labels for human resources strategy and technology strategy have been revised to read simply human resources and technology, respectively. Not one of the organizations in the study created an explicit human resources or technology strategy, nor were these two functions considered to require a strategic plan. Rather, they were used as tools to meet the organizational goals and were largely used in a tactical sense. For example, technology was acquired by the financial services firm to perform a specific task that was identified as a means to meet some strategic goal. The knowledge management system implemented by the financial services firm is a good example of this. It is not driven by any technology strategy that the CTO could identify or articulate, but its development was instrumental in supporting a business strategy of improved customer service.

The most important revision to the model is the removal of KS as a central element and its placement as a modulating factor in the relationship between business strategy and the subdisciplines of human resources, technology, and organizational structure and culture. For the organizations in this study, KS is an abstract, informal, emergent set of beliefs or guidelines that helps to shape the manner in which knowledge is handled by the

Figure 2. Revised research model

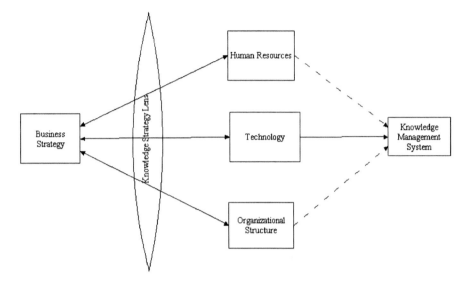

organization. In this form, KS should not occupy a central position in the model, but rather a position that allows it to exercise some influence on the way in which the other disciplines noted are used to carry out the business strategy. Figure 2 displays the revised model.

KS exists in this model as a means of tuning the influence of the business strategy on the disciplines shown such that the use of knowledge is addressed appropriately in the decision-making process. This modulation of the decision-making process is similar to the influence of fiscal strategy or customer service strategy. These are also underlying, fundamental beliefs of the organization that serve to control or guide the decisions made in the various subdisciplines. Rather than existing as a formal, separate strategic plan, they are often implicit and informal and in some cases belong as much to the organizational culture as they do to the managerial process.

One hospital's decision to implement Six Sigma illustrates the revised role of KS. Top management decided that a strategic goal was to streamline the patient care process and reduce the number of information disconnects experienced by the patient as he or she transited the system from admissions to discharge. To accomplish this, the CEO recognized the need for advanced process analysis tools as well as a change in the way his employees addressed their duties. Had there been a formal KS in place, the CEO could have used these guidelines to introduce and implement Six Sigma. However, the KS is an implicit entity, reflecting the beliefs of the top management team about knowledge acquisition and utilization.

The KS of this management team, led by the beliefs of the CEO, includes the viability of a learning organization in which organizational knowledge is developed from within. Knowledge is viewed as organic; it must become part of the organization's fabric if it is to become a strategic asset. Thus, while the initial training of key team members was accomplished externally, the vast majority of the Six Sigma training was accomplished internally by hospital employees who had been thoroughly indoctrinated.

Moreover, the culture of the organization has also become part of the knowledge acquisition effort; employees are excited about the new tools and their language now focuses on the improvement they can make in quality and patient care. This success largely is due to the manner in which the new knowledge was acquired by the organization and spread throughout the ranks. The knowledge building program had unequivocal support from upper management, though the financial support was minimal due to the cost reduction strategy of the organization. But, this limitation was overcome by the strategic use of career-centered inducements and CEO-provided pizza.

The hospital's KS centers on internally developed and delivered knowledge and knowledge synthesis across organizational boundaries. Its predisposition toward tacit knowledge creation played a major role in the actions taken by human resources as well as the changes made in the organizational structure and culture. It also resulted in minimal technology changes, these being limited to increased access to computers with adequate computing power to execute the appropriate statistical analyses. How would a different KS have changed this scenario, and possibly the overall outcome of the business strategy?

An opposite KS might be less proactive in the acquisition of knowledge, preferring to make use of the knowledge that naturally occurs in the organization. It might also rely more heavily on explicit knowledge stored in an intranet or in manuals; rather than educating employees it might be concerned with making sure they knew where to find certain information without making sure they knew what to do with it. Given this reactive approach to knowledge, the organization might have chosen outside instructors to train the employees in the use of certain analytical tools, though the lack of background education and contextual knowledge would likely have reduced the value of this knowledge in some segments of the employee population. If the funding for external trainers was not available, they might have relied on books or documents on the intranet as a substitute for training. However, not everyone learns well from a book, and not everyone in the organization has access to a networked PC. Thus, knowledge would be much less widespread, the excitement generated by the increasing awareness of the importance of analysis, and the substantial

improvements in patient care might have been replaced by a situation where only a few people in the organization had enough training, education, and initiative to utilize the new analysis tools and the organization would not have witnessed the change in the level of conversation regarding quality and process improvement. The KS of the organization influenced the manner in which the human resources, technology, and organizational structure was used to implement the business strategy.

The data collected in this study give ample evidence of the relationship between the human resources, technology, and organizational structure on the one hand and the KS on the other. That relationship still exists in the revised model, but the pathway of the influence is different. Rather than directly driving the KS, these other organizational factors shape the KS as the results of decisions are digested by the organization. In other words, the KS is the result of decisions made regarding knowledge; each decision produces some change in the KS. This mechanism supports the emergent nature of many knowledge strategies.

An organization, whether a for-profit accounting firm or a nonprofit hospital, is a system. Each interaction within this system, for instance between the upper management team and a subdiscipline such as human resources, can be considered a subsystem of the organization. These two entities interact by passing direction and influence from the upper management team to the subdiscipline and by passing information in both directions. When the management team passes directions to the human resources discipline, it passes through a number of lenses before reaching the intended recipient. These lenses impose certain policies or influences upon the directions, such as fiscal policies, beliefs about the use of technology, and guidelines that shape the role of knowledge. Each of these lenses changes the message from the management team to the functional areas so that the directions contained in those messages support upper management's view of how the operation should run. When there is a clearly defined set of policies regarding a particular aspect of the operation, there will likely be only one set of lenses for the message to be passed through. However, when the set of policies is not common throughout the organization, middle-level management might impose their own lenses upon the incoming messages, thus transforming them in some way and possibly changing the message's ability to support the organization's goals.

Like any well-run system, the messages sent by upper management to the functional areas result in some activity taking place, and this activity generates feedback to the originator of the directive. The feedback might be generated by the functional area in the form of reports, or it might be the result of surveillance on the part of management. In either case, the feedback should be in two parts. First, the feedback should include some measurement of the outcome of the directive. This might be something like increase in revenue, reduced costs, increased patient throughput, and so forth. These are important measures to have since they will form the basis for the next set of management decisions. Their measurement plan should be included in the original directive. However, these are not the measurements that are important to us here.

The second area of feedback is that of process. The evaluation of the effectiveness of any set of instructions or directives provides guidance for future decisions. It is in this aspect that we find the influence of the functional area upon KS. By recognizing the role played by knowledge in the implementation of the directive, the functional area is able to provide adjustments to the KS lens that can be used to shape future decisions. The extent to which this adjustment can take place is dependent upon three things. First, the functional area's ability to recognize the role of knowledge in the execution of the business strategy is crucial to the revision of the KS. Without this, there is no basis for any internally directed analysis based upon knowledge. Second, the number of lenses in existence will also have an effect on the degree of adjustment made, since the functional area might

only recognize its own KS lens and not have any idea that others exist. Third, the degree of flexibility in the lens, a metaphor for organizational and managerial flexibility, plays a large role in determining the ability of the organization to adjust its approach to knowledge.

Jennex and Olfman (2005) support this feedback mechanism in their model of knowledge management success evaluation. This model demonstrates the relationship between the net benefits of a KM system and the impact of those benefits on both the user's intent to use the system as well as their satisfaction with the system. The data collected in the present study extends the reach of this feedback to include adjustments to the knowledge strategy and managerial decision-making.

As the KS is influenced from the functional areas by means of process-based feedback, so too is it driven by the business strategy in the form of adjustments made by upper management. As the management team digests the results from previous decisions, as well as changes in the external environment, the knowledge lens through which they view future business decisions will adjust. As with the functional areas, there are also limitations in place to mitigate the amount, direction, and rate of change from the business strategy side. Besides the characteristics of the business environment and the organization's business strategy, the manager's background and style, the degree of alignment between the existing KS and the business strategy, and the number of different lenses between the upper management and the functional area each play a part in determining the changes in the organization's KS.

The relationships among KS, business strategy (embodied in the top management team), and the functional areas of the organization are described as a system with one or more sets of lenses through which data, information, and especially guidance and feedback, must pass. As these messages of guidance and feedback pass back and forth between the parties and through the lenses, they adjust the shape of these lenses such that subsequent decisions will be based upon the newly contoured lenses. In this model, the relationship between the business strategy and the functional areas of the organization is portrayed in a systemic fashion, with KS being an organic entity within the system. It grows and changes in the system and its environment, rather than acting as a bolted-on filtering mechanism as portrayed in much of the previously reviewed literature. Unlike the business strategy, it does not exist as a discrete entity; KS is an integral part of the relationships within the system and is often only evident as an influencer of decisions rather than as a decision in its own right.

Some important distinctions can be drawn between a KS and other organizational characteristics, such as culture, which also act to modulate internal activities. Whereas entities such as culture grow organically due, in large part, to organizational composition and environment (e.g., demographics, location, industry, etc.), a KS tends to result from decisions made by the organization's leaders and members. A more important distinction is that organizational characteristics tend toward significant levels of inertia, in that once created they can be very difficult to change. This is evident in the difficulty many firms face in changing company culture to respond to changes in technology, market requirements, or global competition. However, a KS is, by definition, a dynamic construct. It is created as a result of decisions made during the course of doing business, and continues to evolve even as it influences subsequent decisions. Thus, organizational characteristics such as culture do not exist to further the goals of an organization and often tend to hinder more than help the flow of ideas and knowledge. A KS, on the other hand, is created and shaped by the organization to promote the productive use of knowledge toward the attainment of strategic goals. Therefore, while they might both exist in a manner such as Figure 2, only one of them is the result of a reasoned approach to knowledge flow and is expected to

evolve based upon organizational decisions and their results.

A few examples from the data are in order at this point to help illustrate this concept. I start by finishing the hospital example begun earlier. Influenced by the external marketplace and the strategic objective of operating within strict cost constraints, the hospital decided to acquire certain process analysis tools to enable them to design better, more efficient processes. The KS in place with the top management team, especially the CEO who was the driving force behind the project, was to provide as much training as possible internally, to embody the knowledge within the people as widely and as thoroughly as possible, and to change the culture such that the language of quality and process improvement would become the language of the organization. Thus, the KS in place was concentrated very sharply on the human resources and organizational structure and away from technology.

Large organizations being what they are, and healthcare institutions are no exception, these initiatives were met with some resistance, much of which centered on the acquisition of new knowledge as well as the sharing of existing knowledge (in other words, power). Thus, certain areas of the organization had their own lens through which they viewed knowledge-based decisions, and it was very different from the CEO's lens. However, through the recruiting of key people into the process, a critical mass began to emerge. This group, who had become believers in the ideas of the CEO, began to change the lens through which their portion of the organization viewed knowledge and with those changes, it moved closer to that of the CEO. Human resources also saw the benefit of these new processes and began changing their procedures for evaluation and promotion to include in their decisions the employee's knowledge activities such as training and knowledge sharing. Thus, the organizational structure and culture, as well as human resources, began to influence the organization's KS.

As the results of his decisions were observed, the CEO continued to adjust his KS by taking steps to encourage interdisciplinary knowledge sharing in an effort to remove the silos of knowledge that have formed the foundation of organizational culture in healthcare for years. The strategic directions of the hospital as well as that of the system, along with his observations of the organization, caused the CEO to adjust his approach to knowledge by taking steps to encourage the formation of a culture of continuous learning and process improvement. As it digested these initiatives, the organization continued to adjust its KS until, at present, the institution has a relatively coherent and uniform KS.

A contrasting example is found in the software firm. The KS of this organization is to depend heavily upon technology to gather and distribute knowledge, tending to avoid reliance on the tacit knowledge of individuals. This is the result of the need for many people within the organization to have access to the same customer and market-based knowledge simultaneously to maintain the pace of development as well as a protection against knowledge loss when people leave the company in an industry known for its turnover. The KS lens is thus oriented toward technology and represents a low degree of variability within the organization's approach to knowledge.

The last revision to the original research model is the position of the knowledge management system. Originally driven directly from the KS, as per the literature, it appears that the knowledge management system is almost completely an artifact of the information technology area with guidance from the human resources and organizational structure. The technology function creates the knowledge management system in response to direction from upper management through the KS lens. The evidence from each organization in the study that has a knowledge management system suggests that very little influence comes through either human resources or the organizational structure.

The influence of the KS upon the decision to implement the knowledge management system is apparent in most of the firms that have one. The role of the KS here is to modify the manner in which the business strategy is implemented. For the bank, the financial services firm, and the software development firm, the KS includes a strong inclination to house organizational knowledge in some explicit form as opposed to allowing it to reside within the employees. Thus, it is not surprising that these are the firms that either have, or are creating, a knowledge management system. Organizations that seem to value the tacit knowledge within their employees do not have, or did not stress, a knowledge management system. These organizations, including both healthcare institutions and the insurance firm, approach knowledge as a human asset and view the use of a knowledge management system as an unnecessary tool, at best, or an impediment to the useful application of knowledge in the worst case.

CONCLUSION

KS can take many forms in the organizations that employ it. Kasten (2006) has shown that knowledge strategies can be emergent or formal and can key on one or many knowledge-based activities. The point of this article is not to derive these dimensions of KS or the form it might take. Rather, this article keys on the manner in which a KS manifests itself in an organization. By locating the KS in between business strategy and organizational processes, as well as identifying some dynamics surrounding the role of the KS, this article serves as a starting point for further research on the interactions among these entities.

Evidence derived from the data gathered suggest that the KS is not a centralized entity that is directly influenced, or directly influences, organizational entities such as technology or human resources. Rather, KS acts as more of a mitigating function, or lens, that shapes the organization's interactions along the guidelines contained within the KS. An understanding of the place occupied by KS, an elusive construct at best, will assist in gaining a better picture of how knowledge strategies are created and their role in the creation of competitive advantage for the firm.

With this framework established, the work to extend and solidify has only begun. Future research should include both qualitative and quantitative studies. The qualitative studies will be useful to continue to identify the nuances of the relationship between the knowledge strategy and the organization. These will be necessary to draw a more complete picture of the dynamics of this relationship and to begin the process of theory development.

Once developed, this deeper understanding and basic theory will form the basis for future quantitative studies. Hypotheses regarding the nature of the KS/organization interaction can be studied by gathering data describing the form and function of the KS, the measurable reactions of the organization, and, ultimately, the changes in firm performance brought about by the introduction and implementation of a particular KS in a specific organizational environment.

REFERENCES

Bierly, P. E. III. (1999). Development of a generic knowledge strategy typology. *The Journal of Business Strategy, 16*(1), 1–26.

Bierly, P. E. III, & Chakrabarti, A. (2001). Dynamic knowledge strategies and industry fusion. *International Journal of Manufacturing Technology and Management, 3*(1/2), 31–48. doi:10.1504/IJMTM.2001.001394

Buckley, P. J., & Carter, M. J. (2004). A formal analysis of knowledge combination in multinational enterprises. *Journal of International Business Studies, 35,* 371–384. doi:10.1057/palgrave.jibs.8400095

Chase, R. L. (1997). Knowledge management benchmarks. *Journal of Knowledge Management, 1*(1), 83–92. doi:10.1108/EUM0000000004583

Felton, S. M., & Finnie, W. C. (2003). Knowledge is today's capital: Strategy & leadership interviews Thomas A. Stewart. *Strategy and Leadership, 31*(2), 48–55. doi:10.1108/10878570310464411

Feurer, R., Chaharbaghi, K., & Distel, M. (1995). Dynamic strategy ownership. *Management Decision, 33*(4), 12–21. doi:10.1108/00251749510084635

Girard, J. P. (2005). Taming enterprise dementia in public sector organizations. *International Journal of Public Sector Management, 18*(6/7), 534–545. doi:10.1108/09513550510616751

Gopalakrishnan, S., & Bierly, P. E. III. (2006). The impact of firm size and age on knowledge strategies during product development: A study of the drug delivery industry. *IEEE Transactions on Engineering Management, 53*(1), 3–16. doi:10.1109/TEM.2005.861807

Huang, K. (1997). Capitalizing collective knowledge for winning, execution and teamwork. *Journal of Knowledge Management, 1*(2), 149–156. doi:10.1108/EUM0000000004590

Hughes, A. (1997). Information strategy—Threat or opportunity? *Librarian Career Development, 5*(2), 60. doi:10.1108/09680819710180912

Jang, S., Hong, K., Bock, G. W., & Kim, I. (2002). Knowledge management and process innovation: The knowledge transformation path in Samsung SDI. *Journal of Knowledge Management, 6*(5), 479–485. doi:10.1108/13673270210450582

Jennex, M. E., & Olfman, L. (2005). Assessing knowledge management success. *International Journal of Knowledge Management, 1*(2), 33–49. doi:10.4018/jkm.2005040104

Johannessen, J., Olaisen, J., & Olsen, B. (1999). Strategic use of information technology for increased innovation and performance. *Information Management & Computer Security, 7*(1), 5–22. doi:10.1108/09685229910255133

Kasten, J. E. (2006). *Knowledge strategy drivers: An exploratory study.* Unpublished doctoral dissertation, Long Island University, Brookville, NY.

Kim, Y., Yu, S., & Lee, J. (2003). Knowledge strategy planning: Methodology and case. *Expert Systems with Applications, 24,* 295–307. doi:10.1016/S0957-4174(02)00158-6

Lane, C., & Probert, J. (2007). The external sourcing of technological knowledge by US pharmaceutical companies: Strategic goals and inter-organizational relationships. *Industry and Innovation, 14*(1), 5–25. doi:10.1080/13662710601130574

Laursen, K., & Mahnke, V. (2001). Knowledge strategies, firm types, and complementarity in human-resource practices. *Journal of Management and Governance, 5,* 1–27. doi:10.1023/A:1017985623502

Liebeskind, J. P. (1996). Knowledge, strategy, and the theory of the firm. *Strategic Management Journal, 17,* 93–107.

López, S. P., Peón, J. M., & Vázquez Ordás, C. J. (2004). Managing knowledge: The link between culture and organizational learning. *Journal of Knowledge Management, 8*(6), 93–104. doi:10.1108/13673270410567657

Maier, R., & Remus, U. (2003). Implementing process-oriented knowledge management strategies. *Journal of Knowledge Management, 7*(4), 62–74. doi:10.1108/13673270310492958

Nickerson, J. A., & Silverman, B. S. (1998). Intellectual capital management strategy: The foundation of successful new business generation. *Journal of Knowledge Management, 1*(4), 320–331. doi:10.1108/EUM0000000004603

Ponzi, L., & Koenig, M. (2002). Knowledge management: Another management fad? *Information Research, 8*(1).

Shankar, R., Singh, M. D., Gupta, A., & Narain, R. (2003). Strategic planning for knowledge management implementation in engineering firms. *Work Study, 52*(4), 190–200. doi:10.1108/00438020310479036

Snyman, R., & Kruger, C. J. (2004). The interdependency between strategic management and strategic knowledge management. *Journal of Knowledge Management, 8*(1), 5–19. doi:10.1108/13673270410523871

Southon, F. C. G., Todd, R. J., & Seneque, M. (2002). Knowledge management in three organizations: An exploratory study. *Journal of the American Society for Information Science and Technology, 53*(12), 1047–1059. doi:10.1002/asi.10112

Syed-Ikhsan, S. O. S., & Rowland, F. (2004). Knowledge management in a public organization: A study on the relationship between organizational elements and the performance of knowledge transfer. *Journal of Knowledge Management, 8*(2), 95–111. doi:10.1108/13673270410529145

Ursic, D., Nikl, A., Mulej, M., & Smogave Cestar, A. (2006). System-organizational aspect of a learning organization in companies. *Systemic Practice and Action Research, 19*(1), 81–99. doi:10.1007/s11213-005-9005-1

von Krogh, G., & Roos, J. (1995). A perspective on knowledge, competence and strategy. *Personnel Review, 24*(3), 56–76. doi:10.1108/00483489510089650

Zack, M. H. (1999). Developing a knowledge strategy. *California Management Review, 41*(3), 125–145.

APPENDIX

Basic Interview Script

1. Describe your strategy creation process.
2. Do you have specific substrategies, that is, technology strategy, human resources strategy, knowledge strategy?
3. What drives the use of knowledge in the firm?
4. Does the strategic use of knowledge drive the HR, technology, or organizational plans of the firm?
5. How do the knowledge needs of the firm influence the creation of knowledge management systems?
6. How do the knowledge needs/assets of the firm influence the creation of the business strategy?

This work was previously published in International Journal of Knowledge Management, Volume 5, Issue 3, edited by Murray E. Jennex, pp. 38-53, copyright 2009 by IGI Publishing (an imprint of IGI Global).

Chapter 16
Zooming in on the Effect of National Culture on Knowledge Sharing Behavior

Wei Li
Freddie Mac, USA

ABSTRACT

This research project investigates what are the national cultural factors that influence employees' cross-cultural knowledge sharing in online environments and in what way. The chapter draws on findings from 41 in-depth interviewees conducted with 20 Chinese and 21 American employees who worked for a large multinational corporation. The rich interview data identified three national cultural differences that impacted Chinese and American participants s' knowledge sharing through an online system, namely, language, differences grounded in collectivism/individualism, and different levels of uncertainty avoidance. English created a barrier for Chinese users to post their ideas but it didn't seem to stop them from consuming knowledge. Differences grounded in collectivist/individualist values were mainly reflected in these two cultural groups' different logic regarding the relationship between different working contexts and the need to share. Chinese participants also showed a higher level of uncertainty avoidance than American participants. Together these cultural differences could explain why Chinese shared knowledge less frequently than their American peers. Despite these reported cultural differences, findings from this research suggest that the actual cultural differences were smaller than what literature implies. Possible explanations for fewer cultural differences are explored. Practical implications for knowledge management practitioners are also offered.

INTRODUCTION

The globalization of business over the past two decades has raised awareness of the importance of *knowledge sharing* within subsidiaries located in different countries with differing cultures (Chase, 2004; Gammelgaard & Ritter, 2008; Li, 2010). In his dissertation, Buzan (2005) argued that in the era of increased globalization, the knowledge multinational organizations need in order to keep their competitive advantages is no longer located in

DOI: 10.4018/978-1-60960-555-1.ch016

one central place, usually the headquarters; instead it is dispersed in headquarters and subsidiaries. According to Buzan, the model of knowledge flow from the headquarters to subsidiaries is outdated and should be replaced by the model where subsidiaries also play an important role in the process of knowledge creation and diffusion (pp. 52-53).

In order to leverage the knowledge of employees who are distributed all over the world, multinational organizations, such as Buckman Laboratories and Siemens, have been implementing distributed knowledge sharing systems to help their members access knowledge regardless of space or time (Fulmer, 1999; Heier, Borgman & Manuth, 2005; Stonehouse & Minocha, 2008). In order to encourage employees from different countries to use knowledge sharing systems more effectively and make the systems more fruitful in a global setting, we need to know what factors, particularly what cultural factors influence employees' online knowledge sharing in *cross-cultural* contexts; however, despite the growing importance of cross-cultural considerations in knowledge sharing, the literature is almost silent in its cross-cultural dimensions (Ang & Massingham, 2007; Bhagat, Kedia, Harveston & Triandis, 2002; Glisby & Holden, 2003; Holden, 2001, 2002; Nissen, 2007). Not many studies have explicitly concentrated on the discussion of national cultural factors that influence knowledge sharing (Dulaimi, 2007; Huang, 2005; Jennex, 2006; Kohlbacher & Krähe, 2007; Lai & Lee, 2007; Paik & Choi, 2005; Sackmann & Friesl, 2007; Zhu, 2004), let alone empirical research dedicated to the influence of national cultural differences on virtual knowledge sharing. In order to address this research gap, The author carried out a qualitative study in a multinational corporation and attempt to answer the following research questions:

- What are the cultural differences that influence online knowledge sharing among Chinese and American employees?

- How do cultural differences affect the way Chinese and American employees share knowledge online?

It needs to be pointed out that "knowledge sharing" is defined in this study as the activity in which participants are involved in the joint process of contributing, negotiating and utilizing knowledge. Knowledge sharing is a joint process in nature because participants need to be engaged in the process if they really want to share knowledge. The form of engagement can be contributing their ideas, or negotiating the meaning of knowledge, or absorbing and making sense of others' ideas in order to use them for future tasks; therefore, by this definition both asking questions to seek knowledge and answering questions to provide knowledge are knowledge sharing activities. Other researchers have also argued that knowledge sharing is a two-way process with both knowledge providers and knowledge consumers involved (Barachini, 2009; Hendriks, 1999; Hooff & Ridder, 2004; Koh & Kim, 2004).

LITERATURE REVIEW

This section will review the existing studies that shed light on national cultural impact on knowledge sharing. It begins with reviewing the theoretical perspectives regarding the influence of national cultural values on knowledge sharing, and then reports the empirical studies exploring knowledge sharing in cross-cultural contexts. Hofstede (2001) defines culture as "the collective programming of the mind that distinguishes the members of one group or category of people from another" (p. 9). According to Hofstede, culture manifests itself in different ways including values, norms, symbols and artifacts, but the core element of culture is its value system; culture is a very complex phenomenon and it can present itself at different levels; at the highest level is the culture of a national or regional society, which is called *national culture*.

In the field of national cultural research, scholars who have made significant contributions include Hall (1976), Hofstede (2001), Triandis (1995) and Trompenaars (1994). The five cultural dimensions theorized by Hofstede have been used most widely in cross-cultural studies (Gudykunst & Matsumoto, 1996; Hwang, Francesco & Kessler, 2003; Kurman, 2003). In the area of knowledge sharing, language and three of the five dimensions have been argued to impact cross-cultural knowledge sharing, i.e. collectivism/individualism, uncertainty avoidance and power distance. Language is one of the most obvious indicators of cultural differences (Hofstede, 2001). Although it is possible to share knowledge just through observation (Nonaka, 1994), language is a primary tool humans use to exchange ideas, so a common language can help assist knowledge sharing while different languages create knowledge blocks (Ford & Chan, 2003; Krauss & Chiu, 1998; Li, 2010; Zakaria, Amelinckx & Wilemon, 2004).

According to Hofstede (2001), individualism/ collectivism refers to the degree to which individuals are supposed to look after themselves or remain integrated into groups. Bhagat et al. (2002) argue that collectivism and individualism significantly influence people's cognitive styles. They suggest that individualists tend to have an analytic mode of thinking by analyzing each piece of information at a time while collectivists usually have a holistic mode of thinking by analyzing the whole picture. Trompenaars (1994) uses "specific" versus "diffuse" relationship to describe the same cultural difference. Hall (1976) uses "high-context" versus "low-context" culture to talk about the same phenomenon. According to Hall, in low-context communication among individualists, most of the information is included in the explicit code while in high-context communication among collectivists the mass of the information is embedded in indirect or implicit messages (p. 79). In *cross-cultural knowledge sharing*, the different

level of emphasis collectivists and individualists put on context can cause barriers because they may interpret received knowledge differently (Peltokorpi, 2006).

Collectivism and individualism also influence how people interpret the relationship between "self" and others (Chen, Sun & McQueen, 2010; Lin & Dalkir, 2010). Collectivists tend to see themselves as interdependent with others but individualists tend to see themselves as independent of others (Bhagat et al., 2002). Similarly, Triandis (1995) claims that people in collectivist society have a stronger tendency to form in-groups than individualists and they tend to be more cooperative in order to reach collective goals when compared with individualists. Hofstede (2001) also notices that collectivists often form tight in-groups while individualists do not. The in-group/out-group distinction has double implication for knowledge sharing. It may be easier for collectivists to share with their in-group members for the sake of collective benefit while individualists may not have this motivation since they don't form close in-groups; meanwhile, collectivists may have difficulties in sharing with outsiders due to lack of trust while individualists may not encounter this problem because of the absence of in-group/out-group boundary (Ardichvili, Maurer, Li, Wentling & Stuedemann, 2006). Face is also a factor rooted in collectivism that can influence collectivists' knowledge sharing behavior. Although people from numerous cultures have concern about face, face is a particularly important factor in collectivist society like China (Redding & Wong, 1986). This concern can prevent collectivists from sharing certain types of knowledge (Chow, Deng & Ho, 2000; Tong & Mitra 2009).

Uncertainty avoidance can also influence the knowledge sharing behavior of people from different national cultures (Khalil & Seleim, 2010). Hofstede (2001) defines "uncertainty avoidance" as the degree to which people in a culture prefer structured or unstructured situations. Hofstede's concept of "uncertainty avoidance" is similar to

Triandis' concept of "tolerance for ambiguity" (Triandis, 1995). In cultures with high uncertainty avoidance, people do not feel comfortable with ambiguous situations, so they try to find answers that exactly match their questions; however, in cultures with low uncertainty avoidance, people are used to ambiguous situations and they feel comfortable with taking various types of knowledge and integrating them to create something new (Bhagat et al., 2002; Yoo & Torrey, 2002).

Power distance is another national cultural dimension that might impact knowledge sharing (Chen et al., 2010). This dimension is defined as "the extent to which the less powerful members of organizations and institutions accept and expect that power is distributed unequally" (Hofstede, 2001, p.xix). Triandis' (1995) distinction between vertical and horizontal culture is similar to the concept of power distance. According to Triandis and Hofstede, people in vertical cultures tend to see themselves as different from others in social status, so they expect and accept differences in status rather than value equality; in horizontal cultures, differences in social status are less pronounced and people value equality. Bhagat et al. (2002) argue that these differences can create knowledge sharing barriers between people from horizontal and those from vertical cultures because information in vertical cultures usually flows from the top to the bottom whereas information in horizontal cultures usually flows in both directions.

Several empirical studies have been found that explicitly address the impact of national culture on knowledge sharing in organizational settings (Ardichvili et al., 2006; Chen et al., 2010; Chow et al., 2000; Ford & Chan, 2003; Hong, Heikkinen & Blomqvist, 2010; Husted and Michailova, 2002; Jolly, 2002; Magnier-Watanabe & Senoo, 2010; Peltokorpi, 2006; Su, Li & Chow, 2010; Tong & Mitra, 2009; Yoo & Torrey, 2002). Some are reviewed here as examples. Chow et al. (2000) studied the openness of knowledge sharing in organizational settings by collecting data from 104 American managers and 38 Chinese managers. Their findings indicate that with higher collectivism Chinese nationals were more likely to share knowledge than Americans when there was conflict between self and collective interests, and that Chinese were much less willing to share knowledge with out-group members than Americans although they showed an equal level of willingness to share with in-group members. Jolly (2002) investigated knowledge sharing between Chinese and westerners (from North America and Europe) in Sino-foreign joint ventures and found that language differences created a big sharing barrier, and that different interpretation of the same events due to cultural differences hampered knowledge exchange between Chinese and their western colleagues.

Ford and Chan (2003) did a case study in a Japanese manufacturing subsidiary in the U.S. Their study found that language created knowledge blocks between Japanese and English speakers. Due to high power distance in Japanese culture, Japanese participants tended to seek advice from their supervisors or managers whereas the knowledge flows for North American participants were more diverse including top-down, lateral and bottom up. Peltokorpi (2006) used semi-structured interviews to examine knowledge sharing between Nordic expatriates and Japanese in Japan. Interview data in Peltokorpi's study provided several interesting findings. First, Japanese, who were from a vertical culture, were more sensitive to status hierarchies and less likely to share knowledge with colleagues who were distant in the corporate hierarchy when compared with Nordic expatriates. Second, language differences created a strong barrier for knowledge sharing between Japanese and Nordic expatriates. Third, due to collectivist values, Japanese mainly consulted with in-group members defined on the basis of a common department or language even though more experienced colleagues who were considered as outsiders existed in the same subsidiary. Fourth, Japanese had a different logic regarding interpreting shared knowledge than Nordic expatriates. Japanese tended to reject the knowledge shared by expatriates because they claimed that Japan had unique business practice which made approaches developed in Europe not work in the Japanese context. However, Nordic expatriates were eager to replicate their global best practices with minor modification in order to obtain efficiency.

Together, these studies have contributed insights into national cultural impact on knowledge sharing in organizational environments. However, most of the existing studies (except the studies by Yoo & Torrey, 2002, and Ardichvili et al., 2006) only focused on offline knowledge sharing. More research is needed to help us understand the complex process of cross-cultural knowledge sharing among organizational members through online systems because virtual environments can add another layer of complexity (Li, 2008).

RESEARCH METHOD

This study utilized a qualitative design and was based on semi-structured interviews with 20 Chinese and 21 American employees. These interview participants worked for a multinational corporation (pseudo-named Alpha) which is a world's leading manufacturer. Alpha had a worldwide knowledge sharing system in English called ShareNet (this is a pseudo-name). The ShareNet is structured based on communities of practice (CoPs). Within each CoP, users can make posting in the form of asking questions, answering questions or sharing insights/materials etc. All the interviewees in this study were ShareNet users and each joined one or multiple CoPs.

The analysis reported in this chapter is part of a larger project carried out in two stages. Findings from the first stage show that on average Chinese users contributed knowledge (e.g., posting in the ShareNet to ask/answers questions or share ideas/ materials) much less frequently than Americans (results of the larger study are presented in Li,

2008). This chapter only focuses on the cultural differences identified through data collected in the second-stage, namely in-depth interviews. The Chinese participants were located in Beijing or Shanghai, Alpha's subsidiaries in China, and they were all interviewed face-to-face. The American participants were from four states in the U.S. and they were interviewed face-to-face or over the phone. These interviewees played various job roles and their levels ranged from entry positions to general managers in Alpha.

An interview instrument was developed and pilot-tested to guide the interviews. In order to reduce biases as much as possible, the author only asked culturally-neutral questions during the interview and let cultural differences emerge from the data analysis process. The interview data were coded and analyzed using the qualitative data analysis method proposed by Miles and Huberman (1994), including first-level coding of individual interview data and pattern-coding of the overall interview data. ATLAS.ti (version 5.0) was used to handle the large volume of qualitative data and facilitate the analysis process.

During the data collection stage, the author visited Alpha's headquarters and its subsidiaries in China (Beijing and Shanghai) multiple times in order to gain field experiences, better understand participants' working environments and collect data in locations convenient to participants. When making these field trips, the author also had meetings with Alpha's knowledge sharing representatives at different levels and they helped show me around their offices. In order to increase credibility of the findings from the interview data, the author did member checking (Lincoln & Guba, 1985, p. 314). The member checking was performed at the end of the interview, considering the busy schedule of participants in a business setting for this study. Multiple professors in the field of knowledge sharing were invited to review the study findings. In addition, knowledge sharing managers from Alpha reviewed the findings and acknowledged that the findings were credible. This study didn't intend to claim generalizability by using a large number of participants; instead, it attempted to deepen our understanding of knowledge sharing in online cross-cultural contexts and ensure transferability through describing rich data from in-depth interviews.

FINDINGS

Analysis of the interview data suggests several issues related to national cultural differences that can help explain why Chinese participants contributed knowledge much less frequently than their American peers. What follows is a description of these issues identified as related to national cultural differences.

Language

When asked the question "Do you feel English is a barrier for you in using the ShareNet? If yes, in what way?" 14 out of the 20 (70%) Chinese answered "No". Here are some quotes from those who did not think English created a barrier for them. "My major was English when I was in college." "English is not a barrier for Alpha employees." "It is very easy. We are all fine with reading and writing in English although we are not good at speaking English. We all use Chinese-style English and everybody can understand it."

Although English was not a barrier for these participants, it could be a barrier for other people in Alpha, as explained by a Chinese Certified Public Accountant who had working experience in both China and the U.S. She said: "Language is not a barrier for me. It can be a barrier since most employees prefer to communicate in Chinese. When people have to solve problems in English, people can overcome the language barrier. This is different from a free space without any pressure and target. Under this situation, people do not care and may not be willing to answer. People are concerned whether they can freely express their ideas and whether what they write will be understood as they wish."

The other six (30%) said that English was a barrier for them and all of them were asked to explain in what way the language barrier impacted their participation in the ShareNet. Five of them felt it was easier to read in Chinese than in English or perceived that English decreased their reading speed. All of their quotes are cited below in order to explain the language impact in more detail.

An IT Analyst said: "It is not as easy as reading in my native language, Chinese. But this will not impact my understanding." A Supplier Excellence Manager said: "Frankly speaking, it is easier for me to read in Chinese. I can read much faster in Chinese than in English. If the ShareNet was in Chinese, I might want to do some research there seriously. Since the ShareNet is in English, I will only read what is relevant to my job. If the ShareNet was in Chinese, I might browse more." A Training Consultant explained: "Not a big barrier. Sometimes, I lost patience to read on if the materials are in English. If it is in Chinese, I may be willing to read through. English is a barrier considering that it is not my native language. But these days I do not like reading materials in Chinese, not because my English is very good, but because the translation is awkward and the translated materials are hard to understand. Some training materials in Alpha are harder to understand after being translated. But English in the ShareNet will not influence my usage level, although I hope to read in Chinese."

A Direct Sales Representative said: "It is easier to read in Chinese. There is some barrier, but not a big problem. I have difficulties in identifying some terminology in English. All other systems are in English. We discuss everything in English." A Sales Representative said: "English is not a very big barrier. I would rather read in English. English is easier to understand than Chinese. My reading speed is low in English." But he continued to say: "Working in a foreign company, I am expected to read in English. Also translation is not always good…People here all received higher education, so we can all write in English even if we are poor in speaking and listening in English. Typing in Chinese is slower than typing in English. It takes me more efforts to type in Chinese. We are in an English environment. Using Chinese brings trouble to me and our company. Even among Chinese, we write emails in English. We can all understand well in Chinese-style-English. I can explain my questions clearly in English. English is a requirement during today's hiring process."

One of them said English influenced her understanding. She explained this way: "I can understand 80-90% of the content in English. I can read faster in Chinese. English impacts my reading speed. Chinese is more direct. If it is very professional knowledge, I need to consult others to help me understand. But this will not influence how frequently I use the ShareNet. Reading in English can help me practice English."

Influence of Different Working Contexts on Willingness to Share

Five Chinese stated that they were less willing to ask/answer questions or share materials through the ShareNet because they thought that different working contexts made it not as valuable to share with American peers. Here are three examples. A Market/Administrative Assistant explained why she did not want to raise questions in the ShareNet. She said: "If I ask a question on the ShareNet and get answers from the U. S. or Australia, I do not know whether their answers will be valuable for me considering different situations in different locations. We do different work in different locations." A Sales Representative explained why cultural difference stopped him from answering foreign colleagues' questions. He said: "I do not answer questions. Each area has its own characteristics. People in Asia may not know the background of questions in America. Questions which are simple in my eyes may be very complex. It is not good to comment if you do not know the background

of others' questions. When people ask questions about China, I do not think they can understand what I write even if I reply, so I do not bother to answer. From many years of working experience in Alpha, I don't think it is easy to understand culture-intensive content if you are not an indigene. For example, if I tell others that people in northwest China do not buy Alpha marine engines, they can not understand why. I once tried to explain but found that it was useless to explain. Therefore, I do not even try to explain any more."

A Certified Public Accountant explained why she and possibly other Chinese did not want to share in the ShareNet due to differences in cultural values and practice, based on her observation in both China and the U.S. She commented: "We can not share well with foreign colleagues, so it is still sharing within the Chinese community. Chinese are worried about being blamed for posting in the ShareNet without knowing much. Our practice is different, so it is not necessary to share. Even we share, others will not appreciate this. Others' experience can not be good reference for us either …I will not share because many things here are very special. If shared, they will bring unnecessary confusion. I do not want to create confusion…I am concerned what I share on the ShareNet will be misused."

In addition, another Chinese used a common Chinese proverb to explain why many Chinese did not offer their ideas in the ShareNet. As a high-level Integration Manager, he also had working experience in both China and the U.S. He said: "Some people may be enthusiastic to answer questions while others may think 'it is better to do less than more in order to avoid trouble'. There may be more people in the U.S. who like to answer questions."

In contrast, many American participants thought that it was because of different values and practice that there was a clear need to share with each other. Nineteen of the 21 American interviewees expressed strong interests in reading non-English postings. One respondent did not feel the need at this point in time because he was not in a community where there were multi-language postings. One respondent did not feel the need for himself, but he could see the value of translated postings for others. Among those who were interested in reading non-English postings, five of them used online translation tools or asked bi-lingual colleagues to help translate non-English materials. They were interested in translated postings because postings from other countries could bring unique information and provide access to different ideas and different ways. For example, an IT Analyst remarked: "I find that some unique information comes from areas of the world where people do not use English, from a technical perspective. For example, Chinese and Japanese characters use the double-byte links. They run into that kind of stuff much more often than we do. Sometimes they have specialized information that can be extremely useful. So I look forward to reading some postings from the non-English speaking people."

Perceived Credibility of What Was Posted in the ShareNet

Some American users asked questions in the ShareNet in order to collect inputs from multiple people and then create solutions by using their own judgment to evaluate others' ideas, while it seemed that Chinese did not think of using the ShareNet this way. Eleven American participants shared their perception of the credibility of information/ideas collected through the ShareNet and all of them thought the ShareNet was a fairly credible source for getting opinions as reference. After receiving a variety of responses, they depended on their own analytical skills to make sense of others' ideas and form their own solutions. For example, a Human Resource Manager said: "When a question is asked, typically who responds is someone who is an expert or who knows the subject matter. I don't think I will have a problem to trust the answer that is given." And a

Manager in Strategic Business Planning explained in more detail. He said: "I think whether it is in ShareNet or a Wikipedia type of thing, people in Alpha have enough integrity to give you the best information as they can. The person who receives the information should make a judgment whether this information makes sense in the context of my question…I trust the people who give me the information are giving me the best information as they possibly can and the best information they have. And people would not purposely mislead anyone, nor would they answer if they did not feel they had the authority to answer…. Sometimes the information is simple enough for me to know whether it makes sense or not. If the information is critical, it is my responsibility to either follow up or double check with the person who supplies that information."

Different from these 11 Americans, two Chinese were concerned that information from the ShareNet is not official for them to use. One of them was a Certified Public Accountant and she said: "The biggest concern is that ShareNet is not very official. I can not rely on it." Another was a Direct Sales Representative and she said: "I dare not trust the answers from the ShareNet since people just volunteer to answer questions there. I need someone to answer my question and be responsible for his or her answer. I question the qualification of respondents on the ShareNet… ShareNet can not provide authoritative answers."

In addition to these three issues, three Chinese participants mentioned that they hesitated to raise questions in the ShareNet because of the fear of losing face, that is, they were concerned that their questions were perceived as too simple or they would feel embarrassed if nobody provided answers. A Chinese Market/Administrative Assistant said: "The answer I need is very simple. My questions are simple and preliminary. If I ask questions in the ShareNet, experts will think my questions are too simple. I do not want to ask silly questions." A Chinese Specialist in the Intellectual Property Department said: "When I enter a new working environment, I feel my questions may be stupid." A Chinese Sales Administration Manager commented: "Chinese people worry that others think their questions are simple. They feel embarrassed to let others know they even do not understand simple issues…We are concerned whether my questions will be answered. We feel embarrassed if nobody answers. So I'd better try to solve questions by myself."

Furthermore, two Chinese interviewees commented that personal connection was important for getting help and so they did not think it would be fruitful to ask strangers. The Chinese Specialist in the Intellectual Property Department said: "When I have questions, I ask my friend or people I know. I will not ask strangers." And the Chinese Integration Manager explained in detail: "Only after you have built connections with someone, will that person take your questions seriously and share his/her knowledge…If I am only a stranger and ask a question in a ShareNet community, I may not get an answer. People need to know who you are to be motivated to answer your question."

At the end of this section, the author would like to also report an interesting finding which is not necessarily a national cultural issue but can help understand some of the cultural differences identified in this study. Some Chinese participants tended not to answer questions or share voluntarily due to the lack of confidence in their knowledge. Ten (nine Chinese and one American) participants talked about this point. They did not feel they had advanced knowledge which was not known to American peers yet, or they did not know if what they had would be valuable for others, or they thought their peers outside of China performed better. Quotes from some of these participants are provided below to show their lack of confidence.

A Chinese Service Operation Representative said: "It is not that Chinese do not want to share… they do not know whether what they have is valuable to others. They may think others already know what they know." He also perceived that there was an unspoken rule in the ShareNet "Try not to speak a lot." A Chinese Category Manager said: "There are very few Chinese materials. We are not very open in this sense. I do not know whether what I have is valuable for others… Maybe it is Chinese culture that I am willing to reply or share after I am asked. I am worried my sharing without being requested is a bother to others." A Chinese Supplier Excellence Manager said: "I do not know Alpha as a whole because it is too big. Maybe some people in America or Europe work better than me." A Chinese Sales Representative said: "I have not met cases I have valuable materials for others. In fact, we do not have as many information channels as our American and European colleagues. They have a lot of information sources we do not know. We depend on them to get new information." A Chinese Certified Public Accountant said: "It is a matter of Alpha experience. Overall, people here have less experience on average." A Chinese Service Engineer commented: "If you take a closer took at the technical level in China, you will notice that it is impossible for us to have access to core knowledge. Many times, we do not know much about knowledge in factories. A large amount of knowledge is not available to us. When we ask service engineers in American factories, they told us "This is internal material. We can not share it with you"… I feel what I know is already known by others."

An American Engineer also shared his view when asked why Chinese participants were less active in sharing. He observed: "One reason that keeps Chinese from sharing is the lack of confidence in their own knowledge. They do not want to share if they do not feel they are experts or they are official. The confidence issue can be a cultural thing. I work a lot with contract agencies that have foreign workers. They do not want to feel inferior, so they tend not to respond. They do not want to give the impression that they do not know the answer, do not know what they are talking about."

DISCUSSION AND IMPLICATIONS

Research on knowledge sharing in cross-cultural settings suggests that national cultural values influence people's knowledge sharing behavior (Ardichvili, 2008;

Ardichvili et al., 2006; Bhagat et al., 2002; Chen et al., 2010; Holden, 2001; Hong et al., 2010; Khalil & Seleim, 2010; Li, 2010; Lin & Dalkir, 2010; Magnier-Watanabe & Senoo, 2010; Su et al., 2010; Tong & Mitra, 2009). This study has identified some national culture-related differences between the Chinese and American groups. In the field of national cultural research, Hofstede (2001), Triandis (1995) and Hall (1976) have contributed the most, and thus their theories on national cultural differences are most widely cited (Myers & Tan, 2002). Here, the author will borrow some of the concepts from these well-respected national cultural researchers to interpret the findings on national cultural differences and their impact on knowledge sharing behavior. To be more specific, language, differences grounded in collectivist/individualist values, and different levels of uncertainty avoidance emerged as important factors in this study that influenced Chinese and Americans' knowledge sharing behavior. These factors can explain why the Chinese group contributed less than the American group.

Language

One of the most obvious markers of cultural differences is the existence of different languages (Hofstede, 2001). Krauss and Chiu (1998) have claimed language as the "primary means by which we gain access to the contents of others' mind" (p. 41). Therefore, a common language can help facilitate knowledge sharing while different languages create barriers. Knowledge sharing is not error-free even among people who speak the same language because people can interpret things differently. In addition, knowledge sharing by itself is not an easy process and has to overcome

cognitive barriers (Hinds & Pfeffer, 2003). Therefore, it is not surprising to see difficulties arising from linguistic differences in the cross-cultural knowledge sharing process.

Indeed, previous empirical studies have reported the negative impact of lack of a common language on knowledge sharing (Ford & Chan, 2003; Jolly, 2002; Peltokorpi, 2006; Wei, 2007; Zakaria et al., 2004). Consistent with the existing literature, findings from this study indicate that English created some barriers for Chinese participants to share knowledge. The negative influence of different languages was clearly reflected in Chinese participants' reluctance to post. Although an online environment can help make people feel more comfortable psychologically because they can take time to phrase their thoughts and thus do not experience the pressure in face-to-face communication (Zuboff, 1988, p. 370), Chinese participants in this study didn't want to make extra efforts to express their ideas in a second language when they were not required to do so. In addition, they might be concerned that what they wrote in English would be interpreted differently from what they intended to communicate. This language barrier helps account for why Chinese contributed less than Americans. The strong negative impact of the linguistic barrier on Chinese participants' willingness to contribute suggests that it might be worth allowing Chinese to post in their native language and then translate their postings for circulation to a larger audience, in order to motivate them to share.

However, in terms of consuming knowledge, language didn't seem to be a huge barrier since many Chinese didn't perceive that text only available in English made much difference for them to browse what others posted. One will not be surprised to see language as a smaller barrier here when considering the following two elements. First, most Chinese participants had good English skill, which was a requirement during the hiring process. All the Chinese participants had advanced education (40% with Bachelor's degree and 60% with Master degree) through which they had built sufficiently good reading and writing skills in English. Second, English was the working language in Alpha and Chinese interviewees were used to English for written communication.

Values Rooted in Collectivism/ Individualism

Among the five national cultural dimensions theorized by Hofstede (2001), collectivism/ individualism is arguably the most frequently applied dimension to compare Chinese culture and American culture. For example, Bhagat et al. (2002) argue that collectivism and individualism significantly influence people's cognitive styles. Drawing on evidence from different fields, including ethnography and philosophy, they claim that people in an individualist society tend to adopt the "analytic" mode of thinking while collectivists tend to have a "holistic" mode of thinking (p. 215). The "analytic" mode tends to "analyze each piece of information, taken one at a time, for its unique contribution to knowledge"; however, the "holistic" mode tends to "analyze the entire spectrum of information" which is called "contextualism" (p. 215).

Hall (1976) uses a different concept, high/ low-context culture, to explain the same cultural difference. According to Hall, in high-context cultures (e. g. Chinese culture), "most of the information is either in the physical context or internalized in the person while very little is in the coded, explicit, transmitted part of the message"; in low-context cultures (e.g. American culture), the opposite is true, "the mass of the information is vested in the explicit code" (p. 79). Therefore, Chinese tend to rely more on the context of non-verbal actions and the environmental settings to convey meaning than Americans. Similarly, Nisbett (2003) has also found that people in East Asia are more "holistic" and pay more attention to the whole picture than people in the west; thus East Asians are less likely to use formal logic than westerners since they tend to emphasize context and depend on "dialectical" thinking.

Based on the current literature, Chinese, who are from a collectivist culture, and Americans, who are from an individualist culture, emphasize context to different extents and have different thinking logic. And these differences can make a difference in their knowledge sharing behavior. Placing high weight on context when interpreting knowledge, Chinese may hesitate to borrow knowledge that is gained from a different context. They may also feel more reluctant to share knowledge with people who work in radically different environments.

Therefore, it is not surprising to see that the Chinese participants in this study were less willing to ask or answer questions, or to exchange ideas with American colleagues because Chinese thought that different working contexts made it not as valuable to share with Americans. Besides, they were concerned about the possibility of introducing confusion rather than help by sharing the knowledge they accumulated in the Chinese subsidiary, where practices can be unique to the local business. With a different thinking style, most American users thought that different working contexts made knowledge sharing a necessary and rewarding task. And they usually trusted their own logic to make sense of the knowledge contributed by others before making a decision on how to use the borrowed knowledge. The different perceived connection between diverse working contexts and the necessity to share can explain why Americans asked/answered questions more often and shared personal experiences or insights more often than Chinese users in the ShareNet. Actually, Pelto-korpi (2006) reported a similar knowledge sharing barrier between Japanese, who had an "it cannot work here" attitude and Nordic expatriates (p. 146). Husted and Michailova (2002) also observed this knowledge sharing barrier between Russians, who had the "not invented here" syndrome, and westerners (p. 23).

Collectivist and individualist orientation also influences how people perceive the relationship between "self" and others. Collectivists see themselves as interdependent with others within their immediate social circles but individualists tend to see themselves functioning relatively independently of others (Bhagat et al., 2002, p. 208). Based on the rich research by social psychologists, Zhang, Chintakovid, Sun, Ge and Zhang (2006) have pointed out that although people have the general inclination to form in-groups based on common attributes or interests, the strength of in-group membership is not universal across cultures. Similarly, Triandis (1995) argues that collectivists have a stronger tendency to form in-groups than individualists. Hofstede (2001) also claims that collectivists like to form tightly knit in-groups while the ties among individualists are looser. In addition, Triandis (1995) has observed that collectivists tend to be cooperative due to the value they put on collective accomplishments, but knowledge sharing happens primarily among in-group members. He believes that this is because people in collectivist cultures usually feel the moral obligation to share with in-group members and they show a strong distrust toward those who are considered as out-group members. According to Triandis, people from individualist cultures will share knowledge with relative ease with others within the organization because they don't set clear in-group/out-group boundaries (Triandis, 1995).

The existing literature suggests that Chinese people's collectivist values have a dual impact on their knowledge sharing behavior. On the one hand, they are more willing to share knowledge with members of their cohesive in-groups; on the other hand, they may not want to share with those who are not regarded as intimate in-groups members even if they all work for the same organization. Findings from this study show some traces of Chinese participants' sharp in-group/out-group distinction. Several Chinese remarked that they hesitated to seek help from strangers in the ShareNet as they thought strangers did not know who they were and thus might not feel motivated to lend help. These Chinese felt that the personal connection built among in-group members prior to asking for help was critical for motivating these in-group members to provide what they asked. Without the assurance of prior relationship, they did not think it would be fruitful to seek help through communities of practice in the ShareNet, where they did not know community members personally. This concern helps explain why Chinese rarely asked questions there. However, American users in this study never mentioned any concern about asking strangers. It seems that they did not have reservation to seek help from strangers due to a looser in-group/out-group distinction. Other comparative studies have generated similar findings, saying that people from collectivist cultures, such as Chinese, Japanese and Russians, were much more reluctant to share knowledge with outsiders than westerners (Chow et al., 2000; Husted & Michailova, 2002; Li, Ardichvili, Maurer, Wentling & Stuedemann, 2007; Peltokorpi, 2006).

Face is another factor rooted in collectivism that can influence Chinese people's knowledge seeking behavior. The harmony theory, one of the most influential theories to help understand interpersonal communication in China, stresses the critical importance of face in Chinese communication, where people try to save one's own face and others' face very carefully (Chen, 2001). Chinese people's face-saving goal may impede their willingness to share knowledge if the sharing could damage their face or potentially threaten their social standing (Zhang et al., 2006). Furthermore, some researchers have suggested that it is less likely for individuals who are worried about losing face to ask questions in public simply because they want to avoid losing face (Hwang et al., 2003).

With these theoretical perspectives on the potential impact of face on knowledge sharing in mind, one won't be surprised to find that in this study some Chinese respondents didn't ask questions in the ShareNet because of the fear of losing face. Some would even feel embarrassed if nobody answered their questions. Different from these Chinese, Americans didn't seem to have concern about asking questions that might be simple or stupid in others' opinions. In addition, Americans commented that no answer simply implied that nobody knew the answer or this question was just not interesting, and it was not a big deal in either case. These differences can help explain why on average Chinese asked questions much less frequently. Embarrassment can be a social cost for people from a collectivist culture, and the negative effect of the fear of losing face on tendency to ask questions in public has been reported in previous research (Huang, 2005).

Different Levels of Uncertainty Avoidance

Scholars in national cultural research use uncertainty avoidance as another important dimension to differentiate Chinese culture from American culture (Hofstede, 2001). According to Hofstede, uncertainty avoidance means the degree to which people in a culture prefer structured or unstructured situations. For people in a culture with low uncertainty avoidance, they might be used to taking various types of explicit knowledge and integrating them to create something new, while people with high uncertainty avoidance would seek a precise match or authoritative answers. Hofstede's concept of "uncertainty avoidance" is very similar to what Triandis calls "tolerance for ambiguity" (Triandis, 1995). As an important psychological trait, tolerance for ambiguity has been argued as important in knowledge sharing because both knowledge contributors and knowledge consumers need a certain level of tolerance for ambiguity to start and finish the knowledge sharing process effectively (Bhagat et al., 2002; Lord & Maher, 1990; Szulanski, 1996).

Chinese culture has been described as one with high uncertainty avoidance where people have low tolerance for ambiguous situations, while American culture is the opposite (Hofstede, 2001; Triandis, 1995). The general risk-avoiding psychology of Chinese can be seen from a very popular Chinese saying, "Duo Yi Shi Bu Ru Shao Yi Shi" (It is called "多一事不如少一事" in Chinese), which means "the more one does, the more mistakes; the less one does, the fewer mistakes; if one does nothing, there will be no mistakes at all, which is not bad". In this project, the impact of Chinese participants' high uncertainty avoidance and American participants' low uncertainty avoidance can be found in three related aspects.

First, it is very likely that Chinese people were hesitant to risk making postings due to the uncertainty that posting something improper would bring them unnecessary trouble. Therefore, they did not post much. Second, American users felt comfortable to ask questions through virtual communities of practice in the ShareNet for the purpose of collecting multiple responses from colleagues distributed in various locations. With relatively high tolerance for ambiguity, they wanted to use their own judgment to evaluate others' ideas as reference and then create solutions based on their own analysis. However, Chinese participants seldom thought about asking questions to collect multiple opinions and thus they rarely posted questions. Third, the ShareNet was a free and equal space for members to post voluntarily. For American users, it might be a great resource to tap into since most American users perceived that what's posted in the ShareNet was credible. But some Chinese might not feel as comfortable as their American peers when using the voluntarily shared knowledge since it was not official and thus could not function as precisely matched answers.

Uncertainty avoidance is a common factor documented in existing literature that can affect how people seek and use knowledge (Ardichvili et al., 2006; Yoo & Torrey, 2002). It also provides a sound reason to explain why Chinese contributed postings less often than Americans in this study. Here, the author wants to highlight a relevant issue, the lack of confidence by Chinese in their knowledge. This issue is important because it can explain why Chinese participants tended not to answer questions or share their thoughts. Also, it might have reinforced Chinese participants' risk-avoiding psychology and thus created an extra barrier to prevent them from posting.

Literature has pointed out that modesty can account to some extent for why people from collectivist cultures do not respond to questions even when they know the answers (Kurman, 2003). Here one could argue that Chinese were reluctant to offer up solutions because they did not want to appear to be bragging. However, this study provides solid evidence to show that Chinese users' perceived lack of confidence was more related to the direction of knowledge flow in Alpha rather than caused by the national cultural value of being modest. The evidence comes from two sources.

First, many Chinese and some American respondents mentioned that many times knowledge flowed from the U.S. to China, rather than the opposite. The direction of knowledge flow made Chinese feel that their American colleagues probably had already known what they knew and so there was no need to post what they knew. And this single direction of knowledge flow was hindered to some extent by the intellectual property (IP) issue. The interview data suggest that some Chinese participants formed the perception that American colleagues didn't want to share due to IP-related concerns. Through conversation with Alpha's knowledge sharing managers and the interviewees, the author observed that Alpha had strict IP protection policies and its employees were very mindful regarding their obligation to keep certain knowledge confidential when sharing in general or particularly in the ShareNet. As an important security matter, IP protection was a very legitimate concern for Alpha, but this created certain barriers for its internal knowledge sharing. In fact, IP issues have been reported by other authors (Riege, 2005) to create knowledge sharing barriers. And researchers have pointed

out the tension between IP protection and knowledge sharing, so that organizations need to find a "middle ground" between these two practices (Ryan, 2006, p. 144).

Second, people who answered questions in this study commented that they did so because they had experience on the question's topic. In fact, the interview data indicate that people volunteered to answer others' questions because they had experience on the question topic and were willing to share that in order to help others, as mentioned by seven (two Chinese and five Americans) participants. This suggests that there might be some unspoken rule in the ShareNet that people needed to have certain experience or expertise on the topic in order to feel "qualified" to post. As a matter of fact, on average Chinese had much shorter working history in Alpha than Americans (5.4 versus 16.3 years). With far less experiences in Alpha, it is not surprising to see Chinese participants' felt lack of confidence. However, this does not mean people working in Alpha China did not have much to contribute. In fact, some Americans commented that sometimes they gained unique knowledge from Chinese peers who had unique practices. Considering the strong negative impact of the lack of confidence on Chinese people's willingness to share, multinational corporations should help Chinese members build their confidence if they want to motivate this group to share their knowledge, for example, by finding cases where what Chinese share makes a difference and publicizing these cases.

Why Didn't National Culture Make a Bigger Impact?

This chapter is devoted to the national cultural differences identified in the study and how they hindered Chinese users' willingness to share. One can see that national cultural differences did impact Chinese and Americans' knowledge sharing. And the differences discussed above were significant enough to prevent Chinese from making postings in the ShareNet. However, findings from this study also suggest that cultural differences were smaller than what literature would predict. The cultural differences discussed earlier were only mentioned by some of the Chinese participants. And not all the national cultural dimensions turned out to be important factors. For example, one important dimension of national culture, power distance, didn't seem to make any notable difference in this study, even if literature has pointed out that power distance distinguishes Chinese culture from American culture and can have a profound effect on how Chinese and Americans share knowledge (Ardichvili et al., 2006; Hofstede, 2001). Why did national cultural differences not have bigger impact? There are four possible interpretations in the context of this study.

First, it is possible that the hiring process in Alpha selected Chinese who were more in line with American values than the typical Chinese person in China. Schneider (1987) proposes an attraction-selection-attrition (ASA) cycle as a model for understanding organizations and the causes of the structures and processes within organizations. The ASA model argues that different kinds of organizations attract, select and retain different kinds of people. People behave the way they do as shaped by the organization's expectations because they are attracted to that cultural environment, selected by it and stay with it. Through recruitment and selection procedures, organizations end up choosing individuals who share many common personal attributes which fit the organizational climate.

In the case of Alpha, it hires Chinese who share its values or feel comfortable with western culture. There are within-country differences and not every individual is the same within a single nation. Those who appreciate Alpha's culture will be the most attractive employees. There are many potential Chinese employees to pick from considering the large labor pool in today's China. Only those whose values fit with what Alpha expects will meet the recruitment requirements and

then be selected. Over time, people who stay with Alpha are those who find a good fit between their individual expectations and the reality of Alpha life. Thus, the chance is that the Chinese who work for Alpha enjoy Alpha's culture and behave in the way Alpha expects, at least in the workplace. So the group of Chinese participants in this study might not accurately represent Chinese culture.

Second, the online environment could make a difference. Since this study investigated knowledge sharing through virtual communities of practice, one possible explanation could be that national cultural differences are less salient online than they are in face-to-face contexts. Indeed, there are already some studies showing that electronically facilitated communication may make cross-cultural differences less salient (Ardichvili et al., 2006; Jarvenpaa & Leidner, 1999; Matsumoto, 2002; Singh & Baack, 2004). These are interesting findings on possible interaction between national culture and computer-mediated communication, but these findings are more of an exploratory nature considering the nature and the scale of this study. Future research can further verify the interplay between these two factors based on larger-scale projects, or even measure how strong the interaction is using a quantitative methodology.

Third, there have been national culture changes and generational value shifts in China (Hu & Grove, 1999; Huang, 2005; Lau, 1992; Ralston, Gustafson, Terpstra & Holt, 1995; Ralston, Egri, Stewart, Terpstra & Yu, 1999; Srite, 2006). Most of the Chinese interviewees in this study were younger than 40 and had international experiences, thus it is not very surprising to find them more similar to their western peers than what literature would predict.

Fourth, the overriding organizational culture provides a plausible explanation considering the fact that Alpha has a fairly strong organizational culture. Knowledge sharing can be affected by the interaction of national culture and other contextual factors simultaneously, including organizational culture (Chow et al., 2000; Huang, 2005). Indeed, a couple of other studies have also suggested a similar overriding effect of strong organizational culture (Ford & Chan, 2003; Huang, 2005; King, 2007; Li et al., 2007; Magnier-Watanabe & Senoo, 2010). One of the practical implications from these findings is that multinational corporations can help their culturally diverse members overcome cross-cultural knowledge sharing barriers by building strong organizational culture.

CONCLUSION

Findings from this study show that national cultural differences, including language, diverse values rooted in collectivism/individualism, and different levels of uncertainty avoidance can explain why Chinese contributed less Americans. As a second language, English created a barrier for Chinese users to post their ideas but it didn't seem to stop them from consuming knowledge. Differences grounded in collectivist/individualist orientations made Chinese contribute less than Americans. These differences are reflected in their different logic regarding the relationship between different working contexts and the necessity to share, strong versus loose in-group/out-group distinction, and different levels of concern about face. Chinese also showed a higher level of uncertainty avoidance than Americans and thus it was less likely for Chinese to ask questions to collect responses from strangers. In addition, Chinese users' risk-avoiding psychology might have been reinforced by their lack of confidence in their own knowledge.

The findings in this study of fewer cross-cultural differences than what literature predicts are exciting from the point of view of promoting global knowledge sharing. As national cultural differences decrease, similarities between people from different nations increase. Cross-cultural research tends to focus on differences and this is important because these insights can help us understand what causes miscommunication or creates knowledge blocks when they do happen. But for the purpose of facilitating cross-cultural knowledge sharing, it is also critical to find out what the similarities are because similarities among people from different national cultural backgrounds can help them build common ground that is vital for effective knowledge sharing.

REFERENCES

Ang, Z., & Massingham, P. (2007). National culture and the standardization versus adaptation of knowledge management. *Journal of Knowledge Management*, *11*(2), 5–21. doi:10.1108/13673270710738889

Ardichvili, A. (2008). Learning and knowledge sharing in virtual communities of practice: Motivators, barriers and enablers. *Advances in Developing Human Resources*, *10*(4), 541–554. doi:10.1177/1523422308319536

Ardichvili, A., Maurer, M., Li, W., Wentling, T., & Stuedemann, R. (2006). Cultural influences on knowledge sharing through online communities of practice. *Journal of Knowledge Management*, *10*(1), 94–107. doi:10.1108/13673270610650139

Barachini, F. (2009). Cultural and social issues for knowledge sharing. *Journal of Knowledge Management*, *13*(1), 98–110. doi:10.1108/13673270910931198

Bhagat, R. S., Kedia, B. L., Harveston, P. D., & Triandis, H. C. (2002). Cultural variations in the cross-border transfer of organizational knowledge: An integrative framework. *Academy of Management Review*, *27*(2), 204–221. doi:10.2307/4134352

Buzan, L. R. (2005). *The relationship among cultural distance, social ties, and tacit knowledge sharing in a multinational corporation*. D.M., University of Phoenix.

Chase, R. L. (2004). Knowledge sharing. *Journal of Knowledge Management, 8*(2), 4–5.

Chen, G. (2001). Toward transcultural understanding: A harmony theory of Chinese communication. In Milhouse, V. H., Asante, M. K., & Nwosu, P. O. (Eds.), *Transcultural realities: Interdisciplinary perspectives on cross-cultural relations* (pp. 55–70). Thousand Oaks, CA: Sage Publications.

Chen, J., Sun, P. Y. T., & McQueen, R. J. (2010). The impact of national cultures on structured knowledge transfer. *Journal of Knowledge Management, 14*(2), 228–242. doi:10.1108/13673271011032373

Chow, C. W., Deng, F. J., & Ho, J. L. (2000). The openness of knowledge sharing within organizations: A comparative study in the United States and the People's Republic of China. *Journal of Management Accounting Research, 12*, 65–95. doi:10.2308/jmar.2000.12.1.65

Dulaimi, M. F. (2007). Case studies on knowledge sharing across cultural boundaries. *Engineering, Construction, and Architectural Management, 14*(6), 550–567. doi:10.1108/09699980710829012

Ford, D. P., & Chan, Y. E. (2003). Knowledge sharing in a multi-cultural setting: A case study. *Knowledge Management Research & Practice, 1*(1), 11–27. doi:10.1057/palgrave.kmrp.8499999

Fulmer, W. E. (1999). *Buckman Laboratories (A)*. Case No. 9-800-160. Harvard Business School.

Gammelgaard, J., & Ritter, T. (2008). Virtual communities of practice: a mechanism for efficient knowledge retrieval in MNCs. *International Journal of Knowledge Management, 4*(2), 46–61. doi:10.4018/jkm.2008040104

Glisby, M., & Holden, N. (2003). Contextual constraints in knowledge management theory: The cultural embeddedness of Nonaka's knowledge-creating company. *Knowledge and Process Management, 10*(1), 29–36. doi:10.1002/kpm.158

Gudykunst, W. B., & Matsumoto, Y. (1996). Cross-cultural variability of communication in personal relationships. In Gudykunst, W. B., Ting-Toomey, S., & Nishida, T. (Eds.), *Communication in personal relationships across cultures* (pp. 19–56). Thousand Oaks, CA: Sage Publications.

Hall, E. T. (1976). *Beyond culture* (1st ed.). Garden City, NY: Anchor Press.

Heier, H., Borgman, H. P., & Manuth, A. (2005). Siemens: Expanding the knowledge management system ShareNet to research & development. *Journal of Cases on Information Technology, 7*(1), 92–107. doi:10.4018/jcit.2005010106

Hendriks, P. (1999). Why share knowledge? the influence of ICT on the motivation for knowledge sharing. *Knowledge and Process Management, 6*(2), 91–100. doi:10.1002/(SICI)1099-1441(199906)6:2<91::AID-KPM54>3.0.CO;2-M

Hinds, P. J., & Pfeffer, J. (2003). Why organizations don't "know what they know": Cognitive and motivational factors affecting the transfer of expertise. In Ackerman, M. S., Pipek, V., & Wulf, V. (Eds.), *Sharing expertise: Beyond knowledge management* (pp. 3–26). Cambridge, MA: MIT Press.

Hofstede, G. H. (2001). *Culture's consequences: Comparing values, behaviors, institutions and organizations across nations* (2nd ed.). Thousand Oaks, CA: Sage Publications.

Holden, N. (2001). Knowledge management: Raising the spectre of the cross-cultural dimension. *Knowledge and Process Management, 8*(3), 155–163. doi:10.1002/kpm.117

Holden, N. (2002). *Cross-cultural management: A knowledge management perspective*. Harlow, NY: Financial Times Prentice Hall.

Hong, J., Heikkinen, J., & Blomqvist, K. (2010). Culture and knowledge co-creation in R&D collaboration between MNCs and Chinese universities. *Knowledge and Process Management, 17*(2), 62–73. doi:10.1002/kpm.342

Hooff, B., & Ridder, J. (2004). Knowledge sharing in context: The influence of organizational commitment, communication climate and CMC use on knowledge sharing. *Journal of Knowledge Management, 8*(6), 117–130. doi:10.1108/13673270410567675

Hu, W., & Grove, C. L. (1999). *Encountering the Chinese: A guide for Americans* (2nd ed.). Yarmouth, ME: Intercultural Press.

Huang, H. (2005). *Knowledge sharing in Chinese surgical teams.* Ph.D., University of Southern California.

Husted, K., & Michailova, S. (2002). Knowledge sharing in Russian companies with Western participation. *Management International, 6*(2), 17–28.

Hwang, A., Francesco, A. M., & Kessler, E. (2003). The relationship between individualism-collectivism, face, and feedback and learning processes in Hong Kong, Singapore, and the United States. *Journal of Cross-Cultural Psychology, 34*(1), 72–91. doi:10.1177/0022022102239156

Jarvenpaa, S. L., & Leidner, D. E. (1999). Communication and trust in global virtual teams. *Organization Science, 10*(6), 791–815. doi:10.1287/orsc.10.6.791

Jennex, M. E. (2006). Culture, context, and knowledge management. *International Journal of Knowledge Management, 2*(2), i–iv.

Jolly, D. (2002). Sharing knowledge and decision power in sino-foreign joint ventures. *Asia Pacific Business Review, 9*(2), 81–100. doi:10.1080/713999186

Khalil, O. E. M., & Seleim, A. (2010). Culture and knowledge transfer capacity: A cross-national study. *International Journal of Knowledge Management, 6*(4), 60–86. doi:10.4018/jkm.2010100104

King, W. R. (2007). A research agenda for the relationships between culture and knowledge management. *Knowledge and Process Management, 14*(3), 226–236. doi:10.1002/kpm.281

Koh, J., & Kim, Y. (2004). Knowledge sharing in virtual communities: An e-business perspective. *Expert Systems with Applications, 26*(2), 155–166. doi:10.1016/S0957-4174(03)00116-7

Kohlbacher, F., & Krähe, M. O. B. (2007). Knowledge creation and transfer in a cross-cultural context - empirical evidence from tyco flow control. *Knowledge and Process Management, 14*(3), 169–181. doi:10.1002/kpm.282

Krauss, R. M., & Chiu, C. (1998). Language and social behavior. In Gilbert, D., Lindzey, G., & Fiske, S. T. (Eds.), *The handbook of social psychology* (4th ed., pp. 41–88). Boston: McGraw-Hill.

Kurman, J. (2003). Why is self-enhancement low in certain collectivist cultures?: An investigation of two competing explanations. *Journal of Cross-Cultural Psychology, 34*(5), 496–510. doi:10.1177/0022022103256474

Lai, M., & Lee, G. (2007). Risk-avoiding cultures toward achievement of knowledge sharing. *Business Process Management Journal, 13*(4), 522–537. doi:10.1108/14637150710763559

Lau, S. (1992). Collectivism's individualism: Value preference, personal control, and the desire for freedom among Chinese in mainland China, Hong Kong, and Singapore. *Personality and Individual Differences, 13*(3), 361–366. doi:10.1016/0191-8869(92)90115-6

Li, W. (2008). *Online knowledge sharing in a multinational corporation: Chinese and American practices*. Ph.D., University of Illinois at Urbana-Champaign.

Li, W. (2010). Virtual knowledge sharing in a cross-cultural context. *Journal of Knowledge Management, 14*(1), 38–50. doi:10.1108/13673271011015552

Li, W., Ardichvili, A., Maurer, M., Wentling, T., & Stuedemann, R. (2007). Impact of Chinese culture values on knowledge sharing through online communities of practice. *International Journal of Knowledge Management, 3*(3), 47–60. doi:10.4018/jkm.2007070103

Lin, Y., & Dalkir, K. (2010). Factors affecting KM implementation in the Chinese community. *International Journal of Knowledge Management, 6*(1), 1–22. doi:10.4018/jkm.2010103001

Lincoln, Y. S., & Guba, E. G. (1985). *Naturalistic inquiry*. Beverly Hills, CA: Sage Publications.

Lord, R., & Maher, K. J. (1990). Cognitive theory in industrial and organizational psychology. In Dunnette, M. D., Triandis, H. C., & Hough, L. M. (Eds.), *Handbook of industrial and organizational psychology* (2nd ed., pp. 1–62). Palo Alto, CA: Consulting Psychologists Press.

Magnier-Watanabe, R., & Senoo, D. (2010). Shaping knowledge management: Organization and national culture. *Journal of Knowledge Management, 14*(2), 214–227. doi:10.1108/13673271011032364

Matsumoto, D. R. (2002). *The new Japan: Debunking seven cultural stereotypes*. Yarmouth, ME: Intercultural Press.

Miles, M. B., & Huberman, A. M. (1994). *Qualitative data analysis: An expanded sourcebook* (2nd ed.). Thousand Oaks, CA: Sage Publications.

Myers, M. D., & Tan, F. B. (2002). Beyond models of national culture in information systems research. *Journal of Global Information Management, 10*(1), 24–32. doi:10.4018/jgim.2002010103

Nisbett, R. E. (2003). *The geography of thought: How Asians and Westerners think differently... and why*. New York: Free Press.

Nissen, M. E. (2007). Knowledge management and global cultures: Elucidation through an institutional knowledge-flow perspective. *Knowledge and Process Management, 14*(3), 211–225. doi:10.1002/kpm.285

Nonaka, I. (1994). A dynamic theory of organizational knowledge creation. *Organization Science, 5*(1), 14–37. doi:10.1287/orsc.5.1.14

Paik, Y., & Choi, D. Y. (2005). The shortcomings of a standardized global knowledge management system: The case study of Accenture. *The Academy of Management Executive, 19*(2), 81–84.

Peltokorpi, V. (2006). Knowledge sharing in a cross-cultural context: Nordic expatriates in Japan. *Knowledge Management Research & Practice, 4*(2), 138–148. doi:10.1057/palgrave.kmrp.8500095

Ralston, D. A., Egri, C. P., Stewart, S., & Terpstra, R. H., & Yu, Kaicheng. (1999). Doing business in the 21st century with the new generation of Chinese managers: A study of generational shifts in work values in China. *Journal of International Business Studies, 30*(2), 415–427. doi:10.1057/palgrave.jibs.8490077

Ralston, D. A., Gustafson, D. J., Terpstra, R. H., & Holt, D. H. (1995). Pre-post Tiananmen Square: Changing values of Chinese managers. *Asia Pacific Journal of Management, 12*(1), 1–20. doi:10.1007/BF01733968

Redding, G., & Wong, G. Y. Y. (1986). The psychology of Chinese organizational behaviour. In Bond, M. H. (Ed.), *The psychology of the Chinese people* (pp. 267–295). Hong Kong, New York: Oxford University Press.

Riege, A. (2005). Three-dozen knowledge sharing barriers managers must consider. *Journal of Knowledge Management*, 9(3), 18–35. doi:10.1108/13673270510602746

Ryan, J. J. C. H. (2006). Managing knowledge security. *Vine*, 36(2), 143–145. doi:10.1108/03055720610682942

Sackmann, S. A., & Friesl, M. (2007). Exploring cultural impacts on knowledge sharing behavior in project teams - results from a simulation study. *Journal of Knowledge Management*, 11(6), 142–156. doi:10.1108/13673270710832226

Schneider, B. (1987). The people make the place. *Personnel Psychology*, 40(3), 437–453. doi:10.1111/j.1744-6570.1987.tb00609.x

Singh, N., & Baack, D. W. (2004). Web site adaptation: A cross-cultural comparison of U.S. and Mexican web sites. *Journal of Computer-Mediated Communication*, 9(4). http://jcmc.indiana.edu/vol9/issue4/singh_baack.html.

Srite, M. (2006). Culture as an explanation of technology acceptance differences: An empirical investigation of Chinese and US users. *Australasian Journal of Information Systems*, 14(1), 5–25. doi:10.3127/ajis.v14i1.4

Stonehouse, G., & Minocha, S. (2008). Strategic processes @ Nike—making and doing knowledge management. *Knowledge and Process Management*, 15(1), 24–31. doi:10.1002/kpm.296

Su, W. B., Li, X., & Chow, C. W. (2010). Exploring the Extent and Impediments of Knowledge Sharing in Chinese Business Enterprise. *International Journal of Knowledge Management*, 6(4), 24–46. doi:10.4018/jkm.2010100102

Szulanski, G. (1996). Exploring internal stickiness: Impediments to the transfer of best practice within the firm. *Strategic Management Journal*, 17, 27–43.

Tong, J., & Mitra, A. (2009). Chinese cultural influences on knowledge management practice. *Journal of Knowledge Management*, 13(2), 49–62. doi:10.1108/13673270910942691

Triandis, H. C. (1995). *Individualism and collectivism*. Boulder, CO: Westview Press.

Trompenaars, F. (1994). *Riding the waves of culture: Understanding diversity in global business*. Burr Ridge, IL: Irwin Professional Pub.

Wei, K. (2007). Sharing Knowledge in global virtual teams: How do Chinese team members perceive the impact of national cultural differences on knowledge sharing? In Crowston, K., Sieber, S., & Wynn, E. (Eds.), *International Federation for Information Processing, 236, Virtuality and Virtualization* (pp. 251–265). Boston: Springer.

Yoo, Y., & Torrey, B. (2002). National culture and knowledge management in a global learning organization. In Choo, C. W., & Bontis, N. (Eds.), *The strategic management of intellectual capital and organizational knowledge* (pp. 421–434). Oxford, New York: Oxford University Press.

Zakaria, N., Amelinckx, A., & Wilemon, D. (2004). Working together apart? Building a knowledge-sharing culture for global virtual teams. *Creativity and Innovation Management*, 13(1), 15–29. doi:10.1111/j.1467-8691.2004.00290.x

Zhang, Q., Chintakovid, T., Sun, X., Ge, Y., & Zhang, K. (2006). Saving face or sharing personal information? A cross-cultural study on knowledge sharing. *Journal of Information and Knowledge Management*, 5(1), 73–79. doi:10.1142/S0219649206001335

Zhu, Z. (2004). Knowledge management: Towards a universal concept or cross-cultural contexts? *Knowledge Management Research & Practice, 2*(2), 67–79. doi:10.1057/palgrave.kmrp.8500032

Zuboff, S. (1988). *In the age of the smart machine: The future of work and power.* New York: Basic Books.

Chapter 17
Utilizing the Rasch Model to Develop and Evaluate Items for the Tacit Knowledge Inventory for Superintendents (TKIS)

Christian E. Mueller
University of Memphis, USA

Kelly D. Bradley
University of Kentucky, USA

ABSTRACT

Tacit knowledge was originally introduced into the professional literature by Michael Polanyi and later made popular by researchers in a variety of domains. Measuring this implicit form of procedural knowledge requires multiple approaches to adequately "capture" what is often known, but not easily articulated. The present study combines use of Sternberg et al.'s framework for capturing domain-specific tacit knowledge with that of Rasch modeling to develop and validate items for use on a newly developed tacit knowledge inventory. Development of the Tacit Knowledge Inventory for Superintendents (TKIS) occurred in three phases, including two phases of piloting and Rasch analysis. For illustrative purposes, presentation of results is limited to the Rasch analyses conducted on interpersonal tacit knowledge items. However, the methodology extends its usefulness to researchers and practitioners to guide the development process of similar assessments.

INTRODUCTION

Understanding leadership effectiveness has long been an interest for researchers in both psychology and leadership. Leithwood (1995) has suggested that it is necessary to understand the cognition of the leader to measure leadership effectiveness, because of the important role that cognitive processes play in overall leadership judgment and decision making (Leithwood & Steinbach, 1995). One

DOI: 10.4018/978-1-60960-555-1.ch017

such cognitive construct that is receiving growing interest from researchers in numerous domains is that of *tacit knowledge*. Originally introduced into the professional literature by Michael Polanyi (1946, 1966, 1976), it was not until the later work of others in psychology (e.g., Insch, McIntyre, & Dawley, 2008; Sternberg et al., 2000; Wagner & Sternberg, 1985), leadership (e.g., Hedlund et al., 2003; Rowe & Christie, 2008) and organizational management (e.g., Coff, Coff, & Eastvold, 2006; Nonaka, 1994; Nonaka & Konno, 1998) that researchers gained a better understanding of how tacit knowledge is acquired and utilized as a tangible resource. Despite the ubiquity of tacit knowledge research, however, Taylor (2007) and others (e.g., Ambrosini & Bowman, 2001) have noted that confusion and debate still exist in most research circles regarding the exact nature of tacit knowledge, and more importantly, how to elicit and study tacit knowledge in a useful manner.

Polanyi (1966) originally proposed, "I shall reconsider human knowledge by starting from the fact that we can know more than we can tell" (p. 4). Polanyi certainly could not envision the difficulty and challenges that researchers would encounter in attempting to capture a type of knowledge that was, by some accounts, inarticulatable. In an earlier study linking tacit knowledge with practical intelligence, Wagner and Sternberg (1985) suggested that some forms of tacit knowledge may be inaccessible at the conscious level, and thus, may remain unmeasured using common research methods. In this conception, however, they note, "by our use of tacit in the present context we do not wish to imply that this knowledge is inaccessible to conscious awareness, unspeakable, or unteachable, but merely that it is not taught directly to most of us" (p. 439). Thus, in Wagner and Sternberg's view, an individual's tacit knowledge could be articulated, and as their substantial body of empirical research has shown, could also be measured and used to predict numerous outcomes (e.g., Colonia-Wilner, 1999; Hedlund et al., 2003). Other researchers (e.g., Ambrosini & Bowman, 2001;

Castillo, 2002; Tsoukas, 2003) have also written about the inherent difficulty in measuring or capturing tacit knowledge. For example, Ambrosini and Bowman (2001) have suggested that there are varying degrees of tacit knowledge ranging from "explicit skills" to "deeply ingrained tacit skills" (p. 816). In their estimation, the deeply ingrained tacit skills (which would be of most interest to researchers and practitioners) are inaccessible at the individual conscious level. They further suggest that empirical research already conducted on tacit knowledge has probably tapped only the middle to upper levels, that is, "tacit skills that can be imperfectly articulated" (p. 816).

One reason that researchers continue to show heightened interest in tacit knowledge is the strong predictive validity it has demonstrated in a variety of contexts, including managerial performance (e.g., Sternberg, Wagner, Williams, & Horvath, 1995), leadership effectiveness (Hedlund et al., 2003) and when effectively retained and utilized by organizations, in providing a strategic advantage in business operations (Ambrosini, 2003; Coff et al. 2006). Sternberg et al. (1995), for example, found that tacit knowledge accounted for up to 32% of unique variance in managerial performance, even after controlling for predictors such as IQ and other personality and cognitive constructs. And, Castillo (2002) has noted, "this ubiquitous concept appears across a broad spectrum of writing as either an explanatory construct to numerous psychosocial issues, an intervening variable to a myriad of managerial concerns, or a catalytic element to more complex, organizational-level phenomena" (p.46). Despite the apparent consistency in empirical findings, two issues that remain salient for tacit knowledge researchers are that of operationalization and measurement (Taylor 2005, 2007). It is to these two issues that we turn our attention next.

The Tacit Knowledge Framework

Although most tacit knowledge research can be traced back to the original work of Polanyi, Taylor (2005) notes, there is some confusion in the literature over the exact definition of tacit knowledge and its relationship to similar concepts, such as implicit learning, procedural knowledge and practical intelligence.... In applied management studies, there has been a lack of consistency in the operationalization of the tacit knowledge concept, and on what distinguishes tacit knowledge from explicit knowledge. (p. 26)

One factor contributing to this ongoing confusion is that tacit knowledge is assumed to be context specific (Sternberg et al., 2000; Sternberg & Horvath, 1999; Wagner & Sternberg, 1985). Although there are some characteristics that make tacit knowledge unique (discussed later), it is assumed that tacit knowledge at the individual level manifests differently depending upon the domain or context in which it is studied. Possible reasons given to help explain why tacit knowledge is domain-specific include the constructivist nature of acquiring tacit knowledge, as well as the assumption that successful performance in any given domain is measured using different criteria. Most researchers agree that tacit knowledge is acquired implicitly through personal experiences, rather than through direct training or instruction (Taylor, 2007). That is, tacit knowledge is constructed through an individual's unique interaction with their environment. Further, Sternberg and his colleagues have shown through multiple studies (e.g., Grigorenko, Sternberg, & Strauss, 2006; Sternberg et al., 2001) how individuals rely on different aspects of tacit knowledge to be successful in any given domain. For example, managerial success, or the ability to successfully lead groups of people, requires tacit knowledge related to managing others. Successful performance in another profession might require an individual to draw more from tacit knowledge of managing oneself or of managing tasks in order to be suc-

cessful. In addition to being context-specific, tacit knowledge is assumed to be different than other types of knowledge.

Polanyi originally distinguished between two types of knowledge; practical knowledge and intellectual knowledge. Or, as Gilbert Ryle (1949) phrased it, the "knowing what" and the "knowing how" (Polanyi, 1966, p. 7). This was very similar in structure to what we now call declarative and procedural knowledge (Anderson, 1983). Polanyi's framework for "knowing" proposed that the two types of knowledge complemented each other. Polanyi further claimed that intellectual knowledge had a tacit aspect to it because by itself intellectual knowledge was meaningless. It was the tacit understanding that individuals brought to bear on this intellectual knowledge that gave it its meaning. In this sense, tacit knowledge as Polanyi viewed it was very much a constructivist type of knowledge; the perspective of the individual was important. Currently, individual tacit knowledge is typically studied using the framework proposed by Sternberg and his colleagues (Sternberg et al., 2000), because of their clear definition of tacit knowledge, as well as the extensive body of empirical literature supporting this definition (Taylor, 2005, 2007).

Tacit Knowledge in the Present Study

In the present study, we draw from several areas to construct a workable definition of tacit knowledge, including that of Sternberg et al. (e.g., Sternberg et al., 2000; Wagner & Sternberg, 1985) and Wagner (1987). It is similar to the definition proposed by Taylor (2005) in her discussion of tacit knowledge in the knowledge management literature, which views tacit knowledge as a multidimensional construct. In line with previous conceptions, we view tacit knowledge as being procedural in nature (i.e., knowing "how" vs. knowing "what"), that it is useful in the accomplishment of personally meaningful goals (i.e., can be directly applied in a given setting), and that it is gained through personal experience and without aid from others. Further, we conceptualize individual tacit knowledge manifesting as managing oneself, managing others, and managing tasks (Wagner, 1987). This has also been referred to as intrapersonal, interpersonal, and organizational tacit knowledge in other studies (e.g., Nestor-Baker & Hoy, 2001). And, in line with Nonaka's assertion (e.g., Nonaka, 1994; Nonaka & Konno, 1998) that tacit knowledge has two dimensions: cognitive and technical, Insch, McIntyre, and Dawley (2008) recently characterized these dimensions as cognitive, social, and technical. While this demonstrates the proliferation and continued use of varied terminology, the underlying processes are assumed here to represent the same thing as in the previous studies. The following sections describe these processes in further detail.

Tacit Knowledge is Procedural

Sternberg et al. (1995) suggested that the procedural nature of tacit knowledge could be represented as a form of "condition-action pairs" that took the form of "IF (antecedent condition)-THEN (consequent action)" sequences. Nestor-Baker and Hoy (2001) adapted this for their work with educational leaders by adding another step to the process, in which "BECAUSE" was added to the "IF-THEN" sequence. The "BECAUSE" allowed individuals to articulate their reasoning behind their actions. Ambrosini and Bowman (2001) assert that the way in which tacit knowledge is usually defined is in comparing it with more declarative forms of knowledge. Sternberg and Hedlund (2002) pointed out that tacit knowledge is more than just a set of abstract heuristics or problem-solving strategies, and suggested that tacit knowledge "is context-specific knowledge about what to do in a given situation or class of situations" (p. 147). It is the pairing of several complex decision-making mechanisms that must all be balanced in order to determine the best course of action in any given situation (Sternberg et al., 2000). Described in this way, tacit knowledge could be described as a metaprocedural form of knowledge.

Tacit Knowledge is Practically Useful in Pursuit of Goals

This is a key component in that it distinguishes tacit knowledge from other types of knowledge because of the intentional use on the part of the individual. Clearly, this aspect of tacit knowledge comes, at least in part, from the intent to distinguish it from IQ. Although other forms of knowledge can be used with intention on the part of the individual to achieve goals, it is specifically this aspect that makes tacit knowledge unique. In addition to being a procedural form of knowledge, it is procedural knowledge that helps individuals successfully accomplish their goals. Given the previous description, it is easy to understand why tacit knowledge is considered context-specific; that is, it differs in relation to how professionals in a given field define success for that field, because the types of goals that individuals pursue will depend upon their individual professional roles.

Tacit Knowledge is Gained Through Personal Experience

In suggesting that tacit knowledge is a distinct construct, Sternberg and his colleagues have proposed the process of acquiring tacit knowledge is what distinguishes it from other types of knowledge. Although one could argue that individuals certainly acquire both procedural as well as declarative knowledge in any form of direct training or instruction, the type of knowledge being described here is different. Tacit knowledge, as it is defined here, is that type of metaprocedural knowledge where several decision-making processes are occurring at one time.

The use and utility of tacit knowledge appears to become more sophisticated the longer one remains in a particular role, as supported by the link between tacit knowledge and years of experience on the job (Wagner & Sternberg, 1985). Hence, one of the key ways of studying tacit knowledge is to examine differences between experts and novices in terms of their decision making. Sternberg (1988) further proposed that tacit knowledge acquired in this way is often done without direct environmental support. That is, the individual must pull out the relevant information from their personal experiences that will help guide their decision making in the future. This could explain why not everyone benefits equally from professional experience, and why only some people seem to attain the expertise and knowledge that is associated with the best performers in a particular profession. In this way, tacit knowledge becomes a way to explain why some end up as more effective leaders than others. Sternberg et al. (2000) may have come up with a partial explanation of how this aspect of tacit knowledge acquisition works when they wrote,

When an individual is helped to distinguish more from less important information (selective encoding), to combine elements of information in useful ways (selective combination), and to identify knowledge in memory that is relevant to the present situation (selective comparison), that individual has been supported in acquiring knowledge. In performing real world tasks, individuals often must engage in these processes on their own in order to make sense of and respond to situations. (p. 106)

Tacit Knowledge is Manifested as Managing Self, Others, and Tasks

In their conception of practical intelligence, Wagner and Sternberg (1985) and later Wagner (1987) proposed that tacit knowledge manifests itself as the tacit knowledge of managing oneself, managing others, managing tasks, and managing one's career. The difference in the amount and usefulness of tacit knowledge in these areas becomes apparent when examining differences in the behavior of experts and novices in a particular field. Tacit knowledge about managing oneself is expressed in the ability to prioritize work tasks efficiently, the ability to motivate oneself, and the ability to work efficiently and effectively to maximize one's accomplishments. Tacit knowledge about managing others refers to knowing how best to manage or lead others, which includes being able to play to people's strengths while minimizing weaknesses. It also encompasses the ability to get along well with others. Tacit knowledge about managing tasks is concerned with the larger organizational tasks at hand. Tacit knowledge about managing one's career is concerned with being able to establish a favorable reputation, how to further and enhance that reputation, and how to convince superiors that a reputation is well-earned and well-deserved. In a later work, Wagner expanded this original scope to include two additional ideas. In this later model, the notion of *context* (focus on short-term or long-term goals) and *orientation* (whether a focus on idealistic or practical ideals) were added. Again, it is important to point out here that tacit knowledge in these cases is that form of procedural knowledge that is gained through experience on the job that helps individuals successfully pursue and accomplish the types of tasks just described. It is different from the knowledge gained through formal instruction that would also help individuals in many of these instances, as well.

As discussed previously, and in the current study, tacit knowledge is assumed to be context or domain-specific. Sternberg et al. (2000) have suggested that in order to capture tacit knowledge as it manifests in individuals in any domain requires the development of a new assessment or inventory in order to capture tacit knowledge as it manifests in individuals in any given domain. Examples of tacit knowledge inventories that have been created using the Sternberg et al. (2000) framework include the *Tacit Knowledge Inventory for Military Leaders* (TKML; Hedlund et al., 2003), the Practical Knowledge Inventory for Nurses (PKIN, Fox, 1994, 1999), and the *Tacit Knowledge Inventory for Managers* (TKIM, Wagner & Sternberg, 1991).

Sternberg et al.'s framework combines multiple methods and may be viewed as one of the most effective ways of eliciting and measuring tacit knowledge at the individual level (Taylor, 2005). This framework consists of four main phases: (a) knowledge identification; (b) item selection; (c) assessment construction; and, finally (d) validation of the created assessment. Sternberg and Wagner (1985) and later Wagner (1987) utilized this general framework in creating tacit knowledge inventories for use with academic psychologists and business leaders. Numerous researchers have utilized this methodology in developing other tacit knowledge inventories, including those for use with college populations (Somech & Bogler, 1999), nurses (Fox, 1999) and military leaders (Hedlund et al., 2003). As a part of a larger study conducted to develop a tacit knowledge inventory for use with educational leaders, the researchers in the present study utilized Rasch modeling (Rasch 1960/1980) to validate and refine items that were generated at earlier phases of the larger study (i.e., phases "a," "b," and "c" from Sternberg et al.'s framework). Thus, in the present study, we combined Sternberg et al.'s general framework of developing scenarios and items with that of Rasch modeling to demonstrate how the Rasch model can be utilized to improve the development of tacit knowledge inventories. For those not already familiar with Rasch modeling, a brief description is provided next.

SCALE CONSTRUCTION AND RASCH MODELING

Traditionally, three methods have been applied in the social sciences for the development of psychological, personality, and educational inventories: psychometrics or classical test theory (CTT), item response theory (IRT), and generalizability theory

(Fox, 1999). Wright (1997) and Devillis (1991), among others, have suggested that educational and psychological researchers are most familiar with the principles of psychometrics or CTT, since the majority of research conducted in these fields is grounded in the early work of Karl Pearson and Sir Francis Galton. In CTT, a researcher typically develops a bank of test items based on the use of comparable measures and/or theory. Whether using comparable measures or being guided by relevant theory, the goal in using both of these methods is the same: to develop items that are valid, reliable and measure the underlying theoretical construct of interest (Bond & Fox, 2001). In this process, both construct validity of items and internal reliability is of the utmost importance to the researcher. It is essential that all items measure the same latent construct (construct validity) and that these items correlate highly with one another (internal validity) (Bond & Fox, 2001).

There are inherent flaws, however, in using psychometrics or CTT to develop items for use on psychological, personality, and educational measures (Bond & Fox, 2001; Fox, 1999). First, it is typically accepted that Likert-type scale items are at interval levels of measurement, thus implying an equidistant measure between all response options. In theory, this view may indeed be true; however, in practice it is flawed as there is no systematic way of ensuring this fact. A second assumption of CTT is that each item is of equal importance to the overall measurement of the construct, thus implying no redundancy or overlap of items. Third, it is typically assumed that all respondents are able to interpret directions correctly, that all items are written clearly, and that the items connect to a single latent construct. Lastly, CTT requires complete records in order to make comparisons and to produce a single standard error of measurement. In actuality, all of these assumptions are unstable, and often problematic, in traditional survey research (Sampson & Bradley, 2003).

Item response theory (IRT), including Rasch modeling, attempts to address these limitations through use of a probabilistic mathematical model. McCamey (2002) notes:

IRT promises to overcome circular dependency of CTT which is the situation, as described by Fan (1998), where the person statistic is item dependent and the item statistics examinee (person) dependent...the Rasch model allows tests to be constructed where the measure of a person's ability is independent of the sample of items used and is independent of the norm group used to "calibrate" the test. (p. 4)

In the current study, a one-parameter IRT model known as the Rasch model (Rasch, 1960/1980) was utilized. The Rasch model addresses many of the inherent weaknesses of CTT because, as Bradley and Sampson (2005) explain, "*Rasch analysis begins at the level of measurement, providing diagnostic information on the quality of the measurement tool, in addition to yielding a more comprehensive and informative picture of the construct under measurement as well as the respondents on that measure.*"

The earliest traditional IRT models dealt only with dichotomously scored items but were later applied to polytomously scored items such as Likert-type scales (Thornton, 2002). IRT models can involve multiple parameter estimations, including level of ability (theta), difficulty of item (beta), and probability of guessing. While the Rasch model does not utilize specific parameter estimates for guessing, it deals with this issue by flagging lucky guesses as unexpected responses through the use of specific statistics (i.e., infit and outfit statistics, which are described later) (Hambleton, 1992). The Rasch measurement model mathematically estimates a single parameter, specifically modeling the relationship between the latent ability of an individual and the item difficulty (endorsability) as a probability. Thus, as a person's respective ability increases, their likelihood or probability

of answering correctly, or endorsement, on any select item also increases. When measuring a latent construct where individual ability levels can be mapped alongside item difficulty levels, such as with tacit knowledge (see Figure 2), the utility of the Rasch model becomes evident (Bond & Fox, 2001; Fox & Jones, 1998).

OBJECTIVE

Crucial to construction of new inventories such as the TKIS is the Rasch model, especially in its utility to guide revisions throughout the development process (Fox 1994, 1999; Fox & Jones, 1998). The Rasch model is suitable because of its utility in providing feedback and information that aids researchers interested in improving the precision of the developed instrument, which will ultimately improve overall validity and reliability of results and inferences made from those results (Bond & Fox, 2001; Bradley & Sampson, 2005). The framework in the current study builds on the previous work of many researchers, mainly in the areas of cognition, leadership, and education. It combines elements of the research agenda of Sternberg and his colleagues used in studying tacit knowledge, aspects of the work of Nestor-Baker and her colleagues to push tacit knowledge research into the area of educational leadership, specifically the superintendency, and lastly the efforts of Fox and her colleagues (Fox 1994, 1999; Fox & Jones, 1998) in the use of the Rasch model in developing similar assessments of this type.

METHOD

Development of the TKIS occurred in three phases: (a) generating the initial scenarios and response options; (b) initial piloting, Rasch analysis, and reworking of items; and (c) final piloting and Rasch analysis of reconstructed items. For illustrative purposes, only results of the final phase of the larger study will be presented here. Specifically, results pertaining to the analysis and recalibration of interpersonal tacit knowledge items will be presented and then discussed in order to illustrate the utility of the Rasch model in developing inventories that measure complex cognitive abilities. The decision was made to focus specifically on findings related to the development of the interpersonal tacit knowledge items given the importance of this facet of tacit knowledge in overall superintendent success (Nestor-Baker & Hoy, 2001).

The final version of TKIS is designed to be a scenario-based assessment composed of 40 tacit knowledge items across eight scenarios. Scenarios on the TKIS are designed to represent typical situations in a superintendent's day-to-day professional role and are assigned according to the eight AASA standards (described below). Each scenario presents an issue that has five corresponding response options, which reflect varying degrees of effectiveness in dealing with the issue. Respondents are asked to rate each response option on a 1- to 7-point scale where 1 = *extremely ineffective* to 7 = *extremely effective*. Using expert responses, credit is assigned (0 = no points to 3 = full points) dependent upon how well each of the respondent's choices match the scoring protocol (discussed below). All items and scenarios were analyzed and calibrated according to the expectations of the Rasch model (discussed below).

Sample

Here, the focus is on the final phase of the study where the sampling frame consisted of six graduate students and 29 practicing superintendents, resulting in 35 assessments being included in the final Rasch analysis.[1] During the final phase of the larger study, there were 117 assessments sent out to both graduate students and practicing superintendents. Six of the eight assessments distributed to graduate students were completed and returned, yielding a return rate of 75%. These

responses were included in the final Rasch analysis. For practicing superintendents, there were 109 assessments distributed (via mail); of which a total of 19 were returned yielding a response rate of 17.4%. To improve the overall response rate for practicing superintendents, and to meet the minimum necessary requirements to produce stable results in Rasch analysis (Linacre, 1994), reminder cards (Dillman, 1978) were sent to superintendents who had not yet completed the survey by the requested deadline. This resulted in an additional 10 surveys being returned for a final response rate for the practicing superintendents of 26.6%. Overall response rate for the combined group was 32.1%. Again, only responses (N = 35) pertaining to the interpersonal tacit knowledge items are presented here.

Data Collection Procedures

As discussed previously, the process of developing the items and scenarios for use on the TKIS was completed in three phases. Phase I consisted of development of the initial scenarios by experienced superintendents. These superintendents were identified based upon their expertise in one of the eight American Association of School Administrators (AASA) standards. The eight standards, providing the most comprehensive framework for evaluating effective superintendent performance (Hoyle, Bjork, Collier, & Glass, 2005), include leadership and district culture, policy and governance, communications and community relations, organizational management, curriculum planning and development, instructional management, human resources management, and values and ethics of leadership (Hoyle, 1993). These superintendents were then asked to generate scenarios and response options according to the criteria outlined by the lead researcher. Scenarios were designed to fit into one of three categories of superintendent tacit knowledge: interpersonal, intrapersonal, or organizational (Nestor-Baker & Hoy, 2001). In addition, each scenario was

Figure 1. Tacit knowledge framework for effective superintendents

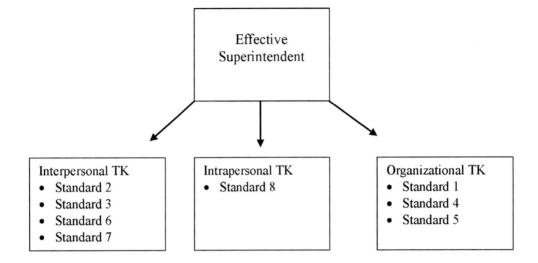

organized according to the AASA professional standards for superintendents.

Figure 1 provides a graphic depiction of the tacit knowledge framework used to organize the scenarios. For those readers not already familiar with Rasch analysis, it may be helpful to provide a more thorough discussion of the Rasch model and how it was used to analyze the interpersonal

tacit knowledge items in the current study. What follows is a general overview of the Rasch model, and in particular the partial-credit Rasch model (Masters, 1982), followed by a description of the specific methods used to analyze and calibrate the interpersonal tacit knowledge items.

Figure 2. Example variable (person/item) map for organizational tacit knowledge

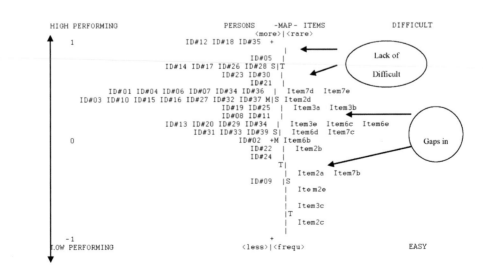

Analysis

Rasch Model

The Rasch model (Rasch, 1960/1980) is particularly suited for use in developing and validating measures of complex cognitive abilities (Bond & Fox, 2001), such as the case with tacit knowledge (Fox, 1999). According to the Rasch model, the relationship between the latent ability of an individual and how difficult an item is can be mathematically modeled as a probability. As an individual's respective ability increases, the probability of answering correctly on any select item also increases. (Bond & Fox, 2001; Fox & Jones, 1998).

The partial-credit Rasch model (Masters, 1982) is an extension of the dichotomous model and is used for polytomously scored items, such as the case with interpersonal tacit knowledge items on the TKIS. The partial-credit Rasch model is expressed as $ln(P_{nij}/P_{ni(j-1)}) = B_n - D_i - F_{ij} = B_n - D_{ij}$, where F_j is the "calibration" measure of category j relative to category $j-1$, the point where categories j and $j-1$ are equally probable relative to the measure of the item (Linacre, 2005, p. 20). Fox (1999) suggested that the use of the partial-credit model is particularly useful in developing assessments of complex cognitive ability, where "graded judgments of performance can be scaled and subsequently assessed for quality of calibrations" (p. 342). Furthermore, she notes, "the partial-credit model can calibrate these ordered levels of performance that represent varying degrees of performance" (p. 342).

Winsteps software, version 3.51(Linacre, 2004), was used to analyze data from both graduate students and experienced superintendents (N=35). Mean responses from the expert prototype were used as the scoring protocol. In the larger study, data were analyzed separately for intrapersonal, interpersonal, and organizational tacit knowledge. The decision to analyze the data separately for each type of tacit knowledge, rather than as a single construct was made for two reasons: theoretical rationale and the assumption of unidimesionality in using the Rasch model. Wagner (1987) and others (e.g., Hedlund et al., 2003) have concluded, rather than an underlying single construct of tacit knowledge, there are essentially three dimensions of tacit knowledge: intrapersonal, interpersonal, and organizational. Wagner used both principal-components analysis and confirmatory factor analysis to provide support for this assumption. Most researchers in the area of tacit knowledge, including Nestor-Baker and Hoy (2001) in their work with superintendents, follow this precedent and study tacit knowledge as having three separate subdimensions.

In addition to the theoretical and empirical support for tacit knowledge being operationalized in this way, the assumption of unidimensionality of the Rasch model contributed to analyses conducted separately for each type of tacit knowledge. If all items on the assessment were analyzed together, the Rasch model would not be fit for the data due to the presumption that all items on the assessment are measuring the same construct and many items would appear to misfit when that may not have necessarily been the case. Secondly, the goal of the study was to use Rasch analysis to create a measure or "ruler" for each of the three subdimensions of tacit knowledge already described. Thus, using this rationale, the decision was made to conduct the analyses as they appear in the present study.

Analysis Procedures

Diagnosing Misfit

In order to determine how well the data fit the expectations of the Rasch model (in this case unidimensionality), Winsteps software produces both infit and outfit statistics (Linacre, 2002a). Infit and outfit statistics are reported in either mean-square (unstandardized) or standardized form, and both are influenced by the pattern of responses on any particular item. Chiu, Fritz,

Light, and Velozo (2006) and Fox (1999) note that fit statistics determine how well each item fits with the construct it is intended to measure. Tennant, McKenna, and Hagell (2004) noted, "when the observed response pattern coincides with or does not deviate greatly from the expected response pattern, the items fit the measurement model and constitute a true Rasch scale" (p. 23). According to the Rasch model, as a person's ability increases, their likelihood of scoring correctly on an item also should increase. As such, misfit statistics provide an indication of how well both persons and items are fitting according to the expectations of the model or the prediction. In developing items for use on the TKIS, infit and outfit statistics were used to indicate how well the individual items were functioning as measures of each type of tacit knowledge.

Infit statistics are inlier-sensitive or information weighted and are more sensitive to unexpected patterns of responses located near a person's or an item's measure (i.e., where the model would predict responses to be). Therefore, if "less able" persons are scoring correctly on the more difficult items on an assessment, then this would not meet the expectations of the Rasch model. Outfit statistics are outlier-sensitive, and are more sensitive to unexpected patterns of responses far from a person or item's measure. For example, an item would indicate a poor outfit statistic if several persons with low ability answered correctly on a more difficult item. This would violate the expectation of the Rasch model that persons with low ability have a lower probability of answering correctly on a more difficult item. In this case, unacceptable outfit statistics will typically indicate either guessing or carelessness on the part of respondents (Linacre, 2002a).

Mean-square fit statistics indicate the amount of randomness in responses on any particular item, and thus show the amount of distortion in measurement. The expected value for the mean-square statistic (infit and outfit) is 1.0. Values that are less than 1.0 indicate that observations or responses are too predictable, or indicate redundancy. In other words, the item does not provide useful information (from a measurement perspective) above and beyond that of the other items contained on the assessment. Tang, Wong, Chiu, Lum, and Ungvari (2005) note that this typically happens either when items are highly correlated or when item responses are dependent on one another. Values that are greater than 1.0 typically indicate unpredictability in responses, such as with items that do not seem to be measuring the same construct. This is usually the result of either poorly worded or ambiguous items (Linacre, 2002b).

Typically, there are acceptable ranges that items can fall for both infit and outfit statistics for the item to still be considered a useful measurement item. Linacre and Wright (1994) note that because the Rasch model is a stochastic, or probabilistic model, the choice of which cutoff scores to use cannot be done with absolute certainty. Linacre and Wright also note that the choice of cutoff values will depend upon the type of Rasch analysis conducted. But, they also go on to suggest that "fit statistics are indicative, not absolute" (Linacre, 1990, p. 80). Linacre further points out that the use of critical values in statistics is very similar to the use of fit statistics in Rasch. In other words, the use of critical values to reject the null hypothesis in statistics is not an absolute either and that the use of $p < .05$ (or whatever the case may be) is simply the accepted level of tolerance for making a Type I error. The difference in Rasch, however, is that the purpose of using fit statistics is only to identify problematic items rather than to make inferences based on the use of critical values as in the case of typical statistical analyses. In the current study, cutoff scores of .6 to 1.5 were used to identify problematic items.

Variable (Person/Item) Maps

Winsteps software also produces a variable map where individuals are mapped alongside items in order to provide a graphic depiction of how well that bank of items is targeting the ability-level of the sample. Figure 2 presents a sample variable map that was taken from the measure for organizational tacit knowledge from the larger study described earlier.

On the left side of the map, it can be seen that there are 39 participants (referred to by "ID#") being measured on their level of organizational tacit knowledge by the items on the right side of the map. There are 13 items on this particular measure (see Figure 2). By placing persons and items side-by-side in this manner, a determination can be made about how well the individual items on the measure are targeting the full range of ability for the participants being sampled.

Bradley and Sampson (2005) liken the variable map, also referred to as a person/item map, to a ruler, noting,

...the items (on the right) act as the measurement units to gauge the ability measures of the persons (on the left). In a well-targeted assessment, mean item and person measures should be approximately equivalent, the difficulty measures of the items should span at least the width of the ability measures of the persons taking the assessment and the items should be distributed such that they accurately measure all persons taking the test. When a group of persons fall in a space between item placements on the ruler, it is comparable to measuring the length of an object with a ruler where the units of measure have been rubbed out at the very length of the object; one could report that the length of the object is between certain units, but could not report the precise length. (p. 13)

From the Rasch measurement perspective, the person/item map contained in Figure 2 has three pressing issues: a) there are not sufficient items near the top of the continuum to measure the highest levels of ability, b) there are gaps between items where certain individuals are not being adequately measured (such as with ID#8 & ID#11), and c) there are redundant items, or items

measuring at the same level of ability (e.g., Items 2a and 7b), contained on the measure. This last point is important because one of the main benefits of using Rasch analysis is to create an assessment that contains the fewest number of items that still provides good measurement information.

Two additional pieces of information needed to understand the variable map is that both person ability (left side of map) and item difficulty (right side of map) are listed on a continuum from least able to most able, and from least difficult to most difficult. Secondly, the map is labeled on both sides with the person and item means (M), and one and two standard deviations above and below the mean (labeled respectively with S and T). Ideally, the means should be roughly equivalent, but on the measure in Figure 2 it can be seen that the mean for persons is almost one standard deviation above the mean for items, thus indicating that the sample in this case found this measure relatively easy.

Scoring Protocol

In order to create the scoring protocol for the TKIS, an expert profile was developed. Similar to the expert profile created in Fox (1999), the present study calculated the expert profile by taking the mean responses of those superintendents who had initially generated the scenarios in a previous step. Of the eight superintendents who were recontacted, two agreed to take the full version of the assessment (containing all 17 scenarios) in order to create the profile, therefore only two experts were available to provide the responses to be used as the scoring protocol. One of these individuals was named outstanding superintendent of the year in the state of Kentucky in 2003. Each of these individuals also had at least 10 years of experience on the job. This last qualifier was important because of previous literature suggesting that at least 10 years of experience is needed to develop expertise in any field (e.g., Chi, Glaser, & Farr, 1988; Ericsson & Crutcher, 1990).

Fox also included three additional criteria in creating her scoring protocol: (a) three of the four experts had to be in agreement to include the item for piloting, (b) responses for the experts had to be on the same side of the 7-pt. continuum, and (c) responses had to be within two points of each other. For example, an item would be excluded from further analysis if only one or two of the experts were in agreement on that item, or if two experts rated the best response as a "3" (*somewhat ineffective*) and another rated the best response as "5" (*somewhat effective*). This would meet the condition of being within 2 points, but would not meet the criteria of being on the same side of the continuum, therefore this particular item would be eliminated from further analysis. This protocol of using mean responses to develop the expert profile follows previous suggestions by Sternberg et al. (2000).

RESULTS

In order to best illustrate the utility of the Rasch model in developing items for the TKIS, only the final results pertaining to the analysis and recalibration of interpersonal tacit knowledge items are presented. Final results presented here reflect some changes that occurred during earlier phases of piloting and initial Rasch analysis. Results for interpersonal tacit knowledge items are presented according to diagnosing misfitting items (infit and outfit statistics), mapping person ability with item difficulty (person/item map), and lastly, providing person and item reliabilities. Details pertaining to individual aspects of the Rasch model are discussed as they apply to analysis of individual interpersonal tacit knowledge items.

Table 1. Fit statistics[2] for interpersonal tacit knowledge (phase III)

Item	Infit MNSQ	Outfit MNSQ
2d	1.24	1.26
2b	1.09	1.22
6d	1.16	1.18
6b	1.12	1.09
3a	1.08	1.07
7e	1.07	1.07
2a	1.06	1.06
7d	1.01	1.03
3c	.96	1.01
7b	.93	.99
2c	.95	.98
6c	.97	.92
3e	.97	.96
2e	.93	.86
6e	.85	.79
7c	.83	.79
3b	.76	.72
Mean	1.01	1.05
S. D.	.19	.47

Interpersonal Tacit Knowledge

Item Misfit

Seventeen interpersonal tacit knowledge items were re-analyzed during the final phase of the study using Winsteps software. Referring to Table 1, it is evident that all items that were re-analyzed and were included on the interpersonal tacit knowledge measure fit the expectations of the Rasch model. Thus, the four items that were re-worded (from the earlier piloting phase) and included as a part of the analysis in the final phase now fit the expectations of the Rasch model. Specifically, items 2e, 7b, 7d, and 7e now had fit statistics within the acceptable limits. Item 5 was added to replace an item that had poor wording in phase II. Items 7b, 7d, and 7e were reworded to remove extraneous information, which seemed to improve the understandability of the items. For example, the wording of item 7b in phase III…

You decide leadership training should begin with the board of education since they are to be held accountable for attainment of district goals.

Had been reworded from its phase II form of…

The board of education is to be held accountable for all goals attainment in the district. Therefore, the primary focus for leadership training needs to begin with the board of education albeit they are removed from day to day classroom activities.

In phase II, there was a lack of expert agreement on the item; therefore, the wording was changed which not only improved agreement between the experts, but also produced acceptable fit statistics in the final Rasch analysis.

Variable Map

First, in examining the final variable map for interpersonal tacit knowledge (see Figure 3), the distribution of items on the interpersonal

tacit knowledge measure seems to have sufficient distribution indicating items measuring various levels of tacit knowledge. Additionally, there is sufficient variability in the items, as evidenced by a wide distribution over the continuum (i.e., spanning up to 2 standard deviations [S and T] above and below the mean [M]). However, a lack of sufficient items near the top of the continuum results in the most able respondents not being adequately measured by this bank of items.

Referring to Figure 3, the graduate students are again highlighted in bold (ID#1-ID#6) on the right side of the variable map to illustrate how these individuals did as compared to the practicing superintendents. It is evident that some of the students did well on the measure for interpersonal tacit knowledge as compared to some of the practicing superintendents. This could again reflect the notion that some of the practicing superintendents have not yet acquired a high level of interpersonal tacit knowledge, or it could be unique to the individuals in this sample. This point is further explored in the discussion portion of the article.

Figure 3. Variable (person/item) map for interpersonal tacit knowledge

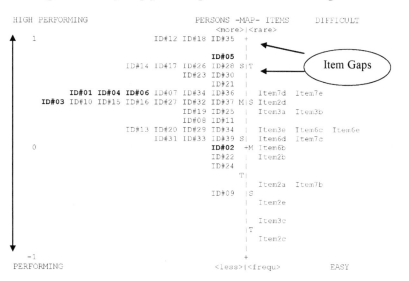

Reliability Estimates (Person and Item)

Reliability in Rasch measurement, as in traditional statistics, indicates "the degree to which test scores are free from measurement error" (Smith, 2004a, p. 94). Similar to their use in true score theory, reliability estimates range from zero to one and are reflective of the inter-item correlation among all of the responses for a particular item, and thus are used as a measure of internal consistency for scores on that item.

Winsteps reports reliability estimates for both persons and items. Linacre (2005) notes that person reliability is equivalent to traditional test reliability. Item reliability has no traditional equivalent. Person reliability is improved when there is a large enough sample size (i.e. greater than 30, Linacre, 1994) and there are sufficient numbers of items to target the full range of abilities being measured; whereas, item reliability estimates are improved when there are sufficient numbers of individuals with varying degrees of ability on the latent construct being measured, including having few or no gaps in items where persons are not being measured. Furthermore, Bradley and Sampson (2005) note,

Rasch measurement models provide a direct estimate of the modeled error variance for each estimate of a person's ability and an item's difficulty, providing a quantification of the precision of every person measure and item difficulty which can "be used to describe the range within which each item's 'true' difficulty or person's 'true' ability falls. (Smith, 2004a, p. 96). (p. 24)

The measure for interpersonal tacit knowledge demonstrated low person (.31) and item (.70) reliability estimates. Referring again to Figure 3, not all levels of ability are being measured (i.e., near the top of the continuum), as well as they could be. This finding also impacts overall item reliability, as there is not a sufficient range of ability levels (i.e., as evidenced by most people

being gathered around the mean). Linacre (1994) notes that measuring individuals who have a wide range of ability on the construct of interest will improve the item reliability estimate, because the items are tapping into a larger distribution.

DISCUSSION

Tacit knowledge is a form of procedural knowledge that is gained primarily from personal experience, rather than through formal training or instruction. Utilizing tacit knowledge to accomplish personally meaningful goals appears to be more important than simply acquiring it (Wagner & Sternberg, 1985). In this sense, more than simply procedural knowledge, tacit knowledge acts as a form of "metaprocedural knowledge" in that it operates at the cognitive level and helps individuals balance many competing demands in their pursuit of these goals. Lastly, tacit knowledge has been explored in the context of many professions, and typically operationalized and measured as intrapersonal (managing self), interpersonal (managing others), and organizational (managing tasks) (e.g., Colonia-Wilner, 1999). Because tacit knowledge is thought to be context specific, it typically requires the development of a new measure before it can be explored in the context of a new profession.

Nestor-Baker and Hoy (2001) conducted preliminary work in this area in the context of superintendents finding evidence that supported that tacit knowledge does take the form of intrapersonal, interpersonal, and organizational. In addition, they further posited that tacit knowledge could be broken down even further into 21 smaller categories, or organized according to different characteristics. In the current study, categories of tacit knowledge were organized according to the eight AASA standards discussed previously. Additional researchers have found that different types of tacit knowledge are more important for success depending upon the context. For example, Nestor-Baker and Hoy found that with school superintendents intrapersonal tacit knowledge is not as important for superintendent success as interpersonal tacit knowledge. Therefore, the final version of the TKIS reflects this finding in that there are more scenarios contained on the assessment for interpersonal than intrapersonal tacit knowledge. Although Nestor-Baker and Hoy's study identified the types of tacit knowledge present in the superintendency, an assessment was never developed (Nestor-Baker & Hoy, 2001).

Thus, the current study was primarily exploratory in nature as it was a first attempt to develop a ready-to-use, paper-and-pencil assessment of tacit knowledge in school superintendents that served as an effective measurement tool (according to the principles of the Rasch model) with solid theoretical rationale in measuring. Again, the usefulness of the Rasch model comes in the way of providing graphic (e.g., variable map), as well as statistical information (e.g., infit and outfit statistics) to help researchers evaluate and refine instrument reliability and validity. Rather than viewing Rasch as a replacement to traditional psychometrics, the researchers in the present study view use of the Rasch model as a complement to psychometrics; mainly because Rasch starts at the level of measurement and is assumed to be sample and item independent (McCamey, 2002). While exploratory in nature, the results of the current study offer promising insight into several important questions related to the development of an inventory that specifically measures tacit knowledge in the context of the superintendency.

Question 1: How well do items on the TKIS Measure Interpersonal Tacit Knowledge in Superintendents?

Reviewing the final results of the Rasch analysis for interpersonal tacit knowledge provides some interesting feedback for these 17 items. First, fit statistics for all of items are within the acceptable limits (i.e., between .6 and 1.5), thus the items are assumed to be measuring the same

latent construct of intrapersonal tacit knowledge. Given that the items were subjected to an earlier round of piloting and Rasch analysis, there exists stronger evidence supporting this conclusion because responses are assumed to be somewhat free of sample bias (Wright, 1977). However, further testing would need to be done before this becomes a foregone conclusion. Nonetheless, these initial findings do provide additional support to earlier findings that interpersonal tacit knowledge is present in this sample of school superintendents.

Second, while there does appear to be adequate variability in this bank of interpersonal tacit knowledge items, they are clustered within +1 to -1 logits of the mean suggesting a need for additional items to measure a broader range of abilities. Either this sample of superintendents truly resembles each other in their overall levels of tacit knowledge, or there are not enough items to measure at different ability levels to make a determination. Referring back to Figure 3, it is evident that there is a clear need to have additional items of increased difficulty included. Another way to interpret the lack of difficult items, as evidenced by the person mean (M) being equivalent to one standard deviation above the item difficulty mean (S), is that this sample of superintendent is simply more able than the items can measure. Again, without administering the assessment to another group, it is unclear which the case is. From a diagnostic standpoint, however, and in order to improve this assessment as a measure of interpersonal tacit knowledge in superintendents, one goal moving forward would be to generate additional items of increased difficulty and possibly administer them to the same group of superintendents, and if possible, another group, as well.

Third, there appears to be quite a bit of redundancy or overlap in some of the items (e.g., items 7d and 7e; 3a and 3b; 3e, 6c, and 6e; and 2a and 7b in Figure 3). Because these items fall on the item distribution at the same point, it is unclear whether they are redundant. Since one goal of good measurement is to include items that significantly contribute to measuring the construct of interest, in this case interpersonal tacit knowledge, Rasch modeling provides diagnostic information to help accomplish this. Whether the groups of items listed above are truly redundant (i.e., do not provide additional measurement information), or whether they simply measure at the same level of ability remains unclear. What is clear in this case, however, is that moving forward, additional information would need to be gathered about the items to answer the question of how adequately each item is functioning as an important measure of tacit knowledge. Lastly, and somewhat disappointing, results showed that the person reliability (.31) and item reliability (.70) for these items were found to be rather low. Linacre (1994) suggests that person reliability is improved when samples are more diverse. In this case, including a greater range of ability levels would probably improve the overall reliability estimate. Because this particular sample of superintendents demonstrates a relatively restricted range (i.e., clustered between -1 and +1 logit around the mean), it is difficult to determine whether the ability of this sample is truly homogenized, or if this simply reflects inadequate items to measure a greater range of ability levels. Linacre also notes that item reliability typically improves when items are measuring at all ability levels, as well as at the higher and lower levels.

In conclusion, to answer the research question, all 17 items functioned according to the expectations of the Rasch model; thus, fit statistics indicated that all 17 measured the theoretical construct of interest. As for the relative distribution of items and persons along the continuum, there was little variance in the distribution of persons and not enough tacit knowledge items measuring at the highest levels. In addition, there seemed to be some overlap or redundancy in the placement of items, which undoubtedly produced the unacceptable person and item reliabilities. Because of the limited range of ability in this sample, and the assumption that tacit knowledge develops with more experience, the sample used here does

not provide an adequate test for distinguishing this fact. On the whole, however, it appears that the efforts at each phase of the study drastically improved items included on the final measure as indicators of interpersonal tacit knowledge.

LIMITATIONS, STRENGTHS, AND FUTURE RESEARCH

Limitations

Limitations of the current study are best characterized as methodological issues—specifically, the sample used, the limited number of experts used to generate the scoring protocol, and the very nature of the scenarios and tacit knowledge items generated. Limitations in the sample include the limited number of graduate students (novices) available, as well as the relative homogenous nature of the sample of experienced superintendents used. While Linacre (1999) notes as few as 10 observations per response offers at least reasonably stable information for polytomously scored items, using at least 30 responses per response in order to provides even more useful and stable estimates (Linacre, 1994). Further, developing items in earlier phases would have increased access to a more diverse and nationally representative sample, providing a greater range of ability levels in which to test the items.

The second notable limitation in the current study is the generation of the scoring protocol used to assign point totals for each response. Fox (1994) used the responses from four experts to generate her scoring protocol, and then utilized agreement between at least three of the four as an additional type of quality control. While efforts were made to contact more than the two experts, the reality is that only two agreed to this aspect of the study. Clearly, future research should address this limitation by ensuring that more responses are utilized to generate the scoring protocol. Regardless, it should be noted that two experts agreeing on an item still provides some interrater reliability to the understanding of what is the "best" way to handle a situation.

Strengths

First of all, this study is the first attempt to develop a ready-to-use, paper-and-pencil tacit knowledge inventory for use exclusively with superintendents. Through the use of the Rasch model with the inclusion of two rounds of data collection and subsequent analysis, the items that were included on the final version of the TKIS should be considered unidimensional items that represent interpersonal tacit knowledge (Smith, 2004b). Secondly, development of scenarios and items were based on the eight professional standards established by the American Association of School Administrators, the best acceptable standards of practice in this area (Hoyle, 1993). Thus, while the efforts in the current study did not produce a completed assessment tool, the present study did at least contribute to this process.

Future Research

To further refine the TKIS as a measurement tool, future researchers should address three limitations in the current study. First, extra effort needs to go into the recruitment of a nationally representative sample spanning the full range of superintendent experience, from novices in graduate training programs to veteran superintendents. A nationally representative sample would provide a more accurate range of tacit knowledge present in the superintendency as a profession, which would improve overall generalizability and overall validity and reliability of the instrument by tapping the highest levels of expertise. Second, priority needs to be placed on recruiting the top superintendents (perhaps at the national level) in order to generate the scoring protocol (expert profile). Lastly, future researchers should consider including interviews with the experts who develop the

initial scenarios and response options in order to better develop these items up front. Perhaps, in addition to recruiting more experts, having some initial feedback during the development of initial tacit knowledge scenarios and items would have reduced the attrition of items at later stages of the present study, as well as having improved the item reliability estimates.

CONCLUSION

This study was an important next step to extend the work of Nestor-Baker and Hoy (2001) in introducing the construct of tacit knowledge into the context of the superintendency; that of designing an assessment tool specifically for use with superintendents. Development of the TKIS used an existing theoretical framework based primarily on the work of Sternberg and his colleagues, as well as use of the partial-credit Rasch model to develop and calibrate the tacit knowledge items contained on the assessment tool. Researchers and practitioners can employ the methodology in this study to produce quality instruments in a variety of contexts. Specific to this research area, the findings and methods (specifically the application of the Rasch model) in the current study offer exciting promise about the study of tacit knowledge in the superintendency. The hope is that by developing a valid and reliable measure, researchers can better understand how tacit knowledge develops and exactly how it influences decision-making in school superintendents. Ideally, in understanding the mechanisms involved in the acquisition and use of tacit knowledge, researchers and practitioners can improve the training and development of new superintendents and ultimately improve the future state of education.

REFERENCES

Ambrosini, V., & Bowman, C. (2001). Tacit knowledge: Some suggestions for operationalization. *Journal of Management Studies, 34,* 811–829. doi:10.1111/1467-6486.00260

Bond, T. G., & Fox, C. M. (2001). *Applying the Rasch model: Fundamental measurement in the human sciences.* Mahwah, NJ: Erlbaum.

Bradley, K. D., & Sampson, S. (2005, Spring). A case for using a Rasch model to assess the quality of measurement in survey research. *The Respondent,* 12-13.

Chi, M. T. H., Glaser, R., & Farr, M. J. (1988). *The nature of expertise.* Hillsdale, NJ: Erlbaum.

Chiu, Y., Fritz, S. L., Light, K. E., & Velozo, C. A. (2006). Use of item response analysis to investigate measurement properties and clinical validity of data for the Dynamic Gait Index. *Physical Therapy, 86*(6), 778–787.

Colonia-Wilner, R. (1999). Investing in practical intelligence: Ageing and cognitive efficiency among executives. *International Journal of Behavioral Development, 23,* 591–614. doi:10.1080/016502599383711

Dillman, D. A. (1978). *Mail and telephone surveys: The total design method.* New York: Wiley.

Ericsson, K. A., & Crutcher, R. J. (1990). The nature of exceptional performance. In Baltes, P. B., Featherman, D. L., & Lerner, R. M. (Eds.), *Life-span development and behavior,10* (pp. 187–217). Hillsdale, NJ: Erlbaum.

Fox, C. (1994). A practical knowledge inventory: Psychometric characteristics and validity of an assessment for nurses (Doctoral dissertation, Kent State University).

Fox, C. (1999). An introduction to the partial credit model for developing nursing assessments. *The Journal of Nursing Education, 38*(8), 340–346.

Fox, C. M., & Jones, J. A. (1998). Uses of Rasch modeling in counseling psychology research. *Journal of Counseling Psychology, 45*(1), 30–45. doi:10.1037/0022-0167.45.1.30

Grigorenko, E. L., Sternberg, R. J., & Strauss, S. (2006). Practical intelligence and elementary-school teacher effectiveness in the United States and Israel: Measuring the predictive power of tacit knowledge. *Thinking Skills and Creativity, 1*(1), 14–33. doi:10.1016/j.tsc.2005.03.001

Hambleton, R. (1992). Hambleton's 9 theses. *Rasch Measurement Transactions, 6,* 215–217.

Hedlund, J., Forsythe, G. B., Horvath, J. A., Williams, W. M., Snook, S., & Sternberg, R. J. (2003). Identifying and assessing tacit knowledge: Understanding the practical intelligence of military leaders. *The Leadership Quarterly, 14,* 117–140. doi:10.1016/S1048-9843(03)00006-7

Hoyle, J. (1993). *Professional standards for the superintendency.* Arlington, VA: American Association of School Administrators.

Hoyle, J. R., Bjork, L. G., Collier, V., & Glass, T. (2005). *The superintendent as CEO: Standards-based performance.* Thousand Oaks, CA: Corwin Press.

Leithwood, K. (1995). Cognitive perspectives on school leadership. *Journal of School Leadership, 5,* 115–135.

Leithwood, K., & Steinbach, R. (1995). *Expert problem solving: Evidence from school and district leaders.* Albany: State University of New York Press.

Linacre, J. M. (1990). Where does misfit begin? *Rasch Measurement Transactions, 3,* 80.

Linacre, J. M. (1994). Sample size and item calibration stability. *Rasch Measurement Transactions, 7,* 328.

Linacre, J. M. (2002a). What do infit and outfit, mean-square and standardized mean? *Rasch Measurement Transactions, 16,* 878.

Linacre, J. M. (2002b). Understanding Rasch measurement: Optimizing rating scale category effectiveness. *Journal of Applied Measurement, 3*(1), 85–106.

Linacre, J. M. (2004). *Winsteps Rasch measurement software version 3.51.*

Linacre, J. M. (2005). *WINSTEPS Rasch measurement computer program.* Chicago: Winsteps.com.

Linacre, J. M., & Wright, B. D. (1994). Chi-square fit statistics. *Rasch Measurement Transactions, 8,* 350.

Masters, G. N. (1982). A Rasch model for partial credit scoring. *Psychometrika, 47,* 149–174. doi:10.1007/BF02296272

McCamey, R. (2002 February 14-16). *A primer on the one-parameter Rasch model.* Paper presented at the meeting of the Annual Meeting of the Southwest Educational Research Association, Austin, TX.

Nestor-Baker, N. (2002). Knowing when to hold 'em and fold 'em: Tacit knowledge of place-bound and career-bound superintendents. *Journal of Educational Administration, 40*(3), 230–256. doi:10.1108/09578230210427163

Nestor-Baker, N., & Hoy, W. K. (2001). Tacit knowledge of school superintendents: Its nature, meaning, and content. *Educational Administration Quarterly, 37*(1), 86–129. doi:10.1177/00131610121969253

Nonaka, I. (1994). A dynamic theory of organizational knowledge creation. *Organization Science, 5*(1), 14–37. doi:10.1287/orsc.5.1.14

Polanyi, M. (1946). *Science, faith, and society.* Chicago: The University of Chicago Press.

Polanyi, M. (1966). *The tacit dimension.* Garden City, NY: Doubleday Anchor.

Polanyi, M. (1976). Tacit knowing. In Marx, M., & Goodson, F. (Eds.), *Theories in contemporary psychology* (2nd ed., pp. 330–344). New York: Macmillan.

Rasch, G. (1980). *Probabilistic models for some intelligence and attainment tests.* Chicago: The University of Chicago Press. (Original work published 1960)

Sampson, S., & Bradley, K. D. (2003). Rasch analysis of educator supply and demand rating scale data: An alternative to the true score model. *Research Methods; The Forum.* Retrieved February 21, 2009, from http://aom.pace.edu/rmd/2003forum.html

Smith, E. V. (2004a). Evidence for the reliability of measures and validity of measure interpretation: A Rasch measurement perspective. In Smith, E. V., & Smith, R. M. (Eds.), *Introduction to Rasch measurement* (pp. 93–122). Maple Grove, MN: JAM Press.

Smith, E. V. (2004b). Detecting and evaluating the impact of multidimensionality using item fit statistics and principal component analysis of residuals. In Smith, E. V., & Smith, R. M. (Eds.), *Introduction to Rasch Measurement* (pp. 575–600). Maple Grove, MN: JAM Press.

Sternberg, R. J., Forsythe, G. B., Hedlund, J., Horvath, J. A., Wagner, R. K., & Williams, W. M. (2000). *Practical intelligence in everyday life.* New York: Cambridge University Press.

Sternberg, R. J., & Hedlund, J. (2002). Practical intelligence, g, and work psychology. *Human Performance, 15*(1/2), 143–160. doi:10.1207/S15327043HUP1501&02_09

Sternberg, R. J., & Horvath, J. A. (Eds.). (1999). *Tacit knowledge in professional practice: Researcher and practitioner perspectives.* Mahwah, NJ: Erlbaum.

Sternberg, R. J., Nokes, C., Geissler, P. W., Prince, R., Okatcha, F., Bundy, D. A., & Grigorenko, E. L. (2001). The relationship between academic and practical intelligence: A case study in Kenya. *Intelligence, 29,* 401–418. doi:10.1016/S0160-2896(01)00065-4

Sternberg, R. J., Wagner, R. K., Williams, W. M., & Horvath, J. A. (1995). Testing common sense. *The American Psychologist, 50*(11), 912–927. doi:10.1037/0003-066X.50.11.912

Tang, W. K., Wong, E., Chiu, H. F. K., Lum, C. M., & Ungvari, G. S. (2005). The geriatric depression scale should be shortened: Results of Rasch analysis. *International Journal of Geriatric Psychiatry, 20,* 783–789. doi:10.1002/gps.1360

Tennant, A., McKenna, S. P., & Hagell, P. (2004). Application of Rasch analysis in the development and application of quality of life instruments. *Value in Health, 7*(1), 22–26. doi:10.1111/j.1524-4733.2004.7s106.x

Thornton, A. (2002 February 1). *A primer on the 2- and 3-parameter item response theory models.* Paper presented at the meeting of the Annual Meeting of the College of Education, University of North Texas, Educational Research Exchange, Denton, TX.

Wagner, R. K. (1987). Tacit knowledge in everyday intelligent behavior. *Journal of Personality and Social Psychology, 52,* 1236–1247. doi:10.1037/0022-3514.52.6.1236

Wagner, R. K., & Sternberg, R. J. (1985). Practical intelligence in real-world pursuits: The role of tacit knowledge. *Journal of Personality and Social Psychology, 49,* 436–458. doi:10.1037/0022-3514.49.2.436

Wagner, R. K., & Sternberg, R. J. (1991). Tacit knowledge: Its uses in identifying, assessing, and developing managerial talent. In Jones, J., Steffy, B., & Bray, D. (Eds.), *Applying psychology in business: The manager's handbook* (pp. 333–344). New York: Human Sciences Press.

Wright, B. D. (1977). Solving measurement problems with the Rasch model. *Journal of Educational Measurement, 14*(2), 97–166. doi:10.1111/j.1745-3984.1977.tb00031.x

Wright, B. D. (1997). A history of social science measurement. *Educational Measurement: Issues and Practice, 16*(4), 33–45. doi:10.1111/j.1745-3992.1997.tb00606.x

Wright, B. D., & Linacre, J. M. (2001). Glossary of Rasch measurement terminology. *Rasch Measurement Transactions, 15,* 824–825.

Wright, B. D., & Tennant, A. (1996). Sample size again. *Rasch Measurement Transactions, 9,* 468.

ENDNOTES

[1] In the larger study, the sampling frame consisted of 176 practicing superintendents and 15 graduate students from two superintendent preparation programs located in a southeastern state.

[2] Items were flagged as problematic if they were outside the acceptable range of .6 to 1.5.

This work was previously published in International Journal of Knowledge Management, Volume 5, Issue 3, edited by Murray E. Jennex, pp. 73-93, copyright 2009 by IGI Publishing (an imprint of IGI Global).

Section 4

Chapter 18

Exploring Qualitative Differences in Knowledge Sources:
A Study of Hierarchical Effects of Judgmental Confidence and Accuracy Performance

Carina Antonia Hallin
University of Stavanger, Norway

Torvald Øgaard
University of Stavanger, Norway

Einar Marnburg
University of Stavanger, Norway

ABSTRACT

Focusing on knowledge management (KM) and strategic decision making in service businesses through the constructs of strategic capital and knowledge sharing, the study investigates qualitative differences in domain-specific knowledge of frontline employees and executives. The study draws on cognitive theory and investigates the extend to which the knowledge of these subject groups is correct with respect to incorporating intuitive judgments by various employee groups into forecasting and following strategic decision making. The authors carried out this investigation through an exploratory study of the subject groups' confidence and accuracy (CA) performance in a constructed knowledge-based forecasting setting. The groups' intuitive judgmental performances were examined when predicting uncertain business and industry-related outcomes. The authors surveyed 39 executives and 38 frontline employees in 12 hotels. The analysis is based on a between-participants design. The results from this setting do not fully confirm findings in earlier CA studies. Their results indicate that there are no significant differences in the accuracy of executives (as experts) and frontline employees (as novices). Although executives dem-

DOI: 10.4018/978-1-60960-555-1.ch018

onstrate overconfidence in their judgments and frontline employees demonstrate underconfidence, in line with earlier CA theory of experts and novices, the differences we find are not significant. Similarly, the CA calibration performance difference between the two groups is not significant. They suggest, among other reasons, that our findings differ from earlier CA studies because of organizational politics and culture by power distance, social capital, misuse of knowledge and the size of the business.

INTRODUCTION

The literature of knowledge management has presented theories and empirical evidences on how knowledge is created, stored, retrieved, shared, and how it may be taken into practice. However, two dimensions have scarcely been addressed; namely how political, cultural, structural and ecological issues can restrain and promote various kind of knowledge (cf. Lawrence, Mauws, Dyck, & Kleysen, 2005), and the issue of qualitative differences in knowledge sources in terms of accuracy, i.e. how correct is the knowledge by various sources in an organization.

Focusing on the latter two dimensions, the emphasis in this study is on how knowledge assets may advance good strategic decision making by top management. In an increasingly uncertain and complex competitive business environment, the need for good strategic decisions is becoming increasingly important for service businesses. This can be seen as a result of major forces driving changes such as continual changes in customer expectations, continuous innovation and the growing internationalization of companies. Subsequently, accurate business forecasts to assist managerial strategic decision making is becoming progressively both more difficult and more important.

Scholars have pointed out the limitations of using solely statistical historical data as the ground for strategic decision making (Ghalia & Wang, 2000; Hogarth & Makridakis, 1981; Lawrence, Edmundson, & O'Connor, 1986; Lawrence, Goodwin, O'Connor, & Önkal, 2006; Wright & Ayton, 1987), and the role of intuition has been pointed out as crucial in forecasting and

following strategic decisions (Ghalia & Wang, 2000; Bennett, 1998; Lawrence et al., 2006). The important role of intuition in knowledge management is demonstrated in the Japanese approach to knowledge management (Nonaka & Takeuchi, 1995). In this line of thought, an organization's success is largely dependent on its social capital, which is shaped by the opinions and insights of the organization's employees through their everyday socialization (Smith, 2005). Nonaka and Takeuchi (1995) proposed that this socialization process is founded on the sharing of both tacit and explicit knowledge and that it is the starting point for new organizational knowledge creation. While explicit knowledge is founded on identifiable facts and is inherently independent of the individual, tacit knowledge is the rich and untapped knowledge that resides in individuals, which cannot be easily externalized as it is shaped by facts, cognitions, feelings and emotions. Building on Nosek's (2004) definitions of categories of organizational knowledge, Smith (2005) defines the tacit and explicit knowledge as the organization's strategic capital, which is shaped by employees' knowledge of changeable and unchangeable facts, opinions and insights through their everyday interactions. Such knowledge and impressions may be used as input in forecasting and strategic decision-making processes by top management in their usage of employees' judgmental and intuitive predictions and is likely to be crucial for the organization's capability to execute strategies successfully in dynamic environments.

Traditionally, executives are considered to be knowledge experts in strategic processes compared with subordinates because of their continuous access to, and handling of, strategic information (Lord & Maher, 1991, 1993). In service businesses, however, the role of frontline employees may be particularly important to strategic decision matters because of their continuous interaction and knowledge sharing with customers, managers, colleagues, employees from other competing businesses within the particular service industry and other interest groups. It is therefore reasonable to expect that important strategic information will be created at particularly two different hierarchical levels in the organization: top management level and at the operational level. However, this information is arguably qualitatively different from the other because it arrives from different knowledge sources resulting from different organizational roles and expectations (Walsh & Ungson, 1991), and will probably also, due to differences in hierarchical status, have a systematic different influence on the organization.

As a parallel to the knowledge management's emphasis on the importance of intuition for strategic decision making, research in metacognition and metamemory in relation to judgmental performance has flourished (e.g., Metcalfe & Shimamura, 1994; Metcalfe, 2000). The study of metamemory processes includes understanding the future judgmental performance of experts versus nonexperts resulting from the confidence with which they hold their knowledge and ability to learn. This theory relates particularly to confidence in the accuracy and comprehensiveness of individuals' memories when they make judgments about a particular event that occurred in the past without having had direct access to it (Brewer & Sampaio, 2006). The accuracy of a person's metamemory can be assessed by examining the relationship between a person's predicted and actual judgmental performance, known as the confidence–accuracy (CA) relationship (Bothwell et al., 1987) and by applying various levels of judgmental task difficulties into such an assessment (Brewer & Sampaio, 2006).

During the last decade, there has also been a growing body of literature on judgmental forecasting and performance related to experts' and lay peoples' confidence and accuracy biases in intuitive judgments (e.g., Brenner et al., 2005; Selart et al., 2006; Vaughan, 1979). The literature has addressed confidence–accuracy issues in cognitive psychology, focusing on: judgmental patterns of experts versus novices (Blais et al., 2005; Griffin & Tversky, 1992); psychology and aging (Touron & Hertzog, 2004); legal and criminological psychology in respect to eyewitness identification (Weber & Brewer, 2004); accounting and finance with a focus on auditor's judgments (Chung & Monroe, 2000); and forecasting, concentrating on probability judgments in combination with statistical and rational models (Hall & Rieck, 2001; Lawrence et al., 2006). These studies, many of them experimentally based, concentrate on calibration performance, which refers to the association between judgments of objective (accuracy) and subjective (confidence) probabilities of the occurrence of an event (Weber & Brewer, 2004, p. 157).

Despite a significant amount of research on judgmental forecasting and CA in laboratory studies, there are few studies so far that have attempted to investigate what effects the confidence and accuracy performance of professionals may have outside the lab for improving judgmental forecasts (Lawrence et al., 2006) as part of strategic decision making and as a consequence of qualitative differences of various employee groups as knowledge sources. Within the research setting of service businesses in a managerial versus employee context, we found no studies on CA.

Our aim is to improve information utilization and processing in strategic decision making; thus, we investigated judgmental CA performance of frontline personnel and executives in order to understand the differences in their intuitive judgmental patterns in uncertain industry-related and firm-related outcomes as related to socialization processes.

We addressed the following research questions: 1) What is the accuracy performance of the two subject groups for different judgmental task difficulties? 2) Are the two subject groups prone to overconfidence or underconfidence in their judgments? 3) What is the calibration performance of the groups? 4) Is there evidence that supports differences in the judgmental patterns between the groups, indicating that the roles as novices differ from those of experts, because of experts' rich knowledge of the industry data in question?

As an example of a service business setting, a survey was conducted of executives and frontline employees in hotel companies. We investigated their intuitive judgments of performance indicator results from 2004 for this industry, distinguishing different geographic proximity levels for several destinations.

Theory Review

In the following review we will first look into the concept of intuitive judgments. Thereafter we will present the relatively new concept of strategic capital within knowledge management which links knowledge management and the usage of knowledge for forecasting and following strategic decision making. We will then put forward theories on the qualitative differences of organizational knowledge sources by top managers and frontline personnel and the consequences these differences may have for intuitive judgmental performance for these groups. The theory review is finalized by reviewing previous research on CA judgmental performance by experts and novices and present theory on task difficulty.

Intuitive Judgments

The concept of intuition embraces a number of related meanings, and no universal definition of the concept exists (Agor, 1989). However, Vaughan (1979) summed up the general definitions of intuition that emerge from the literature, which in most cases contrast intuition in decision making with reason, rationality and logical decision-making processes. He states that intuition is "... knowing without being able to explain how we know" (p. 46). This definition is closely related to Polanyi's (1966, p. 4) discussion of tacit knowledge. As he puts it, "we can know more than we can tell". Tacit knowledge that is anchored in a highly individualized knowledge stock and practical know-how gathered through years of experiences within a specific knowledge domain (Bennett, 1998; Nonaka & Takeuchi, 1995; Polanyi, 1958, 1966; Wagner and Sternberg, 1985) is the breeding ground for intuitive processing and judgments (Bennett, 1998). Reber (1989) proposes that the same elements of focus in studies of complex knowledge-acquiring processes are also identified in studies of intuitive processes. While learning is characterized by an unconscious process and produces abstract knowledge, an intuitive thought is "the end product of an implicit learning experience" (Reber, 1989, p. 232). Intuitive judgments are, therefore, the results of the individual's acquisition of knowledge needed for a particular matter in order to make such intuitive judgments (Shirley & Langan-Fox, 1996). In other words, intuitive processing and judgments are the end product of one's tacit knowledge stock that is stored subconsciously, and intuition and tacit knowledge therefore seem to be interconnected in creating good decisions.

Although the majority of writers on intuition tend to agree that human intuition is driven by intense confidence in one's knowledge stock and intuitive feeling (Nisbett & Wilson, 1977), some authors (e.g., Bowers, 1987; Gilovich et al., 2002; Griffin & Tversky, 1992; Tversky & Kahneman, 1974; Vaughan, 1979) disagree about whether intuitive judgments include the possibility of mistakes.

Intuition may be conceptualized in two distinct ways: as holistic hunch and as automated expertise (Miller & Ireland, 2005). In the holistic hunch conceptualization, intuition corresponds to judgments or choices made through a subconscious synthesis of information drawn from diverse experiences and impressions. Information stored in memory is subconsciously combined in complex ways to produce judgments or choices that feel right; "gut feeling" is often used to describe the final choice (Bastick, 1982; Miller & Ireland, 2005).

Intuition as automated expertise, on the other hand, corresponds to the subconscious recognition of a familiar situation and is a straightforward application of previous learning related to that situation (Miller & Ireland, 2005). This form of intuition develops over time as relevant expertise and tacit knowledge are accumulated within a particular domain (ibid, 2005).

In recent years, there has been particular focus on intuitive judgments by experts versus novices as a result of their domain-specific knowledge (e.g., Lawrence et al., 2006). In strategic decision and forecasting research, it is quite common to warn against human intuitive judgments as a method (Lawrence et al., 2006). Nevertheless, over the past 30 years, there has been a growing acceptance of intuitive judgments in forecasting and a desire to learn how to blend judgments with statistical methods in order to advance accurate forecasts (Hogarth & Makridakis, 1981; Kahneman & Tversky, 1973; Lawrence et al., 2006; Wright & Ayton, 1987).

In the early 1970s, Kahneman and Tversky (e.g., 1972, 1973) introduced the theory of intuition, heuristics and biases in human judgment of frequencies and probabilities, which takes its point of departure in the theory of bounded rationality (e.g., Edwards, 1961). Their research aim was to understand how intuitive judgments can be debiased and improved rather than accepting intuitive predictions or rejecting them.

They revealed that not only are the models of intuitive judgment simpler and more efficient because of their basic computations of the mind in comparison with the demands of rational models, but they are also categorically different (Gilovich et al., 2002, p. 3).

Strategic Capital

Along with growing acceptance on the use of intuitive judgments in strategic decision making and forecasting, the construct of strategic capital has been introduced in the literature dealing with knowledge and strategic management as a way to link the use and management of knowledge assets to strategic decision making (Hughes & Morgan, 2007; Smith, 2005, 2006). Smith (2006, p. 195) defines the organization's strategic capital as "the capability to successfully plan and execute strategies" and suggests that capability depends on the rate of explicit and tacit knowledge sharing of the organization's employees (Smith, 2006, p. 195).

Building on Fitzgerald's (1992) views of knowledge, Nosek (2004, p. 56) proposes that both explicit and tacit knowledge are highly relevant as input in strategic planning processes and for the organization's ability to act. He refers to explicit knowledge as static knowledge, which is developed from knowledge of unchanging facts and which is recognized as being located in the world as discoverable 'truths' independent of the knower and which is identical to explicit knowledge. The other type of knowledge is dynamic, which is created from changeable facts, cognitions, feelings, emotions, and which is of tacit in nature and dependent on the knower. In knowledge sharing between people, individuals tend to draw on both static and dynamic knowledge.

The amount of knowledge sharing capabilities between organizational members is essential for the advancement of strategic capital (Smith, 2005), hence from a knowledge management perspective, it is relevant for management to acknowledge and nurture those factors that result in employees' positive attitudes to knowledge sharing. A positive knowledge sharing climate is influenced by several factors, but three factors seem to be particularly prevalent. These are related to the organization's social capital (Hoffman, Hoelscher & Sherif, 2005; Smith, 2006), organizational culture (e.g., Al-Alawi et al., 2007; Hall & Goody, 2007; Janz

& Prasarnphanich; Schein, 1985) and company size (e.g., Ruiz-Mercader et al., 2006).

The social capital is formed by organizational members' relationship with each other. The social capital may in this context be defined as "the set of resources, tangible or virtual, that accrue to a corporate player through the player's social relationships facilitating the attainment of goals" (Gabbay & Lenders, 1999, p. 3). Social capital may be low as a result of distrust and lack of openness among employees or strong as a consequence of individuals' close relationships.

Organizational culture is acknowledged to be crucial for the development of effective knowledge management and the organization's strategic capital because it determines values, beliefs and work systems that can encourage or impede social capital and knowledge creation. (Alavi & Leidner; 2001; Gold, Malhotra & Segars, 2001; Janz & Prasarnphanich, 2003). In the same fashion, Hall and Goody (2007) proposed that power issues as a part of the management politics and culture are a major obstacle for knowledge sharing, and influence the rate of knowledge sharing between management and staff members.

Another factor that may especially impede the rate of knowledge sharing and knowledge capturing is the size of the company. Ruiz-Mercader, Merõno-Cerdan and Sabater-Sánchez (2006) proposed that in smaller and medium-sized enterprises (SMEs), knowledge capturing and learning are more likely to happen in more informal and less complex ways than in major companies, thus enhancing knowledge sharing among personnel.

In order to advance strategic decision-making processes, a particular challenge for top management is to establish a more employee-inclusive routine for effectively collecting, sharing and exploring the qualitative differences in knowledge needed to implement strategic actions (Smith, 2005). Moreover, it is relevant to understand the implications of top management using such knowledge in strategic decision making in terms of qualitative differences in knowledge sources by various employee groups.

In every service company, frontline employees in particular accumulate both static and dynamic knowledge. In their daily knowledge sharing and interactions with diverse interest groups, they receive impressions of both changeable facts and unchangeable facts that provide a breeding ground for intuitive judgments. Such intuitive judgments by organizational members are of potentially strategic importance to management in terms of their knowledge of the particular service industry and the state of the business. Yet, frontline employees' knowledge is assumed to be qualitatively different from executives' knowledge, and this may be seen as a result of individual, political, cultural, transformation and ecological factors in the organization.

Assumptions about Qualitative Differences in Knowledge Sources and Intuitive Judgments

The above arguments indicate that knowledge of strategic importance may not be attributed to management alone. In service businesses it is also reasonable to expect that frontline employees – those who daily interact with guests/customers and daily observe how the service delivery system works – also possess important knowledge that can contribute information for future predictions and strategic decisions. In fact, it is this *socialization process*, i.e. the learning which occurs in the daily work that Nonaka and Takeuchi (1995) point out as the initial source of knowledge creating.

In the classical work of Walsh & Ungson (1991) on organizational memory there is given a systematic approach of sources for knowledge generation and memory. Organizational members develop cognitive heuristics based on their daily experiences and observations. Walsh & Ungson (1991) state that internal in the organization there may be found five sources of "memory":

the individual, culture, transformations, structure and ecology.

It may be assumed that there are systematic differences in knowledge between top managers and frontline employees in a service organization: Top managers often have more education and longer work experience than frontline employees. What concerns culture, differences will probably mostly be related to the cultural information distributed in the organization (Schein, 1985) and the rate of knowledge sharing between organizational members (e.g., Al-Alawi et al., 2007; Hall & Goody, 2007; Janz & Prasarnphanich), and then particularly across ranks. Organizational structure provides implications for role behavior such as what organizational members expect from each other as a result of their positional status (i.e. the position as frontline employee versus the position as manager). Besides whom gives orders to whom, role behavior also defines external contacts. The external contacts of top managers will embrace other top decision makers while frontline employees will probably have most contact with peers in other parts of the company and colleagues from other service businesses. It is also reasonable to expect that the ecology by the physical structure of the organization (Walsh & Ungson, 1991, p. 65) in respect to size of the business (i.e. a chain hotel corporation versus an individual hotel) will contribute to qualitative differences in knowledge assets for strategic decision making. However, above all factors 'transformation' is likely to represent the major qualitative differences in memory sources. Transformation is defined as an input that is transformed to an output (Walsh & Ungson, 1991, p. 65). The assumption underlying transformation processes is that the retrieval of past information resulting from past transformations guides current transformation processes. In cases where individuals carry out a more analytical approach to problem solving, the transformation process tends to be familiar. On the other hand, if situations, or the task at hand is not familiar, individuals tend rely on experiences, wisdom and intuition which direct problem solving behavior. This complexity characterized by a switch between personal experiences of what seems to be familiar problem on hand, and what is not, is likely to result in the misuse of knowledge (Walsh & Ungson, 1991). In many instances, decisions may results in that a routine decision response is carried out rooted in previous experiences and an analytical approach when actually a non-routine response is required due to a novel situation that is not recognized. The opposite situation is also likely to occur; and in both situations it results in reduced precision in intuitive forecasting and following strategic decisions. In making daily decisions, mangers are habituated with relying on their memory capabilities and carrying out the switch between familiar and unfamiliar situations and may therefore be at particular risk of making wrong decisions.

The daily tasks of top management and employees are not only very different, but in addition to their daily tasks, one of the primary tasks that top managers have is to predict future development internally and externally and make strategic decisions according to these predictions. Due to this last difference, it is reasonable to consider top managers experts in strategic judgments and further consider frontline employees novices in the same respect.

Prior Research on CA Performance of Experts and Novices

Over the past 25 years, a large number of studies have been conducted investigating experts' versus nonexperts' judgmental predictive performance (Lawrence et al., 2006). Most of these studies were experimental and laboratory based, concentrating on probability forecasting in meteorology (Murphy & Winkler, 1984), predictions of earnings (Whitecotton, 1996), exchange rates (Önkal et al., 2003; Wilkie-Thomson et al., 1999), sports games outcomes (Andersson et al., 2005) and stock prices (Muradoglu & Önkal, 1994). In all of these cases, experts provided better probability forecasts than nonexperts.

Experimental studies in the intuition and heuristics tradition have focused on both experts' and laypeople's confidence in probabilistic judgments about financial, medical and personal outcomes. These especially concern the questions of when such probability judgments are likely to be calibrated and how they might be improved (Brenner et al., 2005). In intuitive judgments of probability and frequency, Kahneman and Tversky (1973) and Tversky and Kahneman (1974) have revealed that people use heuristics that are responsive to some features of the information setting but not to others; hence heuristics (such as availability, representativeness, anchoring and adjustments) produce predictable patterns of calibration and miscalibration in judgments (Brenner et al., 2005; Griffin & Tversky, 1992, Massey & Wu, 2005).

Studies of race oddsmakers (Griffith, 1949; Hausch et al., 1981) and expert bridge players (Keren, 1987) have revealed that intuitive judgments by experts are better calibrated than those of novices when they have rich knowledge of the predictability case in question. Yet, when predictability is low, experts have a tendency to be more overconfident than lay people with limited knowledge of the case in question. In areas of financial and economic forecasting, it is also observed that "the combination of overconfidence and optimism is a potent brew, which causes people to overestimate their knowledge, underestimate risks and exaggerate their ability to control events" (Kahneman & Riepe, 1998, p. 54). Studies of managers predicting industry-related and firm-related outcomes have also revealed that experts tend to be overconfident in their judgments (Russo & Schoemaker, 1992).

Task Difficulty

Experimental studies on metamemory (Brewer & Sampaio, 2006) reveal that confidence and accuracy performance depends on the difficulty of the judgmental task. Hence, one way to examine the relationship between confidence and accuracy is to examine survey items that differ in level of difficulty. If participants' confidence is related to the accuracy of their memory, they should demonstrate greater confidence in easy tasks and less confidence in difficult ones.

In the following section, we present the development of our propositions based on theories of accuracy, confidence and calibration performance of executives versus novices.

RESEARCH HYPOTHESES

Accuracy

Judgments are knowledge-dependent because individuals must recall necessary information from their memory in order to perform judgmental tasks (Nelson et al., 1995), hence the match between the information recalled and the task requirement is critical to the accuracy of judgment outcomes.

Findings in studies of the effects on accuracy of audit experience reveal that experience builds up an auditor's abilities to process information, to make mental comparisons between alternative solutions and to take subsequent action (Gibbins, 1984). Libby (1995) suggests that inexperienced auditors have not developed the same abilities as experienced auditors who draw on complex memory structures of information on which they base their decisions.

The consequence of this for executives in the service industry, who engage in strategic decision making in their daily work, is that they are better at judging events accurately than frontline personnel who do not engage in strategic decision making to the same extent. This assumption leads to the following proposition.

Proposition 1: Executives produce more accurate judgments for all difficulty levels of strategic judgmental tasks compared with frontline employees.

Confidence

Within academic psychological literature, the conviction that overconfidence is a factor exercising profound influence on human biases in judgments under uncertainty is generally acknowledged. According to Griffin and Tversky (1992), people tend to attach too much weight to the strength of evidence (for instance, how well a candidate did in an interview) in relation to the actual credibility of that type of evidence (which in this case is limited insight gained from a single interview).

Several studies have revealed the tendency to bias toward overconfidence in judgments. For example, von Winterfeldt and Edwards (1986, p. 539) assert that overconfidence in judgment is a "reliable and reproducible finding". This is supported by Yates (1990, p. 94), who states that "it is often believed that people's judgments are routinely overconfident".

Shiller (2000, p. 142) observed investor behavior in the stock market and commented that "some basic tendency toward overconfidence appears to be a robust human character". Yet Weinstein (1980) concludes that one of the common reasons people overestimate likelihoods of events is that they are generally optimistic about desirable events.

Another significant factor in biases in human judgments is the characteristic of underconfidence, which is a phenomenon that follows the classical Bayesian studies of conservatism addressed by, for example, Phillips and Edwards (1966), who conclude that people tend to overuse the middle values of a given probability scale (e.g., near 0.5) and underuse the extreme values on the scale (near 0 and 1). Accordingly, overconfidence and underconfidence are common patterns in intuitive judgments.

Prior experience is found to influence confidence in judgments. Fazio and Zanna (1978) found that inexperienced decision makers (novices) demonstrated lower confidence levels than experienced decision makers (experts). In comparison with inexperienced decision makers, experienced decision makers' accumulation of focused, domain-specific or task-related knowledge means that their behavior concerning a task within their particular knowledge domain may lead to greater confidence, because the task is subsequently repeated. For the most part, experts tend to be overconfident and novices tend to be underconfident when judging tasks they find difficult.

It is therefore expected that executives in the service industry, who work with strategic decision making on a regular basis, will have greater confidence in judgments concerning tasks related to strategic issues. This discussion leads to the following proposition.

Proposition 2: Executives demonstrate overconfidence for all difficulty levels of strategic judgmental tasks compared with frontline employees, who demonstrate underconfidence.

Calibration

The attitude of the decision maker toward the judgmental task plays an important role in judgmental performance. The ideal is when decision makers who demonstrate low degrees of accuracy in tasks subsequently demonstrate a low degree of confidence (Chung & Monroe, 2000). However, ratings of confidence in forecasting tasks are very rarely perfectly calibrated with accuracy of judgments. There is often a mismatch between attitude and behavior (Chung & Monroe, 2000, p. 137).

Perfect calibration in probability judgments is said to occur when each set of events assigned a common probability judgment, p, is in fact associated with a corresponding relative frequency, p, (Brenner et al., 2005, p. 64). In other words, calibration is a measure of the correspondence between forecast probabilities or frequencies and the realized proportion of accurate predictions and over/underconfidence, depending on the task structure used (Lawrence et al., 2006). Outcomes of overconfidence, underconfidence and accuracy that indicate calibration performance are often presented in an index of subjects' probability assessments, either exceeding or falling short of the attained proportion of correct answers to the events predicted (Lawrence et al., 2006).

Given our preceding discussion on confidence, accuracy and calibration, it is expected that executives are better calibrated than frontline personnel in their CA performance. This is expressed in the following proposition.

Proposition 3: Executives' accuracy in judgments and confidence in knowledge are better calibrated compared with frontline employees.

In the following section, we will describe our methodology, sample of participants, research setting, material and procedures, research design, measures and data analysis.

METHODOLOGY

The Sample of Participants

The survey sample in our study consisted of 77 participants. Thirty-nine of these were hospitality executives who were involved in strategic decision making on a regular basis for their hotel companies. The executives were general managers, hotel managers and functional managers such as human resource managers, key account managers, sales managers, revenue managers and some front office managers. The 38 frontline personnel worked at front desks in the hotel companies. However, only 37 frontline personnel completed the actual survey quiz.

We assumed that the frontline personnel were novices, while the executives were experts. As discussed, frontline employees do not participate in strategic decision making to the same extent as executives in service businesses. It was therefore

assumed that frontline personnel and executives had received different dosages of strategic information at the point of observation. However, in order to group executives in the study as experts and frontline employees as novices, we carried out a manipulation check of their experience of prior knowledge of the type of tasks addressed in the survey quiz. These results are presented in the empirical results.

Both executives and frontline personnel were recruited to our study through personal contact with executives at the hotels included in the study.

Research Setting

The sample of businesses in the study comprised of 12 hotels in Norway. These 12 hotels were drawn from a list of hotels in the city of Stavanger (Stavanger Travel, 2006). All the hotel managers who were contacted and asked to take part in the study volunteered to participate.

The hotels were selected based on their size expressed through the number of employees. We chose size as a criterion for selection of the individual hotel to ensure homogeneity in the sample of hotels. The hotels had between 50 and 250 employees and were therefore medium-sized businesses according to the European Commission definition of SME. The number of employees at the hotels was assumed to play an important role in the division of work among employees and in the amount of accumulated strategic knowledge by frontline employees (Ruiz-Mercader et al., 2006).

The single industry, homogenous company size and homogenous surroundings (single city) of the sample should reduce error variance and thus improve the power of the study. The similarity of the respondents could imply that certain response styles are dominant, but because we measure the dependent variable using a number of different methods, that should not influence the findings.

Material and Procedure

A survey quiz[1] with 43 questions was administered to the participants at their workplace. Participants were asked to take a 15-minute quiz about the hotel industry and performance indicator results for different pairs of destinations from the year 2004. Participants were told to rank orders of two alternatives of economic performance of the lodging industry at the local, regional and European level and then indicate their confidence level in their rankings. The participants had no access to aids when filling out the survey and sat in meeting rooms in the hotels while taking the quiz. We observed the participants while they took the quiz in order to ensure that none of them communicated with each other about their answers.

Design

The source of inspiration for our research design was derived from a study designed by Griffin and Tversky (1992). The present study was characterized by a between-participants design, and both executives and frontline personnel received identical tasks. Task difficulty was operationalized using different performance indicators for this particular service industry and the geographic proximity of results for different destinations in Norway and Europe. In the hotel industry, widely used performance measures are: average room revenue, average RevPar[2] and average occupancy

rate (Horwath Consulting, 2005). Task difficulty in terms of geographic proximity was operationalized using newer economic geographic theory on knowledge formation (Amin & Cohendet, 2005), which provides evidence concerning the importance of geographic proximity between individuals to the transfer of knowledge. According to this theory, local knowledge formation is distinguished from global knowledge formation, suggesting that actors within a local geographic area tend to draw on the knowledge generation of other actors in that area, thus enhancing knowledge formation. While knowledge exchange and relational proximity within a local milieu is likely to enhance actors' knowledge of events in a local area, knowledge exchanges based on long distance and knowledge generation stemming from global events occur less frequently and more formally and often result in a lower domain-specific knowledge (Amin & Cohendet, 2005).

To ensure a representative sampling of performance indicator results for different geographical proximity levels for the three industrial performance indicators, two pairs of destinations for each different geographic level from 2004 were selected at random (i.e., European cities, Norwegian counties and Norwegian cities). This resulted in a matrix of 18 paired destinations as presented in Table 1. The majority of paired destinations and performance results of room revenue, RevPar and occupancy rate at the different geographic levels were drawn from different lists presented

Table 1. Judgmental tasks: Paired destinations performance indicators

Geographic Proximity Level	Performance Indicator 1 (Room Revenue)	Performance Indicator 2 (RevPar)	Performance Indicator 3 (Occupancy Rate)
European city level	Copenhagen – Glasgow 2004 Amsterdam – Brussels 2004	Berlin – Amsterdam 2004 Frankfurt – Copenhagen 2004	Edinburgh – Brussels 2004 Glasgow – Stockholm 2004
Domestic county level	Buskerud – Nordland 2004 Aust-Agder – Sør-Trøndelag 2004	Nord-Trøndelag – Hedmark 2004 Troms – Møre-Romsdal 2004	Hordaland – Østfold 2004 Finmark – Møre-Romsdal 2004
Domestic city level	Trondheim – Bergen 2004 Kristiansand – Bergen 2004	Tromsø – Oslo 2004 Tromsø – Trondheim 2004	Trondheim – Bergen 2004 Stavanger – Bergen 2004

in the Norwegian Hotel Study of 2005 (Horwath Consulting, 2005, pp. 7, 12, 34). For results concerning RevPar at national level, room revenue at regional level and occupancy rate at regional level, we used accommodation statistics from Statistics Norway.

To ensure differences in task difficulties of performance indicators 1, 2 and 3 and the three geographic levels, we carried out a manipulation check and asked subjects to rate their prior knowledge of results for diverse performance indicators and for different geographic proximity levels. Subjects were asked to rate their prior sense of knowledge for each type of task (on a scale from 1 to 7, 1 being no knowledge at all and 7 being well aware).

Measures

The dependent variables used in the study were: accuracy in judgments of tasks, confidence in the accuracy of participants' judgments and CA calibration performance.

The independent variables were based on accuracy tasks addressed in Table 1 and a confidence scale. Accuracy was measured using performance indicator results for different indicators and for different geographic proximity levels. Subjects were asked to choose which of the destinations in each pair had achieved the highest performance results in 2004 for different indicators. After each task, we tested the subjects' confidence in their answers, employing a seven-point confidence scale developed by Brewer and Sampaio (2006). On the scale, 1 was labeled as totally uncertain (a guess) and 7 was labeled as absolutely certain. Participants were instructed to tick 1 if they had absolutely no confidence that their judgments of events were correct and to tick 7 to indicate that they were totally confident that their judgments were correct.

Data Analysis

To test the participants' performance on manipulation tasks, accuracy of judgmental tasks, confidence in their knowledge and calibration performance, descriptive analyses and paired samples statistics were performed using SPSS version 15. Our analytical approach and data presentation was inspired by Griffin & Tversky (1992).

RESULTS

Manipulation Checks

To test the validity of the classes, "expert" for executives and "novice" for frontline personnel, we conducted a t-test of the differences in prior knowledge of tasks between groups. Frontline personnel had a prior knowledge score of M = 3.18, N = 35 of the tasks, while executives had a score of M = 3.69, N = 39. The difference is significant (p <.05) and supports our assumption that the sampled frontline personnel were novices and that the executives were experts.

The manipulation check of the validity of diverse difficulty levels between judgmental tasks was performed using a paired samples t-test. The results of this manipulation check are presented in Table 2.

As the results for the paired performance indicators and the different geographic proximity levels revealed, there were significant differences (p <.05) between the groups' prior knowledge of tasks in 5 out of 6 types of task. The results for indicators 1 and 3 were not significant (t < 2, ns). It should be mentioned that these results indicate only some tendencies because they address subjects' perceptions of their own knowledge, while the actual results of the survey quiz reveal the groups' actual performance across tasks of varying degrees of difficulty.

Table 2. Prior knowledge of task categories

Pairs	Tasks	Mean	N	Sig.
Performance Indicators				
Pair 1	Indicator 1 – Indicator 2	3.64 3.05	74	.000
Pair 2	Indicator 1 – Indicator 3	3.64 3.66	74	.836
Pair 3	Indicator 2 – Indicator 3	3.05 3.66	74	.000
Geographic Proximity				
Pair 1	European cities – Domestic counties	3.14 3.50	74	.013
Pair 2	European cities – Domestic cities	3.14 3.71	74	.000
Pair 3	Domestic counties – Domestic cities	3.50 3.71	74	.009

Participants and Their Job Experience

In the sample of executives and frontline personnel, 67.5% were female and 32.5% were male. The ages of the participants ranged from 18 to 62 years, M = 34.07. The age of front personnel in the sample was M = 29.53 years, while that of executives was M = 38.26.

The frontline personnel's full-time work experience in the hospitality and tourism industry was M = 6.68 years, SD = 6.58 for full-time work and M = 4.29 years and SD = 2.07 for part-time work. For executives, their full-time job experience in the industry was M = 11.26 years and SD = 9.17, while their part-time job work experience was M = 5.36 years and SD = 3.27.

Judgmental Accuracy

We test Proposition I in this section. This proposition postulates that executives demonstrate more accurate judgments at all difficulty levels of strategic judgmental tasks compared with frontline employees.

The testing of this proposition was twofold, using t-tests. First, we tested accuracy in mean judgments for results of different types of industrial performance indicators. Then we examined accuracy in mean judgments for industrial performance indicator results for different geographic proximity levels.

In Figure 1, we have plotted the accuracy of the respondents' judgmental accuracy performance. Although executives seemed to be more accurate than frontline employees for every judgmental task, the differences are not significant. However, looking at the statistical significance of the results between these two groups, the values in mean difference between executives (N = 39) and frontline employees (N = 37) were not significant for occupancy rate (52.99 versus 49.55, t < 2, ns), RevPar (55.98 versus 53.15, t < 2, ns) and room revenue (44.02 versus 42.34, t < 2, ns).

When we turn to the judgmental accuracy grouped by geographic proximity, the differences between the two groups is once again not significant. Yet, the results plotted in Figure 2 indicate an interesting change of pattern in that the executives do not perform better than frontline personnel at the most difficult prior perceived task (assessed in the manipulation test) which concerns European cities. Proposition 1 is therefore not supported.

Figure 1. Average accuracy of judgments of results for different performance indicators

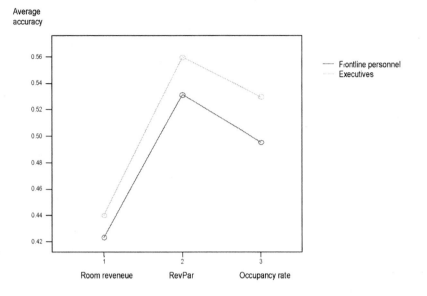

Confidence

Proposition 2 suggests that executives will be over-confident for all judgmental tasks compared with frontline employees, who will be underconfident. To test this proposition, we conducted a t-test.

We investigated each of the groups' judgmental behavior patterns in terms of their tendencies toward over/underconfidence by subtracting mean accuracy values from mean confidence ratings for each task group. Next, we tested the significant difference between task difficulty for

Figure 2. Average accuracy of judgments of performance indicator results for different geographic proximity levels

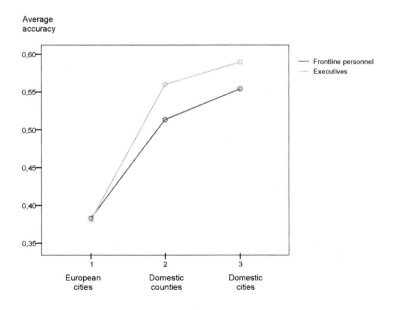

Table 3. Over/underconfidence of frontline employees' judgments of tasks

n = 37	room rev	revpar	occupancy rate	european cities	domestic counties	domestic cities
Confidence	43.82	39.77	42.34	41.25	38.42	46.27
Accuracy	42.34	53.15	49.55	38.29	51.35	55.41
Conf – Acc	1.48	(–)13.38	(–)7.21	2.96	(–)12.93	(–)9.14

Table 4. Over/underconfidence of executives' judgments of tasks

N = 39	Room Rev	RevPar	Occupancy Rate	European Cities	Domestic Counties	Domestic Cities
Confidence	55.37	49.76	56.29	47.44	51.53	62.45
Accuracy	44.02	55.98	52.99	38.03	55.98	58.97
Conf – Acc	11.35	(–)6.22	3.3	9.41	(–)4.45	3.48

each subject group before we proceeded to test differences between the two subject groups for the confidence minus accuracy results.

In Tables 3 and 4, mean values are presented for confidence ratings, accuracy, and results for over/underconfidence of frontline employees' and executives' judgments of all tasks.

Frontline employees' judgments of tasks exhibited underconfidence in 4 out of 6 tasks. However, as for the first group of tasks concerning performance indicators (room revenue, RevPar and occupancy rate), the results indicated that frontline employees only demonstrated significant underconfidence for RevPar in comparison with room revenue (–13.38 versus 1.48, p <.05). For the second group of tasks, with respect to geographic proximity, the statistical results exhibited significant underconfidence for domestic counties versus European cities (–12.93 versus 2.96, p <.05) and for domestic cities versus European cities (–9.14 versus 2.96, p <.05).

On the other hand, executives were overconfidence in four out of six instances. Their confidence ratings exhibited overconfidence in 4 out of 6 tasks. This tendency to overconfidence is also supported in the statistical results, which demonstrated overrated confidence by executives in their ratings of room revenue versus RevPar

(11.35 versus –6.22, p <.05) and of room revenue versus occupancy rate (11.35 versus 3.3, p <.05). Moreover, there was a significant overconfidence in executives' ratings of accuracy judgments of European cities versus domestic counties (9.41 versus –4.45, p <.05).

Although the preceding results demonstrated a tendency to overconfidence by executives and a tendency to underconfidence by frontline employees, the differences in the confidence–accuracy values between frontline personnel and executives, as presented in the third row of Table 3 and 4, needed to be tested.

A t-test revealed that there were no significant differences between executives and frontline personnel for any of the tasks in their over/underconfidence ratings (1.48 versus 11.35; –13.38 versus –6.22; –7.21 versus 3.3; 2.96 versus 9.41; –12.93 versus –4.45; –9.14 versus 3.48 (t < 2, ns). Consequently, we conclude that Proposition 2 is not supported.

Calibration Performance

In the following section, we test Proposition 3, in which it is postulated that executives are better calibrated with respect to their total accuracy and

Table 5. Differences in overall average calibration performance of the groups

Groups	Confidence/Accuracy	Mean	SD
Executives (N = 39)	Confidence Accuracy Actual difference in scale points	53.81 51.00 2.81	18.35 10.65
Frontline personnel (N = 37)	Confidence Accuracy Actual difference in scale points	41.98 48.35 (−)6.37	17.98 10.87

confidence performance compared with frontline employees.

An independent samples t-test of the overall confidence–accuracy value as the dependent variable was performed on the two groups, in order to investigate which group demonstrated the best calibration performance.

The mean values of total accuracy and total confidence were compared for each group, as presented in Table 5. Figure 3 illustrates how the calibration performance for the groups' answers for both accuracy and confidence are scattered in comparison with the linear, fictive and perfect calibration line. The results in Table 5 indicate that the actual difference between them in CA calibration performance is only 9.18 scale points (−6.37 for novices versus 2.81 for executives). This difference between the groups was not significant

($t < 2$, ns) according to a t-test. We can thereby conclude that Proposition 3 is not supported.

DISCUSSION

In this study we empirically tested the qualitative differences in knowledge sources between executives and frontline personnel in service businesses. The study is grounded in knowledge management and cognitive theory with emphasis on investigating the accuracy of knowledge in organizations. The purpose of the study is to bridge the existing gaps in knowledge management literature between judgmental forecasting and following strategic decisions and the application of knowledge assets to advance good strategic decision making.

Figure 3. Scatter plot of differences in calibration performance between groups

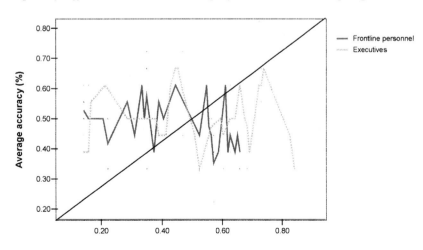

We proposed the new construct of strategic capital within the literature of knowledge management as a way to bridge this gap (Hughes & Morgan, 2007; Smith, 2005, 2006), and emphasized knowledge sharing of tacit and explicit knowledge, social capital and culture as factors contributing to the formation of strategic capital. Focusing on the assumptions of differences in domain-specific knowledge and intuitive judgmental performance by executives and frontline employees, we explored the qualitative differences by hierarchical effects of judgmental CA performance of these groups. Our study estimated the effects of the groups' judgments of strategic tasks related to uncertain business- and industry related outcomes by a survey quiz carried out in real field settings.

We sampled 12 hotel companies as the research setting and the sample of participants included 39 executives classified as "experts" and 38 frontline employees classified as "novices". The assumption of this classification was confirmed in a manipulation check prior to the actual survey questions which indicated that executives had significantly more sense of prior knowledge of tasks than did frontline employees. The subjects were asked to assess performance indicator results from 2004 for this particular industry according to varying levels of task difficulty by three different performance indicators: room revenue, RevPar and occupancy rate, and for different pairs of European cities, domestic counties and domestic cities in Norway. Subjects' prior knowledge of tasks was also tested in a manipulation test to control for subjects' perception of uncertainty in the judgmental tasks but at the same time to ensure they would draw on metamemory processes (Brewer & Sampaio, 2006) where they are likely to experience a sense of knowing. This assumption was confirmed about prior knowledge of tasks as subjects only had a mean prior knowledge score of tasks with M = 3.18 for frontline employees and M = 3.69 for executives using a seven-point scale.

Manipulation checks were also carried out for task difficulty, which revealed a tendency toward differences in perception of difficulty among different performance indicators for different geographic proximity levels.

Participants' actual accuracy of knowledge and confidence in their knowledge were tested by conducting a survey with a number of paired destinations and asking them to rank which of the destinations achieved highest performance for several performance indicators. They were then asked to rate how confident they were in their own judgments for each pair of destinations (tasks).

In the following section, we will first discuss our findings from the perspective of our three propositions in conjunction with earlier studies of CA. We will then proceed to discuss practical implications for knowledge management and strategic capital applications, before we continue to discuss implications for the assumptions of qualitative differences in knowledge sources in service organizations. We will then turn our focus towards considerations concerning the validity of the study before we finalize our discussion in which we consider future research in knowledge management and cognitive theory with specific focus on the area of judgmental performance and qualitative differences in knowledge sources.

Theoretical Implications

Our results for the first proposition did not confirm prior theory (e.g., Muradoglu & Önkal, 1994; Önkal et al., 2003) that suggests that experts produce significantly more accurate judgments than novices because of their knowledge of the case in question. Although experts demonstrated the highest mean sense of prior knowledge in comparison with frontline employees (3.69 versus 3.18) in the manipulation check, the results did not reveal significant differences in accuracy for tasks related to both performance indicators and geographic proximity.

In addition to the first proposition, we investigated a second, in which it was suggested that executives demonstrated overconfidence in judgmental tasks at all difficulty levels compared with frontline employees, who demonstrated underconfidence. Contrary to earlier studies (Russo & Schoemaker, 1992) of decision makers predicting industry and firm-related outcomes, which revealed that experienced decision makers tend to be overconfident and inexperienced decision makers tend to be underconfident (Fazio & Zanna, 1978), our tests revealed that this was not the case. We found no significant differences in confidence–accuracy values for different tasks between executives and frontline personnel.

Finally, we tested our third proposition, in which we proposed that executives' accuracy in knowledge and confidence in knowledge were better calibrated than frontline employees. Again, contrary to earlier studies, we found no significant differences in calibration performance between the groups. For instance, studies of race oddsmakers (Griffith, 1949; Hausch et al., 1981) and expert bridge players (Keren, 1987) revealed that intuitive judgments of experts are better calibrated than novices when they have rich knowledge of the prediction task in question. This indicates that the executives in this study did not have a significantly better sense of 'gut feeling' than the frontline employees about uncertain indicator results in the industry as a result of their domain-specific knowledge.

Practical Implications for Knowledge Management and Strategic Capital Applications

The principal findings of this study reveal that frontline employees' intuitive judgments about uncertain events are not more biased in terms of accuracy in judgments and confidence in knowledge than those of executives. This indicates that executives are not necessarily better performers in a forecasting setting than frontline employees. For management of service businesses, this means that in a knowledge management perspective when incorporating judgmental forecasting as an isolated strategic tool or in combination with statistical forecasting systems to enhance strategic decision making, both executives and frontline employees can be included in the sample as forecasters. These findings may indicate that frontline employees indeed have knowledge repertoires that are of strategic importance to management because of their daily interactions and communications with different groups of people. This may also indicate that employees' knowledge sharing processes are not necessarily qualitatively different from executives.

As proposed in this article, the strategic capital of employees is strongly dependent on knowledge sharing among executives, colleagues and other interest groups (Smith, 2005) and a positive knowledge sharing climate is rooted in the organization's social capital (Hoffman, Hoelscher & Sherif, 2005), culture (Al-Alawi et al., 2007, Schein 1985) by its politics and power distance (Hall & Goody, 2007), but may also be determined by the size of the business (Ruiz-Mercader et al., 2006). Such factors may have influenced the results of our study.

The study was conducted in a Scandinavian business setting, and the organizational structure of Scandinavian companies is characterized by very little power distance between management and other members of the organization compared with other countries (Hofstede, 1993). The small power distance between management and employees in Scandinavian countries was also supported in a study by Smith et al. (2003), who found that Nordic managers rely more on subordinates and less on formal rules and superiors compared with other European managers. Consequently, the social capital resulting from the knowledge sharing between managers and subordinates is likely to be stronger in Scandinavian service businesses as compared with other European countries.

We conducted our study in medium-sized service businesses, where the number of employees ranged between 50 and 250. Studies have revealed that in smaller and medium-sized businesses, knowledge sharing between management and staff occurs on a more regular and less formalized basis (Ruiz-Mercader et al., 2006), which is likely to increase the strategic knowledge pool of staff members.

Overall, the findings of the study lead to consideration of the importance of strategic capital and knowledge management in service businesses. As for the strategic capital, the study has demonstrated that frontline personnel's knowledge, consisting of both explicit and tacit knowledge (Smith, 2005, 2006) is an as strong a strategic capital as that of management. Nevertheless, should this finding be consistent over time with new empirical studies of the topic, it may be worth addressing the following issue: Namely, if new knowledge is generated on a natural and continuous basis that is as reliable input in strategic decision making as leaders' knowledge; and assuming that better and more effective decisions are carried out by management when relying on diverse knowledge pools and intuitive judgments; and thereby promoting competitive advantage, what will the role of management be in managing knowledge? Knowledge processes, knowledge sharing and following knowledge generation happen in an informal way under all circumstances, and this study may have indicated that the way to elicit some of the tacit knowledge stock of employees is by employing intuitive judgments as input in judgmental forecasting and strategic decision making.

Implications for the Assumptions of the Qualitative Differences in Knowledge Sources

In the article, we put forward several assumptions about differences in knowledge sources of memory related to the individual, culture, transformations by the misuse of knowledge, structure and ecology (Walsh & Ungson, 1991). Yet, we found no qualitative differences in executives and frontline personnel as knowledge sources. This may be

seen as a result of the fact that either the groups generate knowledge from the same information sources or that they generate knowledge from different information sources but arrive at the same answer. Nevertheless, if we rely on the assumptions of qualitative differences in knowledge sources between the subject groups resulting from different information sources among other reasons, the findings of this study have indeed indicated the important value of knowledge sharing among various employee groups. Yet, the study has not examined what the underlying qualitative differences are resulting from different knowledge sources. In further studies in knowledge management it would be relevant to empirically address these differences.

When it comes to the individual executive, the practical implication of the findings is related to power and political behavior of top management and power relationship in the organization (Lawrence et al., 2005) which affects the culture of knowledge sharing. In most service companies, top managers tend to have longer education and work experience than frontline personnel. Intuitive judgments made by front line employees, will be incorporated into strategic processes resulting in degrees of ignorance or acceptance, and thereby degrees of final institutionalizations. For instance, top mangers may wish to build an empire, and this is likely to hinder the application of intuitive judgmental input from subordinates. It is also reasonable to assume that the organizational members' awareness of power distribution also affects their long term performance when it comes to if, how, when and why top management accepts externalization of intuitive strategic judgments by frontline employees as the organization's strategic capital.

The assumption of misuse of knowledge in relation to transformation processes is likely to have appeared in the study (Walsh & Ungson, 1991). This would have happened if executives have used a routine answer to the survey items when they were actually required to recognize the novelty of the questions. Such misuse of knowledge in judgmental performance makes it even more important for top management to recognize the usefulness of sampling organizational members collectively for strategic decision making in order to reduce biases and advance the accuracy in forecasting and strategic decisions.

Finally, it is worth mentioning that if the size of the business is an important explanatory factor for the lack of differences in the CA performance of the subject groups, it is relevant to consider how businesses may be structured in order to ensure a high degree of knowledge sharing. In this case, it may well be that the role of knowledge management can particular contribute in the understanding of such ecological processes of organizations.

Validity of the Study

As well as our preceding consideration of the results, it should be noted that our findings may suggest that the tasks addressed in the study lay outside executives' domain-specific knowledge and thus reduce the internal validity of the results. This should be taken into consideration, even though this group engaged in strategic decision-making meetings on a daily basis for their companies and their prior sense of expertise was compared with that of frontline employees. It is likely that performance indicators for the industry are not a common topic of discussion in strategic meetings between executives. This issue may also be reflected in executives' fairly low prior mean knowledge of tasks, which measured 3.69 on the scale. On the other hand, in the research design, it was necessary to create the sense of a real forecasting setting, stressing uncertainty and thereby promoting the use of intuitive judgments.

Research Implications

Our results lead to new considerations and research questions within knowledge management and cognitive theory with focus on intuitive judgmental performance of confidence and accuracy biases of executives and frontline employees. We suggest that further research be carried out to examine the different factors that may influence CA performance between executives and frontline employees in order to understand which organizational factors influence individuals in their knowledge sharing, knowledge generation and following CA performance.

Valuable research on the psychology of judgmental and knowledge-based forecasting has been carried out by Kahneman and Riepe (1998), Kahneman and Tversky (1972, 1973), Tversky and Kahneman (1974) and Gilovich et al. (2002), who investigated the cognitive structures of biases in intuitive judgments. Further research is needed on explanatory variables of the organization that may influence the CA performance of executives and frontline personnel. We suggest possible variables: organizational politics and culture by power distance in organizations, social capital, and transformation processes by the misuse of knowledge and size of business. Many other factors are also relevant when investigating the implications of intuitive judgmental biases in knowledge-based forecasting and strategic decision making, and we encourage research within these topics. Given the findings of this article, we also hope to stimulate further research on the impact of managements' execution of knowledge management activities in relation to strategic capital and the performance of intuitive judgment performance by employees and executives.

CONCLUSION

We have established some findings on executives' and frontline personnel's knowledge abilities by their intuitive judgmental performance aiming at strengthening judgmental forecasting and strategic decision making in service businesses. We investigated qualitative differences between executives and frontline employees' CA biases in judgments of uncertain quantities. Contrary to earlier theory, the empirical evidence we collected found no significant differences between the groups in terms of accuracy, confidence and calibration performance of CA. We found that frontline employees as a knowledge source may be considered as good a strategic capital as executives. We conclude that in a knowledge-based forecasting setting for management of smaller and medium-sized service businesses and in cultures with small power distances between executives and employees with a strong corporate social capital, it is worth sampling both executives and frontline personnel as judgmental forecast performers because of the similarity in their strategic knowledge when it comes to uncertain business and industry outcomes. Yet, management should be aware of the possible misuse of knowledge of strategic experts. The findings of the study also demonstrate that service companies are likely to achieve more accurate estimates if they sample collective knowledge.

REFERENCES

Agor, W. H. (1989). *Intuition in organizations: Leading and managing productivity*. Newbury Park, CA: Sage.

Al-Alawi, A. I., Al-Marzooqi, N. Y., & Mohammed, Y. F. (2007). Organizational culture and knowledge sharing: Critical success factors. *Journal of Knowledge Management, 11*, 22–42. doi:10.1108/13673270710738898

Alavi, M., & Leidner, D. E. (2001). Review: Knowledge management and knowledge management systems: Conceptual foundations and research issues. *MIS Quarterly, 25*(1), 107–136. doi:10.2307/3250961

Amin, A., & Cohendet, P. (2005). Geographies of knowledge formation in firms. *Industry and Innovation, 12*, 465–486. doi:10.1080/13662710500381658

Andersson, P., Edman, J., & Ekman, M. (2005). Predicting the World Cup 2002 in soccer: Performance and confidence of experts and non-experts. *International Journal of Forecasting, 21*, 565–576. doi:10.1016/j.ijforecast.2005.03.004

Bastick, T. (1982). *Intuition: How we think and act*. New York: John Wiley & Sons Inc.

Bennett, R. H. (1998). The importance of tacit knowledge in strategic deliberations and decisions. *Management Decision, 36*(9), 589–597. doi:10.1108/00251749810239478

Blais, A.-R., Thompson, M. M., & Baranski, J. V. (2005). Individual differences in decision processing and confidence judgments in comparative judgment tasks: The role of cognitive styles. *Personality and Individual Differences, 38*, 1701–1713. doi:10.1016/j.paid.2004.11.004

Bothwell, R. K., Deffenbacher, K. A., & Brigham, J. C. (1987). Correlation of eyewitness accuracy and confidence: Optimality hypothesis revisited. *The Journal of Applied Psychology, 72*, 691–695. doi:10.1037/0021-9010.72.4.691

Bowers, K. T. (1987). *Intuition and discovery*. Hillsdale, NJ: Analytical Press.

Brenner, L., Griffin, D., & Koehler, D. J. (2005). Modeling patterns of probability calibration with random support theory: Diagnosing case-based judgment. *Organizational Behavior and Human Decision Processes, 97*, 64–81. doi:10.1016/j.obhdp.2005.02.002

Brewer, W. F., & Sampaio, C. (2006). Processes leading to confidence and accuracy in sentence recognition: A metamemory approach. *Memory (Hove, England), 14*(5), 540–552. doi:10.1080/09658210600590302

Chung, J., & Monroe, G. (2000). The effects of experience and task difficulty on accuracy and confidence assessments of auditors. *Accounting and Finance, 40*, 135–152. doi:10.1111/1467-629X.00040

Edwards, W. (1961). Behavioral decision theory. *Annual Review of Psychology, 12*, 473–498. doi:10.1146/annurev.ps.12.020161.002353

European Commission. (2006, October). *Enterprise and Industry. SME definition*. Available: http://ec.europa.eu/enterprise/enterprise_policy/sme_definition/index_en.htm

Fazio, R. H., & Zanna, M. P. (1978). Attitudinal qualities relating to the strength of the attitude–behavior relationship. *Journal of Experimental Social Psychology, 14*, 398–408. doi:10.1016/0022-1031(78)90035-5

Fitzgerald, J. (1992). *Towards knowledge in writing: Illustrations from revision studies.* New York, NY: Springer-Verlag.

Gabbay, S. M., & Leenders, R. Th. A. J. (1999). The structure of advantage and disadvantage. In R. Th. A. J. Leenders & S. M. Gabbay (Eds), *Corporate social capital and liability* (pp. 1–14). Boston, MA: Kluwer Academic Publishers.

Ghalia, M. B., & Wang, P. P. (2000). Intelligent system to support judgmental business forecasting: The case of estimating hotel room demand. *IEEE transactions on Fuzzy Systems, 8*, 380–397. doi:10.1109/91.868945

Gibbins, M. (1984). Propositions about the psychology of professional judgment in public accounting. *Journal of Accounting Research, 22*, 103–125. doi:10.2307/2490703

Gilovich, T., Griffin, D., & Kahneman, D. (2002). *Heuristics and biases. The psychology of intuitive judgment.* New York, NY: Cambridge University Press.

Gold, A. H., Malhotra, A., & Segars, A. H. (2001). Knowledge management: An organizational capabilities perspective. *Journal of Management Information Systems, 18*(1), 185–214.

Griffin, D., & Tversky, A. (1992). The weighing of evidence and the determinants of confidence. *Cognitive Psychology, 24*, 411–435. doi:10.1016/0010-0285(92)90013-R

Griffith, R. M. (1949). Odds adjustments by American horse-race bettors. *The American Journal of Psychology, 62*, 290–294. doi:10.2307/1418469

Hall, H., & Goody, M. (2007). KM, culture and compromise: Interventions to promote knowledge sharing supported by technology in corporate environments. *Journal of Information Science, 33*, 181–188. doi:10.1177/0165551506070708

Hall, P., & Rieck, A. (2001). Improving coverage accuracy of nonparametric prediction intervals. *Journal of the Royal Statistical Society. Series B, Statistical Methodology, 63*, 717–725. doi:10.1111/1467-9868.00308

Hausch, D. B., Ziemba, W. T., & Rubinstein, M. (1981). Efficiency of the market for racetrack betting. *Management Science, 27*, 1435–1452. doi:10.1287/mnsc.27.12.1435

Hoffmann, J. J., Hoelscher, M. L., & Sherif, K. (2005). Social capital, knowledge management, and sustained superior performance. *Journal of Knowledge Management, 9*(3), 93–100. doi:10.1108/13673270510602791

Hofstede, G. (1993). Cultural dimensions in people management: The socialization perspective. In V. Pucik, N. M. Tichy, & C. K. Barnett (Eds). *Globalizing Management* (pp. 139–158). New York, NY: John Wiley & Sons, Inc.

Hogarth, R. M., & Makridakis, S. (1981). Forecasting and planning: An evolution. *Management Science, 27*(2), 115–216. doi:10.1287/mnsc.27.2.115

Horwath Consulting. (2005). *The Norwegian hotel industry 2005*. Oslo, Norway: Horwath Consulting AS.

Hughes, P., & Morgan, R. E. (2007). A resource-advantage perspective of product-market strategy performance & strategic capital in high technology firms. *Industrial Marketing Management, 36*, 503–517. doi:10.1016/j.indmarman.2006.01.003

Janz, B. D., & Prasarnphanich, P. (2003). Understanding the antecedents of effective knowledge management: The importance of a knowledge-centered culture. *Decision Sciences, 34*(2), 351–384. doi:10.1111/1540-5915.02328

Kahneman, D., & Riepe, M. W. (1998). Aspects of investor psychology. *Journal of Portfolio Management, 24*, 52–65. doi:10.3905/jpm.1998.409643

Kahneman, D., & Tversky, A. (1972). Subjective probability: A judgment of representativeness. *Cognitive Psychology, 3*, 430–454. doi:10.1016/0010-0285(72)90016-3

Kahneman, D., & Tversky, A. (1973). On the psychology of prediction. *Psychological Review, 80*, 237–251. doi:10.1037/h0034747

Keren, G. (1987). Facing uncertainty in the game of bridge: A calibration study. *Organizational Behavior and Human Decision Processes, 39*, 98–114. doi:10.1016/0749-5978(87)90047-1

Lawrence, M., Edmundson, R., & O'Connor, M. (1986). The accuracy of combining judgmental and statistical forecasts. *Management Science, 32*(3), 1521–1532. doi:10.1287/mnsc.32.12.1521

Lawrence, M., Goodwin, P., O'Connor, M., & Önkal, D. (2006). Judgmental forecasting: A review of progress over the last 25 years. *International Journal of Forecasting, 22*, 493–518. doi:10.1016/j.ijforecast.2006.03.007

Lawrence, T. B., Mauws, M. K., Dyck, B., & Kleysen, R. F. (2005). The politics of organizational learning: Integrating power into the 4I framework. *Academy of Management Review, 30*(1), 180–191.

Libby, R. (1995). The role of knowledge and memory in audit judgment. In R.H. Ashton, & A. H. Ashton. (Eds). *Judgment and decision-making research in accounting and auditing* (pp. 176-206). New York, NY: Cambridge University Press.

Lord, R. G., & Maher, K. J. (1991). Cognitive theory in industrial and organizational psychology. In M. D. Dunnette, & L. M. Hough (Eds.). *Handbook of industrial and organizational Psychology* (pp. 1-62). Palo Alto, CA: Consulting Psychologists Press.

Lord, R. G., & Maher, K. J. (1993). *Leadership and information processing: Linking perceptions and performance*. London: Unwin Hyman Inc.

Massey, C., & Wu, G. (2005). Detecting regime shifts: The psychology of under- and overreaction. *Management Science, 51*(6), 932–947. doi:10.1287/mnsc.1050.0386

Metcalfe, J. (2000). Metamemory. In E. Tulving, & F. I. M. Craik (Eds.), *The Oxford handbook of memory* (pp. 197–211). New York, NY: Oxford University Press.

Metcalfe, J., & Shimamura, A. P. (1994). *Metacognition: Knowing about knowing*. Cambridge, MA: MIT Press.

Miller, C. C., & Ireland, R. D. (2005). Intuition in strategic decision making: Friend or foe in the fast-paced 21st century? *The Academy of Management Executive, 19*, 19–30.

Muradoglu, G., & Önkal, D. (1994). An exploratory analysis of portfolio managers' probabilistic forecasts of stock-prices. *Journal of Forecasting, 13*, 565–578. doi:10.1002/for.3980130702

Murphy, A. H., & Winkler, R. (1984). Probability forecasting in meteorology. *Journal of the American Statistical Association, 79,* 489–500. doi:10.2307/2288395

Nelson, M. W., Libby, R., & Bonner, S. E. (1995). Knowledge structure and the estimation of conditional probabilities in audit planning. *Accounting Review, 70,* 27–47.

Nisbett, R. E., & Wilson, T. D. (1977). Telling more than we can know: Verbal reports on mental processes. *Psychological Review, 84,* 231–259. doi:10.1037/0033-295X.84.3.231

Nonaka, I., & Takeuchi, H. (1995). *The knowledge-creating company.* New York, NY: Oxford University Press.

Nosek, J. T. (2004). Group cognition as a basis for supporting group knowledge creation and sharing. *Journal of Knowledge Management, 8,* 54–64. doi:10.1108/13673270410556361

Önkal, D., Yates, J. F., Simga-Mugan, C., & Öztin, S. (2003). Professional vs. amateur judgment accuracy: The case of foreign exchange rates. *Organizational Behavior and Human Decision Processes, 91,* 169–185. doi:10.1016/S0749-5978(03)00058-X

Phillips, L. D., & Edwards, W. (1966). Conservatism in a simple probability inference task. *Journal of Experimental Psychology, 72,* 346–354. doi:10.1037/h0023653

Polanyi, M. (1958). *Personal knowledge: Toward a post-critical philosophy* (1ˢᵗ ed.). Chicago, IL: The University of Chicago Press.

Polanyi, M. (1966). *The tacit dimension.* Gloucester, MA: Doubleday & Company

Reber, A. S. (1989). Implicit learning and tacit knowledge. *Journal of Experimental Psychology. General, 118,* 219–235. doi:10.1037/0096-3445.118.3.219

Ruiz-Mercader, J., Merõno-Cerdan, A. L., & Sabater-Sánchez, R. (2006). Information technology and learning: Their relationship and impact on organisational performance in small businesses. *International Journal of Information Management, 26,* 16–29. doi:10.1016/j.ijinfomgt.2005.10.003

Russo, J. E., & Schoemaker, P. J. H. (1992). Managing overconfidence. *Sloan Management Review, 33,* 7–17.

Schein, E. H. (1985). *Organizational culture and leadership.* San-Francisco, CA: Jossey-Bass.

Selart, M., Kuvaas, B., Boe, O., & Takemura, K. (2006). The influence of decision heuristics and overconfidence on multiattribute choice: A process-tracing study. *The European Journal of Cognitive Psychology, 18,* 437–453. doi:10.1080/09541440500173054

Shiller, R. J. (2000). *Irrational exuberance.* Princeton, NJ: Princeton University Press.

Shirley, D. A., & Langan-Fox, J. (1996). Intuition: A review of the literature. *Psychological Reports, 79,* 563–584.

Smith, P. A. C. (2005). Knowledge sharing and strategic capital: The importance and identification of opinion leaders. *The Learning Organization, 12*(6), 563–574. doi:10.1108/09696470510626766

Smith, P. A. C. (2006). Enhancing strategic capital. *Handbook of Business Strategy, 7*(1), 195–199.

Smith, P. B., Andersen, J. A., Ekelund, B., Graversen, G., & Ropo, A. (2003). In search of Nordic management styles. *Scandinavian Journal of Management, 19,* 491–507. doi:10.1016/S0956-5221(03)00036-8

Stavanger Travel. (2006). Retrieved December 10, 2006 from: http://www.stavangertravel.com

Touron, D. R., & Hertzog. (2004). Distinguishing age differences in knowledge, strategy use, and confidence during strategic skill acquisition. *Psychology and Aging, 19*(3), 452–466. doi:10.1037/0882-7974.19.3.452

Tversky, A., & Kahneman, D. (1974). Judgement under uncertainty: Heuristics and biases. *Science, 185,* 1124–1131. doi:10.1126/science.185.4157.1124

Vaughan, F. E. (1979). *Awakening intuition.* Garden City, NY: Anchor Press, Doubleday.

Von Winterfeldt, D., & Edwards, W. (1986), *Decision analysis and behavioral research.* Cambridge, UK: Cambridge University Press.

Wagner, R. K., & Sternberg, R. J. (1985). Practical intelligence in real-world pursuits: The role of tacit knowledge. *Journal of Personality and Social Psychology, 49,* 436–458. doi:10.1037/0022-3514.49.2.436

Walsh, J. P., & Ungson, G. R. (1991). Organizational memory. *Academy of Management Review, 16*(1), 57–91. doi:10.2307/258607

Weber, N., & Brewer, N. (2004). Confidence–accuracy calibration in absolute and relative face recognition judgments. *Journal of Experimental Psychology. Applied, 10*(3), 156–172. doi:10.1037/1076-898X.10.3.156

Weinstein, N. D. (1980). Unrealistic optimism about future events. *Journal of Personality and Social Psychology, 39,* 806–820. doi:10.1037/0022-3514.39.5.806

Whitecotton, S. M. (1996). The effects of experience and a decision aid on the slope, scatter, and bias of earnings forecasts. *Organizational Behavior and Human Decision Processes, 66*(1), 111–121. doi:10.1006/obhd.1996.0042

Wilkie-Thomson, M. E., Önkal-Atay, D., Pollock, A. C., & Macaulay, A. (1999). The influence of trend strength on directional probabilistic currency predictions. *Technological Forecasting and Social Change, 61,* 79–80.

Wright, G., & Ayton, P. (Eds.). (1987). *Judgmental forecasting.* GB, Wiltshire: John Wiley & Sons Ltd.

Yates, J. T. (1990). *Judgment and decision making.* Englewood Cliffs, NJ: Prentice Hall.

ENDNOTES

[1] The survey instrument is available upon request from carina.a.hallin@uis.no

[2] RevPar is a measure of profit and is calculated as follows: RevPar = Rooms revenue × occupancy rate. In recent years, RevPar has become a common performance indicator in the hotel industry because it is a quick indicator of the competitiveness of the business compared with other hotel businesses. This key measure is used to compare profitability of hotels, regions and markets (Horwarth Consulting, 2005).

This work was previously published in International Journal of Knowledge Management, Volume 5, Issue 4, edited by Murray E. Jennex, pp. 1-25, copyright 2009 by IGI Publishing (an imprint of IGI Global).

Chapter 19
An Experiment of Information Elaboration in Mediated Knowledge Transfer

Kelly J. Fadel
Utah State University, USA

Alexandra Durcikova
The University of Arizona, USA

Hoon S. Cha
Salisbury University, USA

ABSTRACT

Understanding knowledge transfer in computer mediated contexts is becoming essential given that organizations are spread more and more globally. In this chapter, the authors adopt elaboration likelihood theory to investigate knowledge transfer processes in a Knowledge Management System (KMS). They report the results of an exploratory experiment conducted to examine the impact of argument quality, source credibility and validation on knowledge usefulness of a document in a KMS. Their findings indicate that while validation of knowledge in KMS positively affects perceptions of knowledge usefulness, higher argument quality was associated with lower usefulness ratings. Surprisingly, source credibility has no effect on perceptions of knowledge usefulness. The implications of these results for both researchers and practitioners are discussed.

INTRODUCTION

In an effort to exploit their knowledge resources, many companies devote great effort to managing their knowledge capital through centralized knowledge management systems (KMS). The

DOI: 10.4018/978-1-60960-555-1.ch019

role of KMS has become increasingly important as knowledge capital stored in the repository is no longer limited to traditional customer and product data, but also includes valuable "best practices" that can be adopted and reused by individual employees through a meaningful knowledge transfer process. KMS can potentially support and enhance knowledge transfer by providing ready access to knowledge across personal, departmental, and organizational boundaries. However, implementing KMS alone does not ensure that successful knowledge transfer will occur. Rather, this outcome is realized only to the extent that the knowledge KMS provide is effectively processed, adopted, and utilized by individual knowledge users (Markus, 2001).

Researchers have recognized that KMS success depends on the *quality* of KMS use (Jennex, 2008). However, extant literature lacks studies investigating the mechanisms that govern how individuals adopt and internalize KMS knowledge; thus, little guidance is available for KM practitioners seeking to establish or enhance KMS-enabled knowledge transfer processes within their organizations. This paper addresses this void by presenting the results of an exploratory research study that investigates how individuals in an organization process and perceive the usefulness of knowledge retrieved from a knowledge repository. A survey was conducted in an experimental setting where subjects were asked to use a mock KMS to recommend a solution to a given IT authentication problem. We build and test hypotheses based on theories of information influence (Petty & Cacioppo, 1986; Petty, Cacioppo, & Goldman, 1981) and organizational knowledge transfer in mediated contexts (Sussman & Siegal, 2003) to better understand the process by which knowledge in a KMS is evaluated and used by individuals. The results of our experiment offer actionable insights for KM practitioners and point to several directions for future research in KMS-enabled knowledge transfer.

THEORETICAL BACKGROUND AND HYPOTHESES

KMS and Knowledge Transfer

Knowledge is a justified belief that increases an entity's capacity for effective action, and is embodied in both tacit (e.g. insights, intuitions, assumptions) and explicit (e.g. documents, recorded solutions, formal analyses) forms (Alavi & Leidner, 2001). Organizational knowledge transfer involves the conveyance of knowledge from a source to where it is needed in the organization, and has been identified as a critical component of successful knowledge management practice (Alavi & Leidner, 2001; Huber, 2001). Knowledge transfer can occur between and among individuals, departments, teams, and organizations themselves (Alavi & Leidner, 2001; Sussman & Siegal, 2003). In many cases, transfer transpires directly between two knowledge-bearing entities, such as one individual verbally imparting knowledge to another. However, in today's distributed work environment, transfer increasingly takes place across mediated channels of communication in which the knowledge source and knowledge recipient are geographically and temporally disconnected. In such cases, the role of the intervening knowledge medium becomes a key enabler of the knowledge transfer process.

Information technology is an ideal vehicle for supporting mediated knowledge transfer. Knowledge from a source can be stored within an information system for later retrieval and use by one or many knowledge consumers. This function constitutes the essence of KMS, defined herein as information technology based systems designed and implemented to facilitate storage, retrieval, transfer, and application of organizational knowledge (Gray & Meister, 2004; Majchrzak, Cooper, & Neece, 2004). KMS enable and enhance these practices by providing a centralized and accessible knowledge repository from which knowledge consumers can draw, invoking internalization of explicit codified knowledge from an external source to an individual's personal consciousness (Nonaka, 1994). However, while KMS can facilitate the transfer process, access to knowledge in a KMS does not guarantee that transfer will take place. After it is retrieved, knowledge must be processed and evaluated in such a way that it can be applied to the problem at hand. Not all knowledge retrieved from a KMS will undergo equal processing—some may be carefully analyzed, some briefly examined, and some completely disregarded. Understanding the mechanisms underlying this processing is thus critical to enabling and sustaining KMS-supported knowledge transfer.

Relatively few IS studies have focused on the individual information processing underlying knowledge transfer. One notable exception is Sussman and Seigal (2003), who examined adoption of information conveyed in advice-bearing emails. Drawing from the Elaboration Likelihood Model (*ELM*) (Petty & Cacioppo, 1986; Petty, et al., 1981), Sussman and Siegal examined the role of two information characteristics, argument quality and source credibility, on perceptions of information usefulness and subsequent adoption. Though they focus on email as the mechanism of knowledge transfer, Sussman and Siegal suggest that their findings are applicable to other mediated contexts, such as KMS. We therefore draw from their work to explore the mechanisms underlying knowledge transfer in a KMS environment. The next section discusses the ELM and develops the research hypotheses to be tested.

The Elaboration Likelihood Model

The Elaboration Likelihood Model is a theory of information influence developed by Petty and Cacioppo (1986) to account for variations in information influence across individuals and contexts. ELM states that information influence occurs via a process of cognitive elaboration, wherein the recipient attends to and evaluates various characteristics of the information in the process of forming a judgment about its utility. Evaluation of these characteristics is divided into two channels, or "routes" of information influence: the central route and the peripheral route. The central route operates under conditions of high elaboration likelihood, and is characterized by analysis of

the information content itself. Arguments within an informational message are scrutinized and evaluated in context of extant knowledge about the topic in an effort to discern the quality of the information. Intuitively, messages perceived to contain high quality arguments are more likely to exert influence than are those deemed to contain low quality arguments.

Because the central route requires the recipient to engage in focused application of cognitive resources, it does not operate in all circumstances. In cases where high elaboration is too costly, information influence may operate instead through a peripheral route, wherein the recipient evaluates the utility of the information based on decision rules or heuristics rather than on the merits of the arguments themselves. These rules often focus on various meta-characteristics of the information, such as its provenance and/or various attributes of the source itself. For instance, a message received from a trusted individual may be deemed reliable based on characteristics of the individual alone, with little or no regard to the objective quality of the message content.

The central and peripheral routes represent extremes of an elaboration continuum; typical information processing relies on a combination of both types of processing (Petty & Cacioppo, 1986; Sussman & Siegal, 2003). Nevertheless, research has identified several factors that make one route more dominant than the other in certain circumstances. First, elaboration likelihood is influenced by the expertise of the information recipient. Because recipients who are experts in the given domain possess advanced mental models that facilitate argument evaluation, they are more likely to engage in central route processing and less likely to rely on peripheral cues than are novices (Ratneshwar & Chaiken, 1991; Sussman & Siegal, 2003). Second, elaboration likelihood is influenced by the degree to which the message bears personal relevance to the recipient, or the degree to which the recipient is *involved* in the topic. Recipients with a high degree of involvement will be more likely to devote cognitive resources to high-elaboration central route processing, whereas those with low involvement will more readily rely on peripheral cues (Petty & Cacioppo, 1986; Petty, et al., 1981; Stamm & Dube, 1994).

ELM has been utilized to understand the nature of information influence in a wide range of disciplines, including consumer behavior (e.g. Bredahl & Grunert, 1998; Kar Yan & Shuk Ying, 2005; Kim & Benbasat, 2009; Lee, Park, & Han, 2008), communication (e.g. Rucker & Petty, 2006; Wan, 2008), education (e.g. White, Charles, & Nelson, 2008), and many others. In the IS domain, researchers have adopted ELM in seeking to understand the processes by which both systems themselves (Angst & Agarwal, 2009; Bhattacherjee & Sanford, 2006) and information contained in systems (Nah & Benbasat, 2004; Sussman & Siegal, 2003) are adopted and used by individuals. Sussman and Siegal's (2003) study is particularly relevant to this research. Sussman and Siegal integrate ELM with IS adoption theories to investigate how people evaluate and adopt information received in advice-bearing emails. Drawing from ELM, their theoretical model of information adoption (hereafter referred to as MIA) posits that argument quality (a central route characteristic) and source credibility (a peripheral route characteristic) of

an email influence the degree to which the information it contains is considered useful by the recipient. Consistent with IS adoption theories (e.g. Davis, 1989; Venkatesh, Morris, Davis, & Davis, 2003), perceived usefulness of the information, in turn, influences the likelihood of information adoption. In accordance with ELM, the relationships between argument quality and knowledge usefulness, and between source credibility and knowledge usefulness, are moderated by the expertise and involvement of the information recipient. Specifically, high levels of expertise and involvement are expected to intensify the effect of perceived argument quality on knowledge usefulness and decrease the effect of perceived source credibility on knowledge usefulness. The MIA is depicted graphically in Figure 1.

We draw upon the MIA as a theoretical basis for investigating how individuals perceive and process knowledge retrieved from a knowledge repository. First, the MIA suggests that higher perceived argument quality of a piece of information will lead to higher perceptions of its usefulness (central route of information influence). Information quality entails several dimensions, including accuracy, completeness, currency, and format (Nelson, Todd, & Wixom, 2005). A recipient who judges information to possess high

Figure 1. Model of information adoption (Sussman & Siegal, 2003)

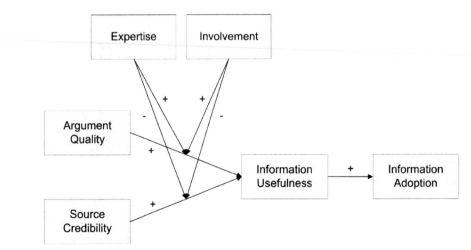

levels of these attributes should logically be more inclined to perceive the information as useful. This relationship is supported by a large body of IS research that has identified information quality as a key antecedent to perceived usefulness of information systems in general (DeLone & McLean, 1992, 2003; Nelson, et al., 2005; Saeed & Abdinnour-Helm, 2008) and KMS in particular (Jennex, 2008; Jennex & Olfman, 2006). Accordingly, we hypothesize that:

H1: The higher the perceived argument quality of a KMS document, the more useful the knowledge in the document will be perceived to be.

In addition to argument quality, the MIA also identifies source credibility as an indicator of information usefulness (the peripheral route of information influence). Early research on information influence argued that knowledge recipients tend to value knowledge more highly when its source is perceived as highly credible, while discounting knowledge from sources that are perceived as having low credibility (Eagley, Wood, & Chaiken, 1978; Mizerski, Golden, & Kernan, 1979). Later research on knowledge transfer in organizations has borne additional support for this relationship. For example, Ko, Kirsch, & King (2005) found that higher perceived credibility of ERP system consultants lead to increased knowledge transfer from the consultants to employees of the hiring firm. Similarly, Joshi, Sarker, & Sarker (2007) showed that source credibility strongly predicted the degree to which knowledge was transferred among members of information systems development teams. Consistent with this work, we hypothesize that:

H2: The higher the perceived credibility of the author of a KMS document, the more useful the knowledge in the document will be perceived to be.

In the context of email (Sussman & Siegal, 2003), argument quality and source credibility are key indicators of the internal validity of an information-bearing message. These attributes are also present in the context of information retrieved from a knowledge repository. However, many knowledge-based systems offer an additional cue that may contribute to the elaboration process: knowledge validation. Knowledge validation refers to the process of "continually monitoring, testing, and refining the knowledge in the knowledge base to suit the existing or potential realities" (Bhatt, 2001 p. 71) faced by the firm, and has been identified as a key component of the knowledge management lifecycle (Bhatt, 2001; Kakabadse, Kakabadse, & Kouzmin, 2003). Validation of knowledge in a KMS is critical in order to avoid the perpetuation of information that is incomplete, incorrect, or obsolete (Goodman & Darr, 1998; Markus, 2001). Validation can be carried out through various mechanisms, including content ratings by knowledge consumers themselves (Poston & Speier, 2005), or analysis and review by a trusted expert or committee to ensure knowledge accuracy (Marwick, 2001).

Knowledge management literature suggests that validation constitutes an important peripheral cue to which information consumers attend in evaluating knowledge contained in a KMS (Poston & Speier, 2005; Shon & Musen, 1999; Wathen & Burkell, 2002). A knowledge recipient may hesitate to adopt knowledge from a source whose trustworthiness is questionable or unknown (Husted & Michailova, 2002). Because validation offers evidence for content accuracy, knowledge that has been validated is expected to more readily influence the knowledge recipient than knowledge that has not been validated. Consider, for example, a consultant who accesses a KMS document recommending a solution to a particular problem. Given the breadth of potential contributors to the KMS, the consultant may know little, if anything, about the credentials of the document's source. However, if the consultant sees that the document has been validated by a trusted third party, she will more likely find the information credible and, hence, useful for addressing the task at hand (Offsey, 1997). Research has indeed indicated that validation can significantly improve the quality of knowledge contained in a repository, thereby enhancing its value to knowledge seekers (Markus, 2001; Offsey, 1997; Zack, 1999). In view of these arguments, we hypothesize that:

H3: A KMS document that is validated will be perceived as more useful as the one that is not validated.

Finally, our model includes the moderating effects of expertise and involvement in the information elaboration process. Research suggests that individuals with greater expertise in a domain are better equipped to thoughtfully analyze information on the merits of its content and arguments, while less experienced recipients must rely more heavily on peripheral cues (Cacioppo & Petty, 1982; Kang & Herr, 2006). Similarly, recipients are more likely to scrutinize information when dealing with a topic that bears personal relevance to them (high involvement), and more likely to attend to peripheral cues when such relevance is low (low involvement) (Petty & Wegener, 1999;

Stamm & Dube, 1994). Therefore, consistent with MIA (Sussman & Siegal, 2003), and ELM (Petty & Cacioppo, 1986; Petty, et al., 1981), we hypothesize that higher expertise and involvement of the KMS knowledge recipient will increase reliance on central-route cues (argument quality) and decrease reliance on peripheral-route cues (source credibility and validation) in the elaboration process. These hypotheses are formalized as follows:

H4: Recipient expertise will positively moderate the influence of argument quality on knowledge usefulness (H4a) and negatively moderate the influence of source credibility (H4b) and validation (H4c) on knowledge usefulness.

H5: Recipient involvement will positively moderate the influence of argument quality on knowledge usefulness (H5a) and negatively moderate the influence of source credibility (H5b) and validation (H5c) on knowledge usefulness.

Figure 2 summarizes the research hypotheses to be tested. The following section describes the development and implementation of a randomized experiment designed to test our hypotheses.

Figure 2. Theoretical model

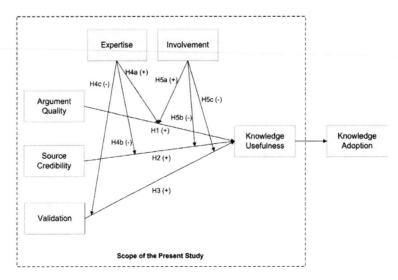

RESEARCH METHODOLOGY

The study was conducted in an experimental setting to control argument quality, source credibility, and validation, as well as to allow measurement of knowledge usefulness and control variables. A between-subjects experiment was designed that covered two levels of each of the three factors (high or low source credibility and argument quality, and present or not present validation of the document), providing a 2x2x2 fully factorial design.

The context of the experiment involved the use of a mock KMS to recommend an Internet authentication solution to a client company of an IT consulting firm. Each participant was asked to assume the role of a junior consultant who had just received a memo from his/her supervisor assigning him/her recommend a method of Internet authentication for an internal order processing system utilized by a client company. The memo also suggested that the participant consult the company's KMS to search for possible Internet authentication solutions recommended to past clients. After reading the memo, participants were directed through a staged KMS "search" that yielded one document outlining four potential Internet authentication solutions. The document was structured as follows: For each solution, a general description was provided, followed by a list of pros and cons and a set of instructions for implementing the solution. Experimental treatments were achieved by manipulating the argument quality, source credibility, and validation of the document as described below.

Following prior research (Bailey & Pearson, 1983; Sussman & Siegal, 2003), argument quality was operationalized by altering the original KMS document along three dimensions: completeness, consistency, and accuracy. Completeness and consistency were manipulated by randomly removing portions of each authentication solution described in the document. Specifically, in the low argument quality conditions, three solutions omitted the discussion of pros, cons or both, while another

solution lacked implementation instructions. Accuracy was manipulated by introducing obvious spelling and grammatical errors, such as letter transpositions (e.g., *authentiaction*), double words (e.g., *that which..*) missing letters (e.g., *usernam*), and errant apostrophes (e.g, *you're web site*). These errors are similar to those utilized in previous IS studies (Everard & Galletta, 2005-2006).

Source credibility was operationalized by indicating the author of the KMS document, as well as providing an experience rating for the author in the form of a five-star scale. In the high source credibility condition, the author was identified the Chief Security Officer of the company who had been MCSE certified and had a 5-star experience rating. The author of the low source credibility condition was identified as a junior analyst with a 1-star experience rating.

Finally, validation was operationalized by indicating whether or not the document had been validated. For the validated condition, the document displayed a prominent indicator stating that the document had been reviewed and validated by the internal IT Security Review Committee. For the non-validated condition, the document displayed a similar field warning that the document had not yet been validated. Figure 3 shows screenshots of source and validation indicators.

The dependent variable of knowledge usefulness, together with control variables of expertise and involvement, were operationalized using scales validated in prior research. The knowledge usefulness scale was adapted from IS usefulness scales used in several IS acceptance studies (e.g. Bhattacherjee & Sanford, 2006; Davis, 1989; Venkatesh & Davis, 2000). Measures of expertise and involvement were adapted from Sussman and Siegal (2003) and Stamm and Dube (1994). The validation measure was developed for this study following the procedure for scale development described in Moore and Benbasat (1991). All items used a 7-point Likert scale format.

A pilot test was conducted prior to the experiment. Fifteen doctoral students participated in the

Figure 3. Document source and validation indicators

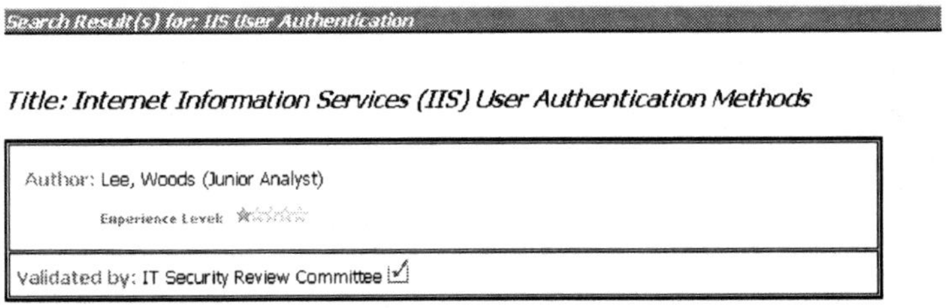

An example of low source credibility but validated document

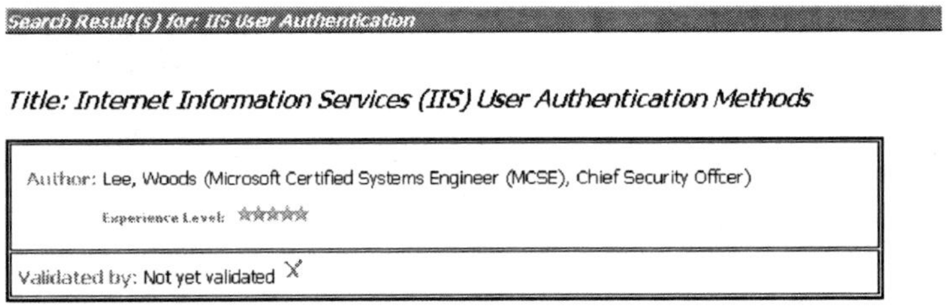

An example of high source credibility but not validated document

pilot test. Pilot participants were asked to provide feedback on the clarity of the experimental materials and the overall experimental design. Based this feedback, some changes were made to the wording of the experimental materials and the questionnaire.

For primary data collection, participation was solicited from 242 undergraduate business majors sampled from the sections of an upper-division undergraduate MIS course at a large U.S. university. Students were informed that the purpose of the study was to learn about how one makes a decision regarding Internet authentication using a knowledge base system, and were offered course extra credit for participation. Those who elected to participate were randomly assigned to one of 8 treatment conditions (high vs. low argument quality x high vs. low source credibility x validation vs. no validation) upon arrival. The experiment then proceeded as follows: Participants first read the memo, after which they accessed the KMS document outlining four Internet authentication solutions. The document content varied by treatment condition as described above. After reading the document, participants were asked to select

one solution to recommend to the client company, together with a rationale for their choice and a confidence rating that they had chosen the best solution. Finally, participants completed an online questionnaire containing measures of experimental and control variables.

RESULTS

Experimental results were screened for outliers as a first step in the data analysis. Nine participants were found to have finished the task in less than 10 minutes, with the lower quartile at 12 minutes. After dropping these participants from the data set, a total of 223 valid answers were retained. 159 were males, 126 females, with an average GPA of 3.35 (st.dev. 0.361).

To make sure that the subjects noticed the treatment we conducted manipulation checks using the scales for validation, source credibility and argument quality. These manipulation checks were significant for all three factors; specifically, for validation the means for the two groups were 3.7 and 4.6 ($F = 20.8$, df 1/231, sig = 0.000), for argument quality the group means were 2.8 and 3.4 (F = 13.4, df 1/231, sig = 0.000), and for source credibility the group means were 4.5 and 4.9 (F = 7.6, df 1/231, sig = 0.006).

Convergent and discriminant validity of measurement scales were assessed through exploratory factor analysis (Table 1) as well as construct correlations and cross-correlations (Table 2). Results confirm that all constructs demonstrate

Table 1. Exploratory factor analysis with varimax rotation

Item	Item Wording	SC	KU	VAL	AQ	EXP	INV
SC4	How reliable is the author? (Not Reliable, Somewhat Reliable, Extremely Reliable)	**0.874**	-0.035	0.188	-0.136	0.096	0.004
SC3	How trustworthy is the author? (Not Trustworthy, Somewhat Trustworthy, Extremely Trustworthy)	**0.867**	-0.054	0.171	-0.076	0.098	0.010
SC5	How credible is the author? (Not Credible, Somewhat Credible, Extremely Credible)	**0.861**	0.005	0.182	-0.109	0.085	0.032
SC2	How would you rate the expertise of the author with respect to IIS authentication? (Low Expertise, Average Expertise, High Expertise)	**0.735**	0.125	-0.040	-0.396	-0.036	0.052
SC1	How knowledgeable about IIS authentication is the author? (Not Knowledgeable, Somewhat Knowledgeable, Extremely Knowledgeable)	**0.663**	0.182	-0.043	-0.282	-0.113	0.049
KU2	The content of the solution document was valuable to me in making my recommendation	0.043	**0.943**	0.110	-0.079	-0.046	0.042
KU1	I found the content of the solution document useful in making my recommendation	0.027	**0.922**	0.113	-0.098	0.046	0.014
KU3	The content of the solution document improved my ability to decide on a solution	0.050	**0.889**	0.151	-0.104	-0.029	0.043
VAL3	The accuracy of the solution document content was verified	0.080	0.075	**0.871**	-0.172	0.038	0.037
VAL2	There is evidence that the content of the solution document was confirmed	0.131	0.082	**0.859**	-0.214	0.012	-0.004
VAL1	The content of the solution document was validated	0.174	0.258	**0.819**	-0.079	0.076	0.008
AQ2	The content of the solution document was: Consistent…Inconsistent	-0.231	-0.093	-0.164	**0.831**	0.015	0.044
AQ1	The content of the solution document was: Complete…Incomplete	-0.308	-0.122	-0.116	**0.749**	-0.071	0.161
AQ3	The content of the solution document was: Accurate…Inaccurate	-0.228	-0.102	-0.317	**0.746**	-0.110	-0.043
EXP2	To what extent are you an expert on the topic of user authentication?	0.057	-0.050	0.124	-0.112	**0.810**	0.269
EXP1	How informed are you on the subject matter of user authentication?	0.054	-0.035	0.023	-0.201	**0.800**	0.241
EXP3	Overall, I consider myself a novice with respect to user authentication.	0.015	0.040	-0.009	0.134	**0.750**	-0.034
INV1	In general, I find the topic of user authentication very interesting.	0.044	0.029	0.044	0.044	0.136	**0.888**
INV2	I've been thinking about authentication issues lately.	0.042	0.064	-0.012	0.077	0.219	**0.843**

Table 2. Descriptive statistics, reliability, AVE, and inter-construct correlations

#	Construct/ Dimension	# of items	Response Mean	Std. Dev.	Cronbach's Alpha	Internal Consistency	AVE	1	2	3	4	5	6
1	Knowledge Usefulness	3	5.68	1.27	0.94	0.94	0.92	**0.92**					
2	Validation	3	4.20	1.51	0.89	0.89	0.72	0.32*	**0.85**				
3	Argument Quality	3	2.95	1.28	0.84	0.83	0.83	-0.22*	-0.39*	**0.79**			
4	Source Credibility	5	4.89	1.05	0.89	0.90	0.80	0.13*	0.30*	-0.54*	**0.80**		
5	Expertise	3	3.25	1.35	0.71	0.84	0.69	0.01	0.11	-0.13*	0.11	**0.81**	
6	Involvement	2	3.48	1.71	0.77	0.86	0.75	0.08	0.04	-0.04	0.09	0.39*	**0.87**

*Correlations greater than 0.125 are significant at 0.05

sufficient convergent and discriminant validity. All Cronbach's alpha scores are above the 0.7 score suggested by Nunnally (1978).

We performed a regression analysis to test our hypotheses. As a first step, summated scales were calculated by averaging the individual responses for each construct. These scales constituted the variables used in the analysis. Correlations among independent variables were less than 0.6; hence, multicollinearity was not deemed a problem (Billings & Wroten, 1978). Variables were standardized

to test for interaction effects. Per Table 3, hypothesis 3 (validation → knowledge usefulness) is supported; however, hypotheses 1 (argument quality → knowledge usefulness) and 2 (source credibility → knowledge usefulness) are not supported. Moreover, neither expertise nor involvement was found to significantly moderate relationships between argument quality, source credibility, and knowledge usefulness, thus failing to support H4a-b and H5a-b. Finally, the influence of validation on knowledge usefulness was posi-

Table 3. Results

	Model 1	Model 2
Constant		
Argument Quality	-0.139*	-0.15**
Source Credibility	-0.033	-0.03
Validation	0.277***	0.281***
Argument Quality * Involvement		-0.009
Argument Quality * Expertise		0.01
Source Credibility * Involvement		0.105
Source Credibility * Expertise		-0.078
Validation * Involvement		-0.142
Validation * Expertise		0.114**
	R-squared = 0.117	R-squared = 0.142
	F change = 10.13 (3/229)	F change = 1.073 (6/223)
	Sig. F change = 0.000	Sig. F change = 0.379
(*** is significant at 0.01, ** is significant at 0.05, and * is significant at 0.1)		

tively moderated by recipient involvement, supporting H5c. However, H4c, positing a negative moderating effect of recipient expertise on the validation-usefulness relationship, was not supported. The percentage of variance explained in the dependent variable (knowledge usefulness) was 14.2%.

DISCUSSION

This paper draws upon theories of elaboration likelihood and information adoption to understand how individuals form perceptions of knowledge usefulness in a KMS environment. According to ELM, a recipient of a message will evaluate this message using two channels: central and the peripheral. The central route focuses on the content itself, e.g. argument quality of the message. The peripheral route focuses on various meta-characteristics of the message, e.g. source credibility and validation of the message. The influence of these two routes can be moderated by the expertise of the recipient and his/her involvement in the message content.

Our experiment yielded some interesting results that point to potential singularities in KMS as a vehicle for mediated knowledge transfer. First, higher values of argument quality *negatively* affected perceived usefulness of the knowledge in the repository. This contrasts with the relationship posited by H1 and the results of Sussman and Siegal (2003), who found that argument quality of emails positively influenced usefulness perceptions of the information they contained. One potential explanation for this may have been the length of the document used in the high argument quality condition. As described earlier, argument quality was operationalized by altering the original document along three dimensions: completeness, consistency, and accuracy. In order to make the document complete, it was fairly long (participants had to scroll down 3 screens to read through the entire document). Implementing inconsistencies

and lowering completeness reduced the document length by approximately one third, which may have made it easier read and comprehend. Information processing theory suggests that humans are limited in their ability to process large amounts of information (Miller, 1956; Miller, Galanter, & Pribram, 1960; Zellner, 1988). The length of a KMS document itself may thus serve as a peripheral cue that affects the degree of processing undertaken by the KMS user.

Second, perceived credibility of the document's source had no significant effect on the perception of usefulness of knowledge in the document (H2). Even though participants differentiated between a high and low source credibility (see manipulation check), this distinction did not affect their perception of knowledge usefulness. This again contrasts with Sussman and Siegal (2003) and others (Joshi, et al., 2007; Ko, et al., 2005), who found that source credibility positively predicted perceptions of knowledge usefulness. This contrast may highlight an important difference between KMS and other forms of knowledge media (e.g. email) as vehicles for mediated knowledge transfer. Information received via email is typically received in response to a knowledge seeker's solicitation for advice from one or more individuals with whom the seeker is acquainted. This was the case in Sussman and Siegal's study, where selected emails had been received in response to a request for information (see Sussman & Siegal, 2003 p. 54 for examples). Knowledge seekers using email are likely to solicit information from individuals with whom they are familiar, or, at minimum, whose proficiency in the subject matter is known. This observation is supported by evidence from the trust literature, which has found that transfer of useful knowledge is enhanced when the knowledge recipient has established a relationship of trust with the knowledge source (Carley, 1991; Mayer, Davis, & Schoorman, 1995). Building on this work, Levin & Cross (2004) found that both competence-based trust (trusting in the competence of the knowledge source) and benevolence-based trust (trusting in the motives of the knowledge source) played a key role in mediating the receipt of useful knowledge from a knowledge source with which the recipient had strong ties. In the case of KMS-mediated knowledge transfer, however, the knowledge recipient may have little opportunity to establish such trust with the knowledge source. Rather, the source may be only remotely familiar, if known at all. Moreover, information retrieved from a KMS may be viewed as less personal than a direct response received from a colleague via email. Taken together, these factors may introduce increased 'distance' between the knowledge source and knowledge recipient, eroding the latter's ability to effectively judge the former's credibility. Supporting this idea, many of our participants reported that, because they had no prior experience with the document author, they had difficulty judging his/her credibility, despite the fact that he/she was identified as expert/novice. This implies that for knowledge retrieved from a KMS, more cues may be needed to judge credibility of a source than just an indication of expertise. Alternatively, it may be the credibility of the system or the credibility of the work processes (such as validation), rather than the credibility of an individual author, that drive the perception of usefulness of KMS knowledge. In this case, spending resources to add more cues about the author may be less important than trying to maximize the credibility of the KMS as whole.

Finally, our results showed that a validated document was perceived to be more useful than one that was not validated (H3). This finding accords with prior knowledge management literature that identifies validation as a valuable signal of knowledge quality (Poston & Speier, 2005; Shon & Musen, 1999; Wathen & Burkell, 2002). Moreover, validation was a stronger determinant of knowledge usefulness when expertise of the knowledge recipient was relatively high. This suggests that validation may be a more important indicator of knowledge usefulness in cases where knowledge seekers are well educated in the topic.

This study points to several implications and questions for future research. First, how does the length of a KMS document affect the recipient's ability or motivation to evaluate the quality of the arguments it contains? As noted above, one possible explanation of our paradoxical results with respect to argument quality is that a lengthy document may divert the reader from examining its content in favor of simply evaluating simpler indicators of its validity. This may be particularly true of novice recipients who lack the cognitive resources necessary to evaluate the quality of the content in the first place (Nah & Benbasat, 2004). Future research should investigate this issue by manipulating the length of the KMS document in order to arrive at an optimum length that renders analysis of argument quality feasible.

Second, future research should examine how various mechanisms enhancing personalization and source familiarity influence processing of information in a KMS and other knowledge transfer media. For example, providing additional information about the document source (e.g. author bios, ratings from other users) may enhance the level of trust that the knowledge recipient places in the information, thereby activating the expected relationship between source credibility and perceived knowledge usefulness. On the other hand, the significant effect of validation on perceived knowledge usefulness vis-à-vis the non-significant effect of source credibility may indicate that validation by a third party is a more salient peripheral cue than are attributes of the source itself. Future research should build upon our results by further examining the influence of validation compared with other, potentially contrasting peripheral cues. In addition, the effect of alternative validation mechanisms (e.g. expert review vs. community ratings) should be investigated to identify consequent nuances in the knowledge elaboration process.

A third area for future research concerns the degree to which different types of information processing lead beyond perceptions of knowledge usefulness to consequent behaviors of knowledge seekers. For example, recent work suggests that access to a KMS can interact with perceived organizational climate to promote not only knowledge reuse, but also knowledge innovation (Durcikova, Fadel, Butler, & Galletta, 2010). However, these outcomes likely depend on the type of information processing undertaken by the recipient. For example, the intensive scrutiny involved central route processing could promote exploration of new, innovative solutions, while reliance on cursory evaluation of peripheral cues might lead to rote re-use of existing solutions. Future research can incorporate the model of information processing presented here to better account for the causes behind these behavioral patterns. Similarly, this model might also be applied to understanding learning outcomes achieved by knowledge seekers who utilize a KMS. Recent evidence suggests that KMS users have a short-term performance advantage in solving structured problems over those who have access to more traditional knowledge sources, such as printed materials (McCall, Arnold, & Sutton, 2008). However, the evidence also suggests that KMS users ultimately may suffer decreased mental encoding of important procedural rules that guide decision making. In other words, use of a KMS may tend to short-circuit the long-term establishment of expertise and internalization of knowledge on the part of knowledge workers even while it supports a "quick fix" for the problem at hand (Gray & Durcikova, 2005-2006). This learning disparity may be directly connected to the information processing routes afforded by a KMS. Specifically, the peripheral cues of knowledge usefulness made readily available by the KMS may induce the knowledge seeker to circumvent a more thoughtful (and permanent) evaluation of the arguments, thereby promoting ongoing dependency on the KMS and eroding long-term development of individual expertise. Future research should examine the learning effects of KMS-based information processing to better

understand how organizations can maximize both short-term performance and long-term learning.

For practitioners, this study highlights critical attributes of KMS knowledge that must be managed so as to enable effective knowledge transfer. Our results indicate that more detail in a KMS document may not always result in increased perceptions of utility, suggesting that practitioners should regulate the length and detail of KMS content. In addition, richer mechanisms may be necessary for adequately conveying source credibility, particularly in environments where the source is likely to be unfamiliar to the knowledge seeker. Finally, our results corroborate the tenet that knowledge validation is an important contributor to perceptions of knowledge usefulness. A recent study on the effect of validation mechanisms on users' perception of knowledge quality in a KMS (Durcikova & Gray, 2009) suggests that transparency and restrictiveness of a validation process increases the perceived knowledge quality. However, duration of the validation process decreases the perception of knowledge quality in a KMS. This suggests that practitioners should seriously consider a mechanism for KMS knowledge validation and the means by which this validation is communicated to the knowledge seeker.

As with any empirical research, limitations of the present study should be recognized. First, the experimental context, while allowing for controlled observation of the study's variables, may decrease the applicability of the findings to real-world KMS scenarios. In addition, using students as participants may limit generalizability of our results to the rest of the population, though underlying elaboration processes are expected to hold for all populations. Second, offering students extra credit may not reflect actual incentives received in the real world, potentially resulting in participants exercising less caution in their behavior than would real-world knowledge workers. However, we sought to mitigate this limitation by making the amount of extra credit received contingent on students' performance. A future study may use employees of real firms that encounter situations like the one in the experiment while performing their job duties. Finally, the task differed somewhat from actual KMS use in that participants were exposed to only one KMS document. In real KMS environments, users would likely research more than one resource before making a recommendation. In a future study, it may be possible to offer more than one entry and allow more time to make a decision in order to better reflect a real work environment.

CONCLUSION

As firms increasingly rely on technology-mediated knowledge transfer, understanding the cognitive processes that govern such transfer becomes paramount. This exploratory study is a first step toward better understanding elaboration processes in the context of KMS-enabled knowledge transfer. The findings from our experiment demonstrate the importance of elaboration mechanisms in judging KMS knowledge utility, and underscore the subtle distinctions between KMS and other knowledge transfer media. Specifically, argument quality and validation were found to negatively and positively influence perceptions of KMS knowledge usefulness, respectively, while source credibility had no significant effect on this perception. We anticipate that future studies will continue to build on this work in an effort to better understand how KMS knowledge transfer is shaped by elaboration processes.

REFERENCES

Alavi, M., & Leidner, D. E. (2001). Review: Knowledge management and knowledge management systems: Conceptual foundations and research issues. *Management Information Systems Quarterly, 25*(1), 107–136. doi:10.2307/3250961

Angst, C. M., & Agarwal, R. (2009). Adoption of Electronic Health Records in the Presence of Privacy Concerns: The Elaboration Likelihood Model and Individual Persuasion. [Article]. *Management Information Systems Quarterly, 33*(2), 339–370.

Bailey, J. E., & Pearson, S. W. (1983). Development of a tool for measuring and analyzing computer satisfaction. *Management Science, 29*(5), 530–545. doi:10.1287/mnsc.29.5.530

Bhatt, G. D. (2001). Knowledge management in organizations: examining the interaction between technologies, techniques, and people. *Journal of Knowledge Management, 4*(1), 68–75. doi:10.1108/13673270110384419

Bhattacherjee, A., & Sanford, C. (2006). Influence processes for information technology acceptance: An elaboration likelihood model. *Management Information Systems Quarterly, 30*(4), 805–825.

Billings, R. S., & Wroten, S. P. (1978). Use of path analysis in industrial/organizational psychology: Criticisms and suggestions. *The Journal of Applied Psychology, 63*, 677–688. doi:10.1037/0021-9010.63.6.677

Bredahl, L., & Grunert, K. G. (1998). Consumer attitudes and decision-making with regard to genetically engineered food products. *Journal of Consumer Policy, 21*(3), 251–277. doi:10.1023/A:1006940724167

Cacioppo, J. T., & Petty, R. E. (1982). The need for cognition. *Journal of Personality and Social Psychology, 42*, 116–131. doi:10.1037/0022-3514.42.1.116

Carley, K. (1991). A Theory of Group Stability. *American Sociological Review, 56*, 331–354. doi:10.2307/2096108

Davis, F. D. (1989). Perceived Usefulness, Perceived Ease of Use and User Acceptance of Information Technology. *MIS Quarterly, 13*(3 (September)), 319-340.

DeLone, W. H., & McLean, E. R. (1992). Information Systems Success: The Quest for the Dependent Variable. *Information Systems Research*, *3*(1), 60–95. doi:10.1287/isre.3.1.60

DeLone, W. H., & McLean, E. R. (2003). The DeLone and McLean model of information systems success: A ten-year update. *Journal of Management Information Systems*, *19*(4), 9.

Durcikova, A., Fadel, K. J., Butler, B. S., & Galletta, D. F. (2010). Knowledge Exploration and Exploitation: The Impacts of Psychological Climate and Knowledge Management System Access. *Information Systems Research*, isre.1100.0286. doi: 10.1287/isre.1100.0286

Durcikova, A., & Gray, P. H. (2009). How Knowledge Validation Processes Affect Knowledge Contribution. *Journal of Management Information Systems*, *25*(4), 81–107. doi:10.2753/MIS0742-1222250403

Eagley, A., Wood, W., & Chaiken, S. (1978). Causal inferences about communicators and their effect on opinion change. *Journal of Personality and Social Psychology*, *36*, 424–443. doi:10.1037/0022-3514.36.4.424

Everard, A., & Galletta, D. F. (2005-2006). How Presentation Flaws Affect Perceived Site Quality, Trust, and Intention to Purchase from an Online Store. *Journal of Management Information Systems*, *22*(3), 55–95.

Goodman, P. S., & Darr, E. D. (1998). Computer-aided systems and communities: Mechanisms for organizational learning in distributed environments. *Management Information Systems Quarterly*, *22*(4), 417–440. doi:10.2307/249550

Gray, P. H., & Durcikova, A. (2005-2006). The Role of Knowledge Repositories in Technical Support Environments: Speed Versus Learning in User Performance. *Journal of Management Information Systems*, *22*(3), 821–834.

Gray, P. H., & Meister, D. B. (2004). Knowledge Sourcing Effectiveness. *Management Science*, *50*(6), 821–834. doi:10.1287/mnsc.1030.0192

Huber, G. P. (2001). Transfer of knowledge in knowledge management systems: unexplored issues and suggested studies. *European Journal of Information Systems*, *10*(2), 72–79. doi:10.1057/palgrave.ejis.3000399

Husted, K., & Michailova, S. (2002). Diagnosing and Fighting Knowledge-Sharing Hostility. *Organizational Dynamics*, *31*(1), 60–73. doi:10.1016/S0090-2616(02)00072-4

Jennex, M. E. (2008). Exploring System Use as a Measure of Knowledge Management Success. *Journal of Organizational and End User Computing*, *20*(1), 50–63. doi:10.4018/joeuc.2008010104

Jennex, M. E., & Olfman, L. (2006). A model of knowledge management success. *International Journal of Knowledge Management*, *2*(3), 51–68. doi:10.4018/jkm.2006070104

Joshi, K. D., Sarker, S., & Sarker, S. (2007). Knowledge transfer within information systems development teams: Examining the role of knowledg source attributes. *Decision Support Systems*, *43*, 322–335. doi:10.1016/j.dss.2006.10.003

Kakabadse, N. K., Kakabadse, A., & Kouzmin, A. (2003). Reviewing the knowledge management literature: Towards a taxonomy. *Journal of Knowledge Management*, *7*(4), 75–91. doi:10.1108/13673270310492967

Kang, Y.-S., & Herr, P. M. (2006). Beauty and the beholder: Toward an integrative model of communication source effects. *The Journal of Consumer Research*, *33*, 123–130. doi:10.1086/504143

Kar Yan, T., & Shuk Ying, H. (2005). Web Personalization as a Persuasion Strategy: An Elaboration Likelihood Model Perspective. [Article]. *Information Systems Research*, *16*(3), 271–291. doi:10.1287/isre.1050.0058

An Experiment of Information Elaboration in Mediated Knowledge Transfer

Kim, D., & Benbasat, I. (2009). Trust-Assuring Arguments in B2C E-commerce: Impact of Content, Source, and Price on Trust. [Article]. *Journal of Management Information Systems, 26*(3), 175–206. doi:10.2753/MIS0742-1222260306

Ko, D. G., Kirsch, L. J., & King, W. R. (2005). Antecedents of Knowledge Transfer from Consultants to Clients in Enterprise System Implementations. *Management Information Systems Quarterly, 29*(1), 36–85.

Lee, J., Park, D.-H., & Han, I. (2008). The effect of negative online consumer reviews on product attitude: An information processing view. *Electronic Commerce Research and Applications, 7*(3), 341–352. doi:10.1016/j.elerap.2007.05.004

Levin, D. Z., & Cross, R. (2004). The strength of weak ties you can trust: The mediating role of trust in effective knowledge transfer. *Management Science, 50*(11), 1477–1490. doi:10.1287/mnsc.1030.0136

Majchrzak, A., Cooper, L. P., & Neece, O. E. (2004). Knowledge Reuse for Innovation. *Management Science, 50*(2), 174–188. doi:10.1287/mnsc.1030.0116

Markus, M. L. (2001). Toward a theory of knowledge reuse: Types of knowledge reuse situations and factors in reuse success. *Journal of Management Information Systems, 18*(1), 57–93.

Marwick, A. D. (2001). Knowledge management technology. *IBM Systems Journal, 40*(4), 814–830. doi:10.1147/sj.404.0814

Mayer, R. C., Davis, J. H., & Schoorman, F. D. (1995). An integration model of organizational trust. *Academy of Management Review, 20*, 709–734. doi:10.2307/258792

McCall, H., Arnold, V., & Sutton, S. G. (2008). Use of knowledge management systems and the impact on the acquisition of explicit knowledge. *Journal of Information Systems, 22*(2), 77–101. doi:10.2308/jis.2008.22.2.77

Miller, G. A. (1956). The magical number seven, plus or minus two: Some limits on our capacity for processing information. *Psychological Review, 63*, 81–97. doi:10.1037/h0043158

Miller, G. A., Galanter, E., & Pribram, K. H. (1960). *Plans and the structure of behavior*. New York: Holt, Rinehart, and Winston. doi:10.1037/10039-000

Mizerski, R., Golden, L., & Kernan, J. (1979). The attributional process in consumer decision making. *The Journal of Consumer Research, 6*, 123–140. doi:10.1086/208756

Moore, G. C., & Benbasat, I. (1991). Development of an Instrument to Measure the Perceptions of Adopting an Information Technology Innovation. *Information Systems Research, 2*(3), 192–223. doi:10.1287/isre.2.3.192

Nah, F., & Benbasat, I. (2004). Knowledge-based Support in a Group Decision Making Context: An Expert-Novice Comparison. [Article]. *Journal of the Association for Information Systems, 5*(3), 125–150.

Nelson, R. R., Todd, P. A., & Wixom, B. H. (2005). Antecedents of information and system quality: An empirical examination within the context of data warehousing. *Journal of Management Information Systems, 21*(4), 199–235.

Nonaka, I. (1994). A Dynamic Theory of Organizational Knowledge Creation. *Organization Science, 5*(1), 14–37. doi:10.1287/orsc.5.1.14

Nunnally, J. C. (1978). *Psychometric Theory* (2nd ed.). New York: McGraw-Hill.

Offsey, S. (1997). Knowledge management: Linking people to knowledge for bottom line results. *Journal of Knowledge Management, 1*(2), 113–122. doi:10.1108/EUM0000000004586

Petty, R. E., & Cacioppo, J. T. (1986). *Communication and Persuation: Central and Peripheral Routes to Attitude Change*. New York: Springer-Verlag.

Petty, R. E., Cacioppo, J. T., & Goldman, R. (1981). Personal involvement as a determinant of argument-based persuasion. *Journal of Personality and Social Psychology, 41*, 847–855. doi:10.1037/0022-3514.41.5.847

Petty, R. E., & Wegener, D. T. (1999). The Elaboration Likelihood Model: Current Status and Controversies. In Gilbert, D. T., Fiske, S. T., & Gardner, L. (Eds.), *Dual-Process Theories in Social Psychology* (pp. 323–390). New York: McGraw-Hill.

Poston, R. S., & Speier, C. (2005). Effective Use of Knowledge Management Systems: A Process Model of Content Ratings and Credibility Indicators. *Management Information Systems Quarterly, 29*(2), 221.

Ratneshwar, S., & Chaiken, S. (1991). Comprehension's role in persuasion: The case of its moderating effect on the persuasive impact of source cues. *The Journal of Consumer Research, 18*, 52–62. doi:10.1086/209240

Rucker, D. D., & Petty, R. E. (2006). Increasing the Effectiveness of Communications to Consumers: Recommendations Based on Elaboration Likelihood and Attitude Certainty Perspectives. *Journal of Public Policy & Marketing, 25*(1), 39–52. doi:10.1509/jppm.25.1.39

Saeed, K. A., & Abdinnour-Helm, S. (2008). Examining the effects of information system characteristics and perceived usefulness on post adoption usage of information systems. *Information & Management, 45*, 376–386. doi:10.1016/j.im.2008.06.002

Shon, J., & Musen, M. A. (1999, November 6-10). *The Low Availability of Metadata Elements for Evaluating the Quality of Medical Knowledge on the Word Wide Web*. Paper presented at the Proceedings of American Medical Informatics Association Symposium, Washington, DC.

Stamm, K., & Dube, R. (1994). The relationship of attitudinal components to trust in media. *Communication Research, 21*(1), 105–123. doi:10.1177/009365094021001006

Sussman, S. W., & Siegal, W. S. (2003). Information Influence in Organizations: An Integrated Approach to Knowledge Adoption. *Information Systems Research, 14*(1), 47–65. doi:10.1287/isre.14.1.47.14767

Venkatesh, V., & Davis, F. D. (2000). A Theoretical Extension of the Technology Acceptance Model: Four Longitudinal Field Studies. *Management Science, 46*(2), 186–204. doi:10.1287/mnsc.46.2.186.11926

Venkatesh, V., Morris, M. G., Davis, G. B., & Davis, F. D. (2003). User acceptance of information technology: Toward a unified view. *Management Information Systems Quarterly, 27*(3), 425.

Wan, H.-H. (2008). Resonance as a Mediating Factor Accounting for the Message Effect in Tailored Communication: Examining Crisis Communication in a Tourism Context. *The Journal of Communication, 58*(3), 472–489. doi:10.1111/j.1460-2466.2008.00395.x

Wathen, C. N., & Burkell, J. (2002). Believe It or Not: Factors Influencing Credibility on the Web. *Journal of the American Society for Knowledge Science and Technology, 53*(2), 134–144. doi:10.1002/asi.10016

White, F. A., Charles, M. A., & Nelson, J. K. (2008). The Role of Persuasive Arguments in Changing Affirmative Action Attitudes and Expressed Behavior in Higher Education. *The Journal of Applied Psychology, 93*(6), 1271–1286. doi:10.1037/a0012553

Zack, M. H. (1999). Managing Codified Knowledge. *Sloan Management Review, 40*(4), 45–58.

Zellner, A. (1988). Optimal Information Processing and Bayes's Theorem. *The American Statistician, 42*, 278–284. doi:10.2307/2685143

Chapter 20

Facilitating Knowledge Transfer and the Achievement of Competitive Advantage with Corporate Universities:
An Exploratory Model Based on Media Richness and Type of Knowledge to be Transferred

M. Suzanne Clinton
University of Central Oklahoma, USA

Kimberly L. Merritt
Oklahoma Christian University, USA

Samantha R. Murray
Lubbock Christian University, USA

ABSTRACT

The knowledge literature suggests that transferring knowledge leads to synergistic cost advantages, better implementation of organizational strategies, and competitive advantage. Organizations are implementing corporate universities to aid in knowledge transfer. There is no standardized definition for corporate universities, but rather models that allow organizations to customize them to meet their training needs. Building on recent work of managing the knowledge transfer process (Murray & Peyrefitte, 2007) and on seminal work on media richness theory (Daft & Lengel, 1986), the authors propose that the type of knowledge to be transferred, and the appropriate media to transfer that knowledge, determine the most beneficial generation of corporate university to achieve competitive advantage. The chapter presents a model and propositions concerning relationships between the type of knowledge to be transferred, appropriate media selection, and generation of corporate university to implement.

DOI: 10.4018/978-1-60960-555-1.ch020

INTRODUCTION

In today's rapidly changing environment, learning for firms is ultimately about staying in business (Miller, Stewart, & Walton, 1999; Sumner, 2003). "Finding ways to embed knowledge in organizational processes and documents, to distribute information and know-how in readily-accessible forms, and to disseminate knowledge and accelerate learning are key challenges facing organizations," (Mohrman & Lawler, 1998, p.438). The ultimate challenge lies in exploiting the knowledge that we have at a faster rate than our competitors (Mohrman & Lawler, 1998).

Research has suggested that knowledge is the primary ingredient in gaining a competitive advantage (e.g., Li, Shen, & Xi, 2010; Subashini, 2010; Chilton & Bloodgood, 2008; Eldin & Hamza, 2009; Mohammadi, Khanlari, & Sohrabi, 2009; Gnyawali, Stewart, & Grant, 1997; Kogut & Zander, 1992) and that knowledge is a firm's main inimitable resource (Grant, 1996). In order for firms to maximize the competitive advantage arising from knowledge, knowledge must be effectively transferred within organizations (Li, Shen, & Xi, 2010; McDonnell, Gunnigle & Lavelle, 2010).

The authors propose that an appropriately designed corporate university can maximize the transfer of corporate knowledge. As illustrated in Figure 1, when designing a corporate university, both the type of knowledge to be transferred and the most appropriate type of media for that transfer must be considered.

The development of a corporate university represents a high-profile, creative corporate commitment both to knowledge transfer and to producing strategic advantages by providing faster learning than the competition (Miller, Stewart, & Walton, 1999; Allen, 2002). Additionally, corporate universities lengthen the shelf life of knowledge and help align training with strategic business goals (Sunoo, 1998).

Corporate universities are vital to the individual employee as well. In the new, flexible, decentralized organizational structure, responsibility and authority are pushed downward and all employees are expected to make decisions and to contribute to competitive advantage. This organization requires a new breed of workers, ones who can think and do for themselves (Estrada, 1995). As such, advanced education and continuous learning are crucial (Allerton, 1998). The key goal for an organization is

Figure 1. Relationship between type of knowledge to be transferred, appropriate media required for knowledge transfer, appropriate generation of corporate university necessary for achieving knowledge transfer and competitive advantage

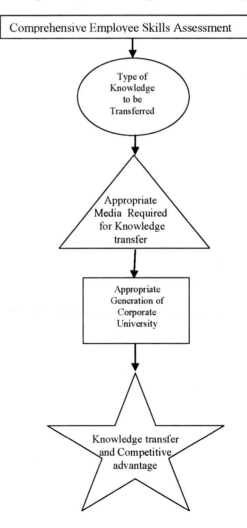

to provide its workers with the ability to retool their skills and knowledge continually (Meister, 1998b). Corporate universities allow employers to provide employees the opportunity to increase their knowledge, and in return, employees will take education from the corporate university and give back to the organization through innovation, efficiency and productivity. Therefore, corporate universities afford benefits to both the employee and the employer (Allen, 2002).

However, in order for corporate universities to aid in the knowledge transfer process successfully, several steps are required. First, the organization's education and training shortcomings must be identified. Second, the organization must decide whether the knowledge to be transferred is explicit or tacit. Third, the organization must select the appropriate communication media for the property or type of knowledge to be transferred. Fourth, the organization must choose an appropriate corporate university model to fit the information processing needs. This process will ensure higher learning outcomes, and therefore help the organization to achieve a competitive advantage.

Although conceptual research convinces us that corporate universities are a viable training tool, what is missing from the literature is instruction in the design of a model. The authors propose that organizations developing a corporate university choose the best fit between media selection and the generation of corporate university, given the type of knowledge to be transferred. Two primary purposes of this chapter are (1) to present a model demonstrating the benefits of a corporate university when used as a knowledge transfer tool and (2) to illustrate how organizations can utilize the model to improve knowledge transfer and achieve competitive advantage for today and for the future.

In the next sections, the authors discuss the literature that addresses knowledge, the appropriate media with which to transfer the knowledge, knowledge transfer, and corporate universities. Corporate university generations are introduced. A model is proposed illustrating the relationships

between the type of knowledge to be transferred, the appropriate media choice for transferring this type of knowledge, and the appropriate generation of corporate university to be implemented. Finally, implications of the model proposed will be discussed.

THEORETICAL BACKGROUND

Knowledge and Knowledge Transfer

For many years, both researchers and practitioners have discussed the importance of knowledge transfer within organizations (e.g., McDonnell, Gunnigle & Lavelle, 2010; Mohammadi, Khanlari, & Sohrabi, 2009; Desenberg, 2000; Govindarajan & Fisher, 1990; Kogut & Zander, 1992; Narasimha, 2000; Zander & Kogut, 1995). In fact, knowledge transfer has become a major component of strategy and the strategic planning process (Liebeskind, 1996). Knowledge has emerged as the most strategically significant resource of the firm (Grant, 1996). Experts propose that rapid knowledge transfer is the foundation for competitive advantage (McDonnell, Gunnigle & Lavelle, 2010; Li, Shen, & Xi, 2010; Mohammadi, Khanlari, & Sohrabi, 2009; Phillips, 2004; Fenn, 1999; Kogut & Zander, 1992). "An increasing number of organizations are concluding that the knowledge and skill of employees and the speed with which employees can increase their knowledge and skill represents what is arguably the only sustainable competitive advantage," (Allen, 2002, p.56).

Although knowledge management researchers have fundamentally different perspectives on the definitions of knowledge, the authors of this chapter will define knowledge as information whose validity has been established through test of proof and can therefore be distinguished from opinion, speculation, beliefs, or other types of unproven information (Liebeskind, 1996). This definition of knowledge consists of two primary classifications, explicit knowledge (information) and tacit knowledge (know-how) (Giju, Badea, Lopez Ruiz, & Nevado Pena, 2010; Nonaka, 1991). This dichotomous view of knowledge has been dominant in the knowledge management literature (Giju, Badea, Lopez Ruiz, & Nevado Pena, 2010; Smedund, 2009) since the publication of the SECI model (Nonaka & Takeuchi, 1995). Although research shows that explict and tacit knowledge form two endpoints of a knowledge continuum with varying degrees of explicitness in between (Giju, Badea, Lopez Ruiz, & Nevado Pena, 2010; Eldin & Hamza, 2009; Taylor, 2007; Klein, Connell & Meyer, 2005), the authors of this chapter will limit their discussion to knowledge that is primarily explicit and primarily tacit.

Explicit knowledge is defined as knowledge that is codified, in the form of books, documents and written procedures (Chilton & Bloodgood, 2008; Smedlund, 2009; Grant 1996). This is "knowledge about things" and that knowledge that can be transmitted without losing the exact meaning. Thus, explicit knowledge implies understanding and being able to communicate the knowledge in written form accurately (Grant, 1996; Nonaka, 1994).

Tacit knowledge is more complex than explicit knowledge. Tacit knowledge is the experience and intuition that allows one to do something efficiently (Subashini, 2010; Chilton & Bloodgood, 2008; Grant, 1996; Nonaka, 1994). Tacit knowledge has a personal quality that makes it difficult to formalize and to communicate because it involves both cognitive and technical elements and is not easy to write down. Where explicit knowledge is codified, tacit knowledge is experience-based (Smedlund, 2009). As the academic discipline of knowledge management has evolved, there has been increasing emphasis on tacit knowledge (Subashini, 2010; Snowden, 2002). In fact, some researchers assert, "that it is tacit knowledge that will determine the degree to which companies remain competitive. The rationale being that while explicit knowledge is more easily managed, tacit knowledge has more value, being derived from

particular circumstances and therefore difficult to imitate externally. Thus, citing the importance of tacit knowledge to prosperity, as well as the lack of evidence for the positive impact of explicit knowledge solutions, researchers are calling for the addition of techniques and cultures to promote tacit knowledge transfer" (Jimes & Lucardie, 2003, p. 24).

Knowledge transfer in organizations has become a primary strategic focus (Chilton & Bloodgood, 2008). There are many reasons that knowledge transfer is vital to organizations. First, high resource sharing and knowledge transfer may yield a synergistic cost advantage, providing a shared resource at a lower cost than if different parts of the organization had produced or created it separately (Brush, 1996; Govindarajan & Fisher, 1990; Gupta & Govindarajan, 1986; Porter, 1987). Second, knowledge transfer enables organizational members to identify and to respond appropriately to critical environmental situations and to adapt more quickly (McDonnell, Gunnigle & Lavelle, 2010; Zajac & Bazerman, 1991). Third, knowledge transfer allows members to obtain more complete information and to make better informed decisions (Gnyawali, *et al*, 1997).

Effective knowledge transfer leads to organizational learning. Varying perspectives of this learning can be found in the literature. One perspective of organizational learning holds that an organization learns if, through its processing of information, its potential behaviors are changed (Jennex & Croasdell, 2003; Croasdell, Jennex, Zhihong, and Christianson, 2003; Jennex, Olfman, and Addo, 2003; Huber, Davenport, and King, 1998). In this chapter, the authors adopt the learning organization perspective of Dodgson (1993) who argues that individuals are the primary learning entity in organizations and that it is the individual who creates organizational forms that encourage learning and knowledge transfer. If individuals transfer knowledge to other organizational members, then the organization has learned. Organizational learning results in associations, cognitive systems, and memories that are shared by organizational members (Fiol & Lyles, 1985).

Corporate University Defined

A review of the literature reveals that there are numerous definitions of a corporate university. For example, Greenberg (1998) says that a corporate university is not a physical place; however, it is a "concept for organized learning that is designed to perpetuate the organization" (p.37). Meister (1998a) defines a corporate university as a strategic umbrella with the purpose of developing and educating the various parts of the organization's value chain in order to help the company achieve its business strategy more efficiently and effectively. Others indicate that a corporate university may be all or any of the following: "a partnership with universities and other suppliers; a focus for learning and development of employees; a system of knowledge management; and/or a center of excellence," (Thomas, 1999 as quoted in Blass, 2001, p.158). Allen (1994) defines a corporate university as an "educational entity that is a strategic tool designed to assist its parent organization in achieving its mission by conducting activities that cultivate both individual and organization knowledge and wisdom," (pp. 58-59). Perhaps Blass (2001, p.156) gives the most inclusive definition by stating that a corporate university is

A set of continua, including, for example: Bricks and mortar through to virtual (Thomas, 1999); Encompasses some employees through to encompasses all employees (Ball, 1999); Produces measurable benefits though to produces a feel-good factor (ibid); Is a corporate training department through to being a system of knowledge management (Blass, 2001); and Is self-contained through to works solely in partnerships (Blass, 2001). Where each organization fits on each continuum is for them to decide...the corporate university is the mechanism by which organizations are trying

to make learning part of everyday activities so that they can become 'learning organizations'...

For the purpose of this chapter, the authors define corporate university as a strategic corporate commitment to learning. The skill-enhancement processes involved in a corporate university are ongoing. Internal and external resources are used both to train new employees and to keep veteran employees' skills ever current (Fenn, 1999). In order for organizations to compete in this rapidly changing environment, knowledge must be disseminated throughout the organization (Greenberg, 1998; Miller, Stewart, & Walton, 1999). Corporate universities can aid this dissemination.

Corporate universities have a strategic focus. They are proactive, centralized, and have a customized, strategically-relevant curriculum for key job families (Cocheo, 2004; Galloway, 2004). Only with clear expectations, roles and objectives, is a corporate university a strategic player (Phillips, 2004). They shape corporate culture and foster the development of intangible skills such as leadership, creative thinking and problem solving (Sunoo, 1998). The development of a corporate university represents a strategic umbrella for the education and development of employees and value chain members such as customers, suppliers, and dealers (Meister, 1998c; Firestone, 2002). Once a company commits to linking corporate education closely to its overall corporate strategy, not just to improving individual work performance, the creation of a corporate university makes sense (Greco, 1997). Defense Acquisition University "recognize[s] that the whole purpose of providing a learning environment is to create competitive advantage," (Salopek, 2004, p.47). They create this advantage with their strategic assets—learning and people. Others argue that organizations should take the "next logical step and put learning at the center of [the] strategy," (Sumner, 2003, p.2).

Although the superordinate factor driving the proliferation of corporate universities is the corporation's ability to compete in today's global marketplace, the literature provides numerous and varied factors that have driven the proliferation of corporate universities. The astronomical growth of corporate universities is due in part to the firm's ability to compete (Greco 1997), desire to receive company-specific training/development (Meister, 1998a), need for continuous learning/ updating of skills (Fenn, 1999; Meister, 1998c; Rosener & Walesh, 1998), corporate downsizing (Mohrman & Lawler, 1998), the change in the United States from a manufacturing to a service economy, and the organization's ability to recruit/ retain employees (Fenn, 1999; Rosener & Walesh, 1998). Therefore, corporate universities are important and appropriate media choice is critical in achieving maximum knowledge transfer and competitive advantage.

Generations of Corporate Universities

The academic literature describes and categorizes corporate universities in various ways, specifically through the use of generation phases or stages. This research will employ Miller, Stewart, and Walton's (1999, p.43) description of corporate universities, which utilizes the metaphor of generations to classify corporate universities:

- First-generation - little more than a repackaging of conventional training and development departments; focus on specific training modules requiring classroom attendance and an emphasis on the acquisition of corporate values
- Second-generation - reflect a broader-based strategy toward organizational learning; often an extension of the total quality management philosophy; based in one campus location
- Third-generation - possess a virtual element to the learning process; encompass a

broad range of strategies for the development of intellectual capital

Implementing Corporate Universities

A corporate university can act as a chameleon in meeting the education and training needs of the organization. According to Greenberg (1998), the average corporate university requires an investment of 2.3% of an organization's payroll, a figure equating to an average operating budget of $10.1 million. Therefore, the stakes are high and it is vital that organizations are creating corporate universities that match their own particular training and educational needs. Organizations face a significant challenge in finding the right formula to be successful. The structure of a corporate university should hinge on the needs of the organization and should fill employee training gaps. Corporate universities can range from contracting with a local university to design a curriculum to develop employees' business principles or leadership skills, to creating an on-site university to educate employees about company-specific knowledge. As previously delineated, in order to choose the correct fit, the organization's education and training needs must be identified and the organization must decide whether the knowledge to be transferred is explicit or tacit. Next, the organization must select the appropriate communication media for the property or type of knowledge to be transferred. Finally, the organization must choose the corporate university model that is congruent with the information processing needs. In the following paragraphs, the authors will present a discussion of these steps and the actions required for addressing them.

Table 1. Matching corporate university generation with media

First-Generation			
Needs	**Knowledge Type**	**Appropriate Media**	**Example of Appropriate Media**
Communicating standardized procedures	Explicit	Lean	Video/ Passive Lecture
Greeting customers	Tacit	Rich	Role Play/ Job Rotation
Second-Generation			
Needs	**Knowledge Type**	**Appropriate Media**	**Example of Appropriate Media**
Enhance employee education	Explicit	Lean	Passive Lecture
Third-Generation			
Needs	**Knowledge Type**	**Appropriate Media**	**Example of Appropriate Media**
Using new software	Explicit	Lean	Lecture
Communicating corporate values	Tacit	Rich	Face-to-face two-way communication
Teaching motivational techniques	Tacit	Richer	Simulation

Source: Original.

THE PROPOSED MODEL

Identify the Organization's Education and Training Shortcomings: Comprehensive Employee Skills Assessment

First, the organization's education and training shortcomings must be identified. Although the literature is full of methods and measures for quantifying education (e.g., Literacy Testing, Michigan Mathematics Leadership Academy Mathematics Assessment, Test of Adult Basic Education, requiring high school or college transcripts) and training (e.g., performance appraisals may illustrate that employees do not know how to perform effectively or that employees cannot demonstrate correct knowledge or behavior, studies of improper use of equipment or injury reports from the Occupational Safety and Health Administration) shortcomings, this topic exceeds the scope of this chapter. The

fact remains that regardless of the methods used to do so, organizations must identify education and training shortcomings.

Decide Whether the Knowledge to be Transferred is Explicit or Tacit

Second, the organization must decide whether the knowledge to be transferred is explicit or tacit. As previously discussed, explicit knowledge is defined as knowledge that is codified in the form of books, documents and written procedures (Chilton & Bloodgood, 2008; Smedlund, 2009; Grant 1996), while tacit knowledge is the experience and intuition that allows one to do something efficiently (Subashini, 2010; Chilton & Bloodgood, 2008; Grant, 1996; Nonaka, 1994). Explicit knowledge is codified, and tacit knowledge is experience-based (Smedlund, 2009). The organization must choose which type of knowledge needs to be transferred to resolve its education and training shortcomings.

Select the Appropriate Communication Media for Transferring the Knowledge

Third, while many factors are involved in transferring knowledge, one that is of particular importance is media selection (Carlson & Davis, 1998). Media differ in richness, which is the ability of information to change understanding within a time interval (Daft & Lengel, 1986, p. 560). Daft and Lengel (1986), in their seminal work on media richness, argued that organizational members could improve performance by matching media characteristics to the needs of the organization. Rich media are personal and involve face-to-face two-way communication while media of lower richness are impersonal and rely on rules, forms, procedures, or data bases. According to media richness theory, messages should be communicated through channels with sufficient and appropriate media richness capacities (Lengel & Daft, 1988). Equivocal messages require media high in immediate feedback (e.g., face-to-face contact or telephone), whereas unequivocal messages can be adequately carried by lean media (such as written documents or passive lecture) (Webster & Trevino, 1995). Messages transferred on channels that are inappropriate to the situation run a higher risk of being ineffective (cf., Carlson & Zmud, 1999). In addition, the richness of the communication media chosen to share knowledge is related to the type of knowledge transferred (explicit knowledge or tacit knowledge) (Murray & Peyrefitte, 2007).

As stated previously, explicit knowledge is defined as knowledge that is codified, and can be transmitted without losing the exact meaning. It follows, then, that these tasks are analyzable. When tasks are analyzable, the uncertainty levels are lower and less complex; therefore, a leaner media selection is sufficient to meet information needs and thus transfer knowledge defined as ex-

plicit knowledge (Daft & Lengel, 1986). Explicit knowledge may be easier to transfer as it can be written down or codified. Training and educational methods that are lower in media richness include videotapes and passive instructional lectures (Murray & Peyrefitte, 2007). These methods involve one-way communication, do not require direct personal contact, and are appropriate media for relaying codifiable knowledge, such as rules and procedures. Therefore, the authors propose the following:

Proposition 1a. Under conditions of explicit knowledge transfer, lean media will lead to better learning outcomes than rich media.

Tacit knowledge is defined as knowledge that is not analyzable, which means that it is difficult to identify and explain because of its complexity and because it encompasses the owner's accumulated experience, intuition, and judgment. Sharing tacit knowledge often increases uncertainty because it may give rise to multiple interpretations and because tacit knowledge is difficult to write down (Grant, 1996). Tasks of this type require rich media (Daft and Lengel, 1986) that allow for rapid feedback and multiple cues so that communicators can align their mental models. The training methods that are higher in media richness include, but are not limited to, mentoring, simulation games, role-playing, and job rotation (Murray & Peyrefitte, 2007). Once again, these methods are considered richer media because they require more face-to-face interaction, rapid feedback, and the ability to transfer complex knowledge or tacit knowledge.

Proposition 1b. Under conditions of tacit knowledge transfer, rich media will lead to better learning outcomes than lean media.

Since the effectiveness of organizational learning in the knowledge transfer process is dependent on the context (Shropshire, 2010; Gnyawali *et al.*, 1997), it may be important to use an appropriate medium at the right time. Thus, a potential problem could be using inappropriate media to transfer explicit knowledge and tacit knowledge. Using lean media to transfer tacit knowledge will not provide face-to-face interactions and therefore, may not be the most efficient way to transfer tacit knowledge. As stated earlier, corporate universities are expensive. If organizations attempt to save money and choose lean media for tacit knowledge, then more than likely, they will fail to transfer the tacit knowledge and there will be a decrease in the quality of learning outcomes. If the corporate university fits the training and educational needs of the organization, then the costs of richer media may be recouped because the result will likely be increased efficiency, production, or other desired outcomes. Likewise, attempting to transfer explicit knowledge via rich media may exhaust the limits of the media and not leave room to transfer tacit knowledge effectively. For example, a training session may be needed to address a new policy, but instead of using a videotape, the organization hires a consultant. In this case, the organization has chosen the wrong media and probably has spent far more money on the training module than necessary. It is likely that failure to transfer complex and important knowledge will be quickly noticed, but the opposite may not be true.

On the other hand, if the appropriate media is used to transfer the correct type of knowledge, better learning outcomes will be achieved, thereby increasing the effectiveness of organizational learning in the knowledge transfer process. Further, this increased organizational learning effectiveness (i.e., superior learning outcomes) will lead the organization to competitive advantage.

Proposition 1c. Increased learning outcomes will lead to competitive advantage for the organization.

For example, if an organization found out through a survey that its employees were unsure what words or actions could constitute sexual harassment, the organization might choose to train its employees on its sexual harassment policies. The goal of communicating an overview of sexual harassment policies or standardized procedures—each examples of more traditional training program—would be to transfer explicit knowledge. Explicit knowledge is best transferred through videotapes and lectures, which are leaner media, since this type of knowledge is easy to communicate and can be codified (Murray & Peyrefitte, 2007). The first- generation corporate university, which mirrors a more traditional training and development program, excels at transferring explicit knowledge with leaner media.

Choose the Appropriate Corporate University Model

To choose the appropriate corporate university model, the organization must conduct a comprehensive employee skills assessment. The results of that assessment will determine the appropriate model of corporate university to be implemented. If the assessment leads an organization to conclude that the primary need is employee development, with the scope of knowledge being individual skills/knowledge and the enhancement of current business practices, a first-generation corporate university would sufficiently fulfill the organization's needs. The first-generation corporate university is basically the repackaging of conventional training and development departments (Miller, Stewart, & Walton, 1999). In this case, the corporate university will be implemented through the traditional training departments.

If the results of the comprehensive skills assessment indicate that the primary knowledge gap is imminent business needs (e.g. learning new software, a new marketing strategy, or learning to support a new strategic business alliance) with the scope of knowledge being on current business practices, then additional education is necessary. Therefore, a second-generation corporate university would be required to fulfill the organization's needs, which reflects a broader-based strategy toward organizational learning. In this instance, a corporate university might involve an organization partnering with a local university to provide instruction in a common body of knowledge. This type of corporate university is often an extension of the total quality management philosophy and is based in a single campus location (Miller, Stewart, & Walton, 1999). College courses would be offered to employees for additional education through means of traditional classroom media, including textbooks, lectures, videotapes, and case studies. For example, GE and Procter and Gamble recently partnered with the University of Michigan Business School in an effort to raise the level of ethics, integrity and corporate global citizenship in business (www.ge.com).

If the results of the comprehensive skills assessment indicate that the primary gap is unknown business development with the scope of knowledge being redefining business to be an industry leader or restructuring with the focus of undefined market potential, then the corporate university may be on-site and provide employees company specific knowledge. This would require the implementation of a third-generation corporate university, which possesses a virtual element to the learning process, and encompasses a broad range of strategies for the development of intellectual capital (Miller, Stewart, & Walton, 1999). An on-site corporate university provides the opportunity to clearly communicate the organizational culture and concretely instill the organization's values and beliefs. For example, McDonald's opened Hamburger University in 1961 and since its inception, training at Hamburger University has emphasized consistent restaurant operations procedures, service, quality and cleanliness (www. McDonalds.com/corp/career/hamburger_university). It has become McDonald's global center of excellence for operations training and leadership development. The curriculum is delivered using a combination of classroom instruction, hands-on-lab activities, goal-based scenarios and computer e-learning modules. Management-level employees are able to build on their leadership and consulting skills, teaching individuals how to operate great restaurants effectively.

Proposition 2. Explicit knowledge will best be transferred through lean media using a First-Generation Corporate university to achieve higher learning outcomes, and therefore, a competitive advantage.

On the other hand, if an organization wanted to teach employees how to customize a customer greeting or close a sale, the organization would need to transfer tacit knowledge. Tacit knowledge should be transferred with richer media such as role-play or job rotation, since this type of knowledge cannot be easily communicated or codified (Murray & Peyrefitte, 2007). Role-play is an effective training and development tool which aids employees in "thinking outside the box". A first-generation corporate university is appropriate for transferring tacit knowledge with richer media.

Proposition 3. Tacit knowledge will best be transferred through rich media using a First-Generation Corporate university to achieve higher learning outcomes, and therefore, a competitive advantage.

If an organization chose to implement statistical process control, its employees may need instruction in mathematics and statistics. Explicit knowledge of this type is best transferred through leaner media since this type of knowledge can be easily communicated and codified (Murray & Peyrefitte, 2007). A second-generation corporate university involves partnering with a local university to enhance employee education on a common body of knowledge. This is accomplished primarily through a classroom setting, which generally involves textbooks, lectures, and case analyses. Thus, the second-generation corporate university transfers mostly explicit knowledge, and would be best suited to this educational need.

Proposition 4. Explicit knowledge will best be transferred through lean media using a Second-Generation Corporate university to achieve higher learning outcomes, and therefore, a competitive advantage.

If Dominos' on-site university wants to train employees in the use of new pizza tracking software, explicit knowledge transfer is needed. Because explicit knowledge is easily communicated and can be codified, lecture is the most appropriate media. The third-generation corporate university, which involves an on-site location and transfers specific company knowledge, will face the challenge of designing a curriculum that transfers the appropriate type of knowledge (explicit) through the appropriate media (lean).

Proposition 5. Explicit knowledge will best be transferred through lean media using a Third-Generation Corporate university to achieve higher learning outcomes, and therefore, a competitive advantage.

However, if GE wants to communicate tacit knowledge such as corporate values of ethics, integrity and global citizenship, then face-to-face communication may be necessary. In this instance, a more rich media might be the best way to transfer this type of knowledge effectively. This is best accomplished through the use of a third-generation corporate university. Proposition 6. Tacit knowledge will best be transferred through rich media using a Third-Generation Corporate university to achieve higher learning outcomes, and therefore, a competitive advantage.

Similarly, if McDonald's desires to share motivational techniques with managers, then role-play might be an effective richer media. Likewise, issues involving strategic initiatives and problem solving would certainly need to be

transferred with face-to-face methods, since such topics are hard to communicate and write down. Third-generation corporate universities are best suited to this type of knowledge transfer.

Proposition 7. Tacit knowledge will best be transferred through richer media using a Third-Generation Corporate university to achieve higher learning outcomes, and therefore, a competitive advantage.

Figure 2 visually depicts the relationship between the type of knowledge to be transferred at the conclusion of the comprehensive employee skills assessment, the appropriate media selection, and the appropriate generation of corporate university to utilize. The figure also delineates each proposition.

SUMMARY

As discussed above, the need for organizations to transfer knowledge has been well documented. The literature has also provided evidence that knowledge transfer leads to better decision making (Gnyawali *et al.*, 1997), and that knowledge sharing increases task effectiveness (Hansen & Haas, 2001). One tool that can help organizations transfer knowledge is corporate universities. Although conceptual research suggests that corporate universities are a viable training tool, what is missing from the literature is instruction in the design of a model. The main contribution of this chapter is a proposed contingency model of the relationships between type of knowledge to be transferred, appropriate media selection, and appropriate generation of corporate university necessary for achieving knowledge transfer and competitive advantage.

Figure 2. Relationships between type of knowledge to be transferred, appropriate media selection, and generation of corporate university necessary for achieving knowledge transfer and competitive advantage

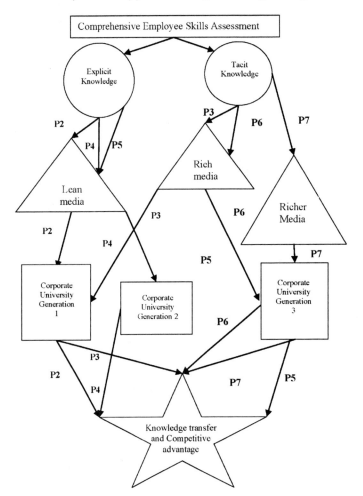

IMPLICATIONS

The implications of this research include the following. Inappropriately matching the type of knowledge to be transferred, the generation of corporate university, and the appropriate media will result in the loss of knowledge transfer efficiency and effectiveness. This loss will lead to losses in employee performance, customer satisfaction, and employee satisfaction, to name a few. Correcting losses and lack of satisfaction most often results in additional supervision, discipline, repeated training, job redesign or the like. The authors assert that an appropriately designed and deployed corporate university, based on the type of knowledge to be transferred and the appropriate media selection, will assist organizations in achieving efficiency and effectiveness in the knowledge transfer process.

SUGGESTIONS FOR FUTURE RESEARCH

Suggestions for future research include an empirical examination of each of the propositions delineated within the model. Such investigations will further assist firms in matching appropriate media richness to knowledge transfer.

Directions in Operationalizing Constructs for Model Variables

A search of the literature for operationalizing constructs for model variables was less than fruitful. In order to assist future researchers, the authors recommend the following as a potential "jumping-off point" for operationalizing the constructs.

Chilton and Bloodgood (2008) measured the degree to which workers rely on tacit knowledge. This study produced an indirect form of measurement that eliminates the need to render the knowledge entirely explicit prior to measurement, and allows the classification of the knowledge along the continuum. Once an organization identifies its training or educational needs, it could utilize a similar process to measure the degree of tacitness in the knowledge that is needed to be transfered.

In order to operationalize explicit and tacit knowledge, Murray and Peyrefitte (2007) conducted one-on-one interviews with employees at various levels of hospitals in which knowledge was being transferred. From the interviews, the variety of knowledge-sharing activities was identified. Preliminary lists of knowledge-sharing activities were refined and knowledge-sharing activity operationalized using common responses from the interviews. The survey was employed to measure the use of various media to transfer explicit and tacit knowledge. For example, they measured the use of videoconferencing for transferring explicit and tacit knowledge as follows:

Participation in videoconferencing allows you to

1. Discuss regulatory information. (Explicit)
2. Solve organizational problems that are easy to identify and explain. (Explicit)
3. Talk to a consultant. (Tacit)
4. Solve organizational problems that are hard to identify and explain. (Tacit)

An organization could utilize a similar process to operationalize the specific explicit and tacit knowledge it needs to transfer once it has identified its training or educational needs.

Muhammed, Doll, & Deng (2009) utilized a similar method to operationalize different forms of knowledge (conceptual, contextual and operational) in their study. One aim of the study was to develop measures of the various forms of knowledge. This study surveyed knowledge workers in a variety of industries and from various sized companies. The survey items consisted of questions requiring the respondents to self-rate their own knowledge on various aspects of knowledge (e.g. to who to go for resources or the reasons behind actions). A similar process could be employed to operationalize the specific explicit and tacit knowledge an organization needs to transfer once it has identified its training or educational needs.

To date, media richness is not something that has been thoroughly measured in the literature. Studies that have examined this question include work by D'Ambra (1995) and Trevino, Lengel, Bodensteiner and Gerloff (1990). Generally, media richness is simply determined by its location on Daft, Lengel, and Trevino's (1987) hierarchy of richness. In other words, media richness is treated as an "invariant objective features" of each communication media (Yu, 1997; Schmitz and Fulk, 1991).

Daft, Lengel, and Trevino (1987) developed a hierarchy of media richness to illustrate a continuum of media richness from low (unaddressed documents such as flyers and bulletins), to medium (written addressed documents and telephone conversations), to high (face to face). Once an organization identifies its training or educational needs, and operationalizes the specific explicit and tacit knowledge it needs to transfer, Daft, Lengel, and Trevino's (1987) hierarchy could be used to identify the media with the appropriate richness necessary to transfer the knowledge.

CONCLUSION

The authors have examined the relationship between the type of knowledge to be transferred and the selection of the appropriate media with which to do so as a foundation for determining the most beneficial generation of corporate university to implement in order to achieve knowledge transfer and competitive advantage. The proposed model can serve as a blueprint for managers hoping to utilize effectively a corporate university in the knowledge transfer process in the pursuit of competitive advantage.

REFERENCES

Allen, M. (2002). *The Corporate University Handbook: Designing, Managing and Growing a Successful Program*. New York: American Management Association.

Allerton, H. (1998). Phi beta company. *Training & Development, 52*(1), 8.

Ball, C. (1999). *Chairman's opening address and closing remarks*. Paper given at the IQPC Conference on the Corporate University in London on 22-23 June.

Blass, E. (2001). What's in a name? A comparative study of the traditional public university and the corporate university. *Human Resource Development International, 4*(2), 153–172. doi:10.1080/13678860121806

Brush, T. H. (1996). Predicted change in operational synergy and post-acquisition performance of acquired businesses. *Strategic Management Journal, 17*, 1–24. doi:10.1002/(SICI)1097-0266(199601)17:1<1::AID-SMJ782>3.0.CO;2-W

Carlson, J. R., & Zmud, R. W. (1999). Channel expansion theory and the experiential nature of media richness perceptions. *Academy of Management Journal, 42*(2), 153–170. doi:10.2307/257090

Carlson, P. J., & Davis, G. B. (1998). An investigation of media selection among directors and managers: From "self" to "other" orientation. *Management Information Systems Quarterly, 22*(3), 335–362. doi:10.2307/249669

Chilton, M., & Bloodgood, J. (2008). The dimensions of tacit and explicit knowledge: A description and measure. *International Journal of Knowledge Management, 4*(2), 75–91. doi:10.4018/jkm.2008040106

Cocheo, S. (2004). If you build it, they will learn. *ABA Banking Journal, 96*(2), 22–24.

Croasdell, D. T., & Jennex, M. Zhihong Yu & Christianson, T. (2003). *A meta-analysis of methodologies for research in knowledge management, organizational learning and organizational memory: Five years at HICSS*. Proceedings of the 36th Annual Hawaii International Conference on System Sciences.

D'Ambra, J. (1995*). A field study of information technology, task equivocality, media richness, and media preference*. PhD Dissertation, University of NSW.

Daft, R. L., & Lengel, R. H. (1986). Organizational information requirements, media richness and structural design. *Management Science, 32*(5), 554–571. doi:10.1287/mnsc.32.5.554

Daft, R. L., Lengel, R. H., & Trevino, L. K. (1987). Message equivocality, media selection, and manager performance: Implications for information systems. *Management Information Systems Quarterly, 11*(3), 355–366. doi:10.2307/248682

Desenberg, J. (2000). Moving past the information age: Getting started with knowledge management. *Public Management, 29*(2), 52–55.

Dodgson, M. (1993). Organizational learning: A review of some literatures. *Organization Studies*, *14*(3), 375–394. doi:10.1177/017084069301400303

Eldin, S., & Hamza, A. (2009). Capturing tacit knowledge from transient workers: Improving the organizational competitiveness. *International Journal of Knowledge Management*, *5*(2), 87–103. doi:10.4018/jkm.2009040106

Estrada, V. (1995). Are your factory workers know-it-alls? *The Personnel Journal*, (September): 128–131.

Fenn, D. (1999). Corporate universities for small companies. *Inc.*, *21*(2), 95–97.

Fiol, C. F., & Lyles, M. A. (1985). Organizational learning. *Academy of Management Review*, *10*(4), 803–813. doi:10.2307/258048

Firestone, G. (2002). An industry starving for cost-effective education. *Healthcare Publishing News*, *26*(9), 50–51.

Galloway, L. (2004). View from the top. *T&D*, *58(*4), 38-43.

Giju, G., Badea, L., Lopez Ruiz, V., & Nevado Pena, D. (2010). Knowledge management – the key resource in the knowledge economy. *Theoretical and Applied Economics*, *17*(6), 27–36.

Gnyawali, D. R., Stewart, A. C. & Grant, J. H. (1997). Creation and utilization of organizational knowledge: An empirical study of the roles of organizational learning on strategic decision making. *Academy of Management Best Paper Proceedings*, 16-20.

Govindarajan, V., & Fisher, J. (1990). Strategy, control systems, and resource sharing: Effects on business-unit performance. *Academy of Management Journal*, *33*(2), 259–285. doi:10.2307/256325

Grant, R. M. (1996). Toward a knowledge-based theory of the firm. *Strategic Management Journal*, *17*, 109–122.

Greco, J. (1997). Corporate home schooling. *The Journal of Business Strategy*, *18*(3), 48–52. doi:10.1108/eb039857

Greenberg, R. (1998). Corporate u. takes the job training field. *Techniques: Making Education & Career Connections*, *73*(7), 36–39.

Gupta, A. K., & Govindarajan, V. (1986). Resource sharing among SBUs: Strategic antecedents and administrative implications. *Academy of Management Journal*, *29*, 695–714. doi:10.2307/255940

Hansen, M. T. & Haas, M. R. (2001). Different knowledge, different benefits: Toward a productivity perspective on knowledge sharing in organizations. *Academy of Management Proceedings*, C1-C6.

Huber, G. P., Davenport, T. H., & King, D. (1998). *Some perspectives on organizational memory.* Unpublished Working Paper for the Task Force on Organizational Memory, F. Burstein, G. Huber, M. Mandviwalla, J. Morrison, and L. Olfman, (eds.) Presented at the 31st Annual Hawaii International Conference on System Sciences.

Jennex, M., & Croasdell, D. (2003). *Knowledge management, organizational memory and organizational learning.* Proceedings of the 36th Annual Hawaii International Conference on System Sciences.

Jennex, M., Olfman, L., & Addo, T. B. A. (2003). *The need for an organizational knowledge management.* Proceedings of the 36th Annual Hawaii International Conference on System Sciences.

Jimes, C., & Lucardie, L. (2003). Reconsidering the tacit-explicit distinction - A move toward functional (tacit) knowledge management. *Journal of Knowledge Management*, *1*(1), 23–32.

Klein, J. H., Connell, N. A. D., & Meyer, E. (2005). Knowledge characteristics of communities of practice. *Knowledge Management Research and Practice, 3*, 106–144. doi:10.1057/palgrave. kmrp.8500055

Kogut, B., & Zander, U. (1992). Knowledge of the firm, combinative capabilities, and the replication of technology. *Organization Science, 3*(3), 383–397. doi:10.1287/orsc.3.3.383

Lengel, R., & Daft, R. (1988). The selection of communication media as an executive skill. *The Academy of Management Executive, 2*(3), 225–232.

Li, Z., Shen, H. & Xi, Y. (2010). Do knowledge characteristics matter? A test of the relationship between knowledge characteristics and performance. *SAM Advanced Management Journal, Spring,* 38-53.

Liebeskind, J. P. (1996). Knowledge, strategy, and the theory of the firm. *Strategic Management Journal, 17,* 93–107.

McDonnell, A., Gunnigle, P., & Lavelle, J. (2010). Learning transfer in multinational companies: Explaining inter-organization variation. *Human Resource Management Journal, 20*(1), 23–43. doi:10.1111/j.1748-8583.2009.00104.x

Meister, J. (1998a). *Corporate universities: Lessons in Building a World-class Work Force.* New York: McGraw-Hill.

Meister, J. (1998b). The quest for lifetime employability. *The Journal of Business Strategy, 19*(3), 25–28. doi:10.1108/eb039933

Meister, J. (1998c). Ten steps to creating a corporate university. *Training & Development, 52*(11), 38–43.

Miller, R., Stewart, J., & Walton, J. (1999). Opened university. *People Management, 5*(12), 42–45.

Mohammadi, K., Khanlari, A., & Sohrabi, B. (2009). Organizational readiness assessment for knowledge management. *International Journal of Knowledge Management, 5*(1), 29–46. doi:10.4018/jkm.2009010103

Mohrman, S., & Lawler, E. (1998). *The New Human Resources Management: Creating the Strategic Business Partnership. Tomorrow's Organization: Crafting Winning Capabilities in a Dynamic World.* San Francisco: Jossey-Bass.

Muhammed, S., Doll, W. J., & Deng, X. (2009). A model of interrelationships among individual level knowledge management success measures. *International Journal of Knowledge Management, 5*(1), 1–15. doi:10.4018/jkm.2009010101

Murray, S., & Peyrefitte, J. (2007). Knowledge type and communication media choice in the knowledge transfer process. *Journal of Managerial Issues, 19*(1), 111–133.

Narasimha, S. (2000). Organizational knowledge, human resource management, and sustained competitive advantage: Toward a framework. *Competitiveness Review, 10*(1), 123–134.

Nonaka, I. (1991). The knowledge-creating company. *Harvard Business Review, 69*(6), 96–104.

Nonaka, I. (1994). A dynamic theory of organizational knowledge creation. *Organization Science, 5*(1), 14–37. doi:10.1287/orsc.5.1.14

Nonaka, I., & Takeuchi, H. (1995). *The Knowledge-creating Company: How Japanese Companies Create the Dynamics of Innovation.* New York: Oxford University Press.

Phillips, J. (2004). Twelve success factors for corporate universities. *Chief Learning Officer, 3*(2), 50–52.

Porter, M. E. (1987). From competitive advantage to corporate strategy. *Harvard Business Review,* (May-June): 43–59.

Roesner, L., & Walesh, S. (1998). Corporate university: Consulting firm case study. *Journal of Management Engineering*, *14*(2), 56–63. doi:10.1061/(ASCE)0742-597X(1998)14:2(56)

Salopek, J. (2004). Targeting the learning organization. *T&D, 58*(3), 46-51.

Schmitz, J., & Fulk, J. (1991). Organizational colleagues, media richness and electronic mail. *Communication Research*, *8*(4), 487–523. doi:10.1177/009365091018004003

Shropshire, C. (2010). The role of the interlocking director and board receptivity in the diffusion of practices. *Academy of Management Review*, *35*(2), 246–264.

Smedlund, A. (2009). Social network structures for explicit, tacit and potential knowledge. *International Journal of Knowledge Management*, Jan-March, 78-87.

Snowden, D. (2002). Complex acts of knowing: Paradox and descriptive self-awareness. *Journal of Knowledge Management*, *6*(2), 100–111. doi:10.1108/13673270210424639

Subashini, R. (2010). Tacit knowledge -The ultimate essence of an organization. *Advances in Management*, *3*(8), 36–39.

Sumner, J. (2003). Making the leap to a learning organization. *KM Review*, *6*(4), 2.

Sunoo, B. (1998). Corporate universities: More and better. *Workforce*, *77*(5), 16–18.

Taylor, H. (2007). Tacit knowledge: Conceptualizations and operationalizations. *International Journal of Knowledge Management*, *3*(3), 60–73. doi:10.4018/jkm.2007070104

Thomas, D. (1999). *The corporate university as a model for organizational and individual learning*. Paper given at the IQPC Conference on the Corporate university in London on 22-23 June.

Trevino, L., Lengel, R., Bodensteiner, W., Gerloff, E., & Muir, N. (1990). The richness imperative and cognitive style: The role of individual differences in media choice behavior. *Management Communication Quarterly*, *4*, 176–197. doi:10.1177/0893318990004002003

Webster, J., & Trevino, L. K. (1995). Rational and social theories as complementary explanations of communication media choices: Two policy-capturing studies. *Academy of Management Journal*, *38*, 1544–1572. doi:10.2307/256843

Yu, R. (1997). *Information Technology and Media Choice of CFO*. Master's Thesis, University of NSW.

Zajac, E. J., & Bazerman, M. N. (1991). Blind spots in industry and competitor analysis: The implications of interfirm perceptions for strategic decisions. *Academy of Management Review*, *16*, 37–56. doi:10.2307/258606

Zander, U., & Kogut, B. (1995). Knowledge and the speed of the transfer and imitation of organizational capabilities: An empirical test. *Organization Science*, *6*(1), 76–92. doi:10.1287/orsc.6.1.76

Chapter 21
Knowledge Management Utilization:
A Case Study of Two Jordanian Universities

Dalal M. Zoubi
Al- Balqa' Applied University, Jordan

ABSTRACT

The interest in KM in Jordan is retalively new, since about 2003. Many Jordanian institutions, including universities are working to understand issues related to this field in order to use KM and achieve excellence and competitiveness. This study tries to highlight some of the factors affecting KM utilization at universities, such as KM awareness and the exercising of its operations, because failure to utilize KM is often due to a lack of awareness, and incrrect exercise of its operations. This study aims at identifying the impact of the workers KM awareness at YU and ANU, and exercising its operations on KM utilization. Data was collected from workers at senior and middle management levels, using a questionnaire consisting of three sub-measures. Several conclusions have been reached, and it is expected that they will contribute to helping universities utilize the KM system successfully.

INTRODUCTION

Knowledge is as old as man, but the new thing in this context is the interest in knowledge management (KM) and its utilization in institutions in the public and private sector in various parts of the world. This interest started to gain momentum by the late eighties, and coincided with the overwhelming wave of globalization. Studies, publications, and conferences related to KM have increased since the late nineties (Tamtana, 2007, p.125). The utilization of KM is one of the ways which institutions can resort to in order to meet the challenges, changes and developments in

DOI: 10.4018/978-1-60960-555-1.ch021

different fields that do not stop at a certain point. Many modern institutions have implemented KM programs to improve institutional performance and achieve a competitive advantage with other institutions (Small & Sage, 2005/2006, p.156; AMIR &USAD, 2003, p.2). Like other institutions, universities are affected by what is going on, and exposed to growing pressure to improve their output and services they provide to the community (Al-Khatib, Maayah, 2006, p.82).

Universities are scientific and intellectual centers that are resorted to in order to solve the most difficult problems facing society, and credited for the superior technological innovation and the highest qualified personnel in the world. Its activity is basically academic, the direct output of which is thought and knowledge that is subject to different principles in its production and marketing compared with other institutions. The investment in this is a long term investment which requires the adopting of an effective management system, such as the KM system so that they can shift from management of the teaching staff and students to the management of knowledge and innovation (Faris, 1426 H, p.1; Mahjoub, 2003, p.25).

The importance of this study is that it addresses one of the issues affecting the essence of institutions in general, which is the utilization of KM. Since Jordanian universities do not apply the KM system formally, it is intended, to see whether KM is informally used, and what factors are influencing this, such as workers' awareness of KM and exercise of its operations. This might help to obtain real information that helps universities management under study, A case study at Yarmouk University (YU) and Amman National University (ANU), to understand and accommodate the reality of KM at universities, and help decision-makers adopt this system formally in the future since failure to use KM in many institutions is due to a lack of adequate awareness of the concept of KM and operations associated with the use of it (Hijazi, 2005a, p.50). In addition, there is a possibility to benefit from the results of this study at other universities, both inside and outside Jordan, as an indication of the importance of awareness of KM and exercising its operations.

STATEMENT OF THE PROBLEM

This study tries to understand and measure how workers' awareness of KM and the exercise of operations related to it, affect the utilization of KM in Jordanian Universities (A case study at YU and ANU). Accordingly, the main query of the research is as follows:

What is the impact of the workers' awareness of KM and exercising its operations in its utilization at YU and ANU?

To answer the research question, the degree of workers' awareness of KM, exercising its operations, and utilizing it have been measured through a questionnaire which was distributed among administrative workers and academics from the senior and middle management levels of YU and ANU.

BACKGROUND

Knowledge Management in Jordan

As a result of globalization and increasing competition between international business organizations, Jordan began to review its economic and social status. This has been done through setting a sustainable comprehensive development plan. One of its highest priorities is to create a knowledge economy emphasizing performance improvement of institutions so that they are able to cope with the growing competition and meet the changing demands in the international business environment.

This cannot be achieved except through a culture of excellence based on knowledge. Hence, the rising interest in KM in Jordan for implementing KM systems. This interest increased after the King Abdullah II Center for Excellence (2006) decided to grant the "King Abdullah II Award for Excellence", which is the highest award at the national level in Jordan. The award is granted to winning institutions from the public and private sectors in order to strengthen the competitiveness of these institutions, and to highlight the outstanding efforts of national institutions and their achievements in developing their systems, products and services, and to encourage them to compete at the national and international level. The importance of this award has encouraged many institutions to increase their interest in KM and its applications as it opens the way for them to compete for the award at a larger scale.

Many leading institutions apply KM in Jordan. For example, the Free Zones Institution which started to adopt the KM system and applied it prior to the approval of the award in 2005 (KM strategy, 2005-2007), and the Ministry Of Industry and Trade's which started to apply KM in July 2006 (KM strategy, 2006), after that it participated in the King Abdullah II Award for excellence where it ranked first among all the ministries. The Jordan Valley Authority -the Ministry of Water and Irrigation also began to apply KM in 2007(KM strategy, 2007), in addition to the Jordanian Royal Medical Services which started to adopt and apply KM in 2008 (KM strategy, 2008-2010).

According to Hijazi - the consultant of KM in Jordan – in a journalistic interview (2010, April 3) "the government and private institutions of Jordan started application of KM initiatives, but it must be said frankly and with great caution that these attempts are still in their infancy and they are far in their application to a large extent on the correct understanding and true KM. For example, there is still considerable confusion between the concept of information and the concept of knowledge, confusion between the concept of technology management and the concept of KM. Many reasons impede the application of KM in our institutions of government and private sectors, notably: lack of awareness of the fact that KM is not management of information and technology held by the institu-

tion, but rather a management philosophy aimed at making the organization smarter and respond to emergency situations and the changing environment, and that the KM used to make a strategic long-term improvements. Because of the lack of awareness of this fact, the required support from senior management for the application of KM is not found, and therefore it does not allocate the necessary financial resources for the application of KM, including efficient trainings".

Researchers in Jordan have begun to pay attention to KM, but on a very limited scale. For example Omary (2004) conducted a study of the Jordanian commercial banks and found out that there was a relationship between the joint use of information technology and KM and the high value of the work in banks. Hijazi (2005a) also conducted a study, aimed at building a model for utilizing KM in public and private sector institutions in Jordan. Moreover, Al- Khalili (2006) conducted a study on KM at the Ministry of Education of Jordan. She found out that the Ministry of Education succeeded to strengthen the concept of KM through practicing activities related to this concept. An applied study on the Ministry of Higher Education in Jordan by Darwazeh (2008) aimed to detecting the relationship between the requirement of KM as defined by the Award of King Abdullah II for Excellence (knowledge needs, knowledge awareness and commitment, external and internal communications), and KM (diagnosis, generation, storing, distribution and application) on one hand, on the institutional performance on the other. The results of the study shows that this relationship does exist.

In addition, some universities started to teach a course in KM for postgraduate students specializing in management information systems (Arab Academy for Banking and Financial Sciences). So, it is clear that the issue of KM in Jordan has not received enough attention in various sectors, either in terms of application or research, and the efforts in this field have been few. Furthermore, this subject has not been adopted or studied so far in Jordanian universities, except for a few studies, the first of which is the field study included in this chapter, where data were collected in late 2007. This study was followed by several studies in the sector of Jordanian universities such as, the study of Al-Hawary and Al-Najar (2008) which examined the impact of the information system utilization technology on knowledge creation and conversion by applying the SECI model. This study was applied to business administration departments in 10 Jordanian Universities. The finding of this study indicates that information systems technology has had a significant impact on knowledge creation and conversion through applying the SECI model. The study by Al-Mahamed (2008) which aimed to reveal the impact of KM on higher education quality assurance, the results of the study indicated that there was no correlation between scientific activities, e-library, internet connection, and education quality assurance, and that there was correlation between equipments saving, external database sharing, library diversification, and education quality assurance.

Kelany & Abu Nady (2008) also held a study aimed at identify the components constructed the organizational culture which support the knowledge participation at public Jordanian universities. The results showed that encouraging individuals to share knowledge, participate in decision-making and setting goals are the most important components. In the field of the successful use of KM application at universities Zoubi & Rousan (2009) presented a paper at INTED conference aimed to come up with a vision for the successful use of KM applications in teaching and learning at Jordanian universities, which was suggested by proposing an integrated framework to regulate the use of KM at all administrative and educational levels of the university, and show the factors affecting the successful use of KM to improve the learning outcomes.

Alzoubi &Alnajar (2010) also held astudy aimed to detect empirically the presence of KM in the Jordanian universities. The research tested a set of variables related to KM, to reach out the main factors constructing KM architecture, aiming to establish a proposed model representing the architecture pillars in higher education institutions. It was revealed based on the results of the study that the pillars of KM architecture in higher education in the Jordanian universities are,Strategy and commitment, Information systems, Culture, and Communications. Zoubi & Kana'an (2010) presented a paper at WICE conference about intellectual capital (IC) in universities, which aimed to adopt the model- that was developed by the Austrian Research Centre for the Austrian universities- to gain information about the IC in the Jordanian universities. Then they adapted the model and the indicators related to it to insure that they fit the profile of the Jordanian universities.

The non- adoption of formal KM systems at universities doesn't necessarity mean that they are not a ware of its importance. Therefore, some universities, YU and ANU (the subjects of this study) made serious attempts to understand KM.

YU is one of the governmental academic institutions that have self-independence, and the number of students who apply to this university is much more than those who are registered, so there is no fear of competition with other universities. The reasons behind this great desire of students to study in such a university are; first, its a formal university supervized directly by the government, second, it has lower fees than private ones, third, it has a good academic reputation and educational inputs and outputs, in addition to a variety of specializations. But in spite of awareness of YU in maintaining distinguished educational quality, it has to follow modern management developments, like KM, which can be achieved through concentration of some activities and elements such as workers corporation, institutional learning, knowledge development, authority empowerment, decentralization, procedures flexibility, and providing an information technology system which is a basic element in supporting KM, and exercising some operations like knowledge generation. To achieve such goals the university has started to inform workers of KM concepts and clarify the importance of implementing it through local meetings, seminars, and work shops in order to adjust workers acceptance of KM when it is formally adopted.

ANU is a private academic, self-financed institution. The competitive situation of this university differs from YU, so it needs to maintain a distinguished and high level in education and specialization quality in order to compete with formal universities. There is a need for modern management methods to compete and keep its continuity, so ANU is aware of planning for the future and laying strategic plans through two basic methods; the first one depends on the adoption of a quality management system in order to have distinguished educational inputs and outputs, the second one is to build an E-learning model through establishing the first center of excellence for E-learning in Jordanian Universities, in order to implement its strategies. ANU realized that to cope with modern management methods and to have successful programs it should have effective administration. The university started to identify KM concepts that deal with information, knowledge, and human recourses, and to achieve this it communicated with other institutions especially within the private sectors to benefit from their experience. The university participates in seminars, workshops, and meetings related to KM, and is providing the infrastructure with machines and equipment, and developing workers skills through specialized courses to be able to implement this system formally in the near future.

Knowledge Management

KM and its utilization are in fact a part of a large trend away from prior assumptions which assume that management is the institution's sole and unique defense. It aims at reaching the stage of relying on the collective knowledge of members of the institution as it is an essential matter

for management. (Tamtana,200, p.125). Warier (2003) identified several reasons that call upon institutions to apply KM:

1. It is the only way for integration of quality and level of service.
2. It helps institutions to grow by focusing on intellectual capital, and provide services that meet the needs of the market.
3. It gives institutions the opportunity for survival and continuity.
4. It uses old knowledge to generate new knowledge.
5. It helps to support effective decisions.
6. It promotes a culture of partnership in the institution, which the information system couldn't achieve.
7. It maintains that the institution's important capabilities are not lost through maintaining the implicit knowledge.

Sajeva & Jucevicius (2006) discussed the factors for the successful use of KM and achievement of competitive advantage. They concluded that institutions that have greater awareness of the importance of applying knowledge will have a greater opportunity to achieve a competitive advantage. This orientation has been confirmed by Zoubi & Rousan (2009) in their paper which aimed to come up with a vision for the successful use of KM applications in teaching and learning at Jordanian universities. Numprasertchai & Poovarawan in their study (2008) addressed the importance of KM to improve efficiency and effectiveness in university mandates and provide many benefits to a university. The initial findings of the study indicate that an information and communication technology (ICT) based KM system significantly enhances the university's performance in terms of its quality of students, research results and innovative community services. And the specific KM practices and projects support different aspects of university mandates.

Rawat (2009) pointed out in his paper - which tries to analyze higher education system in India - that the Success of any KM project basically needs: people, process, content and technology, because today, knowledge and technology are key factors in transforming any organization. KM support is important to offer expanded new web-based offerings with cost effectiveness by making use of suitable technology. Attempt has been made in this chapter to use KM by the Universities to enhance graduation rates and retain and increase more people for lifelong learning and resolve the issues of employees' shortages.

Shoham & Perry in their study (2009) confirmed the importance of technology as it is the main cause of change and a tool for dealing with the change. They examined the organization-wide technological changes that have infiltrated every aspects of life at all universities that are part of the higher education system in Israel during the last 7 years. The study proposes a model for managing organization-wide technological changes in universities. Implementation of the model will make it possible to realize the challenge of transforming the university from a "knowledge institution" to a "learning institution." It will bring life to the extent that the higher education system in Israel, its leaders and decision-makers understand the need for a permanent mechanism to manage change and adopt this rational model in order to establish it.

This study seeks to identify the impact of some factors on utilizing KM, such as the concepts of KM awareness and the exercising of its operations.

Knowledge Management Awareness and Utilization

To achieve the purposes of this study, KM awareness is defined as the extent of knowledge that the study population possesses regarding the concept of KM, its role in building the competitive advantage of the university, the way KM assets are used (tangible and intangible), the goals KM seeks to achieve, the benefits resulting from utilizing KM, the importance of KM leader, and the role and contribution of the prevailing institutional culture at the university in utilization of KM.

Al-Ali, Gendilji, and Omary (2006) defined knowledge as "a set of facts which have credibility and exploratory rules that give users an economic advantage." (p. 25). Kumar & Thondikulam (2005-2006) have emphasized this concept, that is, KM helps to build a competitive advantage for modern institutions. Knowledge is power and wealth, and the power of knowledge characterizes the twenty first century as it is the most important resource which is built accumulatively and does not decrease through use (Al-Ali, Gendilji, and Omary, 2006, p.26).

KM has also been defined as "a system used to develop ways to acquire, evaluate, retrieve, and share assets of knowledge". This does not only include electronic data and documents, but the uncontrolled experience of workers (Hassell, 2007, p.192). Child & Shumate (2007) confirmed that the efficiency of workers is not positively related to the use of stored information, but to their understanding of knowledge and their experience in it.

Tashkandi study (2007) examined the importance and the understanding of the concept of KM and the extent of applying its processes from the point of view of the educational administration directresses and the administrative female supervisor in Makkah and Jeddah (Saudi Arabia). The findings pointed out that the population of the study conceive the important of implementing KM in the educational administration, and that knowledge acquisition and knowledge development are two of the most important processes of KM, but, they think that educational administration in Makkah and Jeddah does not give priority to KM.

Knowledge is divided into two main types: implicit knowledge, and explicit. Explicit knowledge is more formal than the implicit, and it is found in books and databases, and computer programs, while implicit knowledge is personal and individual, resulting from experience, technical skills and the mental model and the beliefs of individuals (Hijazi, 2005b, pp. 65-66; Small & Sage, 2005 /2006, p.154).

Lin (2007) points out that implicit knowledge is influenced by justice among individuals and institutional cooperation more than anything else. At universities, there are two branches of knowledge: scientific knowledge and practical knowledge. Scientific knowledge is explicit and clear through education, research, publishing, and conferences; it moves within the university through the integration of students in learning processes and the scholars' studies of the research results, and cooperation between universities and the labour market. In contrast, practical knowledge is the support provided by workers, which generates explicit knowledge in areas such as computer services, management, research support, and student services (Geng, Townley, Huang & Zhang, 2005, pp.1032-1033). Sanchez's study (2001) examined university information services as part of the university policy of KM and concluded that the use of Web technology is of great importance in the sharing of knowledge.

It can be said that the existing knowledge at modern universities has a great role and there is a great role for KM strategies adopted by these universities in the interaction of the social environment. Likewise, the accumulated scientific and technological knowledge at universities operate as infrastructure for society building. (Vandeburg, 2003, p.1).

The awareness of the institutions that unique knowledge leads to institutional competitive value (Warier, 2003, p.86), comes from the discovery, ownership, protection and use of knowledge assets, making them renewed and innovative institutions, able to use the tangible assets of knowledge and protect the intangible assets (Teece, 2000, p.147). The tangible assets of knowledge is defined as devices, equipment and buildings... etc., while the assets of intangible knowledge is defined as assets of technology and written knowledge,

and assets of human knowledge and other assets such as copyrights and trademarks (Hijazi, 2005 b, pp.73-74).

The most valuable assets of knowledge in institutions of the twentieth century are knowledge workers. Most management contributions to increasing productivity come from the knowledge workers (Al-Ali, and others, 2006, p.26).

Utilization of KM has many benefits. Among these benefits is the creation of innovation that leads to economic growth in society, (Jaime, Gardoni, Mosca & Vinck, 2006, p.1). Other benefits, such as the improvement of the decision-making process and implementation of it in a better way, in addition to improving the ability of workers regarding the knowledge related to their work and to the others work which enables them to put forward initiatives of higher awareness and experience. Jones (2006) discussed the relationship between activities related to KM and stages of decision making. He confirmed that this relationship led to making decisions that reflect on the increase of competitive ability with other institutions.

In order for institutions to utilize KM in an appropriate way to achieve these benefits, there must be a leader for KM as the changing reality in institutions requires the existence of this leader, and the KM strategy capable of working under changing circumstances and is developable. (Newman, 2006).

Many studies have dealt with the impact of KM leadership on the institutional environment operations and institutional performance. They also examined the relationship between the initiatives of KM leadership and the work strategies used to implement these initiatives. They agreed that KM leadership has a clear impact on the institutions' growth and the performance associated with it and that the KM leadership integrates with the work strategies used (Nadeem, 2006; Chia & Sun, 2007; Young & Sun, 2007; Bogner & Bansal, 2007; Choi, Poon & Davis, 2008).

The idea upon which the KM leadership is based upon is that institutions do not progress through the management of what exists, but through leadership which improves what we have inherited from others. (Hassell, 2007, p.193), and through the ability of the KM leader to balance between the effort required for KM and to develop new knowledge that replaces old knowledge (Newman, 2002, p.30). The study by Fullan (2002), which has been applied in schools, emphasized the importance of maintaining the continuation and changing of leadership which is capable of discovering and sharing knowledge through paying attention to the development of the teaching profession. Tamtana (2007) showed that leadership affects the achievement of profits of institutions, rather than that of industry itself in those institutions.

Knowledge Management Operations and Utilization

To achieve the purposes of this study, KM operations are defined as the extent to which universities generate knowledge through interaction between explicit and implicit knowledge, the sharing of such knowledge among workers, and the exercise of institutional learning processes leading to innovation in KM.

Spending time and money to create knowledge may lead to disappointment because the labor force is the party that needs money and time to be spent on them, as individuals are necessary for the production of knowledge operations, simply because they are knowledge themselves, and they only need a little information that management should provide to enable them to produce knowledge (Hassell, 2007, p.193). The study of Baban & Baban (2010) which aimed to offer a perspective on KM employment within a Romanian academic research consortium, pointed out that individuals are using diverse practices of KM, but there is still place for more improvements in sharing of knowledge.

KM systems emphasize the importance of possessing and sharing existing knowledge. In-

stitutions need to adopt systems that can generate knowledge efficiently and effectively through interaction between explicit and implicit knowledge, using knowledge transfer operations, namely:

1. Socialization: means to extract the implicit knowledge from the individual and sharing it with another.
2. Combination: means to transfer explicit knowledge into another explicit one.
3. Internalization: means to transfer explicit knowledge into an implicit one where individuals record their experiences and excersise (Kermalli, 2005, pp.75-77; Despres & Chauvel, 2000, p.90).

Knowledge generation includes creation, acquisition, synthesis, fusion, and adaptation activities. The need for communication and the culture of accepting new ideas is important for most of these activities (Wensley & O'sullivan, 2000, p.118).This idea has been confirmed by Alzoubi & Alnajjar (2010) in their study which tested a set of variables related to KM, to reach out the main factors constructing KM architecture, aiming to establish a proposed model representing the architecture pillars in higher education institutions in Jordan. The results found that the pillars of KM architecture are: culture, communication, information systems, strategy and commitment.

Chen & Mohamed (2007) found that the more powerful the activities of acquisition and use are, the greater institutional knowledge will be. This stimulates the acquisition and use of new implicit knowledge and improves the performance of these institutions.

The implicit knowledge stored in the minds of individuals is of little value unless it is shared by others (Small & Sage, 2005/2006, p.156). Lack of knowledge sharing can be a problem. This is because, at the present time, institutions want to compete in this world of rapid change, and the need to work as a unit is very necessary.One of the most important limitations of knowledge sharing reached by Chieh (2007) in his study is autonomy of task.

Accordingly, workers do not share knowledge due to their belief that keeping knowledge for themselves gives them a sense of power, but sharing knowledge will result in losing power. On the other hand, knowledge can not be considered power if not used (Murray, 2006, p.19). In their study, Vashisth, Kumar and Chandra (2010) examined the barriers and facilitators to KM as perceived from researchers in India. For this purpose, three domains, namely (knowledge gathering, creation, and diffusion) are considered in three dimensions of barriers and facilitators (individual aspects, socio-organizational aspects, and technological aspects). The findings suggest that researchers are more concerned with individual and socio-organizational aspects of KM, rather than the technological aspect. People and their interactions create knowledge and promote the flow of knowledge.

Many researchers studied the importance of knowledge sharing and concluded that sharing knowledge, teamwork and cooperation in the enterprise are positively linked to the level of performance, and generating added value in the institution, sharing knowledge identifies motivations of users (Moss, Kubaki, Hersh & Gunn, 2007; Qureshi, Briggs & Hlupic, 2006; ONeill & Ayda, 2007). According to Peet & Walsh (2010), the leaders of most organizations do not know what they know, and cannot share their knowledge with others. They follow this idea by testing an innovative method of tacit knowledge retrieval known as Generative Knowledge Interviewing with a small group of fund-raising experts at the University of Michigan. The results demonstrated that the tacit knowledge of a retiring leader could be successfully retrieved, documented and fully transferred to new leaders in several interview sessions.

Obviously, this leads to the idea of institutional learning which has become the crucial point for adequacy and capacity (Despress & Chauvel,

2000, p.81). KM assumes that managers are not the only ones possessing useful ideas in the enterprise. So, they must create an effective institutional learning process in order that workers will be able to participate with their ideas (Tamtana, 2007, p.125). This is because learning is brought about by individuals and groups (Newman, 2002, p.128). The results of the study of Kelany & Abu Nady (2008) showed that encouraging individuals to share knowledge, participate in decision-making and setting goals are the most important components constructed the organizational culture which support the knowledge participation at public Jordanian universities. The study by King and Marks (2008) indicates that there is significant impact of system variables regarding the encouragement of sharing idea and using KM.

If the institution is aware of the fact that creativity is essential for its growth and it leads the competitive advantage. So, learning institutions should seek technological development which leads to new knowledge and effective ways of learning. This would achieve and develop performance at all levels of work as collective learning is an essential part of institution development (Warier, 2003, p.86).

RESEARCH DESIGN AND METHODOLOGY

Research Hypotheses

Three hypotheses are derived from the main research query:

H1: There are no significant statistical differences between workers awareness, exercising operations, and utilization of KM at YU and ANU.

H2: Workers awareness of KM has a significant statistical impact on its utilization in YU and ANU.

H3: Workers exercise of KM operations has a significant statistical impact on utilizing it at YU and ANU.

Assessment of Variables

A questionnaire is used to assess:

1. The independent variables: a- The university workers' awareness of KM
    b- The university workers' exercise of KM operations.
2. The dependent variable: Utilization of KM by university workers.

The Study Model

The researcher is seeking to build a model that works on the measurement of independent and dependent variables in line with the hypotheses of the study. Figure 1 shows the prototype of the study, which reflects the impact of the workers awareness of KM, and the workers exercise of KM operations on utilizing it at YU and ANU.

This model will be analyzed and tested in the next section (data analysis and discussion) to

determine the impact of independent variables on the dependent variable

Data Collection

To achieve the objectives of the study, the case study method was used to carry out this research in two Jordanian universities; a public university (YU), and a private one (ANU). The age and location are the criterion used in the selection of these two universities out of 26 universities in Jordan (10 public, 16 private).

ANU is the oldest private university in Jordan, established in 1990 and located in the city of Amman the capital of Jordan. YU is one of the two oldest universities in the country, it was established in 1976 and is located in Irbid city in the northern part of Jordan. Therefore, the author thinks that the selection of the oldest two universities to achieve the purposes of this study might be appropriate as their laws, regulations, instructions, and methods of work have stabilized. The author also thinks that the selection of these two universities which are located in two different locations might be of importance due to cultural and urban differences between the centre and north. In the capital, Amman, most public and private sector

Figure 1. The impact of KM awareness and the exercising of KM operations on KM utilization

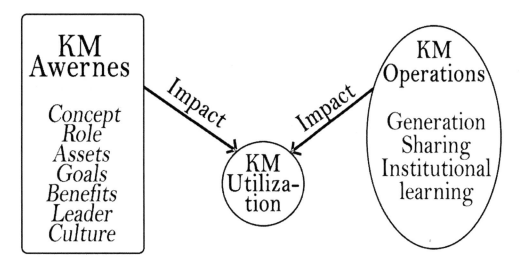

institutions are concentrated there and the investments as well. This is due to the fact that modern and cultural openness in Amman is higher than in Irbid though Irbid is the second biggest city in the country. In addition, there is social diversity in the city of Amman as it houses many different nationalities, unlike Irbid where the majority of its population are Jordanians. So, the difference in location might explain the difference in the status of KM in the two universities.

The study population sample included all employees at the senior management (Vice President, Deans of the Faculties, Directors of Departments), and middle management (Head of Academic Departments, and Head of Administrative Departments) in both Universities. The criterion in light of which the study sample was selected is that top management makes the most important administrative decisions. So, any initiatives or decisions concerning KM have to be taken at senior management level. Those working in middle management level are the linking chain between senior management and employees, and they are concerned with the publication of ideas and decisions of senior management and circulating them to all employees. In addition, they share the senior management in decision-making in many cases. Therefore, information about the utilization of KM and factors influencing this are available at these two levels more than that of the employees or in records and documents. This is because KM system in these universities is not formally applied.

The distribution and collection of the questionnaire took about two months in the summer of 2007. Table 1 shows the study population, and response rate in both universities.

Study Tool

A questionnaire was used by the author to achieve the purpose of the study. It is a part of a tool prepared by Hijazi (2005 a) who aimed at building a model for better use of KM in the public and private institutions in Jordan. The author used this part of the tool, and she amended it to suit the purposes of this study. This tool includes three sub-measures all of which are dealt with in this chapter:

- **First,** The measure of KM awareness. It includes 46 items distributed over seven areas: KM concept, the role of KM, knowledge assets, KM objectives, the benefits of knowledge, capabilities of knowledge leader, the role of institutional culture.
- **Second,** The measure of exercise KM operations. It includes 20 items distributed over three areas: knowledge generation, knowledge sharing, and institutional learning.
- **Third,** The measure of KM utilization. It includes 21 items distributed over three areas: the use of KM, utilization of KM aiming at carrying out institutional operations, utilization of KM based on its importance. (appendix1).

The respondents answers were obtained by using Leckert quintuple scale as follows:

(1) I strongly disagree; (2) I disagree; (3) I agree to some extent; (4) I agree; (5) I strongly agree.

Table 1. Responses ratio in the two universities

University	Population	No. of Responses	% of Responses
Yarmouk	178	118	66.3%
Amman National	42	39	92.8%

Table 2. Means, and T-test for the case of YU and ANU

KM Measures	University	N	Mean	Std.Deviatin	T-test for equality of means t df Sig
KM awareness	YU ANU	118 39	3.49 3.82	0.620 0.472	-3.032 155 0.003*
Exercising of KM operations	YU ANU	118 39	3.09 3.86	0.742 0.435	-6.078 155 0.00*
KM Utilization	YU ANU	118 39	3.12 3.69	0.713 0.486	-4.613 155 0.00*

* P< 0.05

Validity and Reliability

The author has adapted the questionnaire used in this study from a validated tool used in the study of Hijazi (2005a). The validity has been confirmed in his study after being presented to a number of specialized referees. After the author had adapted the questionnaire to suit the study population, and before it was used in this study, it was presented to 12 referees specializing in KM, management information systems, and business administration at YU and Al-Balqa' Applied University. The validity was confirmed again by referees. This means that the questionnaire is able to measure the objectives of this study.

Cronbach's Alpha value was used to assess the internal consistency of the research three sub-measures, which were (0.96), (0.95) and (0.95) for the first, second and the third respectively. These values confirmed the high reliability of the questionnaire.

After data collection, it was analyzed using statistical packages programs of social sciences SPSS, then means and T-test was used to test the first hypothesis, and regression analysis to test the second and third hypotheses.

DATA ANALYSIS AND DISCUSSION

H1: There are no significant statistical differences between workers' awareness, exercising operations, and utilizing of KM at YU and ANU.

To test this hypothesis, means and T-test were reached regarding the three measures shown in Table 2.

Table 2 shows that the mean of KM awareness at YU is slightly higher than the mid-premise which is (3). This reveals that the degree of awareness of KM is high, whereas the mean of exercising KM operations, and the mean of KM utilization is close to the mid-premise. This mean that exercising KM operations and utilizing it at YU is moderate.

This result indicates that the workers awareness of KM is higher than exercising its operations and utilizing it; this might be due to the fact that the study population is from senior and middle management levels. They are supposed to possess information about KM and elements associated with. However, this degree of awareness does not necessarily mean that the university exercises or utilizes KM, because KM is one of the modern issues that have not been adopted yet in most institutions in Jordan, especially universities. This agrees with what Moss, et al (2007) who stated that it is surprising that issues relating to the KM have recently attracted the attention of universities.

The same Table 2 shows that the means of the three measures of KM at ANU are higher than the mid-premise mean which is (3). This reveals that the degree of awareness of KM, exercising KM operations, and utilizing it at ANU, is high.

To see if there is a significant difference between the means of the three measures of KM at the two universities, T value was calculated as shown in Table 2.

T-test shows that there is a significant statistical differences between the means of, awareness of KM (P<0.003), exercising KM operations (P<0.00), and utilization of KM (P<0.00) at YU and ANU.

Discussion

Looking at the mean in Table 2, the difference that the t-test shows means that the degree of KM awareness, exercise of KM operations, and KM utilization at ANU is higher than YU. This result emphasizes the serious steps which ANU has taken to adopt the KM system. As mentioned before in the research literature, ANU is self-financed, and depends on effective resources management in order to compete with other public universities like YU, which deals with this matter in a different manner, and slowly because it is stable financially and academically, and has good reputation, and follows governmental laws and regulations. This change required a lot of time. Perhaps, this result is due to the fact that ANU is a private university, has greater freedom than public universities in terms of being open to the internal or external environment, and communication with different institutions. Openness provides new ideas that can be useful at a large scale. It is also possible that the private university more free in decision making regarding university system. Moreover, the private university needs not follow routine procedures and bureaucracy which usually prevail in public institutions. Also its unique location in the capital Amman gives it greater opportunity to communicate and benefit from large enterprises which have extensive experience in management.

Moreover, it is possible that because YU has not formally adopted the KM system, exercising KM operations and utilization it stems from some activities like the availability of certain facilities, financial and human resources. The existence of these things help achieve certain objectives consistent with the goal of KM in general. So the

result of this hypothesis agrees with the conditions of both universities.

This result partially agrees with the study of Hijazi (2005a), which shows that public and private sector institutions in Jordan realize KM, exercise its operations, and utilize it at a medium level. Also it partially agrees with the study carried out by Khalili (2006) which indicated that the Ministry of Education in Jordan is able to establish the concept of knowledge through practicing most of the related activities at a very high degree. And it agrees with the study of Tashkandi (2007), the findings pointed out that the population of the study conceive the important of implementing KM in the educational administration, and that knowledge acquisition and knowledge development are two of the most important processes of KM. And it agrees with the study of Alzoubi & Alnajar (2010) which shows that institutional culture is one of the pillars of KM architecture. In the domain of knowledge operations, this study agrees with the study of Peet & Walsh (2010) that the tacit knowledge of a retiring leaders could be successfully retrieved, documented and fully transferred to new leaders, and the study of Baban & Baban (2010) which shows that the members of the UNIKM consortium are using diverse practices of KM, but there is still place for more improvements in sharing of knowledge.

H_2: Workers' awareness of KM has a significant statistical impact on its utilization in YU and ANU.

To test this hypothesis, linear regression analysis was used as shown in Tables (3-8).

YU Results

Table 3 shows that the seven areas of KM awareness variable explain 69.3% (R- square value) of the variance of KM utilization variable, while the remaining percentage refers to other unknown variables.

Table 3. Model summary (the impact on KM utilization)

Standard Error	R- Square Change	R- Square	Multi- Correlation Coefficient R	KM Awareness (areas)
0.408	0.673	0.693	0.832	Concept, Role, Assets, Goals, Benefits, Leadership Capabilities, Institutional Culture

To understand if R-square value has statistical significance, regression variance was analyzed Table 4, and it shows the presence of statistical significance at p < 0.000 level regarding the source of the seven areas together. This result confirms that KM awareness might be one of the important variables that could explain KM utilization at YU. However, the impact of KM awareness on KM utilization is clear (Figure 2).

Table 5 shows regression coefficients of the seven areas. It shows a positive statistical significance correlation between the areas of independent variable: KM concept (p<0.009), institutional culture (p<0.000) and the dependent variable of KM utilization. And there is no significant correlation with the other areas. This statistical significance correlation indicated the importance of these areas on utilization of KM at YU. This might mean that if the university workers are unable to understand what KM means, and if there is no proper environment within the institution to help this understanding, KM utilization will not be achieved.

Table 4. Regression variance analysis (KM utilization)

Source of Variance	Sum of Squares	df	Mean Squares	F Value	Sig
Regression	41.230	7	5.890	35.409	0.000*
Remaining	18.298	110	0.166		
Total	59.528	117			

*P < 0.05

Figure 2. The impact of KM awareness on KM utilization at YU and ANU

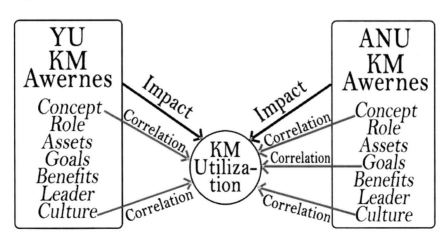

Table 5. Regression coefficients (KM utilization)

KM Awareness (areas)	Non-standard Regression Coefficient		Standard Regression Beta	T Value	Sig
	Normal Regression Coefficient B	Std. Error			
Concept	0.235	0.089	0.234	2.651	0.009*
Role	- 0.178	0.091	-0.152	- 1.954	0.053
Assets	0.154	0.082	0.176	1.878	0.063
Goals	0.063	0.074	0.075	0.850	0.397
Benefits	0.031	0.057	0.037	0.542	0.589
Leader Capabilities	- 0.001	0.057	-0.002	- 0. 021	0.983
Institutional Culture	0.423	0.066	0.541	6.452	0.000*

* P < 0.05

It is also shown that the strength of correlation (Beta value) between the area of institutional culture and the utilization of knowledge is the highest, followed by the area of concept which is natural due to the fact that these areas are the most influential among the seven areas as shown by its statistical significance.

ANU Results

Table 6 shows that the seven areas of KM awareness variable explain 61.8% (R-square value) of the variance of the KM utilization variable,

while the remaining percentage is due to other unknown variables.

To understand whether R-square value has statistical significance, the regression variance was analyzed (Table7). It shows the presence of statistical significance at p<0.000 level regarding the source of the seven areas together. This result confirms that KM awareness might be one of the important variables that might explain the KM utilization at ANU. However, the impact of KM awareness on KM utilization is clear (Figure 2).

Table 8 shows the regression coefficients of the seven areas. It seems that there is positive

Table 6. Model summary (the impact on KM utilization)

KM Awareness (areas)	Multi-Correlation Coefficient – R	R- Square	R- Square Change	Standard Error
Concept, Role, Assets, Goals, Benefits, leadership Capacity, Institutional Culture	0.786	0.618	0.532	0.332

Table 7. Regression variance analysis (KM utilization)

Source of Variance	Sum of Squares	df	Mean Square	F Value	Sig
Regression	5.548	7	0.793	7.179	0.000 *
Remaining	3.422	31	0.110		
Total	8.970	38			

* P < 0.0

Table 8. Regression coefficients (KM utilization)

KM Awareness (areas)	Non-Standard Regression Coefficient		Standard Regression Beta	T Value	Sig
	Normal Regression Coefficient B	Std. Error			
Concept	0.344	0.131	0.373	2.628	0.013*
Role	- 0.023	0.132	- 0.028	- 0.174	0.863
Assets	- 0.048	0.101	-0.075	- 0.474	0.639
Goals	0.308	0.139	0.368	2.211	0.035*
Benefits	- 0.185	0.092	- 0.261	- 2.015	0.053
Leader Capabilities	- 0.068	0.118	- 0.091	- 0.574	0.570
Institutional Culture	0.279	0.090	0.501	3.100	0.004*

*P < 0.05

statistical significance correlation between the area of independent variable: KM concept (p<0.013), goals (p <0.035), institutional culture (p<0.004), and the dependent variable of KM utilization. And there is no significance correlation with the other areas. These statistical significant correlation indicated the importance of these areas of awareness on utilization of KM at ANU. This might mean that if the university workers are unable to understand what KM means, what the goals of KM are and if there is no proper environment within the institution, KM utilization will not be achieved.

It is also shown that the strength of correlation (Beta value) between the area of institutional culture and the utilization of knowledge which is the highest, followed by the area of concept, then the area of goals is natural. This is because these areas are the most influential among the seven areas as shown through statistical significance.

Discussion

The results of this hypothesis show that KM awareness has statistical significance impact on KM utilization at both universities, and that the contribution of KM awareness variable in explaining the variance of the KM utilization at YU (R^2 = 69.3%) is higher than ANU (R^2 =61.8%). This

statistical significance impact emphasizes the importance of awareness in case these universities decide to adopt the KM system. This impact may be explained according to the fact that these universities do not differentiate in having basic sources of capitals and human resources, but the difference stems from whether these universities have or do not have continuous competition advantage, and when intellectual capital becomes a competitive feature of successful institution. Information society will gradually move to be knowledge society as this the basic element that distinguishes one institution from another. These universities realized that this change depends on administrative initiative, learning organization, total quality management, and business reconstruction … etc. Recently, knowledge is looked upon as a corner stone of most projects which will give the vision leading people to thinking rationally.

Also, KM awareness and it's importance refers to the fact that these universities think that the great percentage of knowledge is in the workers' minds. This means that if workers do not realize the importance of such knowledge, they will not be able to use it properly, specially at the low administrative levels. Workers awareness leads them to faster and better decision making. On the other hand, workers will become more aware of their job duties which help in providing initiations that lead to job development. So they may reach better job quality without supervision and get a high level of educational outputs.

The slight difference in variance ratio in KM utilization between the two universities which is slightly higher at YU than ANU. YU being more formal and older than ANU, so its expected that YU has firmer polices and regulations, in addition to job security which gives workers a feeling of relief, and stability more than those in ANU which has an important role in exercising new management initiatives.

Looking at results in Tables 5 and 8, there are similarities between the two universities regarding the most KM awareness effective areas correlated with the KM utilization variable. There were statistical significance correlations between the KM concept, institutional culture and the KM utilization variable in both universities, in addition, the area of knowledge goals was statistical significant at ANU only. This can be explained according to the fact that ANU is much more active than YU in making internal and external initiatives to identify the KM system for workers. So, KM goals are clearer to workers in ANU more than in YU.

The none existence of statistical significance correlation among the rest of the areas of KM awareness variable and KM utilization variable doesn't mean that there is no correlation, but the effect of this correlation is weaker than statistical significant areas. This may refer to the none-adoption of the KM at the two universities, this affects the workers understanding of many facts related to KM like, assets, benefits, and the role of KM in improving universities performance.

Perhaps the result shows that the absence of understanding the meaning of KM, the role of the institutional environment supporting this understanding, and the very clear objectives concerning the goals which the university would like to achieve, means KM will not be utilized in

the right manner to lead to the achievement of the required objectives.

The results of this study agree with Hijazi (2005 a), Kulkarni, Ravindran &Freeze (2006-2007), the study "Mechanisms for KM" (2006), Moss (2007) in that the supporting institutional culture is a direct and an indirect incentive factor in the utilization of knowledge. Likewise, it agrees with the study of Sajeva and Jucevicius, (2006), AL-Khalili (2006), Child and Shumate (2007), Chia&Sun (2007) which showed that awareness of the KM concepts leads to a better utilization to achieve acompetitive advantage. In addition, the challenge of reaching the experience of success is represented by developing a strategy supported by the objectives of the institution to develop common institutional culture. The result, however disagrees with Fullan (2002), Jones (2006), and Nadeem (2006). All of them showed that KM leadership is the driving force of KM initiatives in the organizations of today. The study differs from King and Marks (2008) which showed significant impact of the benefits of knowledge which encourages utilizing KM.

H3: Workers exercise of KM operations has a significant statistical impact on utilizing it atYU and ANU.

To test this hypothesis, linear regression analysis was used as shown in Tables 9-14.

YU Results

Table 9 shows that the three areas of exercising the KM operations variable explain 82.9% (R-square value) of the KM utilization variable, while the remaining percentage is due to other unknown variables.

To understand if R-square value has statistical significance, regression variance was analyzed (Table 10); which shows the presence of statistical significance at p<0.000 level regarding the source of the three areas together. This result

Table 9. Model summary (the impact on KM utilization)

Exercising KM Operations (areas)	Multi Correlation Coefficient R	R -Square	R- Square Change	Standard Error
Knowledge Generation, Knowledge Sharing, Institutional Learning.	0.911	0.829	0.825	0.299

confirms that exercising KM operations might be one of the important variables that might explain KM utilization at YU. However, the impact of exercising KM operations on utilization is clear (Figure 3).

Table 11 shows the regression coefficients for the three areas. It seems a positive statistical significance correlation between all the areas of independent variable: K generation (p<0.000), K sharing (p<0.003), institutional learning (p<0.000), and the dependent variable, KM utilization. These statistical significant correlations indicated the importantce of all the areas on utilization of KM

at YU. This might mean that if exercising all the areas of KM operations, KM utilization will be achieved.

It is existence also shows that the strength of correlation (Beta value) between the area of generation and the utilization of knowledge being the highest, followed by the area of institutional learning, then the area of sharing, is natural because all of these areas have high impact as shown by its statistical significance.

Table 10. Regression variance analysis (KM utilization)

Source of Variance	Sum of Squares	df	Mean Square	F Value	Sig.
Regression	49.366	3	16.455	184.609	0.000 *
Remaining	10.162	114	0.89		
Total	59.528	117			

*P < 0.05

Figure 3. The impact of exercising KM operations on KM utilization at YU and ANU

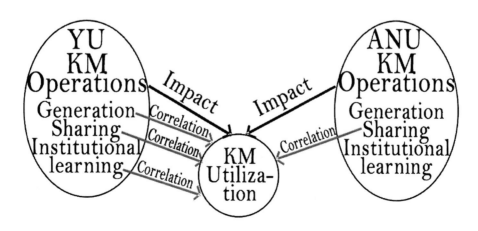

Table 11. Regression coefficients (KM utilization)

Exercising KM Operations (areas)	Non-Standard Regression Coefficient		Standard Regression Beta	T Value	Sig.
	Normal Regression Coefficient B	Std. Error			
Knowledge Generation	0.361	0.049	0.447	7.374	0.000 *
Knowledge Sharing	0.183	0.059	0.208	3.090	0.003 *
Institutional Learning	0.324	0.046	0.374	6.960	0.000 *

* $P < 0.05$

ANU Results

Table 12 shows that the three areas of exercising KM operations variable explain 33.7% (R-square value) of the variance of KM utilization variable, while the remaining percentage is due to other unkown variables.

To understand if R-square value has statistical significance, regression variance was analyzed (Table 13) ; it shows the presence of statistical significance at ($P<0.002$) level regarding the source of the three areas together.This result confirms that exercising the KM operations variable might be one of the important variables that could explain the KM utilization at ANU. However, the impact of exercising KM operations on KM utilization is clear (Figure 3).

Table 14 shows the regression coefficiants of the three areas. It seems a positive statistical significance correlation between the area of knowledge sharing only ($p<0.021$), and the dependent variable KM utilization. And there is no significance correlation with the other areas. This result indicated the importantce of knowledge sharing on utilization of KM at ANU. This might mean that if the university workers are unable to share knowledge, KM utilization will not be achieved.

Its also shows that the strength of correlation (Beta value) between the area of knowledge sharing and the utilization of knowledge being the highest, is natural because this area is the most influential of the three areas as shown by its statistical significance.

Table 12. Model summary (the impact on KM utilization)

Exercising KM Operations (areas)	Multi Correlation Coefficient R	R- square	R Square Change	Standard Error
Knowledge Generation, Knowledge Sharing, Institutional Learning	0.581	0.337	0.280	0.412

Table 13. Regression variance analysis (KM utilization)

Source of Variance	Sum of Squares	df	Mean Square	F value	Sig
Regression	3.023	3	1.008	5.932	0.002*
Remaining	5.947	35	0.170		
Total	8.970	38			

*$P < 0.05$

Table 14. Regression coefficients (KM utilization)

Exercising KM Operations (areas)	Non-Standard Regression Coefficient		Standard Regression Variable Beta	T Value	Sig.
	Normal regression coefficient B	Std. Error			
Knowledge Generation,	0.046	0.152	0.048	0.300	0.766
Knowledge Sharing,	0.303	0.125	0.415	2.421	0.021*
Institutional Learning	0.232	0.137	0.250	1.693	0.099

* $P < 0.05$

Discussion

Hypothesis results show that exercising KM operation has statistical significant impact on KM utilization at both universities and that the role of exercising KM operations variables in explaining the variance of the KM utilization at YU (R^2=82.9%) is much higher than ANU (R^2=33.7%). In spite of the great difference in ratios between the two universities, this statistical significant impact emphasizes the importance of exercising KM operation if these universities decided to formally adopt this system which gives the chance to generate and use knowledge. This leads to innovation and to achievement of continuous competitive advantage that is a basic element for the successful institution. So the kind of knowledge which can be discovered through problem solving may be more useful. Generation of knowledge shows that individuals only can generate knowledge. This means that universities can't generate knowledge without workers. So the polices of universities may be an important factor that affects generation of knowledge by workers and uses it later. In spite of the importance of knowledge generation, it doesn't lead to a superior performance at the university if knowledge transfer is not shared between employees through direct written and readable means, or indirectly through informal relationships between them.

Encouraging both universities to apply knowledge transfer operation was probably the cause of effective role of sharing, using knowledge and generating new knowledge. This leads to the importance of the third operation which is institutional learning of using knowledge. Learning means acquisition and internalization of new knowledge. One of the things that helped the learning operation these universities adopted was a learning method. It aims at developing knowledge throughout the university. The other thing is following universal learning methods and using data instead of assumptions in making decisions, in addition to learning from other previous experience of other universities. When knowledge is generated, spread and shared among individuals, it will have a wide positive effect and this is what the results of testing this hypothesis have showed.

The big difference in variance ratio of the KM utilization variable between the two universities shows that YU is an old formal university, and has well-established laws and regulations, whereas ANU, as a private university, may be exposed to many changes in its polices and administrations. This allows a great change in its internal environment. These factors explain why exercising KM operations do not explain the high ratio of the variance in KM utilization variable.

Looking at the results in Tables 11 and 14 which show that the whole area of exercising KM operation at YU has statistical significance correlation with the KM utilization variable, whereas sharing is the only area at ANU which has statistical significance with the KM utilization, in spite of the high mean of exercising the

KM operation at ANU as was clear in the results of the first hypothesis.

Despite the fact that all operations of KM are important for knowledge utilization, knowledge sharing reflects the institution's ability to transfer implicit and explicit knowledge between workers. If this transfer of knowledge is done successfully, knowledge utilization will be affected significantly. As for the generation of knowledge and institutional learning, they are two operations affected significantly by institution policies and strategies, while sharing is affected by individual activities and their desire to share their knowledge in a better way. Perhaps, administrative policies at ANU have led to limited impact of these two areas. In addition, the lack of formally adopting the KM system at the university may lead to irregular and unplanned exercise of these operations. However, this can be attained through individual efforts of workers in various administrative levels.

Also these results may refer to individuals or institutional obstacles at ANU which have limited the affect of institutional learning and generation operations on using KM such as, workers resistance to use knowledge that has been generated. This is related to their ability to deal with new attitudes, events, information, and structure. Some individuals are unable to acquaint with it because of their feeling of threat caused by job insecurity which is different from that in formal universities.

The results of this study conform with studies by Hijaz1 (2005 a), Sajeva & Jucevicius (2006), Young and Sun, (2007), and Chen and Mohamed (2007), which show that the possession, generation and sharing of knowledge stimulate the process of utilization knowledge and improve performance of institutions. It also agrees with Sanchez (2001), Moss et al (2007), and Kulkarni, et al (2006-2007) in that knowledge sharing is an important factor in its use and reuse. Likewise, it agrees with the study of Bonger&Bansal, (2007) which shows that the growth rate of companies is positively associated with their ability to generate new knowledge of value and use it. Also it agrees with the study

of Jones (2006), which emphasizes KM related activities relationship, such as generation of decision making leading to the use and the best competitive advantage.

Recommendations and Suggestions

Based on the findings of the study, the author recommends:

- That both universities should formally adopt the KM system by establishing a specialized unit to:
  1. Deal formally with KM.
  2. Launch initiatives of KM and follow up its related matters in terms of defining its concept.
  3. Establishing the relationship between KM and personnel, and train them in how to exercise its various operations, and follow up its procedures and functions that are consistent with the objectives of KM.
  4. Facilitate KM utilization in various academic and administrative departments.
- That a course of study be taught in both universities to enable students to understand the concept, objectives and benefits of KM, so that they can be qualified to contribute to the implementation of KM initiatives when joining the labor market.

The author also suggests that:

- Similar studies are carried out in other universities inside and outside Jordan to identify the status of KM in these universities.
- System of rewards at universities should be modified to encourage the generation of knowledge, transfer and sharing.
- Open channels of joint work between the public and private universities with a view to strengthening relationships and partnerships

between them, would enhance the generation of knowledge, transfer and sharing.

CONCLUSION

This study deals with three hypotheses, focusing on the impact of KM awareness, exercising its operations on KM utilization in two Jordanian universities, YU and ANU.

If universities want to use KM successfully in order to achieve excellence and competitiveness, they should pay attention to workers' awareness of KM and their exercise of KM operations that achieve this utilization. On the contrary, the failure of utilizing KM is often due to workers' lack of adequate awareness of concepts associated with KM, and correct exercising of KM operations.

This study aims at starting a practical study on workers' KM awareness, and the extent of exercising its operations at universities (a case study on two universities, a public university and a private one, YU and ANU respectively). It also aims at identifying whether this awareness and the exercising of operations have an impact on the utilization of KM.

Understanding KM status at two Jordanian universities (a public university and a private one) might be an indicator to some extent, for research-ers, and the people interested in this subject to do further research in this field. Data was collected from workers in the two universities at senior and middle management levels, by using a question-naire to measure the three variables of the study (KM awareness, KM operations, KM utilization).

Referring to the outcomes of this study, it is clear that the mean of KM awareness, exercising KM operations and KM utilization at the private university is higher than that at the public one as shown by T-test. In contrast, the impact of KM awareness on KM utilization in both universities is almost the same and has statistical significance, whereas the impact of exercising KM operations on KM utilization at the public university is clearer than that of the private university, although the impact at the two universities is statistically sig-nificant, as shown by the linear regression analysis.

From the foregoing ideas, we can deduce that the status of KM in the two universities is similar in one part, but different in another one. Figure 4 shows the final model of the study based on the results of the two universities (YU and ANU) which illustrates the impact of the independent variables (KM awareness, exercising KM opera-tions) on KM utilization.

This encourages researchers to conduct further research on this subject at Jordanian universities,

Figure 4. The final model of the study (the impact of KM awareness and exercising KM operations on KM utilization at YU and ANU)

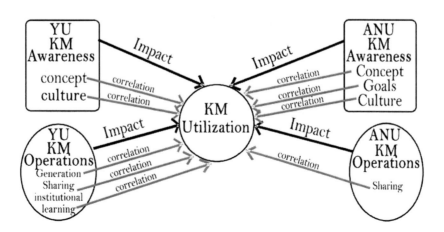

and identify whether these differences exist in public and private universities in general, or only in the universities under study. Furthermore, these results encourage researchers to study this issue in other institutions as it is a relatively new subject that has not been adequately understood.

REFERENCES

AL-Ali. A., Gendilji, A.I. & Omary, G. (2006). *Introduction to knowledge Management*. Dar Alamseera for Publication and Distribution, Amman, Jordan.

AL-hawary, F.A. & Al-najar,F. J. (2008). Impact assessment of I/S technology utilization on knowledge creation and conversion: An empirical study in Jordanian universities. *Journal of Knowledge Management Practice.*, *9*(1), 1–15.

AL-khalili. S.M. (2006). *Knowledge management in the ministry of education, Jordan: Analytic study*. Unpublished master thesis, Yarmouk University, Irbid, Jordan.

AL-Khatib. A.M. & Maayah, A.S. (2006). *Universities Creative Management: New models*. Amman, Jordan: Jadara House for the World Book Publishing and Distribution.

AL-Mahamed. R.J. (2008). *The role of knowledge management in higher education quality assurance: applied study at private Jordanian universities*.Unpublished master thesis, The Middle East University, Amman, Jordan.

Alzoubi, M.R. & Alnajar, F.J. (2010).Knowledge management architecture empirical study on the Jordanian universities. European Journal of Economics, Finance and Administrative Sciences, Issue 21, 101-115.

AMIR & USAID. (2003). *The centers of Excellence Guid book*. Jordan: AMIR Program.

Baban, C. F., & Baban, M. (2010). An exploratory study of knowledge management practices in romanian universities within the UNIKM academic research consortium. [special issue]. *Metalurgia International*, *XV*(9), 157–163.

Bogner, W. C., & Bansal, P. (2007). Knowledge Management as the basis of sustained high performance. *Journal of Management Studies*, *44*(1), 165–188. doi:10.1111/j.1467-6486.2007.00667.x

Chen, L., & Mohamed, Sh. (2007). Empirical Study of Interaction between knowledge management activities. *Engineering, Construction, and Architectural Management*, *14*(3), 242–260. doi:10.1108/09699980710744890

Chia, L. L., & Sun, Q. L. (2007). Performance measurement systems for knowledge management in high technology industries: a balanced score card frame work. *International Journal of Technology Management*, *39*(1/2), 158–176. doi:10.1504/IJTM.2007.013444

Chieh, P. L. (2007). To share or not to share: Modeling knowledge sharing using exchange ideology as a moderator. *Personnel Review*, *36*(3), 457–475. doi:10.1108/00483480710731374

Child, J. T., & Shumate, M. (2007). The impact of communal knowledge repositores and people based knowledge management on awareness of team effectiveness. *Management Communication Quarterly*, *21*(1), 29–54. doi:10.1177/0893318907301987

Choi, B., Poon, S. K., & Davis, J. G. (2008). Effects of knowledge management strategy on organizational performance: Acomplementarity theory based approach. *Omega*, *36*(2), 235–251. doi:10.1016/j.omega.2006.06.007

Darwazeh, S. S. (2008). The *relationship between the requirement of knowledge management and processes and its effect on the excellence of institutional performance: an applied study on the ministry of higher education in Jordan.* Unpublished master thesis, The Middle East University, Amman, Jordan.

Despres, Ch., & Chauvel, D. (Eds.). (2000). *Knowledge Horizons.* Boston, U.S.A: Butterworth Heinemann.

Faris, M. (1426H, *November 18*). *Knowledge management and innovation: The place of Arab universities in these developments.* Paper presented in the strategic management seminar in higher education institutions, King Khalid University, Saudi Arabia.

Free Zones Institution. (2005). *Knowledge Management Strategy 2005-2007.* On line: http://www.free-zones.gov.jo/.

Fullan, M. (2002). The role of leadership in the promotion of knowledge management in schools: Theory and practice. *Teachers and Teaching, 8*(3). doi:10.1080/135406002100000530

Geng. Q. Townley, Ch., Huang, K. & Zhang, J. (2005). Comparative Knowledge management: A pilot study of Chinese and American universities. *Journal of the Society for Information Science and Technology, 56* (10), 1031-1044.

Hassell, L. (2007). A continental philosophy perspective on knowledge management. *Information Systems Journal, 17,* 185–195. doi:10.1111/j.1365-2575.2007.00233.x

Hijazi, H. A. (2005a). *Measuring the impact of knowledge management awareness on knowledge management utilization in Jordanian organizations: a comparative analytical study of public and private sector towards building a model for the knowledge management utilization.* Unpublished doctoral dissertation, Amman Al-Arabia University for Higher Studies, Amman, Jordan.

Hijazi, H. A. (2005b). *Knowledge management.* Amman, Jordan: Al-Ahlia for Publication and Distribution.

Hijazi, H. A. (2010, April3). Knowledge management application in Jordan. *Manbralrai Journal,* On line: http://www.manbaralrai.com.

Jaime, A., Gardoni, M., Mosca, J., & Vinck, D. (2006). From quality management to knowledge management in research organizations. *International Journal of Innovation Management, 10*(2), 197–215. doi:10.1142/S1363919606001430

Jones, K. (2006). Knowledge management as a foundation for decision support systems. *Journal of Computer Information Systems, 46*(4), 116–124.

Jordan Valley Authority. (2007). *Knowledge Management Strategy 2007-2009.* On line: http://www.jva.gov.jo/.

Jordanian Royal Medical Services. (2011), *KM strategy, 2008-2010.* On line: http://www.jrms.gov.jo.

Kelany, A. M., & Abu Nady, M. F. (2008). *Components constructed the organizational culture which support the knowledge participation at public Jordanian universities.* On Line: http://rd08.search.ac2.yahoo.com.

Kermalli, S. (2005). *Knowledge Management: Applied Introductory. Translation by Haytham Hijazy.* Amman, Jordan: Al-Ahlia for Publication and Distribution.

King, W. R., & Marks, P. V. (2008). Motivating knowledge sharing through a knowledge management system. *Omega, 36*(1), 131–146. doi:10.1016/j.omega.2005.10.006

King Abdullah II Center for Excellence. (2006). *King Abdullah II Award for Excellence.* On line: http://jusbp.org/alarabic/aboutus ar.shtm.

Kulkarni, U. R., Ravindran, S., & Freeze, R. (2006-2007). A knowledge management success model: Theoretical development and empirical validation. *Journal of Management Information Systems, 23*(3), 309–347. doi:10.2753/MIS0742-1222230311

Kumar, S., & Thondikulam, G. (2005. (2006). Knowledge management in a collaborative business framework. *Information Knowledge Systems Management, 5*(3), 171–187.

Lin, Ch. P. (2007). To share or not to share: Modeling tacit knowledge sharing, its mediators and antecedents. *Journal of Business Ethics, 70*(4), 411–428. doi:10.1007/s10551-006-9119-0

Mahjoub, B. F. (2003). *Arab Universities Management in the light of International Standards*. Cairo, Egypt: Arab Organization for Administrative Development.

Mechanisms for knowledge Management Systems Effectiveness: Empirical evidence from the silicon valley. (2006). *Academy of Management Proceedings*, 1-6.

Ministry Of Industry and Trade's. (2011). *KM strategy 2006*. On line: http://www.mit.gov. jo.Moss, G., Kubaki, K., Hersh, M. & Gunn, R. (2007). Knowledge Management in higher education: A comparison of individualistic and collectivist cultures. *European Journal of Education, 42*(3), 373-394.

Murray, A. (2007). Building the enterprise of the future means no more secrets. *Knowledge. Management World, 16*(5), 19–19.

Nadeem, M. M. (2006). Knowledge management leadership revolutionizing e-business excellence. *Business Renaissance Quarterly, 1*(2), 81–100.

Newman, V. (2002). *The knowledge management activist's- handbook*. United Kingdom: Capstone Publishing Limited.

Newman, V. (2006). Leadership and strategic knowledge management. *Knowledge Management Review, 9*(4), 12–15.

Numprasertchai, S. & Poovarawan, Y.(2008). Improving university performance through ICT based knowledge management system, *International Journal of Innovation and technology, 5*(2), 167 178.

O'Neill, B. S., & Ayda, M. (2007). Knowledge sharing and the psychological contract: Managing knowledge workers across different stages of employment. *Journal of Managerial Psychology, 22*(4), 411–436. doi:10.1108/02683940710745969

Omary, G. (2004). *Combined utilization of information technology and knowledge management to achieve high quality in commercial bank systems*. Unpublished doctoral dissertation. Amman Al Arabia University for Higher Studies. Amman, Jordan.

Peet, M. R., & Walsh, K. (2010). Generative knowledge interviewing: a method for knowledge transfer and talent management at the University of Michigan. *International Journal of Educational Advancement, 10*, 71–85. doi:10.1057/ijea.2010.10

Qureshi, S., Briggs, R., & Hlupic, V. (2006). Value creation from intellectual capital: Convergence of Knowledge Management and collaboration in the intellectual bandwidth Model. *Group Decision and Negotiation, 15*(3), 197–220. doi:10.1007/s10726-006-9018-x

Rawat, M. S. (2009). Knowledge management leveraging e-learning in universities, Proceedings of the *International conference of on e- learning*, 432-439.

Sajeva, S., & Jucevicius, R. (2006). Challenges to implementation of knowledge Management in small and medium- sized enterprises. *Social Sciences, 54*(4), 50–59.

Sanchez, J.A.P. (2001). Knowledge management in universities. *SCIRE: Representaciony organizacion del Conocimiento, 6*(2) 99-120.

Shoham, S., & Perry, M. (2009). Knowledge management as a mechanism for technological and organizational change management in Israeli universities. *Higher Education, 57,* 227–246. doi:10.1007/s10734-008-9148-y

Small, C.T. & Sage, A.P. (2005/2006). Knowledge Management and knowledge sharing: A review. *Information knowledge Systems, 5,* 153-169.

Tamtana, J. S. (2007). The future of knowledge Management. *Management Learning, 38*(1), 125–126. doi:10.1177/135050760703800109

Tashkandi, Z. M. Q. (2007). *Knowledge management: its importance and the extent of applying its processes from the own point of view of the educational administration directresses and the administrative female supervisor in Makkah and Jeddah.* Unpublished master thesis, Om- Alqura University, Makkah, Saudi Arabia.

Teece, D. J. (2000). Managing Knowledge assets in diverse industrial contexts. In Despres, Ch., & Chauvel, D. (Eds.), *Knowledge Horizons.* U.S.A: Butterworth Heinemann. doi:10.1016/B978-0-7506-7247-4.50009-4

Vandeburg, W. H. (2003). The contemporary university and the poverty of nations: Rethinking the mission of STS. *Bulletin of Science, Technology & Society, 23,* 227–235. doi:10.1177/0270467603256076

Vashisth, R., Kumar, R., & Chandra, A. (2010). Barriers and facilitators to knowledge management: evidence from selected Indian universities. *The IUP Journal of Knowledge Management, VIII*(4), 7–25.

Warier, S. (2003). *Knowledge Management, VIKAS publishing House PVTLTD.* New Delhi: VIKAS Publishing House PVTLID.

Wensley, A. K. P., & O'sullivan, A. V. (2000). Tools for Knowledge Management. In Dspres, Ch., & Chauvel, D. (Eds.), *Knowledge Horizons.* U.S.A: Butterworth Heinemann. doi:10.1016/B978-0-7506-7247-4.50008-2

Young, Ch. L., & Sun, K. L. (2007). Capabilities, Processes, and performance of knowledge management: A structural approach. *Human Factors and Ergonomics in Manufacturing, 17*(1), 21–41. doi:10.1002/hfm.20065

Zoubi, D.M. & Kana'an, R.K. (2010, May 19). Intellectual capital and universities: a future study. Paper presented at *"World International Conference on Education (WICE)"*, Amman, Jordan.

Zoubi, D. M., & Rousan, N. M. (2009, March 9). The use of KM in teaching and learning at universities: improving learning outcomes- a suggested frame work. Paper presented at *"International Technology, Education and Development Conference (INTED)"*, Valancia, Spain.

APPENDIX

A questionnaire of the impact of KM awareness, and exercising KM operations on utilizing it." Adapted from a validated tool used in the study of Hijazi (2005a) ".

The questionnaire paragraphs regarding the three sub-measures responses are classified according to Leckert scale:

(1) I strongly disagree (2) I disagree (3) I agree to some extent (4) I agree (5) I strongly agree.

Part One: The Measure of the Degree of KM Awareness

First area: awareness of KM concept
1. The university believes that knowledge is information.
2. There is a strategic plan for the application of KM at the university.
3. The university gives priority to KM.
4. The university knows that KM adds value to its outcome.

Senior managers at the university believe that one of the objectives of KM is that the university is a place for/to:
5. Stimulation and exchange of information.
6. Dissemination of ideas and learning within the university.
7. Facilitate access to information quickly.
8. The use of previous experiments and experiences as basis for future work.

Second area: the role of KM
9. Our university is among the institutions that develop KM.
10. It is possible to use the existing knowledge in the university as an element to improve Performance.
11. Since the knowledge assets have become more important, we should work hard to use KM in the future.
12. There is a need to hire specialists in KM.
13. I believe that the KM program used is appropriate for the work in the university.
14. The KM program can improve the overall performance of the University.

Third area: knowledge assets
15. The university knows its knowledge assets.
16. The university keeps a record for the knowledge-owned assets.
17. The university is aware that the knowledge assets has adds value to its outcomes.
18. The university gives clear importance to the record that contains knowledge assets.
19. The university assesses the quality of KM assets periodically.
20. The university defines and documents main risks threatening knowledge assets.
21. The university implements management strategy of risks threatening knowledge assets.

Fourth area: KM objectives.
22. The University translates its KM strategy into measurable targets.
23. Workers in the university are involved in developing objectives of KM performance.

24. The University transfers and clarifies objectives to workers.
25. The University requests workers to bear responsibility to achieve goals.
26. The University controls objectives of performance, reviews and evaluates them periodically.
27. The university reconsiders KM strategies based on revision and evaluation of KM objectives.
28. The university informs workers about changes and amendments added to the KM strategy.

Fifth area: the benefits of knowledge
29. KM aims to improve the decision-making process.
30. KM aims to improve skills of workers.
31. KM aims to improve the Universities productivity.
32. KM aims to increase the creativity of workers.
33. KM aims to maintain good qualifications.
34. KM aims to the sharing of best practice.

Sixth area: capabilities of knowledge leader
35. Knowledge Leader is capable of influencing workers to share knowledge.
36. Knowledge leader knows well how to manage knowledge.
37. Knowledge leader acts as a facilitator and guide.
38. Knowledge leader makes information available and encourages the generation of knowledge.
39. Knowledge leader stimulates workers to gain new qualifications and skills.
40. Knowledge leader believes in open communication.

Seventh area: the role of the prevailing institutional culture
41. Senior management constantly informs all personnel with the new developments.
42. Sharing information exists between various university units.
43. One of the university objectives is to make workers share information as much as possible.
44. The university encourages workers to participate in setting objectives.
45. The senior management supports the efforts of KM.
46. The workers evaluation system encourages knowledge sharing.

Part Two: The Measure of the Degree of the University Exercise of KM Operation

First area: knowledge generation.
1. The university identifies gaps related to knowledge in preparation for backfilling
2. The university has clear instructions to retrieve stored knowledge.
3. The university supports good ideas and creativity to develop competitive advantage with other universities.
4. The university helps employees to meet the challenges it faces.
5. The university identifies the best practice in other universities.
6. The university converts implicit knowledge to explicit knowledge.

Second area: practice of knowledge sharing
7. The culture of sharing information prevails among workers.
8. The University requests workers to share their knowledge with others.
9. The universities evaluation of workers performance includes the measurement of sharing their explicit and implicit knowledge.
10. The university rewards workers for sharing knowledge.

11. There is a system at the university to monitor and control the sharing of knowledge.
12. The university seeks to find a variety of means to promote knowledge sharing.
13. KM adds value for the environment that stimulates creativity through sharing ideas.

Third area: practice the institutional learning process

14. The university recognizes that learning is an important means which enhances workers' capabilities, individuality and collectively.
15. Learning-promoting culture is spreading at the university at all levels.
16. The university supports learning.
17. Learning is being supported through IT system.
18. Learning is being supported by record management system.
19. Learning is supported by an effective KM system.
20. Learning is supported by certain personnel's affairs policies.

Part Three: The Measure of the Degree of Knowledge Utilization

First area: the use of knowledge

1. The university encourages workers to make sure that knowledge exists before starting any project.
2. The university encourages workers to take advantage of the stock of knowledge it has.
3. The university encourages workers to develop and update knowledge.
4. The university holds workshops, seminars… etc, that are related to knowledge.
5. The university invites experts to participate in workshops, symposiums and lectures relevant to knowledge.
6. The university uses KM in order to identify the surrounding competition of other universities.
7. The University uses KM to develop the quality of education.

Second area: the use of KM in the implementation of institutional processes

8. The university manages relationship with students in an appropriate manner.
9. The university manages educational process in an appropriate manner.
10. The university manages personnel assessment appropriately.
11. The university controls activities that occur within each administrative operation.
12. Institutional operations focus on information sharing within the university and with partners outside the university.
13. The university listens to students to enhance knowledge.
14. The university listens to beneficiaries of university services to enhance knowledge.

Third area: the utilization of KM regarding importance

15. The university possesses an official system that allows everyone to give his own knowledge issues
16. The university possesses an appropriate budget to support KM.
17. The university has a formal system that reshapes and reformulates the rules and regulations impeding the implementation of KM.
18. The university has a formal system that documents most of policies and procedures related to the implementation of KM.
19. The university has a formal system that encourages workers to simulate the best practices of other universities.

20. The university has a formal system that provides employees with appropriate information during training regarding KM.
21. The university has a formal system that encourages effective participation of workers in decision making.

Compilation of References

Adams, G. L., & Lamont, B. T. (2003). Knowledge management systems and developing sustainable competitive advantage. *Journal of Knowledge Management*, 7(2), 142–154.

Adler, P. (2001). Market, hierarchy, and trust: The knowledge economy and the future of capitalism. *Organization Science*, 12(2), 215–234. doi:10.1287/orsc.12.2.215.10117

Agarwal, R., Krudys, G., & Tanniru, M. (1997). Infusing Learning into an Information Systems Organization. *European Journal of Information Systems*, 6(1), 25–40. doi:10.1057/palgrave.ejis.3000257

Agarwal, R., & Karahanna, E. (2000). Time flies when you're having fun: Cognitive absorption and beliefs about information technology usage. *Management Information Systems Quarterly*, 24(4), 665–694. doi:10.2307/3250951

Agor, W. H. (1989). *Intuition in organizations: Leading and managing productivity*. Newbury Park, CA: Sage.

Ahn, J. H., & Chang, S. G. (2004). Assessing the Contribution of Knowledge to Business Performance: The KP3 Methodology. *Decision Support Systems*, 36, 403–416. doi:10.1016/S0167-9236(03)00029-0

Ajmal, M. M., Kekäle, T., & Takala, J. (2009). Cultural Impacts on Knowledge Management and Learning in Project-based Firms. *Vine*, 39(4), 339–352. doi:10.1108/03055720911013634

Al-Alawi, A. I., Al-Marzooqi, N. Y., & Mohammed, Y. F. (2007). Organizational culture and knowledge sharing: Critical success factors. *Journal of Knowledge Management*, 11, 22–42. doi:10.1108/13673270710738898

AL-Ali. A., Gendilji, A.I. & Omary, G. (2006). *Introduction to knowledge Management*. Dar Alamseera for Publication and Distribution, Amman, Jordan.

Alavi, M., Kayworth, T. R., & Leidner, D. E. (2005). An Empirical Examination of the Influence of Organizational Culture on Knowledge Management Practices. *Journal of Management Information Systems*, 22(3), 191–224. doi:10.2753/MIS0742-1222220307

Alavi, M., & Leidner, D. E. (1999). Knowledge management systems: issues, challenges, and benefits. *Communications of the Association for Information Systems*, 1(7), 1–28.

Alavi, M., & Leidner, D. (2001). Review: Knowledge management and knowledge management systems. *Management Information Systems Quarterly*, 25(1), 107–136. doi:10.2307/3250961

Alavi, M. (2000). Managing organizational knowledge. In Zumd, R. (Ed.), *Framing the domains of it management: projecting the future through the past*. New York: Pinnaflex.

Alavi, M., & Leidner, D. (1999). Knowledge management systems: Emerging views and practices form the field. In *Proceedings of the 32th Hawaii International Conference on System Sciences*, IEEE Computer Society.

Albescu, F., Pugna, I., & Paraschiv, D. (2009). Cross-cultural Knowledge Management. *Informatica Economica*, 13(4), 39–50.

AL-hawary, F.A. & Al-najar,F. J. (2008). Impact assessment of I/S technology utilization on knowledge creation and conversion: An empirical study in Jordanian universities. *Journal of Knowledge Management Practice.*, 9(1), 1–15.

AL-khalili. S.M. (2006). *Knowledge management in the ministry of education, Jordan: Analytic study.* Unpublished master thesis, Yarmouk University, Irbid, Jordan.

AL-Khatib. A.M. & Maayah, A.S. (2006). *Universities Creative Management: New models.* Amman, Jordan: Jadara House for the World Book Publishing and Distribution.

Allee, V. (1997). *The knowledge evolution: Expanding organizational intelligence.* Oxford, UK: Butterworth-Heinemann.

Allen, T. (1993). *Managing the flow of technology: Technology transfer and the dissemination of technological information within the R&D organization.* Cambridge, MA: The MIT Press.

Allen, M. (2002). *The Corporate University Handbook: Designing, Managing and Growing a Successful Program.* New York: American Management Association.

Allerton, H. (1998). Phi beta company. *Training & Development, 52*(1), 8.

AL-Mahamed. R.J. (2008). *The role of knowledge management in higher education quality assurance: applied study at private Jordanian universities.* Unpublished master thesis, The Middle East University, Amman, Jordan.

Almahamid, S., Awwad, A., & McAdams, A. C. (2010). Effects of Organizational Agility and Knowledge Sharing on Competitive Advantage: An Empirical Study in Jordan. *International Journal of Management, 27*(3), 387–404.

Alstyne, M. W. V. (2005). Create Colleagues, not Competitors. *Harvard Business Review, 83*(9), 24–25.

Alzoubi, M.R. & Alnajar, F.J. (2010). Knowledge management architecture empirical study on the Jordanian universities. European Journal of Economics, Finance and Administrative Sciences, Issue 21, 101-115.

Amabile, T. (1996). *Creativity in Context.* Boulder, Colorado: Westview Press.

Ambrosini, V., & Bowman, C. (2001). Tacit knowledge: Some suggestions for operationalization. *Journal of Management Studies, 34,* 811–829. doi:10.1111/1467-6486.00260

Amin, A., & Cohendet, P. (2005). Geographies of knowledge formation in firms. *Industry and Innovation, 12,* 465–486. doi:10.1080/13662710500381658

AMIR & USAID. (2003). *The centers of Excellence Guid book.* Jordan: AMIR Program.

Anderson, J. C., & Gerbing, D. W. (1988). Structural Equation Modeling in Practice: A Review and Recommended Two-step Approach. *Psychological Bulletin, 103*(3), 411–423. doi:10.1037/0033-2909.103.3.411

Anderson, L. W., Krathwohl, D. R., Airasian, P. W., Cruikshank, K. A., Mayer, R. E., & Pintrich, P. R. (1998). *Taxonomy for learning, teaching and assessing: A revision of Bloom's taxonomy of educational objectives.* New York: Longman.

Andersson, P., Edman, J., & Ekman, M. (2005). Predicting the World Cup 2002 in soccer: Performance and confidence of experts and non-experts. *International Journal of Forecasting, 21,* 565–576. doi:10.1016/j.ijforecast.2005.03.004

Andersson, T., & Westterlind, T. (1999). *Sharing Knowledge over Company Borders Managing Knowledge in Key Customer Relations at ABB Sweden.* Master Thesis, Linköpings university, Sweden.

Ang, Z., & Massingham, P. (2007). National culture and the standardization versus adaptation of knowledge management. *Journal of Knowledge Management, 11*(2), 5–21. doi:10.1108/13673270710738889

Angst, C. M., & Agarwal, R. (2009). Adoption of Electronic Health Records in the Presence of Privacy Concerns: The Elaboration Likelihood Model and Individual Persuasion. [Article]. *Management Information Systems Quarterly, 33*(2), 339–370.

APEC. (2006). Asia-Pacific Economic Corporation. http://www.apec.com.

Apostolou, D., & Mentzas, G. (1999a). Managing Corporate Knowledge: A Comparative Analysis of Experiences in Consulting Firms: Part 1. *Knowledge and Process Management, 6*(3), 129–138. doi:10.1002/(SICI)1099-1441(199909)6:3<129::AID-KPM64>3.0.CO;2-3

April, K. D. (2002). Guidelines for developing a k-strategy. *Journal of Knowledge Management, 6*(5), 445–456.

Ardichvili, A., Page, V., & Wentling, T. (2003). Motivation and Barriers to Participation in Virtual Knowledge-sharing Communities of Practice. *Journal of Knowledge Management, 7*(1), 64–78. doi:10.1108/13673270310463626

Ardichvili, A. (2008). Learning and knowledge sharing in virtual communities of practice: Motivators, barriers and enablers. *Advances in Developing Human Resources, 10*(4), 541–554. doi:10.1177/1523422308319536

Ardichvili, A., Maurer, M., Li, W., Wentling, T., & Stuedemann, R. (2006). Cultural influences on knowledge sharing through online communities of practice. *Journal of Knowledge Management, 10*(1), 94–107. doi:10.1108/13673270610650139

Argote, L., McEvily, B., & Reagans, R. (2003). Introduction to the special issue on managing knowledge in organizations: creating, retaining and transferring knowledge. *Management Science, 49*(4), 5–8. doi:10.1287/mnsc.49.4.0.14421

Argote, L., & Ingram, P. (2000). Knowledge transfer: a basis for competitive advantage in firms. *Organizational Behavior and Human Decision Processes, 82*(1), 150–169. doi:10.1006/obhd.2000.2893

Armbrecht, F. R., Chapas, R., Chappelow, C. C., Farris, G. F., Friga, P. N., & Harz, C. A. (2001). Knowledge management in research and development. *Research Technology Management, 44*, 28–48.

AS 5037 (2005). Australian Standard Knowledge Management, Standards Australia.

Ashkenas, R. U., Ulrich, D., Jick, T., & Kerr, S. (1995). *The boundary-less organisation: Breaking the chains of the organisational structure.* San Francisco: Jossey-Bass.

ASME. (2006). Austrian Institute for SME Research. http://www.kmuforschung.ac.at.

Axelrod, R. (1984). *The evolution of cooperation.* New York: Basic Books.

Baban, C. F., & Baban, M. (2010). An exploratory study of knowledge management practices in romanian universities within the UNIKM academic research consortium. [special issue]. *Metalurgia International, XV*(9), 157–163.

Back, A., Enkel, E., & Krogh, G. (Eds.). (2007). *Knowledge networks for business growth.* Heidelberg: Springer Verlag.

Bagozzi, R. P. (1980). The nature and causes of self-esteem, performance, and satisfaction in the sales force: A structural equation approach. *The Journal of Business, 53*, 315–331. doi:10.1086/296088

Bailey, J. E., & Pearson, S. W. (1983). Development of a tool for measuring and analyzing computer satisfaction. *Management Science, 29*(5), 530–545. doi:10.1287/mnsc.29.5.530

Ball, C. (1999). *Chairman's opening address and closing remarks.* Paper given at the IQPC Conference on the Corporate University in London on 22-23 June.

Balmisse, G., Meingan, D., & Passerini, K. (2007). Technology trends in knowledge management tools. *International Journal of Knowledge Management, 3*(2), 118–131. doi:10.4018/jkm.2007040106

Barabasi, A.-L., & Bonabeau, E. (2003). Scale-free networks. *Scientific American, 5*, 60–69. doi:10.1038/scientificamerican0503-60

Barabási, A.-L. (2002). *Linked: The new science of networks.* Cambridge, MA: Perseus Publishing.

Barachini, F. (2009). Cultural and social issues for knowledge sharing. *Journal of Knowledge Management, 13*(1), 98–110. doi:10.1108/13673270910931198

Barna, Z. (2003). *Knowledge management: A critical e-business strategic factor.* Unpublished Masters Thesis, San Diego State University, USA.

Barritt, C., & Alderman, F. (2004). *Creating a Reusable Learning Objects Strategy: Leveraging Information and Learning in a Knowledge Economy.* San Francisco, CA: Pfeiffer.

Barson, R., et al. (2000). *Inter and intra organizational barriers to sharing knowledge in the extended supply chain.* e2000 Conference Proceeding.

Bar-Yam, Y. (1997). *Dynamics of complex systems.* Boulder, CO: Westview Press.

Bastick, T. (1982). *Intuition: How we think and act.* New York: John Wiley & Sons Inc.

Baum, J., van Liere, D., & Rowley, T. (2007). Between closure and holes: Hybrid network positions and firm performance. Working paper, Rotman School of Management, University of Toronto.

Baumann, M. R. (2001). The effects of manipulating salience of expertise and membership change on transactive memory. Unpublished doctoral dissertation: University of Illinois, Urbana-Champaign.

Becerra-Fernandez, I., & Sabherwal, R. (2001). Organizational knowledge management: A contingency perspective. *Journal of Management Information Systems*, *18*(1), 23–25.

Becerra-Fernandez, I., González, A. J., & Sabherwal, R. (2004). Knowledge management: challenges, solutions, and technologies.

Beckman, T. (1999). The current state of knowledge management. In Liebowitz, J. (Ed.), *Knowledge management handbook* (pp. 1–22). Boca Raton, FL: CRC Press.

Bedford, D. A. D. (2004). *Enterprise taxonomies— Context, structures & integration.* Paper presented at the American Society of Indexers Annual Conference, American Society of Indexers, Arlington, VA, USA.

Beijerse, R. (2000). Knowledge management in small and medium-sized companies: Knowledge management for entrepreneurs. *Journal of Knowledge Management*, *4*(2), 162–179. doi:10.1108/13673270010372297

Beitler, M. A., & Mitlacher, L. W. (2007). Information Sharing, Self-directed Learning and its Implications for Workplace Learning: A Comparison of Business Student Attitudes in Germany and the USA. *Journal of Workplace Learning*, *19*(8), 526–536. doi:10.1108/13665620710831191

Belbaly, N., & Benbya, H. (2006). A stage model for NPD process maturity and IKMS implementation. In *Artificial Intelligence and Integrated Intelligent Information Systems: Emerging Technologies and Applications* (pp. 428–447). Hershey, PA: IGI Global. doi:10.4018/9781599042497.ch020

Benkler, Y. (2006). *The wealth of networks: How social production transforms markets and freedom.* New Haven: Yale University Press.

Bennet, A., & Bennet, D. (2003). *The partnership between organizational learning and knowledge management.* In C.W. Holsapple (Ed.), Handbook of Knowledge Management, Volume 1: Knowledge Matters. 439-460. Heildelberg: Springer-Verlag

Bennett, R. H. (1998). The importance of tacit knowledge in strategic deliberations and decisions. *Management Decision*, *36*(9), 589–597. doi:10.1108/00251749810239478

Bhagat, R. S., Kedia, B. L., Harveston, P. D., & Triandis, H. C. (2002). Cultural variations in the cross-border transfer of organizational knowledge: An integrative framework. *Academy of Management Review*, *27*(2), 204–221. doi:10.2307/4134352

Bhatt, G. D. (2001). Knowledge management in organizations: examining the interaction between technologies, techniques, and people. *Journal of Knowledge Management*, *4*(1), 68–75. doi:10.1108/13673270110384419

Bhattacherjee, A., & Sanford, C. (2006). Influence processes for information technology acceptance: An elaboration likelihood model. *Management Information Systems Quarterly*, *30*(4), 805–825.

Bierly, P., & Chakrabarti, A. (1996). Generic knowledge strategies in the U.S. pharmaceutical industry. *Strategic Management Journal*, *17*(10), 123–135.

Bierly, P. E. III. (1999). Development of a generic knowledge strategy typology. *The Journal of Business Strategy*, *16*(1), 1–26.

Bierly, P. E. III, & Chakrabarti, A. (2001). Dynamic knowledge strategies and industry fusion. *International Journal of Manufacturing Technology and Management*, *3*(1/2), 31–48. doi:10.1504/IJMTM.2001.001394

Biggam, J. (2001). Defining knowledge: An epistemological foundation for knowledge management. In *Proceedings of the 34th Hawaii International Conference on System Sciences*, IEEE Computer Society.

Billings, R. S., & Wroten, S. P. (1978). Use of path analysis in industrial/organizational psychology: Criticisms and suggestions. *The Journal of Applied Psychology*, *63*, 677–688. doi:10.1037/0021-9010.63.6.677

Birkinshaw, J., Nobel, R., & Ridderstrale, J. (2002). Knowledge as a Contingency Variable: Do the Characteristics of Knowledge Predict Organization Structure. *Organization Science*, *13*(3), 274–289. doi:10.1287/orsc.13.3.274.2778

Blais, A.-R., Thompson, M. M., & Baranski, J. V. (2005). Individual differences in decision processing and confidence judgments in comparative judgment tasks: The role of cognitive styles. *Personality and Individual Differences*, *38*, 1701–1713. doi:10.1016/j.paid.2004.11.004

Blass, E. (2001). What's in a name? A comparative study of the traditional public university and the corporate university. *Human Resource Development International*, *4*(2), 153–172. doi:10.1080/13678860121806

Bloom, B. (1956). *Taxonomy of Behavioral Objectives: Handbook I: Cognitive Domain*. New York: David McKay.

Bogner, W. C., & Bansal, P. (2007). Knowledge Management as the basis of sustained high performance. *Journal of Management Studies*, *44*(1), 165–188. doi:10.1111/j.1467-6486.2007.00667.x

Bond, T. G., & Fox, C. M. (2001). *Applying the Rasch model: Fundamental measurement in the human sciences*. Mahwah, NJ: Erlbaum.

Bothwell, R. K., Deffenbacher, K. A., & Brigham, J. C. (1987). Correlation of eyewitness accuracy and confidence: Optimality hypothesis revisited. *The Journal of Applied Psychology*, *72*, 691–695. doi:10.1037/0021-9010.72.4.691

Bots, P. W. G., & de Bruijn, H. (2002). Effective knowledge management in professional organizations: Going by the rules. In *Proceedings of the 35th Hawaii International Conference on System Sciences*, IEEE Computer Society.

Bowers, K. T. (1987). *Intuition and discovery*. Hillsdale, NJ: Analytical Press.

Boyd, S. (2006). *Are you ready for social software?* Retrieved October 15, 2008, from http://www.stoweboyd.com/message/2006/10/are_you_ready_f.html

Bradley, K. D., & Sampson, S. (2005, Spring). A case for using a Rasch model to assess the quality of measurement in survey research. *The Respondent*, 12-13.

Brand, A. (1998). Knowledge Management and Innovation at 3M. *Journal of Knowledge Management*, *2*(1). doi:10.1108/EUM0000000004605

Brandon, D. P., & Hollingshead, A. B. (2004). Transactive memory systems in organizations: Matching tasks, expertise, and people. *Organization Science*, *15*, 633–644. doi:10.1287/orsc.1040.0069

Bredahl, L., & Grunert, K. G. (1998). Consumer attitudes and decision-making with regard to genetically engineered food products. *Journal of Consumer Policy*, *21*(3), 251–277. doi:10.1023/A:1006940724167

Brenner, L., Griffin, D., & Koehler, D. J. (2005). Modeling patterns of probability calibration with random support theory: Diagnosing case-based judgment. *Organizational Behavior and Human Decision Processes*, *97*, 64–81. doi:10.1016/j.obhdp.2005.02.002

Brewer, W. F., & Sampaio, C. (2006). Processes leading to confidence and accuracy in sentence recognition: A metamemory approach. *Memory (Hove, England)*, *14*(5), 540–552. doi:10.1080/09658210600590302

Brockman, B. K., & Morgan, R. M. (2003). The Role of Existing Knowledge in New Product Innovativeness and Performance. *Decision Sciences*, *34*(2), 385–420. doi:10.1111/1540-5915.02326

Brown, J., & Duguid, P. (2000). *The social life of information*. Boston, MA: Harvard Business School Press.

Brown, J., Collins, A., & Duguid, P. (1989). Situated Cognition and the Culture of Learning. *Educational Researcher*, *18*, 32–42.

Brown, J., & Duguid, P. (2000). Knowledge and Organization: A Social-Practice Perspective. *Organization Science*, *12*, 198–213. doi:10.1287/orsc.12.2.198.10116

Brown, J., & Duguid, P. (1991). Organizational learning and communities-of-practice: Toward a unified view of working, learning, and innovation. *Organization Science*, *2*(1), 40–57.

Brown, S. L., & Eisenhardt, K. M. (1995). Product development: Past research, present findings, and future directions. *Academy of Management Review*, *20*(2), 343–378. doi:10.2307/258850

Brown, S. R. (1986). Q technique and method: Principles and procedures. In Berry, W. D., & Lewis-Beck, M. S. (Eds.), *New tools for social scientists* (pp. 57–76). Beverly Hills, CA: Sage.

Brush, T. H. (1996). Predicted change in operational synergy and post-acquisition performance of acquired businesses. *Strategic Management Journal, 17*, 1–24. doi:10.1002/(SICI)1097-0266(199601)17:1<1::AID-SMJ782>3.0.CO;2-W

Bryant, S. E. (2003). The role of transformational and transactional leadership in creating, sharing and exploiting organisational knowledge. *Journal of Leadership & Organizational Studies, 9*(4). doi:10.1177/107179190300900403

Buckley, P. J., & Carter, M. J. (2004). A formal analysis of knowledge combination in multinational enterprises. *Journal of International Business Studies, 35*, 371–384. doi:10.1057/palgrave.jibs.8400095

Burns, T., & Stalker, G. (1961). *The management of innovation*. London: Tavistock Publications Ltd.

Burt, R. (1992). *Structural holes: The social structure of competition*. Cambridge, MA: Harvard University Press.

Burt, R. (2004). Structural holes and good ideas. *American Journal of Sociology, 110*(2), 349–399. doi:10.1086/421787

Burt, R. (1997). The contingent value of social capital. *Administrative Science Quarterly, 42*(2), 339–365.

Buzan, L. R. (2005). *The relationship among cultural distance, social ties, and tacit knowledge sharing in a multinational corporation*. D.M., University of Phoenix.

Byrne, M. D., John, B. E., Wehrle, N. S., & Crow, D. C. (1999). The tangled Web we wove: A taskonomy of WWW use. In *Proceedings of the SIGCHI conference on Human Factors in Computing Systems: The CHI Is the Limit*. Pittsburgh, PA: ACM.

Cacioppo, J. T., & Petty, R. E. (1982). The need for cognition. *Journal of Personality and Social Psychology, 42*, 116–131. doi:10.1037/0022-3514.42.1.116

Carley, K. (1991). A Theory of Group Stability. *American Sociological Review, 56*, 331–354. doi:10.2307/2096108

Carlson, J. R., & Zmud, R. W. (1999). Channel expansion theory and the experiential nature of media richness perceptions. *Academy of Management Journal, 42*(2), 153–170. doi:10.2307/257090

Carlson, P. J., & Davis, G. B. (1998). An investigation of media selection among directors and managers: From "self" to "other" orientation. *Management Information Systems Quarterly, 22*(3), 335–362. doi:10.2307/249669

Carneiro, A. (2001). The role of intelligent resources in knowledge management. *Journal of Knowledge Management, 5*(4), 358–367. doi:10.1108/EUM0000000006533

Carneiro, A. (2000). How does knowledge management influence innovation and competitiveness? *Journal of Knowledge Management, 4*(2), 87–98.

Chalmeta, R., & Grangel, R. (2008). Methodology for the implementation of knowledge management systems. *Journal of the American Society for Information Science and Technology, 59*(5), 742–755. doi:10.1002/asi.20785

Chase, R. (1997). The knowledge-based organization: An international survey. *Journal of Knowledge Management, 1*(1), 38–49. doi:10.1108/EUM0000000004578

Chase, R. L. (1997). Knowledge management benchmarks. *Journal of Knowledge Management, 1*(1), 83–92. doi:10.1108/EUM0000000004583

Chase, R. L. (2004). Knowledge sharing. *Journal of Knowledge Management, 8*(2), 4–5.

Chen, J., Sun, P. Y. T., & McQueen, R. J. (2010). The impact of national cultures on structured knowledge transfer. *Journal of Knowledge Management, 14*(2), 228–242. doi:10.1108/13673271011032373

Chen, L., & Mohamed, Sh. (2007). Empirical Study of Interaction between knowledge management activities. *Engineering, Construction, and Architectural Management, 14*(3), 242–260. doi:10.1108/09699980710744890

Chen, G. (2001). Toward transcultural understanding: A harmony theory of Chinese communication. In Milhouse, V. H., Asante, M. K., & Nwosu, P. O. (Eds.), *Transcultural realities: Interdisciplinary perspectives on cross-cultural relations* (pp. 55–70). Thousand Oaks, CA: Sage Publications.

Chi, M. T. H., Glaser, R., & Farr, M. J. (1988). *The nature of expertise*. Hillsdale, NJ: Erlbaum.

Chia, L. L., & Sun, Q. L. (2007). Performance measurement systems for knowledge management in high technology industries: a balanced score card frame work. *International Journal of Technology Management*, *39*(1/2), 158–176. doi:10.1504/IJTM.2007.013444

Chia, H. B., Kamdar, D., Nosworthy, G. J., & Chay, Y. W. (2005). *Motivating Knowledge Sharing*. NUS Business School Research Paper Series, RPS#2005-016.

Chieh, P. L. (2007). To share or not to share: Modeling knowledge sharing using exchange ideology as a moderator. *Personnel Review*, *36*(3), 457–475. doi:10.1108/00483480710731374

Child, J. T., & Shumate, M. (2007). The impact of communal knowledge repositores and people based knowledge management on awareness of team effectiveness. *Management Communication Quarterly*, *21*(1), 29–54. doi:10.1177/0893318907301987

Child, J., & Kieser, A. (1981). Development of organizations over time. In Nystrom, N. C., & Starbuck, W. H. (Eds.), *Handbook of organizational design*. Oxford: Oxford University Press.

Chilton, M., & Bloodgood, J. (2008). The dimensions of tacit and explicit knowledge: A description and measure. *International Journal of Knowledge Management*, *4*(2), 75–91. doi:10.4018/jkm.2008040106

Chiri, K., & Klobas, J. (2010). *Knowledge Sharing and Organisational Enabling Conditions*. Proceedings of the 11ᵗʰ European Conference on Knowledge Management, p246-256. Universidade Lusíada de Vila Nova de Famalicão Portugal.

Chiu, S. H. (2010). Students' Knowledge Resources and Knowledge Sharing in the Design Studio – An Exploratory Study. *International Journal of Technology and Design Education*, *20*(1), 27–42. doi:10.1007/s10798-008-9061-9

Chiu, Y., Fritz, S. L., Light, K. E., & Velozo, C. A. (2006). Use of item response analysis to investigate measurement properties and clinical validity of data for the Dynamic Gait Index. *Physical Therapy*, *86*(6), 778–787.

Choi, B., Poon, S., & Davis, J. (2008). Effects of knowledge management strategy on organizational performance: a complementarity theory-based approach. *Omega*, *36*(2), 235–251. doi:10.1016/j.omega.2006.06.007

Choi, S. Y., Lee, H., & Yoo, Y. (2010). The Impact of Information Technology and Transactive Memory Systems on Knowledge Sharing, Application, and Team Performance: A Field Study. *Management Information Systems Quarterly*, *34*(4), 855–870.

Choi, B., & Lee, H. (2003, Summer). Knowledge management enablers, processes, and organizational performance: An integrative view and empirical examination. *Journal of Management Information Systems*, *20*(1), 179–228.

Choi, B., Poon, S. K., & Davis, J. G. (2008). Effects of knowledge management strategy on organizational performance: A complementarity theory based approach. *Omega*, *36*(2), 235–251. doi:10.1016/j.omega.2006.06.007

Choi, Y. S. (2000). *An Empirical Study of Factors Affecting Successful Implementation of Knowledge Management*. Doctoral Dissertation, University of Nebraska, Lincoln, NE

Chow, C. W., Deng, F. J., & Ho, J. L. (2000). The openness of knowledge sharing within organizations: A comparative study in the United States and the People's Republic of China. *Journal of Management Accounting Research*, *12*, 65–95. doi:10.2308/jmar.2000.12.1.65

CHSME. (2006). SME-Portal of Switzerland. http://www.kmu.admin.ch/index.

Chua, A., & Lam, W. (2005). Why KM projects fail: a multi-case analysis. *Journal of Knowledge Management*, *9*(3), 6–17. doi:10.1108/13673270510602737

Chua, A. (2003). Knowledge Sharing: A Game People Play. *Aslib Proceedings*, *55*(3), 117–129. doi:10.1108/00012530310472615

Chung, H. Y., Ming, H. S., Pin, L. Q., & Tsai, M. L. (2005). Critical Factors In Adopting a Knowledge Management System For The Pharmaceutical Industry. *Industrial Management & Data Systems*, *105*(2), 164–183. doi:10.1108/02635570510583307

Chung, J., & Monroe, G. (2000). The effects of experience and task difficulty on accuracy and confidence assessments of auditors. *Accounting and Finance, 40*, 135–152. doi:10.1111/1467-629X.00040

Ciborra, C., & Patriotta, G. (1998). Groupware and teamwork in R&D: Limits to learning and innovation. *R & D Management, 28*(1), 43–52. doi:10.1111/1467-9310.00080

Cichelli, J. J., & Shimp, R. U. (2007). *Taskonomy vs. taxonomy: Human-centered knowledge management design.* Paper presented at the Interservice/Industry Training, Simulation & Education Conference, Orlando, FL.

Clark, K. B., & Fujimoto, T. (1991). *Product development performance: Strategy, organisation and management in the world auto industry.* Boston: Harvard Business School Press.

Clark, S. W. (2003). *The development of an integrated measure of readiness for change instrument and its application on ASC/PK.* Master Thesis, Department of the air force, Air University, Ohio, USA.

Cleetus, K. J., Cascaval, G. C., & Matsuzaki, K. (1996). PACT – a software package to manage projects and coordinate people. In *Proceedings of the 5th International WET ICE'96.*

Coakes, E., & Clarke, S. (2006). Communities of practice. In Schwartz, D. (Ed.), *Encyclopedia of knowledge management* (pp. 30–33). Hershey, PA: Idea Group Publishing. doi:10.4018/9781591405733.ch005

Cocheo, S. (2004). If you build it, they will learn. *ABA Banking Journal, 96*(2), 22–24.

Cohen, D. (1998). Toward a Knowledge Context: Report on the First Annual U.C. Berkeley Forum on Knowledge and the Firm. *California Management Review, 40*(3), 22–40.

Cohen, D., & Prusak, L. (2001). *In good company: How social capital makes organizations work.* Boston: Harvard Business School Press.

Cohen, W., & Levinthal, D. (1990). Absorptive capacity: A new perspective on learning and innovation. *Administrative Science Quarterly, 15*(1), 128–152. doi:10.2307/2393553

Cohen, W. M., & Levinthal, D. A. (1990). Absorptive capacity: a new perspective on learning and innovation. *Administrative Science Quarterly, 35*, 128–152. doi:10.2307/2393553

Coleman, J. (1988). Social capital in the creation of human capital. *American Journal of Sociology, 94*(1), 95–120. doi:10.1086/228943

Colonia-Wilner, R. (1999). Investing in practical intelligence: Ageing and cognitive efficiency among executives. *International Journal of Behavioral Development, 23*, 591–614. doi:10.1080/016502599383711

Connelly, J. (2007). Eight steps to successful taxonomy design. *Information Management Journal, 41*(6), 40–46.

Coolican, H. (1992). *Research methods and statistics in Psychology.* London: Hodder & Stoughton.

Cooper, R. G., & Kleinschmidt, E. J. (1987). New products: What separates winners from losers? *Journal of Product Innovation Management, 4*, 169–184. doi:10.1016/0737-6782(87)90002-6

Cooper, R. G., & Kleinschmidt, E. J. (1993). Major new products: What distinguishes the winners in the chemical industry? *Journal of Product Innovation Management, 10*, 90–111. doi:10.1016/0737-6782(93)90002-8

Cooper, R. G., & Kleinschmidt, E. J. (1994). Determinants of timeliness in product development. *Journal of Product Innovation Management, 11*, 381–396. doi:10.1016/0737-6782(94)90028-0

Cooper, R. G., & Kleinschmidt, E. J. (1995). New product performance: Keys to success, Profitability and cycle time reduction. *Journal of Marketing Management, 11*, 315–337. doi:10.1080/0267257X.1995.9964347

Corral, K., Griffin, J., & Jennex, M. E. (2005). Expert's perspective: The potential of knowledge management in data warehousing. *Business Intelligence Journal, 10*(1), 36–40.

Côté, J. A. (2005). Knowledge taxonomies. *Information Outlook, 9*(6), 45–52.

Cress, U., & Kimmerle, J. (2008). A systemic and cognitive view on collaborative knowledge building with Wikis. *Computer-Supported Collaborative Learning, 3*, 105–122. doi:10.1007/s11412-007-9035-z

Croasdell, D. T., Jennex, M., Yu, Z., & Christianson, T. (2003), *A Meta-Analysis of Methodologies for Research in Knowledge Management, Organizational Learning and Organizational Memory: Five Years at HICSS*. Proceedings of the 36th Hawaii International Conference on System Sciences

Cross, R., & Cummings, J. N. (2004). Tie and network correlates of individual performance in knowledge-intensive work. *Academy of Management Journal, 47*(6), 928–937. doi:10.2307/20159632

Cross, R., Parker, A., Prusak, L., & Borgatti, S. P. (2001). Knowing what we know: Supporting knowledge creation and sharing in social networks. *Organizational Dynamics, 30*(2), 100–120. doi:10.1016/S0090-2616(01)00046-8

Cross, R., & Baird, L. (2000). Technology is not enough: Improving performance by building organizational memory. *Sloan Management Review, 41*(3), 41–54.

Cyr, S., & Choo, C. W. (2010). The Individual and Social Dynamics of Knowledge Sharing: An Exploratory Study. *The Journal of Documentation, 66*(6), 824–846. doi:10.1108/00220411011087832

Daft, R. L., & Lengel, R. H. (1986). Organizational information requirements, media richness and structural design. *Management Science, 32*(5), 554–571. doi:10.1287/mnsc.32.5.554

Daft, R. L., Lengel, R. H., & Trevino, L. K. (1987). Message equivocality, media selection, and manager performance: Implications for information systems. *Management Information Systems Quarterly, 11*(3), 355–366. doi:10.2307/248682

Damanpour, F. (1991). Organizational innovation: A meta-analysis of effect of determinants and moderators. *Academy of Management Journal, 34*(3), 555–590. doi:10.2307/256406

D'Ambra, J. (1995*). A field study of information technology, task equivocality, media richness, and media preference.* PhD Dissertation, University of NSW.

Damodaran, L., & Olphert, W. (2000). Barriers and facilitators to the use of knowledge management systems. *Behaviour & Information Technology, 19*(6), 405–413. doi:10.1080/014492900750052660

Darwazeh, S. S. (2008). The *relationship between the requirement of knowledge management and processes and its effect on the excellence of institutional performance: an applied study on the ministry of higher education in Jordan.* Unpublished master thesis, The Middle East University, Amman, Jordan.

Davenport, T. (1995). *Process Innovation. Reengineering work through information technology.* Boston: Harvard Business School Press.

Davenport, T. (2004). *Thinking for a Living.* Boston: Harvard Business School Press.

Davenport, T. H., DeLong, D. W., & Beers, M. C. (1998). Successful knowledge management projects. *Sloan Management Review, 39*(2), 43–57.

Davenport, T. H., & Prusak, L. (1998). *Working knowledge: How organizations manage what they know.* Boston, MA: Harvard Business School Press.

Davenport, T. H. (1999). Knowledge management and the broader firm: Strategy, advantage, and performance. In Liebowitz, J. (Ed.), *Knowledge management handbook* (pp. 2-1–2-11). Boca Raton, FL: CRC Press.

Davenport, T. H. (1997). *Some Principles of Knowledge Management* (1997). Retrieved on January 21, 2011 from http://www.itmweb.com/essay538.htm.

Davis, R., Alexander, L., & Yelon, S. (1974). *Learning Systems Design.* New York: McGraw-Hill.

Davis, F. D. (1989). Perceived Usefulness, Perceived Ease of Use and User Acceptance of Information Technology. *MIS Quarterly, 13*(3 (September)), 319-340.

Day, G. S. (1994). The capabilities of market driven organizations. *Journal of Marketing,* 37–52. doi:10.2307/1251915

De Long, D. W., & Fahey, L. (2000). Diagnosing cultural barriers to knowledge management. *The Academy of Management Executive, 14*(4), 113–127.

Defense ammunition center.(2008). Retrieved August 2008, from www.dac.army.mil

DeFillippi, R. J. (2002). Organizational models for collaboration in the New Economy. *HR: Human Resource planning, 25*(4), 7.

Delahaye, D. (2003). Knowledge management at SMEs. *International Journal of Organizational Behavior*, *9*(3), 604–614.

DeLone, W. H., & McLean, E. R. (1992). Information Systems Success: The Quest for the Dependent Variable. *Information Systems Research*, *3*(1), 60–95. doi:10.1287/isre.3.1.60

DeLone, W. H., & McLean, E. R. (2003). The DeLone and McLean model of information systems success: A ten-year update. *Journal of Management Information Systems*, *19*(4), 9.

Demarest, M. (1997). Understanding knowledge management. *Long Range Planning*, *30*(3), 374–384. doi:10.1016/S0024-6301(97)90250-8

Denkin, N. K., & Lincoln, Y. S. (1994). *Handbook of qualitative research*. London: Sage.

Denzin, N. K. (1970). *The research act: A theoretical introduction to sociological methods*. Chicago: Aldine.

Desenberg, J. (2000). Moving past the information age: Getting started with knowledge management. *Public Management*, *29*(2), 52–55.

Desouza, K. C. (2003). Barriers to Effective Use of Knowledge Management Systems in Software Engineering. *Communications of the ACM*, *46*(1), 99–101. doi:10.1145/602421.602458

Despres, Ch., & Chauvel, D. (Eds.). (2000). *Knowledge Horizons*. Boston, U.S.A: Butterworth Heinemann.

Dezouza, K., & Awazu, Y. (2006). Knowledge management at SMEs: Five peculiarities. *Journal of Knowledge Management*, *10*(1), 32–43. doi:10.1108/13673270610650085

Dhaliwal, J., & Benbasat, I. (1996). The Use and Effects of Knowledge-based System Explanations: Theoretical *Foundations and a Framework for Empirical Evaluation. Information Systems Research*, *7*(3), 342–362. doi:10.1287/isre.7.3.342

Dillman, D. A. (1978). *Mail and telephone surveys: The total design method*. New York: Wiley.

Dodgson, M. (1993). Organizational learning: A review of some literatures. *Organization Studies*, *14*(3), 375–394. doi:10.1177/017084069301400303

Donnellan, B., Conboy, K., & Hill, S. (2006). IS to support innovation: Weapons of mass discussion. In Khosrow-Pour, M. (Ed.), *Emerging trends and challenges in information technology management* (pp. 623–626). Hershey, PA: Idea Group Publishing.

Dougherty, J. W. D., & Keller, C. M. (1982). Taskonomy: A practical approach to knowledge structures. *American Ethnologist*, *9*(4), 763–774. doi:10.1525/ae.1982.9.4.02a00090

Drucker, P. (1988). The coming of the new organization. *Harvard Business Review*, *66*(1), 45–53.

Dulaimi, M. F. (2007). Case studies on knowledge sharing across cultural boundaries. *Engineering, Construction, and Architectural Management*, *14*(6), 550–567. doi:10.1108/09699980710829012

Durcikova, A., & Gray, P. H. (2009). How Knowledge Validation Processes Affect Knowledge Contribution. *Journal of Management Information Systems*, *25*(4), 81–107. doi:10.2753/MIS0742-1222250403

Durcikova, A., Fadel, K. J., Butler, B. S., & Galletta, D. F. (2010). Knowledge Exploration and Exploitation: The Impacts of Psychological Climate and Knowledge Management System Access. *Information Systems Research*, isre.1100.0286. doi: 10.1287/isre.1100.0286

Dutta, S. (1997). Strategies for implementing knowledge-based systems. *IEEE Transactions on Engineering Management*, *44*(1), 79–90.

Eagley, A., Wood, W., & Chaiken, S. (1978). Causal inferences about communicators and their effect on opinion change. *Journal of Personality and Social Psychology*, *36*, 424–443. doi:10.1037/0022-3514.36.4.424

Earl, M. (2001). Knowledge Management Strategies: Toward a Taxonomy. *Journal of Management Information Systems*, *18*(1), 215–234.

Earl, M. J. (1999). Opinion: what is a chief knowledge officer? *Sloan Management Review*, *40*(2), 29–38.

Easterby-Smith, M. (1997). Disciplines of Organizational Learning: Contributions and Critiques. *Human Relations*, *50*(9), 1085–1113. doi:10.1177/001872679705000903

EC. (2000). Report of the Meeting of the European Commission 23.03.2000. http://ec.europa.eu/growthandjobs.

Edmondson, A. (1999). Psychological Safety and Learning Behavior in Work Teams. *Administrative Science Quarterly, 44*(2), 350–384. doi:10.2307/2666999

Educational Broadcasting Corporation. (2004). *What are the Benefits of Cooperative and Collaborative Learning?* Retrieved on January 21, 2011 from http://www.thirteen.org/edonline/concept2class/coopcollab/index_sub3.html

Edwards, W. (1961). Behavioral decision theory. *Annual Review of Psychology, 12*, 473–498. doi:10.1146/annurev.ps.12.020161.002353

Edwards, J., & Kidd, J. (2003). Bridging the gap from the general to the specific by linking knowledge management to business process management. In Hlupic, V. (Ed.), *Knowledge and business process management* (pp. 124–132). Hershey, PA: Idea Group Publishing.

Efimova, L. (2004). *Discovering the iceberg of knowledge work: A weblog case.* OKLC 2004.

Ein-Dor, P. (2005). Taxonomies of knowledge. In Schwartz, D. (Ed.), *Encyclopedia of knowledge management* (pp. 848–854). Hershey, PA: Idea Group Publishing.

Eldin, S., & Hamza, A. (2009). Capturing tacit knowledge from transient workers: Improving the organizational competitiveness. *International Journal of Knowledge Management, 5*(2), 87–103. doi:10.4018/jkm.2009040106

Emmer, E. T., & Gerwels, M. C. (2002). Cooperative Learning in Elementary Classrooms: Teaching Practices and Lesson Characteristics. *The Elementary School Journal, 103*(1), 75–92. doi:10.1086/499716

Engestrom, Y., Engestrom, R., & Karkkainen, M. (1995). Polycontextuality and boundary crossing in expert cognition: Learning and problem solving in complex work activities. *Learning and Instruction, 5*(4), 319–336. doi:10.1016/0959-4752(95)00021-6

Engeström, Y. (1987). *Learning by expanding: An activity-theoretical approach to developmental research.* Helsinki: Orienta-Konsultit.

Engeström, Y. (1999). 23 Innovative learning in work teams: Analyzing cycles of knowledge creation in practice. In Engeström, Y., Miettinen, R., & Punamäki-Gitai, R.-L. (Eds.), *Perspectives on activity theory.* Cambridge: Cambridge University Press.

English, M.J., & Baker, W.H. (2006, February). Rapid knowledge transfer: The key to success. *Quality Progress, ASQ,* 41-84.

Epstein, J., & Axtell, R. (1996). *Growing artificial societies: Social science from the bottom up.* Boston: Brookings Institute Press, The MIT Press.

Ericsson, K. A., & Crutcher, R. J. (1990). The nature of exceptional performance. In Baltes, P. B., Featherman, D. L., & Lerner, R. M. (Eds.), *Life-span development and behavior, 10* (pp. 187–217). Hillsdale, NJ: Erlbaum.

Estrada, V. (1995). Are your factory workers know-it-alls? *The Personnel Journal,* (September): 128–131.

European Commission. (2006, October). *Enterprise and Industry. SME definition.* Available: http://ec.europa.eu/enterprise/enterprise_policy/sme_definition/index_en.htm

Eveleth, L. B., Eveleth, D. M., & Sarker, S. (2005). An Emerging On-line "Third Place" for Information Systems (IS) Students: Some Preliminary Observations. *Journal of Information Systems Education, 16*(4), 465–475.

Everard, A., & Galletta, D. F. (2005-2006). How Presentation Flaws Affect Perceived Site Quality, Trust, and Intention to Purchase from an Online Store. *Journal of Management Information Systems, 22*(3), 55–95.

Faraj, S., & Sproull, L. (2000). Coordinating expertise in software development teams. *Management Science, 46*, 1554–1568. doi:10.1287/mnsc.46.12.1554.12072

Faris, M. (1426H, November 18). *Knowledge management and innovation: The place of Arab universities in these developments.* Paper presented in the strategic management seminar in higher education institutions, King Khalid University, Saudi Arabia.

Fazio, R. H., & Zanna, M. P. (1978). Attitudinal qualities relating to the strength of the attitude–behavior relationship. *Journal of Experimental Social Psychology, 14*, 398–408. doi:10.1016/0022-1031(78)90035-5

Feldman, S. (2004). Why CATEGORIZE? *KM World, 13*(9), 8.

Felton, S. M., & Finnie, W. C. (2003). Knowledge is today's capital: Strategy & leadership interviews Thomas A. Stewart. *Strategy and Leadership, 31*(2), 48–55. doi:10.1108/10878570310464411

Fenn, D. (1999). Corporate universities for small companies. *Inc., 21*(2), 95–97.

Feurer, R., Chaharbaghi, K., & Distel, M. (1995). Dynamic strategy ownership. *Management Decision, 33*(4), 12–21. doi:10.1108/00251749510084635

Fichman, R. G. (1992). Information Technology Diffusion: A Review of Empirical Research. *Proceedings of the Thirteenth International Conference on Information Systems*, 195–206.

Fink, K. (2004). *Knowledge potential measurement and uncertainty*. Wiesbaden: Dt. Univ.-Verl.

Fink, K., & Ploder, C. (2007c). Knowledge process modeling in SME and cost-efficient software support: Theoretical framework and empirical studies. In Khosrow-Pour, M. (Ed.), *Managing worldwide operations and communications with information technology* (pp. 479–484). Hershey, PA: IGI Publishing.

Fink, K., Roithmayr, F., & Ploder, C. (2006). Multi-functional stakeholder information system for strategic knowledge management: Theoretical concept and case studies. In Khosrow-Pour, M. (Ed.), *Emerging trends and challenges in information technology management* (pp. 152–155). Hershey, PA: Idea Group Publishing.

Fink, K., & Ploder, C. (2007b). Knowledge diffusion through SME Web sites. In Stary, C., Brarachini, F., & Hawamdeh, S. (Eds.), *Knowledge management: Innovation, technology and cultures* (pp. 91–100). New Jersey: World Scientific. doi:10.1142/9789812770592_0008

Fink, K., & Ploder, C. (2006). The impact of knowledge process modeling on small and medium-sized enterprises. In: K. Tochtermann & H. Maurer (Eds.), *Proceedings of I-KNOW '06: 6th International Conference on Knowledge Management,* (pp. 47-51). Graz: J.UCS.

Fink, K., & Ploder, C. (2007a). A comparative study of knowledge processes and methods in Austrian and Swiss SMEs. In: H. Österle, J. Schelp, & R. Winter (Eds.), *Proceedings of the 15th European Conference on Information Systems (ECIS2007),* (pp. 704-715). St. Gallen.

Fiol, C. F., & Lyles, M. A. (1985). Organizational learning. *Academy of Management Review, 10*(4), 803–813. doi:10.2307/258048

Firestone, G. (2002). An industry starving for cost-effective education. *Healthcare Publishing News, 26*(9), 50–51.

Fitzgerald, J. (1992). *Towards knowledge in writing: Illustrations from revision studies*. New York, NY: Springer-Verlag.

Fitzgerald, M. (2006). Tagging tools offer powerful ways to organize information.

Fong, T. W., Allan, M., Bouyssounouse, X., Bualat, M. G., Deans, M., Edwards, L., et al. (2008). *Robotic site survey at Haughton Crater.* Paper presented at the 9th International Symposium on Artificial Intelligence, Robotics, and Automation in Space.

Fonseca, A. M., Biscaya, J. L., Aires-De-Sousa, J., & Lobo, A. M. (2006, January). Geographical classification of crude oils by Kohonen self-organizing maps. *Analytica Chimica Acta, 556*(2), 374–382. doi:10.1016/j.aca.2005.09.062

Forcadell, F. J., & Cuadamillas, F. (2002). A Case Study on the Implementation of A Knowledge Management Strategy Oriented to Innovation. *Knowledge and Process Management, 9*(3), 162–171. doi:10.1002/kpm.143

Ford, D. P., & Chan, Y. E. (2003). Knowledge sharing in a multi-cultural setting: a case study. *Knowledge Management Research & Practice, 1*(1), 11–27. doi:10.1057/palgrave.kmrp.8499999

Fornell, C., & Larcker, D. F. (1981). Evaluating structural equation models with unobservable variables and measurement error. *JMR, Journal of Marketing Research, 18*(1), 39–50. doi:10.2307/3151312

Fox, C. (1999). An introduction to the partial credit model for developing nursing assessments. *The Journal of Nursing Education, 38*(8), 340–346.

Fox, C. M., & Jones, J. A. (1998). Uses of Rasch modeling in counseling psychology research. *Journal of Counseling Psychology, 45*(1), 30–45. doi:10.1037/0022-0167.45.1.30

Fox, C. (1994). A practical knowledge inventory: Psychometric characteristics and validity of an assessment for nurses (Doctoral dissertation, Kent State University).

Free Zones Institution. (2005). *Knowledge Management Strategy 2005-2007*. On line: http://www.free-zones.gov.jo/.

French, R., & Bazalgette, J. (1996). From 'learning organization' to 'teaching-learning organization'? *Management Learning, 27*(1), 113–128. doi:10.1177/1350507696271007

Fuchs-Kittowsk, E., & Köhler, A. (2002). Knowledge creating communities in the context of work processes. *ACM SIGCSE Bulletin, 2*(3), 8–13.

Fulk, J., Flanagin, A., Kalman, M., Monge, P. R., & Ryan, R. (1996). Connective and communal public goods in interactive communication systems. *Communication Theory, 6*, 60–87. doi:10.1111/j.1468-2885.1996.tb00120.x

Fullan, M. (2002). The role of leadership in the promotion of knowledge management in schools: Theory and practice. *Teachers and Teaching, 8*(3). doi:10.1080/135406002100000530

Fuller, S. (2001). *Knowledge Management Foundations*. Boston: Butterworth-Heinemann Press.

Fulmer, W. E. (1999). *Buckman Laboratories (A)*. Case No. 9-800-160. Harvard Business School.

Furner, C. P., Mason, R. M., Mehta, N., Munyon, T. P., & Zinko, R. (2009). Cultural Determinants of Leaning Effectiveness from Knowledge Management Systems: A Multinational Investigation. *Journal of Global Information Technology Management, 12*(1), 30–51.

Gabbay, S. M., & Leenders, R. Th. A. J. (1999). The structure of advantage and disadvantage. In R. Th. A. J. Leenders & S. M. Gabbay (Eds), *Corporate social capital and liability* (pp. 1–14). Boston, MA: Kluwer Academic Publishers.

Gagne, R., Briggs, L., & Wager, W. (1992). *Principles of Instructional Design* (4th ed.). Fort Worth: Harcourt Brace Jovanovich.

Galloway, L. (2004). View from the top. *T&D, 58*(4), 38-43.

Gammelgaard, J., & Ritter, T. (2008). Virtual communities of practice: a mechanism for efficient knowledge retrieval in MNCs. *International Journal of Knowledge Management, 4*(2), 46–61. doi:10.4018/jkm.2008040104

Garland, G. (2007). *Organizational factors and solutions to be considered when implementing knowledge management in a military e-learning environment*. Canada: Royal Roads University.

Garshol, L. M. (2004). Metadata? Thesauri? Taxonomies? Topic maps! Making sense of it all. *Journal of Information Science, 30*(4), 378–391. doi:10.1177/0165551504045856

Garud, R. (1997). On the Distinction between Know-how, Know-what and Know-why. In Huff, A., & Walsh, J. (Eds.), *Advances in Strategic Management* (pp. 81–101).

Gasson, S. (2005). The Dynamics of Sensemaking, Knowledge, and Expertise in Collaborative, Boundary-Spanning Design. *Journal of Computer-Mediated Communication, 10*(4).

GE. (2008). *GE fact sheet*, Retrieved August 2008 from www.ge.com

Geng. Q. Townley, Ch., Huang, K. & Zhang, J. (2005). Comparative Knowledge management: A pilot study of Chinese and American universities. *Journal of the Society for Information Science and Technology, 56* (10), 1031-1044.

Ghalia, M. B., & Wang, P. P. (2000). Intelligent system to support judgmental business forecasting: The case of estimating hotel room demand. *IEEE transactions on Fuzzy Systems, 8*, 380–397. doi:10.1109/91.868945

Giacoppo, A. S. (2008). Integrating Social Software into a Student Teacher Education Program: Enabling Discourse, Knowledge Sharing, and Development in a Community of Learning. *Dissertation Abstracts International Section A: Humanities and Social Sciences, 68*(9-A), 3811.

Gibbins, M. (1984). Propositions about the psychology of professional judgment in public accounting. *Journal of Accounting Research, 22*, 103–125. doi:10.2307/2490703

Giju, G., Badea, L., Lopez Ruiz, V., & Nevado Pena, D. (2010). Knowledge management – the key resource in the knowledge economy. *Theoretical and Applied Economics, 17*(6), 27–36.

Gilbert, N., & Troitzsch, K. (2005). *Simulation for the social scientist*. Berkshire, England: Open University Press.

Gilchrist, A. (2003). Thesauri, taxonomies and ontologies—An etymological note. *The Journal of Documentation, 59*(1), 7–18. doi:10.1108/00220410310457984

Gilmour, D. (2003). How to fix knowledge management. *Harvard Business Review*, 17–18.

Gilovich, T., Griffin, D., & Kahneman, D. (2002). *Heuristics and biases. The psychology of intuitive judgment.* New York, NY: Cambridge University Press.

Ginsberg, M., & Kambil, A. (1999). Annotate: A Web-based knowledge management support system for document collections. In *Proceedings of the 32nd Hawaii International Conference on System Sciences*, IEEE Computer Society.

Girard, J. P. (2005). Taming enterprise dementia in public sector organizations. *International Journal of Public Sector Management, 18*(6/7), 534–545. doi:10.1108/09513550510616751

Glisby, M., & Holden, N. (2003). Contextual constraints in knowledge management theory: The cultural embeddedness of Nonaka's knowledge-creating company. *Knowledge and Process Management, 10*(1), 29–36. doi:10.1002/kpm.158

Gnyawali, D. R., Stewart, A. C. & Grant, J. H. (1997). Creation and utilization of organizational knowledge: An empirical study of the roles of organizational learning on strategic decision making. *Academy of Management Best Paper Proceedings*, 16-20.

Gold, A. H., Malhotra, A., & Segars, A. H. (2001). Knowledge management: An organizational capabilities perspective. *Journal of Management Information Systems, 18*(1), 185–214.

Golder, S., & Huberman, B. A. (2006). Usage patterns of collaborative tagging systems. *Journal of Information Science, 32*, 198–208. doi:10.1177/0165551506062337

Gonzalez-Reinhart, J. (2005). Wikis and the Wiki way. *Information Systems Research*, 1–22.

Goodman, P. S., & Darr, E. D. (1998). Computer-aided systems and communities: Mechanisms for organizational learning in distributed environments. *Management Information Systems Quarterly, 22*(4), 417–440. doi:10.2307/249550

Gopalakrishnan, S., & Bierly, P. E. III. (2006). The impact of firm size and age on knowledge strategies during product development: A study of the drug delivery industry. *IEEE Transactions on Engineering Management, 53*(1), 3–16. doi:10.1109/TEM.2005.861807

Govindarajan, V., & Fisher, J. (1990). Strategy, control systems, and resource sharing: Effects on business-unit performance. *Academy of Management Journal, 33*(2), 259–285. doi:10.2307/256325

Graff, M. (2006). The Importance of Online Community in Student Academic Performance. *Electronic Journal of e-Learning, 4*(2), 127-131.

Graham, A. B., & Pizzo, V. G. (1996). A question of balance: Case studies in strategic knowledge management. *European Management Journal, 14*(4), 338–346. doi:10.1016/0263-2373(96)00020-5

Granovetter, M. (1985). Economic action and social structure: The problem of embeddedness. *American Journal of Sociology, 91*(3), 481–510. doi:10.1086/228311

Grant, R. M. (1996). Toward a Knowledge-based Theory of the Firm. *Strategic Management Journal, 17*(Special Issue), 109–122.

Grantham, D. (2005). *Understanding Student Learning Styles and Theories of Learning.* Retrieved on January 21, 2011 from: www.ukcle.ac.uk/resources/postgraduate/grantham2.html.

Gray, P. H., & Durcikova, A. (2005-2006). The Role of Knowledge Repositories in Technical Support Environments: Speed Versus Learning in User Performance. *Journal of Management Information Systems, 22*(3), 821–834.

Gray, P. H., & Meister, D. B. (2004). Knowledge Sourcing Effectiveness. *Management Science, 50*(6), 821–834. doi:10.1287/mnsc.1030.0192

Greco, J. (1997). Corporate home schooling. *The Journal of Business Strategy, 18*(3), 48–52. doi:10.1108/eb039857

Greenberg, R. (1998). Corporate u. takes the job training field. *Techniques: Making Education & Career Connections, 73*(7), 36–39.

Griffin, A. (1993). PDMA research on new product development practices: Updating trends and benchmarking best practices. *Journal of Product Innovation Management, 14*(6), 429–458. doi:10.1016/S0737-6782(97)00061-1

Griffin, A., & Hauser, J. R. (1992). Patterns of communication among marketing engineering and manufacturing—A comparison between two new product teams. *Management Science, 38*(3), 360–373. doi:10.1287/mnsc.38.3.360

Griffin, D., & Tversky, A. (1992). The weighing of evidence and the determinants of confidence. *Cognitive Psychology, 24*, 411–435. doi:10.1016/0010-0285(92)90013-R

Griffith, T. L., & Sawyer, J. E. (2006). Supporting technologies and organizational practices for the transfer of knowledge in virtual environments. *Group Decision and Negotiation, 15*, 407–423. doi:10.1007/s10726-006-9048-4

Griffith, T. L., Sawyer, J. E., & Neale, M. A. (2003). Virtualness and knowledge in teams: Managing the love triangle of organizations, individuals, and information technology. *Management Information Systems Quarterly, 27*, 265–287.

Griffith, R. M. (1949). Odds adjustments by American horse-race bettors. *The American Journal of Psychology, 62*, 290–294. doi:10.2307/1418469

Griffith, T. L., & Sawyer, J. E. (2007). *Multilevel knowledge and team performance in a Fortune 100 technology company*. Unpublished manuscript.

Grigorenko, E. L., Sternberg, R. J., & Strauss, S. (2006). Practical intelligence and elementary-school teacher effectiveness in the United States and Israel: Measuring the predictive power of tacit knowledge. *Thinking Skills and Creativity, 1*(1), 14–33. doi:10.1016/j.tsc.2005.03.001

Grover, V., & Davenport, T. H. (2001). General Perspectives on Knowledge Management: Fostering a Research Agenda. *Journal of Management Information Systems, 18*(1), 5–17.

Grunbacher, P., & Briggs, R. O. (2001). Surfacing tacit knowledge in requirements negotiation: Experiences using easy win win. In *Proceedings of the 34th Hawaii International Conference on System Sciences*, IEEE Computer Society.

Gudykunst, W. B., & Matsumoto, Y. (1996). Cross-cultural variability of communication in personal relationships. In Gudykunst, W. B., Ting-Toomey, S., & Nishida, T. (Eds.), *Communication in personal relationships across cultures* (pp. 19–56). Thousand Oaks, CA: Sage Publications.

Gummesson, E. (1991). *Qualitative Methods in Management Research*. London: Sage Publishing.

Guo, Z., & Sheffield, J. (2006). *A Paradigmatic and Methodological Examination of KM Research: 2000 to 2004*. Proceedings of the 39th Annual Hawaii International Conference on System Sciences (HICSS 2006), Hawaii, USA.

Gupta, B., Iyer, L., & Aronson, J. (2000). Knowledge management: Practices and challenges. *Industrial Management & Data Systems, 100*(1), 17–21. doi:10.1108/02635570010273018

Gupta, A. K., & Govindarajan, V. (2000). Knowledge Management's Social Dimension: Lessons from Nucor Steel. *Sloan Management Review, 42*(1), 71–80.

Gupta, A. K., & Govindarajan, V. (1986). Resource sharing among SBUs: Strategic antecedents and administrative implications. *Academy of Management Journal, 29*, 695–714. doi:10.2307/255940

Guptara, P. (2000). *Why Knowledge Management Fails: How to avoid the common pitfalls*. Washington, DC: Melcrum Publishing Ltd.

Gurteen, D. (1998). Knowledge, creativity and innovation. *Journal of Knowledge Management, 2*(1), 5–13. doi:10.1108/13673279810800744

Haas, M. R., & Hansen, M. T. (2007). Different knowledge, different benefits: Toward a productivity perspective on knowledge sharing in organizations. *Strategic Management Journal, 28*, 1133–1153. doi:10.1002/smj.631

Hackerman, J., & Morris, C. (1978). Group tasks, group interaction process, and group performance effectiveness: A review and proposed integration. In Berkowltz, L. (Ed.), *Group Process* (pp. 1–15). New York: Academic Press.

Hackman, J. R., & Oldham, G. R. (1980). *Work redesign.* Reading, Massachusetts: Addison-Wesley.

Hackman, J. R. (2002). *Leading teams: Setting the stage for great performances.* Cambridge, MA: Harvard Business School Press.

Haeussler, C. (2011). Information-sharing in academia and the industry: A comparative study. *Research Policy, 40,* 105–122. doi:10.1016/j.respol.2010.08.007

Hair, J. F., Anderson, R. E., Tatham, R. L., & Black, W. C. (1998). *Multivariate data analysis* (5th ed.). Prentice Hall.

Hall, E. T. (1976). *Beyond culture* (1st ed.). Garden City, NY: Anchor Press.

Hall, H., & Goody, M. (2007). KM, culture and compromise: Interventions to promote knowledge sharing supported by technology in corporate environments. *Journal of Information Science, 33,* 181–188. doi:10.1177/0165551506070708

Hall, P., & Rieck, A. (2001). Improving coverage accuracy of nonparametric prediction intervals. *Journal of the Royal Statistical Society. Series B, Statistical Methodology, 63,* 717–725. doi:10.1111/1467-9868.00308

Hall, J., Sapsed, J., & Williams, K. (2000). Barriers and Facilitators to Knowledge Capture and Transfer in Project-Based Firms.

Hambleton, R. (1992). Hambleton's 9 theses. *Rasch Measurement Transactions, 6,* 215–217.

Hamel, C., & Ryan-Jones, D. (2002). Designing Instruction with Learning Objects. *International Journal of Educational Technology, 3*(1), 111–124.

Hammer, M., & Champy, J. (1993). *Reengineering the corporation: A manifesto for business revolution.* New York: Harper Business.

Hansen, M., Nohria, N., & Tierney, T. (1999). What's your strategy for managing knowledge. *Harvard Business Review,* (March-April): 106–116.

Hansen, M. (1999). The search-transfer problem: The role of weak ties in sharing knowledge across organization subunits. *Administrative Science Quarterly, 44*(1), 82–111. doi:10.2307/2667032

Hansen, M. T. & Haas, M. R. (2001). Different knowledge, different benefits: Toward a productivity perspective on knowledge sharing in organizations. *Academy of Management Proceedings,* C1-C6.

Hart, D., & Warne, L. (2005). Comparing cultural and political perspectives of data, information, and knowledge sharing in organisations. *International Journal of Knowledge Management, 2*(2), 1–15. doi:10.4018/jkm.2006040101

Hasan, H., & Crawford, K. (2007). Knowledge mobilisation in communities through socio-technical system. *Journal of KMRP, 5*(4), 237–248.

Hasan, H. (2001). An overview of techniques for applying activity theory to information systems. In H. Hasan, E. Gould, & P. Larkin (Eds.), *Information systems and activity theory: Vol. 2. Theory and practice* (pp. 3-22). Wollongong University Press.

Hasan, H., & Pfaff, C. C. (2006). Emergent conversational technologies that are democratising information systems in organisations: The case of the corporate Wiki. In *Proceedings of the ISF,* Canberra.

Hasanali, F. (2002). *Critical Success Factors of Knowledge Management.* APQC.

Hassell, L. (2007). A continental philosophy perspective on knowledge management. *Information Systems Journal, 17,* 185–195. doi:10.1111/j.1365-2575.2007.00233.x

Hausch, D. B., Ziemba, W. T., & Rubinstein, M. (1981). Efficiency of the market for racetrack betting. *Management Science, 27,* 1435–1452. doi:10.1287/mnsc.27.12.1435

He, J. (2010). Examining Factors that Affect Knowledge Sharing and Students' Attitude toward their Learning Experience within Virtual Teams. *Dissertation Abstracts International Section A: Humanities and Social Sciences, 71*(3A), 925.

Hedlund, G. (1994). A model of knowledge management and the N-form corporation. *Strategic Management Journal, 15*(5), 73–90.

Hedlund, J., Forsythe, G. B., Horvath, J. A., Williams, W. M., Snook, S., & Sternberg, R. J. (2003). Identifying and assessing tacit knowledge: Understanding the practical intelligence of military leaders. *The Leadership Quarterly, 14,* 117–140. doi:10.1016/S1048-9843(03)00006-7

Heier, H., Borgman, H. P., & Manuth, A. (2005). Siemens: Expanding the knowledge management system ShareNet to research & development. *Journal of Cases on Information Technology, 7*(1), 92–107. doi:10.4018/jcit.2005010106

Hemetsberger, A., & Reinhardt, C. (2006). Learning and knowledge-building in open-source communities - a social-experiential approach. *Management Learning, 37*, 187–214. doi:10.1177/1350507606063442

Henderson & Cockburn. (1996, Spring). Scale, scope, and spillovers: The determinants of research productivity in drug discovery. *RAND Journal of Economics, RAND, 27*(1), 32–59. doi:10.2307/2555791

Hendriks, P. (1999). Why share knowledge? the influence of ICT on the motivation for knowledge sharing. *Knowledge and Process Management, 6*(2), 91–100. doi:10.1002/(SICI)1099-1441(199906)6:2<91::AID-KPM54>3.0.CO;2-M

Higgins, J. M. (1995). Innovate or evaporate: Seven secrets of innovative corporations. *The Futurist, 29*(5), 42–48.

Hijazi, H. A. (2005b). *Knowledge management.* Amman, Jordan: Al-Ahlia for Publication and Distribution.

Hijazi, H. A. (2005a). *Measuring the impact of knowledge management awareness on knowledge management utilization in Jordanian organizations: a comparative analytical study of public and private sector towards building a model for the knowledge management utilization.* Unpublished doctoral dissertation, Amman Al-Arabia University for Higher Studies, Amman, Jordan.

Hijazi, H. A. (2010, April3). Knowledge management application in Jordan. *Manbralrai Journal,* On line: http://www.manbaralrai.com.

Hildreth, P.M., & Kimble, C. (2002, October 1). The duality of knowledge. *Information Research, 8*(1).

Hinds, P. J., & Pfeffer, J. (2003). Why organizations don't "know what they know": Cognitive and motivational factors affecting the transfer of expertise. In Ackerman, M. S., Pipek, V., & Wulf, V. (Eds.), *Sharing expertise: Beyond knowledge management* (pp. 3–26). Cambridge, MA: MIT Press.

Hoffmann, J. J., Hoelscher, M. L., & Sherif, K. (2005). Social capital, knowledge management, and sustained superior performance. *Journal of Knowledge Management, 9*(3), 93–100. doi:10.1108/13673270510602791

Hofstede, G. H. (2001). *Culture's consequences: Comparing values, behaviors, institutions and organizations across nations* (2nd ed.). Thousand Oaks, CA: Sage Publications.

Hofstede, G. (1993). Cultural dimensions in people management: The socialization perspective. In V. Pucik, N. M. Tichy, & C. K. Barnett (Eds). *Globalizing Management* (pp. 139–158). New York, NY: John Wiley & Sons, Inc.

Hogarth, R. M., & Makridakis, S. (1981). Forecasting and planning: An evolution. *Management Science, 27*(2), 115–216. doi:10.1287/mnsc.27.2.115

Holden, N. (2001). Knowledge management: Raising the spectre of the cross-cultural dimension. *Knowledge and Process Management, 8*(3), 155–163. doi:10.1002/kpm.117

Holden, N. (2002). *Cross-cultural management: A knowledge management perspective.* Harlow, NY: Financial Times Prentice Hall.

Hollnagel, E., Hoc, J., & Cacciabue, P. (1995). Expertise and technology: I have a feeling we are not in Kansas anymore. In Hoc, J., Cacciabue, P., & Hollnagel, E. (Eds.), *Expertise and technology* (pp. 279–286). New Jersey: Lawrence Erlbaum Associates Publishers.

Holsapple, C. W., & Jones, K. G. (2007). Knowledge chain activity classes: Impacts on competitiveness and the importance of technology support. *International Journal of Knowledge Management, 3*(3), 2–5.

Holsapple, C. W., & Joshi, K. D. (2000). An investigation of factors that influence the management of knowledge in organizations. *The Journal of Strategic Information Systems, 9*, 235–261.

Holsapple, C. W., & Joshi, K. D. (2001). Knowledge management: A three-fold framework. *The Information Society, 18*(1), 47–64.

Holsapple, C. W., & Singh, M. (2001). The knowledge chain model: Activities for competitiveness. *Expert Systems with Applications, 20*(1), 77–98.

Holsapple, C. W., & Singh, M. (2005). Performance implications of the knowledge chain. *International Journal of Knowledge Management, 1*(4), 1–22.

Holsapple, C. W., & Joshi, K. D. (2001). Organizational knowledge resources. *Decision Support Systems, 31*(1), 39–54. doi:10.1016/S0167-9236(00)00118-4

Holsapple, C. W., & Singh, M. (2000). The knowledge chain. In *Proceedings of the Annual Conference of the Southern Association on Information Systems*, Atlanta, Georgia.

Holt, D. T. (2000). *The measurement of readiness for change: A review of instruments and suggestions for future research* Annual meeting of the Academy of Management, Toronto, Canada.

Holt, D. T., Bartczak, S. E., Clark, S. W., & Trent, M. R. (2004). *The Development of an Instrument to Measure Readiness for Knowledge Management.* Proceedings of the 37th Hawaii International Conference on System Sciences

Hong, J., Heikkinen, J., & Blomqvist, K. (2010). Culture and knowledge co-creation in R&D collaboration between MNCs and Chinese universities. *Knowledge and Process Management, 17*(2), 62–73. doi:10.1002/kpm.342

Hooff, B., & Ridder, J. (2004). Knowledge sharing in context: The influence of organizational commitment, communication climate and CMC use on knowledge sharing. *Journal of Knowledge Management, 8*(6), 117–130. doi:10.1108/13673270410567675

Horwath Consulting. (2005). *The Norwegian hotel industry 2005.* Oslo, Norway: Horwath Consulting AS.

Hoyle, J. (1993). *Professional standards for the superintendency.* Arlington, VA: American Association of School Administrators.

Hoyle, J. R., Bjork, L. G., Collier, V., & Glass, T. (2005). *The superintendent as CEO: Standards-based performance.* Thousand Oaks, CA: Corwin Press.

Hu, L., & Bentler, P. M. (1999). Cutoff Criteria for Fit Indexes in Covariance Structure Analysis: Conventional Criteria versus New Alternatives. *Structural Equation Modeling, 6*(1), 1–55. doi:10.1080/10705519909540118

Hu, A. G. Z., & Jaffe, A. B. (2003). Patent citations and international knowledge flow: the cases of Korea and Taiwan. *International Journal of Industrial Organization, 21*(6), 849–880.

Hu, W., & Grove, C. L. (1999). *Encountering the Chinese: A guide for Americans* (2nd ed.). Yarmouth, ME: Intercultural Press.

Huang, K. (1997). Capitalizing collective knowledge for winning, execution and teamwork. *Journal of Knowledge Management, 1*(2), 149–156. doi:10.1108/EUM0000000004590

Huang, H. (2005). *Knowledge sharing in Chinese surgical teams.* Ph.D., University of Southern California.

Huber, G. P. (2001). Transfer of knowledge in knowledge management systems: unexplored issues and suggested studies. *European Journal of Information Systems, 10*(2), 72–79. doi:10.1057/palgrave.ejis.3000399

Huber, G. P., Davenport, T. H., & King, D. (1998). *Some perspectives on organizational memory.* Unpublished Working Paper for the Task Force on Organizational Memory, F. Burstein, G. Huber, M. Mandviwalla, J. Morrison, and L. Olfman, (eds.) Presented at the 31st Annual Hawaii International Conference on System Sciences.

Huemer, L., Krogh, G., & Johan, R. (1998). Knowledge and the concept of trust. In Krogh, G., Roos, J., & Kleine, D. (Eds.), *Knowing in firms* (pp. 123–145). Thousand Oaks, CA: Sage.

Hughes, A. (1997). Information strategy—Threat or opportunity? *Librarian Career Development, 5*(2), 60. doi:10.1108/09680819710180912

Hughes, P., & Morgan, R. E. (2007). A resource-advantage perspective of product-market strategy performance & strategic capital in high technology firms. *Industrial Marketing Management, 36*, 503–517. doi:10.1016/j.indmarman.2006.01.003

Hung, Y. H., Chen, Y. L., & Chou, S. C. T. (2006). *On the Relationship between Knowledge Management Readiness and Intellectual Capital.* APRU DLI.

Hung, Y. H., & Chou, S. C. (2005). *On Constructing a Knowledge Management Pyramid Model.* The IEEE International Conference on Information Reuse and Integration.

Hurley, R., & Hult, T. (1998). Innovation, market orientation, and organizational learning: An integration and empirical examination. *Journal of Marketing, 62*(3), 42–54. doi:10.2307/1251742

Husted, K., & Michailova, S. (2002). Knowledge sharing in Russian companies with Western participation. *Management International, 6*(2), 17–28.

Husted, K., & Michailova, S. (2002). Diagnosing and Fighting Knowledge-Sharing Hostility. *Organizational Dynamics, 31*(1), 60–73. doi:10.1016/S0090-2616(02)00072-4

Hutchins, E. (1996). *Cognition in the Wild.* Cambridge, MA: MIT press.

Hutt, M., & Reingen, P., & Ronchetto, Jr. (1988). Tracing emergent processes in marketing strategy formation. *Journal of Marketing, 52*(1), 4–19. doi:10.2307/1251682

Hwang, A., Francesco, A. M., & Kessler, E. (2003). The relationship between individualism-collectivism, face, and feedback and learning processes in Hong Kong, Singapore, and the United States. *Journal of Cross-Cultural Psychology, 34*(1), 72–91. doi:10.1177/0022022102239156

Iansiti, M. (1992). *Science-based product development: An empirical study of the mainframe computer industry* (Working paper). Cambridge, MA: Harvard Business School.

Ichijo, K., Krogh, G., & Nonaka, I. (1998). Knowledge enablers. In Krogh, G., Roos, J., & Kleine, D. (Eds.), *Knowing in Firms* (pp. 173–203). Thousand Oaks, CA: Sage.

Isaacs, W. N. (1993). Taking flight: Dialogue, collective thinking, and organizational learning. *Organizational Dynamics, 22*(2), 24–39.

Ithia, A. (2003). UK lawyers spend more on KM. *KM Review, 5*(6), 11.

Jacobs, J. (1961). *The decline and rise of American cities.* New York: Random House.

Jaime, A., Gardoni, M., Mosca, J., & Vinck, D. (2006). From quality management to knowledge management in research organizations. *International Journal of Innovation Management, 10*(2), 197–215. doi:10.1142/S1363919606001430

Jang, S., Hong, K., Bock, G. W., & Kim, I. (2002). Knowledge management and processinnovation: The knowledge transformation path in Samsung SDI. *Journal of Knowledge Management, 6*(5), 479–485. doi:10.1108/13673270210450582

Jansen, K. J. (2000). The emerging dynamics of change: Resistance, readiness, and momentum. *Human Resource Planning, 23*(2), 53–55.

Janz, B. D., & Prasarnphanich, P. (2003). Understanding the Antecedents of Effective Knowledge Management: the Importance of a Knowledge-centered Culture. *Decision Sciences, 34*(2), 351–384. doi:10.1111/1540-5915.02328

Jarvenpaa, S. L., & Leidner, D. E. (1999). Communication and trust in global virtual teams. *Organization Science, 10*(6), 791–815. doi:10.1287/orsc.10.6.791

Jashapara, A. (2004). *Knowledge management: An integrated Approach.* Upper Saddle River, NJ: Prentice Hall.

Jasimuddin, S., Klein, J., & Connell, C. (2005). The paradox of using tacit and explicit knowledge. Strategies to face dilemmas. *Management Decision, 43*(1), 102–112. doi:10.1108/00251740510572515

Jennex, M. E. (2008). *Current Issues in Knowledge Management.* New York, NY: IGI Global.

Jennex, M. E. (2005). What is Knowledge Management? *International Journal of Knowledge Management, 1*(4), 1–15.

Jennex, M., & Olfman, L. (2003). Organizational Memory. *Handbook on Knowledge Management, 1,* 207–234.

Jennex, M. (2005). Editorial preface: Knowledge management systems. *International Journal of Knowledge Management, 1*(2), i–iv.

Jennex, M. E., & Olfman, L. (2005). Assessing knowledge management success. *International Journal of Knowledge Management, 1*(2), 33–49. doi:10.4018/jkm.2005040104

Jennex, M. E., & Olfman, L. (2006). A model of knowledge management success. *International Journal of Knowledge Management, 2*(3), 51–68. doi:10.4018/jkm.2006070104

Jennex, M. E., Smolnik, S., & Croasdell, D. (2007b). Knowledge management success. *International Journal of Knowledge Management, 3*(2), i–vi.

Jennex, M. E. (2005). What is KM? *International Journal of Knowledge Management, 1*(4), i–iv.

Jennex, M. E. (2007). *Knowledge management in modern organizations*. Idea Group Publishing.

Jennex, M. E., & Croashell, D. (2005). Knowledge management: Are we a discipline? *International Journal of Knowledge Management, 1*(1), i–v.

Jennex, M. E. (2006). Culture, context, and knowledge management. *International Journal of Knowledge Management, 2*(2), i–iv.

Jennex, M. E. (2008). Exploring System Use as a Measure of Knowledge Management Success. *Journal of Organizational and End User Computing, 20*(1), 50–63. doi:10.4018/joeuc.2008010104

Jennex, M. E., & Olfman, L. (2000). *Development recommendations for knowledge management/organizational memory systems*. Proceedings of the Information Systems Development Conference.

Jennex, M. E., & Olfman, L. (2002). Organizational memory/knowledge effects on productivity: A longitudinal study. In *Proceedings of the 35th Annual Hawaii International Conference on System Sciences*, IEEE Computer Society.

Jennex, M. E., Olfman, L., Pituma, P., & Yong-Tae, P. (1998). An organizational memory information systems success model: An extension of DeLone and McLean's I/S success model. In *Proceedings of the 31st Annual Hawaii International Conference on System Sciences*, IEEE Computer Society.

Jennex, M. E., Smolnik, S., & Croasdell, D. T. (2007). *Towards Defining Knowledge Management Success*. Proceedings of the 40th Annual Hawaii International Conference on System Sciences (HICSS 2007), Hawaii, USA.

Jennex, M. E., Smolnik, S., & Croasdell, D. (2007). Defining Knowledge Management Success. *Proceedings of the 6th Annual ISOnEworld Conference*, Las Vegas, NV.

Jennex, M. E., Smolnik, S., & Croasdell, D. (2007). Towards Defining Knowledge Management Success. *Proceedings of the 40th Annual Hawaii International Conference on System Sciences*.

Jennex, M. E., Smolnik, S., & Croasdell, D. (2007a, January). Towards defining knowledge management success. In *40th Hawaii International Conference on System Sciences, HICSS40, IEEE Computer Society.*

Jennex, M. E., Smolnik, S., & Croasdell, D. (2008, January). Towards measuring knowledge management success. In *41st Hawaii International Conference on System Sciences, HICSS41, IEEE Computer Society.*

Jennex, M., & Croasdell, D. (2003). *Knowledge management, organizational memory and organizational learning*. Proceedings of the 36th Annual Hawaii International Conference on System Sciences.

Jennex, M., Olfman, L., & Addo, T. B. A. (2003). *The need for an organizational knowledge management*. Proceedings of the 36th Annual Hawaii International Conference on System Sciences.

Jimes, C., & Lucardie, L. (2003). Reconsidering the tacit-explicit distinction - A move toward functional (tacit) knowledge management. *Journal of Knowledge Management, 1*(1), 23–32.

Johannenssen, J.-A., Olsen, B., & Olaisen, J. (1999). Aspects of innovation theory based on knowledge management. *International Journal of Information Management, 19*(2), 121–139. doi:10.1016/S0268-4012(99)00004-3

Johannessen, J., Olaisen, J., & Olsen, B. (2001). The mismatch of tacit knowledge: The importance of tacit knowledge, the dangers of information technology, and what to do about it. *International Journal of Information Management, 21*(1), 3–21. doi:10.1016/S0268-4012(00)00047-5

Johannessen, J., Olaisen, J., & Olsen, B. (1999). Strategic use of information technology for increased innovation and performance. *Information Management & Computer Security, 7*(1), 5–22. doi:10.1108/09685229910255133

Johnson, B., Lorenz, E., & Lundvall, B. A. (2002). Why all this fuss about codified and tacit knowledge? *Industrial and Corporate Change, 11*(2), 245–262. doi:10.1093/icc/11.2.245

Jolly, D. (2002). Sharing knowledge and decision power in sino-foreign joint ventures. *Asia Pacific Business Review, 9*(2), 81–100. doi:10.1080/713999186

Jones, K. (2006). Knowledge management as a foundation for decision support systems. *Journal of Computer Information Systems, 46*(4), 116–124.

Jordan Valley Authority. (2007). *Knowledge Management Strategy 2007-2009*. On line: http://www.jva.gov.jo/.

Jordanian Royal Medical Services. (2011), *KM strategy, 2008-2010*. On line: http://www.jrms.gov.jo.

Joshi, K. D., Sarker, S., & Sarker, S. (2007). Knowledge transfer within information systems development teams: Examining the role of knowledg source attributes. *Decision Support Systems, 43*, 322–335. doi:10.1016/j.dss.2006.10.003

Judge, R. (2008). *Simulating knowledge flows to formulate strategies for implementing Knowledge Management in small organizations*. University Microfilms International, P. O. Box 1764, Ann Arbor, MI, 48106, USA.

Junnarkar, B. (1997). Leveraging collective intellect by building organizational capabilities. *Expert Systems with Applications, 13*(1), 29–40. doi:10.1016/S0957-4174(97)00020-1

Kahneman, D., & Riepe, M. W. (1998). Aspects of investor psychology. *Journal of Portfolio Management, 24*, 52–65. doi:10.3905/jpm.1998.409643

Kahneman, D., & Tversky, A. (1972). Subjective probability: A judgment of representativeness. *Cognitive Psychology, 3*, 430–454. doi:10.1016/0010-0285(72)90016-3

Kahneman, D., & Tversky, A. (1973). On the psychology of prediction. *Psychological Review, 80*, 237–251. doi:10.1037/h0034747

Kakabadse, N. K., Kakabadse, A., & Kouzmin, A. (2003). Reviewing the knowledge management literature: Towards a toxonomy. *Journal of Knowledge Management, 7*(4), 75–91. doi:10.1108/13673270310492967

Kalling, T. (2003). Knowledge management and the occasional links with performance. *Journal of Knowledge Management, 7*(3), 67–81.

Kanawattanachai, P., & Yoo, Y. (2007). The impact of knowledge coordination on virtual team performance over time. *Management Information Systems Quarterly, 31*, 783–808.

Kanevsky, V., & Housel, T. (1998). The learning-knowledge-value cycle. In Krogh, G., Roos, J., & Kleine, D. (Eds.), *Knowing in firms* (pp. 269–284). Thousand Oaks, CA: Sage.

Kang, Y.-S., & Herr, P. M. (2006). Beauty and the beholder: Toward an integrative model of communication source effects. *The Journal of Consumer Research, 33*, 123–130. doi:10.1086/504143

Kang, M., Kim, A., Lo, J., Montrose, B., & Khashnobisch, A. (2006). Ontology-based security specification tools for SOA. In Khosrow-Pour, M. (Ed.), *Emerging trends and challenges in information technology management* (pp. 619–622). Hershey, PA: Idea Group Publishing.

Kaptelinin, V., & Nardi, B. A. (1997). *The activity checklist: A tool for representing the space of context* (Working paper). Umeå University: Dept. of Informatics.

Kar Yan, T., & Shuk Ying, H. (2005). Web Personalization as a Persuasion Strategy: An Elaboration Likelihood Model Perspective. [Article]. *Information Systems Research, 16*(3), 271–291..doi:10.1287/isre.1050.0058

Karkoulian, S., Halawi, L. A., & McCarthy, R. V. (2008). Knowledge management formal and informal mentoring: an empirical investigation in Lebanese banks. *The Learning Organization, 15*(5), 409–420. doi:10.1108/09696470810898384

Kartalia, J. (2000). Managing your most valuable asset: The corporate reputation. Entegra. Retrieved October 18, 2008, from www.senet.com/articles_managing_assest.htm

Kasten, J. E. (2006). *Knowledge strategy drivers: An exploratory study*. Unpublished doctoral dissertation, Long Island University, Brookville, NY.

Katz, M. L., & Shapiro, C. (1986). Technology Adoption in the Presence of Network Externalities. *The Journal of Political Economy, 94*(4), 822–841. doi:10.1086/261409

Keith, M., Goul, M., Demirkan, H., Nichols, J., & Mitchell, M. C. (2006). Contextualizing Knowledge Management Readiness to Support Change Management Strategies. *Proceedings of the 39th Hawaii International Conference on System Sciences*

Kelany, A. M., & Abu Nady, M. F. (2008). *Components constructed the organizational culture which support the knowledge participation at public Jordanian universities.* On Line: http://rd08.search.ac2.yahoo.com.

Kelloway, E. K., & Barling, J. (2000). Knowledge work as organizational behaviour. *International Journal of Management Reviews, 2,* 287–304. doi:10.1111/1468-2370.00042

Keren, G. (1987). Facing uncertainty in the game of bridge: A calibration study. *Organizational Behavior and Human Decision Processes, 39,* 98–114. doi:10.1016/0749-5978(87)90047-1

Kermalli, S. (2005). *Knowledge Management: Applied Introductory. Translation by Haytham Hijazy.* Amman, Jordan: Al-Ahlia for Publication and Distribution.

Khalil, O. E. M., & Seleim, A. (2010). Culture and knowledge transfer capacity: A cross-national study. *International Journal of Knowledge Management, 6*(4), 60–86. doi:10.4018/jkm.2010100104

Kidd, J. A., & Christy, R. T. (1961). Supervisory procedures and work-team productivity. *The Journal of Applied Psychology, 45,* 388–392. doi:10.1037/h0040865

Kim, D. H. (1993). The Link between Individual and Organizational Learning. *Sloan Management Review, 35*(1), 37–51.

Kim, Y., Yu, S., & Lee, J. (2003). Knowledge strategy planning: Methodology and case. *Expert Systems with Applications, 24,* 295–307. doi:10.1016/S0957-4174(02)00158-6

Kim, D., & Benbasat, I. (2009). Trust-Assuring Arguments in B2C E-commerce: Impact of Content, Source, and Price on Trust. [Article]. *Journal of Management Information Systems, 26*(3), 175–206. doi:10.2753/MIS0742-1222260306

King, W. R. (2007). A research agenda for the relationships between culture and knowledge management. *Knowledge and Process Management, 14*(3), 226–236. doi:10.1002/kpm.281

King, W. R., & Marks, P. V. (2008). Motivating knowledge sharing through a knowledge management system. *Omega, 36*(1), 131–146. doi:10.1016/j.omega.2005.10.006

King Abdullah II Center for Excellence. (2006). *King Abdullah II Award for Excellence.* On line: http://jusbp.org/alarabic/aboutus ar.shtm.

Klein, H., & Hirschheim, R. (in press). The structure of the IS discipline reconsidered. *Information and Organization.*

Klein, J. H., Connell, N. A. D., & Meyer, E. (2005). Knowledge characteristics of communities of practice. *Knowledge Management Research and Practice, 3,* 106–144. doi:10.1057/palgrave.kmrp.8500055

Knapp, E. M. (1998). Knowledge Management. *Business and Economic Review, 44*(4), 3–6.

Ko, D. G., Kirsch, L. J., & King, W. R. (2005). Antecedents of Knowledge Transfer from Consultants to Clients in Enterprise System Implementations. *Management Information Systems Quarterly, 29*(1), 36–85.

Kogut, B., & Zander, U. (1992). Knowledge of the Firm, Combinative Capabilities, and the Replication of Technology. *Organization Science, 3*(3), 383–398. doi:10.1287/orsc.3.3.383

Koh, J., & Kim, Y. (2004). Knowledge sharing in virtual communities: An e-business perspective. *Expert Systems with Applications, 26*(2), 155–166. doi:10.1016/S0957-4174(03)00116-7

Kohlbacher, F., & Mukai, K. (2007). Japan's learning communities in Hewlett-Packard consulting and integration: Challenging one-size fits all solutions. *The Learning Organization, 14*(1), 8–20.

Kohlbacher, F., & Krähe, M. O. B. (2007). Knowledge creation and transfer in a cross-cultural context - empirical evidence from tyco flow control. *Knowledge and Process Management, 14*(3), 169–181. doi:10.1002/kpm.282

Koskinen, K. U. (2001). Tacit knowledge as a promoter of success in technology firms. In *Proceedings of the 34th Hawaii International Conference on System Sciences,* IEEE Computer Society.

Kotter, J. P. (1995). *Leading Change: Why Transformation Efforts Fail.* Boston, MA. *Harvard Business Review,* (March-April): 59–67.

Krauss, R. M., & Chiu, C. (1998). Language and social behavior. In Gilbert, D., Lindzey, G., & Fiske, S. T. (Eds.), *The handbook of social psychology* (4th ed., pp. 41–88). Boston: McGraw-Hill.

Kreitner, R., & Kinicki, A. (1992). *Organizational behavior*. Homewood, IL: Richard D. Irwin.

Krentler, K. A., & Flurry, L. A. W. (2005). Does Technology Enhance Actual Student Learning? The Case of Online Discussion Boards. *Journal of Education for Business*, *80*(6), 316–321. doi:10.3200/JOEB.80.6.316-321

Krogh, G. (1998). Care in the knowledge creation. *California Management Review*, *40*(3), 133–153.

Kulkarni, U. R., Ravindran, S., & Freeze, R. (2006-2007). A knowledge management success model: Theoretical development and empirical validation. *Journal of Management Information Systems*, *23*(3), 309–347. doi:10.2753/MIS0742-1222230311

Kulp, S. C., Ofek, E., & Whitaker, J. (2003). Supply chain coordination. In Harrison, T., Lee, H. L., & Neale, J. L. (Eds.), *The Practice of Supply Chain Management: where theory and application converge*. Boston: Kluwer Academic Publishing.

Kumar, S., & Thondikulam, G. (2005. (2006). Knowledge management in a collaborative business framework. *Information Knowledge Systems Management*, *5*(3), 171–187.

Kurman, J. (2003). Why is self-enhancement low in certain collectivist cultures?: An investigation of two competing explanations. *Journal of Cross-Cultural Psychology*, *34*(5), 496–510. doi:10.1177/0022022103256474

Lai, M., & Lee, G. (2007). Risk-avoiding cultures toward achievement of knowledge sharing. *Business Process Management Journal*, *13*(4), 522–537. doi:10.1108/14637150710763559

Lai, H., & Chu, T. H. (2000). Knowledge management: A review of theoretical frameworks and industrial cases. In *Proceedings of the 33th Hawaii International Conference on System Sciences*, IEEE Computer Society.

Lam, W., & Chua, A. (2005). Knowledge management project abandonment: An exploratory examination of root causes. *Communications of the Association for Information Systems*, *16*, 723–743.

Lambkin, M. (1988). Order of entry and performance in new markets. *Strategic Management Journal*, *9*, 127140. doi:10.1002/smj.4250090713

Lane, C., & Probert, J. (2007). The external sourcing of technological knowledge by US pharmaceutical companies: Strategic goals and inter-organizational relationships. *Industry and Innovation*, *14*(1), 5–25. doi:10.1080/13662710601130574

Lang, J. C. (2001). Managerial concerns in knowledge management. *Journal of Knowledge Management*, *5*(1), 43–57. doi:10.1108/13673270110384392

Larry, W. C. (2002). Knowledge management and training the value of collaboration. *Performance Improvement*, *41*(4), 37–43. doi:10.1002/pfi.4140410407

Lau, S. (1992). Collectivism's individualism: Value preference, personal control, and the desire for freedom among Chinese in mainland China, Hong Kong, and Singapore. *Personality and Individual Differences*, *13*(3), 361–366. doi:10.1016/0191-8869(92)90115-6

Laudon, K., & Laudon, J. (2006). *Management information systems: Managing the digital firm* (9., 2. print. ed.). Upper Saddle River, NJ: Pearson Education.

Laursen, K., & Mahnke, V. (2001). Knowledge strategies, firm types, and complementarity in human-resource practices. *Journal of Management and Governance*, *5*, 1–27. doi:10.1023/A:1017985623502

Lave, J., & Wenger, E. (1991). *Situated Learning: Legitimate Peripheral Participation*. Cambridge, UK: Cambridge University Press.

Lawler, A. (2007). Lunar science: Asking for the Moon. *Science*, *315*, 1482–1484. doi:10.1126/science.315.5818.1482

Lawrence, M., Edmundson, R., & O'Connor, M. (1986). The accuracy of combining judgmental and statistical forecasts. *Management Science*, *32*(3), 1521–1532. doi:10.1287/mnsc.32.12.1521

Lawrence, M., Goodwin, P., O'Connor, M., & Önkal, D. (2006). Judgmental forecasting: A review of progress over the last 25 years. *International Journal of Forecasting*, *22*, 493–518. doi:10.1016/j.ijforecast.2006.03.007

Lawrence, T. B., Mauws, M. K., Dyck, B., & Kleysen, R. F. (2005). The politics of organizational learning: Integrating power into the 4I framework. *Academy of Management Review*, *30*(1), 180–191.

Lee, H., & Choi, B. (2003). Knowledge Management Enablers, Processes, an Integrative View and Empirical Examination. *Journal of Management Information Systems*, *20*(1), 179–228.

Lee, H. L., Padmanabhan, V., & Whang, S. (1997). The bullwhip effect in supply chains. *Sloan Management Review*, *38*(3), 93–102.

Lee, H., & Choi, B. (2003). Knowledge management enablers, process, and organizational performance: An integrative view and empirical examination. *Journal of Management Information Systems*, *20*(1), 179–228.

Lee, J., Park, D.-H., & Han, I. (2008). The effect of negative online consumer reviews on product attitude: An information processing view. *Electronic Commerce Research and Applications*, *7*(3), 341–352. doi:10.1016/j.elerap.2007.05.004

Leenders, R., van Engelen, J. M. L., & Kratzer, J. (2003). Virtuality, communication, and new product team creativity: a social network perspective. *Journal of Engineering and Technology Management*, *20*(1-2), 69–92. doi:10.1016/S0923-4748(03)00005-5

Leithwood, K. (1995). Cognitive perspectives on school leadership. *Journal of School Leadership*, *5*, 115–135.

Leithwood, K., & Steinbach, R. (1995). *Expert problem solving: Evidence from school and district leaders*. Albany: State University of New York Press.

Lengel, R., & Daft, R. (1988). The selection of communication media as an executive skill. *The Academy of Management Executive*, *2*(3), 225–232.

Leonard-Barton, D. (1995). *Wellsprings of knowledge: Building and sustaining the sources of innovation*. Boston: Harvard Business School Press.

Lesser, E., & Prusak, L. (1999). Communities of practice, social capital and organizational knowledge. *Information Systems Research*, *1*(1), 3–9.

Levin, D. Z., & Cross, R. (2004). The strength of weak ties you can trust: The mediating role of trust in effective knowledge transfer. *Management Science*, *50*(11), 1477–1490. doi:10.1287/mnsc.1030.0136

Lewis, K. (2003). Measuring transactive memory systems in the field: Scale development and validation. *The Journal of Applied Psychology*, *88*, 587–604. doi:10.1037/0021-9010.88.4.587

Lewis, K. (2004). Knowledge and performance in knowledge-worker teams: A longitudinal study of transactive memory systems. *Management Science*, *50*, 1519–1533. doi:10.1287/mnsc.1040.0257

Lewis, K., Belliveau, M., Herndon, B., & Keller, J. (2007). Group cognition, membership change, and performance: Investigating the benefits and detriments of collective knowledge. *Organizational Behavior and Human Decision Processes*, *103*, 159–178. doi:10.1016/j.obhdp.2007.01.005

Li, C., & Bernoff, J. (2008). *Groundswell: Winning in a world transformed by social technologies*. Boston, MA: Harvard University Press, Forrester Research Inc.

Li, W. (2008). *Online knowledge sharing in a multinational corporation: Chinese and American practices*. Ph.D., University of Illinois at Urbana-Champaign.

Li, W. (2010). Virtual knowledge sharing in a cross-cultural context. *Journal of Knowledge Management*, *14*(1), 38–50. doi:10.1108/13673271011015552

Li, W., Ardichvili, A., Maurer, M., Wentling, T., & Stuedemann, R. (2007). Impact of Chinese culture values on knowledge sharing through online communities of practice. *International Journal of Knowledge Management*, *3*(3), 47–60. doi:10.4018/jkm.2007070103

Li, Z., Shen, H. & Xi, Y. (2010). Do knowledge characteristics matter? A test of the relationship between knowledge characteristics and performance. *SAM Advanced Management Journal, Spring*, 38-53.

Liang, D. W., Moreland, R., & Argote, L. (1995). Group versus individual training and group performance: The mediating role of transactive memory. *Personality and Social Psychology Bulletin*, *21*, 384–393. doi:10.1177/0146167295214009

Libby, R. (1995). The role of knowledge and memory in audit judgment. In R.H. Ashton, & A. H. Ashton. (Eds). *Judgment and decision-making research in accounting and auditing* (pp. 176-206). New York, NY: Cambridge University Press.

Liebeskind, J. P. (1996). Knowledge, strategy, and the theory of the firm. *Strategic Management Journal, 17,* 93–107.

Liebowitz, J., & Wright, K. (1999). Does measuring knowledge make "cents"? *Expert Systems with Applications, 17*(5), 99–103. doi:10.1016/S0957-4174(99)00027-5

Liebowitz, J., & Wilcox, L. (1997). *Knowledge management and its integrative elements.* CRC Press.

Lin, L., & Kwok, L. (2006). Challenges to KM at Hewlett Packard China. *KM Review, 9*(1), 20–23.

Lin, Y., & Dalkir, K. (2010). Factors affecting KM implementation in the Chinese community. *International Journal of Knowledge Management, 6*(1), 1–22. doi:10.4018/jkm.2010103001

Lin, Ch. P. (2007). To share or not to share: Modeling tacit knowledge sharing, its mediators and antecedents. *Journal of Business Ethics, 70*(4), 411–428. doi:10.1007/s10551-006-9119-0

Linacre, J. M. (1990). Where does misfit begin? *Rasch Measurement Transactions, 3,* 80.

Linacre, J. M. (1994). Sample size and item calibration stability. *Rasch Measurement Transactions, 7,* 328.

Linacre, J. M. (2002a). What do infit and outfit, mean-square and standardized mean? *Rasch Measurement Transactions, 16,* 878.

Linacre, J. M. (2002b). Understanding Rasch measurement: Optimizing rating scale category effectiveness. *Journal of Applied Measurement, 3*(1), 85–106.

Linacre, J. M., & Wright, B. D. (1994). Chi-square fit statistics. *Rasch Measurement Transactions, 8,* 350.

Linacre, J. M. (2004). *Winsteps Rasch measurement software version 3.51.*

Lincoln, J., Hanada, M., & McBride, K. (1986). Organizational structures in Japanese and U.S. manufacturing. *Administrative Science Quarterly, 31*(3), 338–364. doi:10.2307/2392827

Lincoln, Y. S., & Guba, E. G. (1985). *Naturalistic inquiry.* Beverly Hills, CA: Sage Publications.

Linden, R. (2003). Learning to manage horizontally: The promise and challenge of collaboration. *Public Management, 85*(7), 8.

Lindsey, K. (2002). Measuring knowledge management effectiveness: A task-contingent organizational capabilities perspective. In *Proceedings of the Eighth Americas Conference on Information Systems.*

Linger, H., & Warne, L. (2001). Making the invisible visible: Modelling social learning in a knowledge management context [Special issue on knowledge management]. *Australian Journal of Information Systems,* 56-66.

Loch, C., Stein, L., & Terweisch, C. (1996). Measuring development performance in the electronics industry. *Journal of Product Innovation Management, 13*(1), 3–20. doi:10.1016/0737-6782(95)00089-5

Long, D., & Fahey, L. (2000). Diagnosing cultural barriers to knowledge management. *The Academy of Management Executive, 14*(4), 113–127.

Long, D. D. (1997). Building the knowledge-based organizations: How culture drives knowledge behaviours. *Working Paper of the Center for Business Innovation,* Cambridge, MA: Ernst & Young LLP.

López, S. P., Peón, J. M., & Vázquez Ordás, C. J. (2004). Managing knowledge: The link between culture and organizational learning. *Journal of Knowledge Management, 8*(6), 93–104. doi:10.1108/13673270410567657

Lord, R., & Maher, K. J. (1990). Cognitive theory in industrial and organizational psychology. In Dunnette, M. D., Triandis, H. C., & Hough, L. M. (Eds.), *Handbook of industrial and organizational psychology* (2nd ed., pp. 1–62). Palo Alto, CA: Consulting Psychologists Press.

Lord, R. G., & Maher, K. J. (1993). *Leadership and information processing: Linking perceptions and performance.* London: Unwin Hyman Inc.

Louis, M. R., & Sutton, R. I. (1991). Switching cognitive gears: From habits of mind to active thinking. *Human Relations, 44*, 55–76. doi:10.1177/001872679104400104

Ma, W. W. K., & Yuen, A. H. K. (2011). Understanding Online Knowledge Sharing: An Interpersonal Relationship Perspective. *Computers & Education, 56*(1), 210–219. doi:10.1016/j.compedu.2010.08.004

MacDonald, S. (1998). *Information for Innovation: Managing Change from an Information Perspective*. Oxford, UK: Oxford University Press.

Madhavan, R., & Grover, R. (1998). From embedded knowledge to embodied knowledge: New product development as knowledge management. *Journal of Marketing, 62*(4), 1–12. doi:10.2307/1252283

Madjar, N., Oldham, G. R., & Pratt, M. G. (2002). There's No Place Like Home? The Contributions of Work and Nonwork Creativity Support to Employees' Creative Performance. *Academy of Management Journal, 45*(4), 757–768. doi:10.2307/3069309

Mager, R. (1997). *Preparing Instructional Objectives: A Critical Tool in the Development of Effective Instruction* (3rd ed.). Atlanta: The Center for Effective Performance.

Magnier-Watanabe, R., & Senoo, D. (2008). Organizational characteristics as prescriptive factors of knowledge management initiatives'. *Journal of Knowledge Management, 12*(1), 21–36. doi:10.1108/13673270810852368

Magnier-Watanabe, R., & Senoo, D. (2010). Shaping knowledge management: Organization and national culture. *Journal of Knowledge Management, 14*(2), 214–227. doi:10.1108/13673271011032364

Mahjoub, B. F. (2003). *Arab Universities Management in the light of International Standards*. Cairo, Egypt: Arab Organization for Administrative Development.

Maier, R. (2002). *Knowledge management systems: Information and communication technologies for knowledge management*. Berlin, Germany: Springer- Verlag.

Maier, R., & Remus, U. (2003). Implementing process-oriented knowledge management strategies. *Journal of Knowledge Management, 7*(4), 62–74. doi:10.1108/13673270310492958

Majchrzak, A., Jarvenpaa, S. L., & Hollingshead, A. B. (2007). Coordinating expertise among emergent groups responding to disasters. *Organization Science, 18*, 147–161. doi:10.1287/orsc.1060.0228

Majchrzak, A., Cooper, L. P., & Neece, O. E. (2004). Knowledge Reuse for Innovation. *Management Science, 50*(2), 174–188. doi:10.1287/mnsc.1030.0116

Majid, S., & Wey, S. M. (2009). Perceptions and Knowledge Sharing Practices of Graduate Students in Singapore. *International Journal of Knowledge Management, 5*(2), 21–32. doi:10.4018/jkm.2009040102

Majid, S., & Kowtha, R. (2008). *Utilizing Environmental Knowledge for Competitive Advantage*. International Conference on Information Resources Management (Conf-IMR), 18-20 May, 2008: Niagara Falls, Canada.

Majid, S., & Mokhtar, I. A. (2007). *From Virtual to Real Discourse: Relating Online Student Participation and their Academic Performance*. 3rd International Conference on Open and Online Learning (ICOOL), 11-14 June, 2007: Penang, Malaysia.

Majid, S., & Tina, R. R. (2009). *Perceptions of LIS Graduate Students of Peer Learning*. Asia-Pacific Conference on Library & Information Education and Practice (A-LIEP): Preparing Information professional for International Collaboration, 6-8 March 2009, Japan.

Majid, S., & Yuen, T. J. (2006). Information and Knowledge Sharing by Undergraduate Students in Singapore. In M.K. Pour (ed.), *IRMA International Conference: Proceedings of the 17th IRMA International Conference*. Hershey, PA: Idea Group Publishing.

Mäkelä, K., & Brewster, C. (2009). Interunit Interaction Contexts, Interpersonal Social Capital, and the Differing Levels of Knowledge Sharing. *Human Resource Management, 48*(4), 591–613. doi:10.1002/hrm.20300

Malhotra, A., Gosain, S., & El Sawy, O. (2005). Absortive capacity configurations in supply chains: Gearing for partner-enabled market knowledge creation. *Management Information Systems Quarterly, 29*(1), 145–187.

Malhotra, Y. (2004). Why KMS fail? Enablers and constraints of KM in human enterprises. In M.E.D. Koenig & T. Kanti Srikantaiah (Eds.), *KM lessons learned: What works and what doesn't* (pp. 87-112). American Society for Information Science and Technology Monograph Series: Information Today Inc.

Mandviwalla, M., Eulgem, S., Mould, C., & Rao, S. V. (1998). *Organizational memory systems design.* Unpublished Working Paper for the Task Force on Organizational Memory. In F. Burstein, Massey, A.P., Montoya-Weiss, M.M., & O'Driscoll, T. M. (2002). Knowledge management in pursuit of performance: Insights from Nortel Networks. *Management Information Systems Quarterly, 26*(3), 269–289.

March, J. G. (1991). Exploration and Exploitation in Organizational Learning. *Organization Science, 2*(1), 71–87. doi:10.1287/orsc.2.1.71

Markus, M. L. (2001). Toward a theory of knowledge reuse: Types of knowledge reuse situations and factors in reuse success. *Journal of Management Information Systems, 18*(1), 57–93.

Marshall, L. (2008). The usefulness of chronological arrangement for subheadings in book indexes: An examination of the literature (Part 2). *Key Words, 16*(2), 56–59.

Marsick, V., & Watkins, K. (1994). The Learning Organization: An Integrative Vision for HRD. *Human Resource Development Quarterly, 5*(4), 353–360. doi:10.1002/hrdq.3920050406

Marwick, A. D. (2001). Knowledge Management Technology. *IBM Systems Journal, 40*(4), 814–831. doi:10.1147/sj.404.0814

Mascarenhas, B. (1992). Order of entry and performance in international markets. *Strategic Management Journal, 13*, 499–510. doi:10.1002/smj.4250130703

Massey, C., & Wu, G. (2005). Detecting regime shifts: The psychology of under- and overreaction. *Management Science, 51*(6), 932–947. doi:10.1287/mnsc.1050.0386

Masters, G. N. (1982). A Rasch model for partial credit scoring. *Psychometrika, 47*, 149–174. doi:10.1007/BF02296272

Mathi, K. (2004). *Key success factors for knowledge management.* Retrieved from http://www.dmreview.com/whitepaper.

Matsumoto, D. R. (2002). *The new Japan: Debunking seven cultural stereotypes.* Yarmouth, ME: Intercultural Press.

Mayer, R. C., Davis, J. H., & Schoorman, F. D. (1995). An integration model of organizational trust. *Academy of Management Review, 20*, 709–734. doi:10.2307/258792

Mayr, E. (1969). *Principles of systematic zoology.* New York: McGraw-Hill.

McAdam, R., & Reid, R. (2001). SME and large organization perception of knowledge management: Comparison and contrast. *Journal of Knowledge Management, 5*(3), 231–241. doi:10.1108/13673270110400870

McCall, H., Arnold, V., & Sutton, S. G. (2008). Use of knowledge management systems and the impact on the acquisition of explicit knowledge. *Journal of Information Systems, 22*(2), 77–101. doi:10.2308/jis.2008.22.2.77

McCamey, R. (2002 February 14-16). *A primer on the one-parameter Rasch model.* Paper presented at the meeting of the Annual Meeting of the Southwest Educational Research Association, Austin, TX.

McDermott, R., & O'Dell, C. (2001). Overcoming cultural barriers to sharing knowledge. *Journal of Knowledge Management, 5*(1), 76–85. doi:10.1108/13673270110384428

McDermott, R., & O'Dell, C. (2001). Overcoming cultural barriers to sharing knowledge. *Journal of Knowledge Management, 5*(1), 76–85.

McDonnell, A., Gunnigle, P., & Lavelle, J. (2010). Learning transfer in multinational companies: Explaining inter-organization variation. *Human Resource Management Journal, 20*(1), 23–43. doi:10.1111/j.1748-8583.2009.00104.x

McEvily, S. K., & Chakravarthy, B. (2002). The persistence of knowledge-based advantage: an empirical test for product performance and technological knowledge. *Strategic Management Journal, 23*(4), 285–305. doi:10.1002/smj.223

McKeown, B. F., & Thomas, D. B. (1988). *Q methodology. Quantitative applications in the social sciences.* Newbury Park, CA: Sage.

McLaughlin, S., & Paton, R. A. (2008). Identifying Barriers that Impact Knowledge Creation and Transfer within complex organisations. *Journal of Knowledge Management, 12*(2), 107–123. doi:10.1108/13673270810859550

McLaughlin, S., Paton, R. A., & Macbeth, D. (2006). Managing Change within IBM's complex supply chain. *Management Decision, 44*(8), 1002–1019. doi:10.1108/00251740610690586

Mechanisms for knowledge Management Systems Effectiveness: Empirical evidence from the silicon valley. (2006). *Academy of Management Proceedings,* 1-6.

Meister, J. (1998a). *Corporate universities: Lessons in Building a World-class Work Force.* New York: McGraw-Hill.

Meister, J. (1998b). The quest for lifetime employability. *The Journal of Business Strategy, 19*(3), 25–28. doi:10.1108/eb039933

Meister, J. (1998c). Ten steps to creating a corporate university. *Training & Development, 52*(11), 38–43.

Meloche, J., & Crawford, K. (1998). A metaphorical approach to information seeking, a Q study. In *14th Annual Conference of the Internal Society for the Scientific Study of Subjectivity,* Seoul Korea.

Metcalfe, J. (2000). Metamemory. In E. Tulving, & F. I. M. Craik (Eds.), *The Oxford handbook of memory* (pp. 197–211). New York, NY: Oxford University Press.

Metcalfe, J., & Shimamura, A. P. (1994). *Metacognition: Knowing about knowing.* Cambridge, MA: MIT Press.

Miles, M. B., & Huberman, A. M. (1994). *Qualitative data analysis: An expanded sourcebook* (2nd ed.). Thousand Oaks, CA: Sage Publications.

Miller, D. A. (1996). A preliminary typology of organizational learning: Synthesizing the literature. *Journal of Management, 22*(3), 484–505. doi:10.1177/014920639602200305

Miller, C. C., & Ireland, R. D. (2005). Intuition in strategic decision making: Friend or foe in the fast-paced 21st century? *The Academy of Management Executive, 19,* 19–30.

Miller, G. A. (1956). The magical number seven, plus or minus two: Some limits on our capacity for processing information. *Psychological Review, 63,* 81–97. doi:10.1037/h0043158

Miller, G. A., Galanter, E., & Pribram, K. H. (1960). *Plans and the structure of behavior.* New York: Holt, Rinehart, and Winston. doi:10.1037/10039-000

Miller, R., Stewart, J., & Walton, J. (1999). Opened university. *People Management, 5*(12), 42–45.

Ministry Of Industry and Trade's. (2011). *KM strategy 2006.* On line: http://www.mit.gov.jo.Moss, G., Kubaki, K., Hersh, M. & Gunn, R. (2007). Knowledge Management in higher education: A comparison of individualistic and collectivist cultures. *European Journal of Education, 42*(3), 373-394.

Mizerski, R., Golden, L., & Kernan, J. (1979). The attributional process in consumer decision making. *The Journal of Consumer Research, 6,* 123–140. doi:10.1086/208756

Moffett, S., McAdam, R., & Parkinson, S. (2002). Developing a model for technology and cultural factors in knowledge management: a factor analysis. *Knowledge and Process Management, 9*(4), 237–255. doi:10.1002/kpm.152

Mohammadi, K., Khanlari, A., & Sohrabi, B. (2009). Organizational readiness assessment for knowledge management. *International Journal of Knowledge Management, 5*(1), 29–46. doi:10.4018/jkm.2009010103

Mohrman, S., & Lawler, E. (1998). *The New Human Resources Management: Creating the Strategic Business Partnership. Tomorrow's Organization: Crafting Winning Capabilities in a Dynamic World.* San Francisco: Jossey-Bass.

Monavvarian, A. & Kasaei, M. (2007).KM model for public administration: the case of Labour Ministry.*VINE: The journal of information and knowledge management systems, 37* (3), pp. 348-67.

Monge, P. R., Rothman, L. W., Eisenberg, E. M., Miller, K. I., & Kirste, K. K. (1985). The Dynamics of Organizational Proximity. *Management Science, 31*(9), 1129–1141. doi:10.1287/mnsc.31.9.1129

Monnavarian, A., & Amini, A. (2009). Do interactions within networks lead to knowledge management? *Business Strategy Series, 10*(3), 139–155. doi:10.1108/17515630910956561

Moore, G. C., & Benbasat, I. (1991). Development of an Instrument to Measure the Perceptions of Adopting an Information Technology Innovation. *Information Systems Research, 2*(3), 192–223. doi:10.1287/isre.2.3.192

Moreland, R. L., & Myaskovsky, L. (2000). Explaining the performance benefits of group training: Transactive memory or improved communication? *Organizational Behavior and Human Decision Processes, 82*, 117–133. doi:10.1006/obhd.2000.2891

Moreland, R. L., Argote, L., & Krishnan, R. (1998). Training people to work in groups. In Tindale, R. S., Heath, L., Edwards, J., Posvoc, E. J., Bryant, F. B., & Suarez-Balcazar, Y. (Eds.), *Applications of theory and research on groups to social issues* (*Vol. 4*, pp. 37–60). New York: Plenum.

Moreland, R. L., & Levine, J. M. (1992). Problem identification by groups. In Worchel, S., Wood, W., & Simpson, J. A. (Eds.), *Group process and productivity*. Newbury Park, CA: Sage.

Moss, D., Ashford, R., & Shani, N. (2003). The forgotten sector: Uncovering the role of public relations in SMEs. *Journal of Communication Management, 8*(2), 197–210. doi:10.1108/13632540410807655

Muczyk, J. P., & Reimann, B. C. (1987). The case for directive leadership. *Academy of Management Review, 12*, 637–647.

Muhammed, S., Doll, W. J., & Deng, X. (2009). A model of interrelationships among individual level knowledge management success measures. *International Journal of Knowledge Management, 5*(1), 1–15. doi:10.4018/jkm.2009010101

Muradoglu, G., & Önkal, D. (1994). An exploratory analysis of portfolio managers' probabilistic forecasts of stock-prices. *Journal of Forecasting, 13*, 565–578. doi:10.1002/for.3980130702

Murnighan, J. K., & Conlon, D. E. (1991). The dynamics of intense work groups: A study of British string quartets. *Administrative Science Quarterly, 36*, 165–186. doi:10.2307/2393352

Murphy, T., & Jennex, M. E. (2006a). Knowledge management, emergency response, and hurricane Katrina. *International Journal of Intelligent Control and Systems, 1*(4), 199–208.

Murphy, T., & Jennex, M. E. (2006b). Knowledge management and hurricane Katrina response. *International Journal of Knowledge Management, 2*(4), 52–66.

Murphy, A. H., & Winkler, R. (1984). Probability forecasting in meteorology. *Journal of the American Statistical Association, 79*, 489–500. doi:10.2307/2288395

Murray, S., & Peyrefitte, J. (2007). Knowledge type and communication media choice in the knowledge transfer process. *Journal of Managerial Issues, 19*(1), 111–133.

Murray, A. (2007). Building the enterprise of the future means no more secrets. *Knowledge. Management World, 16*(5), 19–19.

Murray, P. (1996). Information, knowledge and document management technology. *Knowledge Management Briefs, 1*(2), Retrieved October 18, 2008, from http://www.ktic.com/resource/km2/Information,%20knowledge,%20and%20document%20management%20technology.htm

Myers, M. D., & Tan, F. B. (2002). Beyond models of national culture in information systems research. *Journal of Global Information Management, 10*(1), 24–32. doi:10.4018/jgim.2002010103

Nadeem, M. M. (2006). Knowledge management leadership revolutionizing e-business excellence. *Business Renaissance Quarterly, 1*(2), 81–100.

Nah, F., & Benbasat, I. (2004). Knowledge-based Support in a Group Decision Making Context: An Expert-Novice Comparison. [Article]. *Journal of the Association for Information Systems, 5*(3), 125–150.

Nahapiet, J., & Ghoshal, S. (1998). Social capital, intellectual capital, and the organizational advantage. *Academy of Management Review*, *23*(2), 246–266. doi:10.2307/259373

Nakra, P. (2000). Knowledge management: The magic is in the culture. *Competitive Intelligence Review*, *11*(2), 53–60. doi:10.1002/(SICI)1520-6386(200032)11:2<53::AID-CIR8>3.0.CO;2-W

Narasimha, S. (2000). Organizational knowledge, human resource management, and sustained competitive advantage: Toward a framework. *Competitiveness Review*, *10*(1), 123–134.

Nayir, D. Z., & Uzuncarsili, U. (2008). A Cultural Perspective of Knowledge Management: The Success Story of Sarkuysan Company. *Journal of Knowledge Management*, *12*(2), 141–155. doi:10.1108/13673270810859578

Nelson, R., & Winter, S. (1982). *An evolutionary theory of economic change*. Cambridge, MA: Belknap.

Nelson, K. M., & Cooprider, J. G. (1996). The contribution of shared knowledge to IS group performance. *Management Information Systems Quarterly*, *20*(4), 409–429. doi:10.2307/249562

Nelson, M. W., Libby, R., & Bonner, S. E. (1995). Knowledge structure and the estimation of conditional probabilities in audit planning. *Accounting Review*, *70*, 27–47.

Nelson, R. R., Todd, P. A., & Wixom, B. H. (2005). Antecedents of information and system quality: An empirical examination within the context of data warehousing. *Journal of Management Information Systems*, *21*(4), 199–235.

Nemeth, Cook, O'Connor, & Klock. (2004). Using Cognitive Artifacts to Understand Distributed Cognition. *IEEE Transactions on Systems, Man, and Cybernetics*, *34*(6), 726–735. doi:10.1109/TSMCA.2004.836798

Nestor-Baker, N. (2002). Knowing when to hold 'em and fold 'em: Tacit knowledge of place-bound and career-bound superintendents. *Journal of Educational Administration*, *40*(3), 230–256. doi:10.1108/09578230210427163

Nestor-Baker, N., & Hoy, W. K. (2001). Tacit knowledge of school superintendents: Its nature, meaning, and content. *Educational Administration Quarterly*, *37*(1), 86–129. doi:10.1177/00131610121969253

Neto, M., & Correia, A. M. (2009). *BIWiki – Using a Business Intelligence Wiki to Form a Virtual Community of Practice for Portuguese Master's students*. Proceedings of the 10ᵗʰ European Conference on Knowledge Management, 570-577. Università Degli Studi Di Padova, Vicenza, Italy.

Nevo, D., & Wand, Y. (2005). Organizational memory information systems: A transactive memory approach. *Decision Support Systems*, *39*, 549–562. doi:10.1016/j.dss.2004.03.002

Newman, V. (2002). *The knowledge management activist's- handbook*. United Kingdom: Capstone Publishing Limited.

Newman, V. (2006). Leadership and strategic knowledge management. *Knowledge Management Review*, *9*(4), 12–15.

Nickerson, J. A., & Silverman, B. S. (1998). Intellectual capital management strategy: The foundation of successful new business generation. *Journal of Knowledge Management*, *1*(4), 320–331. doi:10.1108/EUM0000000004603

Nisbett, R. E. (2003). *The geography of thought: How Asians and Westerners think differently... and why*. New York: Free Press.

Nisbett, R. E., & Wilson, T. D. (1977). Telling more than we can know: Verbal reports on mental processes. *Psychological Review*, *84*, 231–259. doi:10.1037/0033-295X.84.3.231

Nissen, M. E. (2006). *Harnessing knowledge dynamics: Principled Organizational Knowing and Learning*. IRM Press.

Nissen, M. E. (2007). Knowledge management and global cultures: Elucidation through an institutional knowledge-flow perspective. *Knowledge and Process Management*, *14*(3), 211–225. doi:10.1002/kpm.285

Nissen, M. E., & Levitt, R. E. (2004). Agent-based modeling of knowledge flows: illustration from the domain of information systems design. *System Sciences, 2004. Proceedings of the 37th Annual Hawaii International Conference on*, 8.

Nonaka, I., & Takeuchi, H. (1995). *The knowledge creating company. How Japanese create the dynamics of innovation*. New York, Oxford: Oxford University Press.

Nonaka, I., & Toyama, R. (2000). SECI, Ba and Leadership: a Unified Model of Dynamic Knowledge Creation. *Long Range Planning*, *33*, 5–34. doi:10.1016/S0024-6301(99)00115-6

Nonaka, I. (1994). A dynamic theory of organizational knowledge creation. *Organization Science*, *5*(1), 14–37. doi:10.1287/orsc.5.1.14

Nonaka, I., Byosiere, P., & Konno, N. (1994). Organizational knowledge creation theory: A first comprehensive test. *International Business Review*, *3*(4), 337–351. doi:10.1016/0969-5931(94)90027-2

Nonaka, I., & Konno, N. (1998). The Concept of "Ba": Building a foundation for knowledge creation. *California Management Review*, *40*(3), 40–54.

Nonaka, I. (1991). The knowledge-creating company. *Harvard Business Review*, *69*(6), 96–104.

Norrgren, F., & Schaller, J. (1999). Leadership style: Its impact on cross-functional product development. *Journal of Product Innovation Management*, *16*, 377–384. doi:10.1016/S0737-6782(98)00065-4

Norton, R. C. (2003). Projects that succeed: seven habits of IT executives who understand how to prevent project failure. *The E-business Executive Daily*, available at: http://www.strategit.com/Pdfs/Boardroom_ProjectsThatSucceed.pdf (accessed 10 August 2004).

Nosek, J. T. (2004). Group cognition as a basis for supporting group knowledge creation and sharing. *Journal of Knowledge Management*, *8*, 54–64. doi:10.1108/13673270410556361

Numprasertchai, S. & Poovarawan, Y.(2008). Improving university performance through ICT based knowledge management system, *International Journal of Innovation and technology*, *5*(2), 167 178.

Nunnally, J. (1978). *Psychometric Theory*. New York, NY: McGraw-Hill.

Nunnally, J. C. (1978). *Psychometric Theory* (2nd ed.). New York: McGraw-Hill.

O'Brien, F., & Ali, I. (2006). Formal and informal networks during emergency situations: The impact for information strategy. In *Proceeding of 11ᵗʰ ICCRTS.*

O'Dell, C., & Grayson, J. (1999). Knowledge transfer: Discover your value proposition. *Strategy and Leadership*, *27*(2), 10–15. doi:10.1108/eb054630

O'Leary, D. E. (1998). Enterprise knowledge management. *IEEE Computer*, *31*(3), 54–61.

OECD. (2005). OECD SME and Entrepreneurship Outlook 2002/2005. Retrieved November 4, 2006, from http://www.oecd.org/document/.

Ofek, E., & Sarvary, M. (2001). Leveraging the customer base: Creating competitive advantage through knowledge management. *Management Science INFORMS*, *47*(11), 1441–1456.

Offsey, S. (1997). Knowledge management: Linking people to knowledge for bottom line results. *Journal of Knowledge Management*, *1*(2), 113–122. doi:10.1108/EUM0000000004586

Oldham, G. R., & Cummings, A. (1996). Employee Creativity: Personal and Contextual Factors at Work. *Academy of Management Journal*, *39*(3), 607–635. doi:10.2307/256657

Omary, G. (2004). *Combined utilization of information technology and knowledge management to achieve high quality in commercial bank systems.* Unpublished doctoral dissertation. Amman Al Arabia University for Higher Studies. Amman, Jordan.

O'Neill, B. S., & Ayda, M. (2007). Knowledge sharing and the psychological contract: Managing knowledge workers across different stages of employment. *Journal of Managerial Psychology*, *22*(4), 411–436. doi:10.1108/02683940710745969

Önkal, D., Yates, J. F., Simga-Mugan, C., & Öztin, S. (2003). Professional vs. amateur judgment accuracy: The case of foreign exchange rates. *Organizational Behavior and Human Decision Processes*, *91*, 169–185. doi:10.1016/S0749-5978(03)00058-X

Ordanini, A. (2006). *Information technology and small businesses: Antecedents and consequences of technology adoption.* MA: Edward Elgar Publishing.

Osterlund, C., & Carlile, P. (2005). Relations in Practice: Sorting Through Practice Theories on Knowledge Sharing in Complex Organizations. *The Information Society*, *21*, 91–107. doi:10.1080/01972240590925294

Pack, T. (2002). *Taxonomy's role in content management. EContent* (p. 26). Information Today.

Paik, Y., & Choi, D. Y. (2005). The shortcomings of a standardized global knowledge management system: The case study of Accenture. *The Academy of Management Executive, 19*(2), 81–84.

Peet, M. R., & Walsh, K. (2010). Generative knowledge interviewing: a method for knowledge transfer and talent management at the University of Michigan. *International Journal of Educational Advancement, 10*, 71–85. doi:10.1057/ijea.2010.10

Peltokorpi, V. (2006). Knowledge sharing in a cross-cultural context: Nordic expatriates in Japan. *Knowledge Management Research & Practice, 4*(2), 138–148. doi:10.1057/palgrave.kmrp.8500095

Petty, R. E., & Cacioppo, J. T. (1986). *Communication and Persuasion: Central and Peripheral Routes to Attitude Change*. New York: Springer-Verlag.

Petty, R. E., Cacioppo, J. T., & Goldman, R. (1981). Personal involvement as a determinant of argument-based persuasion. *Journal of Personality and Social Psychology, 41*, 847–855. doi:10.1037/0022-3514.41.5.847

Petty, R. E., & Wegener, D. T. (1999). The Elaboration Likelihood Model: Current Status and Controversies. In Gilbert, D. T., Fiske, S. T., & Gardner, L. (Eds.), *Dual-Process Theories in Social Psychology* (pp. 323–390). New York: McGraw-Hill.

Pfaff, C. C., & Hasan, H. (2006a). Overcoming organizational resistance to using Wiki technology for knowledge management. In *Proceedings of the 10ᵗʰ Pacific Asian Conference on Information Systems.*

Pfaff, C. C., & Hasan, H. (2006b). The Wiki: A tool to support the activities of the knowledge worker. In *Proceedings of the Transformational Tools for 21st Century (TT21C) Conference 2006* (pp. 38-48).

Pfeffer, J., & Sutton, R. I. (1999). Knowing 'what' to do is not enough: Turning knowledge into action. *California Management Review, 42*(1), 83–109.

Phillips, L. D., & Edwards, W. (1966). Conservatism in a simple probability inference task. *Journal of Experimental Psychology, 72*, 346–354. doi:10.1037/h0023653

Phillips, J. (2004). Twelve success factors for corporate universities. *Chief Learning Officer, 3*(2), 50–52.

Phillips, L. W., & Bagozzi, R. P. (1986). On measuring organizational properties of distribution channels: methodological issues in the use of key informants. In L. Bucklin & J. M. Carman (Eds.), *Research in Marketing, 8*, 313-369.

Pisano, G. P. (1996). *The development factory: Unlocking the potential of process innovation*. Harvard Business School Press.

Plass, J., & Salisbury, M. (2002). A Living System Approach to the Development of Knowledge Management Systems. *Educational Technology Research and Development, 50*(1), 35–57. doi:10.1007/BF02504960

Ploder, C., & Fink, K. (2007). An orchestration model for knowledge management tools in SMEs. In: K. Tochtermann & H. Maurer (Eds.), *Proceedings of I-KNOW '07: 7ᵗʰ International Conference on Knowledge Management,* (pp. 176-183). Graz: J.UCS.

Podolny, J. (1994). Market uncertainty and the social character of economic exchange. *Administrative Science Quarterly, 39*(3), 458. doi:10.2307/2393299

Podolny, J., & Baron, J. (1997). Resources and relationships: Social networks and mobility in the workplace. *American Sociological Review, 62*(5), 673–693. doi:10.2307/2657354

Polanyi, M. (1966). *The tacit dimension*. London: Routledge & Kegan.

Polanyi, M. (1962). Tacit Knowing: Its Bearing on Some Problems of Philosophy. *Reviews of Modern Physics, 34*(4), 601–616. doi:10.1103/RevModPhys.34.601

Polanyi, M. (1954). *Personal knowledge: towards a post-critical philosophy*. Chicago, IL: University of Chicago Press.

Polanyi, M. (1946). *Science, faith, and society*. Chicago: The University of Chicago Press.

Polanyi, M. (1976). Tacit knowing. In Marx, M., & Goodson, F. (Eds.), *Theories in contemporary psychology* (2nd ed., pp. 330–344). New York: Macmillan.

Politis, J. D. (2001). The relationship of various leadership styles to knowledge management. *Leadership and Organization Development Journal, 22*(8), 354–364. doi:10.1108/01437730110410071

Polkinghorne, D. (1988). *Narrative Knowing and the Human Sciences*. Albany, NY: State University of New York Press.

Pomerol, J., Brezillon, P., & Pasquier, L. (2002). Operational Knowledge Representation for Practical Decision-Making. *Journal of Management Information Systems, 18*(4), 101–115.

Ponzi, L., & Koenig, M. (2002). Knowledge management: Another management fad? *Information Research, 8*(1).

Porter, M. E., & Millar, V. E. (1985). How information gives you competitive advantage. *Harvard Business Review*, (Jul-Aug): 149–161.

Porter, M. E. (1987). From competitive advantage to corporate strategy. *Harvard Business Review*, (May-June): 43–59.

Portes, A. (1998). Social capital: Its origins and applications in modern sociology. *Annual Review of Sociology, 24*, 1–24.

Poston, R. S., & Speier, C. (2005). Effective Use of Knowledge Management Systems: A Process Model of Content Ratings and Credibility Indicators. *Management Information Systems Quarterly, 29*(2), 221.

Powell, W., Kogut, K., & Smith-Doerr, L. (1996). Inter-organizational collaboration and the locus of innovation: Networks of learning in biotechnology. *Administrative Science Quarterly, 41*(1), 116–145. doi:10.2307/2393988

PRNewswire. (2005). INPUT predicts federal knowledge management spending will reach $1.3 billion by FY10; Katrina-highlighted weaknesses spur OMB and Congress to push agencies to develop more information sharing processes and systems. *PRNewswire*, Reston, VA.

Probst, G., Raub, S., & Romhardt, K. (2002). *Managing knowledge: Building blocks for success*. Chichester, UK: Wiley.

Prusak, L. (2001). Where did Knowledge Management come from? *IBM Systems Journal, 40*(4), 1002–1007. doi:10.1147/sj.404.01002

Psarras, J. E. (2007). Education and training in the knowledge-based economy: The application of knowledge management. *International Journal of Information Technology & Management, 6*(1), 6–6.

Pumareja, D. T., & Sikkel, K. (2005). *The Role of Dissonance in Knowledge Exchange: A Case Study of a Knowledge Management System Implementation*. Proceedings of the 38th Hawaii International Conference on System Sciences, 42b.

Quinn, J. B., Anderson, P., & Finkelstein, S. (1996). Leveraging intellect. *The Academy of Management Executive, 10*(3), 7–27.

Qureshi, S., Briggs, R., & Hlupic, V. (2006). Value creation from intellectual capital: Convergence of Knowledge Management and collaboration in the intellectual bandwidth Model. *Group Decision and Negotiation, 15*(3), 197–220. doi:10.1007/s10726-006-9018-x

Rabinovitch, E. (2008). WEB 2.0 is here and ready for use. *IEEE Communications Magazine, 46*(3), 24–24. doi:10.1109/MCOM.2008.4463764

Ralston, D. A., Egri, C. P., Stewart, S., & Terpstra, R. H., & Yu, Kaicheng. (1999). Doing business in the 21st century with the new generation of Chinese managers: A study of generational shifts in work values in China. *Journal of International Business Studies, 30*(2), 415–427. doi:10.1057/palgrave.jibs.8490077

Ralston, D. A., Gustafson, D. J., Terpstra, R. H., & Holt, D. H. (1995). Pre-post Tiananmen Square: Changing values of Chinese managers. *Asia Pacific Journal of Management, 12*(1), 1–20. doi:10.1007/BF01733968

Raman, M., Ryan, T., & Olfman, L. (2006). Knowledge management systems for emergency preparedness: The Claremont University consortium experience. *International Journal of Knowledge Management, 2*(3), 51–68. doi:10.4018/jkm.2006070103

Rao, L., & Osei-Bryson, K. M. (2007). Towards defining dimensions of knowledge systems quality. *Expert Systems with Applications, 33*, 368–378. doi:10.1016/j.eswa.2006.05.003

Rapoport, A., & Guyer, M. (1978). A taxonomy of 2x2 Games. *General Systems, XXIII*, 125–136.

Rasch, G. (1980). *Probabilistic models for some intelligence and attainment tests*. Chicago: The University of Chicago Press. (Original work published 1960)

Ratneshwar, S., & Chaiken, S. (1991). Comprehension's role in persuasion: The case of its moderating effect on the persuasive impact of source cues. *The Journal of Consumer Research, 18*, 52–62. doi:10.1086/209240

Ratten, V., & Suseno, Y. (2006). Knowledge development, social capital and alliance learning. *International Journal of Educational Management, 20*(1), 60–72. doi:10.1108/09513540610639594

Rawat, M. S. (2009). Knowledge management leveraging e-learning in universities, Proceedings of the *International conference of on e- learning, 432-439.*

Raybould, B. (1995). Performance Support Engineering: An Emerging Development Methodology for Enabling Organizational Learning. *Performance Improvement Quarterly, 8*(1), 7–22. doi:10.1111/j.1937-8327.1995.tb00658.x

Reagans, R., Argote, L., & Brooks, D. (2005). Individual experience and experience working together: Predicting learning rates from knowing who knows what and knowing how to work together. *Management Science, 51*, 869–881. doi:10.1287/mnsc.1050.0366

Reber, A. S. (1989). Implicit learning and tacit knowledge. *Journal of Experimental Psychology. General, 118*, 219–235. doi:10.1037/0096-3445.118.3.219

Rech, J., Bogner, C., & Haas, V. (2007). Using Wikis to tackle reuse in software projects. *IEEE Software, 24*, 99–104. doi:10.1109/MS.2007.183

Redding, G., & Wong, G. Y. Y. (1986). The psychology of Chinese organizational behaviour. In Bond, M. H. (Ed.), *The psychology of the Chinese people* (pp. 267–295). Hong Kong, New York: Oxford University Press.

Rehak, D. (2003). *SCORM Best Practice Guide for Content Developers*. Pittsburg: Learning Systems Architecture Lab at Carnegie-Mellon.

Ren, Y., Carley, K. M., & Argote, L. (2006). The contingent effects of transactive memory: When is it more beneficial to know what others know? *Management Science, 52*, 671–682. doi:10.1287/mnsc.1050.0496

Render, B. (2003). *Stair, R. and Balakrishnan, N. (2003) Managerial Decision Modeling with Spreadsheets*. Prentice Hall.

Resnick, M. (1997). *Turtles, termites, and traffic jams: Explorations in massively parallel microworlds*. Cambridge, MA: The MIT Press.

Rich, P. (1992). The organizational taxonomy: Definition and design. *Academy of Management Review, 17*(4), 758–781. doi:10.2307/258807

Rich, E., & Duchessi, P. (2000). Models for understanding the dynamics of organizational knowledge in consulting firms. In *Proceedings of the Hawaii International Conference on System Sciences*.

Richter-von Hagen, C., Ratz, D., & Povalej, R. (2005). Towards self-organizing knowledge- intensive processes. *Journal of Universal Knowledge Management, 0*(2), 148–169.

Riege, A. (2005). Three-dozen knowledge-sharing barriers managers must consider The Authors. *Journal of Knowledge Management, 9*(3), 18–35. doi:10.1108/13673270510602746

Robson, R. (2002). SCORM Steps Up. *E-learning, 3*(8), 48–50.

Roesner, L., & Walesh, S. (1998). Corporate university: Consulting firm case study. *Journal of Management Engineering, 14*(2), 56–63. doi:10.1061/(ASCE)0742-597X(1998)14:2(56)

Rosenau, M. D. (1988). Speeding your product to market. *Journal of Consumer Marketing, 5*, 23–40.

Rosenbach, W. T. (1993). *Contemporary issues in leadership* (3rd ed.). Boulder, CO: Westview.

Ross, M. V., & Schulte, W. D. (2005). Knowledge Management in a Military Enterprise: a Pilot Case Study of the Space and Warfare Systems Command. In Stankosky, M. (Ed.), *Creating the Discipline of Knowledge Management: The Latest in University Research, 157-70*. London, UK: Elsevier/Butterworth-Heinemann. doi:10.1016/B978-0-7506-7878-0.50014-4

Rothwell, W., & Kazanas, H. (2004). *Mastering the Instructional Design Process*. San Francisco, CA: Pfeiffer.

Rucker, D. D., & Petty, R. E. (2006). Increasing the Effectiveness of Communications to Consumers: Recommendations Based on Elaboration Likelihood and Attitude Certainty Perspectives. *Journal of Public Policy & Marketing, 25*(1), 39–52. doi:10.1509/jppm.25.1.39

Ruggels, R. (1997). *Knowledge management tools*. Boston: Butterworth-Heinemann.

Ruggles, R. (1998). The state of the notion: Knowledge management in practice. *California Management Review, 40*(3), 80–89.

Ruikar, K., Anumba, C. J., & Carrillo, P. M. (2006). VERDICT-An e-readiness assessment application for construction companies. *Automation in Construction, 15*(1). doi:10.1016/j.autcon.2005.02.009

Ruiz-Mercader, J., Merõno-Cerdan, A. L., & Sabater-Sánchez, R. (2006). Information technology and learning: Their relationship and impact on organisational performance in small businesses. *International Journal of Information Management, 26*, 16–29. doi:10.1016/j.ijinfomgt.2005.10.003

Rulke, D. L., & Galaskiewicz, J. (2000). Distribution of Knowledge, Group Network Structure, and Group Performance. *Management Science, 46*(5), 612–625. doi:10.1287/mnsc.46.5.612.12052

Ruppel, C. P., & Harrington, S. J. (2001). Sharing Knowledge through Intranets: A Study of Organizational Culture and Intranet Implementation. *IEEE Transactions on Professional Communication, 44*(1), 37–52. doi:10.1109/47.911131

Russo, J. E., & Schoemaker, P. J. H. (1992). Managing overconfidence. *Sloan Management Review, 33*, 7–17.

Ryan, J. J. C. H. (2006). Managing knowledge security. *Vine, 36*(2), 143–145. doi:10.1108/03055720610682942

SA. (2006). Statistical Yearbook of Austria. http://www.statistik.at.

Sackmann, S. A., & Friesl, M. (2007). Exploring cultural impacts on knowledge sharing behavior in project teams - results from a simulation study. *Journal of Knowledge Management, 11*(6), 142–156. doi:10.1108/13673270710832226

Saeed, K. A., & Abdinnour-Helm, S. (2008). Examining the effects of information system characteristics and perceived usefulness on post adoption usage of information systems. *Information & Management, 45*, 376–386. doi:10.1016/j.im.2008.06.002

Sajeva, S., & Jucevicius, R. (2006). Challenges to implementation of knowledge Management in small and medium-sized enterprises. *Social Sciences, 54*(4), 50–59.

Salisbury, M. (2000). Creating a Process for Capturing and Leveraging Intellectual Capital. *Performance Improvement Quarterly, 13*(3), 202–219. doi:10.1111/j.1937-8327.2000.tb00182.x

Salisbury, M. (2003). Putting Theory into Practice to Build Knowledge Management Systems. *Journal of Knowledge Management, 7*(2), 128–141. doi:10.1108/13673270310477333

Salisbury, M. (2009). *iLearning: How to Create an Innovative Learning Organization*. San Francisco, CA: Pfeiffer (Imprint of Wiley).

Salisbury, M., & Plass, J. (2001). A Conceptual Framework for a Knowledge Management System. *Human Resource Development International, 4*(4), 451–464. doi:10.1080/13678860010016913

Salisbury, M. Dickinson, M (2006). *The Team Collaboration System: An E-Mail Based Collaborative Work System*. US Department of Energy's 2006 Annual Information Management Conference (AIMC), Austin TX.

Salojärvi, S., Furu, P., & Sveiby, K. (2005). Knowledge management and growth in Finnish SMEs. *Journal of Knowledge Management, 9*(2), 103–122. doi:10.1108/13673270510590254

Salomon, G. (1996). *Distributed Cognitions*. Cambridge, UK: Cambridge University Press.

Salopek, J. (2004). Targeting the learning organization. *T&D, 58*(3), 46-51.

Sambamurthy, V., & Subramani, M. (2005). Special issue on information technologies and knowledge management. *Management Information Systems Quarterly, 29*, 1–7.

Sampson, S., & Bradley, K. D. (2003). Rasch analysis of educator supply and demand rating scale data: An alternative to the true score model. *Research Methods; The Forum*. Retrieved February 21, 2009, from http://aom.pace.edu/rmd/2003forum.html

Sanchez, J.A.P. (2001). Knowledge management in universities. *SCIRE: Representaciony organization del Conocimiento, 6*(2) 99-120.

Sarvary, M. (1999). Knowledge management and competition in the consulting industry. *California Management Review, 41*(2), 95–107.

Scharmer, C. (2001). Self-transcending knowledge: Organizing around emerging realities. In Nonaka, I., & Teece, D. (Eds.), *Managing industrial knowledge: Creation, transfer and utilization*. London: Sage Publications.

Schein, E. H. (1992). *Organizational culture and leadership* (2nd ed.). San Francisco: Jossey-Bass.

Schein, E. H. (1993). How can organizations learn faster? The challenge of entering the green room. *Sloan Management Review, 34*(2), 84–92.

Schilling, M., & Phelps, C. (2007). Interfirm collaboration networks: The impact of large-scale network structure on firm innovation. *Management Science, 52*(11), 1113–1126. doi:10.1287/mnsc.1060.0624

Schmitz, J., & Fulk, J. (1991). Organizational colleagues, media richness and electronic mail. *Communication Research, 8*(4), 487–523. doi:10.1177/009365091018004003

Schneider, B. (1987). The people make the place. *Personnel Psychology, 40*(3), 437–453. doi:10.1111/j.1744-6570.1987.tb00609.x

Schultze, U., & Leidner, D. (2002). Studying Knowledge Management in Information Systems Research: Discourses and Theoretical Assumptions. *Management Information Systems Quarterly, 26*(3), 213–242. doi:10.2307/4132331

Schutte, M., & Snyman, M. (2006). Knowledge flow elements within a context—a model. *South African Journal of Information Management, 8*(2).

Scott, S. G., & Bruce, R. A. (1994). Determinants of Innovative Behavioral Path Model of Individual Innovation in the Workplace. *Academy of Management Journal, 37*(3), 580–607. doi:10.2307/256701

Scott, J. E. (2000). Facilitating interorganizational learning with information technology. *Journal of Management Information Systems, 17*(2), 81.

Selamat, M. H., & Choudrie, J. (2007). Using meta-abilities and tacit knowledge for developing learning based systems: A case study approach. *The Learning Organization, 14*(4), 321–344.

Selart, M., Kuvaas, B., Boe, O., & Takemura, K. (2006). The influence of decision heuristics and overconfidence on multiattribute choice: A process-tracing study. *The European Journal of Cognitive Psychology, 18*, 437–453. doi:10.1080/09541440500173054

Senge, P. (1994). *The fifth discipline: The art and practice of the learning organization*. Currency/Doubleday.

Shankar, R., Singh, M. D., Gupta, A., & Narain, R. (2003). Strategic planning for knowledge management implementation in engineering firms. *Work Study, 52*(4), 190–200. doi:10.1108/00438020310479036

Sharda, R., Biros, D., Lucca, J., & Upton, S. (2008). *A knowledge representation model for lessons learned knowledge*. Stillwater: Oklahoma State University.

Sharkie, R. (2003). Knowledge creation and its place in the development of sustainable competitive advantage. *Journal of Knowledge Management, 7*(1), 20–31.

Sharp, D. (2003). Knowledge management today: Challenges and opportunities. *Information Systems Management*, (Spring): 32–37. doi:10.1201/1078/43204.20.2.20030301/41468.6

Sherif, K. (2006). An adaptive strategy for managing knowledge in organizations. *Journal of Knowledge Management. Kempston, 10*(4), 72.

Shiller, R. J. (2000). *Irrational exuberance*. Princeton, NJ: Princeton University Press.

Shirley, D. A., & Langan-Fox, J. (1996). Intuition: A review of the literature. *Psychological Reports, 79*, 563–584.

Shoham, S., & Perry, M. (2009). Knowledge management as a mechanism for technological and organizational change management in Israeli universities. *Higher Education, 57*, 227–246. doi:10.1007/s10734-008-9148-y

Shon, J., & Musen, M. A. (1999, November 6-10). *The Low Availability of Metadata Elements for Evaluating the Quality of Medical Knowledge on the Word Wide Web.* Paper presented at the Proceedings of American Medical Informatics Association Symposium, Washington, DC.

Shropshire, C. (2010). The role of the interlocking director and board receptivity in the diffusion of practices. *Academy of Management Review, 35*(2), 246–264.

Siakas, K. V., Georgiadou, E., & Balstrup, B. (2010). Cultural Impacts on Knowledge Sharing: Empirical Data from EU Project Collaboration. *The Journal of Information & Knowledge Management Systems, 40*(3/4), 376–389.

Siemieniuch, C. E., & Sinclair, M. A. (2004). A framework for organizational readiness for knowledge management. *International Journal of Operations & Production Management, 24*(1), 79–98. doi:10.1108/01443570410511004

Sigmund, K., Fehr, E., & Nowak, M. (2002). The economics of fair play. *Scientific American, 286*(1). doi:10.1038/scientificamerican0102-82

Simon, N. J. (1996). Meeting the challenge of change: The issue of readiness. *Competitive Intelligence Review, 7*(2), 86-88.

Simonin, B. L. (1999). Ambiguity and the process of knowledge transfer in strategic alliances. *Strategic Management Journal, 20*(7), 595–623. doi:10.1002/(SICI)1097-0266(199907)20:7<595::AID-SMJ47>3.0.CO;2-5

Simons, R. (2005). *Leavers of Organizational Design.* Boston: Harvard Business School Press.

Singh, N., & Baack, D. W. (2004). Web site adaptation: A cross-cultural comparison of U.S. and Mexican web sites. *Journal of Computer-Mediated Communication, 9*(4). http://jcmc.indiana.edu/vol9/issue4/singh_baack.html.

Skyrme, D. (1999). *Knowledge networking. Creating the collaborative enterprise.* Oxford: Butterworth-Heinemann.

Skyrme, D. J., & Amidon, D. M. (1997). *Creating the knowledge based business.* London: Business Intelligence.

Skyrme, D. J. (2002). *The 3Cs of Knowledge Sharing: Culture, Competition and Commitment.* Retrieved on January 21, 2011 from: http://www.skyrme.com/updates/u64_f1.htm.

Small, C.T. & Sage, A.P. (2005/2006). Knowledge Management and knowledge sharing: A review. *Information knowledge Systems, 5*, 153-169.

Smedlund, A. (2009). Social network structures for explicit, tacit and potential knowledge. *International Journal of Knowledge Management*, Jan-March, 78-87.

Smith, T. W. (1983). The Hidden 25 Percent: an Analysis of Nonresponse on the 1980 General Social Survey. *Public Opinion Quarterly, 47*(3), 386–404. doi:10.1086/268797

Smith, P. A. C. (2005). Knowledge sharing and strategic capital: The importance and identification of opinion leaders. *The Learning Organization, 12*(6), 563–574. doi:10.1108/09696470510626766

Smith, P. B., Andersen, J. A., Ekelund, B., Graversen, G., & Ropo, A. (2003). In search of Nordic management styles. *Scandinavian Journal of Management, 19*, 491–507. doi:10.1016/S0956-5221(03)00036-8

Smith, E. V. (2004a). Evidence for the reliability of measures and validity of measure interpretation: A Rasch measurement perspective. In Smith, E. V., & Smith, R. M. (Eds.), *Introduction to Rasch measurement* (pp. 93–122). Maple Grove, MN: JAM Press.

Smith, E. V. (2004b). Detecting and evaluating the impact of multidimensionality using item fit statistics and principal component analysis of residuals. In Smith, E. V., & Smith, R. M. (Eds.), *Introduction to Rasch Measurement* (pp. 575–600). Maple Grove, MN: JAM Press.

Smith, H. A., & McKeen, J. D. (2003). *Instilling a Knowledge-sharing Culture.* Retrieved on January 21, 2011 from: http://business.queensu.ca/centres/monieson/docs/working/working_03-11.pdf.

Smith, P. A. C. (2006). Enhancing strategic capital. *Handbook of Business Strategy, 7*(1), 195–199.

Smith, P. A. C., & McLaughlin, M. (2003). Succeeding with knowledge management: Getting the people-factors right. In *Proceedings of the 6th World Congress on Intellectual Capital and Innovation*, McMaster University, Hamilton.

Smolnik, S., Kremer, S., & Kolbe, L. (2005). Continuum of context explication: Knowledge discovery through process-orientated portal. *International Journal of Knowledge Management, 1*(1), 27–46. doi:10.4018/jkm.2005010102

Smolnik, S., Kremer, S., & Kolbe, L. (2007). The role of context and its explication for fostering knowledge transparency in modern organizations. In Jennex, M. (Ed.), *Knowledge management in modern organizations* (pp. 256–277). Hershey, PA: Idea Group Publishing. doi:10.4018/9781599042619.ch014

Snowden, D. (2002). Complex acts of knowing: Paradox and descriptive self-awareness. *Journal of Knowledge Management, 6*(2), 100–111. doi:10.1108/13673270210424639

Snyman, R., & Kruger, C. J. (2004). The interdependency between strategic management and strategic knowledge management. *Journal of Knowledge Management, 8*(1), 5–19. doi:10.1108/13673270410523871

Sohail, M.S., Daud. S., (2009).Knowledge sharing in higher education institutions: Perspectives from Malaysia. *VINE: The journal of information and knowledge management systems*, 39 (2), 125-142.

Soliman, F., & Spooner, K. (2000). Strategies for implementing knowledge management: role of human resources management. *The Journal of Knowledge Management,* 14), 337-345.

Southon, F. C. G., Todd, R. J., & Seneque, M. (2002). Knowledge management in three organizations: An exploratory study. *Journal of the American Society for Information Science and Technology, 53*(12), 1047–1059. doi:10.1002/asi.10112

Spender, J.-C. (1996). Organizational knowledge, learning and memory: Three concepts in search of a theory. *Journal of Organizational Change Management, 9*, 63–78.

Spender, J.-C. (1996). Making knowledge the basis of a dynamic theory of the firm. *Strategic Management Journal, 17*(Winter Special Issue), 45-62.

Srite, M. (2006). Culture as an explanation of technology acceptance differences: An empirical investigation of Chinese and US users. *Australasian Journal of Information Systems, 14*(1), 5–25. doi:10.3127/ajis.v14i1.4

Stamm, K., & Dube, R. (1994). The relationship of attitudinal components to trust in media. *Communication Research, 21*(1), 105–123. doi:10.1177/009365094021001006

Stavanger Travel. (2006). Retrieved December 10, 2006 from: http://www.stavangertravel.com

Stenmark, D. (2000). Turning tacit knowledge tangible. In *Proceedings of the 33rd Hawaii International Conference on System Sciences*, IEEE Computer Society.

Stephenson, W. (1953). Postulates of behaviorism. *Philosophy of Science, 20*, 110–120. doi:10.1086/287250

Sterman, J. (2000). *Business dynamics: Systems thinking and modeling for a complex world*. Boston: Irwin.

Sternberg, R. J., Forsythe, G. B., Hedlund, J., Horvath, J. A., Wagner, R. K., & Williams, W. M. (2000). *Practical intelligence in everyday life*. New York: Cambridge University Press.

Sternberg, R. J., & Hedlund, J. (2002). Practical intelligence, g, and work psychology. *Human Performance, 15*(1/2), 143–160. doi:10.1207/S15327043HUP1501&02_09

Sternberg, R. J., & Horvath, J. A. (Eds.). (1999). *Tacit knowledge in professional practice: Researcher and practitioner perspectives*. Mahwah, NJ: Erlbaum.

Sternberg, R. J., Nokes, C., Geissler, P. W., Prince, R., Okatcha, F., Bundy, D. A., & Grigorenko, E. L. (2001). The relationship between academic and practical intelligence: A case study in Kenya. *Intelligence, 29*, 401–418. doi:10.1016/S0160-2896(01)00065-4

Sternberg, R. J., Wagner, R. K., Williams, W. M., & Horvath, J. A. (1995). Testing common sense. *The American Psychologist, 50*(11), 912–927. doi:10.1037/0003-066X.50.11.912

Stewart, T. (2001). *The wealth of knowledge: Intellectual capital and the twenty-first century organization*. New York: Doubleday.

Stogdill, R. M. (1963). *Manual for leadership behavior. Description Questionnaire Form, 12*. Columbus, OH: Bureau of Business Research.

Stonehouse, G. H., & Pemberton, J. D. (1999). Learning and knowledge management in the intelligent organization. *Participation & Empowerment: An International Journal, 7*(5), 131–144. doi:10.1108/14634449910287846

Stonehouse, G., & Minocha, S. (2008). Strategic processes @ Nike—making and doing knowledge management. *Knowledge and Process Management, 15*(1), 24–31. doi:10.1002/kpm.296

Storey, J., & Barnett, E. (2000). Knowledge management initiatives: learning from failure. *Journal of Knowledge Management, 4*(2), 145. doi:10.1108/13673270010372279

Streels, N. (2000). Success factors for virtual libraries. *Wilton, 23*(5), 68–71.

Su, W. B., Li, X., & Chow, C. W. (2010). Exploring the Extent and Impediments of Knowledge Sharing in Chinese Business Enterprise. *International Journal of Knowledge Management, 6*(4), 24–46. doi:10.4018/jkm.2010100102

Subashini, R. (2010). Tacit knowledge -The ultimate essence of an organization. *Advances in Management, 3*(8), 36–39.

Sum, C., Kow, L. S., & Chen, C. (2004). A Taxonomy of Operations Strategies of High Performing Small and Medium Enterprises in Singapore. *International Journal of Operations & Production Management, 24*(3/4), 321–345. doi:10.1108/01443570410519051

Sumner, J. (2003). Making the leap to a learning organization. *KM Review, 6*(4), 2.

Sunassee, N. N., & Sewry, D. A. (2003). *A Theoretical Framework for Knowledge Management Implementation* Proceedings of the 2002 annual research conference of the South African institute of computer scientists and information technologists on Enablement through technology, Port Elizabeth, South Africa.

Sunoo, B. (1998). Corporate universities: More and better. *Workforce, 77*(5), 16–18.

Sussman, S. W., & Siegal, W. S. (2003). Information Influence in Organizations: An Integrated Approach to Knowledge Adoption. *Information Systems Research, 14*(1), 47–65. doi:10.1287/isre.14.1.47.14767

Sveiby, K. (1997). *The new organizational wealth: Managing and measuring knowledge-based assets.* San Francisco: Berrett-Koehler.

Swieringa, J., & Wierdsma, A. (1992). *Becoming a learning organization: Beyond the learning curve.* Wokingham, UK: Addison-Wesley.

Swisher, K. (2004, July 29). Boomtown: Wiki may alter how employees work together. *Wall Street Journal,* p. B1.

Syed-Ikhsan, S. O. S., & Rowland, F. (2004). Knowledge management in a public organization: A study on the relationship between organizational elements and the performance of knowledge transfer. *Journal of Knowledge Management, 8*(2), 95–111. doi:10.1108/13673270410529145

Szulanski, G. (2003). *Sticky Knowledge: barriers to knowing in the firm.* Sage Publications Inc.

Szulanski, G. (1996). Exploring internal stickiness: Impediments to the transfer of best practice within the firm. *Strategic Management Journal, 17*(10), 27–43.

Talebi, K., Mohammadi, H. R., & Rahimi, M. (2008). *Framework for implementing knowledge management in small and medium sized enterprises'.*Paper presented at 1st Iranian Knowledge Management Conference, Tehran, Iran, February 2/3.

Tamtana, J. S. (2007). The future of knowledge Management. *Management Learning, 38*(1), 125–126. doi:10.1177/135050760703800109

Tan, M. (2008). Metadata and its applications in the digital library: Approaches and practices. *Journal of Academic Librarianship, 34*(3), 271–271. doi:10.1016/j.acalib.2008.03.019

Tang, W. K., Wong, E., Chiu, H. F. K., Lum, C. M., & Ungvari, G. S. (2005). The geriatric depression scale should be shortened: Results of Rasch analysis. *International Journal of Geriatric Psychiatry, 20,* 783–789. doi:10.1002/gps.1360

Tashkandi, Z. M. Q. (2007). *Knowledge management: its importance and the extent of applying its processes from the own point of view of the educational administration directresses and the administrative female supervisor in Makkah and Jeddah.* Unpublished master thesis, Om-Alqura University, Makkah, Saudi Arabia.

Tatikonda, M. V., & Rosenthal, S. R. (2000). Technology novelty, project complexity, and product development execution success. *IEEE Transactions on Engineering Management, 47,* 74–87. doi:10.1109/17.820727

Taylor, W. A., & Wright, G. H. (2004). *Organizational Readiness for Successful Knowledge Sharing: Challenges for Public Sector Managers.* Hershey, PA: Idea Group Inc.

Taylor, H. (2007). Tacit knowledge: Conceptualizations and operationalizations. *International Journal of Knowledge Management, 3*(3), 60–73. doi:10.4018/jkm.2007070104

Teece, D. (1986). Profiting from technological innovation: Implications for integration, collaboration, licensing and public policy. *Research Policy, 15*(6), 285–305. doi:10.1016/0048-7333(86)90027-2

Teece, D. J. (1998). Capturing value from knowledge assets: the new economy, markets for know how, and intangible assets. *Californian. Management Review, 40*(3), 55–78.

Teece, D. J. (2000). Managing Knowledge assets in diverse industrial contexts. In Despres, Ch., & Chauvel, D. (Eds.), *Knowledge Horizons*. U.S.A: Butterworth Heinemann. doi:10.1016/B978-0-7506-7247-4.50009-4

Tennant, A., McKenna, S. P., & Hagell, P. (2004). Application of Rasch analysis in the development and application of quality of life instruments. *Value in Health, 7*(1), 22–26. doi:10.1111/j.1524-4733.2004.7s106.x

Thomas, D. (1999). *The corporate university as a model for organizational and individual learning*. Paper given at the IQPC Conference on the Corporate university in London on 22-23 June.

Thornton, A. (2002 February 1). *A primer on the 2- and 3-parameter item response theory models*. Paper presented at the meeting of the Annual Meeting of the College of Education, University of North Texas, Educational Research Exchange, Denton, TX.

Thursby, M., Thursby, J., & Haeussler, C. Jiang., L. (2009). Do academic scientists freely share information? Not necessarily. *Vox News* Nov 29, 2009. Retrieved from http://www.voxeu.org/index.php?q=node/4264 (accessed 30.11.09).

Titus, N., Subrahmanian, E., & Ramani, K. (2007). *Folksonomy and designing: An exploration*. Paper presented at the ASME 2007 International Design Engineering Technical Conferences & Computers and Information in Engineering Conference.

Tiwana, A. (2002). *The knowledge management toolkit: Orchestrating IT, strategy, and knowledge platforms* (2nd ed.). Upper Saddle River, N.J.: Prentice Hall.

Tomasello, W. (1999). *The cultural origins of human cognition*. Boston, London: Harvard University Press.

Tong, J., & Mitra, A. (2009). Chinese cultural influences on knowledge management practice. *Journal of Knowledge Management, 13*(2), 49–62. doi:10.1108/13673270910942691

Touron, D. R., & Hertzog. (2004). Distinguishing age differences in knowledge, strategy use, and confidence during strategic skill acquisition. *Psychology and Aging, 19*(3), 452–466. doi:10.1037/0882-7974.19.3.452

Trevino, L., Lengel, R., Bodensteiner, W., Gerloff, E., & Muir, N. (1990). The richness imperative and cognitive style: The role of individual differences in media choice behavior. *Management Communication Quarterly, 4*, 176–197. doi:10.1177/0893318990004002003

Triandis, H. C. (1995). *Individualism and collectivism*. Boulder, CO: Westview Press.

Trompenaars, F. (1994). *Riding the waves of culture: Understanding diversity in global business*. Burr Ridge, IL: Irwin Professional Pub.

Trompenaars, F., & Hampden-Turner, C. (2006). *Riding the waves of culture: Understanding cultural diversity in business* (2. reprint. with corr. ed.). London: Brealey.

Troyer, C. R. (1995). Smart movers in supply chain coordination. *Transport and Distribution, 36*(9), 55.

Tsai, W. (2002). Social Structure of 'Coopetition' Within a Multiunit Organization: Coordination, Competition, and Intraorganizational Knowledge Sharing. *Organization Science, 13*(2), 179–190. doi:10.1287/orsc.13.2.179.536

Tsoukas, H. (1996). The firm as a distributed knowledge system: A constructivist approach. *Strategic Management Journal, 17*, 11–25.

Tversky, A., & Kahneman, D. (1974). Judgement under uncertainty: Heuristics and biases. *Science, 185*, 1124–1131. doi:10.1126/science.185.4157.1124

Ulrich, K. T., & Eppinger, S. D. (2004). *Product design and development* (3rd ed.). McGraw-Hill.

Ursic, D., Nikl, A., Mulej, M., & Smogave Cestar, A. (2006). System-organizational aspect of a learning organization in companies. *Systemic Practice and Action Research, 19*(1), 81–99. doi:10.1007/s11213-005-9005-1

Uzzi, B. (1996). The sources and consequences of embeddedness for the economic performance of organizations: The network effect. *American Sociological Review, 61*(4), 674–698. doi:10.2307/2096399

Uzzi, B., & Spiro, J. (2005). Collaboration and creativity: The small world problem. *American Journal of Sociology, 111*(2), 447–504. doi:10.1086/432782

Van De Ven, A. (1986). Central Problems in the Management of Innovation. *Management Science, 32*(5), 570–607. doi:10.1287/mnsc.32.5.590

Van Weele, A. J. (2002). *Purchasing and Supply Chain Management* (3rd ed.). London: Thompson Publishing.

Vandeburg, W. H. (2003). The contemporary university and the poverty of nations: Rethinking the mission of STS. *Bulletin of Science, Technology & Society, 23*, 227–235. doi:10.1177/0270467603256076

Vashisth, R., Kumar, R., & Chandra, A. (2010). Barriers and facilitators to knowledge management: evidence from selected Indian universities. *The IUP Journal of Knowledge Management, VIII*(4), 7–25.

Vaughan, F. E. (1979). *Awakening intuition.* Garden City, NY: Anchor Press, Doubleday.

Venkatesh, V., & Davis, F. D. (2000). A Theoretical Extension of the Technology Acceptance Model: Four Longitudinal Field Studies. *Management Science, 46*(2), 186–204. doi:10.1287/mnsc.46.2.186.11926

Venkatesh, V., Morris, M. G., Davis, G. B., & Davis, F. D. (2003). User acceptance of information technology: Toward a unified view. *Management Information Systems Quarterly, 27*(3), 425.

Vogel, C. (2003). A roadmap for proper taxonomy design part 1 of 2. *Computer Technology Review, 23*(7), 42–44.

Von Hayek, F. (1952). *The counter revolution in science.* Chicago: University of Chicago Press.

von Krogh, G., & Roos, J. (1995). A perspective on knowledge, competence and strategy. *Personnel Review, 24*(3), 56–76. doi:10.1108/00483489510089650

Von Krogh, G., Nonaka, I., & Ichijo, K. (2000). *Enabling Knowledge Creation: New Tools for Unlocking the Mysteries of Tacit Understanding.* New York City, NY:xOxford University Press.

Von Winterfeldt, D., & Edwards, W. (1986), *Decision analysis and behavioral research.* Cambridge, UK: Cambridge University Press.

Vygotsky, L. S. (1978). *Mind and society.* Cambridge, MA: Harvard University Press.

Wagner, C., & Bolloju, N. (2005). Supporting Knowledge Management in Organizations with Conversational Technologies: Discussion Forums, Weblogs, and Wikis. *Journal of Database Management, 16*(2), 1–8.

Wagner, C. (2004). Wiki: A technology for conversational knowledge management and group collaboration. *Communications of the Association for Information Systems, 13*, 265–289.

Wagner, R. K. (1987). Tacit knowledge in everyday intelligent behavior. *Journal of Personality and Social Psychology, 52*, 1236–1247. doi:10.1037/0022-3514.52.6.1236

Wagner, R. K., & Sternberg, R. J. (1985). Practical intelligence in real-world pursuits: The role of tacit knowledge. *Journal of Personality and Social Psychology, 49*, 436–458. doi:10.1037/0022-3514.49.2.436

Wagner, R. K., & Sternberg, R. J. (1991). Tacit knowledge: Its uses in identifying, assessing, and developing managerial talent. In Jones, J., Steffy, B., & Bray, D. (Eds.), *Applying psychology in business: The manager's handbook* (pp. 333–344). New York: Human Sciences Press.

Walczak, S. (2005). Organizational knowledge management structure. *The Learning Organization, 12*(4), 330–339. doi:10.1108/09696470510599118

Walker, G., Kogut, B., & Shan, W. (1997). Social capital, structural holes and the formation of an industry network. *Organization Science, 8*(2), 109–125.

Walsh, J. P., & Ungson, G. R. (1991). Organizational memory. *Academy of Management Review, 16*(1), 57–91. doi:10.2307/258607

Wan, H.-H. (2008). Resonance as a Mediating Factor Accounting for the Message Effect in Tailored Communication: Examining Crisis Communication in a Tourism Context. *The Journal of Communication*, *58*(3), 472–489. doi:10.1111/j.1460-2466.2008.00395.x

Wang, H., & Wang, S. (2008). A knowledge management approach to data mining process for business intelligence. *Industrial Management & Data Systems*, *108*(5), 622–634. doi:10.1108/02635570810876750

Wang, F., & Plaskoff, J. (2002). An integrated development model for KM. In Bellaver, R., & Lusa, J. (Eds.), *Knowledge management strategy and technology* (pp. 113–134). Boston: Artech House.

Warier, S. (2003). *Knowledge Management, VIKAS publishing House PVTLTD*. New Delhi: VIKAS Publishing House PVTLID.

Warne, L., Hasan, H., & Ali, I. (2005). Transforming organizational culture to the ideal inquiring organization. In Courtney, J., Haynes, J., & Paradice, D. (Eds.), *Inquiring organizations: Moving from knowledge management to wisdom* (pp. 316–336). Hershey, PA.

Wasko, M., & Farja, S. (2000). It is what one does: Why people participate and help others in electronic communities of practice. *The Journal of Strategic Information Systems*, *9*, 155–173. doi:10.1016/S0963-8687(00)00045-7

Wasko, M., & Faraj, S. (2005). Why Should I Share? Examining Social Capital and Knowledge Contribution in Electronic Networks of Practice. *Management Information Systems Quarterly*, *29*(1), 35–37.

Wathen, C. N., & Burkell, J. (2002). Believe It or Not: Factors Influencing Credibility on the Web. *Journal of the American Society for Knowledge Science and Technology*, *53*(2), 134–144. doi:10.1002/asi.10016

Weber, B., & Weber, C. (2007). Corporate venture capital as a means of radical innovation: relational fit, social capital, and knowledge transfer. *Journal of Engineering and Technology Management*, *24*(1/2), 11–35. doi:10.1016/j.jengtecman.2007.01.002

Weber, O. R., & Aha, W. D. (2003). Intelligent delivery of military lessons learned. *Decision Support Systems*, *34*(3), 287. doi:10.1016/S0167-9236(02)00122-7

Weber, R. (2007). Knowledge management in call centres. *Electronic Journal of Knowledge Management*, *5*(3), 333–346.

Weber, N., & Brewer, N. (2004). Confidence–accuracy calibration in absolute and relative face recognition judgments. *Journal of Experimental Psychology. Applied*, *10*(3), 156–172. doi:10.1037/1076-898X.10.3.156

Webster, J., & Trevino, L. K. (1995). Rational and social theories as complementary explanations of communication media choices: Two policy-capturing studies. *Academy of Management Journal*, *38*, 1544–1572. doi:10.2307/256843

Wegner, D. (1987). Transactive memory: A contemporary analysis of the group mind. In Mullen, B., & Goethals, G. R. (Eds.), *Theories of group behavior* (pp. 185–208). New York: Springer-Verlag.

Wei, K. (2007). Sharing Knowledge in global virtual teams: How do Chinese team members perceive the impact of national cultural differences on knowledge sharing? In Crowston, K., Sieber, S., & Wynn, E. (Eds.), *International Federation for Information Processing, 236, Virtuality and Virtualization* (pp. 251–265). Boston: Springer.

Weinstein, N. D. (1980). Unrealistic optimism about future events. *Journal of Personality and Social Psychology*, *39*, 806–820. doi:10.1037/0022-3514.39.5.806

Weiser, M. (1993, October). Hot topics: Ubiquitous computing. *IEEE Computer*, 71-72.

Wenger, E., Mcdermott, R., & Snyder, W. M. (2002). *Cultivating communities of practice: A guide to managing knowledge*. Boston: Harvard Business School Press.

Wensley, A. K. P., & O'sullivan, A. V. (2000). Tools for Knowledge Management. In Dspres, Ch., & Chauvel, D. (Eds.), *Knowledge Horizons*. U.S.A: Butterworth Heinemann. doi:10.1016/B978-0-7506-7247-4.50008-2

Wheelwright, S., & Clark, K. (1992). *Revolutionizing new product development*. New York: Free Press.

White, F. A., Charles, M. A., & Nelson, J. K. (2008). The Role of Persuasive Arguments in Changing Affirmative Action Attitudes and Expressed Behavior in Higher Education. *The Journal of Applied Psychology*, *93*(6), 1271–1286. doi:10.1037/a0012553

Whitecotton, S. M. (1996). The effects of experience and a decision aid on the slope, scatter, and bias of earnings forecasts. *Organizational Behavior and Human Decision Processes*, *66*(1), 111–121. doi:10.1006/obhd.1996.0042

Wiig, K. (1997). *Leveraging knowledge for business performance*. Pretoria, USA: Wits Business School.

Wiig, K. (1997). Knowledge Management: An Introduction and Perspective. *Journal of Knowledge Management*, *1*(1), 6–14. doi:10.1108/13673279710800682

Wiig, K., & Jooste, A. (2004). *Chapter 45: Exploiting Knowledge for Productivity Gains*. In C. W. Holsapple (Eds.), Handbook on Knowledge Management Vol.2: Knowledge Directions, 289-308. B.V.: Springer Science and Business Media.

Wilemon, D., & Thamhain, H. (1983, June). Team building in project management. *Project Management Quarterly*, 73-80.

Wiley, D. (2004). Overcoming the Limitations of Learning Objects. *Journal of Educational Multimedia and Hypermedia*, *13*(4), 507–521.

Wilkie-Thomson, M. E., Önkal-Atay, D., Pollock, A. C., & Macaulay, A. (1999). The influence of trend strength on directional probabilistic currency predictions. *Technological Forecasting and Social Change*, *61*, 79–80.

Wills-Johnson, N. (2008). The networked firm: a framework for RBV. *Journal of Management Development*, *27*(2), 214–224. doi:10.1108/02621710810849344

Winter, S. (1987). Knowledge and competence as strategic assets. In Teece, D. (Ed.), *The competitive challenge: Strategies for industrial innovation and renewal*. Centre for Research Management.

WirelessNews. (2007). *AMR research: Spending on knowledge management will hit $73B in 2007*. AMR Research.

Wolfe, C., & Loraas, T. (2008). Knowledge Sharing: The Effects of Incentives, Environment, and Person. *Journal of Information Systems*, *22*(2), 53–76. doi:10.2308/jis.2008.22.2.53

Wong, K. (2005). Critical success factors for implementing knowledge management in small and medium enterprises. *Industrial Management & Data Systems*, *105*(3), 261–279. doi:10.1108/02635570510590101

Wong, K., & Aspinwall, E. (2005). An empirical study of the important factors for knowledge—management adoption in the SME sector. *Journal of Knowledge Management*, *9*(3), 64–82. doi:10.1108/13673270510602773

Wright, B. D. (1977). Solving measurement problems with the Rasch model. *Journal of Educational Measurement*, *14*(2), 97–166. doi:10.1111/j.1745-3984.1977.tb00031.x

Wright, B. D. (1997). A history of social science measurement. *Educational Measurement: Issues and Practice*, *16*(4), 33–45. doi:10.1111/j.1745-3992.1997.tb00606.x

Wright, B. D., & Linacre, J. M. (2001). Glossary of Rasch measurement terminology. *Rasch Measurement Transactions*, *15*, 824–825.

Wright, B. D., & Tennant, A. (1996). Sample size again. *Rasch Measurement Transactions*, *9*, 468.

Wright, G., & Ayton, P. (Eds.). (1987). *Judgmental forecasting*. GB, Wiltshire: John Wiley & Sons Ltd.

Wu, W., & Munir, S. B. (2010). Why Should I Share? Examining Consumers' Motives and Trust on Knowledge Sharing. *Journal of Computer Information Systems*, *50*(4), 11–19.

Wunram, M., Weber, F., Pawar, K. S., & Gupta, A. (2002). Proposition of a Human-centred Solution Framework for KM in the Concurrent Enterprise. *Proceedings of the 8th International Conference on Concurrent Enterprising–Ubiquitous Engineering in the Collaborative Economy, Rome, Italy, 17*, 151–158.

Yates, J. T. (1990). *Judgment and decision making*. Englewood Cliffs, NJ: Prentice Hall.

Yeung, A. K., Ulrich, D. O., Nason, S. W., & von Glinow, M. A. (1999). *Organizational learning capability*. New York: Oxford University Press.

Yin, R. K. (2002). *Case Study Research* (3rd ed.). London: Sage Publications.

Yoo, Y., & Torrey, B. (2002). National culture and knowledge management in a global learning organization. In Choo, C. W., & Bontis, N. (Eds.), *The strategic management of intellectual capital and organizational knowledge* (pp. 421–434). Oxford, New York: Oxford University Press.

Yoshioka, T., Herman, G., Yates, J., & Orlikowski, W. J. (2001). Genre Taxonomy: A Knowledge Repository of Communicative Actions. *ACM Transactions on Information Systems, 19*(4), 431–456. doi:10.1145/502795.502798

Young, Ch. L., & Sun, K. L. (2007). Capabilities, Processes, and performance of knowledge management: A structural approach. *Human Factors and Ergonomics in Manufacturing, 17*(1), 21–41. doi:10.1002/hfm.20065

Yu, R. (1997). *Information Technology and Media Choice of CFO.* Master's Thesis, University of NSW.

Yu, S.-H., Kim, Y.-G., & Kim, M.-Y. (2004). Linking organizational knowledge management drivers to knowledge management performance: An exploratory study. In *Proceedings of the 37th Hawaii International Conference on System Sciences*, IEEE Computer Society.

Yuan, Y. C., Fulk, J., & Monge, P. R. (2007). Access to information in connective and communal transactive memory systems. *Communication Research, 34*.

Zack, M. H. (1999). Developing a knowledge strategy. *California Management Review, 41*(3), 125–145.

Zack, M. H. (1999). Managing Codified Knowledge. *Sloan Management Review, 40*(4), 45–58.

Zahn, G. L. (1991). Face-to-Face Communication in an Office Setting: The Effects of Position, Proximity, and Exposure. *Communication Research, 18*(6), 737. doi:10.1177/009365091018006002

Zajac, E. J., & Bazerman, M. N. (1991). Blind spots in industry and competitor analysis: The implications of interfirm perceptions for strategic decisions. *Academy of Management Review, 16*, 37–56. doi:10.2307/258606

Zakaria, N., Amelinckx, A., & Wilemon, D. (2004). Working together apart? Building a knowledge-sharing culture for global virtual teams. *Creativity and Innovation Management, 13*(1), 15–29. doi:10.1111/j.1467-8691.2004.00290.x

Zander, D., & Kogut, B. (1995). Knowledge and the speed of the transfer and imitation of organizational capabilities: An empirical test. *Organization Science, 6*(1), 76–92. doi:10.1287/orsc.6.1.76

Zellner, A. (1988). Optimal Information Processing and Bayes's Theorem. *The American Statistician, 42*, 278–284. doi:10.2307/2685143

Zhang, Q., Chintakovid, T., Sun, X., Ge, Y., & Zhang, K. (2006). Saving Face or Sharing Personal Information? A Cross-cultural Study on Knowledge Sharing. *Journal of Information & Knowledge Management, 5*(1), 73–79. doi:10.1142/S0219649206001335

Zhou, Y. R., Knoke, D., & Sakamoto, I. (2010). Rethinking Silence in the Classroom: Chinese Students' Experiences of Sharing Indigenous Knowledge. *International Journal of Inclusive Education, 9*(3), 287–311. doi:10.1080/13603110500075180

Zhu, Z. (2004). Knowledge management: Towards a universal concept or cross-cultural contexts? *Knowledge Management Research & Practice, 2*(2), 67–79. doi:10.1057/palgrave.kmrp.8500032

Zoubi, D. M., & Rousan, N. M. (2009, March 9). The use of KM in teaching and learning at universities: improving learning outcomes- a suggested frame work. Paper presented at "*International Technology, Education and Development Conference (INTED)*", Valancia, Spain.

Zoubi, D.M. & Kana'an, R.K. (2010, May 19). Intellectual capital and universities: a future study. Paper presented at "*World International Conference on Education (WICE)*", Amman, Jordan.

Zuboff, S. (1988). *In the age of the smart machine: The future of work and power.* New York: Basic Books.

About the Contributors

Murray E. Jennex is an associate professor at San Diego State University, Editor-in-Chief of the International Journal of Knowledge Management, Editor-in-Chief of IGI Global book series, Co-Editor in Chief of the International Journal of Information Systems for Crisis Response and Management, and President of the Foundation for Knowledge Management (LLC). Dr. Jennex specializes in knowledge management, system analysis and design, IS security, e-commerce, and organizational effectiveness. Dr. Jennex serves as the Knowledge Management Systems Track Co-Chair at the Hawaii International Conference on System Sciences. He is the author of over 100 journal articles, book chapters, and conference proceedings on knowledge management, end user computing, international information systems, organizational memory systems, ecommerce, security, and software outsourcing. He holds a BA in chemistry and physics from William Jewell College, a MBA and a MS in software engineering from National University, and a MS in telecommunications management and a PhD in information systems from the Claremont Graduate University. Dr. Jennex is also a registered professional mechanical engineer in the state of California and a Certified Information Systems Security Professional (CISSP).

***

Mark B. Allan is a Senior Software Engineer with the Intelligent Robotics Group at NASA Ames Research Center. Mark has been a contractor in the Intelligent Systems Division for over 10 years, and is currently employed by Perot Systems Government Services. He specializes in data visualization and has worked in the areas of ground control systems for remote exploration, novel human/computer interfaces, massively parallel data flow architectures, and flight simulators. Mark holds a M.S. in Information Systems from the Leavey School of Business at Santa Clara University and a B.S. in Biology from U.C. Santa Barbara. Current topics of interest include the use of technology to enhance individual and team effectiveness, the use of virtual worlds to effectively explore remote worlds, and architectures that enable efficient human-robotic coordination.

Nassim Belbaly, (PhD, MA) is an Associate Professor and Dean of academic affairs at GSCM-Montpellier Business School. His research areas are focused on Knowledge Management and NPD development. He is author of several articles published in peer review journals and as book chapters in KM and other books. Dr. Belbaly serves as a KM minitrack co-chair at the Hawaii International Conference on System Sciences.

David Biros is an Assistant Professor of Management Science and Information Systems at Oklahoma State University. He is a retired United State Air Force Lieutenant Colonel who worked in the fields of communications and information assurance. His research interests included knowledge management, information assurance, deception detection and system trust. He has been published MIS Quarterly, Decision Support Systems, Group Decision and Negotiation, MISQ Executive, and the Journal of Digital Forensics Security and Law. He is also an associate editor for the Journal of Digital Forensics Security and Law and is an adjunct professor at Edith Cowen University in Australia.

Kelly D. Bradley - Associate Professor of Educational Policy Studies and Evaluation, University of Kentucky. Current research interests are anchored in quantitative evaluation and measurement, with specific application to the math and science teaching profession, specifically supply and demand issues, including professional development and quality in the classroom.

Hoon S. Cha is an Assistant Professor of Information & Decision Sciences at the Franklin P. Perdue School of Business, Salisbury University. He holds a M.S. and Ph.D. in Management Information Systems from the University of Arizona. His research examines the impact of IT outsourcing on firm knowledge and the business value of IT investment. His work has appeared in MIS Quarterly, Journal of Management Information Systems, Communications of the ACM, Information Technology and People, and International Journal of Knowledge Management.

M. Suzanne Clinton has a doctorate in Business Administration from Mississippi State University and is certified as a Senior Professional in Human Resources and a Certified Personnel Consultant. Suzanne is Assistant Dean of the CBA and Professor of Management at the University of Central Oklahoma. She serves as a human resource consultant/business advisor to Cowherd Family Medical Center in Heber Springs, AR. She has published in numerous management-related journals and has won several Teaching Excellence and Motivation Awards. Suzanne has published in the Journal of Advertising Research, Southern Law Journal, Issues in Information Systems, Western Journal of Human Resource Management, Journal of Business and Behavioral Sciences, Business Journal for Entrepreneurs, Southwest Business and Economics Journal, Academy of Strategic and Organizational Leadership Journal, The Journal of Education for Business, Southwest Oklahoma Economic Review, and Technical Training.

Xiaodong Deng is an Associate Professor of Management Information Systems at Oakland University. He received his Ph.D. in Manufacturing Management and Engineering from The University of Toledo. His research has appeared in Journal of Management Information Systems, Decision Sciences, Information and Management, Information Resources Management Journal, and Journal of Intelligent Manufacturing. His research interests are in post-implementation information technology learning, information systems benchmarking, and information technology acceptance and diffusion.

William J. Doll is a Professor of MIS and Strategic Management at the University of Toledo. Dr. Doll holds a doctoral degree in Business Administration from Kent State University. He has published extensively on information system and manufacturing issues in academic and professional journals including Management Science, Journal of Management Information Systems, Communications of the ACM, MIS Quarterly, Academy of Management Journal, Decision Sciences, Journal of Operations Management, Information Systems Research, Omega, and Information & Management.

Alexandra Durcikova is an Assistant Professor at the Eller College of Management, the University of Arizona. She received her PhD from the University of Pittsburgh. She has worked as an experimental physics researcher in the area of superconductivity and as an instructor of MBA and executive MBA students prior to returning to academia to pursue her PhD. Her research interests include knowledge management and knowledge management systems, the role of organizational climate in the use of knowledge management systems, knowledge management system characteristics, governance mechanisms in the use of knowledge management systems; and human compliance with security policy and characteristics of successful phishing attempts within the area of network security. Her work appeared or will appear in Information Systems Research, Journal of MIS, Communications of ACM, International Journal of Knowledge Management, Electronic Journal of Knowledge Management, as well as various national and international conference proceedings. She has been teaching classes on Information Technology Strategy and Business Data Communications and Networking for both undergraduate and graduate students.

Kelly J. Fadel is an Assistant Professor of Management Information Systems at the Huntsman School of Business at Utah State University. He received his PhD from The University of Arizona. His research areas include knowledge management, end-user learning, and post-adoptive technology use. His research has appeared in journals such as Information Systems Research, Communications of the AIS, Data Base for Advances in Information Systems, and International Journal of Knowledge Management. His work has also been presented with recognition at several international IS conferences.

Kerstin Fink is University Professor at Innsbruck University/School of Management and head of the Department of Information Systems, Operational Management and Logistics. Kerstin Fink conducts research in the field of knowledge management and measurement as well as modeling of knowledge-intensive processes with special focus on small and medium-sized enterprises (SMEs). She was visiting researcher at Stanford University and the University of New Orleans and is currently guest professor at the University of Linz (Austria). Kerstin Fink was awarded with the Tyrolean Chamber of Commerce Prize, the Otto-Beisheim Prize and the Innsbruck Scientific Award for excellent research in the field of Knowledge Management.

Terri L. Griffith is a Professor of Management and Breetwor Fellow in Santa Clara University's Leavey School of Business. Professor Griffith received her M.S. and Ph.D. from Carnegie Mellon's Graduate School of Industrial Administration (now Tepper School of Business). Her B.A. in Psychology was granted by the University of California, Berkeley. Her research interests include the implementation and effective use of new technologies and organizational practices – especially focused on virtual teams, virtual work, knowledge transfer in global settings, triggers for technological sensemaking, and the "negotiated implementation" of organizational change. Most recently this work has been in two Fortune 100 tech firms, sponsored by the National Science Foundation. In 2000, she co-edited the book, "Research on Managing Groups and Teams: Technology." She also authors the blog "Technology and Organizations" http://www.TerriGriffith.com/blog.

Carina Antonia Hallin, MSc., is a Ph.D. candidate in Strategy and Knowledge Management at the University of Stavanger, Stavanger, Norway. Her publications and research interests include studies of knowledge management and strategy as applied to the service industry. Topics are: judgmental forecasting, cognitive theory, exploring the strategic impact of tacit knowledge in relation to economic firm performance and exploring how management deals strategically with uncertainty in change and innovation activities. Moreover, she has teaching experience and has spoken on diverse topics in knowledge management and strategy. She holds an international Master of Science degree in hotel and tourism administration from Cornell University, Johnson Business School and Cornell School of Hotel Administration, and University of Stavanger, Norwegian School of Hotel Management. Hallin has practical experience from diverse service industries within administration and sales including the hospitality sector, the consulting sector of language teaching and banking.

Salah Eldin Adam Hamza is a quality manager, consultant of engineering & technology management, and expert of engineering & project management best practices. He is the author of several journal articles, and conference proceedings on knowledge management, business process analysis and engineering, organizational development, six sigma, and benchmarking. He holds a B.Sc. (1st class honors) and an M.Sc. in surveying engineering from the University of Khartoum, and an M.Sc. in total quality & performance management from Bradford University. Salah Hamza is also a senior member of the American Society for Quality (ASQ) and a member of the American Statistical Association (ASA).

Helen Hasan is an Associate Professor in Information Systems in the Faculty of Commerce at the University of Wollongong. She has a Masters in Physics followed by a PhD in Information Systems, is a member of the Australian Standards Committees on Knowledge Management and Small to Medium Enterprises. She has published extensively in the areas of Human Computer Interaction, Decision Support Systems (DSS) and Knowledge Management (KM) and more recently Network-Centric Organisation. Helen is Director of the Activity Theory Usability Laboratory at the University of Wollongong and a founding member of the cross-institutional Socio-Technical Activity Research (STAR) Group on Knowledge Management that is funded until 2007 by a Discovery Grant from the Australian Research Council. Currently, she is working with the Defence Scientific and Technology organisation on a simulation game to research and train for team-building in the network-centric paradigm.

Subramanian Rama Iyer is a PhD student in Finance in the Spears School of Business at Oklahoma State University. He received his MBA from Oklahoma State University in 2008. While in the MBA program he was awarded several scholarships. He has worked in India for the banking industry. He has also served as an Adjunct Faculty in the Institute of Management Studies (IMS), India. He has published in Expert Systems with Applications. His research interests include shareholder activism, corporate governance, and banking.

Richard Jolly is currently pursuing a joint Systems Science and Business Administration PhD at Portland State University. Richard's academic focus is the application of systems science methodologies to complex business problems – with a current focus on knowledge management. Richard currently works full time at Intel Corporation in the planning of server components. In 2006 he was awarded the Intel Achievement Award – Intel's highest honor. Richard has 26 years of computer industry experience.

He has authored or co-authored 14 publications in the field of electronics and has one patent granted. Richard has received an MS in Systems Science from Portland State University in 2007, an MBA from Portland State University in 1990, an MS in EECS from the University of California, Berkeley in 1980 and a BS in EECS from University of California, Berkeley in 1978.

Robert Judge holds undergraduate degrees in Biology and Botany, an MBA, and a PhD in the Management of Information Systems and Technology from Claremont Graduate University. His career spans the semiconductor, aerospace, consumer electronics, and Internet Service industries at mid-management and executive levels. He has held functional responsibilities that include Materiel, Manufacturing, Information Systems, Marketing, Project Management and Customer Support. Throughout the last 20+ years of his career, he has served both San Diego State University and the University of San Diego as an adjunct professor teaching graduate and undergraduate courses in Operations, Supply Chain Management, Manufacturing Planning and Control Systems, Project Management and Information Systems. His current research interests lie in understanding how barriers to knowledge flow arise as small organizations grow, and also in how Knowledge Management Systems in Supply Chains can influence innovation and the flow of non-logistical knowledge.

Joseph Kasten is the Chair of the Computer Information Systems Department in the Townsend School of Business at Dowling College. He earned his Ph. D. in Information Science from Long Island University. Prior to joining academia, Professor Kasten was an engineer in the defense industry, working in both aircraft and information systems design. His current research interests center on the creation and implementation of knowledge strategy as well as the leveraging of knowledge management systems to create competitive advantage and increased firm performance. Recent research has been published in Knowledge Organization, as chapters in KM texts, and in the proceedings of various I.T. conferences. When not teaching or writing, Joe and his family can be found camping, hiking, and canoeing the mountains and waterways of upstate New York.

Amir Khanlari is Ph. D student of Marketing Management in the school of management at the University of Tehran in Iran. He received a master Degree from University of Tehran in information technology management. His research interests include customer relationship management, Knowledge Management, and business intelligence. He has published his papers in the Journal of Computers and Industrial Engineering, Iranian Journal of Accounting & Auditing Review and several local journals.

Anthony A. Korolis is a database products specialist with the IBM Corporation. He received his M.S. in Information Systems from Santa Clara University's Leavey School of Business. His B.A. in Business Administration was granted by the University of Washington. He has worked for IBM, Hitachi Global Storage Technologies and Gap Inc. in a number of operational, supply chain and information technology roles. In those roles, he focused on data warehousing infrastructure and on designing supply chain models related to inventory levels and warranty returns. His interests include knowledge management, data warehousing, business intelligence software, forecasting and supply chain modeling.

Wei Li holds Ph.D. from the Graduate School of Library & Information Science at the University of Illinois at Urbana-Champaign and a Master Degree in Information Science from Beijing University.

Her research interests include knowledge management, cross-cultural knowledge sharing, international entrepreneurship, and risk management in the financial industry. She has carried out extensive research on cross-cultural knowledge sharing among Chinese and American employees through online communities of practice. Ms. Li has presented papers and organized panel discussions at multiple conferences. She has published peer-reviewed articles in both knowledge management and entrepreneurship fields. Her work has been included by well-respected journals, such as the Journal of Knowledge Management, the International Journal of Knowledge Management, and the Journal of Developmental Entrepreneurship. In addition, Dr. Li is a Certified Public Accountant (CPA) and a Certified Internal Auditor (CIA). Currently, she works in the area of model risk management with Freddie Mac. She also pursues research in risk knowledge management, which is an increasingly important area for both academic scholars and industry practitioners.

Joyce Lucca completed a Ph.D. in Management Science and Information Systems from Oklahoma State University. While pursuing her degree she held the position of Institute Associate at the Institute for Research in Information Systems (IRIS) at Oklahoma State. Her work with IRIS involved proposal development, institute promotion, and research seminar organization. Her research interests include collaborative learning, knowledge management, and cross cultural issues with respect to Information Systems. Dr. Lucca has been published in Journal of Management Information Systems and several book chapters and conference proceedings. Her chapter in Mobile/Pervasive Computing entitled "Coordinating Technologies for Virtual Organizations" was awarded best student paper. Dr. Lucca is currently working as a post doctoral research fellow at IRIS on a large military grant involving cutting edge knowledge management projects.

Shaheen Majid is Associate Professor at the Division of Information Studies, Wee Kim Wee School of Communication and Information, Nanyang Technological University (NTU), Singapore. He is Programme Director for MSc (Information Studies) programme. He is Associate Editor of Singapore Journal of Library & Information Management. He did his MSc (Botany) from the University of the Punjab (Pakistan), MLIS from the University of Western Ontario (Canada), and PhD from City University, London (UK). He has written over 60 articles in reputable refereed journals and presented more than 50 papers in international conferences. He has provided consultancy services in Singapore, Malaysia, Vietnam and Pakistan. His research interests include information and knowledge sharing, environment scanning, information literacy, and information needs and information seeking patterns.

Einar Marnburg, Ph.D., is Professor of Tourism Management at Norwegian School of Hotel Management, University of Stavanger. Presently he is also a Vice Dean of the Faculty of Social Sciences at the same university. Professor Marnburg was trained in economics, business administration and psychology at Copenhagen Business School (b. Economics and Business Administration, M.Sc.) and Copenhagen University (B.Sc.), and received his Ph.D. in 1997 from the Norwegian University of Technology and Science. The Ph.D. thesis concerns business ethics with focus on managerial practice and strategy. Before joining academia, professor Marnburg held different management positions in service businesses for 10 years. Later, besides his job as a professor, he has continuously worked as a consultant and advisor for various private companies and public organizations. Professor Marnburg gives courses in leadership, strategy, organizational behavior at all levels, bachelor, master and Ph.D. He has written and edited several textbooks and textbook sections in organizational development, leadership, consultation and business ethics. His research interests are within leadership, strategy, knowledge management, organizational psychology and business ethics, and he has published international research articles within all of these fields. He is member of the Journal of Business Ethics' Board of Editors, is Associate Editor of the Journal of Scandinavian Hospitality and Tourism, and does reviews for several research journals.

Stephen McLaughlin is Head of Research and Development at the Innovation Value Institute and an honorary Adam Smith Senior Research Fellow at the University of Glasgow. Dr McLaughlin's research areas of interest concern knowledge transfer and how it can effectively impact innovation specifically within service orientated industries. He has recently had articles published in the Journal of Knowledge Management, the International Journal of Knowledge and Process Management, and the European Management Journal. He holds a B.Eng (Hons) from the Royal Naval Engineering College, and a MSc (IT), MBA, and PhD from the University of Glasgow. Dr McLaughlin is also a Chartered Engineer as recognised by the Council of Engineers (UK) and a Fellow of the Institute of Engineering and Technology.

Joseph Meloche, is with the School of Management & Marketing, at the University of Wollongong, NSW Australia. Dr Meloche has worked in the field of Knowledge Management and has applied Activity Theory and Q Methodology to a variety of research problems and has published widely in the field of Information Seeking, and Knowledge Management. Dr Meloche works closely with the International Society for the Scientific Study of Subjectivity, (ISSSS) and is an editorial member for their main journal Operant Subjectivity. ISSSS is the society that supports research using Q Methodology. Dr Meloche is also a Member of International Society for Cultural and Activity Research (ISCAR).More recently Dr Meloche has been a visiting scholar at the CHAT, Centre for Human Activity Theory, research at Kansai University in Osaka Japan and a visiting scholar at Kent State University.

Kimberly L. Merritt has a doctorate in Business Administration from Argosy University and is an Associate Professor of Business at Oklahoma Christian University. During thirteen years at Cameron University, Kimberly served as the Director of Faculty Development and received the School of Business Outstanding Teaching Award. Her teaching includes courses in economics and information systems at both the undergraduate and graduate levels. Kimberly's research interests include user satisfaction in information systems, knowledge transfer, corporate universities, and effective teaching strategies for both traditional and online courses. She has published in the International Journal of Knowledge Management, Issues in Information Systems, the Southwest Business and Economics Journal, and the Journal of Internet Commerce.

Christian E. Mueller - Assistant Professor of Educational Psychology, University of Memphis. Current research interests include giftedness and talent development (over the lifespan), and measurement issues in psychology and education. Current research projects focus on exploring resiliency in gifted students, and developing assessments of complex cognitive abilities utilizing the Rasch measurement model.

Shahnawaz Muhammed is Assistant Professor of Operations Management and Director of Academic Operations at American University of the Middle East, Kuwait. Dr. Muhammed teaches operations management and information systems courses in his current position in addition to his administrative role. His research interests include knowledge management, knowledge representation, information systems for knowledge management and knowledge management in supply chains. He holds a B.Tech. in Mechanical Engineering from the University of Calicut, India and a Ph.D. in Manufacturing Management from The University of Toledo. His work experience prior to his academic life includes engineering design, software development and software testing. He is a Certified Supply Chain Professional (CSCP) by APICS.

Samantha Rice Murray has a doctorate in Business Administration from Mississippi State University. She is currently a Graduate Professor at Lubbock Christian University. Her seminal work is in the area of knowledge transfer and has published several articles in this area in Journals such as Journal of Managerial Issues. She also serves on the Board of several Non-profit organizations.

Torvald Øgaard, Ph.D., is professor of Service Marketing and Management at the University of Stavanger. His present teaching includes research methods and service management. He is also professor at the Norwegian School of Economics and Business Administration where he teaches service management. He has a Ph.D. from the Norwegian School of Economics and Business Administration. His main research areas include organizational culture and climate, service quality, service recovery and justice, customer and employee risk perceptions, occupational bullying and health, and creativity and innovation. He has been particularly interested in the interplay between employees and the organizations they work in (multilevel modelling), and the interactions between employees and customers in service industries. Professor Øgaard publishes regularly in international journals.

Charmaine Celeste Pfaff has a Master of Information Systems (Distinction) and Postgraduate Diploma in Information Systems from the University of Wollongong. She has a Bachelor of Science, Honours, in Politics and International Relations from the University of Southampton, U.K. and a Certificate in Education, Institute of Singapore, Singapore. She has just completed her PhD entitled "Harnessing Wiki Technology for Knowledge Management in Learning Organisations" from which several papers have already been published.

Christian Ploder is a Research Assistant at the Department of Information Systems, Operational Management and Logistics at the University of Innsbruck/School of Management and Ph.D. student. In his Ph.D. thesis he is developing a model for diagnosing knowledge intensive business processes. Since working at the Department he is a lecturer for Information System Basic Course, Project & Knowledge Management, author of different journals and papers presented on international conferences. His research interests include knowledge management focused on small and medium-sized enterprises as well as the topic of knowledge intensive processes.

Mark Salisbury has over 25 years of experience in designing and developing human performance solutions. He is the author of iLearning: How to Create an Innovative Learning Organization and has published many articles related to knowledge management in engineering, business, and education journals. He has a master's degree in computer and information science and a Ph.D. in curriculum and instruction from the University of Oregon. Dr. Salisbury also holds a master of arts in teaching economics from Western Oregon University. After completing his graduate studies, he worked for eleven years at The Boeing Company on developing software to improve human performance. His time at Boeing was split between research and development efforts and commercial products. After leaving Boeing, he founded Vitel, Inc. a knowledge management solution provider that developed knowledge management systems for the U.S. Department of Defense (DOD), U.S. Department of Energy (DOE), the national laboratories, and public utility companies. Currently, Dr. Salisbury is a professor in the Organizational Learning and Instructional Technology program at the University of New Mexico where he teaches graduate courses and conducts research in the area of knowledge management.

Ramesh Sharda earned his MBA and PhD from University of Wisconsin-Madison. He is widely recognized for his contributions to Decision Support Systems, optimization software, data mining, and managing information overload. He started OSU's M.S. in Telecommunications Management degree program. His research in the use of neural networks for firm failure prediction and forecasting success of movies has been highly publicized. He is a co-author of several books including Business Intelligence: A Managerial Approach, Decision Support and Business Intelligence Systems. He is also Co Editor-in-Chief of Annals of Information Systems, and on editorial boards of several other major journals. He and his colleagues are working on a project with Defense Ammunition Center that involves knowledge management, learning systems, and advanced technologies. Ramesh is also co-founder of a company (iTradeFair.com, Inc.) that produces virtual trade fairs.

Upton R. Shimp is the Director of Training at the Defense Ammunition Center (DAC), McAlester, Oklahoma. Dr. Shimp earned a Bachelor of Science degree in Education (Mathematics and Elementary Education) from the University of Missouri. For several years after graduation, Dr. Shimp worked in the Missouri public schools as a secondary and elementary education teacher. Dr. Shimp also holds a Master's of Science degree in management from Southern Nazarene University and the Doctor of Philosophy in Education from the Oklahoma State University. Mr. Shimp began his career as a civilian employee of the U.S. Army in January 1980. During his twenty-nine years in federal service, Dr. Shimp's awards include two Meritorious Civilian Service Awards, the Superior Civilian Service Award, the Commanders Award for Civilian Service, the European Association of the United States Army Commendation, Ammunition Manager of the Year, and numerous Special Service Awards.

Anssi Smedlund is a M.Sc. (Econ.) and Lic.Sc. (Tech.). He is a Senior Researcher in the Innovation Management Institute (IMI) at Helsinki University of Technology, and a Research Associate in the Department of Value and Decision Science at Tokyo Institute of Technology, in the Graduate School of Decision Science and Technology. His previous research has concentrated on the topics of intellectual capital and inter-firm networks in regions. In the field of knowledge management, his research interests are in network analysis of flows of knowledge in professional service firms. In his research projects, he also works in close collaboration with companies concentrating on business model development and optimization in industrial services.

Babak Sohrabi is Associate Professor in Department of Information Technology Management, Faculty of Management at University of Tehran, Iran. He received his PhD degree in Management Science, from Lancaster University, England in 2000. He is the Editor-in-Chief of Knowledge management Journal at University of Tehran. His research interests include Artificial Intelligence, Knowledge management, electronic commerce, decision support systems and organizational impact of information technology. His research has appeared in Journal of Interdisciplinary Mathematics, International Journal of Engineering, Journal of operational Research Society, International Journal of production Research, Computers & Industrial Engineering, Review of business information systems and others.

Yan Qi holds a Master of Information Systems and a Graduate Diploma in Information System from the University of Wollongong. She is currently undertaking research for her PhD entitled "Knowledge Management Practices: A metaphorical study of Play as a way to enhance work practices".

Wayne Wakeland was granted a B.S. in Engineering and Master of Engineering in from Harvey Mudd College in 1973, and in 1977 he was granted a Ph.D. in Systems Science from PSU. He became an adjunct member of the core faculty of the Systems Science Ph.D. program and began teaching a sequence of courses on modeling and simulation. This sequence evolved considerably over the years. In 2000, he became an Associate Professor of Systems Science. In parallel with teaching, from 1978 to 2000, Wayne held managerial positions in information systems or manufacturing at Tektronix, Photon Kinetics, Magni Systems, Epson, and Leupold & Stevens. Wayne's research interests include biomedical dynamics, the software development process, criminal justice systems, sustainability, supply chain management, organizational dynamics and systems thinking and simulation & optimization methods using simulation languages such as STELLA, Vensim, Arena, Extend, ProModel, Netlogo, and Simulink.

Miss Sim Mong Wey graduated from the National University of Singapore (NUS) with a Bachelor's degree in Business Administration (Finance) and obtained her Masters of Science in Information Studies from Wee Kim Wee School of Communication and Information, Nanyang Technological University (NTU), Singapore in 2006. She is currently working as an Assistant Manager at the Singapore Medical Council.

David Willis is Manager Research Services at BlueScope Steel Research, Port Kembla, Australia. He manages a team of twenty who provide technical and administrative services to support the research efforts of about ninety scientists, engineers and technologists. David has a PhD in physical metallurgy from the University of NSW and has thirty-two years experience as a researcher and project leader. In 1999 he became Manager Metallic Coatings Research and in 2004 he moved to essentially his current position. David's research interests have been in the metallurgy of metallic coated sheet steel including the metallurgy of the hot-dip process and the product properties and corrosion performance of metallic coated steel. He has a particular responsibility and interest in knowledge management. David has published 45 scientific papers and two patents.

Dalal M. Zoubi is an assistant Professor in the Educational Science Department, Irbid College, Albalqa Applied University, Jordan. He graduated from Amman Arab University for Graduate Students, with a PhD in Educational Administration. His main research interests are in the field of Higher Education Studies, such as university management, academic issues, student learning. Dr. Zoubi has published several papers and has taught several research methods courses. Dr. Zoubi has occupied the position of assistant dean for students affairs, financial affairs, educational affairs in Irbid College, Al-Balqa Applied University for ten years.

Index

A

AASA standards 271, 278

active participants 128

Activity Theory 89, 126-127, 130-132, 137, 140-141

agent-based simulation (ABS) 22

American Association of School Administrators (AASA) 271, 278

Amman National University (ANU) 346-347, 349-350, 354-355, 357-368

argument quality 311, 313-322, 324

artificial environment 22

Asia-Pacific Economic Cooperation (APEC) 50, 61

asynchronous sensemaking 152

attraction-selection-attrition (ASA) model 257

average variance extracted (AVE) 10-12, 218, 320

B

bug tracking systems 150

business borders 53

business environment 172, 178, 183, 237, 287, 347

business process modeling 53

business strategy 44, 58, 227-230, 232-240, 242, 309, 333, 343-344

C

CA calibration performance difference 287

CA judgmental performance 289

captured enemy ammunition (CEA) 198, 206

CA studies 286-287

CA theory of experts and novices 287

Chi-square test 9, 14

classical test theory (CTT) 269-270

codified systems 163-164, 167, 169

cognitive skills 59, 66

Coleman-Burt debate 82

collaborative cognition model 64, 67-69, 76-77

collaborative culture 214

collectivism 243, 245-246, 253-254, 258, 260, 262

combination 22, 82, 94, 122, 150, 199, 210, 212-213, 226, 240, 268, 288, 293, 303, 313, 338, 353

communication channels 116, 120

communities of practice (CoP) 29, 56, 61, 75, 94, 96, 110, 123, 175-176, 186, 224, 247, 254-255, 257-259, 261, 344

comparative fit index (CFI) 11-12

competitive advantage 2, 20, 31-34, 92-93, 113, 123-124, 157, 164, 169-170, 172-173, 175-177, 184, 187, 215, 228, 240, 304, 329-331, 333-334, 337-340, 342, 344, 347, 350-351, 354, 365-366, 374

computer assisted design and drafting (CADD) 182

conceptual knowledge 1-2, 4-7, 10, 12, 14, 16, 67, 72-74

conceptual research 40, 331, 339

Concourse 131-134

confidence–accuracy (CA) 288

content organization 190

contextual knowledge 1-2, 4-5, 7-8, 10, 12-16, 236

contextual task-knowledge 9

contingency theory 84-85

contingency variable 31, 41

controlled vocabulary 192

cooperative learning activities 114

corporate culture 126, 333

corporate hierarchy 246

corporate knowledge 41, 94, 126, 128-129, 134, 137, 139, 141, 330

corporate knowledge workers (CKW) 134, 137

corporate universities 329-331, 333-334, 337, 339, 343-345

corrected item-total correlation (CITC) 8

critical success factors (CSF) 3, 13, 30, 32-35, 42, 63, 93, 127, 129, 139, 306

Cronbach's alpha 8, 10, 35, 218, 320, 357

cross-cultural contexts 244, 248, 263

cross-cultural knowledge sharing 243, 245, 247, 252, 258

cultural differences 243-248, 251-252, 256-258, 262

cultural perspective 1-2, 18

culture-based perspective 2

customer service strategy 235

D

DAC personnel 198, 202, 206

data collection 8-9, 16, 53, 55, 113, 116, 122, 127, 130, 247, 271, 281, 318, 355, 357

data packets 92, 94, 96-107, 109

Defense Ammunition Center (DAC) 198

distance learning (DL) 202

dynamic groups 144, 152-154

dynamic knowledge 79, 240, 290-291

dynamic task environments 153

E

educational outreach programs 148

education quality assurance 349, 368

elaboration likelihood model (ELM) 311, 313-314, 316, 321

e-learning 79, 124, 193, 208, 338, 350, 371

e-library 349

European Union (EU) 50, 61, 124, 307

Europe, Middle East and Africa (EMEA) 158

explicit skills 265

external information repositories 149

externalization 94, 97-102, 104-107, 210, 212-213, 226, 304

F

face-to-face communication 96, 112, 119-120, 181, 252, 339

first-generation corporate university 337-338

fiscal strategy 235

flexible organizational culture 219

freeware 54-55

G

game theoretic analysis 19

game theory 19, 21, 27

GE capital 197

General Electric (GE) 125, 197, 208, 254, 262, 338-339

generalizability theory 269

globalization 243, 346-347

gross domestic product (GDP) 50

H

human knowledge 16, 265, 352

human resources (HR) 178, 181, 221, 242

human resources strategy 229-230, 232, 234, 242

I

ICT solutions 163

ICT systems 163, 167

iGrafx simulation software 97

individualism 15, 243, 245, 253, 258, 260, 262

information-bearing message 315

information technology (IT) 2, 14-16, 25-36, 44, 55-56, 63-69, 77-78, 92-94, 98-101, 109, 122-123, 136-140, 156-159, 163, 169-170, 177-178, 190-191, 198-201, 206-208, 220, 234-239, 248-258, 272-281, 297, 302, 310, 317, 328, 336-338, 346-368,

information transfer mechanisms 157

in-groups 245, 254

institutional culture 351, 356, 358-362, 374

institutional learning 349, 353-354, 356, 363-366, 375

instructional systems design (ISD) 66, 72

instruction approaches 113-114

integrated information systems 159

integrated supply chain (ISC) 158, 160-161, 169

intellectual capital (IC) 349

intellectual knowledge 266

intelligent agents 163

Intelligent Robotics Group (IRG) 144-145, 147-152

internalization 69, 94, 210, 212-213, 226, 312, 323, 353, 365

intuitive judgmental performance 289, 302, 305

intuitive judgments 286, 288-291, 293-294, 303-305

ISO/IEC 9126 norm 54, 56

IT authentication problem 312

item response theory (IRT) model 269-270

IT management 41, 216

J

job rotation 225, 231, 336, 338

Joint Munitions Command (JMC) 198

judgmental forecasting 288, 301, 303-305, 308, 310

K

KM awareness 346, 351, 355-362, 367-368, 373

KM concept 356, 359, 361-362, 373

KM initiatives 2, 31, 34, 127-128, 177, 348, 362, 366

KM leadership 352, 362

KM operations 353, 355-358, 362-365, 367-368, 373

KMscape 19, 22-23, 25-26

KMS knowledge 312, 316, 322-324

KMS quality 176

KM status 367

KM success/failure factors 173

KM success models? 34, 173, 175

KM systems 40, 163, 347, 349, 353

KM utilization 346, 355-368

knowledge abilities 305

knowledge access 4

knowledge acquisition process 49, 52-53, 56, 209, 229, 231-232, 235, 268, 351, 358

knowledge application 4, 15, 32

knowledge assessment process 52-53

knowledge assets 31, 68, 74-76, 78, 81-82, 84, 87-88, 170, 183, 187, 191, 193, 196-199, 215, 230, 287, 290, 292, 301, 352, 356, 371, 373

knowledge base 4-5, 49, 86, 93, 149, 178, 180, 182, 229-230, 315, 318

knowledge-based activities 227-228, 232, 239

knowledge-based decisions 227, 238

knowledge-based economy 113, 208

knowledge-based forecasting 286, 305-306

knowledge-based resources 93, 228

knowledge capture 4, 110, 163

knowledge capturing 291

knowledge consumers 244, 255, 312, 315

knowledge continuum insight 82

knowledge creation 4, 15, 44, 67, 69, 79, 82-83, 89, 94, 96, 110, 112, 140, 158, 160, 169-170, 174, 187, 210-216, 218-219, 222-223, 225, 230, 236, 244, 260-261, 283, 287, 291, 309, 326, 344, 349, 368

knowledge creation modes 212

knowledge creation processes 210, 212, 219, 225

knowledge dessemination process 65

knowledge development process 44, 52, 149, 194, 209, 229, 234, 349, 351, 358

knowledge distribution process 49, 52-53, 56, 193

knowledge dynamics 19, 44

knowledge-enabled organization 227

knowledge exchange 44, 102, 153, 178, 214-215, 246, 296

knowledge, explicit 20, 31-34, 68, 77, 81-89, 93, 126, 160, 163, 165, 167, 172, 174, 184, 212-213, 224, 236, 255, 266, 287, 290, 302, 326, 329, 331-332, 335-339, 342, 351-353, 366, 374

knowledge flow barriers 94

knowledge flows 19, 31, 93-94, 96-97, 108-109, 111, 145, 246

knowledge gap 163, 337

knowledge gathering 227, 229, 354

knowledge generation 291, 296, 304-305, 349, 353, 356, 365, 374

Knowledge goals 52-53, 362

knowledge, implicit 350-353, 374

knowledge, individual 1-2, 6-7, 15, 32, 108, 312

knowledge institution 351

knowledge lifecycle management (KLM) 34

knowledge literature 329

knowledge management activities 114, 305, 368

knowledge management culture 172

knowledge management enablers 43, 210-213, 221-222, 225

knowledge management (KM) 1-7, 13, 15-20, 29-45, 49-53, 55-56, 58-64, 79-83, 86-88, 90, 92-93, 97, 100, 108-114, 117, 123-130, 133, 139, 141-145, 147, 154, 156, 160, 163, 165, 167, 169-177, 183-188, 190-194, 197, 206-213, 216, 218-227, 230-232, 234, 237, 239-243, 258-263, 266, 284, 286-291, 301-312, 315, 322, 324-327, 331-333, 342-371, 373-376

knowledge management processes 34, 40, 230, 232

knowledge management pyramid model (KMPM) 34

knowledge management readiness 32-33, 35, 37, 40, 42-43

knowledge management, resistance to 32

knowledge management systems (KMS) 2-3, 15-17, 33-34, 41-44, 50-51, 58, 61, 79, 92-94, 96-102, 104-105, 108-110, 124, 127-130, 139-143, 145, 174-176, 183-186, 190, 193-194, 220, 242, 306, 311-313, 315-318, 321-327, 370

knowledge management tools 61-63, 193, 230, 232

knowledge maps 56, 191

knowledge nugget organization 199-200

knowledge nuggets (KN) 199, 206

knowledge, organizational 15, 23, 25, 32, 41, 44-45, 60, 67, 69-70, 93, 110, 126-128, 130, 143, 145, 147, 173, 178, 184, 186-188, 212, 219-220, 222-223, 227, 235, 239, 258, 261-262, 283, 287, 289, 312, 326, 343-344

knowledge organization scheme 191-192, 206-207

knowledge, potential 28, 81-88, 345

knowledge power 31

knowledge preservation process 49, 52, 54, 56, 65

knowledge processing flows 94

knowledge process modeling 51, 53, 59, 61-62

knowledge products 66, 68, 72, 151

knowledge recipient 312, 315-316, 321-322

knowledge repositories 96, 99, 127-128, 193-194, 325

knowledge sharing 4, 15, 19-20, 22-23, 27-28, 32-33, 44-45, 49, 59, 79, 110, 113-126, 137-138, 141, 144, 152, 154-155, 159-160, 165, 173, 176, 183, 187, 193, 209, 229-232, 238-239, 243-248, 252-262, 286, 288, 290-292, 302-307, 309, 339, 343, 353-354, 356, 364-366, 368, 370-371, 374-375

knowledge sharing behavior 113, 115-116, 119, 122-123, 243, 245, 252-254, 262

knowledge sharing culture 114, 121

knowledge sharing, explicit 160

knowledge sources 286-289, 291, 301-302, 304, 323

knowledge spiral 67-69, 77, 83

knowledge strategy (KS) 34, 225-226, 228-240

knowledge, tacit 18, 20, 31-33, 65, 68, 73, 77, 81-88, 93-94, 100, 128, 147, 159, 163, 167-168, 170, 172-174, 176-179, 183-187, 191, 195, 213, 216, 224, 229, 236, 239, 258, 264-284, 287, 289-290, 304, 306, 309-310, 332, 335-339, 341, 343, 345, 354, 358, 370

knowledge, tacit, domain-specific 264

knowledge transfer 34, 45, 60, 111, 148, 157, 159-160, 163-169, 172, 179, 185, 192-193, 196, 223, 241, 259-260, 311-313, 315, 321-326, 329-332, 334, 336-337, 339-342, 344, 353, 365, 370

knowledge transfer process 179, 311-312, 329, 331, 336-337, 340, 342, 344

knowledge, ubiquitous 128, 140

knowledge usefulness 311, 314, 316-317, 320-324

knowledge utilization process 31, 52, 209, 366, 375

knowledge workers 2, 8-9, 15, 33, 50, 60, 68, 76, 78, 128, 139, 232, 323, 341, 352, 370

KS creation 228, 231

L

leadership effectiveness 264-265

lean media 329, 336-339

learning culture 173, 175-176, 214

learning environment 115, 333

learning institution 351

lessons learned knowledge (LLK) 192, 194

M

media selection 329, 331, 336, 339-340, 342

mediated knowledge transfer 311-312, 321

metaknowledge 5, 147

micro-SMEs 50

misuse of knowledge 287, 292, 304-306

mock KMS 312, 317

model of information adoption (MIA) 314-316

multicultural organizations 183

multinational organizations 243-244

N

Nanyang Technological University 113, 116

NASA Ames Research Center 144, 148, 150

NASA IRG environment 152

National Aeronautics and Space Administration (NASA) 144, 148, 150, 152, 154

new product development (NPD) 210-216, 219-220, 226

NPD context 210-213

NPD knowledge 211

NPD performance 210-213, 215-216, 219-220, 226

O

online environments 243

online system 243

ontology 152, 190-192, 194

open-door policy 172, 183

operational knowledge 1-2, 4-10, 12, 14, 16, 18

order flow process (OFP) 159-168

Organisation for Economic Co-operation and Development (OECD) 50, 62

organizational boundaries 236, 312

organizational context 2, 4, 13, 152-153, 229

organizational culture 1-3, 15-16, 21, 44, 143, 172-173, 176, 183, 187, 211-213, 219, 231-232, 235, 239, 257-258, 290-291, 306, 309, 338, 349, 354, 369

organizational environments? 23, 240, 247

organizational learning (OL) 175-176

organizational memory 6, 42-43, 94, 109-110, 156, 175, 184, 186, 209, 291, 310, 342-343

organizational memory information system (OMS) 175

organizational resources? 33, 39

organizational strategies 329

organizational structure 50, 81, 97, 100, 108, 147, 211, 227, 229-232, 234, 236, 238-239, 292, 303, 330

out-group 116, 245-246, 254, 258

P

peer production information commons 128

Peer Review 137, 172, 178-180, 183

people strategy 219

Polanyi, Michael 83, 89, 93, 111, 158, 163, 170, 173-174, 187, 264-266, 283, 289, 309

practical knowledge 215, 266, 268, 282, 352

Practical Knowledge Inventory for Nurses (PKIN) 268

prisoner's dilemma 19, 21, 25-27

prisoner's dilemma analysis 19, 25

process improvements? 65, 157-159, 168-169, 234, 236, 238-239

process re-engineering 157

product knowledge 216

product realization process (PRP) 65

professional knowledge 1, 8-9, 249

professional literature 264-265

proprietary knowledge 20, 115

PRP Online Website 65

Q

Q methodology 126-127, 130-132, 140, 142
quality plan 66, 68-69, 71-72, 75-76
Quick Start TMS 149-152, 154

R

Rasch analysis 264, 270-277, 279, 283-284
Rasch model 264, 269-274, 276, 279-284
Rasch modeling 264, 269, 279, 282
relationships 2, 4, 6-7, 12, 22, 52, 81, 84-85,
        88-89, 96, 113-114, 118, 121-122, 131,
        162, 165, 177, 192, 211, 214, 216, 218-
        219, 230, 233, 237-238, 241, 259-260,
        291, 314, 320, 329, 331, 339-340, 365,
        367
rich media 329, 336-339
root mean square error of approximation (RM-
        SEA) 11-12

S

scientific knowledge 352
SCM tools 150
sensemaking 17, 151-152
service innovation 157
sexual harassment 337
sexual harassment policies 337
shareware 54-55
short messaging service (SMS) 99, 120
skill-enhancement 333
small and medium-sized enterprises (SME) 40,
        45, 49-51, 53-56, 58-63, 92-94, 96, 100-
        101, 108, 111-112, 195-197, 202-203,
        206, 291, 295, 307
Small Business Administration (SBA) 51, 93
SME, knowledge processes for 55
SME knowledge toolkit 51, 58-59
social capital 42, 44-45, 89, 124, 184, 186-187,
        223, 287, 290-291, 302-303, 305-307
social collaboration tools 115
socialization 93-94, 96-101, 210, 212-213,
        225, 287-288, 291, 307, 353
socialization, externalization, combination, &
        internalization (SECI) model 79, 82-83,
        94, 210, 212, 332, 349
social network analysis 161-162

social networks 81-82, 88-89, 110, 231
social network structure, centralized 82, 85
social network structure, decentralized 82
social network structure, distributed 82
social network structures 81-82, 84-86, 88, 345
social technologies 127-128, 137, 142
social work situation 20
software configuration management (SCM)
        150-151
software development discussions 151
source credibility 311, 313-324
static knowledge 290
strategic advantages 330
strategic capital 187, 286-287, 289-291, 302-
        306, 308-309
strategic decision making 286-295, 301, 303-
        305, 308, 343
strategy drivers 227, 241
structural complexity 20
structural equation 1, 8, 16-17, 220-221
structural equation model 1
success measures 1-2, 15-16, 344
supply chain 157-160, 163, 165, 167, 169-171
synergistic cost advantages 329
systems science 19

T

tacit knowledge creation 236
tacit knowledge harvesting 172
Tacit Knowledge Inventory for Military Lead-
        ers (TKML) 268
Tacit Knowledge Inventory for Superintendents
        (TKIS) 264, 270-271, 273-276, 278-279,
        281
tacit knowledge research 265-266, 270
tacit knowledge sharing 159, 183, 258, 290,
        370
task knowledge 1-6, 9-10, 12-13, 15-16, 145,
        153
taxonomy 17-18, 21, 29, 67-68, 72, 74, 78,
        125, 152, 174-175, 190-192, 194-196,
        198-204, 207-208
team collaboration system (TCS) 65
technical business practices (TBP) 65
technology-based perspective 2

technology encyclopaedia (TE) wiki 130-134, 136-139
technology strategies 227
technology support system 144
temporal view 197-198, 202
tolerance for ambiguity 246, 255
transactive memory systems (TMS) 144-154
transfer mechanisms 157, 163, 165-167, 169
trust 88, 96, 114, 118, 121-122, 125, 148, 165, 210, 212, 214-215, 218-220, 222, 225, 245, 250, 260, 321-322, 325-327
T-shaped skills 210, 212, 215, 218-219, 225

U

uncertainty avoidance 15, 243, 245-246, 252, 255, 258
United States Department of Energy (DOE) 64-66, 196

V

validation of knowledge 311, 315

value accelerators 92, 96-97, 99-100, 108-109
value creation 81-88, 370
Vygotsky, Lev 131, 143

W

Web 2.0 149, 151, 153, 190, 197, 208
Wiki environment 152-153
Wikis 115, 119, 125-130, 139-141, 144, 149, 153-154, 156
Wiki software 153

Y

Yarmouk University (YU) 42, 174, 176, 188, 229, 241, 257, 261, 341-342, 345-347, 349-350, 354-355, 357-363, 365-368

Z

ZING Technology 133

CPSIA information can be obtained at www.ICGtesting.com

262421BV00008B/77-140/P